We are shaped and fashioned by what
Johann Wolfgang von

TO KNOW HISTORY
IS TO
LOVE HISTORY

Welcome to Prentice Hall's **T.L.C. Edition**.
That's **T**eaching and **L**earning **C**lassroom Edition.

Dear Student,

Your instructor already knows—and loves—history. *Do you?* **Welcome to the new and exciting T.L.C. Edition—** this is the book that will change the way you feel about history. Prentice Hall developed this text to bring history to you with more visual appeal than ever. This is the book that you will want to read because it is interesting. You will think about what you're reading because it has relevance to your life. With this book and the multimedia tools we crafted to accompany it, you will truly experience history's dramatic trials and passionate triumphs in a way that adds meaning to your own life.

And you will score better on tests because preparation will be easier and less time consuming than you ever dreamed possible.

Read on and find out why this book is just the T.L.C. you need to say "I DO" know—and love—history.

TO KNOW HISTORY
IS TO LOVE HISTORY

Imagine if you could make sense of all the names, dates, events, and people who made history?
Imagine putting it all into a context that made you rethink your world, your life, yourself—
with the fascinating perspective that only history provides? All it takes is the T.L.C. you are now

holding in your hand.
Here's what makes
this T.L.C. Edition
different...

■ You will be compelled
to **READ** this
dramatically different,
vividly illustrated,
less dense textbook
because it is not at
all overwhelming.

■ You will be inspired to
THINK about *what* you
are reading *as* you
are reading.

■ You will come to class
READY to take notes
with your automatically
bundled, portable, and
easy-to-use *HistoryNotes*.

OVERVIEW
MAJOR INDIAN TREATIES AND LEGISLATION OF THE LATE NINETEENTH CENTURY

1863	Nez Percé Treaty	Signed illegally on behalf of the entire tribe in which the Nez Percé abandoned 6 million acres of land in return for a small reservation in northeastern Oregon. Led to Nez Percé wars, which ended in 1877 with the surrender of Chief Joseph.
1867	Medicine Lodge Treaty	Assigned reservations in existing Indian Territory to Comanches, Plains (Kiowa), Apaches, Kiowas, Cheyennes, and Arapahoes, bringing these tribes together with Sioux, Shoshones, Bannocks, and Navajos.
1868	Treaty of Fort Laramie	Successfully ended Red Cloud's war by evacuating federal troops from Sioux Territory along the Bozeman Trail; additionally granted Sioux ownership of the

AMERICAN COMMUNITIES
Communities Struggle with Diversity
in Seventeenth-Century Santa Fé

IT WAS A HOT AUGUST DAY IN 1680 WHEN THE FRANTIC MESSEN-GERS rode into the small mission outpost of El Paso with the news that the Pueblo Indians to the north had risen in revolt. The corpses of more than 400 colonists lay bleeding in the dust. Two thousand Spanish survivors huddled inside the Palace of Governors in Santa Fé, surrounded by 3,000 angry warriors. The Pueblo leaders had sent two crosses into the palace—white for surrender, red for death. Which would the Spaniards choose?

Spanish colonists had been in New Mexico for nearly a century. Franciscan priests came first, followed by a military expedition from Mexico in search of precious metals. In 1609, high in the picturesque foothills of the Sangre de Cristo Mountains, the colonial authorities founded La Villa Real de la Santa Fé de San Francisco—"the royal town of the holy faith of St. Francis"—soon known simply as Santa Fé. Colonization efforts included the conversion of the Pueblo Indians to Christianity, making them subjects of the king of Spain, and forcing them to work for the colonial elite who lived in the town.

In the face of overwhelming Spanish power, the Pueblos adopted a flexible attitude. Twenty thousand of them converted to Christianity, but most of these thought of the new

eral years before, the Spanish governor had executed three Pueblo religious leaders and publicly whipped dozens more for secretly practicing their religion. One of those leaders, Popé of San Juan Pueblo, vowed to overthrow the regime. During the next several years he carefully organized a conspiracy among more than twenty Indian towns.

Popé's job was not difficult, for there were plenty of local grievances. The Hopis of northern Arizona, for example, still tell of a missionary who capped his ever-escalating demands on them with the order that all the young women of the village be brought to live with him. When the revolt began, the Hopis surrounded the missionary's house. "I have come to kill you," the chief announced. "You can't kill me," the priest cried from behind his locked door. "I will come [back] to life and wipe out your whole tribe." But the chief shouted back, "my gods have more power than you have." He and his men broke down the door, hung the missionary from the beams, and lit a fire beneath his feet.

When the Indians demanded the surrender of the Spanish inside Santa Fé's Palace of Governors, the besieged colonists sent back the red cross, signaling defiance. But after a siege lasting five days, the

To be able to be caught up into the world of thought—that is to be educated.
Edith Hamilton

QUICK REVIEW

Jim Crow

- Neither major party addressed problem of racism and nativism in campaign of 1896.
- Local and state governments in the South codified racism in Jim Crow laws.
- The Supreme Court upheld the new discriminatory legislation.

18-9
Booker T. Washington, Atlanta Exposition Address (1895)

Nativism   Favoring the interests and culture of native-born inhabitants over those of immigrants.

Jim Crow laws   Segregation laws that became widespread in the South during the 1890s.

Segregation   A system of racial control that separated the races, initially by custom but increasingly by law during and after Reconstruction.

African-American Representation in Congress, 1867–1900
Black men served in the U.S. Congress from 1870 until 1900. All were Republicans.

McKinley's triumph ended the popular challenge to the nation's governing system. With prosperity returning by 1898 and nationalism rising swiftly, McKinley encouraged Americans to go for "a full dinner pail," the winning Republican slogan of the 1900 presidential election.

NATIVISM AND JIM CROW

Campaign rhetoric aside, McKinley and Bryan differed only slightly on the major problems facing the nation in 1896. Neither Bryan the reformer nor McKinley the prophet of prosperity addressed the escalation of racism and **nativism** (anti-immigrant feeling) throughout the nation.

Toward the end of the century, many political observers noted, the nation's patriotic fervor took on a strongly nationalistic and antiforeign tone. Striking workers and their employers alike tended to blame "foreigners" for the hard times. Semisecret organizations such as the American Protective Association sprang up to defend American institutions. Fourth of July orators continued to celebrate freedom and liberty but more often boasted about the might and power of their nation.

In the South, local and state governments codified racist ideology by passing discriminatory and segregationist legislation, which became known as **Jim Crow laws**. The phrase, dating from the early decades of the nineteenth century, was made popular by a white minstrel in black face who used the name "Jim Crow" to characterize all African Americans. Before the Civil War, abolitionists described segregated railroad cars as "Jim Crow." By the end of the century, "Jim Crow" referred to the customs of **segregation** that were becoming codified by law and practice throughout the South. With nine of every ten black Americans living in this region, the significance of this development was sweeping.

"The supremacy of the white race of the South," New South promoter Henry W. Grady declared in 1887, "must be maintained forever . . . because the white race is the superior race." To secure their privileges, Grady and other white Southerners acted directly to impose firm standards of segregation and domination and to forestall any appearance of social equality. State after state in the South enacted new legislation to cover facilities such as restaurants, public transportation, and even drinking fountains. Signs "White Only" and "Colored" appeared over theaters, parks, rooming houses, and toilets. In banks, post offices, and stores, blacks were required to wait until all whites had been served, and special rules prohibited such common practices as trying on shoes or hats before purchasing them.

The United States Supreme Court upheld the new discriminatory legislation. Its decisions in the *Civil Rights Cases* (1883) overturned the Civil Rights Act of 1875, and in *Plessy v. Ferguson* (1896) the Court upheld a Louisiana state law formally segregating railroad cars on the basis of the "separate but equal" doctrine. In *Cumming v. Richmond County Board of Education* (1899), the Court allowed separate schools for blacks and whites, even where facilities for African American children did not exist.

Southern states enacted new literacy tests and property qualifications for voting, demanding proof of $300 to $500 in property and the ability to read and write. Loopholes permitted poor whites to vote even under these conditions, except where they threatened the Democratic Party's rule. "**Grandfather clauses,**" invented in Louisiana, exempted from all restrictions those who had been entitled to vote on January 1, 1867, together with their sons and grandsons, a measure that effectively enfranchised whites while

With T.L.C. comes all the FREE resources you need to succeed in History.

Q: Wondering why *HistoryNotes* was bound free with your text?
A: BETTER TEST SCORES!

This new tool replaces your traditional study guide, and offers you an incredible, portable system for taking and organizing notes, and for doing practice activities. *HistoryNotes* provides for every chapter of this T.L.C. text:

- Map exercises
- Review/study activities
- Practice tests
- Space on each page for note taking.

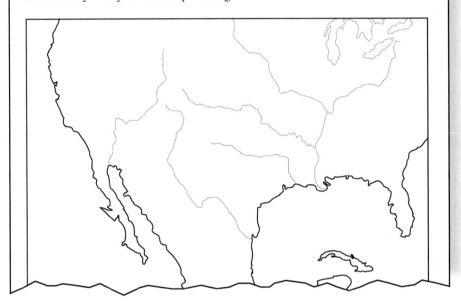

Map Exercise 15-B

Outline and label the following areas or places:

1. independent republic of Texas, 1836
2. Gadsden Purchase, 1853
3. Mexico after 1853
4. ceded to Texas 1845
5. ceded by Treaty of Guadelupe Hidalgo 1848

Everything you need to succeed —all in one place.

Everything you need to succeed—*all in one place.*

With OneKey, you can get a better grade!
You will study smarter using the interactive E-book version of this text, which allows you to take pre-tests and quizzes by chapter, and then incorrect answers are linked directly to the portion of the text where you need further review/study. Interactive flashcards and crossword puzzles also offer a fun way to master concepts.

You will see the text come to life.
All maps from this text become interactive to illustrate the important relationship between what happened—and where it happened. Audio and video clips animate dramatic speeches and events from the text, and biographies introduce you to people who made an impression on history.

AND INCLUDED IN EVERY NEW COPY OF THIS TEXT:
United States History Documents CD-ROM

Organized chronologically according to main periods within U.S. history, this tool offers access to more than 300 authentic primary source documents in an easily navigable .pdf file.

Out of Many

A HISTORY OF THE AMERICAN PEOPLE

TEACHING AND LEARNING CLASSROOM EDITION

BRIEF FOURTH EDITION

VOLUME TWO

John Mack Faragher
YALE UNIVERSITY

Mary Jo Buhle
BROWN UNIVERSITY

Daniel Czitrom
MOUNT HOLYOKE COLLEGE

Susan H. Armitrage
WASHINGTON STATE UNIVERSITY

PEARSON
Prentice
Hall

Upper Saddle River, New Jersey 07458

Library of Congress Cataloging-in-Publication Data

Out of many: a history of the American People / John Mack Faragher . . . — [et al.], Brief
  4th TLC ed.
    p. cm.
  Includes bibliographical references and index.
  ISBN 0-13-193339-6 (v. 1) — ISBN 0-13-193338-8 (v2) — ISBN 0-13-193337-X (combined v.)
  1. United States—History.   I. Faragher, John Mack, 1945–
  E178.1.0935   2005b
  973—dc22   2004060756

VP, Editorial Director: Charlyce Jones Owen
Associate Editor: Emsal Hasan
Editorial Assistant: Maureen Diana
Editor-in-Chief, Development: Rochelle Diogenes
Senior Development Editor: Roberta Meyer
Senior Media Editor: Deborah O'Connell
**AVP, Director of Production
  and Manufacturing:** Barbara Kittle
Managing Editor: Joanne Riker
Production Editor: Randy Pettit
Prepress and Manufacturing Manager: Nick Sklitsis
Prepress and Manufacturing Buyer: Benjamin Smith
Director of Marketing: Heather Shelstad
Marketing Assistant: Cherron Gardner
Creative Design Director: Leslie Osher

Cover Design: Kathy Mrozek
Interior Designer: Anne DeMarinis
Director, Image Resource Center: Melinda Reo
Manager Visual Research: Beth Brenzel
Manager, Rights and Permissions: Zina Arabia
**Manager, Cover Visual Research and
  Permissions:** Karen Sanatar
Color Scanning Services: Joe Conti, Cory Skidds,
  Greg Harrison, Rob Uibelhoer, Ron Walko
Image Permission Coordinator: Michelina Viscusi
Compositor: Preparé, Inc.
Printer/Binder: Courier Companies, Inc.
Cover Printer: The Lehigh Press, Inc.
Cover Art: (top) Library of Congress, (bottom) Library of
  Congress, (rear) Library of Congress

Credits and acknowledgments borrowed from other sources and reproduced, with permission, in this textbook appear on appropiate page within text or on page C-1.

Pearson Education Ltd., London
Pearson Education Australia Pty., Limited, Sydney
Pearson Education Singapore, Pte., Ltd.
Pearson Education North Asia Ltd., Hong Kong

Pearson Education Canada, Ltd., Toronto
Pearson Educación de Mexico, S.A. de C.V.
Pearson Education — Japan, Tokyo
Pearson Education Malaysia, Pte., Ltd.

10 9 8 7 6 5 4 3 2

ISBN 0-13-193338-8
Revised Printing: ISBN 0-13-195128-9

To our students,
our sisters,
and our brothers

BRIEF CONTENTS

CONTENTS

1

A CONTINENT OF VILLAGES, TO 1500   2

2

WHEN WORLDS COLLIDE, 1492–1590   26

3

PLANTING COLONIES IN NORTH AMERICA, 1588–1701   48

4 SLAVERY AND EMPIRE, 1441–1770   70

5 THE CULTURES OF COLONIAL NORTH AMERICA, 1700–1780   100

6 FROM EMPIRE TO INDEPENDENCE, 1750–1776   130

VISUALIZING THE PAST
The Rattlesnake as a National Symbol   160

7

THE CREATION OF THE UNITED STATES, 1776–1786   162

AMERICAN COMMUNITIES: *A National Community Evolves
  at Valley Forge   164*

8

THE UNITED STATES OF NORTH AMERICA, 1786–1800   188

AMERICAN COMMUNITIES: *Mingo Creek Settlers Refuse to
  Pay the Whiskey Tax   190*

9

AN AGRARIAN REPUBLIC, 1790–1824   214

10

THE GROWTH OF DEMOCRACY, 1824–1840   242

11

THE SOUTH AND SLAVERY, 1790S–1830   272

12

INDUSTRY AND THE NORTH, 1790S–1840S   302

13

COMING TO TERMS WITH THE NEW AGE, 1820S–1850S   322

14

THE TERRITORIAL EXPANSION OF THE UNITED STATES, 1830S–1850S   346

15

THE COMING CRISIS, THE 1850S   372

16

THE CIVIL WAR, 1861–1865   400

VISUALIZING THE PAST

17

RECONSTRUCTION, 1863–1877   432

18

CONQUEST AND SURVIVAL, THE TRANS–MISSISSIPPI WEST, 1860–1900   466

VISUALIZING THE PAST
Mythologizing the "Wild West"   500

19

THE INCORPORATION OF AMERICA, 1865–1900   502

20

COMMONWEALTH AND EMPIRE, 1870–1900   530

21

URBAN AMERICA AND THE PROGRESSIVE ERA, 1900–1917   560

22

WORLD WAR I, 1914–1920   586

23

THE TWENTIES, 1920–1929   614

VISUALIZING THE PAST
Advertising and the Modern Woman   640

24

THE GREAT DEPRESSION AND THE NEW DEAL, 1929–1940   642

28

THE CIVIL RIGHTS MOVEMENT, 1945–1966   760

29

WAR ABROAD, WAR AT HOME, 1965–1974   790

VISUALIZING THE PAST
Iconic Images of the Vietnam Era 828

30

THE CONSERVATIVE ASCENDANCY, 1974–1987 830

31

TOWARD A TRANSNATIONAL AMERICA, SINCE 1988 864

MAPS

OVERVIEW TABLES

PREFACE

Out of Many: A History of the American People, offers a distinctive and timely approach to American history, highlighting the experiences of diverse communities of Americans in the unfolding story of our country. The stories of these communities offer a way of examining the complex historical forces shaping people's lives at various moments in our past. The debates and conflicts surrounding the most momentous issues in our national life—independence, emerging democracy, slavery, westward settlement, imperial expansion, economic depression, war, technological change—were largely worked out in the context of local communities. Through communities we focus on the persistent tensions between everyday life and those larger decisions and events that continually reshape the circumstances of local life. Each chapter opens with a description of a representative community. Some of these portraits feature American communities struggling with one another: African slaves and English masters on the rice plantations of colonial Georgia, or *Tejanos* and Americans during the Texas war of independence. Other chapters feature portraits of communities facing social change: the feminists of Seneca Falls, New York, in 1848, or the African Americans of Montgomery, Alabama, in 1955. As the story unfolds we find communities growing to include ever larger groups of Americans: the soldiers from every colony who forged the Continental Army into a patriotic national force at Valley Forge during the American Revolution, or the moviegoers who aspired to a collective dream of material prosperity and upward mobility during the 1920s.

Out of Many is also the only American history text with a truly continental perspective. With community vignettes from New England to the South, the Midwest to the far West, we encourage students to appreciate the great expanse of our nation. For example, a vignette of seventeenth-century Sante Fé , New Mexico, illustrates the founding of the first European settlements in the New World. We present territorial expansion into the American West from the viewpoint of the Mandan villagers of the upper Missouri River of North Dakota. We introduce the policies of the Reconstruction era through the experience of African Americans in Hale County, Alabama. A continental perspective drives home to students that American history has never been the preserve of any particular region.

In these ways *Out of Many* breaks new ground, but without compromising its coverage of the traditional turning points that we believe are critically important to an understanding of the American past. Among these watershed events are the Revolution and the struggle over the Constitution, the Civil War and Reconstruction, and the Great Depression and World War II. In *Out of Many*, however, we seek to integrate the narrative of national history with the story of the nation's many diverse communities. The Revolutionary and Constitutional period tested the ability of local communities to forge a new unity, and success depended on their ability to build a nation without compromising local identity. The Civil War and Reconstruction formed a second great test of the balance between the national ideas of the Revolution and the power of local and sectional communities. The Depression and the New Deal demonstrated the importance of local communities and the growing power of national institutions during the

greatest economic challenge in our history. *Out of Many* also looks back in a new and comprehensive way—from the vantage point of the beginning of a new century and the end of the cold war—at the salient events of the last fifty years and their impact on American communities. The community focus of *Out of Many* weaves the stories of the people and the nation into a single compelling narrative.

Out of Many includes expanded coverage of our diverse heritage. Our country is appropriately known as "a nation of immigrants," and the history of immigration to America, from the seventeenth to the twenty-first centuries, is fully integrated into the text. There is sustained and close attention to our place in the world, with special emphasis on our relations with the nations of the Western Hemisphere, especially our near neighbors, Canada and Mexico. In a completely new final chapter we consider the promises and the risks of American diversity in the new century. The statistical data has been completely updated with the results of the 2000 census. We have also incorporated new scholarship on the South, popular culture, science and technology, and the Cold War.

THE TEACHING AND LEARNING CLASSROOM EDITION

With each edition of *Out of Many* we have sought to strengthen its unique integration of the best of traditional American history with its innovative community-based focus and strong continental perspective. This new version is no exception. A wealth of special features and pedagogical aids reinforces our narrative and helps students grasp key issues.

NEW Single Column Design. The new **Teaching and Learning Classroom Edition** of *Out of Many* offers a new inviting look and format designed to provide an easy-to-read visual and textual learning experience.

NEW Pedagogical Support. The **Teaching and Learning Classroom Edition** introduces students to new pedagogical tools to help reinforce chapter content and provide easy access to important concepts for review.

- **Chapter-opening Questions.** These inquiry-based preview questions correspond to the major sections of the chapter and are repeated within the chapter with these sections to provide a roadmap for study and review.

- **Quick Reviews.** Found at key places within the margins of each chapter, these brief summaries of events and concepts provide an at-a-glance list of the important topics discussed in the text.

- **Marginal Glossary and Key Terms.** Within each chapter key terms are boldfaced in the text and repeated in the margin with a definition or description. A list of the key terms identified in the chapter is also provided at the end of the chapter.

- **Map Questions.** To stress the importance of map literacy and exploration, each map includes a question suitable for assignment that encourages students to fully review and analyze its content.

Community and Diversity. *Out of Many* opens with an introduction, titled "Community and Diversity," that acquaints students with the major themes of the book, providing them with a framework for understanding American history.

Map Explorations. Several maps in each chapter are highlighted and provided in an interactive format on the new *ONEKEY* website available with the text. They provide interactive exploration of key geographical, chronological, and thematic concepts to reinforce the content contained in the maps and the text. Students can access each map individually using the url provided with the map or find them within chapters when exploring the website.

Overview tables. Overview tables provide students with a summary of complex issues.

Graphs, charts, and tables. Every chapter includes one or more graphs, charts, or tables that help students understand important events and trends.

Photos and Illustrations. The abundant illustrations in *Out of Many*, include many that have never before been used in an American history text. None of the images is anachronistic—each one dates from the historical period under discussion. Extensive captions treat the images as visual primary source documents from the American past, describing their source and explaining their significance. In addition, each chapter opens with a stunning visual collage of images that relate to the chapter content and introduce students to the importance of visual documents in the study of history. An image key is included to place each image in its historical context.

Chronologies. A chronology at the end of each chapter helps students build a framework of key events.

Review Questions. Review questions at the end of chapters help students review, reinforce, and retain the material in each chapter and encourage them to relate the material to broader issues in American history.

Recommended Readings. The works in the short, annotated Recommended Reading list at the end of each chapter have been selected with the interested introductory student in mind.

TEACHING AND LEARNING CLASSROOM RESOURCES

In classrooms across the country, many instructors encounter students who perceive history as merely a jumble of names, dates, and events. *Out of Many* brings our dynamic past alive for these students with a text and accompanying print and multimedia classroom resources that combine sound scholarship, engaging narrative, and a rich array of cutting-edge pedagogical tools.

PRINT SUPPLEMENTS

INSTRUCTOR'S RESOURCE BINDER

New to this edition, this resource is a true time-saver in developing and preparing lecture presentation. The binder contains the full array of resources available for use in and out of the classroom, all organized by chapter. In addition, a copy of the *Instructor's Resource Center on CD-ROM* is included which provides electronic access to the print resources in the binder as well as all the maps, graphs, and illustrations from the text that can be easily downloaded for use in the classroom. Contents of the binder include:

- *Instructor's Resource Manual:* Contains chapter outlines, detailed chapter overviews, lecture topics, discussion questions, readings, and information about audio-visual resources.

- *Test Item File:* Offers more than 1,500 multiple-choice, identification, matching, true-false, and essay test questions and 10–15 questions per chapter on the maps found in each chapter. The guide includes a collection of blank maps that can be photocopied and used for map testing purposes or for other class exercises. In addition, there is a special file of questions on the interactive maps, primary source documents offered with the text, and *Exploring America* activities from the accompanying website.

- *Prentice Hall TestGenerator:* This commercial-quality computerized test management program, available for Windows and Macintosh environments, allows instructors to select items from the *Test Item File* and design their own exams.

- *Transparency Package:* Includes full-color transparency acetates of all the maps, charts, and graphs in the text for use in the classroom. Each transparency is accompanied by a page of descriptive material and discussion questions.

HISTORY NOTES, VOLUMES I AND II

History Notes is a new type of study aid that tests for each chapter that students can use to assess their level of understanding of chapter material. It includes identification terms, multiple-choice questions, short essay questions, and map questions. *History Notes* is available free when packaged with *Out of Many*.

DOCUMENTS SET, VOLUMES I AND II

This collection of more than 300 primary source documents directly relates to the themes and content of the text. Each document is approximately two pages long and includes a brief introduction and study questions intended to encourage students to analyze the document critically and relate it to the content of the text. The *Documents Set* is available at a substantial discount when packaged with *Out of Many*.

RETRIEVING THE AMERICAN PAST

Written and developed by leading historians and educators, this reader is an on-demand history database that offers 300 primary source documents on key topics in American History. Each module includes an introduction, several primary documents and secondary sources, follow-up questions, and recommendations for further reading. By deciding which modules to include and the order in which they will appear, instructors can compile a custom reader to fit their needs. Contact your local Prentice Hall representative for more information about this exciting custom publishing option.

MANY LIVES, MANY STORIES: BIOGRAPHIES IN AMERICAN HISTORY

This two-volume collection of sixty-two biographies in American history was written specifically to match the chapter sequence and themes of *Out of Many*. Introductions, pre-reading questions, suggested readings, and a special prologue about the role of biography in the study of American history enrich this important new supplement. Available free when packaged with *Out of Many*.

PRENTICE HALL'S *OneSearch* WITH *Research Navigator*™

This brief guide introduces students to tools for finding, evaluating and using resourcese on the internet. It includes a section of avoiding plagiarism and using sources effectively, tips for finding information related to history on the internet and for documenting electronic sources, and an access code to the *Research Navigator*™ website. *OneSearch* is available for free when packaged with *Out of Many*. Contact your local Prentice Hall representative for details.

PRENTICE HALL AND PENGUIN BUNDLE PROGRAM

Prentice Hall and Penguin are pleased to provide adopters of *Out of Many* with an opportunity to receive significant discounts when orders for *Out of Many* are bundled together with Penguin titles in American history. Please contact your local Prentice Hall representative for details.

MULTIMEDIA SUPPLEMENTS

U.S. HISTORY DOCUMENTS CD-ROM

Bound into every copy of *Out of Many* and organized according to the main periods in American History, this document CD-ROM contains over 300 primary source documents in an easily-navigated PDF file. Each document is accompanied by essay questions that can be answered via the CD-ROM or via a dedicated website.

OneKey

A unique online resource, *OneKey* lets you and your students access the many teaching and learning resources for *Out of Many* all in one place. For students, it means access to documents, quizzes, map explorations, interactive learning activities, video, audio, e-book portions of the text, and other pedagogical material organized by major sections within chapters to reinforce and apply what they are learning in class and from the text. For instructors, it means access to the student's resources, *and* all of the instructional material available to use in teaching with the text, including instructor's manual material, test questions from the test item file, additional documents for assignment, images, maps, charts, and graphs from the text, video and audio clips, and Powerpoint™ presentations and questions for use with *Personal Response* technology in the classroom. Access to this unique website is free to students when packaged with the text. For more information about this exciting new resource, contact your local Prentice Hall representative for a tour.

COMPANION WEBSITE™
www.prenhall.com/faragher

With the *Out of Many Companion Website*™ students can take full advantage of the Web in tandem with the text to enrich their study of American history. The *Companion Website*™ features chapter review tests, learning objectives, and study questions that students can use to assess their comprehension of chapter content.

INSTRUCTOR'S RESOURCE CENTER ON CD-ROM

This CDROM, like the OneKey website, includes all of the print supplements, multimedia resources, and images and art from *Out of Many*. It is provided in the *Instructor's Resource Binder*.

RESEARCH NAVIGATOR™

This unique resource helps your students make the most of their research time. From finding the right articles and journals, to citing sources, drafting and writing effective papers, and completing research assignments, **Research Navigator**™ simplifies and streamlines the entire process. Access to **Research Navigator**™ is available with every copy of the *OneSearch* guide and with the *OneKey* website. For more information, contact your local Prentice Hall representative.

ACKNOWLEDGMENTS

In the years it has taken to bring *Out of Many* from idea to reality and to improve it in successive editions, we have often been reminded that although writing history sometimes feels like isolated work, it actually involves a collective effort. We want to thank the dozens of people whose efforts have made the publication of this book possible.

We wish to thank our many friends at Prentice Hall for their efforts in creating this new Teaching and Learning Edition of *Out of Many*: Yolanda de Rooy, President; Charlyce Jones Owen, Editorial Director; Heather Shelstad, Director of Marketing; Leslie Osher, Creative Design Director; Randy Pettit, Production Editor; Anne DeMarinis and Kathy Mzorek, Interior and Cover Designers, and Martha Williams, Copy Editor.

Historians around the country greatly assisted us by reading and commenting on chapters for this and previous editions. We want to thank each of them for the commitment of their valuable time.

Each of us depended on a great deal of support and assistance with the research and writing that went into this book. We want to thank: Kathryn Abbott, Nan Boyd, Krista Comer, Jennifer Cote, Crista DeLuzio, Keith Edgerton, Carol Frost, Jesse Hoffnung Garskof, Pailin Gaither, Jane Gerhard, Todd Gernes, Mark Krasovic, Melani McAlister, Cristiane Mitchell, J. C. Mutchler, Keith Peterson, Alan Pinkham, Tricia Rose, Gina Rourke, Jessica Shubow, Gordon P. Utz, Jr., and Maura Young.

Our families and close friends have been supportive and ever so patient over the many years we have devoted to this project. But we want especially to thank Paul Buhle, Meryl Fingrutd, Bob Greene, and Michele Hoffnung.

ABOUT THE AUTHORS

Chris Freitag

John Mack Faragher

John Mack Faragher is Arthur Unobskey Professor of American History and Director of the Howard R. Lamar Center for the Study of Frontiers and Borders at Yale University. Born in Arizona and raised in southern California, he received his B.A. at the University of California, Riverside, and his Ph.D. at Yale University. He is the author of *Women and Men on the Overland Trail* (1979), which won the Frederick Jackson Turner Award of the Organization of American Historians, *Sugar Creek: Life on the Illinois Prairie* (1986), *Daniel Boone: The Life and Legend of an American Pioneer* (1992), and (with Robert V. Hine) *The American West: A New Interpretive History* (2000).

Mari Jo Buhle

Mari Jo Buhle is William R. Kenan Jr. University Professor and Professor of American Civilization and History at Brown University, specializing in American women's history. She received her B.A. from the University of Illinois, Urbana–Champaign, and her Ph.D. from the University of Wisconsin, Madison. She is the author of *Women and American Socialism, 1870–1920* (1981) and *Feminism and Its Discontents: A Century of Struggle with Psychoanalysis* (1998). She is also coeditor of *Encyclopedia of the American Left*, second edition (1998). Professor Buhle held a fellowship (1991–1996) from the John D. and Catherine T. MacArthur Foundation.

Daniel Czitrom

Daniel Czitrom is Professor of History at Mount Holyoke College. Born and raised in New York City, he received his B.A. from the State University of New York at Binghamton and his M.A. and Ph.D. from the University of Wisconsin, Madison. He is the author of *Media and the American Mind: From Morse to McLuhan* (1982), which won the First Books Award of the American Historical Association and has been translated into Spanish and Chinese. He has served as a historical consultant and a featured on-camera commentator for several documentary film projects, including two recent PBS series, *New York: A Documentary Film* and *American Photography: A Century of Images.*

Susan H. Armitage

Susan H. Armitage is Claudius O. and Mary R. Johnson Distinguished Professor of History at Washington State University. She earned her Ph.D. from the London School of Economics and Political Science. Among her many publications on western women's history are three coedited books, *The Women's West* (1987), *So Much To Be Done: Women on the Mining and Ranching Frontier* (1991), and *Writing the Range: Race, Class, and Culture in the Women's West* (1997). She currently serves as an editor of a series of books on women and American history for the University of Illinois Press. She is the editor of *Frontiers: A Journal of Women's Studies.*

COMMUNITY & DIVERSITY

One of the most characteristic features of our country has always been its astounding variety. The American people include the descendants of native Indians, colonial Europeans, Africans, and migrants from virtually every country and continent. Indeed, as we enter a new century the United States is absorbing a flood of immigrants from Latin America and Asia that rivals the great tide of people from eastern and southern Europe one hundred years ago. What's more, our country is one of the world's most spacious, incorporating more than 3.6 million square miles of territory. The struggle to meld a single nation out of our many far-flung communities is what much of American history is all about. That is the story told in this book.

Every human society is made up of communities. A community is a set of relationships linking men, women, and their families to a coherent social whole that is more than the sum of its parts. In a community people develop the capacity for unified action. In a community people learn, often through trial and error, how to transform and adapt to their environment. The sentiment that binds the members of a community together is the mother of group identity and ethnic pride. In the making of history, communities are far more important than even the greatest of leaders, for the community is the institution most capable of passing a distinctive historical tradition to future generations.

Communities bind people together in multiple ways. They can be as small as local neighborhoods, in which people maintain face-to-face relations, or as large as the nation itself. This book examines American history from the perspective of community life—an ever-widening frame that has included larger and larger groups of Americans.

Networks of kinship and friendship, and connections across generations and among families, establish the bonds essential to community life. Shared feelings about values and history establish the basis for common identity. In communities, people find the power to act collectively in their own interest. But American communities frequently took shape as a result of serious conflicts among groups, and within communities there has often been significant fighting among competing groups or classes. Thus the term community, as we use it here, includes tension and discord as well as harmony and agreement.

For years there have been persistent laments about the "loss of community" in modern America. But community has not disappeared—it is continually being reinvented. Until the late eighteenth century, community was defined primarily by space and local geography. But in the nineteenth century communities began to be reshaped by new and powerful historical forces such as the marketplace, industrialization, the corporation, mass immigration, mass media, and the growth of the nation-state. In the twentieth century, Americans have struggled to balance commitments to several communities simultaneously. These were defined not simply by local spatial arrangements, but by categories as varied as racial and ethnic groups, occupations, political affiliations, and consumer preferences.

The "American Communities" vignettes that open each chapter reflect this shift. Most of the vignettes in the pre–Civil War chapters focus on geographically defined communities, such as the ancient Indian city at Cahokia, or the experiment in industrial urban planning in early nineteenth-century Lowell, Massachusetts. In the post–Civil War chapters different and more modern kinds of communities make their appearance. In the 1920s, movies and radio offered a new kind of community—a community of identification with dreams of freedom, material success, upward mobility, youth and beauty. In the 1950s, rock'n'roll music helped germinate a new national community of teenagers, with profound effects on the culture of the entire country in the second half of the twentieth century. In the late 1970s, fear of nuclear accidents like the one at Three Mile Island brought concerned citizens together in communities around the country and produced a national movement opposing nuclear power.

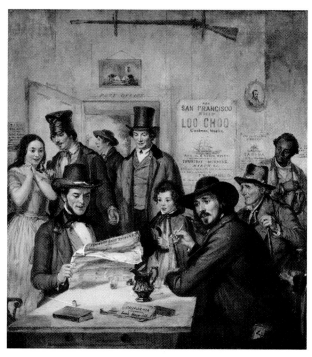

William Sidney Mount (1807–1868) *California News* 1850. Oil on canvas. The Long Island Museum of American Art, History and Carriages. Gift of Mr. and Mrs. Ward Melville, 1955.

The title for our book was suggested by the Latin phrase selected by John Adams, Benjamin Franklin, and Thomas Jefferson for the Great Seal of the United States: E *Pluribus Unum*—"Out of Many Comes Unity." These men understood that unity could not be imposed by a powerful central authority but had to develop out of mutual respect among Americans of different backgrounds. The revolutionary leadership expressed the hope that such respect could grow on the basis of a remarkable proposition: "We hold these truths to be self-evident, that all men are created equal; that they are endowed by their Creator with certain unalienable rights; that among these are life, liberty, and the pursuit of happiness." The national government of the United States would preserve local and state authority but would guarantee individual rights. The nation would be strengthened by guarantees of difference.

"Out of Many"—that is the promise of America, and the premise of this book. The underlying dialectic of American history, we believe, is that as a people we need to locate our national unity in the celebration of the differences that exist among us; these differences can be our strength, as long as we affirm the promise of the Declaration. Protecting the "right to be different," in other words, is absolutely fundamental to the continued existence of democracy, and that right is best protected by the existence of strong and vital communities. We are bound together as a nation by the ideal of local and cultural differences protected by our common commitment to the values of our Revolution.

Today those values are endangered by terrorists using the tactics of mass terror. In the wake of the September 11, 2001, attack on the United States, and with the continuing threat of biological, chemical, or even nuclear assaults, Americans can not afford to lose faith in our historic vision. The United States is a multicultural and transnational society. The thousands of victims buried in the smoking ruins of the World Trade Center included people from dozens of different ethnic and national groups. We must fight to protect and defend the promise of our diverse nation.

Our history shows that the promise of American unity has always been problematic. Centrifugal forces have been powerful in the American past, and at times the country has seemed about to fracture into its component parts. Our transformation from a collection of groups and regions into a nation has been marked by painful and often violent struggles. Our past is filled with conflicts between Indians and colonists, masters and slaves, Patriots and Loyalists, Northerners and

Harvey Dinnerstein, *Underground, Together* 1996, oil on canvas, 90" x 107". Photograph courtesy of Gerold Wunderlich & Co., New York, NY.

Southerners, Easterners and Westerners, capitalists and workers, and sometimes the government and the people. War can bring out our best, but it can also bring out our worst. During World War II thousands of Japanese American citizens were deprived of their rights and locked up in isolated detention centers simply because of their ethnic background. Americans often appear to be little more than a contentious collection of peoples with conflicting interests, divided by region and background, race and class.

Our most influential leaders have also sometimes suffered a crisis of faith in the American project of "liberty and justice for all." Thomas Jefferson not only believed in the inferiority of African Americans, but he feared that immigrants from outside the Anglo-American tradition might "warp and bias" the development of the nation "and render it a heterogeneous, incoherent, distracted mass." We have not always lived up to the American promise, and there is a dark side to our history. It took the bloodiest war in American history to secure the human rights of African Americans, and the struggle for full equality for all our citizens has yet to be won. During the great influx of immigrants in the early twentieth century, fears much like Jefferson—s led to movements to Americanize the foreign born by forcing them, in the words of one leader, "to give up the languages, customs, and methods of life which they have brought with them across the ocean, and adopt instead the language, habits, and customs of this country, and the general standards and ways of American living." Similar thinking motivated Congress at various times to bar the immigration of Africans, Asians, and other ethnic groups and people of color into the country, and to force assimilation on American Indians by denying them the freedom to practice their religion or even to speak their own language. Such calls for restrictive unity still resound in our own day.

But other Americans have argued for a more fulsome version of Americanization. "What is the American, this new man?" asked the French immigrant Michel Crèvecoeur in 1782. "A strange mixture of blood which you will find in no other country." In America, he wrote, "individuals of all nations are melted into a new race of men." A century later Crèvecoeur was echoed by historian Frederick Jackson Turner, who believed that "in the crucible of the frontier, the immigrants were Americanized, liberated, and fused into a mixed race, English in neither nationality nor characteristics. The process has gone on from the early days to our own."

The process by which diverse communities have come to share a set of common American values is one of the most fundamental aspects of our history. It did not occur, however, because of compulsory Americanization programs, but because of free public education, popular participation in democratic politics, and the impact of popular culture. Contemporary America does have a common culture: We share a commitment to freedom of thought and expression, we join in the aspirations to own our own homes and send our children to college, we laugh at the same television programs.

To a degree that too few Americans appreciate, this common culture resulted from a complicated process of mutual discovery that took place when different ethnic and regional groups encountered one another. Consider just one small and unique aspect of our culture: the barbecue. Americans have been barbecuing since before the beginning of written history. Early settlers adopted this technique of cooking from the Indians—the word itself comes from a native term for a framework of sticks over a fire on which meat was slowly cooked. Colonists typically barbecued pork, fed on Indian corn. African slaves lent their own touch by introducing the use of hot sauces. The ritual that is a part of nearly every American family's Fourth of July silently celebrates the heritage of diversity that went into making our common culture.

The American educator John Dewey recognized this diversity early in the last century. "The genuine American, the typical American, is himself a hyphenated character," he declared, "international and interracial in his make-up." The point about our "hyphenated character," Dewey believed, "is to see to it that the hyphen connects instead of separates." We, the authors of *Out of Many*, share Dewey's perspective on American history. "Creation comes from the impact of diversity," wrote the American philosopher Horace Kallen. We also endorse Kallen's vision of the American promise: "A democracy of nationalities, cooperating voluntarily and autonomously through common institutions, . . . a multiplicity in a unity, an orchestration of mankind." And now, let the music begin.

Thomas Satterwhite Noble, *Last Sale of Slaves on the Courthouse Steps*, 1860, oil on canvas, Missouri Historical Society.

The war passed from words to stones which the white children began to hurl at the colored. Several colored children were hurt and, as they had not resented the rock throwing . . . , the white children became more aggressive and abusive.

— *T. Thomas Fortune, from* Norfolk Journal and Guide, *1866*

Mississippi Freedman School, 1866. Noon at the primary school for Freedmen at Vicksburg, Mississippi.

17

RECONSTRUCTION
1863–1877

WHAT WAS Lincoln's vision of Reconstruction in the South?

WHAT WERE the most important changes in the lives of African Americans in the years immediately following the war?

WHAT MAJOR groups made up the Southern Republicans?

WHAT PRECIPITATED the electoral crisis of 1876?

AMERICAN COMMUNITIES

Hale County, Alabama: From Slavery to Freedom in a Black Belt Community

ON A BRIGHT SATURDAY MORNING IN MAY 1867, 4,000 FORMER slaves eagerly streamed into the town of Greensboro, bustling seat of Hale County in west-central Alabama. They came to hear speeches from two delegates to a recent freedmen's convention in Mobile and to find out about the political status of black people under the Reconstruction Act just passed by Congress. Tensions mounted in the days following this unprecedented gathering as military authorities began supervising voter registration for elections to the upcoming constitutional convention that would rewrite the laws of Alabama. On June 13, John Orrick, a local white, confronted Alex Webb, a politically active freedman, on the streets of Greensboro. Webb had recently been appointed a voter registrar for the district. Orrick swore he would never be registered by a black man and shot Webb dead. Hundreds of armed and angry freedmen formed a posse to search for Orrick but failed to find him. Galvanized by Webb's murder, 500 local freedmen formed a chapter of the Union League, the Republican Party's organizational arm in the South. The chapter functioned as both a militia company and a forum to agitate for political rights.

Violent political encounters between black people and white people were common in Southern communities in the wake of the Civil War. The war had destroyed slavery and the Confederacy but left the political and economic status of newly emancipated African Americans unresolved. Communities throughout the South struggled over the meaning of freedom in ways that reflected their particular circumstances. The 4 million freed people constituted roughly one-third of the total Southern population, but the black–white ratio in individual communities varied enormously. In some places the Union army had been a strong presence during the war, hastening the collapse of the slave system and encouraging experiments in free labor. Other areas had remained relatively untouched by the fighting. In some areas small farms prevailed; in others, including Hale County, large plantations dominated economic and political life.

West-central Alabama had emerged as a fertile center of cotton production just two decades before the Civil War. There, African Americans, as throughout the South's black belt, constituted more than three-quarters of the population. The region was virtually untouched by fighting until the very end of the Civil War. But with the arrival of federal troops in the spring of 1865, African Americans in Hale County, like their counterparts elsewhere, began to challenge the traditional organization of plantation labor.

One owner, Henry Watson, found that his entire work force had deserted him at the end of 1865. "I am in the midst of a large and fertile cotton growing country," Watson wrote to a

partner. "Many plantations are entirely without labor, many plantations have insufficient labor, and upon none are the laborers doing their former accustomed work." Black women refused to work in the fields, preferring to stay home with their children and tend garden plots. Nor would male field hands do any work, such as caring for hogs, that did not directly increase their share of the cotton crop.

Above all, freed people wanted more autonomy. Overseers and owners, thus, grudgingly allowed them to work the land "in families," letting them choose their own supervisors and find their own provisions. The result was a shift from the gang labor characteristic of the antebellum period, in which large groups of slaves worked under the harsh and constant supervision of white overseers, to the sharecropping system, in which African American families worked small plots of land in exchange for a small share of the crop. This shift represented less of a victory for newly freed African Americans than a defeat for plantation owners, who resented even the limited economic independence it forced them to concede to their black work force.

Only a small fraction—perhaps 15 percent—of African American families were fortunate enough to be able to buy land. The majority settled for some version of sharecropping, while others managed to rent land from owners, becoming tenant farmers. Still, planters throughout Hale County had to change the old routines of plantation labor. Local African Americans also organized politically. In 1866 Congress had passed the Civil Rights Act and sent the Fourteenth Amendment to the Constitution to the states for ratification; both promised full citizenship rights to former slaves. Hale County freedmen joined the Republican Party and local Union League chapters. They used their new political power to press for better labor contracts, demand greater autonomy for the black work force, and agitate for the more radical goal of land confiscation and redistribution. "The colored people are very anxious to get land of their own to live upon independently; and they want money to buy stock to make crops," reported one black Union League organizer. "The only way to get these necessaries is to give our votes to the [Republican] party . . . making every effort possible to bring these blessings about by reconstructing the State." Two Hale County former slaves, Brister Reese and James K. Green, won election to the Alabama state legislature in 1869.

It was not long before these economic and political gains prompted a white counterattack. In the spring of 1868, the Ku Klux Klan—a secret organization devoted to terrorizing and intimidating African Americans and their white Republican allies—came to Hale

Greensboro

County. *Disguised in white sheets, armed with guns and whips, and making nighttime raids on horseback, Klansmen flogged, beat, and murdered freed people. They intimidated voters and silenced political activists. Planters used Klan terror to dissuade former slaves from leaving plantations or organizing for higher wages.*

With the passage of the Ku Klux Klan Act in 1871, the federal government cracked down on the Klan, breaking its power temporarily in parts of the former Confederacy. But no serious effort was made to stop Klan terror in the west Alabama black belt, and planters there succeeded in reestablishing much of their social and political control.

The events in Hale County illustrate the struggles that beset communities throughout the South during the Reconstruction era after the Civil War. The destruction of slavery and the Confederacy forced African Americans and white people to renegotiate their old economic and political roles. These community battles both shaped and were shaped by the victorious and newly expansive federal government in Washington. In the end, Reconstruction was only partially successful. Not until the "Second Reconstruction" of the twentieth-century civil rights movement would the descendants of Hale County's African Americans begin to enjoy the full fruits of freedom—and even then not without challenge.

THE POLITICS OF RECONSTRUCTION

When General Robert E. Lee's men stacked their guns at Appomattox, the bloodiest war in American history ended. Although President Abraham Lincoln insisted early on that the purpose of the war was to preserve the Union, by 1863 it had evolved as well into a struggle for African American liberation. Indeed, the political, economic, and moral issues posed by slavery were the root cause of the Civil War, and the war ultimately destroyed slavery, although not racism, once and for all.

The Civil War also settled the Constitutional crisis provoked by the secession of the Confederacy and its justification in appeals to states' rights. The name "United States" would from now on be understood as a singular rather than a plural noun, signaling an important change in the meaning of American nationality. The old notion of the United States as a voluntary union of sovereign states gave way to the new reality of a single nation in which the federal government took precedence over the individual states.

WHAT WAS Lincoln's vision of Reconstruction in the South?

THE DEFEATED SOUTH

The white South paid an extremely high price for secession, war, and defeat. In addition to the battlefield casualties, the Confederate states sustained deep material and psychological wounds. Much of the best agricultural land lay waste. Many towns and cities—including Richmond, Atlanta, and Columbia, South Carolina—were in ruins. By 1865, the South's most precious commodities, cotton and African American slaves, were no longer measures of wealth and prestige. Retreating Confederates destroyed most of the South's cotton to prevent its capture by federal troops. What remained was confiscated by Union agents as contraband of war. The former slaves, many of whom had fled to Union lines during the latter stages of the war, were determined to chart their own course in the reconstructed South as free men and women.

It would take the South's economy a generation to overcome the severe blows dealt by the war. In 1860 the South held roughly 25 percent of the nation's wealth; a decade later it controlled only 12 percent.

Many white Southerners resented their conquered status, and white notions of race, class, and "honor" died hard. A white North Carolinian, for example, who had lost almost everything dear to him in the war—his sons, home, and slaves—recalled in 1865 that in spite of all his tragedy he still retained one thing. "They've

16–2
Carl Schurz, Report on the Condition of the South (1865)

IMAGE KEY

for pages 432–433

a. A young African American boy with new clothes and a book provided by the Freedmen's Bureau.

b. Rocks and stones like those used to hurl at slaves.

c. A colored engraving (1866) depicting noon at the primary school for Freedmen at Vicksburg, Mississippi.

d. Two members of the Ku Klux Klan holding guns and wearing hoods and long robes, pictured in *Harper's Weekly*.

e. Pages 44 and 45 from the New England primer show the religious content of the work.

f. The dead at Gettysburg were strewn across the battlefield.

g. Freedmen (freed black slaves) vote in 1867 while standing in line. The Stars and Stripes hang overhead.

h. Three white men decry the Reconstruction Acts of Congress as "usurpations and unconstitutional, revolutionary, and void" while clasping hands above the fallen body of a black man.

i. The "tramp" became a symbol of the misery caused by industrial depression as seen in this *Harper's Weekly* illustration, "The Tramp," September 2, 1876.

16–9
The Nation, "The State of the South" (1872)

"Decorating the Graves of Rebel Soldiers," *Harper's Weekly*, August 17, 1867. After the Civil War, both Southerners and Northerners created public mourning ceremonies honoring fallen soldiers. Women led the memorial movement in the South which, by establishing cemeteries and erecting monuments, offered the first cultural expression of the Confederate tradition. This engraving depicts citizens of Richmond, Virginia, decorating thousands of Confederate graves with flowers at the Hollywood Memorial Cemetery on the James River. A local women's group raised enough funds to transfer over 16,000 Confederate dead from Northern cemeteries for reburial in Richmond.

The Granger Collection (4E1090.99)

left me one inestimable privilege—to hate 'em. I git up at half-past four in the morning, and sit up till twelve at night, to hate 'em."

Emancipation proved the most bitter pill for white Southerners to swallow, especially the planter elite. Conquered and degraded, and in their view robbed of their slave property, white people responded by regarding African Americans more than ever as inferior to themselves. Emancipation, however, forced white people to redefine their world. The specter of political power and social equality for African Americans made racial order the consuming passion of most white Southerners during the Reconstruction years. In fact, racism can be seen as one of the major forces driving Reconstruction and, ultimately, undermining it.

ABRAHAM LINCOLN'S PLAN

By late 1863, Union military victories had convinced President Lincoln of the need to fashion a plan for the reconstruction of the South (see Chapter 16). Lincoln based his reconstruction program on bringing the seceded states back into the Union as quickly as possible. His Proclamation of Amnesty and Reconstruction of December 1863 offered "full pardon" and the restoration of property, not including slaves, to white Southerners willing to swear an oath of allegiance to the United States and its laws, including the Emancipation Proclamation. Prominent Confederate military and civil leaders were excluded from Lincoln's offer, though he indicated that he would freely pardon them.

The president also proposed that when the number of any Confederate state's voters who took the oath of allegiance reached 10 percent of the number who had voted in the election of 1860, this group could establish a state government that Lincoln would recognize as legitimate. Fundamental to this Ten Percent Plan was acceptance by the reconstructed governments of the abolition of slavery. Lincoln's plan was designed less as a blueprint for reconstruction than as a way to shorten the war and gain white people's support for emancipation.

Lincoln's amnesty proclamation angered those Republicans—known as **Radical Republicans**—who advocated not only equal rights for the freedmen, but also a tougher stance toward the white South. In July 1864, Senator Benjamin F. Wade of Ohio and Congressman Henry W. Davis of Maryland, both Radicals, proposed a harsher alternative to the Ten Percent Plan. The Wade-Davis bill required 50 percent of a seceding state's white male citizens to take a loyalty oath before elections could be held for a convention to rewrite the state's constitution. The Radical Republicans saw reconstruction as a chance to effect a fundamental transformation of Southern society. They thus wanted to delay the process until war's end and to limit participation to a small number of Southern Unionists. Lincoln viewed Reconstruction as part of the larger effort to win the war and abolish slavery. He wanted to weaken the Confederacy by creating new state governments that could win broad support from Southern white people. The Wade-Davis bill threatened his efforts to build political consensus within the Southern states, and Lincoln, therefore, pocket-vetoed it, by refusing to sign it within ten days of the adjournment of Congress.

As Union armies occupied parts of the South, commanders had improvised a variety of arrangements involving confiscated plantations and the African American labor force. For example, in 1862 General Benjamin F. Butler began a policy of transforming slaves on Louisiana sugar plantations into wage laborers under the close supervision of occupying federal troops. Butler's policy required slaves to remain on the estates of loyal planters, where they would receive wages according to a fixed schedule, as well as food and medical care for the aged and sick. Abandoned plantations would be leased to Northern investors.

In January 1865, General William T. Sherman issued Special **Field Order 15**, setting aside the Sea Islands off the Georgia coast and a portion of the South Carolina low-country rice fields for the exclusive settlement of freed people. Each family would receive forty acres of land and the loan of mules from the army—the origin, perhaps, of the famous call for "forty acres and a mule" that would soon capture the imagination of African Americans throughout the South. Sherman's intent was not to revolutionize Southern society but to relieve the demands placed on his army by the thousands of impoverished African Americans who followed his march to the sea. By the summer of 1865 some 40,000 freed people, eager to take advantage of the general's order, had been settled on 400,000 acres of "Sherman land."

Conflicts within the Republican Party prevented the development of a systematic land distribution program. Still, Lincoln and the Republican Congress supported other measures to aid the emancipated slaves. In March 1865 Congress established the **Freedmen's Bureau**. Along with providing food, clothing, and fuel to destitute former slaves, the bureau was charged with supervising and managing "all the abandoned lands in the South and the control of all subjects relating to refugees and freedmen." The act that established the bureau also stated that forty acres of abandoned or confiscated land could be leased to freed slaves or white Unionists, who would have an option to purchase after three years and "such title thereto as the United States can convey."

Radical Republicans   A shifting group of Republican congressmen, usually a substantial minority, who favored the abolition of slavery from the beginning of the Civil War and later advocated harsh treatment of the defeated South.

Field Order 15   Order by General William T. Sherman in January 1865 to set aside abandoned land along the southern Atlantic coast for forty-acre grants to freedmen; rescinded by President Andrew Johnson later that year.

Freedmen's Bureau   Agency established by Congress in March 1865 to provide social, educational, and economic services, advice, and protection to former slaves and destitute whites; lasted seven years.

On April 14, 1865, while attending the theater in Washington, President Lincoln was shot by John Wilkes Booth. At the time of his assassination, Lincoln's reconstruction policy remained unsettled and incomplete. In its broad outlines the president's plans had seemed to favor a speedy restoration of the Southern states to the Union and a minimum of federal intervention in their affairs. But with his death the specifics of postwar Reconstruction had to be hammered out by a new president, Andrew Johnson of Tennessee, a man whose personality, political background, and racist leanings put him at odds with the Republican-controlled Congress.

ANDREW JOHNSON AND PRESIDENTIAL RECONSTRUCTION

Andrew Johnson, a Democrat and former slaveholder, was a most unlikely successor to the martyred Lincoln. By trade a tailor, educated by his wife, Johnson overcame his impoverished background and served as state legislator, governor, and U.S. senator. Throughout his career Johnson had championed yeoman farmers and viewed the South's plantation aristocrats with contempt.

In 1864 the Republicans, in an appeal to Northern and border state "War Democrats," nominated Johnson for vice president. But despite Johnson's success in Tennessee and in the 1864 campaign, many Radical Republicans distrusted him. In the immediate aftermath of Lincoln's murder, however, Johnson appeared to side with those Radical Republicans who sought to treat the South as a conquered province. But support for Johnson quickly faded as the new president's policies unfolded. Johnson defined Reconstruction as the province of the executive, not the legislative branch, and he planned to restore the Union as quickly as possible. He blamed individual Southerners—the planter elite—rather than entire states for leading the South down the disastrous road to secession.

In the spring of 1865 Johnson granted amnesty and pardon, including restoration of property rights except slaves, to all Confederates who pledged loyalty to the Union and support for emancipation. Fourteen classes of Southerners, mostly major Confederate officials and wealthy landowners, were excluded. But these men could apply individually for presidential pardons. During his tenure Johnson pardoned roughly 90 percent of those who applied. Significantly, he instituted this plan while Congress was not in session. Johnson also appointed provisional governors for seven of the former Confederate states and set highly favorable terms for readmission in the Union. By the fall of 1865 ten of the eleven Confederate states claimed to have met Johnson's requirements to reenter the Union.

Andrew Johnson used the term "restoration" rather than "reconstruction." A lifelong Democrat with ambitions to be elected president on his own in 1868, Johnson hoped to build a new political coalition composed of Northern Democrats, conservative Republicans, and Southern Unionists. Firmly committed to white supremacy, he opposed political rights for the freedmen. Johnson's open sympathy for his fellow white Southerners, his antiblack bias, and his determination to control the course of Reconstruction placed him on a collision course with the powerful Radical wing of the Republican Party.

THE RADICAL REPUBLICAN VISION

Most Radicals were men whose careers had been shaped by the slavery controversy. At the core of their thinking lay a deep belief in equal political rights and equal economic opportunity, both guaranteed by a powerful national government.

QUICK REVIEW

Johnson's Reconstruction Plan

- Johnson extended pardons to Southerners who swore an oath of allegiance.
- He restored property rights to Southerners who swore an oath of allegiance.
- His plan had nothing to say about the voting and civil rights of former slaves.

THE FIFTEENTH AMENDMENT

"The Fifteenth Amendment," 1870. The Fifteenth Amendment, ratified in 1870, stipulated that the right to vote could not be denied "on account of race, color, or previous condition of servitude." This illustration expressed the optimism and hopes of African Americans generated by this Constitutional landmark aimed at protecting black political rights. Note the various political figures (Abraham Lincoln, John Brown, Frederick Douglass) and movements (abolitionism, black education) invoked here, providing a sense of how the amendment culminated a long historical struggle.

Courtesy of the Library of Congress

They argued that once free labor, universal education, and equal rights were implanted in the South, that region would be able to share in the North's material wealth, progress, and fluid social mobility.

In the Radicals' view, the power of the federal government would be central to the remaking of Southern society, especially in guaranteeing civil rights and suffrage for freedmen. In the most far-reaching proposal, Representative Thaddeus Stevens of Pennsylvania called for the confiscation of 400 million acres belonging to the wealthiest 10 percent of Southerners to be redistributed to black and white yeomen and Northern land buyers. "The whole fabric of Southern society must be changed," Stevens told Pennsylvania Republicans in September 1865, "and never can it be done if this opportunity is lost. How can republican institutions, free schools, free churches, free social intercourse exist in a mingled community of nabobs and serfs? If the South is ever to be made a safe republic let her lands be cultivated by the toil of the owners."

Northern Republicans were especially outraged by the stringent "**black codes**" passed by South Carolina, Mississippi, Louisiana, and other states. These were designed to restrict the freedom of the black labor force and keep freed people as close to slave status as possible. Laborers who left their jobs before contracts expired would forfeit wages already earned and be subject to arrest by any white citizen. Vagrancy, very broadly defined, was punishable by fines and involuntary plantation labor. Apprenticeship clauses obliged black children to work without pay for employers. Some states attempted to bar African Americans from land ownership. Other laws specifically denied African Americans equality with white people in civil rights, excluding them from juries and prohibiting interracial marriages.

The black codes underscored the unwillingness of white Southerners to accept the full meaning of freedom for African Americans. The Radicals, although not a majority of their party, were joined by moderate Republicans as growing numbers of Northerners grew suspicious of white Southern intransigence

16–4
Mississippi Black Code (1865)

16–3
Clinton B. Fisk, Plain Counsels for Freedmen (1865)

Black codes Laws passed by states and municipalities denying many rights of citizenship to free black people before the Civil War.

and the denial of political rights to freedmen. When the Thirty-ninth Congress convened in December 1865, the large Republican majority prevented the seating of the white Southerners elected to Congress under President Johnson's provisional state governments. Republicans also established the Joint Committee on Reconstruction. After hearing extensive testimony from a broad range of witnesses, it concluded that not only were old Confederates back in power in the South, but also that black codes and racial violence required increased protection for African Americans.

As a result, in the spring of 1866, Congress passed two important bills designed to aid African Americans. The landmark Civil Rights bill, which bestowed full citizenship on African Americans, overturned the 1857 *Dred Scott* decision and the black codes. It defined all persons born in the United States (except Indian peoples) as national citizens, and it enumerated various rights, including the rights to make and enforce contracts, to sue, to give evidence, and to buy and sell property. Under this bill, African Americans acquired "full and equal benefit of all laws and proceedings for the security of person and property as is enjoyed by white citizens."

Congress also voted to enlarge the scope of the Freedmen's Bureau, empowering it to build schools and pay teachers, and also to establish courts to prosecute those charged with depriving African Americans of their civil rights. The bureau achieved important, if limited, success in aiding African Americans. Bureau-run schools helped lay the foundation for Southern public education. The bureau's network of courts allowed freed people to bring suits against white people in disputes involving violence, nonpayment of wages, or unfair division of crops. The very existence of courts hearing public testimony by African Americans provided an important psychological challenge to traditional notions of white racial domination.

An angry President Johnson vetoed both of these bills. But his intemperate attacks on the Radicals—he damned them as traitors unwilling to restore the Union—united moderate and Radical Republicans and they succeeded in overriding the vetoes. Congressional Republicans, led by the Radical faction, were now unified in challenging the president's power to direct Reconstruction and in using national authority to define and protect the rights of citizens.

In June 1866, fearful that the **Civil Rights Act** might be declared unconstitutional and eager to settle the basis for the seating of Southern representatives, Congress passed the Fourteenth Amendment. The amendment defined national citizenship to include former slaves ("all persons born or naturalized in the United States") and prohibited the states from violating the privileges of citizens without due process of law. It also empowered Congress to reduce the representation of any state that denied the suffrage to males over twenty-one. Republicans adopted the Fourteenth Amendment as their platform for the 1866 congressional elections and suggested that Southern states would have to ratify it as a condition of readmission. President Johnson, meanwhile, took to the stump in August to support conservative Democratic and Republican candidates. His unrestrained speeches often degenerated into harangues, alienating many voters and aiding the Republican cause.

For their part, the Republicans began an effective campaign tradition known as "waving the bloody shirt"—reminding Northern voters of the hundreds of thousands of Yankee soldiers left dead or maimed by the war. In the November 1866 elections, the Republicans increased their majority in both the House and the Senate and gained control of all the Northern states. The stage was now set for a battle between the president and Congress. Was it to be Johnson's "restoration" or **Congressional Reconstruction**?

16–7
The Fourteenth Amendment (1868)

Civil Rights Act 1866 act that gave full citizenship to African Americans.

Congressional Reconstruction Name given to the period 1867–1870 when the Republican-dominated Congress controlled Reconstruction-era policy.

CONGRESSIONAL RECONSTRUCTION AND THE IMPEACHMENT CRISIS

United against Johnson, Radical and moderate Republicans took control of Reconstruction early in 1867. In March, Congress passed the first **Reconstruction Act** over Johnson's veto. This act divided the South into five military districts subject to martial law. To achieve restoration, Southern states were first required to call new constitutional conventions, elected by universal manhood suffrage. Once these states had drafted new constitutions, guaranteed African American voting rights, and ratified the Fourteenth Amendment, they were eligible for readmission to the Union.

Congress also passed several laws aimed at limiting Johnson's power. One of these, the **Tenure of Office Act**, stipulated that any officeholder appointed by the president with the Senate's advice and consent could not be removed until the Senate had approved a successor. In this way, congressional leaders could protect Republicans, such as Secretary of War Edwin M. Stanton, entrusted with implementing Congressional Reconstruction. In August 1867, with Congress adjourned, Johnson suspended Stanton and appointed General Ulysses S. Grant interim secretary of war. This move enabled the president to remove generals in the field that he judged to be too radical and replace them with men who were sympathetic to his own views. It also served as a challenge to the Tenure of Office Act. In January 1868, when the Senate overruled Stanton's suspension, Grant broke openly with Johnson and vacated the office. Stanton resumed his position and barricaded himself in his office when Johnson attempted to remove him once again.

Outraged by Johnson's relentless obstructionism, and seizing upon his violation of the Tenure of Office Act as a pretext, radical and moderate Republicans in the House of Representatives again joined forces and voted to impeach the president by a vote of 126 to 47 on February 24, 1868, charging him with eleven counts of high crimes and misdemeanors. To ensure the support of moderate Republicans, the articles of impeachment focused on violations of the Tenure of Office Act, leaving unstated the Republicans' real reasons for wanting the president removed: Johnson's political views and his opposition to the Reconstruction Acts.

An influential group of moderate Senate Republicans feared the damage a conviction might do to the constitutional separation of powers. They also worried about the political and economic policies that might be pursued by Benjamin Wade, the president pro tem of the Senate and a leader of the Radical Republicans, who, because there was no vice president, would succeed to the presidency if Johnson were removed from office. Behind the scenes during his Senate trial, Johnson agreed to abide by the Reconstruction Acts. In May, the Senate voted 35 for conviction, 19 for acquittal—one vote shy of the two-thirds necessary for removal from office. Johnson's narrow acquittal established the precedent that only criminal actions by a president—not political disagreements—warranted removal from office.

MAP EXPLORATION
To explore an interactive version of this map, go to
http://www.prenhall.com/faraghertlc/map17.1

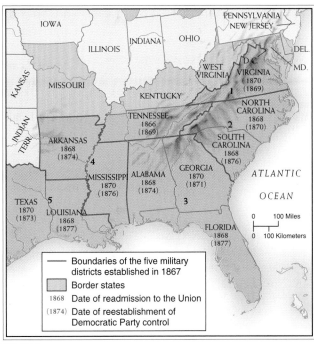

MAP 17-1

Reconstruction of the South, 1866–1877 Dates for the readmission of former Confederate states to the Union and the return of Democrats to power varied according to the specific political situations in those states.

WHAT WERE the competing plans for reconstructing the Southern states?

16–1
"Address from the Colored Citizens of Norfolk, Virginia, to the People of the United States" (1865)

Reconstruction Act 1877 act that divided the South into five military districts subject to martial law.

Tenure of Office Act Act stipulating that any officeholder appointed by the president with the Senate's advice and consent could not be removed until the Senate had approved a successor.

16–8
Albion W. Tourgee, Letter on
Ku Klux Klan Activities (1870)

Susan B. Anthony (1820–1906) and
Elizabeth Cady Stanton (1815–1902),
the two most influential leaders of the
woman suffrage movement, ca. 1892.
Anthony and Stanton broke with their
longtime abolitionist allies after the Civil
War when they opposed the Fifteenth
Amendment. They argued that the doctrine of universal manhood suffrage it
embodied would give constitutional
authority to the claim that men were the
social and political superiors of women.
As founders of the militant National
Woman Suffrage Association, Stanton and
Anthony established an independent
woman suffrage movement with a broader
spectrum of goals for women's rights and
drew millions of women into public life
during the late nineteenth century.

The Susan B. Anthony House, Rochester, NY

THE ELECTION OF 1868

By the summer of 1868, seven former Confederate states (Alabama, Arkansas,
Florida, Louisiana, North Carolina, South Carolina, and Tennessee) had ratified
the revised constitutions, elected Republican governments, and ratified the Fourteenth Amendment. They had thereby earned readmission to the Union. Though
Georgia, Mississippi, Texas, and Virginia still awaited readmission, the presidential election of 1868 offered some hope that the Civil War's legacy of sectional
hate and racial tension might finally ease.

Republicans nominated Ulysses S. Grant, the North's foremost military hero.
Grant enjoyed tremendous popularity after the war, especially when he broke with
Johnson. Totally lacking in political experience, Grant admitted after receiving the
nomination that he had been forced into it in spite of himself.

Significantly, at the very moment that the South was being forced to enfran-
chise former slaves as a prerequisite for readmission to the Union, the Republicans rejected a campaign plank endorsing black suffrage in the North. Their
platform left "the question of suffrage in all the loyal States . . . to the people of
those States." State referendums calling for black suffrage failed in eight Northern states between 1865 and 1868, succeeding only in Iowa and Minnesota. The
Democrats, determined to reverse Congressional Reconstruction, nominated Hor-
atio Seymour, former governor of New York and a longtime foe of emancipation
and supporter of states' rights.

The **Ku Klux Klan**, founded as a Tennessee social club in 1866, threatened,
whipped, and murdered black and white Republicans to prevent them from voting.
This terrorism enabled the Democrats to carry Georgia and Louisiana,
but it ultimately cost the Democrats votes in the North. In the final tally,
Grant carried twenty-six of the thirty-four states for an electoral college
victory of 214 to 80. But he received a popular majority of less than 53
percent, beating Seymour by only 306,000 votes. Significantly, more than
500,000 African American voters cast their ballots for Grant, demonstrating their overwhelming support for the Republican Party. The Republicans also retained large majorities in both houses of Congress.

In February 1869, Congress passed the **Fifteenth Amendment**,
providing that "the right of citizens of the United States to vote shall not
be denied or abridged . . . on account of race, color, or previous condition of servitude." To enhance the chances of ratification, Congress
required the three remaining unreconstructed states—Mississippi, Texas,
and Virginia—to ratify both the Fourteenth and Fifteenth Amendments
before readmission. They did so and rejoined the Union in early 1870.
The Fifteenth Amendment was ratified in February 1870. In the narrow
sense of simply readmitting the former Confederate states to the Union,
Reconstruction was complete.

WOMAN SUFFRAGE AND RECONSTRUCTION

Many women's rights advocates had long been active in the abolitionist movement. The Fourteenth and Fifteenth Amendments, which
granted citizenship and the vote to freedmen, both inspired and frustrated these activists. For example, Elizabeth Cady Stanton and Susan
B. Anthony, two leaders with long involvement in both the antislavery
and feminist movements, objected to the inclusion of the word "male"
in the Fourteenth Amendment. "If that word 'male' be inserted," Stanton predicted in 1866, "it will take us a century at least to get it out."

OVERVIEW
RECONSTRUCTION AMENDMENTS TO THE CONSTITUTION, 1865–1870

Amendment and Date Passed by Congress	Main Provisions	Ratification Process (3/4 of all states including ex-Confederate states required)
13 (January 1865)	■ Prohibited slavery in the United States	December 1865 (27 states, including 8 Southern states)
14 (June 1866)	■ Conferred national citizenship on all persons born or naturalized in the United States ■ Reduced state representation in Congress proportionally for any state disfranchising male citizens ■ Denied former Confederates the right to hold state or national office ■ Repudiated Confederate debt	July 1868 (after Congress makes ratification a prerequisite for readmission of ex-Confederate states to the Union)
15 (February 1869)	■ Prohibited denial of suffrage because of race, color, or previous condition of servitude	March 1870 (ratification required for readmission of Virginia, Texas, Mississippi, and Georgia)

Insisting that the causes of the African American vote and the women's vote were linked, Stanton, Anthony, and Lucy Stone founded the American Equal Rights Association in 1866. The group launched a series of lobbying and petition campaigns to remove racial and sexual restrictions on voting from state constitutions. Throughout the nation, the old abolitionist organizations and the Republican Party emphasized passage of the Fourteenth and Fifteenth Amendments and withdrew funds and support from the cause of woman suffrage. Disagreements over these amendments divided suffragists for decades.

The radical wing, led by Stanton and Anthony, opposed the Fifteenth Amendment, arguing that ratification would establish an "aristocracy of sex," enfranchising all men while leaving women without political privileges. They argued for a Sixteenth Amendment that would secure the vote for women. Other women's rights activists, including Lucy Stone and Frederick Douglass, asserted that "this hour belongs to the Negro." They feared a debate over woman suffrage at the national level would jeopardize passage of the two amendments.

By 1869 woman suffragists had split into two competing organizations: the moderate American Woman Suffrage Association (AWSA), which sought the support of men, and the more radical all-female National Woman Suffrage Association (NWSA). For the NWSA, the vote represented only one part of a broad spectrum of goals inherited from the Declaration of Sentiments manifesto adopted at the first women's rights convention held in 1848 at Seneca Falls, New York (see Chapter 13).

Although women did not win the vote in this period, they did establish an independent suffrage movement that eventually drew millions of women into political life. The NWSA in particular demonstrated that self-government and

16–10
Susan B. Anthony and the "New Departure" for Women (1873)

Ku Klux Klan   Perhaps the most prominent of the vigilante groups that terrorized black people in the South during Reconstruction era, founded by the Confederate veterans in 1866.

Fifteenth Amendment   Passed by Congress in 1869, guaranteed the right of American men to vote, regardless of race.

democratic participation in the public sphere were crucial for women's emancipation. The failure of woman suffrage after the Civil War was less a result of factional fighting than of the larger defeat of Radical Reconstruction and the ideal of expanded citizenship.

THE MEANING OF FREEDOM

The deep desire for independence from white control formed the underlying aspiration of newly freed slaves. For their part, most Southern white people sought to restrict the boundaries of that independence. As individuals and as members of communities transformed by emancipation, former slaves struggled to establish economic, political, and cultural autonomy. They built on the twin pillars of slave culture—the family and the church—to consolidate and expand African American institutions and thereby laid the foundation for the modern African American community.

Emancipation greatly expanded the choices available to African Americans. It helped build confidence in their ability to effect change without deferring to white people. Freedom also meant greater uncertainty and risk. But the vast majority of African Americans were more than willing to take their chances.

MOVING ABOUT

The first impulse of many emancipated slaves was to test their freedom. The simplest, most obvious way to do this involved leaving home. By walking off a plantation, coming and going without restraint or fear of punishment, African Americans could savor freedom. Throughout the summer and fall of 1865, observers in the South noted enormous numbers of freed people on the move.

Yet many who left their old neighborhoods returned soon afterward to seek work in the general vicinity, or even on the plantation they had left. Many wanted to separate themselves from former owners but not from familial ties and friendships. Others moved away altogether, seeking jobs in nearby towns and cities. Many former slaves left predominantly white counties, where they felt more vulnerable and isolated, for new lives in the relative comfort of predominantly black communities. Many African Americans, attracted by schools, churches, and fraternal societies as well as the army, preferred the city. Between 1865 and 1870, the African American population of the South's ten largest cities doubled, while the white population increased by only 10 percent.

Disgruntled planters had difficulty accepting African American independence. During slavery, they had expected obedience, submission, and loyalty from African Americans. Now many could not understand why so many former slaves wanted to leave despite urgent pleas to continue working at the old place. Many freed people went out of their way to reject the old subservience. Moving about freely was one way of doing this, as was refusing to tip one's hat to white people, ignoring former masters or mistresses in the streets, and refusing to step aside on sidewalks. After encountering an African American who would not step aside, Eliza Andrews, a Georgia plantation mistress, complained, "It is the first time in my life that I have ever had to give up the sidewalk to a man, much less to negroes!" When freed people staged parades, dances, and picnics to celebrate their new freedom, as they did, for example, when commemorating the Emancipation Proclamation, white people invariably condemned them angrily for "insolence," "outrageous spectacles," or "putting on airs."

WHAT WERE the most important changes in the lives of African Americans in the years immediately following the war?

THE AFRICAN AMERICAN FAMILY

Emancipation allowed freed people to strengthen family ties. For many former slaves, freedom meant the opportunity to reunite with long-lost family members. To track down relatives, freed people trekked to faraway places, put ads in newspapers, sought the help of Freedmen's Bureau agents, and questioned anyone who might have information about loved ones. Many thousands of family reunions, each with its own story, took place after the war.

Thousands of African American couples who had lived together under slavery streamed to military and civilian authorities and demanded to be legally married. By 1870, the two-parent household was the norm for a large majority of African Americans.

Emancipation brought changes to gender roles within the African American family as well. Black men could now serve on juries, vote, and hold office; black women, like their white counterparts, could not. Freedmen's Bureau agents designated the husband as household head and established lower wage scales for women laborers. African American editors, preachers, and politicians regularly quoted the biblical injunction that wives submit to their husbands.

African American men asserted their male authority, denied under slavery, by insisting their wives work at home instead of in the fields. Yet African American women continued to work outside the home, engaging in seasonal field labor for wages or working a family's rented plot. Most rural black families barely eked out a living and, thus, the labor of every family member was essential to survival. The key difference from slave times was that African American families themselves, not white masters and overseers, decided when and where women and children worked.

AFRICAN AMERICAN CHURCHES AND SCHOOLS

The creation of separate African American churches proved the most lasting and important element of the energetic institution building that went on in postemancipation years. Before the Civil War, Southern Protestant churches had relegated slaves and free African Americans to second-class membership. Black worshipers

An overflow congregation crowds into Richmond's First African Baptist Church in 1874. Despite their poverty, freed people struggled to save, buy land, and erect new buildings as they organized hundreds of new black churches during Reconstruction. As the most important African American institution outside the family, the black church, in addition to tending to spiritual needs, played a key role in the educational and political life of the community.

Wood engraving. The Granger Collection (4E1090.98)

were required to sit in the back during services, they were denied any role in church governance, and they were excluded from Sunday schools. Even in larger cities, where all-black congregations sometimes built their own churches, the law required white pastors. In rural areas, slaves preferred their own preachers to the sermons of local white ministers who quoted Scripture to justify slavery and white supremacy.

In communities around the South, African Americans now pooled their resources to buy land and build their own churches. Before these structures were completed, they might hold services in a railroad boxcar, where Atlanta's First Baptist Church began, or in an outdoor arbor, the original site of the First Baptist Church of Memphis. By late 1866 Charleston's African American community could boast of eleven churches in the city—five Methodist, two Presbyterian, two Episcopalian, one Baptist, and one Congregational. In rural areas, different denominations frequently shared the same church building. Churches became the center not only for religious life but for many other activities that defined the African American community: schools, picnics, festivals, and political meetings. They also helped spawn a host of organizations devoted to benevolence and mutual aid, such as burial societies, Masonic lodges, temperance clubs, and trade associations.

The church became the first social institution fully controlled by African Americans. In nearly every community ministers, respected for their speaking and organizational skills, were among the most influential leaders. By 1877 the great majority of black Southerners had withdrawn from white-dominated churches and belonged to black Baptist or Methodist churches.

African American communities received important educational aid from outside organizations. By 1869 the Freedmen's Bureau was supervising nearly 3,000 schools serving over 150,000 students throughout the South. Over half the roughly 3,300 teachers in these schools were African Americans, many of whom had been free before the Civil War. Other teachers included dedicated Northern white women volunteers. Throughout the South in 1865 and 1866, African Americans raised money to build schoolhouses, buy supplies, and pay teachers. Black artisans donated labor for construction, and black families offered room and board to teachers.

LAND AND LABOR AFTER SLAVERY

Most newly emancipated African Americans aspired to quit the plantations and to make new lives for themselves. Leaving the plantation was not as simple as walking off. Some freed people did find jobs in railroad building, mining, ranching, or construction work. Others raised subsistence crops and tended vegetable gardens as squatters. The majority hoped to become self-sufficient farmers. Many former slaves believed they were entitled to the land they had worked throughout their lives. General Oliver O. Howard, chief commissioner of the Freedmen's Bureau, observed that many "supposed that the Government [would] divide among them the lands of the conquered owners, and furnish them with all that might be necessary to begin life as an independent farmer." This perception was not merely a wishful fantasy. Frequent reference in the Congress and the press to the question of land distribution made the idea of "forty acres and a mule" not just a pipe dream but a matter of serious public debate.

Above all, African Americans sought economic autonomy, and ownership of land promised the most independence. "Give us our own land and we take care of ourselves," was how one former slave saw it. "But widout land, de ole massas can hire us or starve us, as dey please." At the Colored Convention in Montgomery, Alabama, in May 1867, delegates argued that the property now owned by planters had been "nearly all earned by the sweat of our brows, not theirs. It has been forfeited to the government by the treason of its owners, and is liable to be confiscated

QUICK REVIEW

Black Churches

- Many African Americans found inspiration and courage in their religious faith.
- Most black churches split from white-dominated congregations after the war.
- Black churches created a variety of organizations that served the black community.

whenever the Republican Party demands it." But by 1866 the federal government had already pulled back from the various wartime experiments involving the breaking up of large plantations and the leasing of small plots to individual families.

16–5
James C. Beecher, Report on Land Reform in the South Carolina Islands (1865, 1866)

 MAP EXPLORATION

To explore an interactive version of this map, go to **http://www.prenhall.com/faraghertlc/map17.2**

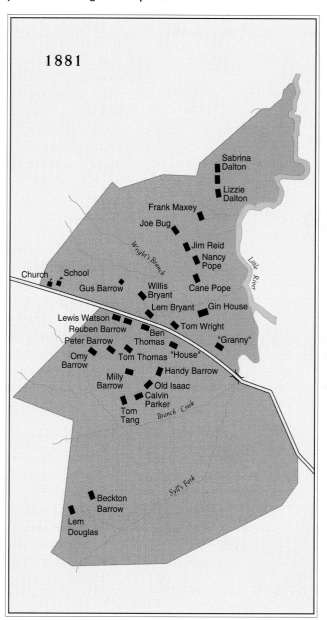

MAP 17-2

The Barrow Plantation, Oglethorpe County, Georgia, 1860 and 1881 (approx. 2,000 acres) These two maps, based on drawings from *Scribner's Monthly*, April 1881, show some of the changes brought by emancipation. In 1860 the plantation's entire black population lived in the communal slave quarters, right next to the white master's house. In 1881 black sharecropper and tenant families lived on individual plots, spread out across the land. The former slaves had also built their own school and church.

WHAT CHANGES in the lives of Black Southerners are reflected in the two maps of the Barrow Plantation?

President Johnson directed General Howard of the Freedmen's Bureau to evict tens of thousands of freed people settled on confiscated and abandoned land in southeastern Virginia, Southern Louisiana, and the Georgia and South Carolina low country. These evictions created a deep sense of betrayal among African Americans. A former Mississippi slave, Merrimon Howard, bitterly noted that African Americans had been left with "no land, no house, not so much as a place to lay our head. . . . We were friends on the march, brothers on the battlefield, but in the peaceful pursuits of life it seems that we are strangers."

By the late 1860s, **sharecropping** had emerged as the dominant form of working the land. Sharecropping represented a compromise between planters and former slaves. Under sharecropping arrangements, individual families contracted with landowners to be responsible for a specific plot. Large plantations were thus broken into family-sized farms. Generally, sharecropper families received one-third of the year's crop if the owner furnished implements, seed, and draft animals, or one-half if they provided their own supplies. African Americans preferred sharecropping to gang labor, as it allowed families to set their own hours and tasks and offered freedom from white supervision and control. For planters, the system stabilized the work force by requiring sharecroppers to remain until the harvest and to employ all family members. It also offered a way around the chronic shortage of cash and credit that plagued the postwar South.

By 1880 about 80 percent of the land in the black belt states—Mississippi, Alabama, and Georgia—had been divided into family-sized farms. Nearly three-quarters of black Southerners were sharecroppers. Through much of the black belt, family and community were one. Often several families worked adjoining parcels of land in common, pooling their labor in order to get by. Men usually oversaw crop production. Women went to the fields seasonally during planting or harvesting, but they mainly tended to household chores and child care. In addition, women frequently held jobs that might bring in cash, such as raising chickens or taking in laundry. The cotton harvest engaged all members of the community, from the oldest to the youngest.

THE ORIGINS OF AFRICAN AMERICAN POLITICS

Inclusion rather than separation was the objective of early African American political activity. In 1865 and 1866, African Americans throughout the South organized scores of mass meetings, parades, and petitions that demanded civil equality and the right to vote. In the cities, the growing web of churches and fraternal societies helped bolster early efforts at political organization.

Hundreds of African American delegates, selected by local meetings or churches, attended statewide political conventions held throughout the South in 1865 and 1866. Previously free African Americans, as well as black ministers, artisans, and veterans of the Union army, tended to dominate these proceedings, setting a pattern that would hold throughout Reconstruction. Convention debates sometimes reflected the tensions within African American communities, such as friction between poorer former slaves and better-off free black people, or between lighter- and darker-skinned African Americans. But most of these state gatherings concentrated on passing resolutions on issues that united all African Americans. The central concerns were suffrage and equality before the law.

The passage of the first Reconstruction Act in 1867 encouraged even more political activity among African Americans. The military started registering the South's electorate, ultimately enrolling approximately 735,000 black and 635,000

16–12
A Sharecrop Contract (1882)

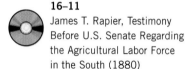

16–11
James T. Rapier, Testimony Before U.S. Senate Regarding the Agricultural Labor Force in the South (1880)

QUICK REVIEW

Southern Republicans

◆ African American voters.

◆ White Northerners called "carpetbaggers" by white Southerners.

◆ Native whites pejoratively termed "scalawags."

Sharecropping Labor system that evolved during and after Reconstruction whereby landowners furnished laborers with a house, farm animals, and tools and advanced credit in exchange for a share of the laborers' crop.

white voters in the ten unreconstructed states. Five states— Alabama, Florida, Louisiana, Mississippi, and South Carolina— had black electoral majorities. Fewer than half the registered white voters participated in the elections for state constitutional conventions in 1867 and 1868. In contrast, four-fifths of the registered black voters cast ballots in these elections. Much of this new African American political activism was channeled through local **Union League** chapters throughout the South.

Begun during the war as a Northern, largely white middle-class patriotic club, the Union League now became the political voice of the former slaves. Union League chapters brought together local African Americans, soldiers, and Freedmen's Bureau agents to demand the vote and an end to legal discrimination against African Americans. It brought out African American voters, instructed freedmen in the rights and duties of citizenship, and promoted Republican candidates.

In 1867 and 1868, the promise of Radical Reconstruction enlarged the scope of African American political participation and brought new leaders to the fore. Many were teachers, preachers, or others with useful skills, such as literacy. For most ordinary African Americans, politics was inseparable from economic issues, especially the land question. Grass-roots political organizations frequently intervened in local disputes with planters over the terms of labor contracts. African American political groups closely followed the congressional debates over Reconstruction policy and agitated for land confiscation and distribution. Perhaps most important, politics was the only arena where black and white Southerners might engage each other on an equal basis.

W. L. Sheppard, "Electioneering at the South," *Harper's Weekly*, July 25, 1868. Throughout the Reconstruction-era South, newly freed slaves took a keen interest in both local and national political affairs. The presence of women and children at these campaign gatherings illustrates the importance of contemporary political issues to the entire African American community.

Courtesy of the Library of Congress

SOUTHERN POLITICS AND SOCIETY

By the summer of 1868, when the South had returned to the Union, the majority of Republicans believed the task of Reconstruction to be finished. Ultimately, they put their faith in a political solution to the problems facing the vanquished South. That meant nurturing a viable two-party system in the Southern states, where no Republican Party had ever existed. If that could be accomplished, Republicans and Democrats would compete for votes, offices, and influence, just as they did in Northern states.

Yet over the next decade the political structure created in the Southern states proved too restricted and fragile to sustain itself. Federal troops were needed to protect Republican governments and their supporters from violent opposition. Congressional action to monitor Southern elections and protect black voting rights became routine. Despite initial successes, Southern Republicanism proved an unstable coalition of often conflicting elements, unable to sustain effective power for very long. By 1877, Democrats had regained political control of all the former Confederate states.

SOUTHERN REPUBLICANS

Three major groups composed the fledgling Republican coalition in the postwar South. The first group, African American voters, made up a large majority of Southern Republicans throughout the Reconstruction era.

WHAT MAJOR groups made up the Southern Republicans?

Union League   Republican party organizations in Northern cities that became an important organizing device among freedmen in Southern cities after 1865.

The second group consisted of white Northerners, derisively called "**carpetbaggers**" by native white Southerners. Most carpetbaggers combined a desire for personal gain with a commitment to reform the "unprogressive" South by developing its material resources and introducing Yankee institutions such as free labor and free public schools. Most were veterans of the Union army who stayed in the South after the war. Others included Freedmen's Bureau agents and businessmen who had invested capital in cotton plantations and other enterprises. Although they made up a tiny percentage of the population, carpetbaggers played a disproportionately large role in Southern politics. They won a large share of Reconstruction offices, particularly in Florida, South Carolina, and Louisiana and in areas with large African American constituencies.

The third major group of Southern Republicans were the native white residents pejoratively termed "**scalawags**." They had even more diverse backgrounds and motives than the Northern-born Republicans. Loyalists during the war and traditional enemies of the planter elite (most were small farmers), these white Southerners looked to the Republican Party for help in settling old scores and relief from debt and wartime devastation.

Deep contradictions strained the alliance of these three groups. Southern Republicans touted themselves as the "party of progress and civilization" and promised a new era of material progress for the region. Republican state conventions in 1867 and 1868 voiced support for internal improvements, public schools, debt relief, and railroad building. Yet few white Southerners identified with the political and economic aspirations of African Americans. Moderate elements more concerned with maintaining white control of the party and encouraging economic investment in the region, outnumbered and defeated "confiscation radicals" who focused on obtaining land for African Americans.

RECONSTRUCTING THE STATES: A MIXED RECORD

With the old Confederate leaders barred from political participation, and with carpetbaggers and newly enfranchised African Americans representing many of the plantation districts, Republicans managed to dominate the ten Southern constitutional conventions of 1867–1869. Most of these conventions produced constitutions that expanded democracy and the public role of the state. The new documents guaranteed the political and civil rights of African Americans, and they abolished property qualifications for officeholding and jury service, as well as imprisonment for debt. They created the first state-funded systems of education in the South, to be administered by state commissioners. The new constitutions also mandated establishment of orphanages, penitentiaries, and homes for the insane. In 1868, only three years after the end of the war, Republicans came to power in most of the Southern states. By 1869, new constitutions had been ratified in all the old Confederate states. "These constitutions and governments," one South Carolina Democratic newspaper vowed bitterly, "will last just as long as the bayonets which ushered them into being, shall keep them in existence, and not one day longer."

Republican governments in the South faced a continual crisis of legitimacy that limited their ability to legislate change. They had to balance reform against the need to gain acceptance, especially by white Southerners. Their achievements were thus mixed. In the realm of race relations there was a clear thrust toward equal rights and against discrimination. Republican legislatures followed up the

Carpetbaggers   Northern transplants to the South, many of whom were Union soldiers who stayed in the South after the war.

Scalawags   Southern whites, mainly small landowning farmers and well-off merchants and planters, who supported the Southern Republican party during Reconstruction.

The Ku Klux Klan emerged as a potent political and social force during Reconstruction, terrorizing freed people and their white allies. An 1868 Klan warning threatens Louisiana governor Henry C. Warmoth with death. Warmoth, an Illinois-born "carpetbagger," was the state's first Republican governor. Two Alabama Klansmen, photographed in 1868, wear white hoods to hide their identities.

(a) University of North Carolina Southern Historical Collection; (b) Rutherford B. Hayes Presidential Center

federal Civil Rights Act of 1866 with various antidiscrimination clauses in new constitutions and laws prescribing harsh penalties for civil rights violations. African Americans could now be employed in police forces and fire departments, serve on juries, school boards, and city councils, and they could hold public office at all levels of government.

Segregation, though, became the norm in public school systems. African American leaders often accepted segregation because they feared that insistence on integrated education would jeopardize funding for the new school systems. African Americans opposed constitutional language requiring racial segregation in schools; most African Americans were less interested in the abstract ideal of integrated education than in ensuring educational opportunities for their children and employment for African American teachers.

Segregation in railroad cars and other public places was more objectionable to African Americans. By the early 1870s, as black influence and assertiveness grew, laws guaranteeing equal access to transportation and public accommodation were passed in many states. By and large, though, such civil rights laws were difficult to enforce in local communities.

In economic matters, Republican governments failed to fulfill African Americans' hopes of obtaining land. Few former slaves possessed the cash to buy land in the open market, and they looked to the state for help. Republicans tried to weaken the plantation system and promote black ownership by raising taxes on land. Yet even when state governments seized land for nonpayment of taxes, the property was never used to help create black homesteads.

Republican leaders envisioned promoting Northern-style capitalist development—factories, large towns, and diversified agriculture—through state aid. Much Republican state lawmaking was devoted to encouraging railroad construction. Between 1868 and 1872 the Southern railroad system was rebuilt and over 3,000 new miles of track added, an increase of almost 40 percent. But in spite of all the new laws, it proved impossible to attract significant amounts of Northern and European investment capital. The obsession with railroads withdrew resources from education and other programs. As in the North, it also opened the doors to widespread corruption and bribery of public officials. Railroad failures eroded public confidence in the Republicans' ability to govern. The "gospel of prosperity" ultimately failed to modernize the economy or solidify the Republican Party in the South.

White Resistance and "Redemption"

The emergence of a Republican Party in the reconstructed South brought two parties but not a two-party system to the region. The opponents of Reconstruction, the Democrats, refused to acknowledge Republicans' right to participate in Southern political life. In their view, the Republican Party, supported primarily by the votes of former slaves, was the partisan instrument of the Northern Congress. Since Republicans controlled state governments, this denial of legitimacy meant, in effect, a rejection of state authority itself.

From 1870 to 1872 the Ku Klux Klan fought an ongoing terrorist campaign against Reconstruction governments and local leaders. Although not centrally organized, the Klan was a powerful presence in nearly every Southern state. It acted as a kind of guerrilla military force in the service of the Democratic Party, the planter class, and all those who sought the restoration of white supremacy. In October 1870, after Republicans carried Laurens County in South Carolina, bands of white people drove 150 African Americans from their homes and murdered 13 black and white Republican activists. In March 1871, three African Americans were arrested in Meridian, Mississippi, for giving "incendiary" speeches. At their court hearing, Klansmen killed two of the defendants and the Republican judge, and thirty more African Americans were murdered in a day of rioting. The single bloodiest episode of Reconstruction era violence took place in Colfax, Louisiana, on Easter Sunday 1873. Nearly 100 African Americans were murdered after they failed to hold a besieged courthouse during a contested election.

Southern Republicans looked to Washington for help. In 1870 and 1871 Congress passed three Enforcement Acts designed to counter racial terrorism. These declared that interference with voting was a federal offense. The acts provided for federal supervision of voting, and authorized the president to send the army and to suspend the writ of habeas corpus in districts declared to be in a state of insurrection. The most sweeping measure was the Ku Klux Klan Act of April 1871, which made the violent infringement of civil and political rights a federal crime punishable by the national government. Attorney General Amos T. Akerman prosecuted hundreds of Klansmen in North Carolina and Mississippi. In October 1871 President Grant sent federal troops to occupy nine South Carolina counties and rounded up thousands of Klan members. By the election of 1872, the federal government's intervention had helped break the Klan and restore a semblance of law and order.

The Civil Rights Act of 1875 outlawed racial discrimination in theaters, hotels, railroads, and other public places, but the law proved more an assertion of principle than a direct federal intervention in Southern affairs. Enforcement required African Americans to take their cases to the federal courts, a costly and time-consuming procedure.

As wartime idealism faded, Northern Republicans became less inclined toward direct intervention in Southern affairs. They had enough trouble retaining political control in the North. In 1874 the Democrats gained a majority in the House of Representatives for the first time since 1856. Key Northern states also began to fall to the Democrats. Northern Republicans slowly abandoned the freedmen and their white allies in the South.

Gradually, conservative Democrats "redeemed" one state after another. Virginia and Tennessee led the way in 1869, North Carolina in 1870, Georgia in 1871, Texas in 1873, and Alabama and Arkansas in 1874. In Mississippi, white conservatives employed violence and intimidation to wrest control in 1875 and "redeemed" the state the following year. Republican infighting in Louisiana in 1873 and 1874 led to a series of contested election results, including bloody clashes between black militia and armed whites, and finally to "redemption" by the Democrats in 1877. Once these states returned to Democratic rule, African Americans faced obstacles to voting, more stringent controls on plantation labor, and deep cuts in social services.

Several Supreme Court rulings involving the Fourteenth and Fifteenth Amendments effectively constrained federal protection of African American civil rights. In the so-called **Slaughterhouse cases** of 1873, the Court issued its first ruling on the Fourteenth Amendment. The cases involved a Louisiana charter that gave a New Orleans meat-packing company a monopoly over the city's butchering business on the grounds of protecting public health. A rival group of butchers had sued, claiming the law violated the Fourteenth Amendment, which prohibited states from depriving any person of life, liberty, or property without due process of law. The Court held that the Fourteenth Amendment protected only the former slaves, not butchers, and that it protected only national citizenship rights, not the regulatory powers of states. The ruling in effect denied the original intent of the Fourteenth Amendment—to protect against state infringement of national citizenship rights as spelled out in the Bill of Rights.

Three other decisions curtailed federal protection of black civil rights. In *United States* v. *Reese* (1876) and *United States* v. *Cruikshank* (1876), the Court restricted congressional power to enforce the Ku Klux Klan Act. Future prosecution would depend on the states rather than on federal authorities. In these rulings the Court held that the Fourteenth Amendment extended the federal power to protect civil rights only in cases involving discrimination by states; discrimination by individuals or groups was not covered. The Court also ruled that the Fifteenth Amendment did not guarantee a citizen's right to vote; it only barred certain specific grounds for denying suffrage—"race, color, or previous condition of servitude." This interpretation opened the door for Southern states to disfranchise African Americans for allegedly nonracial reasons. States back under Democratic control began to limit African American voting by passing laws restricting voter eligibility through poll taxes and property requirements.

Slaughterhouse cases   Group of cases resulting in one sweeping decision by the U.S. Supreme Court in 1873 that contradicted the intent of the Fourteenth Amendment by decreeing that most citizenship rights remained under state, not federal, control.

Finally, in the 1883 *Civil Rights Cases* decision, the Court declared the Civil Rights Act of 1875 unconstitutional, holding that the Fourteenth Amendment gave Congress the power to outlaw discrimination by states, but not by private individuals. The majority opinion held that black people must no longer "be the special favorite of the laws." Together, these Supreme Court decisions marked the end of federal attempts to protect African American rights until well into the next century.

WHITE YEOMEN, WHITE MERCHANTS, AND "KING COTTON"

The Republicans' vision of a "New South" remade along the lines of the Northern economy failed to materialize. Instead, the South declined into the country's poorest agricultural region. Cotton growing had defined the economic life of large plantations in the coastal regions and black belt communities of the antebellum South. In the post–Civil War years "King Cotton" expanded its realm, as greater numbers of small white farmers found themselves forced to switch from subsistence crops to growing cotton for the market.

MAP EXPLORATION

To explore an interactive version of this map, go to **http://www.prenhall.com/faraghertlc/map17.3**

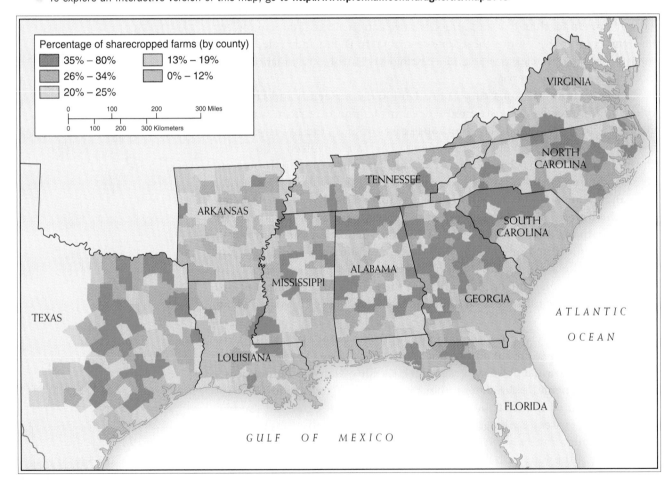

MAP 17-3

Southern Sharecropping and the Cotton Belt, 1880 The economic depression of the 1870s forced increasing numbers of Southern farmers, both white and black, into sharecropping arrangements. Sharecropping was most pervasive in the cotton belt regions of South Carolina, Georgia, Alabama, Mississippi, and east Texas.

HOW DID this new form of labor affect the lives of former slaves?

The spread of the "crop lien" system as the South's main form of agricultural credit forced more and more farmers into cotton growing.

A chronic shortage of capital and banking institutions made local merchants and planters the sole source of credit. They advanced loans to sharecroppers and tenant farmers only in exchange for a lien, or claim, on the year's cotton crop, and they often charged usurious interest rates on advances, while marking up the prices of the goods they sold in their stores. Thus, at the end of the year, sharecroppers and tenants found themselves deep in debt to stores (many owned by Northerners) for seed, supplies, and clothing.

The near total dominance of "King Cotton" inhibited economic growth across the region. Unlike Midwestern and Western farm towns burgeoning from trade in wheat, corn, and livestock, Southern communities found themselves almost entirely dependent on the price of one commodity as more and more farmers turned to cotton growing as the only way to obtain credit. Expanding production depressed prices. Competition from new cotton centers in the world market, such as Egypt and India, accelerated the downward spiral. As cotton prices declined alarmingly, from roughly 11 ¢ per pound in 1875 to 5 ¢ in 1894, per capita wealth in the South fell steadily; by the 1890s it equaled only one-third that of the East, Midwest, or West. Cotton dependency also prevented planters from acquiring the capital to purchase the farm equipment needed to profitably cultivate wheat or corn.

By 1880 about one-third of white farmers and nearly three-quarters of African American farmers in the cotton states were sharecroppers or tenants. Many former slaves and poor white people had tried subsistence farming in the undeveloped backcountry. Yet to obtain precious credit, most found themselves forced to produce cotton for market and, thus, became enmeshed in the debt-ridden crop lien system. In the upcountry and newer areas of cultivation, cotton-dominated commercial agriculture, with landless tenants and sharecroppers as the main work force, had replaced the more diversified subsistence economy of the antebellum era.

With their power based on control of credit and marketing, merchants emerged as a new economic elite unconnected to the antebellum planters whose power had rested on the ownership of land and slaves. But within both the new towns and the old planter elite, white families increasingly defined their social position by celebrating a certain type of ideal household. Women found meaning in their role as upholders of domestic virtue by creating a comfortable home environment and tending to the needs of children and husbands. Men were to be of strong moral fiber and to provide material support for the family. These elite ideals, articulated in magazines, schools, sermons, and other public discourse, rested on a belief that one's ability to reach the standards of womanhood and manhood rested solely upon moral character and individual choice.

RECONSTRUCTING THE NORTH

Abraham Lincoln liked to cite his own rise as proof of the superiority of the Northern system of "free labor" over slavery. But the triumph of the North brought with it fundamental changes in the economy, labor relations, and politics that brought Lincoln's ideal vision into question. The spread of the factory system, the growth of large and powerful corporations, and the rapid expansion of capitalist enterprise all hastened the development of a large unskilled

WHAT PRECIPITATED
the electoral crisis of 1876?

and routinized work force. Rather than becoming independent producers, more and more workers found themselves consigned permanently to wage labor.

The old Republican ideal of a society bound by a harmony of interests had become overshadowed by a grimmer reality of class conflict. A violent national railroad strike in 1877 was broken only with the direct intervention of federal troops. Northern society, like the society of the South, appeared more hierarchical than equal. That same year the last federal troops withdrew from their Southern posts, marking the end of the Reconstruction era. By then, the North had undergone its own "reconstruction" as well.

THE AGE OF CAPITAL

In the decade following Appomattox, the North's economy continued the industrial boom begun during the Civil War. By 1873, America's industrial production had grown 75 percent over the 1865 level. By that time, too, the number of nonagricultural workers in the North had surpassed the number of farmers. Between 1860 and 1880 the number of wage earners in manufacturing and construction more than doubled, from 2 million to over 4 million.

The railroad business both symbolized and advanced the new industrial order. Shortly before the Civil War, enthusiasm mounted for a transcontinental line. Private companies took on the huge and expensive job of construction, but the federal government funded the project, providing the largest subsidy in American history. An 1864 act bestowed a subsidy of $15,000 per mile of track laid over smooth plains country and varying larger amounts up to $48,000 per mile in the foothills and mountains of the Far West. The Union Pacific employed gangs of Irish American and African American workers to lay track heading west from Omaha, while the Central Pacific brought in more than 10,000 men from China to handle the difficult work in the Sierra Nevada mountain region. On May 10, 1869, Leland Stanford, the former governor of California and president of the Central Pacific Railroad, traveled to Promontory Point in Utah Territory to hammer a ceremonial golden spike, marking the finish of the first transcontinental line.

Completion of the transcontinental railroad, May 10, 1869, as building crews for the Union Pacific and Central Pacific meet at Promontory Point, Utah. The two locomotive engineers salute each other, while the chief engineers for the two railroads shake hands. Construction had begun simultaneously from Omaha and Sacramento in 1863, with the help of generous subsidies from Congress. Work crews, consisting of thousands of ex-soldiers, Irish immigrants, and imported Chinese laborers, laid nearly 1,800 miles of new track.

The Granger Collection, New York (4E377.23)

Railroads paved the way for the rapid settlement of the West, and both rural and urban areas grew dramatically over the next several decades. The combined population of Minnesota, the Dakotas, Nebraska, and Kansas, for example, jumped from 300,000 in 1860 to over 2 million in 1880. In the fifty years after 1870, the nation's railroad system expanded to more than a quarter million miles—more than all the rest of the world's railroad track combined.

Railroad corporations became America's first big businesses. Railroads required huge outlays of investment capital, and their growth increased the economic power of banks and investment houses centered on Wall Street. Bankers often gained seats on the boards of directors of these railroad companies, and their access to capital sometimes gave them the real control of railways. A new breed of aggressive entrepreneur sought to ease cutthroat competition by absorbing smaller companies and forming "pools" that set rates and divided the market. A small group of railroad executives, including Cornelius Vanderbilt, Jay Gould, Collis P. Huntington, and James J. Hill, amassed unheard-of fortunes. When he died in 1877, Vanderbilt left his son $100 million. By comparison, a decent annual wage for working a six-day week was around $350.

Railroad promoters, lawyers, and lobbyists became ubiquitous figures in Washington and state capitals, wielding enormous influence among lawmakers. Railroads benefited enormously from government subsidies. Between 1862 and 1872, Congress alone awarded more than 100 million acres of public lands to railroad companies and provided them over $64 million in loans and tax incentives.

Some of the nation's most prominent politicians routinely accepted railroad largesse. The worst scandal of the Grant administration grew out of corruption involving railroad promotion. As a way of diverting funds for the building of the Union Pacific Railroad, an inner circle of Union Pacific stockholders created the dummy Crédit Mobilier construction company. In return for political favors, a group of prominent Republicans received stock in the company. When the scandal broke in 1872, it politically ruined Vice President Schuyler Colfax and led to the censure of two congressmen.

Other industries also boomed in this period, especially those engaged in extracting minerals and processing natural resources. Railroad growth stimulated expansion in the production of coal, iron, stone, and lumber, and these also received significant government aid. For example, under the National Mineral Act of 1866, mining companies received millions of acres of free public land. Oil refining enjoyed a huge expansion in the 1860s and 1870s. As with railroads, an early period of fierce competition soon gave way to concentration. By the late 1870s, John D. Rockefeller's Standard Oil Company controlled almost 90 percent of the nation's oil-refining capacity.

LIBERAL REPUBLICANS AND THE ELECTION OF 1872

With the rapid growth of large-scale, capital-intensive enterprises, Republicans increasingly identified with the interests of business rather than the rights of freedmen or the antebellum ideology of "free labor." The old Civil War–era Radical Republicans had declined in influence. State Republican parties now organized themselves around the spoils of federal patronage rather than grand causes such as preserving the Union or ending slavery. Despite the Crédit Mobilier affair, Republicans had no monopoly on political scandal. In 1871 New York City newspapers reported the shocking story

Liberal Republicans Disaffected Republicans that emphasized the doctrines of classical economics.

MAP EXPLORATION

To explore an interactive version of this map, go to
http://www.prenhall.com/faragherlic/map17.4

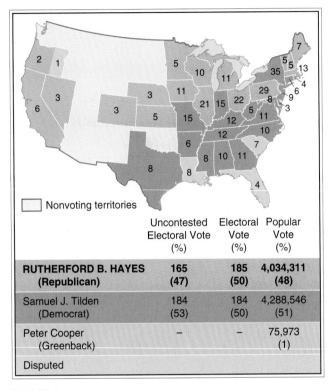

	Uncontested Electoral Vote (%)	Electoral Vote (%)	Popular Vote (%)
RUTHERFORD B. HAYES (Republican)	**165 (47)**	**185 (50)**	**4,034,311 (48)**
Samuel J. Tilden (Democrat)	184 (53)	184 (50)	4,288,546 (51)
Peter Cooper (Greenback)	–	–	75,973 (1)
Disputed			

MAP 17-4

The Election of 1876 The presidential election of 1876 left the nation without a clear-cut winner.

WHAT LED to the electoral crisis of 1876?

of how Democratic Party boss William M. Tweed and his friends had systematically stolen tens of millions from the city treasury. The "Tweed Ring" had received enormous bribes and kickbacks from city contractors and businessmen. But to many, the scandal represented only the most extreme case of the routine corruption that now plagued American political life.

By the end of President Grant's first term, a large number of disaffected Republicans sought an alternative. The **Liberal Republicans**, as they called themselves, emphasized the doctrines of classical economics, stressing the law of supply and demand, free trade, defense of property rights, and individualism. They called for a return to limited government, arguing that bribery, scandal, and high taxes all flowed from excessive state interference in the economy.

Liberal Republicans were also suspicious of expanding democracy. They believed that politics ought to be the province of "the best men"—educated and well-to-do men like themselves, devoted to the "science of government." They proposed civil service reform as the best way to break the hold of party machines on patronage.

Although most Liberal Republicans had enthusiastically supported abolition, the Union cause, and equal rights for freedmen, they now opposed continued federal intervention in the South. The national government had done all it could for the former slaves; they must now take care of themselves. "Root, Hog, or Die" was the harsh advice offered by Horace Greeley, editor of the *New York Tribune*. In the spring of 1872 a diverse collection of Liberal Republicans nominated Greeley to run for president. A longtime foe of the Democratic Party, Greeley nonetheless won that party's presidential nomination as well. He made a new policy for the South the center of his campaign against Grant. All Americans, Greeley urged, must put the Civil War behind them and "clasp hands across the bloody chasm."

Grant easily defeated Greeley, carrying every state in the North and winning 56 percent of the popular vote. Most Republicans were not willing to abandon the regular party organization, and "waving the bloody shirt" was still a potent vote-getter. But the 1872 election accelerated the trend toward federal abandonment of African American citizenship rights. The Liberal Republicans quickly faded as an organized political force. But their ideas helped define a growing conservative consciousness among the Northern public. Their agenda included retreat from the ideal of racial justice, hostility toward trade unions, suspicion of working-class and immigrant political power, celebration of competitive individualism, and opposition to government intervention in economic affairs.

THE DEPRESSION OF 1873

In the fall of 1873 the postwar boom came to an abrupt halt as a severe financial panic triggered a deep economic depression. The collapse resulted from commercial overexpansion, especially speculative investing in the nation's railroad system. By 1876 half the nation's railroads had defaulted on their bonds. Over the next two years more than 100 banks folded and 18,000 businesses shut their doors. The depression that began in 1873 lasted sixty-five months—the longest economic contraction in the nation's history until then.

The human toll of the depression was enormous. As factories began to close across the nation, the unemployment rate soared to about 15 percent. In many cities the jobless rate was much higher; roughly one-quarter of New York City workers were unemployed in 1874. Many thousands of men took to the road in search of work, and the "tramp" emerged as a new and menacing figure on the social landscape. The Pennsylvania Bureau of Labor Statistics noted that never before had "so many of the working classes, skilled and unskilled . . . been moving from place to place seeking employment that was not to be had." Farmers were also hard hit by the depression. Agricultural output continued to grow, but prices and land values fell sharply. As prices for their crops fell, farmers had a more difficult time repaying their fixed loan obligations; many sank deeper into debt.

Mass meetings of workers in New York and other cities issued calls to government officials to create jobs through public works. But these appeals were rejected. Indeed, many business leaders and political figures denounced even meager efforts at charity. They saw the depression as a natural, if painful, part of the business cycle, one that would allow only the strongest enterprises (and workers) to survive.

The depression of the 1870s prompted workers and farmers to question the old free-labor ideology that celebrated a harmony of interests in Northern society. More people voiced anger at and distrust of large corporations that exercised great economic power from outside their communities.

THE ELECTORAL CRISIS OF 1876

With the economy mired in depression, Democrats looked forward to capturing the White House in 1876. New scandals plaguing the Grant administration also weakened the Republican Party. In 1875, a conspiracy surfaced between distillers and U.S. revenue agents to cheat the government out of millions in tax revenues. The government secured indictments against more than 200 members of this "Whiskey Ring," including Orville E. Babcock, Grant's private secretary. Though acquitted, thanks to Grant's intervention, Babcock resigned in disgrace. In 1876, Secretary of War William W. Belknap was impeached for receiving bribes for the sale of trading posts in Indian Territory, and he resigned to avoid conviction.

Democrats nominated Governor Samuel J. Tilden of New York, who brought impeccable reform credentials to his candidacy. In 1871 he had helped expose and prosecute the "Tweed Ring" in New York City. As governor he had toppled the "Canal Ring," a graft-ridden scheme involving inflated contracts for repairs on the Erie Canal. In their platform, the Democrats linked the issue of corruption to an attack on Reconstruction policies. They blamed the Republicans for instituting "a corrupt centralism."

Republican nominee Rutherford B. Hayes, governor of Ohio, also sought the high ground. As a lawyer in Cincinnati he had defended runaway slaves. Later he had distinguished himself as a general in the Union army. Hayes promised, if elected, to support an efficient civil service system, to vigorously prosecute officials who betrayed the public trust, and to introduce a system of free universal education.

On an election day marred by widespread vote fraud and violent intimidation, Tilden received 250,000 more popular votes than Hayes. But Republicans refused to concede victory, challenging the vote totals in the electoral college. Tilden garnered 184 uncontested electoral votes, one shy of the majority required to win, while Hayes received 165. The problem centered in 20 disputed votes from Florida, Louisiana, South Carolina, and Oregon. In each of the three Southern states two sets of electoral votes were returned. In Oregon, which Hayes had unquestionably carried, the Democratic governor nevertheless replaced a disputed Republican elector with a Democrat.

The crisis was unprecedented. In January 1877 Congress moved to settle the deadlock, establishing an Electoral Commission composed of five senators, five representatives, and five Supreme Court justices; eight were Republicans and seven were Democrats. The commission voted along strict partisan lines to award all the contested electoral votes to Hayes. Outraged by this decision, Democratic congressmen threatened a filibuster to block Hayes's inauguration. Violence and stalemate were avoided when Democrats and Republicans struck a compromise in February. In return for Hayes's ascendance to the presidency, the Republicans promised to appropriate more money for Southern internal improvements, to appoint a Southerner to Hayes's cabinet, and to pursue a policy of noninterference ("home rule") in Southern affairs.

Shortly after assuming office, Hayes ordered removal of the remaining federal troops in Louisiana and South Carolina. Without this military presence to sustain them, the Republican governors of those two states quickly lost power to Democrats. "Home rule" meant Republican abandonment of freed people, Radicals, carpetbaggers, and scalawags. It also effectively nullified the Fourteenth and Fifteenth Amendments and the Civil Rights Act of 1866. The **Compromise of 1877** completed repudiation of the idea, born during the Civil War and pursued during Congressional Reconstruction, of a powerful federal government protecting the rights of all American citizens.

CONCLUSION

Reconstruction succeeded in the limited political sense of reuniting a nation torn apart by the Civil War. The Radical Republican vision, emphasizing racial justice, equal civil and political rights guaranteed by the Fourteenth and Fifteenth Amendments, and a new Southern economy organized around independent small farmers, never enjoyed the support of the majority of its party or the Northern public. The federal government's failure to pursue land reform left former slaves without the economic independence needed for full emancipation. Yet the newly autonomous black family, along with black-controlled churches, schools, and other social institutions, provided the foundations for the modern African American community.

Even as the federal government retreated from the defense of equal rights for black people, it took a more aggressive stance as the protector of business interests. The Hayes administration responded decisively to one of the worst outbreaks of class violence in American history by dispatching federal troops to several Northern cities to break the Great Railroad Strike of 1877. In the aftermath of Reconstruction, the struggle between capital and labor had clearly replaced "the Southern question" as the number one political issue of the day. "The overwhelming labor question has dwarfed all other questions into nothing," wrote an Ohio Republican. "We have home questions enough to occupy attention now."

Compromise of 1877 The Congressional settling of the 1876 election which installed Republican Rutherford B. Hayes in the White House and gave Democrats control of all state governments in the South.

CHRONOLOGY

1865   Freedmen's Bureau established.

Abraham Lincoln assassinated.

Andrew Johnson begins presidential Reconstruction.

Black codes begin to be enacted in Southern states.

Thirteenth Amendment ratified.

1866   Civil Rights Act passed.

Congress approves Fourteenth Amendment.

Ku Klux Klan founded.

1867   Reconstruction Acts, passed over President Johnson's veto, begin congressional Reconstruction.

Tenure of Office Act.

Southern states call constitutional conventions.

1868   President Johnson impeached by the House but acquitted in Senate trial.

Fourteenth Amendment ratified.

Most Southern states readmitted to Union.

Ulysses S. Grant elected president.

1869   Congress approves Fifteenth Amendment.

Union Pacific and Central Pacific tracks meet at Promontory Point in Utah Territory.

Suffragists split into National Woman.

Suffrage Association and American Woman Suffrage Association.

1870   Fifteenth Amendment ratified.

1871   Ku Klux Klan Act passed.

"Tweed Ring" in New York City exposed.

1872   Liberal Republicans break with Grant and Radicals, nominate Horace Greeley for president.

Crédit Mobilier scandal.

Grant reelected president.

1873   Financial panic and beginning of economic depression.

Slaughterhouse cases.

1874   Democrats gain control of House for first time since 1856.

1875   Civil Rights Act.

1876   Disputed election between Samuel Tilden and Rutherford B. Hayes.

1877   Electoral Commission elects Hayes president.

President Hayes dispatches federal troops to break Great Railroad Strike and withdraws last remaining federal troops from the South.

SUMMARY

The Politics of Reconstruction   The end of the Civil War answered some questions about the nation's future but raised serious issues about dealing with the South and the four million ex-slaves. Disagreement arose between the plans of Presidents Lincoln and Johnson versus those of Congress. The Radical Republicans succeeded in implementing their program, including constitutional amendments to guarantee the rights of African Americans.

The Meaning of Freedom   The end of slavery created new opportunities and new challenges for African Americans. The first impulse was to move freely about the country. It soon gave way to attempts to build new communities, to accommodate their new status and conditions. Family, churches, and schools served as cornerstones of the new communities, but economic realities of the postwar South severely limited job options. The first attempts to build political power bases also occurred.

Southern Politics and Society Republicans constituted a minority in the South and faced great challenges in developing the party. Issues also arose over attempts to reconstruct the South and also stimulated a strong conservative Democratic resistance that eventually redeemed state governments from Republican rule. A variety of factors plagued attempts to build a "New South" following Northern economic trends.

Reconstructing the North Following the Civil War, the Northern economy followed its path of the expansion of industrialization and the growth of large corporations. The spearhead of development was railroad construction. Economic growth influenced Republicans to ally with businesses, neglecting Radical Republican causes. The depression of 1873 caused great distress and increased tension between labor and capital. Scandals and corruption hurt Republicans in the 1876 election where a stalemate was avoided by a compromise that ended Reconstruction.

REVIEW QUESTIONS

1. How did various visions of a "reconstructed" South differ? How did these visions reflect the old political and social divisions that had led to the Civil War?

2. What key changes did emancipation make in the political and economic status of African Americans? Discuss the expansion of citizenship rights in the post–Civil War years. To what extent did women share in the gains made by African Americans?

3. What role did such institutions as the family, the church, the schools, and the political parties play in the African American transition to freedom?

4. How did white Southerners attempt to limit the freedom of former slaves? How did these efforts succeed, and how did they fail?

5. Evaluate the achievements and failures of Reconstruction governments in the Southern states.

6. What were the crucial economic changes occurring in the North and South during the Reconstruction era?

KEY TERMS

Black Codes (p. 439)

Carpetbaggers (p. 450)

Civil Rights Act (p. 440)

Congressional Reconstruction (p. 440)

Compromise of 1877 (p. 460)

Field Order 15 (p. 437)

Fifteenth Amendment (p. 443)

Freedmen's Bureau (p. 437)

Ku Klux Klan (p. 443)

Liberal Republicans (p. 457)

Radical Republicans (p. 437)

Reconstruction Act (p. 441)

Scalawags (p. 450)

Sharecropping (p. 448)

Slaughterhouse cases (p. 453)

Tenure of Office Act (p. 441)

Union League (p. 449)

RECOMMENDED READING

Paul A. Cimbala and Randall M. Miller, eds., *The Freedmen's Bureau and Recon-struction* (1999). A wide-ranging collection of the latest scholarship, with special attention to recapturing the historical voices of freed people.

Jane Dailey, *Before Jim Crow: The Politics of Race in Post Emancipation Virginia* (2000). A fine study that focuses on the tension between the drive to establish white supremacy and the struggle for biracial coalitions in post–Civil War Virginia politics.

Laura F. Edwards, *Gendered Strife and Confusion: The Political Culture of Reconstruc-tion* (1997). An ambitious analysis of how gender ideologies played a key role in shaping the party politics and social relations of the Reconstruction-era South.

Michael W. Fitzgerald, *The Union League Movement in the Deep South* (1989). Uses the Union League as a lens through which to examine race relations and the close connections between politics and economic change in the post–Civil War South.

Eric Foner, *Reconstruction: America's Unfinished Revolution, 1863–1877* (1988). The most comprehensive and thoroughly researched overview of the Reconstruction era.

William Gillette, *Retreat from Reconstruction: A Political History, 1867–1878* (1979). Covers the national political scene, with special attention to the abandon-ment of the ideal of racial equality.

Jacqueline Jones, *Labor of Love, Labor of Sorrow* (1985). Includes excellent material on the work and family lives of African American women in slavery and freedom.

Leon Litwack, *Been in the Storm So Long: The Aftermath of Slavery* (1979). A richly detailed analysis of the transition from slavery to freedom; excellent use of African American sources.

Scott Reynolds Nelson, *Iron Confederacies: Southern Railways, Klan Violence, and Reconstruction* (1999). Pathbreaking analysis of how conservative Southern and Northern business interests rebuilt the South's railroad system and also achieved enormous political power within individual states.

Edward Royce, *The Origins of Southern Sharecropping* (1993). A sophisticated, tightly argued work of historical sociology that explains how sharecrop-ping emerged as the dominant form of agricultural labor in the post–Civil War South.

"IS *THIS* A REPUBLICAN FORM OF GOVERNMENT? IS *THIS* PROTECTING LIFE, LIBERTY, OR PROPERTY? IS *THIS* THE EQUAL PROTECTION OF THE LAWS?"

MR. LAMAR (*Democrat, Mississippi*). "In the words of the inspired Poet, 'Thy Gentleness has made thee Great.'" [Did Mr. LAMAR mean the Colored Race?]

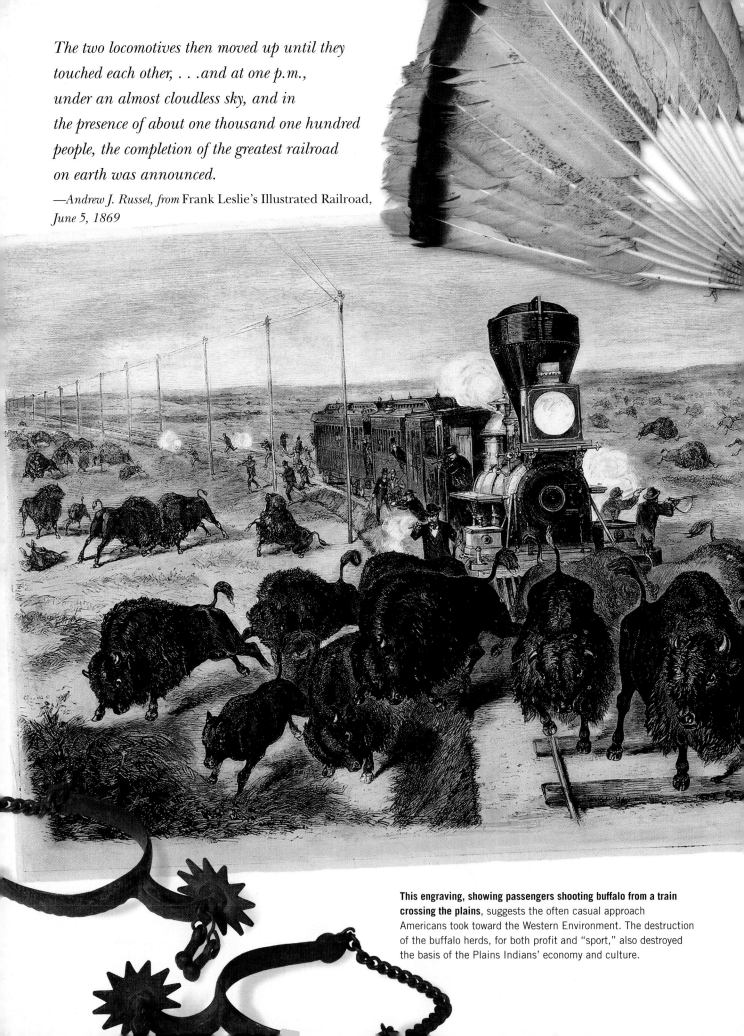

The two locomotives then moved up until they touched each other, . . .and at one p.m., under an almost cloudless sky, and in the presence of about one thousand one hundred people, the completion of the greatest railroad on earth was announced.

—*Andrew J. Russel, from* Frank Leslie's Illustrated Railroad, *June 5, 1869*

This engraving, showing passengers shooting buffalo from a train crossing the plains, suggests the often casual approach Americans took toward the Western Environment. The destruction of the buffalo herds, for both profit and "sport," also destroyed the basis of the Plains Indians' economy and culture.

18

CONQUEST AND SURVIVAL
THE TRANS-MISSISSIPPI WEST, 1860–1900

HOW DID the slaughter of the buffalo affect the Plains Indians?

HOW DID the mining industry develop in the United States?

WHAT WAS life like for a cowboy in the late nineteenth century?

WHO TOOK advantage of the Homestead Act?

HOW DID agribusiness differ from more traditional forms of farming?

WHAT PLACE did the West hold in the national imagination?

WHAT KIND of Indian society did reformers envision?

AMERICAN COMMUNITIES

The Oklahoma Land Rush

DECADES AFTER THE EVENT, COWBOY EVAN G. BARNARD VIVIDLY recalled the preparations made by settlers when Oklahoma territorial officials announced the opening of No Man's Land to the biggest "land rush" in American history. "Thousands of people gathered along the border. . . . As the day for the race drew near, the settlers practiced running their horses and driving carts." Finally the morning of April 22, 1889, arrived. "At ten o'clock people lined up . . . ready for the great race of their lives." Like many others, Barnard displayed his guns prominently on his hips, determined to discourage competitors from claiming the 160 acres of prime land that he intended to grab for himself.

Evan Barnard's story was one strand in the larger tale of the destruction and creation of communities in the trans-Mississippi West. In the 1830s, the federal government designated what was to become the state of Oklahoma as Indian Territory, reserved for the Five Civilized Tribes (Cherokees, Chickasaws, Choctaws, Creeks, and Seminoles) who had forcibly been removed from their eastern lands. All five tribes had reestablished themselves as sovereign republics in Indian Territory. The Cherokees and Chocktaws became prosperous cotton growers. The Creeks managed large herds of hogs and cattle, and the Chickasaws grazed not only cattle, but also sheep and goats on their open fields. The Five Tribes also ran sawmills, gristmills, and cotton gins. Indian merchants were soon dealing with other tribespeople as well as licensed white traders and even contracting with the federal government.

The Civil War, however, took a heavy toll on their success. Some tribes, slaveholders themselves, sided with the Confederacy; others with the Union. When the war ended, more than 10,000 people—nearly one-fifth of the population of Indian Territory—had died. To make matters worse, new treaties required the Five Civilized Tribes to cede the entire western half of the territory, including the former northern Indian territory of Nebraska and Kansas, for the resettlement of tribes from other regions.

Western Oklahoma thereby became home to thousands of newly displaced peoples, including the Pawnees, Peorias, Ottawas, Wyandots, and Miamis. Many small tribes readily took to farming and rebuilt their communities. But the nomadic, buffalo-hunting Kiowas, Cheyennes, Comanches, and Arapahoes did not settle so peacefully. They continued to traverse the plains until the U.S. Army finally forced them onto reservations. Eventually, more than 80,000 tribespeople were living on twenty-one separate reservations in western Oklahoma, all governed by agents appointed by the federal government.

Indian Territory (Oklahoma)

The opening of the unassigned far western district of Oklahoma known as No Man's Land to non-Indian homesteading, however, signaled the impending end of Indian sovereignty. Many non-Indians saw this almost 2 million acre strip as a Promised Land, perfect for dividing into thousands of small farms. African Americans, many of whom were former slaves of Indian planters, appealed to the federal government for the right to stake claims there. Another group of would-be homesteaders, known as "Boomers," quickly tired of petitioning and invaded the district in 1880, only to be booted out by the Tenth Cavalry. Meanwhile, the railroads, seeing the potential for lucrative commerce, put constant pressure on the federal government to open No Man's Land for settlement. In 1889 the U.S. Congress finally gave in.

Cowboy Barnard was just one of thousands to pour into No Man's Land on April 22, 1889. Many homesteaders simply crossed the border from Kansas. Southerners, dispossessed by warfare and economic ruin in their own region, were also well represented. Market-minded settlers claimed the land nearest the railroads, and by nightfall of April 22 they had set up tent cities along the tracks. In a little over two months, after 6,000 homestead claims had been filed, the first sod houses appeared, sheltering growing communities of non-Indian farmers, ranchers, and other entrepreneurs.

Dramatic as it was, the land rush of 1889 was only one in a series of events that soon dispossessed Oklahoma's Indians of their remaining lands. First, the federal government broke up the estates held collectively by various tribes in western Oklahoma, assigning to individuals the standard 160-acre allotment and allowing non-Indian homesteaders to claim the rest. Then, in 1898, Congress passed the Curtis Act, formally dissolving Indian Territory and dispossessing the Five Tribes. Members of the former Indian nations were directed to dismantle their governments, abandon their estates, and join the ranks of other homesteaders. They nevertheless retained many of their tribal customs and managed to regain their sovereign status in 1977.

Later generations of Oklahomans often celebrated their historic ties to the Indian nations. At formal ceremonies marking statehood, just before the newly elected governor took the oath of office, a mock wedding ceremony united a tough and virile cowboy with a demure and submissive Indian maiden. By this time, in 1907, tribespeople were outnumbered in Oklahoma by ten to one.

By this time also, nearly one-quarter of the entire population of the United States lived west of the Mississippi River.

Hundreds of new communities, supported primarily by cattle ranching, agriculture, mining, or other industries, had not only grown with the emerging national economy but also helped to shape it in the process. The newcomers displaced communities that had formed centuries earlier. They also drastically transformed the physical landscape. Through their activities and the support of Easterners, the United States realized an ambition that John L. O'Sullivan had described in 1845 as the nation's "manifest destiny to overspread the continent" and remake it in a new image.

INDIAN PEOPLES UNDER SIEGE

The tribespeople living west of the Mississippi River keenly felt the pressure of the gradual incorporation of the West into the nation. The Oregon Trail opened the Northwest to large numbers of non-Indian settlers. In 1846 the United States reached an agreement with Great Britain for the division of the Oregon Country. Then came the addition of the vast territories taken from Mexico following the Mexican-American War. California quickly became a state in 1850, Oregon in 1859. Congress consolidated the national domain in the next decades by granting territorial status to Utah, New Mexico, Washington, Dakota, Colorado, Nevada, Arizona, Idaho, Montana, and Wyoming. The purchase of Alaska in 1867 added an area twice the size of Texas and extended the nation beyond its contiguous borders so that it reached almost to Russia and the North Pole. The federal government made itself the custodian of all these thinly settled regions, permitting limited self-rule, with appointed governors supervising the transition from territorial status to statehood.

Competition for the land and its resources was central to this encounter. Unlike the settlers wedded to the principles of private property, the tribespeople mainly believed that the land belongs to those who revere it across many generations. Their prospects to preserve their ways of life amid this contest dimmed considerably following the discovery of gold in California in 1848, the opening of western lands to homesteaders in 1862, and the completion of the transcontinental railroad in 1869. White settlers, hoping to build a new life for themselves, rushed into these new territories and repeatedly invaded Indian lands west of the Mississippi. Violent outbreaks between white emigrants and Indian peoples became increasingly commonplace. Since the Jefferson administration, federal officials had promoted the assimilation of Indian peoples; they now became even more determined to break up their tribal councils and to bring them into the American mainstream.

ON THE EVE OF CONQUEST

Before the European colonists reached the New World, tribespeople of the Great Plains, Southwest, and Far West had occupied the lands for more than 20,000 years. Hundreds of tribes, totaling perhaps a million members, had adapted to such extreme climates as the desert aridity of present-day Utah and Nevada, the bitter cold of the northern Great Plains, and the seasonally heavy rain of the Pacific Northwest. Many cultivated maize (corn), foraged for wild plants, fished, or hunted game. Several tribes built cities with several thousand inhabitants and traded across thousands of miles of western territory.

Invasion by the English, Spanish, and other Europeans brought disease, religious conversion, and new patterns of commerce. But geographic isolation

HOW DID the slaughter of the buffalo affect the Plains Indians?

IMAGE KEY
for pages 466–467

a. A feather fan carried by Yuchi dancers.
b. Passengers and the train crew shooting buffalo on the line of the Kansas-Pacific Railroad in this colored line engraving of 1871.
c. Confederate cavalry spurs from the American Civil War.
d. An old fashioned steam locomotive engine.
e. Wooly Head's wife and child.
f. A Chinese mine worker steadies a water cannon in a shallow riverbed in Idaho with a fellow laborer standing nearby.
g. Buffalo Bill Cody from an 1899 poster for his "Wild West Show."
h. Nebraska homesteaders in 1886.
i. Thirty-three horse team harvester, cutting, threshing, and sacking wheat, c. 1902.

 17–6
Congressional Report on Indian Affairs (1887)

MAP EXPLORATION

To explore an interactive version of this map, go to **http://www.prenhall.com/faraghertlc/map18.1**

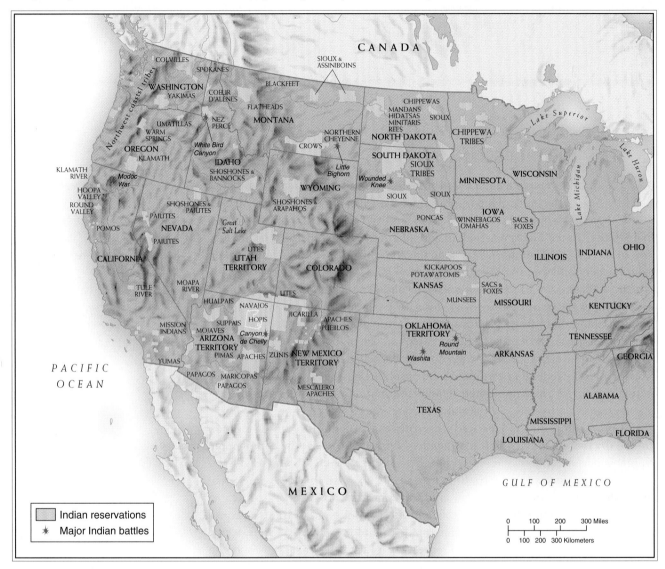

MAP 18-1

Major Indian Battles and Indian Reservations, 1860–1900   As commercial routes and white populations passed through and occupied Indian lands, warfare inevitably erupted. The displacement of Indians to reservations opened access by farmers, ranchers, and investors to natural resources and to markets.

WHY WERE the Indians forcibly removed to reservations?

still gave many tribes a margin of survival unknown in the East. At the close of the Civil War, approximately 360,000 Indian people still lived in the trans-Mississippi West, the majority of them on the Great Plains.

The surviving tribes adapted to changing conditions. The Plains Indians learned to ride the horses and shoot the guns introduced by Spanish and British traders. Even before they were uprooted and moved across the Mississippi River, the Cherokees had learned English, converted to Christianity, established a constitutional republic, and become a nation of farmers.

Legally, the federal government had long regarded Indian tribes as autonomous nations residing within American boundaries and had negotiated numerous treaties with them over land rights and commerce. But pressured by land-hungry whites, several states had violated these federal treaties so often that the U.S. Congress passed the Indian Removal Act of 1830 (see Chapter 10), which provided funds to relocate all eastern tribes by force if necessary. The Cherokees challenged this legislation, and the Supreme Court ruled in their favor in *Cherokee Nation* v. *Georgia* (1831). Ignoring the Court's decision, President Andrew Jackson, known as a hardened Indian fighter, forced many tribes to cede their land and remove to Indian Territory. There, it was believed, they might live undisturbed by whites and gradually adjust to "civilized" ways. But soon, the onslaught of white settlers, railroad entrepreneurs, and prospectors rushing for gold pressured tribes to cede millions of their acres to the United States. In 1854, to open the Kansas and Nebraska Territories for white settlement, the federal government simply abolished the northern half of Indian Territory. As demand for resources and land accelerated, the entire plan for a permanent Indian Territory fell apart.

RESERVATIONS AND THE SLAUGHTER OF THE BUFFALO

As early as the 1840s, highly placed officials had outlined a plan to subdue the intensifying rivalry over natural resources and land. Under the terms of their proposal, individual tribes would agree to live within clearly defined zones— reservations—and, in exchange, the Bureau of Indian Affairs would provide guidance while U.S. military forces ensured protection. By the end of the 1850s eight western reservations had been established where Indian peoples were induced to speak English, take up farming, and convert to Christianity.

Several tribes signed treaties, although often under duress. High-handed officials, such as governor Isaac Stevens of Washington Territory, made no attempt at legitimate negotiations, choosing instead to intimidate or deceive Indian peoples into signing away their lands. State officials moved the Indians onto three reservations after their leaders signed away 45,000 square miles of tribal land. The Suquamish leader Seattle admitted defeat but warned the governor: "Your time of decay may be distant, but it will surely come."

Those tribes that moved to reservations often found federal policies inadequate to their needs. The Medicine Lodge Treaty of 1867 assigned reservations in existing Indian Territory to Comanches, Plains (Kiowa) Apaches, Kiowas, Cheyennes, and Arapahoes, bringing these tribes together with Sioux, Shoshones, and Bannocks. All told, more than 100,000 people found themselves competing intensely for survival. Over the next decade, a group of Quakers appointed by President Ulysses S. Grant attempted to mediate differences among the tribes and to supply the starving peoples with food and seed. At the same time, white prospectors and miners continued to flood the Dakota Territory. Corrupt officials of the Bureau of Indian Affairs routinely diverted funds for their own use and reduced food supplies, a policy promoting malnutrition, demoralization, and desperation.

The nomadic tribes that traditionally hunted and gathered over large territories saw their freedom sharply curtailed. The Lakotas, or Western Sioux, a loose confederation of bands scattered across the northern Great Plains, were one of the largest and most adaptive of all Indian nations. Seizing buffalo-hunting territory from their rivals, the Pawnees and the Crows, the Sioux had learned to follow the herds on horseback. The Sioux were also vision seekers. Young men and women pursued dreams that would provide them guidance for a lifetime; elders themselves followed dreams that might guide the destiny of the entire tribe or nation.

QUICK REVIEW

White Migration and the Plains Indians

- Desire by whites for land led to violations of treaties.
- Buffalo were eliminated from tribal hunting grounds.
- Many Indian peoples decided they could only fight or die.

Chief Red Cloud in an 1868 photograph. The Oglala Sioux spiritual leader is seen with Red Dog, Little Wound, interpreter John Bridgeman (on his right), American Horse, and Red Shirt (on his left). He ventured to Washington with his delegation to discuss with President Ulysses S. Grant the various provisions of the peace treaty, just signed, to end the violent conflict over the Bozeman Trail.

National Anthropological Archives/Smithsonian Institution (3238/E)

The mass slaughter of the buffalo brought the crisis provoked by the increasing restriction of the nomadic Plains peoples to a peak. In earlier eras, vast herds of buffalo had literally darkened the western horizon. As gunpowder and the railroad came to the range, the number of buffalo fell rapidly. Non-Indian traders avidly sought fur for coats, hide for leather, bones for fertilizer, and heads for trophies. New rifles, like the .50-caliber Sharps, could kill at 600 feet; one sharpshooter bragged of killing 3,000 buffalo. Army commanders encouraged the slaughter, accurately predicting that starvation would break tribal resistance to the reservation system. With their food sources practically destroyed, diseases such as smallpox and cholera (brought by fur traders) sweeping through their villages, and their way of life undermined, many Great Plains tribes, including many Sioux, concluded that they could only fight or die.

THE INDIAN WARS

Under these pressures, a handful of tribes organized themselves and their allies to resist both federal policies and the growing wave of white settlers. The overwhelming majority of tribespeople did not take up arms. But settlers, thousands of them Civil War veterans with weapons close at hand, responded to real or imaginary threats with their own brands of violence.

Large-scale war erupted in 1864. Having decided to terminate all treaties with tribes in eastern Colorado, territorial governor John Evans encouraged a group of white civilians, the Colorado Volunteers, to stage raids through Cheyenne campgrounds. Seeking protection, Chief Black Kettle brought a band of 800 Cheyennes to a U.S. fort and received orders to set up camp at Sand Creek. Feeling secure in this arrangement, Black Kettle sent out most of his men to hunt. Several weeks later, on November 29, 1864, the Colorado Volunteers and soldiers attacked. While Black Kettle held up a U.S. flag and a white truce banner, a disorderly group of 700 men, many of them drunk, slaughtered 105 Cheyenne women and children and 28 men. They mutilated the corpses and took scalps back to Denver to exhibit as trophies. Iron Teeth, a Cheyenne woman who survived, remembered seeing a woman "crawling along on the ground, shot, scalped, crazy, but not yet dead." Months after the **Sand Creek Massacre**, bands of Cheyennes, Sioux, and Arapahoes were still retaliating, burning civilian outposts and sometimes killing whole families.

The Sioux played the most dramatic roles in the Indian Wars. In 1851, believing the U.S. government would recognize their own rights of conquest over other Indian tribes, the Sioux relinquished large tracts of land as a demonstration of good faith. But within a decade, a mass invasion of miners and the construction of military forts along the Bozeman Trail in Wyoming, the Sioux's principal buffalo range, threw the tribe's future into doubt. During the Great Sioux War of 1865–1867, the Oglala Sioux warrior Red Cloud fought the U.S. Army to a stalemate and forced the government to abandon its forts, which the Sioux then burned to the ground. The **Treaty of Fort Laramie**, signed in 1868, created the Great Sioux Reservation, which included the present state of South Dakota west of the Missouri River, but restored only a temporary peace to the region.

The Treaty of Fort Laramie granted the Sioux the right to occupy the Black Hills, or Paha Sapa, their sacred land, "as long as the grass shall grow," but the discovery of gold soon undermined this guarantee. White prospectors hurriedly invaded the territory. Directed to quash rumors of fabulous deposits of the precious metal, Lieutenant Colonel George Armstrong Custer organized a surveying expedition to the Black Hills during the summer of 1874, but, contrary to plan, the Civil War hero described rich veins of ore that could be cheaply extracted. The U.S. Congress then

Sand Creek Massacre   The near annihilation in 1864 of Black Kettle's Cheyenne band by Colorado troops under Colonel John Chivington's orders to "kill and scalp all, big and little."

Treaty of Fort Laramie   The treaty acknowledging U.S. defeat in the Great Sioux War in 1868 and supposedly guaranteeing the Sioux perpetual land and hunting rights in South Dakota, Wyoming, and Montana.

Kiowa Preparing for a War Expedition, ca. 1887. This sketch on paper was made by an Indian artist, Silverhorn, who had himself taken part in the final revolt of the Kiowas in 1874. He later became a medicine man, and then served as a private in the U.S. Cavalry at Fort Sill, Oklahoma Territory.

Silverhorn, Native American, *Kiowa Preparing for a War Expedition*. From Sketchbook, 1887. Graphite ink and crayon. Gift of Mrs. Terrell Bartlett. Collection of the McNay Art Museum pushed to acquire the territory for Americans. To protect their land, Sioux, Cheyenne, and Arapaho warriors, ranging between 2,000 and 9,000 in number, moved into war camps during the summer of 1876 and prepared for battle.

After several months of skirmishes and battles between the U.S. Army and Sioux warriors, Lieutenant Colonel Custer decided to rush ahead to a site in Montana that was known to white soldiers as Little Bighorn and to Lakotas as Greasy Grass. This foolhardy move offered the allied Cheyenne and Sioux warriors a perfect opportunity to cut off Custer's logistical and military support. On June 25, 1876, Custer and his troops were wiped out by one of the largest Indian contingents ever assembled, an estimated 2,000 to 4,000 warriors.

"Custer's Last Stand" gave Indian-haters the emotional ammunition to whip up public excitement. After Custer's defeat, spiritual leader Sitting Bull reportedly said, "Now they will never let us rest." By 1877, Sioux leadership in the Indian Wars was ended.

Among the last to hold out against the reservation system were the Apaches in the Southwest. Most Apache bands, unable to tolerate the harsh conditions on the reservation, returned to their old ways of seizing territory and stealing cattle.

Pursued by the U.S. Army, the Apaches earned a reputation as intrepid warriors. Their brilliant strategists and horse-riding braves became legendary for lightning-swift raids followed by quick disappearances. The Kiowas and the Comanches, both powerful tribes, joined the Apaches in one of the bloodiest conflicts, the Red River War of 1874–1875. The U.S. Army ultimately prevailed less by military might than by denying Indians access to food. Even after the Red River War, small-scale warfare sputtered on. Not until September 1886, his band reduced to only thirty people, did Geronimo finally surrender, ending the Indian Wars.

THE NEZ PERCÉ

The Nez Percé (meaning "pierced nose") had been given their name by French Canadian fur trappers, who thought they had seen members of the tribe wearing shells in their septums. For generations the Nez Percé had regarded themselves as good friends to white traders and settlers. Living in the plateau where Idaho, Washington, and Oregon now meet, they had saved the Lewis and Clark expedition from starvation in 1803. The Nez Percé had occasionally assisted American armies against hostile tribes, and many of them were converts to Christianity.

But the discovery of gold on Nez Percé territory in 1860 changed their relations with whites for the worse. Pressed by prospectors and mining companies, government commissioners, in the treaty of 1863, demanded the Nez Percé cede 6 million acres, nine-tenths of their land, at less than 10 ¢ per acre. Some of the Nez Percé leaders agreed to the terms of the treaty, which had been fraudulently signed on behalf of the entire tribe, but others refused. At first, federal officials listened to Nez Percé complaints against the treaty and decided to allow them to remain on their land. But responding to pressure from settlers and politicians, however, they almost immediately reversed their decision, ordering the Nez Percé, including Chief Joseph and his followers, to sell their land and to move onto a reservation.

Intending to comply, Chief Joseph's band set out from the Wallowa Valley with their livestock and all the possessions they could carry. Along the way, some young members of another Indian band traveling with them rode away from camp to avenge the death of one of their own by killing several white settlers. Hoping to explain the situation, a Nez Percé truce team approached U.S. troops. The troops opened fire, and the Indian riders fired back, killing one-third of the soldiers. Brilliantly outmaneuvering vengeful U.S. troops sent to intercept them, the 750 Nez Percé retreated for some 1,400 miles into Montana and Wyoming through mountains and prairies, and across the Bitterroot Range. Over the three and a half months of their journey, Nez Percé braves fought 2,000 regular U.S. troops and eighteen Indian auxiliary detachments in eighteen separate engagements and two major battles. U.S. troops finally trapped the Nez Percé in the Bear Paw Mountains of northern Montana, just 30 miles from the Canadian border. Suffering from hunger and cold, they surrendered.

Promised they would be returned to Oregon, the Nez Percé were sent instead to disease-ridden bottomland near Fort Leavenworth in Kansas, and then to Oklahoma. Arguing for the right of his people to return to their Oregon reservation, Joseph spoke eloquently, through an interpreter, to Congress in 1879. "Treat all men alike. Give them all the same law. Give them all an even chance to live and grow. All men were made by the same Great Spirit Chief," Joseph pleaded. The last remnant of Joseph's band were deported under guard to a non–Nez Percé reservation in Washington, where Chief Joseph died in 1904 "of a broken heart," and where his descendants continue to live in exile to this day.

THE INTERNAL EMPIRE

Since the time of Christopher Columbus, the Americas had inspired in Europeans visions of a land of incredible wealth, free for the taking. In the nineteenth century, the North American continent, stretching across scarcely populated territories toward the Pacific Ocean, revived this fantasy. Determined to make their fortunes, be it from copper in Arizona, wheat in Montana, or oranges in California, numerous adventurers traveled west. As a group they carried out the largest migration and greatest commercial expansion in American history.

But the settlers themselves also became the subjects of a huge "internal empire" whose financial, political, and industrial centers of power remained in the East. Only a small number of settlers actually struck it rich in the great extractive industries—mining, lumbering, ranching, and farming—that ruled the Western economy. Meanwhile, older populations—Indian peoples, Hispanic peoples, and more recently settled communities like the Mormons—struggled to create places for themselves in this new order.

MINING TOWNS

The discovery of gold in California in 1848 roused fortune seekers from across the United States, Europe, and as far away as Chile and China. Within a year, prospecting parties overran the western territories, setting a pattern for intermittent rushes for gold, silver, and copper that extended from the Colorado mountains to the Arizona deserts, from California to Oregon and Washington, and from Alaska to the Black Hills of South Dakota. Mining camps and boomtowns soon dotted what had once been thinly settled regions. The population of California alone jumped from 14,000 in 1848 to 223,856 just four years later. More than any other industry or commercial enterprise, mining fostered western expansion.

The mining industry quickly grew from its treasure-hunt origins into a grand corporate enterprise. The most successful mine owners bought out the smaller claims and built an entire industry around their stakes. They found investors to finance their expansion and used the borrowed capital to purchase the latest in extractive technology, such as new explosives, compressed-air or diamond-headed rotary drills, and wire cable. They gained access to timber to fortify their underground structures and water to feed the hydraulic pumps that washed down mountains. They built smelters to refine the crude ore into ingots and often financed railroads to transport the product to distant markets. By the end of the century,

HOW DID the mining industry develop in the United States?

QUICK REVIEW

Technology and Mining

♦ Mining began as an individual enterprise.

♦ Deeper mining required expensive equipment.

♦ As mining became more complex and costly, it came under corporate control.

MAP EXPLORATION

To explore an interactive version of this map, go to **http://www.prenhall.com/faraghertlc/map18.2**

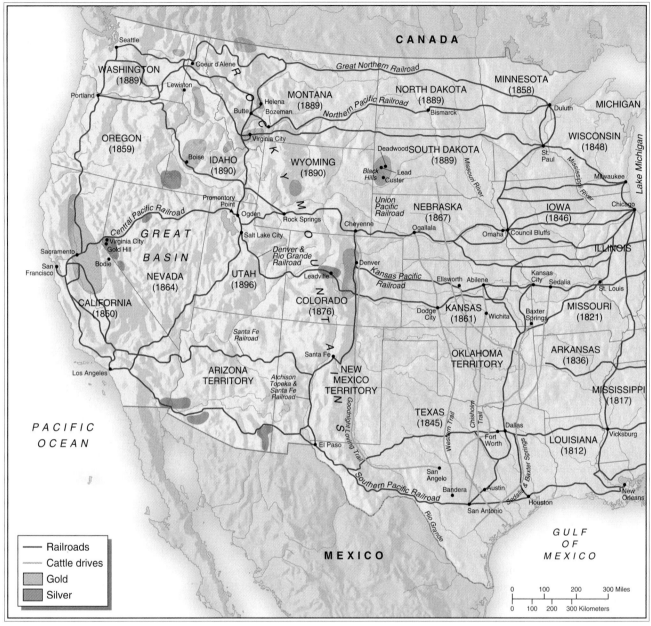

MAP 18-2

Railroad Routes, Cattle Trails, Gold and Silver Rushes, 1860–1900   By the end of the nineteenth century, the vast region of the West was crosscut by hundreds of lines of transportation and communication. The trade in precious metals and cattle helped build a population almost constantly on the move, following the rushes for gold or the herds of cattle.

Encyclopedia of American Social History.

HOW DID the growth of railroads and mining impact the environment and the lives of native peoples?

the Anaconda Copper Mining Company, which had mining interests throughout the West, had expanded into hydroelectricity to become one of the most powerful corporations in the nation.

The mining corporations laid the basis for a new economy as well as an interim government and established many of the region's first white settlements. Before the advent of railroads, ore had to be brought out of, and supplies brought into, mining areas by boats, wagons, and mules traveling hundreds of miles over rough territory. The railroad made transportation of supplies and products easier and faster. The shipping trade meanwhile grew into an important industry of its own, employing thousands of merchants, peddlers, and sailors. Gold Hill and nearby Virginia City, Nevada, began as a cluster of small mining camps and by the early 1860s became a thriving urban community of nearly 6,000 people. A decade later, the population had quadrupled, but it subsequently fell sharply as the mines gave out. Men outnumbered women by as much as ten to one, and very few lived with families or stayed very long. They often bunked with male kin and worked alongside friends or acquaintances from their hometown. Some lived unusually well, feasting on oysters trucked in at great expense. The town center was usually the saloon, where, as one observer complained, men "without the restraint of law, indifferent to public opinion, and unburdened by families, drink whenever they feel like it, whenever they have the money to pay for it, and whenever there is nothing else to do."

The western labor movement began in these camps, partly as a response to dangerous working conditions. In the hardrock mines of the 1870s, one of every thirty workers was disabled, one of eighty killed. Miners began to organize in the 1860s, demanding good pay for dangerous and life-shortening work. By the end of the century they had established the strongest unions in the West.

When mine owners' private armies "arrested" strikers or fought their unions with rifle fire, miners burned down the campsites, seized trains loaded with ore, and sabotaged company property. The miners' unions also helped to secure legislation mandating a maximum eight-hour day for certain jobs and workers' compensation for injuries. Such laws were enacted in Idaho, Arizona, and New Mexico by the 1910s, long before similar laws in most Eastern states.

The unions fought hard, but they did so exclusively for the benefit of white workers. The native-born and the Irish and Cornish immigrants (from Cornwall, England) far outnumbered other groups before the turn of the century, when Italians, Slavs, and Greeks began to replace them. Labor unions eventually admitted these new immigrants but refused Chinese, Mexican, and Indian workers.

When prices and ore production fell sharply, not even unions could stop the owners from shutting down the mines and leaving ghost towns in their wake. Often they also left behind an environmental disaster. Hydraulic mining, which used water cannons to blast hillsides and expose gold deposits, drove tons of rock and earth into the rivers and canyons. By the late 1860s southern California's rivers were clogged, producing floods that wiped out towns and farms. In 1893, Congress finally passed the **Caminetti Act**, giving the state the power to regulate the mines. (The act also created the Sacramento River Commission, which began to replace free-flowing rivers with canals and dams.) Underground mining continued unregulated, using up whole forests for timbers and filling the air with dangerous, sulfurous smoke.

A "hard rock" miner demonstrates the tiring and often dangerous task of hammering a drill into a rock to prepare a blasting hole. New technologies, such as diamond-headed drills, quickly revolutionized the extractive process, but potentially lethal hazards, including cave-ins and poisonous gases, remained great.

Artist unknown, *Miners Underground*, 1897. Glass plate negative. Photograph by Timothy O'Sullivan. Courtesy Colorado Historical Society

Caminetti Act   1893 act giving the state the power to regulate the mines.

MAP EXPLORATION

To explore an interactive version of this map, go to
www.prenhall.com/faraghertlc/map18.3

MAP 18-3
Mormon Cultural Diffusion, ca. 1883

WHY WERE many western parks and national Forests established before eastern ones.

Edmunds Act 1882 act that effectively disfranchised those who believed in or practiced polygamy and threatened them with fines and imprisonment.

Edmunds-Tucker Act 1887 act which destroyed the temporal power of the Mormon Church by confiscating all assets over $50,000 and establishing a federal commission to oversee all elections in the Utah territory.

MORMON SETTLEMENTS

The Mormons (members of the Church of Jesus Christ of Latter-Day Saints) had fled western New York in the 1830s for Illinois and Missouri, only to face greater persecution in the Midwest. When their founder, Joseph Smith, was murdered after proclaiming the doctrine of polygamy (the taking of more than one wife), the community sought refuge in the West. Led by their new prophet, Brigham Young, the Mormons migrated in 1846–1847 to the Great Basin in present-day Utah and formed an independent theocratic state called Deseret. However, their dream was cut short in 1850 when Congress set up Utah Territory. In 1857 President James Buchanan declared the Mormons to be in "a state of substantial rebellion" (for being an independent state within U.S. territory) and sent the U.S. Army to occupy the territory.

Although federal troops remained until the outbreak of the Civil War in 1861, the Mormon population continued to grow. By 1870, more than 87,000 Mormons lived in Utah Territory. Contrary to federal law, church officials forbade the selling of land. Mormons instead held property in common. They created sizable settlements complemented by satellite villages joined to communal farmlands and a common pasture. Relying on agricultural techniques learned from local Indian tribes, the Mormons built dams for irrigation and harvested a variety of crops from desert soil. Eventually nearly 500 Mormon communities spread from Oregon to Idaho to northern Mexico.

But as territorial rule tightened, the Mormons saw their unique way of life once again threatened. Preceded by prohibitory federal laws enacted in 1862 and 1874, the Supreme Court finally ruled against polygamy in the 1879 case of *United States* v. *Reynolds*, which granted the freedom of belief but not the freedom of practice. In 1882, Congress passed the **Edmunds Act**, which effectively disfranchised those who believed in or practiced polygamy and threatened them with fines and imprisonment. Equally devastating was the **Edmunds-Tucker Act**, passed five years later, which destroyed the temporal power of the Mormon Church by confiscating all assets over $50,000 and establishing a federal commission to oversee all elections in the territory. By the early 1890s, Mormon leaders officially renounced the practice of plural marriage.

BORDERLAND COMMUNITIES

The Treaty of Guadalupe Hidalgo, which ended the Mexican-American War, allowed the Hispanic people north of the Rio Grande to choose between immigrating to Mexico or staying in what was now the United States. But the new Mexican-American border, one of the longest unguarded boundaries in the world, could not successfully sever communities that had been connected for centuries. What gradually emerged was an economically and socially interdependent zone, the Anglo-Hispanic borderlands linking the United States and Mexico.

Although under the treaty all Hispanics were formally guaranteed citizenship and the "free enjoyment of their liberty and property," local "Anglos" (as the Mexicans called white Americans) often violated these provisions and, through fraud or coercion, took control of the land. The Sante Fe Ring, a group of lawyers, politicians, and land speculators, stole millions of acres from the public domain and grabbed over 80 percent of the Mexicano landholdings in New Mexico alone. More often, Anglos used new federal laws for their own benefit.

For a time, Arizona and New Mexico seemed to hold out hope for a mutually beneficial interaction between Mexicanos and Anglos. A prosperous class of Hispanic landowners, with long-standing ties to Anglos through marriage, had established itself in cities like Albuquerque and Tucson, old Spanish towns that had been founded in the seventeenth and eighteenth centuries. In Las Cruces, New Mexico, an exceptional family such as the wealthy Amadors could shop by mail from Bloomingdales, travel to the World's Fair in Chicago, and send their children to English-language Catholic schools. These Mexican elites, well integrated into the emerging national economy, continued to wield political power as ranchers, landlords, and real estate developers until the end of the century. They secured passage of bills for education in their regions and often served as superintendents of local schools. Several prominent merchants became territorial delegates to Congress.

But the majority of Mexicans, who had lived in the mountains and deserts of the Southwest for well over two centuries, were less prepared for these changes. Most had worked outside the commercial economy, farming and herding sheep for their own subsistence. Before 1848 they had few contacts with the outside world. With the Anglos came land closures as well as commercial expansion prompted by railroad, mining, and timber industries. Many poor families found themselves crowded onto plots too small for subsistence farming. Many turned to seasonal labor on the new Anglo-owned commercial farms, where they became the first of many generations of poorly paid migratory workers. Other Mexicanos adapted by taking jobs on the railroad or in the mines. By the end of the century Mexicanos had become a predominantly urban population, dependent on wages for survival.

Mexican Americans in San Antonio continued to conduct their traditional market bazaar well after the incorporation of this region into the United States. Forced off the land and excluded from the better paying jobs in the emerging regional economy, many Mexicanos and especially women sought to sell the products of their own handiwork for cash or for bartered food and clothing.

Thomas Allen, *Market Plaza*, 1878–1879. Oil on canvas, 26" × 39". Witte Museum, San Antonio, Texas (36–65/8P)

Women were quickly drawn into the expanding network of market and wage relations. They tried to make ends meet by selling produce from their backyard gardens; more often they worked as seamstresses or laundresses. Formerly at the center of a communal society, Mexicanas found themselves with fewer options in the cash economy. What wages they could now earn fell below even the low sums paid to their husbands, and women lost status within both the family and community.

Occasionally, Mexicanos organized to reverse these trends or at least to limit the damage done to their communities. In the border town of Brownsville, Texas, in 1859, Juan Nepomuceno Cortina, known as the Red Robber of the Rio Grande, and sixty of his followers pillaged white-owned stores and killed four Anglos who had gone unpunished for murdering several Mexicans. "Cortina's War" marked the first of several sporadic rebellions. Other Mexicanos organized more peacefully. *El Alianzo Hispano-Americano* (the **Hispanic-American Alliance**) was formed "to protect and fight for the rights of Spanish Americans" through political action. *Mutualistes* (mutual aid societies) provided sickness and death benefits to Mexican families.

Despite many pressures, Mexicanos preserved much of their cultural heritage. The Roman Catholic Church retained its influence in the community, and most Mexicans continued to turn to the church to baptize infants, to celebrate the feast day of their patron saints, to marry, and to bury the dead. Special saints like the Virgin of Guadalupe and distinctive holy days like the Day of the Dead survived along with fiestas celebrating the change of seasons. Many communities continued to commemorate Mexican national holidays, such as *Cinco de Mayo* (the Fifth of May), marking the Mexican victory over French invaders in the battle of Puebla in 1862. Spanish language and Spanish place names continued to distinguish the Southwest.

Americans had brought in commercial capitalism, their political and legal systems, as well as many of their social and cultural institutions. Ironically, though, even after statehood, white settlers would still be only distant representatives of an empire whose financial, political, and industrial centers remained in the Northeast. Embittered Westerners, along with Southerners, would form the core of a nationwide discontent that would soon threaten to uproot the American political system.

Hispanic-American Alliance
Organization formed to protect and fight for the rights of Spanish Americans.

WHAT WAS life like for a cowboy in the late nineteenth century?

QUICK REVIEW

Cattle Ranching

◆ Indian removal and the arrival of the railroad opened land for ranching.

◆ High profits in the industry attracted speculative capital and large companies.

◆ The industry collapsed in the 1880s due to overgrazing.

THE CATTLE INDUSTRY

The slaughter of the buffalo made way for the cattle industry, one of the most profitable businesses in the West. Texas longhorns, introduced by the Spanish, numbered over 5 million at the close of the Civil War and represented a potentially plentiful supply of beef for Eastern consumers. The Kansas Pacific Railroad provided crucial transportation links to slaughtering and packing houses and commercial distributors in Kansas City, St. Louis, and Chicago.

Drovers pushed herd after herd north from Texas through Oklahoma on the trail marked out by part-Cherokee trader Jesse Chisholm. Great profits were made on Texas steers bought for $7–$9 a head and sold in Kansas for upward of $30. In 1880 nearly 2 million cattle were slaughtered in Chicago alone. For two decades, cattle represented the West's bonanza industry.

COWBOYS

The great cattle drives depended on the cowboy, a seasonal or migrant worker. After the Civil War, cowboys—one for every 300–500 head of cattle on the trail—rounded up herds of Texas cattle and drove them as many as 1,500 miles north to grazing ranches or to the stockyards where they were readied for shipping by rail to eastern markets. The boss supplied the horses, the cowboy his own bedroll, saddle, and spurs. The workday lasted from sunup to sundown, with short night shifts for guarding the cattle. Scurvy, a widespread ailment, could be traced to the basic chuckwagon menu of sowbelly, beans, and coffee, a diet bereft of fruits and vegetables. The cowboy worked without protection from rain or hail, and severe dust storms could cause temporary blindness.

In return for his labor, the cowboy received at the best of times about $30 per month. Wages were usually paid in one lump sum at the end of a drive, a policy that encouraged cowboys to spend their money quickly and recklessly. When wages began to fall along with the price of beef, many Texas cowboys struck for higher wages; nearly all Wyoming cowboys struck in 1886. Aided by the legendary camaraderie fostered in the otherwise desolate conditions of the long drive, cowboys, along with miners, were among the first western workers to organize against employers.

Like other parts of the West, the cattle range was ethnically diverse. Between one-fifth and one-third of all workers were Indian, Mexican, or African American. Some African American cowboys were sons of former slaves who had been captured from the African territory of Gambia, where cattle raising was an age-old art. Unlike Mexicans, they earned wages comparable to those paid to Anglos and especially during the early years worked in integrated drover parties. By the 1880s, as the center of the cattle industry shifted to the more settled regions around the northern ranches, African Americans were forced out, and they turned to other kinds of work. The majority of Anglo cowboys also came from the South and remained loyal to the racial hierarchy of the Confederacy.

COWGIRLS AND PROSTITUTES

Although few women worked as trail hands, they did find jobs on the ranches, usually in the kitchen or laundry. The majority of women attended to domestic chores, caring for children and maintaining the household. Their daughters, however, enjoyed better prospects. By the end of the century, women, who as girls had accompanied their fathers in outside chores, were riding astride, "clothespin style," roping calves, branding cattle or cutting their ears to mark them, and castrating bulls.

In cattle towns as well as mining camps, many women worked as prostitutes. During the first cattle drive to Abilene in 1867, a few women were so engaged, but by the following spring, Cowman Joseph McCoy's assistant recalled, "they came in swarms, and as the weather was warm 4 or 5 girls could huddle together in a tent very comfortably." Although some women worked in trailside "hoghouses," the best-paid prostitutes congregated in "brothel districts" or "tenderloins." Dodge city had two: one with white prostitutes for white patrons; another with black prostitutes for both white and black men.

Perhaps 50,000 women engaged in prostitution west of the Mississippi during the second half of the nineteenth century. Like most cowboys, most prostitutes were unmarried and in their teens or twenties. Often fed up with underpaid jobs in dressmaking or domestic service, they found few alternatives to prostitution in the cattle towns, where the cost of food and lodging was notoriously high. Still, earnings in prostitution were slim. In the best of times, a fully employed Wichita prostitute might earn $30 per week, nearly two-thirds of which would go for room and board.

COMMUNITY AND CONFLICT ON THE RANGE

The combination of prostitution, gambling, and drinking discouraged the formation of stable communities. Personal violence was notoriously commonplace on the streets and in the barrooms of cattle towns and mining camps populated mainly by

17–3
Horace Greeley, *An Overland Journey* (1860)

17–4
Joseph G. McCoy, *Historic Sketches of the Cattle Trade of the West and Southwest* (1874)

young, single men. But contrary to popular belief, gunfights were relatively rare. Local police officers, such as Wyatt Earp and James "Wild Bill" Hickok, worked mainly to keep order among drunken cowboys.

After the Civil War, violent crime, assault, and robbery rose sharply throughout the United States. In the West, the most prevalent crimes were horse theft and cattle rustling, which peaked during the height of the open range period and then decreased by the 1890s. Death by legal hanging or illegal **lynching**—at "necktie parties" in which the victims were "jerked to Jesus"—was the usual sentence.

The "range wars" of the 1870s produced violent conflicts. By this time, both farmers and sheepherders were encroaching on the fields where cattle had once grazed freely. Sheep chew grass down to its roots, making it practically impossible to raise cattle on land they have grazed. Farmers meanwhile set about building fences to protect their domestic livestock and property. Great cattle barons fought back against farmers by ordering cowboys to cut the new barbed-wire fences.

The cattle barons, eager for greater profits and often backed by foreign capital, overstocked their herds, and eventually the cattle began to deplete the limited supply of grass. Finally, during 1885–1887, a combination of summer drought and winter blizzards killed 90 percent of the cattle on the northern Plains. Many big ranchers fell into bankruptcy. Along the way, they often took out their grievances against the former cowboys who had gathered small herds for themselves. They charged these small ranchers with cattle rustling, taking them to court or, in some cases, rounding up lynching parties. As one historian has written, violence was "not a mere sideshow" but "an intrinsic part of western society."

Lynching Execution, usually by a mob, without trial.

FARMING COMMUNITIES ON THE PLAINS

The vision of a huge fertile garden extending from the Appalachians to the Pacific Ocean had inspired Americans since the early days of the republic. But the first explorers who actually traveled through the Great Plains quashed this dream. "The Great Desert" was the name they gave to the region stretching west from Kansas and Nebraska, north to Montana and the Dakotas, and south again to Oklahoma and Texas. Few trees fended off the blazing sun of summer or promised a supply of lumber for homes and fences. The occasional river or stream flowed with "muddy gruel" rather than pure, sweet water. Economically, the entire region appeared as hopelessly barren as it was vast. It took massive improvements in both transportation and farm technology—as well as unrelenting advertising and promotional campaigns—to open the Great Plains to widescale agriculture.

THE HOMESTEAD ACT

■ ■ ■ ■ ■ ■ ■ ■ ■ ■

WHO TOOK advantage of the Homestead Act?

■ ■ ■ ■ ■ ■ ■ ■ ■ ■

The **Homestead Act of 1862** offered the first incentive to prospective white farmers. This act granted a quarter section (160 acres) of the public domain free to any settler who lived on the land for at least five years and improved it; or a settler could buy the land for $1.25 per acre after only six months' residence. Restricting its provisions to unmarried women, the Homestead Act encouraged adventurous and hard-working women to file between 5 and 15 percent of the claims, which allowed approximately 400,000 households to build farms for themselves.

Homesteaders achieved their greatest success in the central and upper Midwest where the soil was rich and weather relatively moderate. But those settlers lured to the Great Plains by descriptions of land "carpeted with soft grass—a sylvan paradise" found themselves locked in a fierce struggle with the harsh climate and arid soil.

Homestead Act of 1862 1862 act which granted a quarter section (160 acres) of the public domain free to any settler who lived on the land for at least five years and improved it.

Rather than filing a homestead claim with the federal government, most settlers acquired their land outright. State governments and land companies usually held the most valuable land near transportation and markets, and the majority of farmers were willing to pay a hefty price for these benefits. A few women speculators did very well, particularly in the Dakotas, where they acquired acreage under the generous terms of the Homestead Act, not to farm but to sell when prices for land increased. The big-time land speculators gained even more, plucking choice locations at bargain prices. Although the Homestead Act did spark the largest migration in American history, it did not lay the foundation for a nation of prosperous family farms.

POPULATING THE PLAINS

The rapid settlement of the West could not have taken place without the railroad. Although the Homestead Act offered prospective farmers free land, it was the railroad that promoted settlement, brought people to their new homes, and carried crops and cattle to Eastern markets. The railroads, therefore, wielded tremendous economic and political power throughout the West. Their agents—reputed to know every cow in the district—made major decisions regarding territorial welfare. In designing routes and locating depots, railroad companies put whole communities "on the map," or left them behind.

The Western railroads directly encouraged settlement. Unlike the railroads built before the Civil War, which followed the path of villages and towns, the Western lines preceded settlement. Bringing people west became their top priority, and the railroad companies conducted aggressive promotional and marketing campaigns. Agents enticed Easterners and Europeans alike with long-term loans and free transportation by rail to distant points in the West. The railroads also sponsored land companies to sell parcels of their own huge allotments from the federal government.

More than 2 million Europeans, many recruited by professional promoters, settled the Great Plains between 1870 and 1900. Some districts in Minnesota seemed to be virtual colonies of Sweden; others housed the largest number of Finns in the New World. Nebraska, whose population as early as 1870 was 25 percent foreign-born, concentrated Germans, Swedes, Danes, and Czechs. But Germans outnumbered all other immigrants by far. A smaller portion of European immigrants reached Kansas, still fewer the territories to the south where Indian and Hispanic peoples and African Americans remained the major ethnic populations.

Many immigrants found life on the Great Plains difficult but endurable. The German-speaking Russians who settled the Dakotas discovered soil similar to that of their homeland, but weather that was even more severe. Having earlier fled religious persecution in Germany for Russia, they brought with them heavy coats and the technique of using sun-dried bricks to build houses in areas where lumber was scarce. These immigrants often provided examples for other settlers less familiar with such harsh terrain.

Having traveled the huge distance with kin or members of their Old World villages, immigrants tended to form tight-knit communities on the Great Plains. Many married only within their own group. For example, only 3 percent of Norwegian men married women of a different ethnic background. Like many Mexicanos in the Southwest, several immigrant groups retained their languages well into the twentieth century, usually by sponsoring parochial school systems and publishing their own newspapers. A few groups closed their communities to outsiders. The Poles who migrated to central Nebraska in the 1880s, for example, formed an exclusive settlement; and the German Hutterites, who disavowed private property, lived as much as possible in seclusion in the Bon Homme colony of South Dakota, established in 1874.

Among the native-born settlers of the Great Plains, the largest number had migrated from states bordering the Mississippi River. Settling as individual families rather than as whole communities, they faced an exceptionally solitary life on the Great Plains. The prospect of doing better, which brought most homesteaders to the Great Plains in the first place, caused many families to keep seeking greener pastures. Mobility was so high that between one-third and one-half of all households pulled up stakes within a decade.

Communities eventually flourished in prosperous towns, like Grand Island, Nebraska; Coffeyville, Kansas; and Fargo, North Dakota, that served the larger agricultural region. Built alongside the railroad, they grew into commercial centers, home to banking, medical, legal, and retail services. But closeness did not necessarily promote social equality or even friendship. A social hierarchy based on education (for the handful of doctors and lawyers) and, more important, investment property (held mainly by railroad agents and bankers) governed relationships between individuals and families. Reinforced by family ties and religious and ethnic differences, this hierarchy often persisted across several generations.

WORK, DAWN TO DUSK

By the 1870s the Great Plains, once the home of buffalo and Indian hunters, was becoming a vast farming region populated mainly by immigrants from Europe and white Americans from east of the Mississippi. In place of the first one-room shanties, sod houses, and log cabins stood substantial frame farmhouses, along with a variety of other buildings like barns, smokehouses, and stables. But the built environment took nothing away from the predominating vista—the expansive fields of grain.

Most farm families survived, and prospered if they could, through hard work, often from dawn to dusk. Men's activities in the fields tended to be seasonal, with heavy work during planting and harvest; at other times, their labor centered on construction or repair of buildings and on taking care of livestock. Women's activities were usually far more routine, week in and week out: cooking and canning of seasonal fruit and vegetables, washing, ironing, churning cream for butter, and keeping chickens for their eggs. Women might occasionally take in boarders, usually young men working temporarily in railroad construction, and they tended to the young children. Many women complained about the ceaseless drudgery, especially when they watched their husbands invest in farm equipment rather than in domestic appliances. Others, relished the challenge.

Milking the cows, hauling water, and running errands to neighboring farms could be done by the children, once they had reached the age of nine or so. The "one-room school," where all

These homesteaders in Nebraska, 1886, confronted the typically harsh conditions of treeless plains by erecting sod huts. They often brought with them an assortment of seeds and seedlings for spring plantings and a small number of livestock. A good fall harvest would provide the cash for building more substantial frame houses and outbuildings and encourage other homesteaders to settle near them. Communities eventually grew from these crude beginnings.

Sylvester Rawding Family sod house, 1884. Nebraska State Historical Society, Solomon D. Butcher Collection (RG2608–1784)

grades learned together, taught the basics of literacy and arithmetic that a future farmer or commercial employee would require.

The harsh climate and unyielding soil nevertheless forced all but the most reclusive families to seek out friends and neighbors. Neighbors might agree to work together haying, harvesting, and threshing grain. They also traded their labor, calculated by the hour, for use of equipment or for special assistance. A well-to-do farmer might "rent" his threshing machine in exchange for a small cash fee and, for instance, three days' labor. His wife might barter her garden produce for her neighbor's bread and milk or for help during childbirth or disability.

Much of this informal barter, however, resulted from lack of cash rather than a lasting desire to cooperate. When annual harvests were bountiful, even the farm woman's practice of bartering goods with neighbors and local merchants—butter and eggs in return for yard goods or seed—diminished sharply, replaced by cash transactions. Still, wheat production proved unsteady in the last half of the nineteenth century, and few farm families could remain reliant wholly on themselves.

For many farmers, the soil simply would not yield a livelihood, and they often owed more money than they took in. Start-up costs, including the purchase of land and equipment, put many farmers deep in debt to local creditors. Some lost their land altogether. By the turn of the century, more than one-third of all farmers in the United States were tenants on someone else's land.

Again and again foreclosures wiped out the small landowner through dips in commodity prices, bad decisions, natural disasters, or illness. The swift growth of rural population soon ended. Although writers and orators alike continued to celebrate the family farm as the source of virtue and economic well-being, the hard reality of big money and political power told a far different story.

THE WORLD'S BREADBASKET

During the second half of the nineteenth century commercial farms employed the most intensive and extensive methods of agricultural production in the world. Hard-working farmers brought huge numbers of acres under cultivation, while new technologies allowed them to achieve unprecedented levels of efficiency in the planting and harvesting of crops. As a result, Western agriculture became increasingly tied to international trade, and modern capitalism soon ruled Western agriculture, as it did the mining and cattle industries.

NEW PRODUCTION TECHNOLOGIES

Only after the trees had been cleared and grasslands cut free of roots could the soil be prepared for planting. But as farmers on the Great Plains knew so well, the sod west of the Mississippi did not yield readily to cultivation and often broke the cast-iron plows typically used by Eastern farmers. Farther west, some farmers resorted to drills to plant seeds for crops such as wheat and oats. Even in the best locations, where loamy, fertile ground had built up over centuries into eight or more inches of decayed vegetation, the preliminary breaking, or "busting," of the sod required hard labor. But, as a North Dakota settler wrote to his wife back in Michigan, after the first crop the soil became as "soft as can be, any team [of men and animals] can work it."

In 1837 John Deere had designed his famous "singing plow" that easily turned prairie grasses under and turned up even highly compacted soils. Around the

HOW DID agribusiness differ from more traditional forms of farming?

QUICK REVIEW

Changes in Farming

- Increased emphasis on production for exchange.
- International demand for wheat supported wheat farming in U.S.
- New technology encouraged the consolidation of land into large farms.

This "thirty-three horse team harvester" was photographed at the turn of the century (ca. 1902) in Walla Walla, Washington. Binding the grain into sheaves before it could hit the ground, the "harvester" cut, threshed, and sacked wheat in one single motion.

Courtesy of the Library of Congress

same time, Cyrus McCormick's reaper began to be used for cutting grain; by the 1850s his factories were turning out reapers in mass quantities. The harvester, invented in the 1870s, drew the cut stalks upward to a platform where two men could bind them into sheaves; by the 1880s an automatic knotter tied them together. Drastically reducing the number of people traditionally required for this work, the harvester increased the pace many times over. The introduction of mechanized corn planters and mowing or raking machines for hay all but completed the technological arsenal.

In the 1890s, the U.S. commissioner of labor measured the impact of technology on farm productivity. Before the introduction of the wire binder in 1875, he reported, a farmer could not plant more than 8 acres of wheat if he were to harvest it successfully without help; by 1890 the same farmer could rely on his new machine to handle 135 acres with relative ease and without risk of spoilage. The improvements in the last half of the century allowed an average farmer to produce up to ten times more than was possible with the old implements.

Scientific study of soil, grain, and climatic conditions was another factor in the record output. Beginning in the mid-nineteenth century, federal and state governments added inducements to the growing body of expertise, scientific information, and hands-on advice. Through the **Morrill Act of 1862**, "land-grant" colleges acquired space for campuses in return for promising to institute agricultural programs. The Department of Agriculture, which attained cabinet-level status in 1889, and the Weather Bureau (transferred from the War Department in 1891) also made considerable contributions to farmers' knowledge. The federal Hatch Act of 1887, which created a

Morrill Act of 1862 Act by which "land-grant" colleges acquired space for campuses in return for promising to institute agricultural programs.

series of state experimental stations, provided for basic agricultural research, especially in the areas of soil minerals and plant growth. Many states added their own agricultural stations, usually connected with state colleges and universities.

Hand versus Machine Labor on the Farm, about 1880

Crop	Time Worked (in hours)		Labor Cost	
	Hand	Machine	Hand	Machine
Wheat	61	3	$3.55	$0.66
Corn	39	15	3.62	1.51
Oats	66	7	3.73	1.07
Loose Hay	21	4	1.75	0.42
Baled Hay	35	12	3.06	1.29

Nature nevertheless often reigned over technological innovation and seemed in places to take revenge against these early successes. West of the 98th meridian—a north-south line extending through western Oklahoma, central Kansas and Nebraska, and eastern Dakota—perennial dryness due to an annual rainfall of less than 20 inches constantly threatened to turn soil into dust and to break plows on the hardened ground. Summer heat burned out crops and ignited grass fires. Mountains of winter snows turned rivers into spring torrents that flooded fields; heavy fall rains washed crops away. Even good weather invited worms and flying insects to infest the crops. During the 1870s grasshoppers in clouds a mile long ate everything organic, including tree bark and clothes.

PRODUCING FOR THE MARKET

Farming changed in important ways during the last third of the nineteenth century. Although the family remained the primary source of labor, farmers tended to put more emphasis on production for exchange rather than for home use. They continued to plant vegetable gardens and often kept fowl or livestock for the family's consumption, but farmers raised crops mainly for the market and measured their own success or failure in terms of cash products.

Wheat farmers in particular prospered. With the world population increasing at a rapid rate, the international demand for wheat was enormous, and American farmers made huge profits from the sale of this crop. Wheat production ultimately served as a barometer of the agricultural economy in the West. Farmers in all corners of the region, from Nebraska to California, expanded or contracted their holdings and planned their crops according to the price of wheat.

The new machines and expanding market did not necessarily guarantee success. Land, draft animals, and equipment remained very expensive, and start-up costs could keep a family in debt for decades. A year of good returns often preceded a year of financial disaster. Weather conditions, international markets, and railroad and steamship shipping prices all proved equally unpredictable and heartless.

The new technology and scientific expertise favored the large, well-capitalized farmer over the small one. The majority of farmers with fewer resources expanded at more modest rates. Between 1880 and 1900, average farm size in the seven leading grain-growing states increased from 64.4 acres to more than 100 acres.

CALIFORNIA AGRIBUSINESS

The trend toward big farms reached an apex in California, where farming as a business surpassed farming as a way of life. Farms of nearly 500 acres dominated the California landscape in 1870; by the turn of the century, two-thirds of the state's arable land was in 1,000-acre farms. As land reformer and social commentator Henry George noted, California was "not a country of farms but a country of plantations and estates."

This scale of production made California the national leader in wheat production by the mid-1880s, but it also succeeded dramatically with fruit and vegetables. Large- and medium-sized growers, shrewdly combined in cooperative marketing associations during the 1870s and 1880s, used the new refrigerator cars to ship their produce in large quantities to the East and even to Europe. By 1890, cherries, apricots, and oranges, packed with mountains of ice, made their way into homes across the United States.

By 1900, California had become the model for American agribusiness, not the home of self-sufficient homesteaders, but the showcase of heavily capitalized farm factories. Machines soon displaced animals and even many people. Many Californios tried to hold onto their traditional forms of labor if not their land, only to become the backbone of the state's migrant work force. Intense battles in the state legislature over land and irrigation rights underscored the message that powerful forces had gathered in California to promote large-scale agricultural production.

THE TOLL ON THE LAND

The new inhabitants often looked past the existing flora and fauna toward a landscape remade strictly for commercial purposes. The changes they produced in some areas were nearly as cataclysmic as those that occurred during the Ice Age.

Banishing many existing species, farmers "improved" the land by introducing exotic plants and animals—that is, biological colonies indigenous to other regions and continents. Farmers also unintentionally introduced new varieties of weeds, insect pests, and rats. Surviving portions of older grasslands and meadows eventually could be found only alongside railroad tracks, in graveyards, or inside national parks.

Numerous species disappeared altogether or suffered drastic reduction. The grizzly bear, for example, an animal exclusive to the West, could once be found in large numbers from the Great Plains to California and throughout much of Alaska; by the early decades of the twentieth century, one nature writer estimated that only 800 survived, mostly in Yellowstone National Park. At the same time the number of wolves declined from perhaps as many as 2 million to just 200,000. By the mid-1880s, no more than 5,000 buffalo survived in the entire United States, and little remained of the once vast herds but great heaps of bones sold for $7.50 per ton.

The slaughter of the buffalo had a dramatic impact, not only on the fate of the species, but also on the grasslands of the Great Plains. Over all, the biological diversity of the region had been drastically reduced. Having killed off the giant herds, ranchers and farmers quickly shifted to cattle and sheep production. Unlike the roaming buffalo, these livestock did not range widely and soon devoured the native grasses down to their roots. With the ground cover destroyed, the soil eroded and became barren. By the end of the century, huge dust storms formed across the windswept plains.

In 1873 the U.S. Congress passed the **Timber Culture Act**, which allotted homesteaders an additional 160 acres of land in return for planting and cultivating forty acres of trees. Because residence was not required, and because tree planting could not be assessed for at least thirteen years, speculators filed for several claims at once, then turned around and sold the land without having planted a single tree. Although some forests were restored, neither the weather nor the soil improved.

Large-scale commercial agriculture also took a heavy toll on inland waters. Before white settlement, rainfall had drained naturally into lakes and underground aquifers, and watering spots were abundant throughout the Great Plains. Farmers

Timber Culture Act 1873 act which allotted homesteaders an additional 160 acres of land in return for planting and cultivating 40 acres of trees.

mechanically rerouted and dammed water to irrigate their crops, causing many bodies of water to disappear and the water table to drop significantly. Successful farmers pressed for ever greater supplies of water. In 1887 the state of California formed irrigation districts, securing bond issues for the construction of canals, and other western states followed. But by the 1890s, irrigation had seemed to reach its limit without federal support. The Newlands or **National Reclamation Act** of 1902 added 1 million acres of irrigated land, and state irrigation districts added more than 10 million acres. Expensive to taxpayers, and ultimately benefiting corporate farmers rather than small landowners, these projects further diverted water and totally transformed the landscape.

Although Western state politicians and federal officials debated water rights for decades, they rarely considered the impact of water policies on the environment. The need to maintain the water supply indirectly led to the creation of national forests and the Forest Service. Western farmers supported the **General Land Revision Act of 1891**, which gave the president the power to establish forest reserves to protect watersheds against the threats posed by lumbering, overgrazing, and forest fires. In the years that followed, President Benjamin Harrison

National Reclamation Act 1902 act which added 1 million acres of irrigated land to the United States.

General Land Revision Act of 1891 Act which gave the president the power to establish forest reserves to protect watersheds against the threats posed by lumbering, overgrazing, and forest fires.

 MAP EXPLORATION

To explore an interactive version of this map, go to **www.prenhall.com/faraghertlc/map18.4**

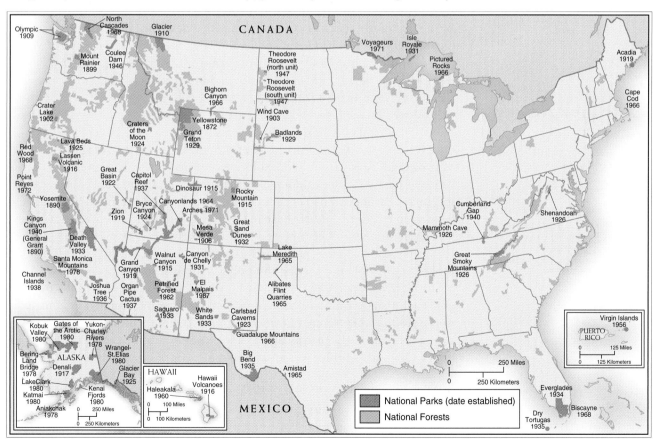

MAP 18-4
The Estabilishment of National Parks and Forests

WHAT IF ANY factors in the West provided a more conducive environment in which the Mormons could flourish.

established fifteen forest reserves exceeding 16 million acres, and President Grover Cleveland added more than 21 million acres. But only in 1897 did the secretary of the interior finally gain the authority to regulate the use of these reserves.

The **Forest Management Act** of 1897 and the National Reclamation Act of 1902 set the federal government on the path of large-scale regulatory activities. The Forest Service was established in 1905, and in 1907 forest reserves were transferred from the Department of the Interior to the Department of Agriculture. The federal government would now play an even larger role in economic development of the West, dealing mainly with corporate farmers and ranchers eager for improvements.

Forest Management Act 1897 act which, along with the National Reclamation Act, set the federal government on the path of large-scale regulatory activities.

WHAT PLACE did the West hold in the national imagination?

THE WESTERN LANDSCAPE

The public east of the Mississippi craved stories about the West and visual images of its sweeping vistas. Artists and photographers built their reputations in what they saw and imagined. Scholars, from geologists and botanists to historians and anthropologists, toured the trans-Mississippi West in pursuit of new data. The region and its peoples came to represent what was both unique and magnificent about the American landscape.

NATURE'S MAJESTY

By the end of the century, scores of writers had described spectacular, breathtaking natural sites like the Grand Tetons and High Sierras, vast meadows of waving grasses and beautiful flowers, expansive canyons and rushing white rivers, and exquisite deserts covered with sagebrush or dotted with flowering cactus and enticing precisely for their stark qualities.

Moved by such evidence, the federal government began to set aside huge tracts of land as nature reserves. In 1864 Congress passed the Yosemite Act, which placed the spectacular cliffs and giant sequoias under the management of the state of California. Meanwhile, explorers returned to the East awestruck by the varied terrain of the Rocky Mountains, the largest mountain chain in North America. In 1872 Congress named Yellowstone the first national park. Yosemite and Sequoia in California, Crater Lake in Oregon, Mount Ranier in Washington, and Glacier in Montana all became national parks between 1890 and 1910.

Landscape painters, particularly the group that became known as the Rocky Mountain School, also piqued the public's interest in western scenery. In the 1860s, German-born Albert Bierstadt, equipped with a camera, traveled the Oregon Trail. Using his photographs as inspiration, Bierstadt painted mountains so wondrous that they seemed nearly surreal, projecting a divine aura behind the majesty of nature. His "earthscapes"—huge canvases with exacting details of animals and plants—thrilled viewers and sold for tens of thousands of dollars.

THE LEGENDARY WILD WEST

By the end of the century, many Americans, rich and poor alike, imagined the West as a land of promise and opportunity and, above all, of excitement and adventure. Future president Theodore Roosevelt helped promote this view. Soon after his election to the New York State Assembly in 1882, Roosevelt was horrified to see himself lampooned in the newspapers as a dandy and weakling. A year later, after buying a ranch in South Dakota, he began to reconstruct his public image. He wrote three books recounting his adventures in the West, claiming that they had not only instilled in him personal bravery and "hardihood" but also self-reliance. The

QUICK REVIEW

National Parks

- 1864: Congress passed the Yosemite Act placing area under management of state of California.
- 1872: Yellowstone named first national park.
- Five new national parks named between 1890 and 1910.

Buffalo Bill's "Wild West Show" poster from 1899. William Cody's theatrical company toured the United States and Europe for decades, reenacting various battles and occasionally switching to football (cowboys versus Indians). Cody's style set the pace for both rodeos and Western silent films.

Courtesy of the Library of Congress

West, as Roosevelt insisted, meant "vigorous manhood."

The first "westerns," the "dime novels" that sold in the 1860s in editions of 50,000 or more, reflected these myths. Competing against stories about pirates, wars, crime, and sea adventures, westerns outsold the others. Edward Zane Carroll Judson's *Buffalo Bill, the King of the Border Men*, first published in 1869, spawned hundreds of other novels, thousands of stories, and an entire magazine devoted to Buffalo Bill. Real-life African American cowboy Nat Love lived on in the imaginations of many generations as Edward L. Wheeler's dime novel hero "Deadwood Dick," who rode the range as a white cowboy in black clothes in over thirty stories. His girlfriend "Calamity Jane"—"the most reckless buchario in ther Hills"—also took on mythic qualities.

Railroad promoters and herd owners actively promoted these romantic and heroic images. Cowman Joseph McCoy staged Wild West shows in St. Louis and Chicago, where Texas cowboys entertained prospective buyers by roping calves and breaking horses. Many cowboys played up this imaginary role, dressing and talking to match the stories told about them. The first professional photographers often made their living touring the West, setting up studios where cowboys and prostitutes posed in elaborate costumes.

The former Pony Express rider, army scout, and famed buffalo hunter William F. Cody hit upon the idea of an extravaganza that would bring the legendary West to those who could never experience it in person. "Buffalo Bill" Cody made sharpshooter Annie Oakley a star performer. Entrancing crowds with her stunning accuracy with pistol or rifle, Oakley shot dimes in midair and cigarettes from her husband's mouth. Cody also hired Sioux Indians and hundreds of cowboys to perform in mock stagecoach robberies and battles. With far less fanfare, many veteran cowboys enlisted themselves on "dude ranches" for tourists or performed as rope twirlers or yodeling singers in theaters across the United States.

THE "AMERICAN PRIMITIVE"

New technologies of graphic reproduction encouraged painters and photographers to provide new images of the West, authentic as well as fabricated. A young German American artist, Charles Schreyvogel, saw Buffalo Bill's tent show in

Buffalo and decided to make the West his life's work. His canvases depicted Indian warriors and U.S. cavalry fighting furiously but without blood and gore. Charles Russell, a genuine cowboy, painted the life he knew but also indulged in imaginary scenarios, producing paintings of buffalo hunts and first encounters between Indian peoples and white explorers.

Frederic Remington, the most famous of all the Western artists, left Yale Art School to visit Montana in 1881, became a Kansas sheep herder and tavern owner, and then returned to painting. Painstakingly accurate in physical details, especially of horses, his paintings celebrated the "winning of the West" from the Indian peoples.

Painters and photographers led the way for scholarly research on the various Indian societies. The early ethnographer and pioneer of fieldwork in anthropology Lewis Henry Morgan devoted his life to the study of Indian family or kinship patterns, mostly of eastern tribes such as the Iroquois, who adopted him into their Hawk Clan.

One of the most influential interpreters of the cultures of living tribespeople was the pioneering ethnographer Alice Cunningham Fletcher. In 1879, Fletcher met Suzette (Bright Eyes) La Flesche of the Omaha tribe, who was on a speaking tour to gain support for her people, primarily to prevent their removal from tribal lands. Well known as an expert on Omaha music, Fletcher also supported the Omahas' campaign to gain individual title to tribal lands, eventually drafting legislation that was enacted by Congress as the **Omaha Act of 1882**.

While white settlers and the federal government continued to threaten the survival of tribal life, Indian lore became a major pursuit of scholars and amateurs alike. Adults and children delighted in turning up arrowheads. Fraternal organizations such as the Elks and Eagles borrowed tribal terminology. The Boy Scouts and Girl Scouts, the nation's premier youth organizations, used tribal lore to instill strength of character. And the U.S. Treasury stamped images of tribal chiefs and buffalo on the nation's most frequently used coins.

Omaha Act of 1882 Act which allowed the establishment of individual title to tribal lands.

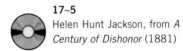

WHAT KIND of Indian society did reformers envision?

17–5
Helen Hunt Jackson, from *A Century of Dishonor* (1881)

THE TRANSFORMATION OF INDIAN SOCIETIES

In 1871, the U.S. government formally ended the treaty system, eclipsing without completely abolishing the sovereignty of Indian nations. Still, the tribes persisted. Using a mixture of survival strategies from farming and trade to the leasing of reservation lands, they both adapted to changing conditions and maintained old traditions.

REFORM POLICY AND POLITICS

For decades, reformers, mainly from the Protestant churches, had lobbied Congress for a program of salvation through assimilation, and they looked to the Board of Indian Commissioners, created in 1869, to carry out this mission. The board often succeeded in mediating conflicts among the various tribes crowded onto reservations but made far less headway in converting them to Christianity or transforming them into prosperous farming communities. The majority of Indian peoples lived in poverty and misery, deprived of their traditional means of survival and more often than not subjected to fraud by corrupt government officials and private suppliers. Reformers who observed these conditions firsthand nevertheless remained unshaken in their belief that tribespeople must be raised out of the darkness of ignorance into the light of civilization.

Some reformers were genuinely outraged by the government's continuous violation of treaty obligations and the military enforcement of the reservation pol-

OVERVIEW

MAJOR INDIAN TREATIES AND LEGISLATION OF THE LATE NINETEENTH CENTURY

1863	Nez Percé Treaty	Signed illegally on behalf of the entire tribe in which the Nez Percé abandoned 6 million acres of land in return for a small reservation in northeastern Oregon. Led to Nez Percé wars, which ended in 1877 with the surrender of Chief Joseph.
1867	Medicine Lodge Treaty	Assigned reservations in existing Indian Territory to Comanches, Plains (Kiowa) Apaches, Kiowas, Cheyennes, and Arapahoes, bringing these tribes together with Sioux, Shoshones, Bannocks, and Navajos.
1868	Treaty of Fort Laramie	Successfully ended Red Cloud's war by evacuating federal troops from Sioux Territory along the Bozeman Trail; additionally granted Sioux ownership of the western half of South Dakota and rights to use Powder River county in Wyoming and Montana.
1871		Congress declares end to treaty system.
1887	Dawes Severalty Act	Divided communal tribal land, granting the right to petition for citizenship to those Indians who accepted the individual land allotment of 160 acres. Successfully undermined sovereignty.

icy. One of the most influential was Helen Hunt Jackson, a noted poet and author of children's stories. Her book-length exposé, *A Century of Dishonor*, published in 1881, detailed the plight of Indian peoples.

The **Dawes Severalty Act**, passed by Congress in 1887, established federal Indian policy for decades to come. The act allowed the president to distribute land not to tribes but to individuals legally "severed" from their tribes. Those individuals who accepted the land allotment of 160 acres and agreed to allow the government to sell unallotted tribal lands (with some funds set aside for education) could petition to become citizens of the United States. A little over a decade after its enactment, many reformers believed that the Dawes Act had resolved the basis of the "Indian problem." Hollow Horn Bear, a Sioux chief, offered a different opinion, judging the Dawes Act to be "only another trick of the whites."

The Dawes Act successfully undermined tribal sovereignty but offered little compensation. Indian religions and sacred ceremonies were banned, the telling of legends and myths forbidden, and shaman and medicine men imprisoned or exiled for continuing their traditional practices. "Indian schools" forbade Indian languages, clothing styles, and even hair fashions in order to "kill the Indian . . . and save the man," as one schoolmaster put it.

Treated as savages, Indian children fled most white schools. Nor did adults receive much encouragement to become property holders. Government agencies allotted them inferior farmland, inadequate tools, and little training for agricultural self-sufficiency. Seeing scant advantage in assimilating, only a minority of adults dropped their tribal religion for Christianity or their communal ways for the accumulation of private property. Within the next forty years, the Indian peoples lost 60 percent of the reservation land remaining in 1887 and 66 percent of the land allotted to them as homesteaders. The tenets of the Dawes Act were not reversed until 1934. In that year, Congress passed the Indian Reorganization Act, which affirmed the integrity of Indian cultural institutions and returned some land to tribal ownership (see Chapter 24).

Dawes Severalty Act An 1887 law terminating tribal ownership of land and allotting some parcels of land to individual Indians with the remainder opened for white settlement.

THE GHOST DANCE

After the passage of the Dawes Severalty Act, one more cycle of rebellion remained for the Sioux. In 1888, the Paiute prophet Wovoka, ill with scarlet fever, had a vision during a total eclipse of the sun. In his vision, the Creator told him that if the Indian peoples learned to love each other, they would be granted a special place in the afterlife. The Creator also gave him the Ghost Dance, which the prophet performed for others and soon spread throughout the tribe. The Sioux came to believe that when the day of judgment came, all Indian peoples who had ever lived would return to their lost world and white peoples would vanish from the earth.

White Americans took the Ghost Dance as a warning of tribal retribution rather than a religious ceremony. As thousands of Sioux danced to exhaustion, local whites intolerantly demanded the practice be stopped. A group of the Sioux led by Big Foot, now fearing mass murder, moved into hiding in the Bad Lands of South Dakota. After a skirmish, the great leader Sitting Bull and his young son lay dead.

The Seventh Cavalry pursued the Sioux Ghost Dancers and 300 undernourished Sioux, freezing and without horses, to Wounded Knee Creek on the Pine Ridge Reservation. There, on December 29, 1890, while the peace-seeking Big Foot, who had personally raised a white flag of surrender, lay dying of pneumonia, they were surrounded by soldiers armed with automatic guns. The U.S. troops expected the Sioux to surrender their few remaining weapons, but an accidental gunshot from one deaf brave who misunderstood the command caused panic on both sides.

Within minutes, 200 Sioux had been cut down and dozens of soldiers wounded, mostly by their own cross fire. For two hours soldiers continued to shoot at anything that moved—mostly women and children straggling away.

Black Elk later recalled, "I can see that something else died there in the bloody mud, and was buried in the blizzard. A people's dream died there. It was a beautiful dream. . . . The nation's hoop is broken and scattered. There is no center any longer, and the sacred tree is dead."

ENDURANCE AND REJUVENATION

Not even an insular, peaceful agricultural existence on semiarid, treeless terrain necessarily provided protection. Nor did a total willingness to peacefully accept white offers prevent attack. The Pimas of Arizona, for instance, had a well-developed agricultural system adapted to a scarce supply of water, and they rarely warred with other tribes. After the arrival of white settlers, they integrated Christian symbolism into their religion, learned to speak English, and even fought with the U.S. cavalry against the Apaches. Still, the Pimas saw their lands stolen, their precious waterways diverted, and their families impoverished.

A majority of tribes, especially smaller ones, sooner or later reached numbers too low to maintain their collective existence. The Quapaws, for example, formally disbanded in the aftermath of the Dawes Severalty Act. Later generations petitioned the federal government and regained tribal status, established ceremonial grounds and cultural centers (or bingo halls), and built up one of the most durable powwows in the state. Even so, much of the tribal lore that had underpinned distinct identity had simply vanished.

A small minority of tribes, grown skillful in adapting to dramatically changing circumstances, managed to persist and even grow. The Cheyennes had found themselves caught geographically between aggressive tribes in the Great Lakes region and had migrated into the Missouri area, where they split into small village-sized communities. By the mid-nineteenth century they had become expert horse traders on the Great Plains, well prepared to meet the massive influx of white settlers by shifting their location frequently. They avoided the worst of the pestilence that spread from the dis-

17–7
Tragedy at Wounded Knee (1890)

17–8
Benjamin Harrison, Report on Wounded Knee Massacre and the Decrease in Indian Lane Acreage (1891)

QUICK REVIEW

Adaptation

- Cheyenne became expert horse traders.
- Navajos turned to crafts for survival.
- Interest of influential whites helped Hopis fend off threats.

eases white people carried, and likewise survived widespread intermarriage with the Sioux in the 1860s and 1870s. Instructed to settle, many Cheyenne took up elements of the Christian religion and became farmers, also without losing their tribal identity.

The Navajos experienced an extraordinary renewal, largely because they built a life in territory considered worthless by whites. Having migrated to the Southwest from the northwestern part of the continent perhaps 700 years ago, the Diné ("the People"), as they called themselves, had already survived earlier invasions by the Spanish. In 1863 they had been conquered again through the cooperation of hostile tribes led by the famous Colonel Kit Carson. Their crops burned, their fruit trees destroyed, 8,000 Navajo were forced in the 300-mile "Long Walk" to the desolate Bosque Redondo reservation, where they nearly starved. Four years later, the Indian Bureau allowed the severely reduced tribe to return to a fraction of its former lands.

By 1880 the Navajos' population had returned to nearly what it had been before their conquest by white Americans. Quickly depleting the deer and ante- lope on their hemmed-in reservation, they had to rely on sheep alone as a food reserve during years of bad crops. With their wool rugs and blankets much in demand in the East, the Navajos increasingly turned to crafts, including eventu- ally silver jewelry as well as weaving, to survive. Although living on the economic margin, they persevered to become the largest Indian nation in the United States.

The nearby Hopis, like the Navajos, survived by stubbornly clinging to lands unwanted by white settlers and by adapting to drastically changing conditions. A

CHRONOLOGY

1848	Treaty of Guadalupe Hidalgo.
1849–1860s	California Gold Rush.
1853	Gadsden Purchase.
1858	Comstock Lode discovered.
1859	Cortina's War in South Texas.
1862	Homestead Act makes free land available.
	Morrill Act authorizes "land-grant" colleges.
1865–1867	Great Sioux War.
1866	Texas cattle drives begin.
	Medicine Lodge Treaty established reservation system.
	Alaska purchased.
1869	Board of Indian Commissioners created.
	Buffalo Bill, the King of the Border Men, sets off "Wild West" publishing craze.
1870s	Grasshopper attacks on the Great Plains.
1872	Yellowstone National Park created.
1873	Timber Culture Act.
	Red River War.
1874–1875	Sioux battles in Black Hills of Dakotas.
1876	Custer's Last Stand.
1877	Defeat of the Nez Percé.
1881	Helen Hunt Jackson, *A Century of Dishonor.*
1882	Edmunds Act outlaws polygamy.
1885–1887	Droughts and severe winters cause the collapse of the cattle boom.
1887	Dawes Severalty Act.
1890	Sioux Ghost Dance movement.Massacre of Lakota Sioux at Wounded Knee.
	Census Bureau announces the end of the frontier line.
1887	Forest Management Act gives the federal government authority over forest reserves.

famous tribe of "desert people," the Hopis had lived for centuries in their cliff cities. Their highly developed theological beliefs, peaceful social system, sand paintings, and kachina dolls interested many educated and influential whites. The resulting publicity helped them gather the public supporters and financial resources needed to fend off further threats to their reservations.

Fortunate northwestern tribes remained relatively isolated from white settlers until the early twentieth century, although they had begun trading with white visitors centuries earlier. Northwestern peoples relied largely on salmon and other resources of the region's rivers and bays. In potlatch ceremonies, leaders redistributed tribal wealth and maintained their personal status and the status of their tribe by giving lavish gifts to invited guests. Northwest peoples also made intricate wood carvings, including commemorative "totem" poles, that recorded their history and identified their regional status. Northwestern peoples maintained their cultural integrity in part through connections with kin in Canada, as did southern tribes with kin in Mexico. In Canada and Mexico, native populations suffered less pressure from new populations and retained more tribal authority than in the United States.

Indian nations approached their nadir as the nineteenth century came to a close. The descendants of the great pre-Columbian civilizations had been conquered by foreigners, their population reduced to fewer than 250,000. Under the pressure of assimilation, the remaining tribespeople became known to non-Indians as "the vanishing Americans." It would take several generations before Indian sovereignty experienced a resurgence.

Conclusion

In 1890 the director of the U.S. Census announced that the nation's "unsettled area has been so broken into by isolated bodies of settlement that there can hardly be said to be a frontier line." The development of the West met the nation's demands for mineral resources for its expanding industries and agricultural products for the people of the growing cities. Envisioning the West as a cornucopia whose boundless treasures would offer themselves to the willing pioneer, most of the new residents failed to calculate the odds against their making a prosperous livelihood as miners, farmers, or petty merchants. Nor could they appreciate the long-term consequences of the violence they brought with them from the battlefields of the Civil War to the far reaches of the West.

Summary

Indian Peoples Under Siege The expansion of the United States created stresses on Indian culture already trying to adapt to the introduction of the Europeans into the Americas. United States policy and practices, including war, severely affected the viability of Indian populations and their lifestyles.

The Internal Empire Stimulated by the discovery of gold, silver, and copper, mining became a large corporate enterprise. Conditions fostered labor conflicts. Mormons built a strong, thriving society in the Utah desert. On the borderlands, ethnic conflicts arose between Americans and Hispanics.

The Cattle Industry In the two decades following the Civil War, cattle was the West's bonanza industry. A culture arose around the cowboy and cattle towns that grew up to serve the burgeoning industry in beef. Weather, market conditions, and the depletion of grass caused severe problems in the cattle industry.

Farming Communities on the Plains Improvements in transportation and farming technology opened the Great Plains to settlement. Easterners and Europeans developed farms leading a hard life that yielded little return.

The World's Breadbasket Open lands, new production technology, and the railroad helped make the West the world's breadbasket. Large-scale farming stimulated the rise of agribusiness. Greater production, however, damaged the environment.

The Western Landscape The beauty and grandeur of the western landscape attracted artists and led the United States to set aside huge areas of nature reserves. Legends of the Wild West were fueled by dime novels and shows. Artists and photographers captured Western life and Indian culture.

The Transformation of Indian Societies Government policy attempted to destroy tribal culture and assimilate Indian people into mainstream culture with many negative results. The Ghost Dance represented a last attempt to resist American policies and practices. Throughout the nation, Indian tribes adjusted to their circumstances with mixed results.

REVIEW QUESTIONS

1. Discuss the role of federal legislation in accelerating and shaping the course of westward expansion.

2. How did the incorporation of western territories into the United States affect Indian nations such as the Sioux or the Nez Percé? Discuss the causes and consequences of the Indian Wars. Discuss the significance of reservation policy and the Dawes Severalty Act for tribal life.

3. What were some of the major technological advances in mining and agriculture that promoted the development of the western economy?

4. Describe the unique features of Mexicano communities in the Southwest before and after the mass immigration of Anglos. How did changes in the economy affect the patterns of labor and the status of women in these communities?

5. What role did the Homestead Act play in western expansion? How did farm families on the Great Plains divide chores among their members? What factors determined the likelihood of economic success or failure?

6. Describe the responses of artists, naturalists, and conservationists to the western landscape. How did their photographs, paintings, and stories shape perceptions of the West in the East?

KEY TERMS

Caminetti Act (p. 477)

Dawes Severalty Act (p. 493)

Edmunds Act (p. 478)

Edmunds-Tucker Act (p. 478)

Forest Management Act (p. 490)

General Land Revision Act of 1891 (p. 489)

Hispanic-American Alliance (p. 480)

Homestead Act of 1862 (p. 482)

Lynching (p. 482)

Morrill Act of 1862 (p. 486)

National Reclamation Act (p. 489)

Omaha Act of 1882 (p. 492)

Sand Creek Massacre (p. 473)

Timber Culture Act (p. 488)

Treaty of Fort Laramie (p. 473)

RECOMMENDED READING

William Cronon, George Miles, and Jay Gitlin, eds., *Under an Open Sky: Rethinking America's Western Past* (1992). A useful collection of essays. Reinterpreting older evidence and adding new data, these essays stress the bitter conflicts over territory, the racial and gender barriers against democratic community models, and the tragic elements of Western history.

Jon Gjerde, *The Minds of the West: Ethnocultural Evolution in the Rural Middle West, 1830–1914* (1997). A combination cultural and economic history that weighs the importance of ethnicity in the shaping of American identities in the farming regions of the Midwest. Gjerde pays close attention to the religious institutions and systems of belief of European immigrants as the basis of community formation.

Lisbeth Haas, *Conquests and Historical Identities in California, 1769–1936* (1995). A multiethnic history, centered in San Juan Capistrano, that examines the political intersection of geography and community formation. The author studies the processes of Americanization among the Spanish and Indian populations who settled this land.

Robert V. Hine and John Mack Faragher, *The American West: A New Interpretive History* (2000). A sweeping, amply illustrated survey of Western history with reference to recent scholarship. The authors emphasize Native Americans and include rich material on ethnicity, the environment, and the role of women.

John C. Hudson, *Making the Corn Belt: A Geographical History of Middle-Western Agriculture* (1994). An ecologically oriented study of corn growing that traces its development from Indians to Southerners moving westward.

Andrew C. Isenberg, *The Destruction of the Bison: An Environmental History, 1750–1920* (2000). A rich study of the forces behind the near-extinction of the bison with special attention to the interplay among Indians, Euroamericans, and the environment of the Great Plains. Isenberg constructs a narrative that is as much cultural as economic in framing the problem.

Karl Jacoby, *Crimes Against Nature: Squatters, Poachers, Thieves, and the Hidden History of American Conservation* (2001). A complex analysis of the origins of national parks in the Adirondacks, Yellowstone, and the Grand Canyon. Rather than focusing on the individuals and groups that led the conservation of vast public lands, Jacoby switches perspective to focus on those who were dispossessed by the process.

Elizabeth Jameson and Susan Armitage, eds., *Writing the Range* (1997). A collection of essays on women in the West that presents an inclusive historical narrative based on the experiences of women of differing backgrounds, races, and ethnic groups.

Katherine M. B. Osburn, *Southern Ute Women: Autonomy and Assimilation on the Reservation, 1887–1934* (1998). Presents a careful analysis of the impact of the Dawes Act on the role and status of women among the Southern Ute. Osburn acknowledges the changes brought by the Office of Indian Affairs programs on the reservations but emphasizes the resistance of the Ute and the retention of old ways.

Glenda Riley, *Building and Breaking Families in the American West* (1996). Essays covering the variety of cultures in the American West, organized topically to highlight courtship, marriage and intermarriage, and separation and divorce.

Thomas E. Sheridan, *Los Tucsonenses: The Mexican Community in Tucson, 1854–1941* (1986). A highly readable account of Mexican-American communities in the Southwest. Sheridan shows how a midcentury accommodation of Anglos and Mexicanos faded with the absorption of the region into the national economy and with the steady displacement of Mexicano community from its agricultural landholdings.

Liping Zhu, *A Chinaman's Chance: The Chinese on the Rocky Mountain Mining Frontier* (1997). Studies the mining communities of Chinese in the Boise Basin of Idaho. Zhu emphasizes the success the Chinese enjoyed not only as miners, but also as merchants in the face of discriminatory practices and laws.

Mythologizing the "Wild West"

WHAT ELEMENTS do the Remington sculptures, the Curtis photograph, and the "dime novel" illustrations have in common? What, to judge from these images, made the West "wild"? How much do you think these images match up with reality?

One artist, Frederic Remington, deserves much of the credit for creating the West of our imagination. In Montana in 1881 an "old-timer" told him that "there is no more West." Remington decided to "try to record some facts around me." He recorded them first in a series of illustrations, then in paintings, and then in sculpture. Another who determined to "record some facts" was Edward S. Curtis who produced the twenty volume collection, *The North American Indian*, between 1906 and 1930. Curtis persuaded Native American peoples to reenact traditional practices, such as hunting or war parties. Often there was a twenty to fifty year gap between the reenactment and the practice itself. In contrast to Remington and Curtis who sought to (re)capture the truth about the West, "dime novels" sought simply to provide thrills. The "Wild West" is still part of our imaginative landscape.

Edward S. Curtis, "On the Warpath — Atsina," from The North American Indian, v.04; Curtis notes: "These grim-visaged old warriors made a thrilling picture as they rode along, breaking out now and then into wild song of the chase or raid." The image recreates a raiding party. Note the headdress on the party's leader, fourth from left. The photograph was taken in 1908.

▼

Frederick Remington, "The Cheyenne," a 1901 bronze statue, now at the Amon Carter Museum, Fort Worth, Texas. Remington loved to portray action; here a warrior is galloping on his pony into battle.

Frederick S. Remington, "The Cheyenne," 1901, cast 1904. Amon Carter Museum

http://memory.loc.gov/ammem/award98/ienhtml/curthome.html

Frederick Remington, "The Rattlesnake," (1905) Bronze (Height 23 7/8 inches), now at Amon Carter Museum, Fort Worth, Texas. Note how the rattlesnake has reverted from national symbol to natural menace as the cowboy's horse rears up and threatens to throw its rider.

Frederick S. Remington, "The Rattlesnake," 1905. Amon Carter Museum

◄ **"Dime novels" purported to tell true tales of western adventure.** Jesse James was an historical figure, even if the stories in this "Log Cabin Library" edition bore no resemblance to his actual deeds. "The King of the Wild West" was a purely fictional creation.

From the Library of Congress's American Memory site
http://www.loc.gov/exhibits/treasures/tri015.html

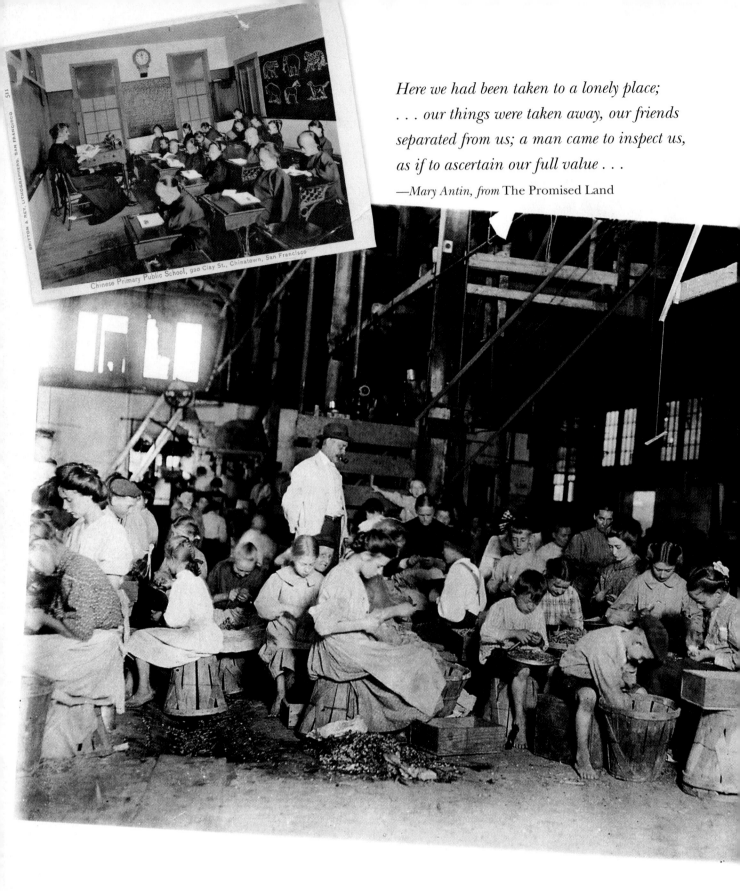

Chinese Primary Public School, 920 Clay St., Chinatown, San Francisco

Here we had been taken to a lonely place;
. . . our things were taken away, our friends
separated from us; a man came to inspect us,
as if to ascertain our full value . . .
—*Mary Antin, from* The Promised Land

Noted urban photographer Lewis Hines captures the cramped working conditions
and child labor in this late nineteenth-century canning factory. Women and children
provided a cheap and efficient work force for labor-intensive industries.

19

THE INCORPORATION OF AMERICA
1865–1900

WHAT WERE the major tenets of the Gospel of Wealth?

WHO WERE the members of the American Federation of Labor?

HOW DID the development of Southern industry affect the lives of African Americans living in the South?

WHAT CONTRIBUTED to the growing population of American cities?

WHAT LED Mark Twain to label the late nineteenth century the Gilded Age?

WHAT ROLE did public spaces play in late nineteenth–century popular culture?

AMERICAN COMMUNITIES
Packingtown, Chicago, Illinois

APPROACHING PACKINGTOWN, THE NEIGHBORHOOD ADJOINING THE Union Stockyards, the center of Chicago's great meatpacking industry, one noticed first the pungent odor, a mixture of smoke, fertilizer, and putrid flesh, blood, and hair from the slaughtered animals. A little closer, the stench of the uncovered garbage dump blended in. Finally one crossed "Bubbly Creek," a lifeless offshoot of the Chicago River, aptly named for the effect of the carbolic acid gas that formed from the decaying refuse poured in by the meatpacking plants. Railroads crisscrossed the entire area, bringing in thousands of animals each day and carrying out meat for sale in markets across the country.

Packingtown occupied about one square mile of land bounded by stockyards, packing plants, and freight yards. With a population of 30,000 to 40,000 at the end of the nineteenth century, it was a rapidly growing community of old and new immigrants who depended on the meatpacking industry for their livelihood. An average household included six or seven people—parents, two or three children, and two or three boarders. They lived typically in wooden houses divided into four or more flats. Although Irish, Germans, Bohemians, Poles, Lithuanians, and Slovaks were squeezed together in this solidly working-class neighborhood, strong ethnic identities persisted. Few households included residents of more than one nationality, and interethnic marriages were rare. Nearly everyone professed the Roman Catholic faith, yet each ethnic group maintained its own church and often its own parochial school, where children were taught in their parents' language. Political organizations, fraternal societies, and even gymnastic clubs and drama groups reflected these ethnic divisions.

The one local institution that bridged the different groups was the saloon. Located on virtually every street corner, saloons offered important services to the community, hosting weddings and dances, providing meeting places for trade unions and fraternal societies, and cashing paychecks. During the frequent seasons of unemployment, Packingtown workers spent a lot of time in saloons. Here they often made friends across ethnic divisions, an extension of their common work experience in the nearby stockyard and packinghouses.

Most of the meatpacking industry's first "knife men"—the skilled workers in the "killing gangs" who managed the actual slaughtering and cutting operations—were German and Irish. Many had learned their butcher's craft in the Old Country. Below them were the common laborers, mainly recent immigrants from eastern Europe. Having no previous experience in meatpacking, these workers found themselves in the lowest-paid jobs,

such as the by-product manufacturing of glue and oleo. A sizable portion had never before earned wages. They soon discovered, as one Lithuanian laborer put it, that "money was everything and a man without money must die." But the money available—a daily wage of $2 (or less)—was often not enough. The death rate from tuberculosis in Packingtown was thought to be the highest in Chicago and among the highest in the nation.

The Packingtown community, small and insular as it seemed to the residents, was bound into an elaborate economic network that reached distant parts of the United States, transforming the way farmers raised livestock and grains, railroads operated, and consumers ate their meals. These workers helped make Chicago a gateway city, a destination point for raw materials coming in from the West as well as a point of export for products of all kinds.

Chicago meatpackers, led by the "big five" of Armour, Cudahy, Morris, Schwarzschild and Sulzberger, and Swift, expanded more than 900 percent between 1870 and 1890, dominating the national market for meat and establishing a standard for monopoly capitalism in the late nineteenth century. In the process, they also became the city's largest manufacturing employer. They built huge, specialized factories during the 1860s and 1870s that speeded the killing process and—thanks to mountains of ice brought by rail from ponds and lakes—operated year round. The introduction of an efficiently refrigerated railroad car in the 1880s made it possible to ship meat nationwide. Consumers had long believed that only meat butchered locally was safe to eat, but now cheap Chicago-packed beef and pork began to appear on every meateater's table. Local packinghouses throughout the Midwest succumbed to the ruthless competition from Chicago.

Chicago's control of the mass market for meat affected all aspects of the industry. Midwestern farmers practically abandoned raising calves on open pastures. Instead, they bought two-year-old steers from the West and fattened them on homegrown corn in feedlots, making sure that bulk went into edible parts rather than muscle and bone. The feedlot—a kind of rural factory—replaced pasture just as pasture had earlier supplanted prairie grasslands.

Few of the workers in Chicago's stockyards had seen a farm since they left their homelands. But as the working hands of what poet Carl Sandburg would later call the "Hog butcher for the world, . . . City of the big shoulders," they played their part, along with the farmer, the grain dealer, the ironworker, the teamster, and many others in bringing together the neighboring countryside, distant regions, and the city in a common endeavor.

Chicago

The Rise of Industry, the Triumph of Business

At the time of the Civil War, the typical American business firm was a small enterprise, owned and managed by a single family, and producing goods for a local or regional market. By the turn of the century, businesses depending on large-scale investments had organized as corporations and grown to unforeseen size. These mammoth firms could afford to mass-produce goods for national and even international markets. At the helm stood unimaginably wealthy men such as Andrew Carnegie, Philip Danforth Armour, Jay Gould, and John D. Rockefeller, all powerful leaders of a new national business community.

A Revolution in Technology

In the decades after the Civil War, American industry transformed itself into a new wonder of the world. The Centennial Exposition of 1876, held in Philadelphia, celebrated not so much the American Revolution 100 years earlier as the industrial and technological promise of the century to come. Its central theme was power. In the main building—at the time the largest on earth—the visiting emperor of Brazil marked the opening day by throwing a switch on a giant steam engine. Examining the telephone, which he had never before seen in operation, he gasped, "My God, it talks!" Patented that year by Alexander Graham Bell, the telephone signaled the rise of the United States to world leadership in industrial technology.

The year 1876 also marked the opening of Thomas Alva Edison's laboratory in Menlo Park, New Jersey. Three years later, his research team hit upon its most marketable invention, an incandescent lamp that burned for more than thirteen hours. By 1882 the Edison Electric Light Company had launched its service in New York City's financial district. By this time American inventors, who had filed nearly half a million patents since the close of the Civil War, were previewing the marvels of the next century. Henry Ford, working as an electrical engineer for the Detroit Edison Company, was already experimenting with the gasoline-burning internal combustion engine and designing his own automobile. By 1900 American companies had produced more than 4,000 automobiles. The prospect of commercial aviation emerged in 1903 when Wilbur and Orville Wright staged the first airplane flight near Kitty Hawk, North Carolina.

A major force behind economic growth was the vast transcontinental railroad, completed in 1869. The addition of three more major rail lines (the Southern Pacific, the Northern Pacific, and the Atchison, Topeka, and Santa Fe) in the early 1880s, and the Great Northern a decade later, completed the most extensive transportation network in the world. As the nation's first big business, railroads linked cities in every state and served a nationwide market for goods. Freight trains carried the bountiful natural resources, such as iron, coal, and minerals that supplied the raw materials for industry, as well as food for the growing urban populations.

The monumental advances in transportation and communication facilitated the progressively westward relocation of industry. The geographic center of manufacturing (as computed by the gross value of products) was near the middle of Pennsylvania in 1850, in western Pennsylvania by 1880, and near Mansfield, Ohio, in 1900.

Industry grew at a pace that was not only unprecedented, but also previously unimaginable. In 1865 the annual production of goods was estimated at $2 billion; by 1900 it stood at $13 billion, transforming the United States from fourth to first in the world in terms of productivity.

WHAT WERE the major tenets of the Gospel of Wealth?

IMAGE KEY

for pages 502–503

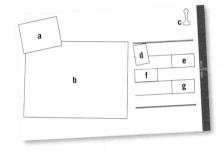

a. A classroom at work in the Chinese Public Primary School in Chinatown, San Francisco, with a Caucasian teacher.

b. A crowd of children at work in a nineteenth-century canning factory. The children sit on overturned baskets while poring over their work under the gaze of an adult male supervisor in their midst.

c. A replica of the first light bulb.

d. Joseph Keppler's *The Two Philanthropists*, caricatures magnates Jay Gould and Cornelius Vanderbilt. The cartoon was published February, 1888 in *Puck* magazine.

e. The Sixth Maryland Militia in Baltimore fires into a hostile crowd of laborers chucking rocks during the Great Railroad Strike of 1877.

f. Humorous drawing of Thomas Edison's laboratories in Menlo Park, New Jersey, around 1880.

g. Fashionable people crowded the Boardwalk in Atlantic City each Easter Sunday to see and be seen in the early twentieth century.

QUICK REVIEW

Growth of Industry

- 1865: $2 billion annual production of goods.
- 1900: $13 billion annual production of goods.
- Revolutions in technology and transportation made growth possible.

MAP EXPLORATION

To explore an interactive version of this map, go to **http://www.prenhall.com/faraghertlc/map19.1**

MAP 19-1

Patterns of Industry, 1900 Industrial manufacturing concentrated in the Northeast and Midwest, while the raw materials for production came mostly from other parts of the nation.

WHY DID industrial patterns differ from region to region?

MECHANIZATION TAKES COMMAND

This second industrial revolution depended on many factors, but none was more important than the application of new technologies to increase the productivity of labor and the volume of goods. Machines, factory managers, and workers together created a system of continuous production by which more could be made, and faster, than anywhere else on earth. Higher productivity depended not only on machinery and technology, but also on economies of scale and speed, reorganization of factory labor and business management, and the unparalleled growth of a market for goods of all kinds.

All these changes depended in turn on anthracite coal, a new source of fuel, which was widely used after 1850. Reliable and inexpensive sources of energy made possible dramatic changes in the industrial uses of light, heat, and motion. Equally important, coal fueled the great open-hearth furnaces and mills of the iron and steel industry. By the end of the century, the U.S. steel industry was the world's largest.

New systems of mass production replaced wasteful and often chaotic practices and speeded up the delivery of finished goods. In the 1860s meatpackers set up one of the earliest production lines. This "disassembly line" displaced patterns of hand labor that were centuries old. The production line became standard in most areas of manufacturing.

Sometimes the invention of a single machine could instantly transform production, mechanizing every stage from processing the raw material to packaging the product. The cigarette-making machine, patented in 1881, shaped the tobacco, encased it in an endless paper tube, and snipped off the tube at cigarette-length intervals. This machine could produce more than 7,000 cigarettes per hour, replacing the worker who at best made 3,000 per day. After a few more improvements, fifteen machines could meet the total demand for American cigarettes. Within a generation, continuous production also revolutionized the making of furniture, cloth, grain products, soap, and canned goods; the refining, distilling, and processing of animal and vegetable fats; and eventually the manufacture of automobiles.

THE EXPANDING MARKET FOR GOODS

To distribute the growing volume of goods, businesses demanded new techniques of marketing and merchandising. For generations, legions of sellers, or "drummers," had worked their routes, pushing goods, especially hardware and patent medicines, to individual buyers and retail stores. The appearance of mail-order houses after the Civil War accompanied the consolidation of the railroad lines and the expansion of the postal system. Rates were lowered for freight and postage alike, and railroad stations opened post offices and sold money orders. By 1896 rural free delivery had reached distant communities.

Growing directly out of these services, the successful Chicago-based mail-order houses drew rural and urban consumers into a common marketplace. Sears, Roebuck and Company and Montgomery Ward offered an enormous variety of goods, from shoes to buggies to gasoline stoves and cream separators. The Sears catalog offered Armour's summer sausage as well as Aunt Jemima's Pancake Flour and Queen Mary Scotch Oatmeal, both made of grains that came from the agricultural heartland. In turn, the purchases made by farm families through the Sears catalog sent cash flowing into Chicago.

The chain store achieved similar economies of scale. By 1900, a half-dozen grocery chains had sprung up. The largest was A&P, originally named the Great Atlantic and Pacific Tea Company to celebrate the completion of the transcontinental railroad. Frank and Charles Woolworth offered inexpensive variety goods in five-and-ten-cent stores. Hurt financially by this competition, community-based retailers headed the lobby for antichain legislation.

Opening shortly after the Civil War, department stores began to take up much of the business formerly enjoyed by specialty shops, offering a spectrum of services that included restaurants, rest rooms, ticket agencies, nurseries, reading rooms, and post offices. Elegantly appointed with imported carpets, sweeping marble staircases, and crystal chandeliers, the department store raised retailing to new heights. By the close of the century, the names of Marshall Field of Chicago, Filene's of Boston, The Emporium of San Francisco, Wanamaker's of Philadelphia, and Macy's of New York had come to represent the splendors of those great cities as well as the apex of mass retailing.

Advertising lured customers to the department stores, the chains, and the independent neighborhood shops. The advertising revolution began in 1869, when Francis Wayland Ayer founded the earliest advertising agency, but the firm did not hire its first full-time copy writers until 1891. Ayer's handled the accounts

Vertical integration The consolidation of numerous production functions, from the extraction of the raw materials to the distribution and marketing of the finished products, under the direction of one firm.

Horizontal combination The merger of competitors in the same industry.

of such companies as Montgomery Ward, Procter & Gamble, and the National Biscuit Company. With the help of this new sales tool, gross revenues of retailers raced upward from $8 million in 1860 to $102 million in 1900.

INTEGRATION, COMBINATION, AND MERGER

The business community aspired to exercise greater control of the economy and to enlarge the commercial empire. From the source of raw materials to the organization of production, from the conditions of labor to the climate of public opinion, business leaders acted shrewdly. Economic cycles alternating between rapid growth and sharp decline also promoted the rise of big business. Major economic setbacks in 1873 and 1893 wiped out weaker competitors, allowing the strongest firms to rebound swiftly and to expand their sales and scale of operation during the recovery period.

Businesses grew in two distinct, if overlapping, ways. Through *vertical integration* a firm gained control of production at every step of the way—from raw materials through processing to transport and merchandising of the finished items. In 1899 the United Fruit Company began to build a network of wholesale houses, and within two years it had opened distribution centers in twenty-one major cities. Eventually it controlled an elaborate system of Central American plantations and temperature-controlled shipping and storage facilities for its highly perishable bananas. The firm became one of the nation's largest corporations.

The second means of growth, *horizontal combination*, entailed gaining control of the market for a single product. The most famous case was the Standard Oil Company, founded by John D. Rockefeller in 1870. Operating out of Cleveland in a highly competitive but lucrative field, Rockefeller first secured preferential rates from railroads eager to ensure a steady supply of oil. He then convinced or coerced other local oil operators to sell their stock to him. The Standard Oil Trust, established in 1882, controlled over 90 percent of the nation's oil-refining industry.

In 1890 Congress passed the Sherman Antitrust Act to restore competition by encouraging small business. Ironically, the courts interpreted the law in ways that inhibited the organization of trade unions (on the ground that they restricted the free flow of labor) and actually helped the consolidation of business. More than 2,600 firms vanished between 1898 and 1902 alone. By 1910 the

John D. Rockefeller, who formed the Standard Oil Company in 1870, sought to control all aspects of the industry, from the transportation of crude oil to the marketing and distribution of the final products. This cartoon, published in *Puck* in 1904, shows the stranglehold Standard Oil had on government and industry alike. In 1911, in response to an antitrust suit, the Supreme Court ordered the company to break up.

Courtesy of the Library of Congress (LCUS264-435)

industrial giants that would dominate the American economy until the last half of the twentieth century—U.S. Rubber, Goodyear, American Smelting and Refining, Anaconda Copper, General Electric, Westinghouse, Nabisco, Swift and Company, Armour, International Harvester, Eastman Kodak, and American Can—had already formed.

THE GOSPEL OF WEALTH

Ninety percent of the nation's business leaders were Protestant, and the majority attended church services regularly. They attributed their personal achievement to hard work and perseverance and made these the principal tenets of a new faith that imbued the pursuit of wealth with old-time religious zeal.

One version of this "**gospel of wealth**" justified the ruthless behavior of entrepreneurs who accumulated unprecedented wealth and power through shady deals and conspiracies. Speculator Jay Gould wrung his fortune, it was widely believed, from the labor of others. He rose quickly from his modest origins through a series of unsavory financial maneuvers and such high-handed measures as sending armed employees to seize a factory.

Speculation in railroads proved to be Gould's forte. He took over the Erie Railroad, paying off New York legislators to get the state to finance its expansion, and he acquired the U.S. Express Company by pressuring and tricking its stockholders. When threatened with arrest, Gould sold off his shares for $9 million and moved on to the Union Pacific, where he cut wages, precipitated strikes, and manipulated elections in the Western and Plains states. Tired of being caricatured in the press as a great swindler, he bought the leading newspapers.

Andrew Carnegie offered a strikingly different model. A poor immigrant from Scotland, Carnegie spent his boyhood studying bookkeeping at night while working days in a textile mill. In 1852 he became the personal secretary of the superintendent of the Pennsylvania Railroad's western division. He learned quickly and soon stepped into the superintendent's job. While improving passenger train service, he invested brilliantly to build funds for his next venture.

Carnegie built an empire in steel. A genius at vertical integration, he undercut his competitors by using the latest technology and designing his own system of cost analysis. By 1900 Carnegie managed the most efficient steel mills in the world, which accounted for one-third of the nation's output. When he sold out to J. P. Morgan's new United States Steel Corporation in 1901, his personal share of the proceeds came to $225 million.

Carnegie was well known as a civic leader. From one point of view, he was a factory despot who underpaid his employees and ruthlessly managed their working conditions. But to the patrons of the public libraries, art museums, concert halls, colleges, and universities that he funded, Carnegie appeared to be the single greatest philanthropist of the age. By the time he died, he had given away his massive personal fortune.

Gospel of wealth   Thesis that hard work and perseverance lead to wealth, implying that poverty is a character flaw.

LABOR IN THE AGE OF BIG BUSINESS

Like the gospel of wealth, the "gospel of work" affirmed the dignity of hard work, the virtue of thrift, and the importance of individual initiative. But unlike business leaders, the philosophers of American working people did not believe in riches as the proof of work well done, or in the lust for power as the driving force of progress. On the contrary, they contended that honesty and competence should become the badge of the morally responsible citizen.

WHO WERE the members of the American Federation of Labor?

This faith inspired a slender minority, less than 3 percent of the work force, to form unions in various trades and industries. Despite its small size, the labor movement represented the most significant and lasting response of workers to the rise of big business and the consolidation of corporate power.

THE WAGE SYSTEM

The accelerating growth of industry, especially the steady mechanization of production, dramatically changed employer-employee relations and created new categories of workers. Both in turn fostered competition among workers and created conditions often hazardous to health.

For most craft workers, the new system destroyed long-standing practices, chipped away at their customary autonomy. Frederick Winslow Taylor, the pioneer of scientific management, explained that managers must "take all the important decisions . . . out of the hands of workmen." Teams of ironworkers, for example, had previously set the rules of production as well as their wages while the company supplied equipment and raw materials. Once steel replaced iron, most companies gradually introduced a new system. Managers now constantly supervised workers, set the pace of production and rate of payment, and introduced new, faster machinery that made many skills obsolete. In the woodworking trades, highly skilled cabinetmakers, who for generations had brought their own tools to the factory, were largely replaced with "green hands"— immigrants, including many women—who with only minimal training and close supervision could operate new woodworking machines at cheaper rates of pay.

Not all trades conformed to this pattern. The garment industry, for example, retained older systems of labor along with the new. The highly mechanized factories employed hundreds of thousands of young immigrant women, while the outwork system, established well before the Civil War, contracted ever-larger numbers of families to work in their homes on sewing machines or by hand. Paid by the piece, all workers labored faster and longer to forestall a dip in wages.

Industrial expansion also offered new opportunities for women to work outside the home. African American and immigrant women found employment in trades least affected by technological advances, such as domestic service. In contrast, English-speaking white women moved into the better-paying clerical and sales positions in the rapidly expanding business sector. After the typewriter and telephone came into widespread use in the 1890s, the number of women employed in office work rose even faster. At the turn of the century, 8.6 million women worked outside their homes—nearly triple the number in 1870.

By contrast, African American men found themselves excluded from many fields. In Cleveland, for example, the number of black carpenters declined after 1870, just as the volume of construction was rapidly increasing. African American men were also systematically driven from restaurant service and barred from newer trades such as boilermaking, plumbing, electrical work, and paperhanging, which European immigrants secured for themselves.

Discriminatory or exclusionary practices fell hardest on workers recruited earlier from China to work in the mines, in the construction of the railroads, and in market gardening. From the 1860s on, many Chinese established laundries and restaurants in west coast cities where they were viewed as potential competitors by white workers and proprietors of small businesses. A potent and racist anti-Chinese movement organized to protest "cheap Chinese labor" and to demand a halt to Chinese immigration. By the late 1870s white rioters were insistently calling for deportation measures and razing Chinese neighborhoods. In 1882 Congress passed the **Chinese Exclusion Act**, which suspended Chinese immigration, limited the civil rights of resident Chinese, and forbade their naturalization.

Chinese Exclusion Act Act which suspended Chinese immigration, limited the civil rights of resident Chinese, and forbade their naturalization.

For even the best-placed wage earners, the new workplace could be unhealthy, even dangerous. Meatpacking produced its own hazards—the dampness of the pickling room, the sharp blade of the slaughtering knife, and the noxious odors of the fertilizer department. Factory owners often failed to mark high-voltage wires, locked fire doors, and allowed the emission of toxic fumes. Extractive workers, such as coal and copper miners, labored in mineshafts where the air could suddenly turn poisonous and where cave-ins were possible and deadly.

Except for federal employees, who had been granted the eight-hour day in 1868, most workers still toiled upward of ten or twelve hours daily.

Moreover, steady employment was rare. Between 1866 and 1897, fourteen years of prosperity stood against seventeen of hard times. The major depressions of 1873–1879 and 1893–1897 were the worst in the nation's history up to that time. Three "minor" recessions (1866–1867, 1883–1885, and 1890–1891) did not seem insignificant to the millions who lost their jobs.

THE KNIGHTS OF LABOR

The Noble and Holy Order of the **Knights of Labor**, founded by a group of Philadelphia garment cutters in 1869, grew to become the largest labor organization in the nineteenth century. Led by Grand Master Workman Terence V. Powderly, the order sought to bring together all wage earners regardless of skill. The Knights endorsed a variety of reform measures—child labor reform, a graduated income tax, more land set aside for homesteading, the abolition of contract labor, and monetary reform—to offset the power of the industrialists. They believed that the "producing classes," once freed from the grip of corporate monopoly and the curses of ignorance and alcohol, would transform the United States into a genuinely democratic society.

The Knights promoted economic cooperation as the alternative to the wage system and advocated a system of producers' cooperatives. In these factories workers collectively made all decisions on prices and wages and shared all the profits.

 19-1
Memorial of the Chinese Six Companies to U.S. Grant, President of the United States (1876)

Knights of Labor Labor union founded in 1869 that included skilled and unskilled workers irrespective of race or gender.

18-5
Address by George Engle, Condemned Haymarket Anarchist (1886)

The Knights also ran small cooperative cigar shops and grocery stores, often housed in their own assembly buildings. Successful for a time, most cooperatives could not compete against the heavily capitalized enterprises and ultimately failed.

The Knights reached their peak during the great campaign for a shorter workday. The Eight-Hour League, led by Ira Steward, advocated a "natural" rhythm of eight hours for work, eight hours for sleep, and eight hours for leisure. After staging petition campaigns, marches, and a massive strike in New York City, the movement collapsed during the economic recession of the 1870s. The Knights helped revive it in the next decade, and this time the campaign aroused widespread support from consumers, who boycotted brands of beer, bread, and other products made in longer-hour shops. Finally, during the first weeks of May 1886, more than a third of a million workers walked off their jobs. Approximately 200,000 of them won shorter hours.

The eight-hour campaign swelled the ranks of the Knights of Labor. The organization grew from a few thousand in 1880 to nearly three-quarters of a million six years later. Nearly 3,000 women formed their own "ladies assemblies" or joined mixed locals. Leonora Barry, appointed to organize women, helped to increase their share of membership to 10 percent. African Americans also joined the Knights— 20,000 to 30,000 nationally—mainly in separate assemblies within the organization.

In Chicago, the shorter-hours campaign ended in tragedy. On May 4, 1886, following a series of confrontations between strikers and authorities, a protest against police violence at Haymarket Square seemed to be ending quietly until someone threw a bomb that killed one policeman and left seven others fatally wounded. Police responded by firing wildly into the crowd, killing an equal number. After Chicago authorities arrested anarchist leaders, a sensational trial ended in death sentences, although no evidence linked the accused to the bombing. Four of the convicted were hanged, one committed suicide, and three other "Haymarket Martyrs," as they were called, remained jailed until pardoned in 1893 by Illinois governor John Peter Altgeld.

The Knights of Labor had suffered an irreparable setback. Employers' associations successfully pooled funds to rid their factories of troublesome organizers and announced that companies would no longer bargain with unions. The wage system had triumphed.

THE AMERICAN FEDERATION OF LABOR

The events of 1886 also signaled the rise of a very different kind of organization, the **American Federation of Labor (AFL).** Unlike the Knights, the AFL accepted the wage system. Following a strategy of "pure and simple unionism," the AFL sought to gain recognition of its union status to bargain with employers for better working conditions, higher wages, and shorter hours. In return, it offered compliant firms the benefit of amenable day-to-day relations with the most highly skilled wage earners. Only if companies refused to bargain in good faith would union members strike.

The new federation, with twelve national unions and 140,000 affiliated members, declared war on the Knights of Labor. In the wake of the Haymarket tragedy and the collapse of the eight-hour movement, the AFL pushed ahead of its rival by organizing craft workers. AFL president Samuel Gompers refused to include unskilled workers, racial minorities, women, and immigrants, believing they were impossible to organize and even unworthy of equal status. Under his leadership, the AFL member became the "aristocrat of labor," the best paid worker in the world.

Although craft unionism represented only a small minority of working Americans—about 10 percent at the end of the century—local federations of skilled workers often played important roles in their communities. They may not have been able to slow the steady advance of mechanization, which diminished the craft

American Federation of Labor (AFL)
Union formed in 1886 that organized skilled workers along craft lines and emphasized a few workplace issues rather than a broad social program.

worker's autonomy and eliminated some of the most desirable jobs, but AFL members managed to make their presence felt. Local politicians courted their votes, and Labor Day, first celebrated in the 1880s, became a national holiday in 1894.

THE NEW SOUTH

At the turn of the century Southern industries lagged far behind enterprises in other regions of the country. Their progress was held back by dependence on Northern finance capital, continued reliance on cotton production, and the legacy of slavery.

AN INTERNAL COLONY

In the 1870s a vocal and powerful new group of Southerners headed by Henry Woodfin Grady, editor of the *Atlanta Constitution,* insisted that the region enjoyed a great potential in its abundant natural resources of coal, iron, turpentine, tobacco, and lumber. Arguing against those planters who aspired to rejuvenate the agricultural economy based on the cultivation of a few staple crops, this group forcefully promoted industrial development and welcomed Northern investors.

Northern investors secured huge concessions from Southern state legislatures, including land, forest, and mineral rights and large tax exemptions. Exploiting the incentives, railroad companies laid over 22,000 miles of new track, connecting the region to national markets and creating new cities. By 1890 a score of large railroad companies, centered mainly in New York, held more than half of all the track in the South.

Northerners also employed various means to protect their investments from Southern competition. By the late 1870s, Southern merchants, with help from foreign investors, had begun to run iron factories around Birmingham, Alabama. Southern iron production was soon encroaching on the Northeastern market. To stave off this competition, Andrew Carnegie ordered the railroads to charge higher freight fees to Birmingham's iron producers. New York bankers later succeeded in expatriating Birmingham's profits through stock ownership in Southern firms. After the turn of the century, U.S. Steel simply bought out the local merchants and took over much of Birmingham's production.

The production of cotton textiles followed a similar course. Powerful merchants and large landowners, realizing that they could make high profits by controlling the cotton crop from field to factory, promoted the vertical integration of the cotton industry. The number of mills in the South grew from 161 in 1880 to 400 in 1900. Southern investors supplied large amounts of the capital for the industrial expansion and technological improvements. The latest machines ran the new mills, and the South boasted the first factory fully equipped with electricity. Production in the four leading cotton-manufacturing states—North Carolina, South Carolina, Georgia, and Alabama—skyrocketed, far outpacing the New England mills.

Recognizing the potential for great profit in these new factories with their cheap labor, Northern manufacturers, including many New England mill owners, shifted their investments to the South. By the 1920s, Northern investors held much of the South's wealth, including the major textile mills, but returned through employment or social services only a small share of the profits to the region's people.

The governing role of capital investments from outside the region reinforced long-standing relationships. Even rapid industrialization—in iron, railroads, and textiles—did not carry the same consequences achieved in the North. The rise of the New South reinforced, rather than diminished, the region's status as the nation's internal colony.

HOW DID the development of Southern industry affect the lives of African Americans living in the South?

QUICK REVIEW

Race and Labor

◆ Advances in Southern industry did little to help African Americans.

◆ Southern workers rarely united across race lines.

◆ Wages throughout the South were low for both whites and blacks.

SOUTHERN LABOR

The advance of Southern industry did little to improve the working lives of most African Americans. African American men did find work with the railroads; in booming cities like Atlanta they even gained skilled positions in the construction trades and worked as bricklayers, carpenters, and painters. For the most part, however, African Americans were limited to unskilled, low-paying jobs. In the textile mills and cigarette factories, which employed both black and white workers, the work force was rigidly segregated. African Americans were assigned mainly to janitorial jobs and rarely worked alongside the white workers who tended the machines. Nearly all African American women who earned wages did so as household workers.

Locals of the all-white carpenters' union maintained a segregation policy so absolute that if too few members were available for a job, the union would send for out-of-town white workers rather than employ local members of the black carpenters' union. In an Atlanta mill in 1897, 1,400 white women operatives went on strike when the company proposed to hire two black spinners.

Only at rare moments did Southern workers unite across racial lines. In the 1880s, the Knights of Labor briefly organized both black and white workers. But when white politicians and local newspapers began to raise the specter of black domination, the Knights were forced to retreat. Across the region their assemblies collapsed. Other unions remained the exclusive preserve of white skilled workers.

Wages throughout the South were low for both black and white workers. In the 1880s, when investors enjoyed profits ranging from 30 percent to 75 percent, Southern mill workers earned as little as 12 cents per hour. Black men earned at or below the poverty line of $300 per year, while black women rarely earned more than $120, and white women about $220, annually. The poorest paid workers were children, the mainstay of Southern mill labor.

The processing of raw tobacco employed thousands of African American women, who sorted, stripped, stemmed, and hung tobacco leaves as part of the redrying process. After mechanization was introduced, white women took jobs as cigarette rollers, but black women kept the worst, most monotonous jobs in the tobacco factories. The women shown in this photograph are stemming tobacco in a Virginia factory while their white male supervisor oversees their labor.

Cook Collection, Valentine Museum/Richmond History Center

As industry expanded throughout the nation, so too did the number of children earning wages. This was especially so in the South. In 1896 only one in twenty Massachusetts mill workers was younger than sixteen, but one in four North Carolina cotton mill operatives was that age or younger. Traditions rooted in the agricultural economy reinforced the practice of using the labor of all family members, even the very young. Seasonal labor, such as picking crops or grinding sugarcane, put families on the move, making formal education all but impossible. Not until well into the twentieth century did compulsory school attendance laws effectively restrict child labor in the South.

A system of convict labor also thrived in the South. Bituminous coal mines and public work projects of all kinds, especially in remote areas, employed disciplinary methods and created living and working conditions reminiscent of slavery. African Americans constituted up to 90 percent of the convict work force. Transported and housed like animals—chained together by day and confined in portable cages at night—these workers suffered high mortality rates. Southern leaders took pride in what they called the "good roads movement"—the chief use of convict labor—as proof of regional progress.

THE TRANSFORMATION OF PIEDMONT COMMUNITIES

The impact of the New South was nowhere greater than in the Piedmont, the region extending from southern Virginia and the central Carolinas into northern Alabama and Georgia. After 1870, long-established farms and plantations gave way to railroad tracks, textile factories, numerous mill villages, and a few sizable cities. By the turn of the century, five Piedmont towns had populations over 10,000. Even more dramatic was the swelling number of small towns with populations between 1,000 and 5,000—from fourteen in 1870 to fifty-two in 1900. Once the South's backcountry, the Piedmont now surpassed New England in the production of yarn and cloth to stand first in the world.

Rural poverty and the appeal of a new life encouraged many farm families to strike out for a mill town. Those with the least access to land and credit—mainly widows and their children and single women—were the first to go into the mills. Then families sent their children. As the agricultural crisis deepened, more and more people abandoned the countryside entirely for what they called "public work."

A mill community typically comprised rows of single-family houses, a small school, several churches, a company-owned store, and the home of the superintendent who governed everyone's affairs. Millworkers frequently complained that they had no private life at all. A federal report published shortly after the turn of the century concluded that "all the affairs of the village and the conditions of living of all the people are regulated entirely by the mill company. Practically speaking, the company owns everything and controls everything, and to a large extent controls everybody in the mill village."

Mill superintendents also relied on schoolteachers and clergy to set the tone of community life. They hired and paid the salaries of Baptist and Methodist ministers to preach a faith encouraging workers to be thrifty, orderly, temperate, and hardworking. The schools, similarly subsidized by the company, reinforced the lesson of moral and social discipline required of industrial life and encouraged students to follow their parents into the mill. But it was mainly young children between six and eight years old who attended school. When more hands were needed in the mill, superintendents plucked out these youngsters and sent them to join their older brothers and sisters who were already at work.

Piedmont mill villages like Greenville, South Carolina, and Burlington, Charlotte, and Franklinville, North Carolina, nevertheless developed a cohesive character typical of isolated rural communities. The new residents maintained many aspects of their agricultural pasts, tilling small gardens and keeping chickens, pigs, and cows in their yards. Factory owners rarely paved roads or sidewalks or provided adequate sanitation. Mud, flies, and diseases such as typhoid fever flourished. Mill-workers endured poverty and health hazards by strengthening community ties through intermarriage. Within a few generations, most of the village residents had, according to one study, "some connection to each other, however distant, by marriage," blood, or both. Even the men and women without families boarded in households where privacy was scarce and collective meals created a familylike atmosphere. Historians have called this complex of intimate economic, family, and community ties the customs of incorporation.

THE INDUSTRIAL CITY

WHAT CONTRIBUTED

to the growing population of American cities?

Before the Civil War, manufacturing had centered in the countryside, in burgeoning factory towns such as Lowell, Massachusetts, and Troy, New York. By the end of the nineteenth century, 90 percent of all manufacturing took place in cities. The metropolis stood at the center of the growing industrial economy, a magnet drawing raw material, capital, and labor, and a key distribution point for manufactured goods. The industrial city inspired both great hope and great trepidation. Civic leaders often bragged about its size and rate of growth; immigrants wrote to their countryfolk of its pace, both exciting and exhausting.

POPULATING THE CITY

The population of cities grew at double the rate of the nation's population as a whole. In 1860 only sixteen cities had more than 50,000 residents. By 1890 one-third of all Americans were city dwellers. Eleven cities claimed more than 250,000 people.

QUICK REVIEW

Big Cities

♦ Cities grew at double the rate of the nation as a whole.

♦ Immigrants and their children were the major source of urban population growth.

♦ After the Civil War, most new immigrants settled in cities.

The nation's largest cities—New York, Chicago, Philadelphia, St. Louis, Boston, and Baltimore—achieved international fame for the size and diversity of their populations. Many of their new residents had migrated from rural communities within the United States. Between 1870 and 1910, an average of nearly 7,000 African Americans moved north each year, hoping to escape the poverty and oppression prevailing in the South and to find better paying jobs. By the end of the century, nearly 80 percent of African Americans in the North lived in urban areas.

Immigrants and their children were the major source of urban population growth in the late nineteenth century. Most of those in the first wave of immigration, before the Civil War, had settled in the countryside. In contrast, after the war it was the industrial city that drew the so-called new immigrants, who came primarily from eastern and southern Europe. By the turn of the century Chicago had more Germans than all but a few German cities and more Poles than most Polish cities; New York had more Italians than a handful of the largest Italian cities, and Boston had nearly as many Irish as Dublin. In almost every group except the Irish, men outnumbered women.

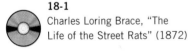

18-1
Charles Loring Brace, "The Life of the Street Rats" (1872)

Like rural migrants, immigrants came to the American city to take advantage of the expanding opportunities for employment. While many hoped to build a new home in the land of plenty, many others intended to work hard, save money, and return to their families in the Old Country. In the 1880s, for example, nearly half of all Italian, Greek, and Serbian men returned to their native lands. Others could not return to their homelands or did not wish to. Jews, for instance, had emigrated to escape persecution in Russia and Russian-dominated Polish and Roman-

MAP EXPLORATION

To explore an interactive version of this map, go to **http://www.prenhall.com/faraghertlc/map19.2**

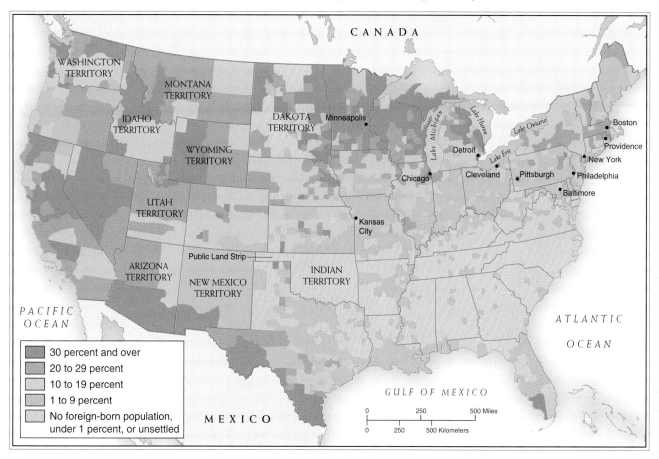

MAP 19-2

Population of Foreign Birth by Region, 1880 European immigrants after the Civil War settled primarily in the industrial districts of the northern Midwest and parts of the Northeast. French Canadians continued to settle in Maine, Cubans in Florida, and Mexicans in the Southwest, where earlier immigrants had established thriving communities.

Clifford L. Lord and Elizabeth H. Lord, *Lord & Lord Historical Atlas of the United States* (New York: Holt, 1953).

WHY DID immigrants tend to settle in some regions and not in others?

ian lands. A Yiddish writer later called this generation the "Jews without Jewish memories. . . . They shook them off in the boat when they came across the seas. They emptied out their memories."

Of all groups, Jews had the most experience with urban life. Forbidden to own land in most parts of Europe and boxed into *shtetls* (villages), Jews had also formed thriving urban communities in Vilna, Berlin, London, and Vienna. Many had worked in garment manufacturing, in London's East End, for example, and followed a path to American cities like New York, Rochester, Philadelphia, or Chicago where the needle trades flourished.

Bohemians settled largely in Chicago, Pittsburgh, and Cleveland. French Canadians, a relatively small group of a few hundred thousand, emigrated from Quebec and settled almost exclusively in New England and upper New York State. Finding work mainly in textile mills, they transformed smaller industrial cities like Woonsocket, Rhode Island, into French-speaking communities. Cubans, themselves often first- or second-generation immigrants from Spain, moved to Ybor

City, a section of Tampa, Florida, to work in cigar factories. Still other groups tended toward cities dominated by fishing, shoemaking, or even glassblowing, a craft carried directly from the Old Country. Italians, the most numerous among the new immigrants, settled mainly in northeastern cities, laying railroad track, excavating subways, and erecting buildings.

Resettlement in an American city did not necessarily mark the end of the immigrants' travels. Newcomers, both native-born and immigrant, moved frequently from one neighborhood to another and from one city to another. American cities experienced a total population turnover three or four times during each decade of the last half of the century.

THE URBAN LANDSCAPE

Faced with a population explosion and an unprecedented building boom, the cities encouraged the creation of many beautiful and useful structures, including commercial offices, sumptuous homes, and efficient public services. At the same time, cities did little to improve the conditions of the majority of the population who worked in dingy factories and lived in crowded **tenements**. Open space rapidly decreased as American cities grew.

American streets customarily followed a simple gridiron pattern. Builders leveled hills, filled ponds, and pulled down any farms or houses in the way. City officials usually lacked any master plan save the idea of endless expansion. Factories often occupied the best sites, typically near waterways, where goods could easily be transported and chemical wastes dumped.

Built by the thousands after the Civil War, the tenement was designed to maximize the use of space. A typical tenement sat on a lot 25 feet by 100 feet and rose to five stories. There were four families on each floor, each with three rooms. By 1890 New York's Lower East Side packed more than 700 people per acre into back-to-back buildings, producing one of the highest population densities in the world.

At the other end of the urban social scale, New York's Fifth Avenue, St. Paul's Summit Avenue, Chicago's Michigan Avenue, and San Francisco's Nob Hill fairly gleamed with new mansions and town houses. Commonwealth Avenue marked Boston's fashionable Back Bay district, built on a filled-in 450-acre tidal flat. State engineers planned this community, with its magnificent boulevard, uniform five-story brownstones, and back alleys designed for deliveries. Back Bay opened onto the Fenway Park system designed by the nation's premier landscape architect, Frederick Law Olmsted.

The industrial city established a new style of commercial and civic architecture. Using fireproof materials, expanded foundations, and internal metal construction, the era's talented young architects focused on the factory and office building. Concentrating as many offices as possible in the downtown areas, they fashioned hundreds of buildings from steel, sometimes decorating them with elaborate wrought-iron facades. The office building could rise seven, ten, even twenty stories high.

In the 1890s, influenced by American wealth and its enhanced role in the global economy, city planners turned to the monumental or imperial style, laying grand concrete boulevards at enormous public cost. New sports amphitheaters spread pride in the city's accomplishments, and huge new art galleries, museums, and concert halls promoted urban excitement as well as cultural uplift. The imperial style also increased congestion and noise, making the city a more desirable place to visit than to live in.

The city also inspired other architectural marvels. Opened in 1883, the Brooklyn Bridge won wide acclaim as the most original American construction. Designed by John Roebling, who died from an accident early in its construction, and by his son Washington Roebling, who became an invalid during its construction, the bridge was considered an aesthetic and practical wonder.

Tenements Four- to six-story residential dwellings, once common in New York, built on tiny lots without regard to providing ventilation or light.

In his watercolor *The Bowery at Night*, painted in 1885, W. Louis Sonntag Jr. shows a New York City scene transformed by electric light. Electricity transformed the city in other ways as well, as seen in the electric streetcars and elevated railroad.

The Bowery at Night, 1885. Watercolor. Museum of the City of New York

Like the railroad but on a smaller scale, streetcars and elevated railroads changed business dramatically because they moved traffic of many different kinds—information, people, and goods—faster and farther than before. By 1895 more than 800 communities operated systems of electrically powered cars or trolleys. In 1902 New York opened its subway system, which would grow to become the largest in the nation.

THE CITY AND THE ENVIRONMENT

By making it possible for a great number of workers to live in communities distant from their place of employment, mass transportation also allowed the metropolitan region to grow dramatically. By the end of the nineteenth century, suburban trains were bringing nearly 100,000 riders daily into the city of Chicago. Outside Boston, suburbs like Dorchester and Brookline sprang up, offering many professional workers quiet residential retreats from the city's busy downtown.

Electric trolleys eliminated the tons of waste from horsecars that had for decades fouled city streets. But the new rail systems also increased congestion and created new safety hazards for pedestrians. Elevated trains, designed to avoid these problems, placed entire communities under the shadow of noisy and rickety wooden platforms. Despite many technological advances, the quality of life in the nation's cities did not necessarily improve.

18-10
United States Sanitary
Commission, Sketch
of Its Purposes (1864)

Modern water and sewer systems now constituted a hidden city of pipes and wires mirroring the growth of the visible city above ground. These advances did not, however, eradicate serious environmental or health problems. Most cities continued to dump sewage into nearby bodies of water. Moreover, rather than outlawing upriver dumping by factories, municipal governments usually moved to establish separate clean-water systems through the use of reservoirs. But downriver communities began to complain about the unendurable stench from the diverted flow.

The unrestricted burning of coal to fuel the railroads and to heat factories and homes after 1880 greatly intensified urban air pollution. Noise levels continued to rise in the most compacted living and industrial areas. Overcrowded conditions and inadequate sanitary facilities bred tuberculosis, smallpox, and scarlet fever, among other contagious diseases. Children's diseases like whooping cough and measles spread rapidly through many poor neighborhoods. Only after the turn of the century, amid an intensive campaign against municipal corruption, did laws and administrative practices address the serious problems of public health (see Chapter 21).

Meanwhile the distance between the city and the countryside narrowed. Naturalists had hoped for large open spaces—a buffer zone—to preserve farmland and wild areas, protect future water supplies, and diminish regional air pollution. However, nearby rural lands not destined for private housing or commercial development became sites for water treatment and sewage plants, garbage dumps, and graveyards—services essential to the city's growing population.

Culture and Society in the Gilded Age

■ ■ ■ ■ ■ ■ ■ ■ ■ ■

WHAT LED Mark Twain
to label the late nineteenth century
the Gilded Age?

■ ■ ■ ■ ■ ■ ■ ■ ■ ■

The growth of industry and spread of cities had a profound impact on all regions of the United States. During the final third of the nineteenth century the standard of living climbed, although unevenly and erratically. Real wages (pay in relation to the cost of living) rose, fostering improvements in nutrition, clothing, and housing. More and cheaper products were within the reach of all but the very poor. Food from the farms became more abundant and varied—grains for bread or beer; poultry, pork, and beef; fresh fruits and vegetables from California. Although many Americans continued to acknowledge the moral value of hard work, thrift, and self-sacrifice, the explosion of consumer goods and services promoted sweeping changes in behavior and beliefs.

"Conspicuous Consumption"

18-3
The Gilded Age (1880)

Gilded Age Term applied to late nineteenth-century America that refers to the shallow display and worship of wealth characteristic of that period.

Conspicuous consumption Highly visible displays of wealth and consumption.

Labeled the "**Gilded Age**" by humorist and social critic Mark Twain, the era following the Civil War favored the growth of a new class united in its pursuit of money and leisure. The well-to-do enjoyed great status throughout the nineteenth century, but only after the war did upper-class Americans form national networks to consolidate their power. Business leaders built diverse stock portfolios and often served simultaneously on the boards of several corporations. Similarly, they intertwined their interests by joining the same religious, charitable, athletic, and professional societies. Their wives and children vacationed together in the sumptuous new seashore and mountain resorts, while they themselves made deals at their leisure in new downtown social clubs and on the golf links of suburban country clubs. Just as Dun and Bradstreet ranked the leading corporations, the Social Register identified the 500 families that controlled most of the nation's wealth.

According to economist and social critic Thorstein Veblen, the rich had created a new style of "**conspicuous consumption.**" A vice president of the Chicago & Northwestern Railroad, Perry H. Smith, built his marble palace in the style of the Greek Renaissance. Its ebony staircase was trimmed in gold, its butler's pantry equipped with faucets not only for hot and cold water, but also for iced champagne. The women who oversaw these elaborate households themselves served as measures of their husbands' status, according to Veblen, by adorning themselves in jewels, furs, and dresses of the latest Paris design.

Perhaps no display of wealth matched the ostentation of the "cottages" of Newport, Rhode Island, where the rich created a summer community centering on consumption. Architect H. H. Richardson and his protégés built manor houses more magnificent than the English homes they mimicked. Here wealthy young men and women engaged in new amateur sports such as polo, rowing, and lawn tennis. Young and old alike joined in yachting and golf tournaments.

The wealthy also became the leading patrons of the arts as well as the chief importers of art treasures from Europe and Asia. They provided the bulk of funds for the new symphonies, operas, and ballet companies, which soon rivaled those of continental Europe. Nearly all major museums and art galleries were founded during the last decades of the nineteenth century.

18-6
Edward Bellamy, from *Looking Backward* (1888)

GENTILITY AND THE MIDDLE CLASS

A new middle class, very different from its predecessor, formed during the last half of the century. The older middle class comprised the owners or superintendents of small businesses, doctors, lawyers, teachers, and ministers and their families. The new middle class included these professionals as well as the growing number of salaried employees—the managers, technicians, clerks, and engineers who worked in the complex web of corporations and government. Long hours of labor earned their families a modest status and sufficient income to live securely in style and comfort. For as little as $10 a month, a family could finance the construction of a suburban retreat from the noise, filth, and dangers of the city. Assisted by modern transportation systems, men often traveled one to two hours each day, five or six days a week, to their city offices and back again. Women and children stayed behind.

Middle-class women found themselves devoting a large part of their day to housework. They frequently employed one or two servants but relied increasingly on the many new household appliances to get their work done. Improvements in the kitchen stove, such as the conversion from wood fuel to gas, saved a lot of time. Yet, simultaneously, with the widespread circulation of cookbooks and recipes in newspapers and magazines, as well as the availability of new foods, the preparation of meals became more complex and time-consuming. Similarly, the new carpet sweepers surpassed the broom in efficiency, but the fashionable high-napped carpeting demanded more care. Rather than diminishing with technological innovation, household work expanded to fill the time available.

Almost exclusively white, Anglo-Saxon, and Protestant, the new middle class embraced "culture" not for purposes of conspicuous consumption but as a means of self-improvement and moral uplift. Whole families visited the new museums and art galleries. The middle class also provided the bulk of patrons for the new public libraries.

Middle-class families applied the same standards to their leisure activities. Hiking was a favorite among both men and women. Roller skating and ice skating, which became crazes shortly after the Civil War, took place in specially designed rinks in almost every major town. By the 1890s, the "safety" bicycle had also been marketed. It replaced the large-wheel variety, which was difficult to keep upright. A good-quality "bike" cost $100 and, like the piano, was a symbol of middle-class status.

Leisure became the special province of middle-class childhood. Removed from factories and shops and freed from many domestic chores, children enjoyed creative play and physical activity. The toy market boomed, and lower printing

QUICK REVIEW

The New Middle Class

◆ Middle-class women devoted a large portion of their day to housework.

◆ The new middle class embraced "culture" as means of self-improvement.

◆ Leisure activities reflected middle-class values.

prices helped children's literature flourish. Uplifting classics such as *Little Women* and *Black Beauty* were popular.

LIFE IN THE STREETS

Immigrants often weighed the material abundance they found in the United States against their memories of the Old Country. One could "live better" here, but only by working much harder. In letters home, immigrants described the riches of the new country but warned friends and relatives not to send weaklings, who would surely die of stress and strain amid the alien and intense commercialism of American society. In many immigrant communities, alcoholism and suicide rates soared. Embittered German immigrants called their new land *Malhuerica,* "misfortune"; Jews called it *Ama Reka,* Hebrew for "without soul"; and Slavs referred to it as *Dollerica.*

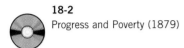

18-2
Progress and Poverty (1879)

Many newcomers, having little choice about their place of residence, concentrated in districts marked off by racial or ethnic lines. In San Francisco, city ordinances prevented Chinese from operating laundries in most of the city's neighborhoods, effectively confining the population to Chinatown. In Los Angeles and San Antonio, Mexicans lived in distinctive barrios. In most cities, African American families were similarly compelled to remain in the dingiest, most crime-ridden, and dangerous sections of town.

The working-class home did not necessarily ensure privacy or offer protection from the dangers of the outside world. In the tenements, families often shared their rooms with other families or paying boarders. During the summer heat, adults, children, and boarders alike competed for a sleeping place on the fire escape or roof, and all year round noise resounded through paper-thin walls. But so complex and varied were income levels and social customs that no single pattern emerged. Packingtown's Slovaks, Lithuanians, and Poles, for example, frequently took in boarders, yet Bohemians rarely did. Neither did the skilled iron rollers who worked at the Carnegie Steel Company in Homestead, Pennsylvania. These well-paid craft workers often owned their own homes, boasting parlors and

The intersection of Orchard and Hester Streets on New York's Lower East Side, photographed ca. 1905. Unlike the middle classes, who worked and played hidden away in offices and private homes, the Jewish lower-class immigrants who lived and worked in this neighborhood spent the greater parts of their lives on the streets.

Oil over a photograph. The Granger Collection (4E534.23)

even imported Belgian carpets. At the other extreme, Italian immigrants, who considered themselves fortunate to get work with a shovel, usually lived in over-crowded rented apartments, just a paycheck away from eviction.

Whether it was a small cottage or a tenement flat, the working-class home involved women and children in routines of household labor without the aid of the new mechanical devices. In addition to cooking and cleaning, women used their cramped domestic space for work that provided a small income. They gathered their children—and their husbands after a hard day's labor—to sew garments, wrap cigars, string beads, or paint vases for a contractor who paid them by the piece. And they cooked and cleaned for the boarders whose rent supplemented the family income.

Despite working people's slim resources, their combined buying power created new and important markets for consumer goods. Often they bought shoddy replicas of products sold to the middle class: cheaper canned goods, inferior cuts of meat, and partially spoiled fruit. Several leading clothing manufacturers specialized in inexpensive ready-to-wear items, usually copied from patterns designed for wealthier consumers but constructed hastily from flimsy materials. Patent medicines for ailments caused by working long periods in cramped conditions sold well in working-class communities, where money for doctors was scarce. Their high alcohol content might lift a person's spirits, if only temporarily.

The close quarters of the urban neighborhood allowed immigrants to preserve many Old World customs. In immigrant communities such as Chicago's Packingtown, Pittsburgh's Poletown, New York's Lower East Side, or San Francisco's Chinatown, people usually spoke their native language while visiting their friends and relatives. In good weather they walked and talked, an inexpensive pastime common in European cities. Immigrants also re-created Old World religious institutions such as the temple, church, or synagogue, or secular institutions such as German family-style taverns or Russian Jewish tearooms. They replicated their native cuisine and married, baptized children, and buried their dead according to Old World customs.

In the cosmopolitan cities, immigrants, by being innovative entrepreneurs as well as the best customers, helped to shape the emerging popular culture. Ragtime, for example, quickly found its way north from Storyville, the red-light district of New Orleans. Created by African American and creole bands, ragtime captivated those teenage offspring of immigrants who rushed to the new dance halls.

When developers realized that "wholesome fun" for the masses could pay better than upper-class leisure or lower-class vice, they decided to transform Coney Island into a magnificent seaside park filled with ingenious amusements such as water slides, mechanized horse races, carousels, roller coasters, and fun houses. Here, millions of working-class people enjoyed cheap thrills that offset the hardships of their working lives.

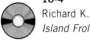

18-4
Richard K. Fox, from *Coney Island Frolics* (1883)

Cultures in Conflict, Culture in Common

The new commercial entertainments gave Americans from various backgrounds more in common than they would otherwise have had. On New York's Lower East Side, for instance, theater blossomed with dramas that Broadway would adopt years later, while children dreamed of going "uptown" where the popular songs they heard on the streets were transcribed onto sheet music and sold in stores throughout the city.

WHAT ROLE did public spaces play in late nineteenth-century popular culture?

EDUCATION

Business and civic leaders realized that the welfare of society now depended on an educated population, one possessing the skills and knowledge required to keep both industry and government running. In the last three decades of the nineteenth century, the idea of universal free schooling, at least for white children, took hold. Kindergartens in particular flourished. St. Louis, Missouri, opened the first public school kindergarten in 1873, and by the turn of the century more than 4,000 similar programs throughout the country enrolled children between the ages of three and seven. The number of public high schools increased from 160 in 1870 to 6,000 by the end of the century.

Agricultural colleges formed earlier in the century developed into institutes of technology and took their places alongside the prestigious liberal arts colleges. The Morrill Federal Land Grant Act of 1862 funded a system of state colleges and universities for teaching agriculture and mechanics "without excluding other scientific and classic studies." One of the most important developments occurred in the area of research and graduate studies, pioneered in this country in 1876 by Johns Hopkins University. By the end of the century several American universities, including Stanford University and the University of Chicago, offered advanced degrees in the arts and sciences.

This expansion benefited women, who had previously had little access to higher education. After the Civil War, a number of women's colleges were founded, beginning in 1865 with Vassar, which set the academic standard for the remainder of the century. Smith and Wellesley followed in 1875, Bryn Mawr in 1885. By the end of the century, 125 women's colleges offered a first-rate education comparable to that given to men at Harvard, Yale, or Princeton. Meanwhile, coeducation grew at an even faster rate; women constituted 21 percent of undergraduate enrollments in 1870, 32 percent in 1880, and 40 percent in 1910.

An even greater number of women enrolled in vocational courses. The first training school for nurses opened in Boston in 1873, followed in 1879 by a diet kitchen that taught women to become cooks in the city's hospitals. Founded in 1877, the **Women's Educational and Industrial Union** offered a multitude of classes to Boston's wage-earning women, ranging from elementary French and German, to drawing, watercoloring, and oil and china painting, to dressmaking and millinery, stenography and typing, as well as crafts less familiar to women, such as upholstering, cabinetmaking, and carpentry. In the early 1890s, when the entering class at a large women's college like Vassar still averaged under 100, the Boston Women's Educational and Industrial Union reported that its staff of 83 served an estimated 1,500 clients per day. By that time, one of its most well-funded programs was a training school for domestic servants.

The leaders of the business community had also begun to promote manual training for working-class and immigrant boys. Craft unionists in several cities actively opposed this development, preferring their own methods of apprenticeship to training programs they could not control. But local associations of merchants and manufacturers lobbied hard for "industrial education" and raised funds to supplement the public school budget. By 1895 all elementary and high schools in the city offered courses that trained working-class boys for future jobs in industry and business.

The expansion of education did not benefit all Americans or benefit them all in the same way. Because African Americans were prohibited from enrolling in colleges attended by white students, special colleges were founded in the southern states shortly after the Civil War. All-black Atlanta and Fisk universities both soon offered a rigorous curriculum in the liberal arts. Educator Booker T.

Women's Educational and Industrial Union Boston organization offering classes to wage-earning women.

Washington encouraged African Americans to resist "the craze for Greek and Latin learning" and to strive for practical instruction. In 1881 he founded the Tuskegee Institute in Alabama to provide industrial education and moral uplift. Black colleges, including Tuskegee, trained so many teachers that by the century's end the majority of black schools were staffed by African Americans.

17-11
W.E.B. Du Bois from "Of Mr. Booker T. Washington and Others" (1903)

LEISURE AND PUBLIC SPACE

Most large cities set aside open land for leisure-time use by residents. New York's Central Park opened for ice skating in 1858, providing a model for urban park systems across the United States. The parks were rolling expanses, cut across by streams and pathways and footbridges and set off by groves of trees, ornamental shrubs, and neat flower gardens. According to the designers' vision, the urban middle class might find here a respite from the stresses of modern life.

The working classes had their own ideas about the use of parks and open land. Trapped in overcrowded tenements or congested neighborhoods, they wanted space for sports, picnics, and lovers' trysts. Young people openly defied ordinances that prohibited play on the grassy knolls, while their elders routinely voted against municipal bonds that did not include funds for more recreational space in their communities. Immigrant ward representatives on the Pittsburgh city council, for instance, argued that band shells for classical music meant little to their constituents, while spaces suitable for sports meant much.

Public drinking of alcoholic beverages, especially on Sunday, provoked similar disputes. Pittsburgh's "blue laws," forbidding businesses to open on Sunday, were rigidly enforced when it came to neighborhood taverns, while large firms like the railroads enjoyed exemptions. Nevertheless, many working people, especially beer-loving German immigrants, continued to treat Sunday as their one day of relaxation and gathered in large numbers for picnics in the city's parks.

NATIONAL PASTIMES

Toward the end of the century, middle-class urban dwellers began to seek out ragtime bands and congregated in nightclubs and even on the rooftops of posh hotels to listen and dance and even to drink.

Vaudeville, the most popular form of commercial entertainment since the 1880s, also bridged middle- and working-class tastes. Drawing on a variety-show tradition of singers, dancers, comedians, jugglers, and acrobats, who had entertained Americans since colonial days, "vaude" became a big business that made ethnic and racial stereotypes and the daily frustrations of city life into major topics of amusement.

Sports, however, outdistanced all other commercial entertainments in appealing to all kinds of fans and managing to create a sense of national identity. No doubt the most popular parks in the United States were the expanses of green surrounded by grandstands and marked by their unique diamond shape—the baseball field. Baseball clubs formed in many cities, and shortly after the Civil War traveling teams with regular schedules made baseball a professional sport. The formation of the National League in 1876 encouraged other spectator sports, but for generations baseball remained the most popular.

Rowdy behavior gave the game a working-class ambience. Team owners, themselves often proprietors of local breweries, counted heavily on beer sales in the parks. To attract more subdued middle-class fans, the National League raised admission prices, banned the sale of alcohol, and observed Sunday blue laws. Catering to a working-class audience, the American Association kept the price of admission low, sold liquor, and played ball on Sunday.

CHRONOLOGY

1862	Morrill Act authorizes "land-grant" colleges.
1869	Knights of Labor founded.
1870	Standard Oil founded.
1871	Chicago Fire.
1873	Financial panic brings severe depression.
1876	Baseball's National League founded.
	Alexander Graham Bell patents the telephone.
1879	Thomas Edison invents the incandescent bulb.
	Depression ends.
1881	Tuskegee Institute founded.
1882	Peak of immigration to the United States (1.2 million) in the nineteenth century.
	Chinese Exclusion Act passed.

	Standard Oil Trust founded.
1883	William Graham Sumner published the social Darwinist classic *What Social Classes Owe to Each Other*.
1886	Campaigns for eight-hour workday peak.
	Haymarket riot and massacre discredit the Knights of Labor.
	American Federation of Labor founded.
1890	Sherman Antitrust Act passed.
1893	Stock market panic precipitates severe depression.
1895	Coney Island opens.
1896	Rural free delivery begins.
1900	Andrew Carnegie's *Gospel of Wealth* recommends honesty and fair dealing.
1901	U.S. Steel Corporation formed.

Entrepreneur Albert G. Spalding brought order to often chaotic baseball, but at a price. Manager and then president of the Chicago White Stockings, Spalding quickly came to see baseball as a source of multiple profits. He procured the exclusive rights to manufacture the official ball and the rule book, while producing large varieties of other sporting equipment. Meanwhile, he built impressive baseball parks in Chicago with seating for 10,000 and special private boxes above the grandstands for the wealthy.

Spalding also succeeded in tightening the rules of participation in the sport. He prevented players from negotiating a better deal and leaving the team that originally signed them. He encouraged his player-manager "Cap" Anson to forbid the White Stockings from playing against any team with an African American member, effectively setting a segregation standard for professional baseball. African Americans organized their own traveling teams. In the 1920s they formed the Negro Leagues, which produced some of the nation's finest ballplayers.

As attendance continued to grow, the enthusiasm for baseball straddled major social divisions, bringing together Americans of many backgrounds, if only on a limited basis. Although it interested relatively few women, sports news riveted the attention of men from all social classes. Loyalty to the "home team" helped to create an urban identity, while individual players became national heroes.

CONCLUSION

By the end of the nineteenth century, industry and the growing cities had opened a new world for Americans. Fresh from Europe or from the native countryside, ordinary urban dwellers struggled to form communities of fellow newcomers through work and leisure, in the factory, the neighborhood, the ballpark, and the public school. Meanwhile, their "betters," the wealthy and the new middle class, made and executed the decisions of industry and marketing, established the era's grand civic institutions, and set the tone for high fashion and art.

Rich and poor alike shared many aspects of the new order. Yet inequality persisted and increased, as much a part of the new order as the Brooklyn Bridge or advertising. During the mostly prosperous 1880s, optimists believed that unfair treatment based on region, on class, and perhaps even on race and gender might ease in time. By the depressed 1890s, however, these hopes had worn thin, and the lure of overseas empire appeared as one of the few goals that held together a suffering and divided nation.

SUMMARY

The Rise of Industry, The Triumph of Business Advances in technology, mechanization, and an expanded market for goods contributed to new strategies of business organization. The trend was toward large corporations and a philosophy of wealth rationalized the methods used by business leaders to secure their wealth.

Labor in the Age of Big Business Economic development profoundly affected the conditions of employment and work. While the number of jobs expanded, discrimination limited the opportunities of certain groups. Seeking improvement, workers formed unions that provided a variety of services and representation with mixed results.

The New South The movement to promote industrialization and the exploitation of resources of the South achieved limited success. Labor opportunities largely followed racial lines and were not affected by European immigration. The Piedmont was most affected by the New South movement. Its industry was organized around mill towns.

The Industrial City Industrialization fueled the growth of cities that were populated by migrants from rural areas and foreign immigrants. Architectural and transportation advances influenced urban development. Rapid, expansive growth caused environmental and health problems that were ameliorated by medical discoveries and public health campaigns.

Culture and Society in the Gilded Age Between approximately 1875 and 1900, the standard of living rose though unevenly. The newly rich industrialist formed a new class based on wealth and conspicuous consumption. At the same time, new middle and working classes emerged that also developed their own values and cultures.

Cultures in Conflict, Culture in Common The growth of cities and industries led to the expansion of the education system, the development of urban parks, and the increased appeal of popular entertainment and spectator sports. Different values and behavior created tensions among classes but changes were made to accommodate.

REVIEW QUESTIONS

1. Discuss the sources of economic growth in the decades after the Civil War. Historians often refer to this period as the era of the "second industrial revolution." Do you agree with this description?

2. Describe the impact of new technologies and new forms of production on the routines of industrial workers. How did these changes affect African American and women workers in particular? What role did trade unions play in this process?

3. Choose one major city, such as Boston, New York, Chicago, Birmingham, or San Francisco, and discuss changes in its economy, population, and urban space in the decades after the Civil War.

4. Discuss the role of Northern capital in the development of the New South. How did the rise of industry affect the lives of rural Southerners? Analyze these changes from the point of view of African Americans.

5. How did urban life change during the Gilded Age? How did economic development affect residential patterns? How did the middle class aspire to live during the Gilded Age? How did their lifestyles compare with those of working-class urbanites?

6. How did the American educational system change to prepare children for their adult roles in the new industrial economy?

7. How did the rise of organized sports and commercial amusements reflect and shape social divisions at the end of the century? Which groups were affected most (or least) by new leisure activities?

KEY TERMS

American Federation of Labor (AFL) (p. 512)

Chinese Exclusion Act (p. 510)

Conspicuous consumption (p. 520)

Gilded Age (p. 520)

Gospel of wealth (p. 509)

Horizontal combination (p. 508)

Knights of Labor (p. 511)

Tenements (p. 518)

Vertical integration (p. 508)

Women's Educational and Industrial Union (p. 524)

RECOMMENDED READING

Cindy S. Aron, *Working at Play: A History of Vacations in the United States* (1999). Covers the expansion of vacations from wealthy families to the middle class in the nineteenth century. Aron examines several types of settings, ranging from the grand summer hotels and posh resorts to camping vacations in the new national parks.

James R. Barrett, *Work and Community in the Jungle* (1987). A very close study of the Packingtown district of Chicago, Illinois, at the turn of the century. Barrett describes the transformation of animals to meat in great stockyards and processing plants. He also provides rich documentation of neighborhood life.

Alfred D. Chandler Jr., *The Visible Hand: The Managerial Revolution in American Business* (1977). A highly acclaimed study of corporate management. Chandler shows how the rapid growth in the scale of business, as well as its influence in public life, brought about a new type of executive with skills for national decision making and close links with others of his kind.

William Cronon, *Nature's Metropolis* (1991). Analyzes the changing economic and political relationship between the city of Chicago and the surrounding countryside. Cronon demonstrates through a variety of evidence the tight interdependence of urban and rural regions.

Herbert G. Gutman, *Work, Culture and Society in Industrializing America: Essays in American Working-Class and Social History* (1977). Influential essays on the formation of working-class communities in the nineteenth century. Gutman focuses on the role of immigrants in transforming the values and belief systems of working-class Americans in the throes of industrialization.

Alice Kessler-Harris, *Out to Work: A History of Wage-Earning Women in the United States* (1982). A comprehensive survey of women's increasing participation in the labor force. Kessler-Harris documents women's role in trade unions and the impact on family patterns and ideas about women's roles in American society.

Kenneth L. Kusmer, *A Ghetto Takes Shape, Black Cleveland, 1870–1930* (1976). A keen analysis of a long-standing African American community. Kusmer shows how blacks suffered downward mobility and increased segregation as their skilled jobs and small-business opportunities were given to European immigrants.

Lawrence H. Larsen, *The Rise of the Urban South* (1985). Studies of the changing South. In Larson's view, the true New South was the city, for relatively few had lived there before the late nineteenth century, but rural values remained vital, especially in religious life and voting patterns.

David F. Noble, *America by Design: Science, Technology and the Rise of Corporate Capitalism* (1977). A view of scientific advancement and its connections with the expanding economy. Noble shows how scientific breakthroughs were often created for, but especially adapted to, corporate purposes.

Dave Roediger and Franklin Rosemont, eds., *Haymarket Scrapbook* (1986). A large, beautifully illustrated book about the events and consequences of the Haymarket tragedy.

Roy Rosenzweig, *Eight Hours for What We Will: Workers and Leisure in an Industrial City, 1870–1920* (1983). Analyzes class and cultural conflicts over recreational space. This valuable book treats the city park as the arena for conflict over whether public community life should be uplifting (devoted to nature walks and concerts) or entertaining (for drinking, courting, and amusement).

Alan Trachtenberg, *The Incorporation of America: Culture and Society in the Gilded Age* (1982). One of the best and most readable overviews of the post–Civil War era. Trachtenberg devotes great care to describing the rise of the corporation as the defining institution of national life, and the reorientation of culture to reflect the new middle classes employed by the corporation.

*Dear Father, In the 5th, 8th, and 19th Wards . . .
the negroes were driven away from the polls,
beaten and wounded . . . No colored votes were
polled in those precincts after twelve o'clock.*

—William Taft, October 22, 1894

Presidential Campaign, 1988. Grover Cleveland and Allen G. Thurman
as the Democratic Party candidates for President and Vice President
on a lithograph campaign poster by Kurz & Allison, 1888.

20

1888

COMMONWEALTH AND EMPIRE
1870–1900

WHAT FACTORS
contributed to the growth of government in the late nineteenth century?

WHAT WERE the goals of the Grange?

WHO PREACHED
the social gospel?

WHAT POLICIES
did the Populists advocate?

HOW DID proponents
of imperialism justify colonization?

WHAT CRITIQUES
of empire were put forward
in the years after
the Spanish-American War?

AMERICAN COMMUNITIES

The Cooperative Commonwealth

Edward Bellamy's Looking Backward *(1888), the century's bestselling novel after Harriet Beecher Stowe's* Uncle Tom's Cabin, *tells the story of a young man who awakens in the year 2000 after a sleep lasting more than 100 years. He is surprised to learn that Americans had solved their major problems. Poverty, crime, war, taxes, air pollution—even housework—no longer exist. Nor are there politicians, capitalists, bankers, or lawyers. Most amazing, gone is the great social division between the powerful rich and the suffering poor. In the year 2000 everyone lives in material comfort, happily and harmoniously. No wonder Bellamy's hero shudders at the thought of returning to the late nineteenth century, a time of "worldwide bloodshed, greed and tyranny."*

Community and cooperation are the key concepts in Bellamy's utopian tale. The nation's businesses, including farms and factories, have been given over to the collective ownership of the people. Elected officials now plan the production and distribution of goods for the common well-being. With great efficiency, they even manage huge department stores and warehouses full of marvelous manufactured goods and oversee majestic apartment complexes with modern facilities for cooking, dining, and laundering. To get the necessary work done, an industrial army enlists all adult men and women, but automated machinery has eliminated most menial tasks. The workday is only four hours; vacations extend to six months of each year. At forty-five everyone retires to pursue hobbies, sports, and culture.

Bellamy envisioned his technological utopia as promoting the "highest possible physical, as well as mental, development for everyone." There was nothing fantastic in this plan, the author insisted. It simply required Americans to share equally the abundant resources of their land. If the nation's citizens actually lived up to their democratic ideals, Bellamy declared, the United States would become a "cooperative commonwealth," that is, a nation governed by the people for their common welfare.

Bellamy, a journalist and writer of historical fiction from Chicopee Falls, Massachusetts, moved thousands of his readers to action. His most ardent fans endorsed his program for a "new nation" and formed the Nationalist movement, which by the early 1890s reached an apex of 165 clubs. Terence V. Powderly of the Knights of Labor declared himself a Nationalist. Many leaders of the woman suffrage movement also threw in their support. They endorsed Looking Backward's *depiction of marriage as a union of "perfect equals" and admired Bellamy's sequel,* Equality *(1897), which*

showed how women might become "absolutely free agents" by ending their financial dependence on men.

During the 1890s Bellamy's disciples actually attempted to create new communities along the lines set forth in Looking Backward. *The best known and longest lasting of these settlements was established in Point Loma, California, in 1897. Situated on 330 acres, with avenues winding through gardens and orchards newly planted with groves of eucalyptus trees, Point Loma was known for its physical beauty. Many young married couples chose to live in small bungalows, which were scattered throughout the colony's grounds; others opted for private rooms in a large communal building. Either way, they all met twice daily to share meals and usually spent their leisure hours together. On the ocean's edge the residents constructed an outdoor amphitheater and staged plays and concerts.*

The colony's founder, Katherine Tingley, described Point Loma as "a practical illustration of the possibility of developing a higher type of humanity." No one earned wages, but all 500 residents lived comfortably. They dressed simply in clothes manufactured by the community's women. The majority of the men worked in agriculture. They conducted horticultural experiments that yielded new types of avocados and tropical fruits and eventually produced over half of the community's food supply. Children, who slept in a special dormitory from the time they reached school age, enjoyed an outstanding education. They excelled in the fine arts, including music and drama, and often demonstrated their talents to audiences in nearby San Diego.

The Point Loma community never met all its expenses, but with the help of donations from admirers across the country it remained solvent for decades. Baseball entrepreneur Albert Spalding, who lived there during his retirement, helped make up the financial deficit. As late as the 1950s the community still had some seventy-five members living on about 100 acres of land.

Even relatively successful cooperative communities such as Point Loma, however, could not bring about the changes that Bellamy hoped to see, and he knew it. Only a mobilization of citizens nationwide could overturn the existing hierarchies and usher in the egalitarian order depicted in Looking Backward. *Without such a rigorous challenge, the economic and political leadership that had been emerging since the Civil War would continue to consolidate its power and become even further removed from popular control.*

The last quarter of the nineteenth century saw just such a challenge, producing what one historian calls "a moment of

Point Loma

democratic promise." Ordinary citizens sought to renew the older values of community through farm and labor organizations as well as philanthropic and charitable societies. They could not clearly see, however, that the fate of the nation *depended increasingly on events beyond its territorial boundaries. Business leaders and politicians had proposed their own vision of the future: an American empire extending to far distant lands.*

TOWARD A NATIONAL GOVERNING CLASS

The basic structure of government changed dramatically in the last quarter of the nineteenth century. Mirroring the fast-growing economy, public administration expanded at all levels—municipal, county, state, and federal—and took on greater responsibility for regulating society, especially market and property relations.

This expansion offered ample opportunities for politicians who were eager to compete against one another for control of the new mechanisms of power. Political campaigns, especially those staged for the presidential elections, became mass spectacles, and votes became precious commodities. The most farsighted politicians attempted to rein in the growing corruption and to promote both efficiency and professionalism in the expanding structures of government.

THE GROWTH OF GOVERNMENT

Before the Civil War, local governments attended mainly to the promotion and regulation of trade and relied on private enterprise to supply vital services such as fire protection and water supply. As cities became more responsible for their residents' well-being, they introduced professional police and firefighting forces and began to finance school systems, public libraries, and parks. This expansion demanded huge increases in local taxation.

At the national level, mobilization for the Civil War and Reconstruction had demanded an unprecedented degree of coordination, and the federal government continued to expand under the weight of new tasks and responsibilities. Federal revenues also skyrocketed, from $257 million in 1878 to $567 million in 1900. The administrative bureaucracy also grew dramatically, from 50,000 employees in 1871 to 100,000 only a decade later.

The modern apparatus of departments, bureaus, and cabinets took shape amid this upswing. The Department of Agriculture was established in 1862 to provide information to farmers and to consumers of farm products. The Department of the Interior, which had been created in 1849, grew into the largest and most important federal department after the Post Office. It came to comprise more than twenty agencies, including the Bureau of Indian Affairs, the U.S. Geological Survey, and the Bureau of Territorial and International Affairs. The Department of the Treasury, responsible for collecting federal taxes and customs as well as printing money and stamps, grew from 4,000 employees in 1873 to nearly 25,000 in 1900.

The nation's first independent regulatory agency took charge of the nation's most important industry. The **Interstate Commerce Commission (ICC)** was created in 1887 to bring order to the growing patchwork of state laws concerning railroads. The five-member commission appointed by the president approved freight and passenger rates set by the railroads. The ICC could take public testimony on possible violations, examine company records, and generally oversee enforcement

WHAT FACTORS contributed to the growth of government in the late nineteenth century?

IMAGE KEY
for pages 530–531

a.   1892 Benjamin Harrison presidential campaign ribbon.

b.   Susan B. Anthony medal for the New York State Suffrage Assn. Convention.

c.   1988 presidential campaign poster for the Democratic party candidates Cleveland and Thurman.

d,e. Campaign buttons for William McKinley, 1896.

f.   A Benjamin Harrison presidential campaign souvenir.

g.   Madison Square Garden during the Democratic National Convention of 1888.

h.   A poster of Grange artists, from *Kingfisher Reformer*, May 3, 1894.

i.   Coxey's Army marching with a band.

j.   William Jennings Bryan at the 1896 Democratic Convention.

k.   Chinese refugee women studying with a Protestant missionary.

l.   An 1898 American magazine cover honoring the U.S.A.'s victory in the Spanish-American War.

m,n. Campaign paraphernalia.

Interstate Commerce Commission (ICC)
The 1887 law that expanded federal power over business by prohibiting pooling and discriminatory rates by railroads and establishing the first federal regulatory agency, the Interstate Commerce Commission.

This wooden noisemaker was designed for Grover Cleveland's presidential campaign in 1892. Pursuing the voters, political campaigners devised ingenious signs, buttons, and other miscellaneous novelties for supporters to display, especially at public demonstrations. When shaken vigorously, noisemakers literally demanded the attention of bystanders.

Cleveland campaign noisemaker, 1892. Museum of American Political Life, University of Hartford. Photo by Sally Andersen-Bruce

19–10
William T. Riordon, from *Plunkitt of Tammany Hall* (1905)

of the law. This set a precedent for future regulation of trade as well as for positive government—that is, for the intervention of the government into the affairs of private enterprise.

THE MACHINERY OF POLITICS

Only gradually did Republicans and Democrats adapt to the demands of governmental expansion. The Republican Party continued to run on its Civil War record, pointing to its achievements in reuniting the nation and in passing new reform legislation. Democrats, by contrast, sought to reduce the influence of the federal government, slash expenditures, repeal legislation, and protect states' rights. While Republicans held on to their longtime constituencies, Democrats gathered support from Southern white voters and immigrants newly naturalized in the North, but neither party commanded a clear majority of votes until the century drew to a close.

Presidents in the last quarter of the century—Rutherford B. Hayes (1877–1881), James A. Garfield (1881), Chester A. Arthur (1881–1885), Grover Cleveland (1885–1889), Benjamin Harrison (1889–1893), and Cleveland again (1893–1897)—did not espouse a clear philosophy of government. They willingly yielded power to Congress and the state legislatures. Only 1 percent of the popular vote separated the presidential candidates in three of five elections between 1876 and 1892. Congressional races were equally tight, less than 2 percentage points separating total votes for Democratic and Republican candidates in all but one election in the decade before 1888.

Both political parties operated essentially as state or local organizations. Successful politicians responded primarily to the particular concerns of their constituents. To please local voters, Democrats and Republicans repeatedly crosscut each other by taking identical positions on controversial issues.

The rising costs of maintaining local organizations and orchestrating mammoth campaigns drove party leaders to seek ever-larger sources of revenue. Winners often seized and added to the "spoils" of office through an elaborate system of payoffs. Legislators who supported government subsidies for railroad corporations, for instance, commonly received stock in return and sometimes cash bribes. At the time, few politicians or business leaders regarded these practices as unethical.

At the local level, powerful bosses and political machines dominated both parties. Democrats William Marcy Tweed of New York's powerful political organization, Tammany Hall, and Michael "Hinky Dink" Kenna of Chicago specialized in giving municipal jobs to loyal voters and holiday food baskets to their families.

A large number of federal jobs, meanwhile, changed hands each time the presidency passed from one party to another. More than 50 percent of all federal jobs were patronage positions—nearly 56,000 in 1881—jobs that could be awarded to loyal supporters as part of the "spoils" of the winner. Observers estimated that decisions about congressional patronage filled one-third of all legislators' time. No wonder Bellamy's utopian community operated without politicians and political parties.

THE SPOILS SYSTEM AND CIVIL SERVICE REFORM

As early as 1865, Republican representative Thomas A. Jenckes of Rhode Island proposed a bill for civil service reform. Congress feared that such a measure would hamper candidates in their relentless pursuit of votes. Finally, a group consisting of mainly professors, newspaper editors, lawyers, and ministers organized the Civil Service Reform Association and enlisted Democratic Senator George H. Pendleton to sponsor reform legislation.

In January 1883, a bipartisan congressional majority passed the **Pendleton Civil Service Reform Act**. This measure allowed the president to create, with Senate approval, a three-person commission to draw up a set of guidelines for executive and legislative appointments. The commission established a system of standards for various federal jobs. The Pendleton Act also barred political candidates from soliciting campaign contributions from government workers. Patronage did not disappear, but public service did improve.

Many departments of the federal government took on a professional character similar to that which doctors, lawyers, and scholars were imposing on their fields through regulatory societies such as the American Medical Association and the American Historical Association. At the same time, the federal judiciary began to act more aggressively to establish the parameters of government. With the Circuit Courts of Appeals Act of 1891, Congress granted the U.S. Supreme Court the right to review all cases at will.

Despite these reforms, many observers still viewed government as a reign of outsiders, people pulling the levers of the party machinery or spending money to influence important decisions. Edward Bellamy agreed. He advised Americans to organize their communities for the specific purpose of wresting control of government from the hands of politicians.

Farmers and Workers Organize Their Communities

In the late 1860s farmers and workers began to organize their respective communities. Though short on financial resources, farmers and workers waged the most significant challenge to the two-party system since the Civil War: the **populist movement**.

The Grange

In many farming communities, the headquarters of the fraternal society, known as the **Grange** (a word for "farm"), became the center of social activity, the site of summer dinners and winter dances.

The Grange movement spread rapidly, especially in areas where farmers were experiencing their greatest hardships. Great Plains farmers barely survived the blizzards, grasshopper infestations, and droughts of the early 1870s. Meanwhile, farmers throughout the trans-Mississippi West and the South watched the prices for grains and cotton fall year by year in the face of growing competition from producers in Canada, Australia, Argentina, Russia, and India. In the hope of improving their condition through collective action, many farmers joined their local Grange. The Patrons of Husbandry soon swelled to more than 1.5 million members.

Grangers blamed hard times on a band of "thieves in the night"—especially railroads and banks—that charged exorbitant fees for service. They fumed at American farm equipment manufacturers, such as Cyrus McCormick, who sold farm equipment more cheaply in Europe than in the United States. To purchase equipment and raw materials, farmers borrowed money and accrued debts averaging twice those of Americans not engaged in business.

WHAT WERE the goals of the Grange?

Pendleton Civil Service Reform Act A law of 1883 that reformed the spoils system by prohibiting government workers from making political contributions and creating the Civil Service Commission to oversee their appointment on the basis of merit rather than politics.

Populist movement A major third party of the 1890s formed on the basis of the Southern Farmers' Alliance and other reform organizations.

Grange The National Grange of the Patrons of Husbandry, a national organization of farm owners formed after the Civil War.

The symbols chosen by Grange artists represented their faith that all social value could be traced to honest labor and most of all to the work of the entire farm family. The hardworking American required only the enlightenment offered by the Grange to build a better community.

Kingfisher Reformer, May 3, 1894, Library of Congress

Granger laws State laws enacted in the Midwest in the 1870s that regulated rates charged by railroads, grain elevator operators, and other middlemen.

Farmers' Alliance A broad mass movement in the rural South and West during the late nineteenth century, encompassing several organizations and demanding economic and political reforms.

Southern Farmers' Alliance The largest of several organizations that formed in the post-Reconstruction South to advance the interests of beleaguered small farmers.

Grangers mounted their greatest assault on the railroad corporations. By bribing state legislators, railroads enjoyed a highly discriminatory rate policy, commonly charging farmers more to ship their crops short distances than over long hauls. In 1874 several Midwestern states responded to pressure and passed a series of so-called **Granger laws** establishing maximum shipping rates. Grangers also complained to their lawmakers about the price-fixing policies of grain wholesalers, warehousers, and operators of grain elevators. In 1873 the Illinois legislature passed a Warehouse Act establishing maximum rates for storing grains.

Determined to buy less and produce more, Grangers established local grain elevators, set up retail stores, and even manufactured some of their own farm machinery.

The deepening depression of the late 1870s wiped out most of these cooperative programs. By 1880 Grange membership had fallen to 100,000. Meanwhile, the Supreme Court overturned most of the key legislation regulating railroads. Despite these setbacks, the Patrons of Husbandry had nonetheless promoted a model of cooperation that would remain at the heart of agrarian protest movements until the end of the century.

THE FARMERS' ALLIANCE

Agrarian unrest did not end with the downward turn of the Grange but instead moved South. In the 1880s farmers organized in communities where both poverty and the crop-lien system prevailed (see Chapter 17).

In 1889, several regional organizations joined forces to create the National **Farmers' Alliance** and Industrial Union. Within a year the combined movement claimed 3 million white members. Separately, the Colored Farmers' Alliance and Cooperative Union grew from its beginnings in Texas and Arkansas in 1888 and quickly spread across the South to claim more than a million members of its own.

In the South, the falling price of cotton underscored the need for action, and farmers readily translated their anger into intense loyalty to the one organization pledged to improve their lot. With more than 500 chapters in Texas alone, and cooperative stores complemented by the cooperative merchandising of crops, the **Southern Farmers' Alliance** became a viable alternative to the capitalist marketplace—if only temporarily.

The Northern Farmers' Alliance took shape in the Great Plains states, drawing upon larger organizations in Minnesota, Nebraska, Iowa, Kansas, and the Dakota Territory. During 1886 and 1887, summer drought followed winter blizzards and ice storms, reducing wheat harvests by one-third on the Plains. Locusts and cinch bugs ate much of the rest. As if this were not enough, prices on the world market fell sharply for what little remained. By 1890 the Kansas Alliance alone claimed 130,000 members.

Grangers had pushed legislation that would limit the salaries of public officials, provide public school students with books at little or no cost, establish a program of teacher certification, and widen the admissions policies of the new state colleges, but only rarely did they put up candidates for office. In comparison, the Farmers' Alliance had few reservations about taking political stands or entering electoral races. By 1890 the alliances had gained control of the Nebraska legislature and held the balance of power in Minnesota and South Dakota.

WORKERS SEARCH FOR POWER

The depression following the Panic of 1873, which produced 25 percent unemployment in many cities, served as a catalyst for workers to organize their communities.

The railroad, which played a key role in the industrial and urban transformations following the Civil War, became the focus of protests by workers and farmers alike. Nonetheless, the railroad corporations were unprepared for the **Great Uprising** of 1877, the first nationwide strike. The strike began in Martinsburg, West Virginia, where workers protesting a 10 percent wage cut uncoupled all engines. No trains would run, they promised, until wages were restored. Within a few days, the strike had spread along the railroad routes to New York, Buffalo, Pittsburgh, Chicago, Kansas City, and San Francisco. In all these cities, workers in various industries and masses of the unemployed formed angry crowds, defying armed militia ordered to disperse them by any means. The crowds halted train traffic, sometimes pulling up entire rails and seizing carloads of food for hungry families. Energized by the activity, workers in St. Louis even took over the city's administration.

The rioting persisted for nearly a week. Fearing a "national insurrection," President Hayes set a precedent by calling in the U.S. Army to suppress the strike. In Pittsburgh, federal troops equipped with semiautomatic machine guns fired into a crowd and killed more than twenty people. By the time the strike finally ended, more than 100 people were dead.

Memories of the Uprising of 1877 haunted business and government officials for decades, prompting the creation of the National Guard and the construction of armories in working-class neighborhoods. Workers also drew lessons from the events. Before the end of the century, more than 6 million workers would strike in industries ranging from New England textiles to Southern tobacco factories to Western mines.

MAP EXPLORATION

To explore an interactive version of this map, go to **http://www.prenhall.com/faraghertlc/map20.1**

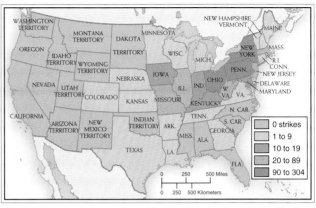

MAP 20-1

Strikes by State, 1880   Most strikes after the Uprising of 1877 could be traced to organized trades, concentrated in the manufacturing districts of the Northeast and Midwest.

Carville Earle, *Geographical Inquiry and American Historical Problems* (Stanford, CA: Stanford University Press, 1992).

HOW DID the federal government respond to the strikes in the 1880.

Great Uprising   Unsuccessful railroad strike of 1877 to protest wage cuts and the use of federal troops against strikers; the first nationwide work stoppage in American history.

The Great Uprising of 1877, which began as a strike of railroad workers, spread rapidly to communities along the railroad routes. Angry crowds defied the armed militia and the vigilantes hired to disperse them. In Philadelphia, for example, strikers set fire to the downtown, destroying many buildings before federal troops were brought in to stop them. More than a hundred people died before the strike ended, and the railroad corporations suffered about $10 million loss in property.

Contemporary engraving. The Granger Collection, New York (0008654)

While the Farmers' Alliance put up candidates in the South and Plains states, workers launched labor parties in dozens of industrial towns and cities.

In New York City, popular economist and land reformer Henry George, with the ardent support of the city's Central Labor Council and the Knights of Labor, put himself forward in 1886 as candidate for mayor on the United Labor Party ticket. His bestselling book *Progress and Poverty* (1879) advocated a sweeping tax on all property to generate enough revenue to allow all Americans to live in comfort.

Tammany Hall delivered many thousands of the ballots cast for George straight into the Hudson River. Nevertheless, George managed to finish a respectable second with 31 percent of the vote, running ahead of young patrician Theodore Roosevelt. Although his campaign ended in defeat, George had issued a stern warning to the entrenched politicians. Equally important, his impressive showing encouraged labor groups in other cities to form parties.

In the late 1880s labor parties won seats on many city councils and state legislatures. The Milwaukee People's Party elected the mayor, a state senator, six assemblymen, and one member of Congress. In smaller industrial towns where workers outnumbered the middle classes, labor parties did especially well. In Rochester, New Hampshire, with a population of only 7,000, workers, mainly shoemakers, elected a majority slate, from city council to mayor.

WOMEN BUILD ALLIANCES

Women helped build both the labor and agrarian protest movements while campaigning for their own rights as citizens. With perhaps 65,000 women members at its peak, the Knights of Labor ran day-care centers for the children of wage-earning mothers and occasionally even set up bakery cooperatives to reduce the drudgery of cooking.

The Grangers issued a charter to a local chapter only when women were well represented on its rolls, and in the 1870s delegates to its conventions routinely gave speeches endorsing woman suffrage and even dress reform. In both the Northern and Southern Alliances, women made up perhaps one-quarter of the membership, and several advanced through the ranks to become leading speakers and organizers.

Women in both the Knights of Labor and the Farmers' Alliance found their greatest leader in Frances E. Willard, the most famous woman of the nineteenth century. Willard assumed that women, who guarded their families' physical and spiritual welfare, would, if granted the right to vote, extend their influence throughout the whole society. From 1878 until her death in 1897, Willard presided over the **Woman's Christian Temperance Union (WCTU)**, at the time the largest organization of women in the world, and encouraged her numerous followers to "do everything." She mobilized nearly 1 million women to, in her words, "make the whole world HOMELIKE." WCTU members preached total abstinence from the consumption of alcohol, but they also worked to reform the prison system, eradicate prostitution, and eliminate the wage system.

Under Willard's leadership, the WCTU grew into the major force behind the campaign for woman suffrage, far surpassing the American Woman Suffrage Association and the National Woman Suffrage Association. By 1890, when the two rival suffrage associations merged to form the **National American Woman Suffrage Association**, the WCTU had already pushed the heart of the suffrage campaign into the Great Plains states and the West. In Iowa, Nebraska, Colorado, and especially Kansas, agitation for the right to vote provided a political bridge among women organized in the WCTU, Farmers' Alliance, Knights of Labor, and various local suffrage societies.

FARMER–LABOR UNITY

In December 1890 the Farmers' Alliance called a meeting at Ocala, Florida, to press for a national third-party movement. This was a risky proposition because the Southern Alliance hoped to capture control of the Democratic Party, whereas many farmers in the Plains states voted Republican. In some areas, however, the Farmers' Alliance established its own parties, put up full slates of candidates for local elections, won majorities in state legislatures, and even sent a representative to Congress. Reviewing these successes, delegates at Ocala decided to push ahead and form a national party, and they appealed to other farm, labor, and reform organizations to join them. In February 1892, representatives from the Farmers' Alliance, the Knights of Labor, and the National Colored Farmers' Alliance, among others, met in St. Louis. The 1,300 delegates adopted a platform for the new People's Party. It called for government ownership of railroads, banks, and telegraph lines, prohibition of large landholding companies, a graduated income tax, an eight-hour workday, and restriction of immigration. The People's Party convened again in Omaha in July 1892 and nominated James Baird Weaver of Iowa for president and, to please the South, the Confederate veteran James Field from Virginia for vice president.

The Populists, as supporters of the People's Party styled themselves, quickly became a major factor in American politics. Although Democrat Grover Cleveland regained the presidency in 1892 (he had previously served from 1885 to 1889), Populists scored a string of local victories. They elected three governors, ten representatives to Congress, and five senators. Despite poor showings among urban workers east of the Mississippi, Populists looked forward to the next round of state elections in 1894. But the great test would come with the presidential election in 1896.

THE CRISIS OF THE 1890s

A series of events in the 1890s shook the confidence of many citizens in the reigning political system. But nothing was more unsettling than the severe economic depression that consumed the nation and lasted for five years. Many feared—while others hoped—that the entire political system would topple.

19–5
The People's Party Platform (1892)

Woman's Christian Temperance Union (WCTU)   Women's organization whose members visited schools to educate children about the evils of alcohol, addressed prisoners, and blanketed men's meetings with literature.

National American Woman Suffrage Association (NAWSA)   The organization, formed in 1890, that coordinated the ultimately successful campaign to achieve women's right to vote.

WHO PREACHED

the social gospel?

FINANCIAL COLLAPSE AND DEPRESSION

The collapse of the Philadelphia and Reading Railroad, followed by the downfall of the National Cordage Company, precipitated a crash in the stock market and sent waves of panic splashing over banks across the country. In a few months, more than 150 banks went into receivership and hundreds more closed; nearly 200 railroads and more than 15,000 businesses also slipped into bankruptcy. Agricultural prices continued to plummet until they reached new lows. The economy slowly began to pick up again in 1897, but the new century arrived before prosperity returned.

In many cities, unemployment rates reached 25 percent; Samuel Gompers, head of the American Federation of Labor (AFL), estimated nationwide unemployment at 3 million. Few people starved, but millions suffered. Inadequate diets prompted a rise in communicable diseases, such as tuberculosis and pellagra. Unable to buy food, clothes, or household items, families learned to survive with the barest minimum.

Tens of thousands "rode the rails" or went "on the tramp" to look for work, hoping that their luck might change in a new city or town. Vagrancy laws (enacted during the 1870s) forced many into prison. In New York City alone, with more than 20,000 homeless people, thousands ended up in jail. Newspapers warned against this "menace" and blamed the growing crime rates on the "dangerous classes."

Another Populist, Jacob Sechler Coxey, decided to gather the masses of unemployed into a huge army and then to march to Washington, D.C., to demand from Congress a public works program. On Easter Sunday, 1894, Coxey left Massillon, Ohio, with several hundred followers. Communities across the country welcomed the marchers, but U.S. attorney general Richard C. Olney, a former lawyer for the railroad companies, conspired with state and local officials to halt them. Only 600 men and women reached the nation's capital, where the police first clubbed and then arrested the leaders for trespassing on the grass. **Coxey's Army** quickly disbanded, but not before voicing the public's growing impatience with government apathy toward the unemployed.

STRIKES AND LABOR SOLIDARITY

Meanwhile, in several locations the conflict between labor and capital had escalated to the brink of civil war. Wage cuts in the silver and lead mines of northern Idaho led to one of the bitterest conflicts of the decade. To put a brake on organized labor, mineowners had formed a **protective association**, and in March 1892 they announced a lower wage scale throughout the Coeur d'Alene district. After the miners' union refused to accept the cut, the owners locked out all union members and brought in strikebreakers by the trainload. Unionists tried peaceful methods of protest, but after three months of stalemate, they loaded a railcar with explosives and blew up a mine. Strikebreakers fled while mineowners appealed to the Idaho governor for assistance. More than 300 union members were herded into bullpens, where they were kept under unsanitary conditions for several weeks before their trial. Ore production meanwhile resumed with "scab" labor, and by November, when the troops were withdrawn, the mineowners declared a victory. But the miners' union survived, and most members eventually regained their jobs.

At Homestead, Pennsylvania, members of the Amalgamated Iron, Steel and Tin Workers, the most powerful union of the AFL, had carved out an admirable position for themselves in the Carnegie Steel Company. Well paid, proud of their skills, the unionists customarily directed their unskilled helpers without undue influence of company supervisors. But, determined to gain control over every

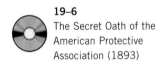

19–6
The Secret Oath of the American Protective Association (1893)

Coxey's Army A protest march of unemployed workers, led by Populist businessman Jacob Coxey, demanding inflation and a public works program during the depression of the 1890s.

Protective association
Organizations formed by mine owners in response to the formation of labor unions.

Jacob Coxey's "Commonwealth of Christ Army," April 1894. Attracting the sympathetic attention of working people and the hostility of most of the wealthier classes, "Industrial Armies" marched through U.S. cities en route to the nation's capital.

Library of Congress

stage of production, Carnegie and his chairman, Henry C. Frick, decided not only to lower wages but also to break the union.

In 1892, when the Amalgamated's contract expired, Frick announced a drastic wage cut. He also ordered a wooden stockade built around the factory, with grooves for rifles and barbed wire on top. When Homestead's city government refused to assign police to disperse the strikers, Frick dispatched a barge carrying a private army armed to the teeth. Gunfire broke out and continued throughout the day. After the governor sent the Pennsylvania National Guard to restore order, Carnegie's factory reopened, with strikebreakers doing the work.

After four months, the union was forced to concede a crushing defeat, not only for itself, but also, in effect, for all steelworkers. The Carnegie company reduced its work force by 25 percent, lengthened the workday, and cut wages 25 percent for those who remained on the job. If the Amalgamated Iron, Steel and Tin Workers, known throughout the industry as the "aristocrats of labor," could be brought down, less-skilled workers could expect little from the corporate giants. Within a decade, every major steel company operated without union interference.

But the spirit of labor solidarity did not die. Just two years after the strikes at Coeur d'Alene and Homestead, the greatest railway strike since 1877 again dramatized the extent of collusion between the government and corporations to crush the labor movement.

Pullman, Illinois, just south of Chicago, had been constructed as a model industrial community. Its creator and proprietor, George M. Pullman, had manufactured luxurious "sleeping cars" for railroads since 1881. He built his company as a self-contained community, with the factory at the center, surrounded by modern cottages, a library, churches, parks, an independent water supply, even its own cemetery, but no saloons. The Pullman Palace Car Company deducted rent, library fees, and grocery bills from each worker's weekly wages. In good times workers

In 1894, to protest a cut in wages, the workers of the Pullman Palace Car Company struck. Eugene V. Debs, president of the American Railway Union, ordered a nationwide boycott against the Pullman Company. The United States Cavalry was brought in to escort the trains run by "scab" laborers.

Library of Congress (49255/3526)

THE GREAT RAILWAY STRIKES—THE FIRST MEAT TRAIN LEAVING THE CHICAGO STOCK-YARDS UNDER ESCORT OF UNITED STATES CAVALRY, JULY 10, 1894.

enjoyed a decent livelihood, although many resented Pullman's autocratic control of their daily affairs.

When times grew hard, the company cut wages by as much as one-half, in some cases down to less than $1 a day. Charges for food and rent remained unchanged. Furthermore, factory supervisors sought to make up for declining profits by driving workers to produce more. In May 1894, after Pullman fired members of a committee that had drawn up a list of grievances, workers voted to strike.

Pullman workers found their champion in Eugene V. Debs, who had recently formed the American Railway Union (ARU) in order to bring railroad workers across the vast continent into one organization. Debs, the architect of the ARU's victory over the Great Northern rail line just one month earlier, advised caution, but delegates to an ARU convention voted to support a nationwide boycott of all Pullman cars. This action soon turned into a sympathy strike by railroad workers across the country. Support for the strike was especially strong in the Western states.

Compared to the Uprising of 1877, the orderly Pullman strike at first produced little violence. ARU officials urged strikers to ignore all police provocations and hold their ground peacefully. But Attorney General Richard C. Olney, claiming that the ARU was disrupting mail shipments (actually Debs had banned such interference), issued a blanket injunction against the strike. On July 4, President Cleveland sent federal troops to Chicago, over Illinois governor John Peter Altgeld's objections. After a bitter confrontation that left thirteen people dead and more than fifty wounded, the army dispersed the strikers. For the next week, railroad workers in twenty-six other states resisted federal troops, and a dozen more people were killed. On July 17, the strike finally ended when federal marshals arrested Debs and other leaders.

Assailing the arrogance of class privilege that encouraged the government to use brute force against its citizens, Debs concluded that the labor movement could not regain its dignity under the present system. An avid fan of Bellamy's *Looking Backward*, he came out of jail committed to the ideals of socialism and in 1898 helped to form a political party dedicated to its principles.

Tens of thousands of people supported Debs. Declining nomination on the Populist ticket in 1896, he ran for president as a socialist in 1900 and in four subsequent elections. The odds against him grew with the scale of the booming economy, but Debs made his point on moral grounds.

THE SOCIAL GOSPEL

Like Edward Bellamy, a growing number of Protestant and Catholic clergy and lay theologians noted a discrepancy between the ideals of Christianity and prevailing attitudes toward the poor. Like Bellamy, they could no longer sanction an economic system that allowed so many to toil long hours under unhealthy conditions and for subsistence wages. They demanded that the church lead the way to a new cooperative order.

Ministers called for civil service reform and the end of child labor. Supporting labor's right to organize and, if necessary, to strike, they petitioned government officials to regulate corporations and place a limit on profits. Local Protestant ministers and community leaders sought to restore what they considered the true spirit of Christianity. Although the social gospel spread most rapidly through the Northern industrial cities, Southern African Americans espoused their own version. They reinterpreted the Gospel as Jesus' promise to emancipate their race from satanic white power brokers. The biblical republic of "Beulahland" became their model of redemption.

Catholics, doctrinally more inclined than Protestants to accept poverty as a natural condition, joined the social gospel movement in smaller numbers. In the early 1880s Polish Americans broke away from the Roman Catholic Church to form the Polish National Church, which was committed to the concerns of working people. Irish Americans, especially prominent in the Knights of Labor, encouraged priests to ally themselves with the labor movement. Pope Leo XIII's encyclical *Rerum Novarum* (1891) endorsed the right of workers to form trade unions.

Women guided the social gospel movement in their communities. In nearly every city, groups of women affiliated with various evangelical Protestant sects raised money to establish small, inexpensive residential hotels for working women, whose low wages rarely covered the price of safe, comfortable shelter. Many of these groups joined to form the Young Women's Christian Association (YWCA), which by 1900 had more than 600 local chapters. The "Y" sponsored a range of services for needy Christian women, ranging from homes for the elderly and for unmarried mothers to elaborate programs of vocational instruction and physical fitness. Meanwhile Catholic lay women and nuns served the poor women of their faith, operating numerous schools, hospitals, and orphanages.

POLITICS OF REFORM, POLITICS OF ORDER

The severe hardships of the 1890s, following a quarter of a century of popular unrest and economic uncertainty, led to a crisis in the two-party system, making the presidential election of 1896 a turning point in American politics.

THE FREE SILVER ISSUE

Grover Cleveland owed his victory in 1892 over Republican incumbent Benjamin Harrison to the predictable votes of the Democratic "**solid South**" and to the unanticipated support of such Northern states as Illinois and Wisconsin, whose German-born voters turned against the increasingly nativist Republicans. But when the economy collapsed the following year, Cleveland and the Democrats who controlled

---

QUICK REVIEW

The Social Gospel

◆ Growing number of clergy called for reconciliation of social reality with Christian ideals.

◆ Catholics joined social gospel movement in smaller numbers than Protestants.

◆ Women played key roles in the movement.

WHAT POLICIES did the Populists advocate?

Solid South The one-party (Democratic) political system that dominated the South from the 1890s to the 1950s.

Congress faced a public eager for action. Convinced that the economic crisis was "largely the result of financial policy . . . embodied in unwise laws," the president called a special session of Congress to reform the nation's currency.

For generations, reformers had advocated "soft" currency—that is, an increase in the money supply that would loosen credit. During the Civil War the federal government took decisive action, replacing state bank notes with a national paper currency popularly called "greenbacks" (from the color of the bills). Then in 1873 the Coinage Act tightened the money supply by eliminating silver from circulation, prompting farmers who depended on credit to call it "the Crime of '73." This measure actually had little real impact on the economy but opened the door to yet more tinkering.

The **Sherman Silver Purchase Act** of 1890 directed the Treasury to increase the amount of currency coined from silver mined in the West and also permitted the U.S. government to print paper currency backed by the silver. In turn, Westerners who stood to benefit most from this reform, agreed to support the McKinley Tariff of 1890 that, in establishing the highest import duties yet on foreign goods, pleased the business community.

Following the crash of 1893, as the economy fell into ruins, a desperate President Cleveland demanded the repeal of the Sherman Act, insisting that only the gold standard could pull the nation out of depression. By exerting intense pressure on congressional Democrats, Cleveland succeeded in October 1893, but not without ruining his chances for renomination. The midterm elections in 1894 brought the largest shift in congressional power in American history: the Republicans gained 117 seats, while the Democrats lost 113. The "Silver Democrats" of Cleveland's own party vowed revenge and began to look to the Populists, mainly Westerners and farmers who favored "**free silver**"—that is, the unlimited coinage of silver. Republicans confidently began to prepare for the presidential election of 1896, known as the "battle of the standards."

POPULISM'S LAST CAMPAIGNS

Populists had been buoyed by the 1894 election, which delivered to their candidates nearly 1.5 million votes, a gain of 42 percent over their 1892 totals. They made impressive inroads into several Southern states. Still, even in the Midwest where Populists doubled their vote, they managed to win less than 7 percent of the total.

As Populists prepared for the 1896 election, they found themselves at a crossroad: What were they to do with the growing popularity of Democrat William Jennings Bryan? A spellbinding orator, Bryan won a congressional seat in 1890. After seizing the Populist slogan "Equal Rights to All, Special Privilege to None," Bryan became a major contender for president of the United States.

Noting the surging interest in free silver, Bryan became its champion. For two years before the 1896 election, Bryan wooed potential voters in a speaking tour that took him to every state in the nation. Pouring new life into his divided party, Bryan pushed Silver Democrats to the forefront.

At the 1896 party convention, the thirty-six-year-old orator thrilled delegates with his evocation of agrarian ideals. "Burn down your cities and leave our farms," Bryan preached, "and your cities will spring up again as if by magic; but destroy our farms and the grass will grow in the streets of every city in the country." What became one of the most famous speeches in American political history closed on a yet more dramatic note. Spreading his arms to suggest the crucified Christ figure, Bryan pledged to answer all demands for a gold standard by saying, "You shall not press down upon the brow of labor this crown of thorns, you shall not crucify mankind upon a cross of gold." The next day, Bryan won the Democratic presidential nomination.

The Populists feared that the growing emphasis on currency would overshadow their more important planks calling for government ownership of the

Sherman Silver Purchase Act 1890 act which directed the Treasury to increase the amount of currency coined from silver mined in the West and also permitted the U.S. government to print paper currency backed by the silver.

Free silver Philosophy that the government should expand the money supply by purchasing and coining all the silver offered to it.

nation's railroads and communications systems. As the date of their own convention approached, delegates divided over strategy: they could endorse Bryan and give up their independent status; or they could run an independent campaign and risk splitting the silver vote.

In the end, the Populists nominated Bryan for president and chose one of their own ranks, the popular Georgian Tom Watson, for the vice presidential candidate. Most of the state Democratic Party organizations, however, refused to put the "fusion" ticket on the ballot, and Bryan and his Democratic running mate Arthur Sewall simply ignored the Populist campaign.

THE REPUBLICAN TRIUMPH

After Cleveland's blunders, Republicans anticipated an easy victory in 1896, but Bryan's nomination, as party stalwart Mark Hanna warned, "changed everything." Luckily, they had their own handsome, knowledgeable, courteous, and ruthless candidate, Civil War veteran William McKinley.

The Republican campaign in terms of sheer expense and skill of coordination outdid all previous campaigns and established a precedent for future presidential elections. Hanna guided a strategy that raised up to $7 million and outspent Bryan more than ten to one. Using innumerable pamphlets, placards, hats, and parades, Republicans advertised their promise to "rebuild out of the ruins of the last four years the stately mansions of national happiness, prosperity and self-respect." McKinley even invited voters to his home, managing to attract as many as 750,000 people to his famous "Front Porch." In the campaign's final two weeks, organizers dispatched 1,400 speakers to spread the word. Fearful that the silver issue could divide their own ranks, Republicans stepped around it while emphasizing the tariff. Delivering a hard-hitting negative campaign, they consistently cast adversary Bryan as a dangerous naysayer.

McKinley triumphed in the most important presidential election since Reconstruction. Bryan managed to win 46 percent of the popular vote but failed to carry the Midwest, West Coast, or Upper South. Moreover, the free silver campaign rebuffed traditionally Democratic urban voters who feared that soft money would bring higher prices. Many Catholics uncomfortable with Bryan's Protestant moral piety also deserted the Democrats. Finally, neither the reform-minded middle classes nor impoverished blue-collar workers were convinced that Bryan's grand reform vision really included them. The Populist following, disappointed and disillusioned, dwindled away.

Once in office, McKinley promoted a mixture of probusiness and expansionist measures. He supported the **Dingley Tariff of 1897**, which raised import duties to an all-time high. In 1897 McKinley also encouraged Congress to create the United States Industrial Commission, which would plan business regulation; in 1898 he promoted a bankruptcy act that eased the financial situation of small businesses; and he proposed the Erdman Act of the same year, which established a system of arbitration to avoid rail strikes. The Supreme Court ruled in concert with the president, finding eighteen railways in violation of antitrust laws and granting states the right to regulate hours of labor under certain circumstances.

Dingley Tariff of 1897 Act which raised import duties to an all-time high.

MAP EXPLORATION
To explore an interactive version of this map, go to
http://www.prenhall.com/faraghertlc/map20.2

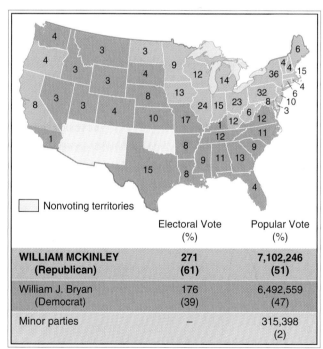

	Electoral Vote (%)	Popular Vote (%)
WILLIAM MCKINLEY (Republican)	**271 (61)**	**7,102,246 (51)**
William J. Bryan (Democrat)	176 (39)	6,492,559 (47)
Minor parties	–	315,398 (2)

MAP 20-2
Election of 1896   Democratic candidate William Jennings Bryan carried most of rural America but could not overcome Republican William McKinley's stronghold in the populous industrial states.

WHAT WHERE the most important elements of McKinle's campaign platform?

Nativism Favoring the interests and culture of native-born inhabitants over those of immigrants.

Jim Crow laws Segregation laws that became widespread in the South during the 1890s.

Segregation A system of racial control that separated the races, initially by custom but increasingly by law during and after Reconstruction.

18-9
Booker T. Washington, Atlanta Exposition Address (1895)

QUICK REVIEW

Jim Crow

- Neither major party addressed problem of racism and nativism in campaign of 1896.
- Local and state governments in the South codified racism in Jim Crow laws.
- The Supreme Court upheld the new discriminatory legislation.

African-American Representation in Congress, 1867–1900
Black men served in the U.S. Congress from 1870 until 1900. All were Republicans.

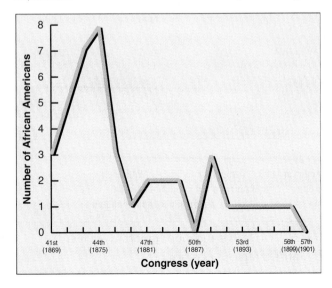

McKinley's triumph ended the popular challenge to the nation's governing system. With prosperity returning by 1898 and nationalism rising swiftly, McKinley encouraged Americans to go for "a full dinner pail," the winning Republican slogan of the 1900 presidential election.

NATIVISM AND JIM CROW

Campaign rhetoric aside, McKinley and Bryan differed only slightly on the major problems facing the nation in 1896. Neither Bryan the reformer nor McKinley the prophet of prosperity addressed the escalation of racism and **nativism** (anti-immigrant feeling) throughout the nation.

Toward the end of the century, many political observers noted, the nation's patriotic fervor took on a strongly nationalistic and antiforeign tone. Striking workers and their employers alike tended to blame "foreigners" for the hard times. Semisecret organizations such as the American Protective Association sprang up to defend American institutions. Fourth of July orators continued to celebrate freedom and liberty but more often boasted about the might and power of their nation.

In the South, local and state governments codified racist ideology by passing discriminatory and segregationist legislation, which became known as **Jim Crow laws**. The phrase, dating from the early decades of the nineteenth century, was made popular by a white minstrel in black face who used the name "Jim Crow" to characterize all African Americans. Before the Civil War, abolitionists described segregated railroad cars as "Jim Crow." By the end of the century, "Jim Crow" referred to the customs of **segregation** that were becoming codified by law and practice throughout the South. With nine of every ten black Americans living in this region, the significance of this development was sweeping.

"The supremacy of the white race of the South," New South promoter Henry W. Grady declared in 1887, "must be maintained forever . . . because the white race is the superior race." To secure their privileges, Grady and other white Southerners acted directly to impose firm standards of segregation and domination and to forestall any appearance of social equality. State after state in the South enacted new legislation to cover facilities such as restaurants, public transportation, and even drinking fountains. Signs "White Only" and "Colored" appeared over theaters, parks, rooming houses, and toilets. In banks, post offices, and stores, blacks were required to wait until all whites had been served, and special rules prohibited such common practices as trying on shoes or hats before purchasing them.

The United States Supreme Court upheld the new discriminatory legislation. Its decisions in the *Civil Rights Cases* (1883) overturned the Civil Rights Act of 1875, and in **Plessy v. Ferguson** (1896) the Court upheld a Louisiana state law formally segregating railroad cars on the basis of the "separate but equal" doctrine. In *Cumming v. Richmond County Board of Education* (1899), the Court allowed separate schools for blacks and whites, even where facilities for African American children did not exist.

Southern states enacted new literacy tests and property qualifications for voting, demanding proof of $300 to $500 in property and the ability to read and write. Loopholes permitted poor whites to vote even under these conditions, except where they threatened the Democratic Party's rule. "**Grandfather clauses**," invented in Louisiana, exempted from all restrictions those who had been entitled to vote on January 1, 1867, together with their sons and grandsons, a measure that effectively enfranchised whites while barring African Americans. In 1898, the Supreme Court ruled that **poll taxes** and literacy requirements enacted in order to prevent blacks (and some poor whites) from voting were a proper means of restricting the ballot to "qualified" voters. By this time, only 5 percent of the Southern black electorate voted, and African Americans were barred from public office and jury service.

Racial violence escalated. Not only race riots but also thousands of lynchings took place. Between 1882 and the turn of the century, the number of lynchings usually exceeded 100 each year; 1892 produced a record 230 deaths (161 black, 69 white). Mobs often burned or dismembered victims in order to drag out their agony and entertain the crowd of onlookers. Announced in local newspapers, lynchings became public spectacles for entire white families, and railroads sometimes offered special excursion rates for travel to these events.

Antilynching became the one-woman crusade of Ida B. Wells, the young editor of a black newspaper in Memphis. After three local black businessmen were lynched in 1892, Wells vigorously denounced the outrage, blaming the white business competitors of the victims. Her stand fanned the tempers of local whites, who destroyed her press and forced the outspoken editor to leave the city.

Wells launched an international movement against lynching, lecturing across the country and in Europe, demanding an end to the silence about this barbaric crime. Her work also inspired the growth of a black women's club movement. The National Association of Colored Women was founded in 1896.

THE SPREAD OF DISFRANCHISEMENT		
1889	Florida	Poll tax
	Tennessee	Poll tax
1890	Mississippi	Poll tax, literacy test, understanding clause
1891	Arkansas	Poll tax
1893, 1901	Alabama	Poll tax, literacy test, grandfather clause
1894, 1895	South Carolina	Poll tax, literacy test, understanding clause
1894, 1902	Virginia	Poll tax, literacy test, understanding clause
1897, 1898	Louisiana	Poll tax, literacy test, grandfather clause
1899, 1900	North Carolina	Poll tax, literacy test, grandfather clause
1902	Texas	Poll tax
1908	Georgia	Poll tax, literacy test, understanding clause, grandfather clause

18–8
Ida B. Wells-Barnett, from
A Red Record (1895)

"Imperialism of Righteousness"

Many Americans attributed the crisis of 1893–1897 not simply to the collapse of the railroads and the stock market, but also to basic structural problems: an overbuilt economy and an insufficient market for goods. Profits from total sales of manufactured and agricultural products had grown substantially over the level achieved in the 1880s, but output increased even more rapidly. While the number of millionaires shot up from 500 in 1860 to more than 4,000 in 1892, the majority of working people lacked enough income to buy back a significant portion of what they produced. As Republican Senator Albert J. Beveridge of Indiana put it, "We are raising more than we can consume . . . making more than we can use. Therefore, we must find new markets for our produce, new occupation for our capital, new work for our labor."

THE WHITE MAN'S BURDEN

In 1893 historian Frederick Jackson Turner read his famous essay, "The Significance of the Frontier in American History," at the meeting of the American Historical Association, which was held in Chicago at the time of the World's Fair, less than two months after the nation's economy had collapsed. A complex of more than 400 buildings, newly constructed in beaux arts design, commemorated the four hundredth anniversary of Columbus's landing.

Agriculture Hall showcased the production of corn, wheat, and other crops and featured a gigantic globe encircled by samples of American-manufactured

HOW DID proponents of imperialism justify colonization?

Plessy v. *Ferguson* Supreme Court decision holding that Louisiana's railroad segregation law did not violate the Constitution as long as the railroads or the state provided equal accommodations.

Grandfather clauses Rules that required potential voters to demonstrate that their grandfathers had been eligible to vote; used in some Southern states after 1890 to limit the black electorate.

Poll taxes Taxes imposed on voters as a requirement for voting.

farm machinery. The symbolism was evident: all eyes were on worldwide markets for American products. Another building housed a model of a canal cut across Nicaragua, suggesting the ease with which American traders might reach Asian markets if transport ships could travel directly from the Caribbean to the Pacific.

The World's Fair also "displayed" representatives of the people who populated foreign lands. The Midway Plaisance, a strip nearly a mile long and more than 600 feet wide, was an enormous sideshow of re-created Turkish bazaars and South Sea island huts. There were Javanese carpenters, Dahomean drummers, Egyptian swordsmen, and Hungarian Gypsies as well as Eskimos, Syrians, Samoans, and Chinese. Very popular was the World Congress of Beauty, parading "40 Ladies from 40 Nations" dressed in native costume.

By celebrating the brilliance of American industry and simultaneously presenting the rest of the world's people as a source of exotic entertainment, the planners of the fair delivered a powerful message. Former abolitionist Frederick Douglass, who attended the fair on "Colored People's Day," objected to the stark contrast setting off Anglo-Saxons from people of color, an opposition between "civilization" and "savagery."

The Chicago World's Fair gave material shape to prevalent ideas about the superiority of American civilization and its racial order. At the same time, by showcasing American industries, it made a strong case for commercial expansion abroad. Social gospeler Josiah Strong, a Congregational minister who had begun his career trying to convert Indians to Christianity, provided a timely synthesis. Linking economic and spiritual expansion, Strong advocated an "imperialism of righteousness" by the white Americans, who were best suited to "Christianizing" and civilizing others with their "genius for colonizing." It was the white American, Strong argued, who had been "divinely commissioned to be, in a peculiar sense, his brother's keeper." Many newspaper reporters and editorialists agreed that it would be morally wrong for Americans to shirk what the British poet Rudyard Kipling called the "White Man's Burden."

20–1
Josiah Strong, from *Our Country* (1885)

FOREIGN MISSIONS

The push for overseas expansion coincided with a major wave of religious evangelism and foreign missions. Early in the nineteenth century, Protestant missionaries, hoping to fulfill what they believed to be a divine command to carry God's message to all peoples and to win converts for their church, had focused on North America. Many disciples, like Josiah Strong himself, headed west and stationed themselves on Indian reservations. Others worked among the immigrant populations of the nation's growing cities. As early as the 1820s, however, a few missionaries had traveled to the Sandwich Islands (Hawai'i) in an effort to supplant the indigenous religion with Christianity. After the Civil War, following the formation of the Women's Union Missionary Society of Americans for Heathen Lands, the major evangelical Protestant denominations all sponsored missions directed at foreign lands.

By the 1890s, college campuses blazed with missionary excitement, and the intercollegiate Student Volunteers for Foreign Missions spread rapidly. Young Protestant women rushed to join foreign missionary societies. By 1915, more than 3 million women had enrolled in forty denominational missionary societies, surpassing in size all other women's organizations in the United States.

By 1898 Protestants claimed to have made Christians of more than 80,000 Chinese, a tiny portion of the population, but a significant stronghold for American interests in their nation. The missionaries did more than spread the gospel. They taught school, provided rudimentary medical care, offered vocational training programs, and sometimes encouraged young men and women to pursue a college education in preparation for careers in their homelands.

Outside the churches proper, the YMCA and YWCA, which had set up nonde-nominational missions for the working poor in many American cities, also embarked on a worldwide crusade to reach non-Christians. A close observer ironically suggested that the United States had three great occupying forces: the army, the navy, and the "Y."

Missionaries played an important role both in generating public interest in foreign lands and in preparing the way for American economic expansion. As Josiah Strong aptly put it, "Commerce follows the missionary."

20–6
The Boxer Rebellion (1900)

AN OVERSEAS EMPIRE

Business and political leaders had also set their sights on distant lands. In the 1860s, Secretary of State William Henry Seward, under Abraham Lincoln and then under Andrew Johnson, correctly predicted that foreign trade would play an increasingly important part in the American economy. Between 1870 and 1900

20–2
Henry Cabot Lodge, "The Business World vs. the Politicians" (1895)

MAP EXPLORATION

To explore an interactive version of this map, go to **http://www.prenhall.com/faraghertlc/map20.3**

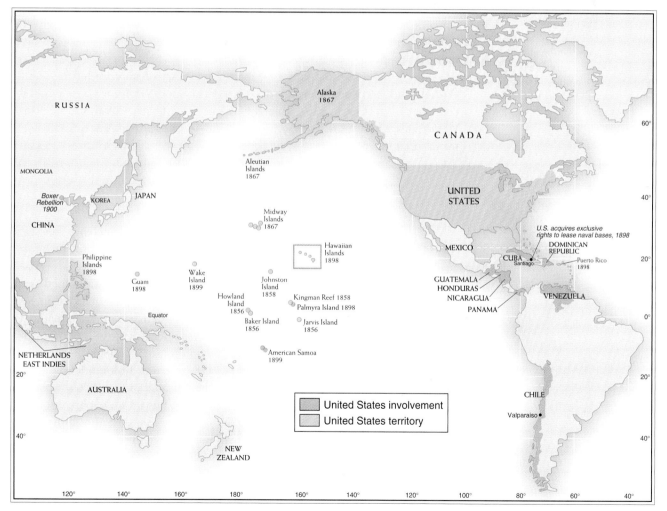

MAP 20-3
The American Domain, ca. 1900   The United States claimed numerous islands in the South Pacific and intervened repeatedly in Latin America to secure its economic interests.

WHAT FUELED America's expansion overseas?

exports more than tripled, from about $400 million to over $1.5 billion, with textiles and agricultural products leading the way. But as European markets for American goods began to contract, business and political leaders of necessity looked more eagerly to Asia as well as to lands closer by.

Since the American Revolution, many Americans had regarded all nearby nations as falling naturally within their own territorial realm, destined to be acquired when opportunity allowed. Seward advanced these imperialist principles in 1867 by negotiating the purchase of Alaska (known at the time as Seward's Icebox) from Russia for $7.2 million. Meanwhile, with European nations launched on their own imperialist missions in Asia and Africa, the United States increasingly viewed the Caribbean as an "American lake" and all of Latin America as a vast potential market for U.S. goods. The crisis of the 1890s transformed this long-standing desire into a perceived economic necessity. Unlike European imperialists, powerful Americans dreamed of empire without large-scale permanent military occupation and costly colonial administration.

Americans focused their expansionist plans on the Western Hemisphere, determined to dislodge the dominant power, Great Britain. In 1867, when Canada became a self-governing dominion, American diplomats hoped to annex their northern neighbor, believing that Great Britain would gladly accede in order to concentrate its imperial interests in Asia. But Great Britain refused to give up Canada, and the United States backed away. Central and South America proved more accommodating to American designs.

Republican stalwart James G. Blaine, secretary of state under Presidents Garfield and Harrison, determined to work out a Good Neighbor policy (a phrase coined by Henry Clay in 1820). Bilateral treaties with Mexico, Colombia, the British West Indies, El Salvador, and the Dominican Republic allowed American business to dominate local economies, importing their raw materials at low prices and flooding their local markets with goods manufactured in the United States. Often American investors simply took over the principal industries of these small nations, undercutting national business classes.

The Good Neighbor policy depended, Blaine knew, on peace and order in the Latin American states. In 1883, wishing to enforce treaties and protect overseas investments, Congress appropriated funds to build up American seapower. Beginning with ninety small ships, over one-third of them wooden, the navy grew quickly to include modern steel fighting ships. The hulls of these ships were painted a gleaming white, and the armada was known as the Great White Fleet.

The annexation of Hawai'i on July 7, 1898, followed nearly a century of economic penetration and diplomatic maneuver. American missionaries, who had arrived in the 1820s to convert Hawai'ians to Christianity, began to buy up huge parcels of land and to subvert the existing feudal system of landholding. They also encouraged American businesses to buy into sugar plantations, and by 1875 U.S. corporations dominated the sugar trade. In 1887 a new treaty allowed the United States to build a naval base at Pearl Harbor on the island of Oahu.

The next year, American planters took a step further, arranging the overthrow of the weak king Kalakaua and securing a new government allied to their economic interests. In 1891, the new ruler, Queen Liliuokalani, struck back by issuing a constitution granting her more discretionary power. The U.S. minister, prompted by the pineapple magnate Sanford B. Dole, responded

20–3
Albert Beveridge, "The March of the Flag" (1898)

Brought to power with the assistance of American businessmen, Queen Liliuokalani nevertheless sought to limit the outsiders' influence. American marines, Christian missionaries, and sugar planters joined in 1893 to drive her from her throne. A century later, the U.S. government apologized to native Hawai'ians for this illegal act.

Library of Congress

by calling for military assistance. On January 16, 1893, U.S. sailors landed on Hawai'i to protect American property. Liliuokalani was deposed, a new provisional government was installed, and Hawai'i was proclaimed an American protectorate (a territory protected and partly controlled by the United States). President Cleveland refused to consider annexation, but five years later McKinley affirmed a joint congressional resolution under which Hawai'i would become an American territory in 1900. The residents of Hawai'i were not consulted about this momentous change in their national identity.

Hawai'i was often viewed as a steppingstone to the vast Asian markets. To accelerate railroad investment and trade, a consortium of New York bankers created the American China Development Company in 1896. They feared, however, that the tottering Manchu dynasty would fall to European, Russian, and Japanese colonial powers, which would then prohibit trade with the United States. Secretary of State John Hay responded in 1899 by proclaiming the Open Door policy. According to this doctrine, outlined in notes to six major powers, the United States enjoyed the right to advance its commercial interests anywhere in the world, at least on terms equal to those of the other imperialist nations. The Chinese marketplace was too important to lose.

THE SPANISH-AMERICAN WAR

During his 1896 campaign, William McKinley firmly committed himself to the principle of economic expansion. It was for him the proper alternative to Edward Bellamy's program for a cooperative commonwealth. Indeed, he once described his "greatest ambition" as achieving American supremacy in world markets. As president, McKinley not only reached out for markets but also took his nation into war while proclaiming its humanitarian and democratic goals.

A "SPLENDID LITTLE WAR" IN CUBA

Before the Civil War, Southerners hoped to acquire Cuba, still owned by Spain, for the expansion of slavery in its sugar mills, tobacco plantations, and mines. After attempting several times to buy the island outright, the United States settled for the continuation of the status quo. Throughout the nineteenth century, the United States resolved to protect Spain's sovereignty over Cuba against the encroachment of other powers, including Cuba itself.

In Cuba, a movement for independence began in the mid-1860s when Spain, its empire in ruins, began to impose stiff taxes on the island. After defeat during the Ten Years War of 1868–1878 and yet another series of setbacks, the insurgents rallied under the nationalist leadership of José Martí. In May 1895 Spanish troops ambushed and killed Martí, turning him into a martyr and fanning the flames of rebellion. By July, the rebels declared Cuba a republic and established a rudimentary government. Meanwhile, the war for independence moved closer to Havana, the island's seat of power.

Many Americans supported the movement for *Cuba Libre*. President Cleveland refused to back the Cuban revolutionaries and instead urged Spain to grant the island a limited autonomy. Even when Congress passed a resolution in 1896 welcoming the future independence of Cuba, Cleveland and his advisers demurred.

After he took over the office, President McKinley also drew back. In his Inaugural Address he declared, "We want no wars of conquest; we must avoid the temptation of territorial aggression." The tide turned, however, when Spain appeared unable to maintain order. In early 1898 public indignation, whipped up by tabloid

WHAT CRITIQUES

of empire were put forward in the years after the Spanish-American War?

20–4
The Spanish-American War (1898)

Charles Post, *Spanish Civil War.* Badly supplied Cuban insurrectos had practiced guerrilla warfare against the Spanish colonizers since the mid-1890s, but after the explosion on the USS *Maine,* American forces took over the war and abandoned the cause of Cuban self-determination. This picture, by the young U.S. volunteer, was one of a series of sketches later transformed into watercolor and oil paintings.

Library of Congress. Courtesy of Mrs. Charles Johnson Post and Miss Phyllis B. Post

press headlines and sensational stories, turned into frenzy on February 15, when an explosion ripped through the battleship USS *Maine,* stationed in Havana harbor ostensibly to rescue American citizens.

McKinley, suspecting war was close, had already begun to prepare for intervention. Newspapers ran banner headlines charging a Spanish conspiracy, although there was no proof. The impatient public meanwhile demanded revenge for the death of 266 American sailors.

Finally, on April 11, McKinley asked Congress for a declaration of war against Spain. Yet Congress barely passed the war resolution on April 25, and only with

MAP EXPLORATION

To explore an interactive version of this map, go to **http://www.prenhall.com/faraghertlc/map20.4**

MAP 20-4A   **MAP 20-4B**

The Spanish-American War   In two theaters of action, the United States used its naval power adeptly against a weak foe.

WHAT DID the United States gain from victories in each of these conflicts?

the inclusion of an amendment by Senator Henry Teller of Colorado that dis-claimed "any disposition or intention to exercise sovereignty, jurisdiction or con-trol over said island, except for the pacification thereof." By the end of April, the fighting had begun.

Ten weeks later the war was all but over. On land, Lieutenant Colonel Theodore Roosevelt—who boasted of killing Spaniards "like jackrabbits"—led his Rough Riders to victory. On July 3, the main Spanish fleet near Santiago Bay was destroyed; two weeks later Santiago itself surrendered, and the war drew to a close. Although fewer than 400 Americans died in battle, disease and the inept treat-ment of the wounded created a medical disaster, spreading sickness and disease to more than 20,000 in the regiments. Roosevelt nevertheless felt invigorated by the conflict, agreeing with John Hay that it had been a "splendid little war."

On August 12, at a small ceremony in McKinley's office marking Spain's sur-render, the United States secured Cuba's independence from Spain, but not its own sovereignty. American businesses proceeded to tighten their hold on Cuban sugar plantations, while U.S. military forces oversaw the formation of a constitutional convention that made Cuba a protectorate of the United States. Under the Platt Amendment, sponsored by Republican senator Orville H. Platt of Connecticut in 1901, Cuba was required to provide land for American bases; to devote national revenues to pay back debts to the United States; to sign no treaty that would be detrimental to American interests; and to acknowledge the right of the United States to intervene at any time to protect its interests in Cuba. After American troops withdrew from Cuba, the terms of the Platt amendment were incorporated into the Cuban-American Treaty of 1903. This treaty, which remained in place until 1934, paved the way for American domination of the island's sugar industry and contributed to anti-American sentiment among Cuban nationalists.

WAR IN THE PHILIPPINES

The Philippines, another of Spain's colonies, seemed an especially attractive prospect, its 7,000 islands a natural way station to the markets of mainland Asia. In 1897 Assistant Secretary of the Navy Theodore Roosevelt and President McKinley had discussed the merits of taking the Pacific colony in the event of war with Spain. At the first opportunity, McKinley acted to bring these islands into the U.S. strategic orbit. Shortly after Congress declared war on Spain, on May 4, the president dispatched 5,000 troops to occupy the Philippines. George Dewey, a Civil War veteran who commanded the American Asiatic Squadron, was ordered to "start offensive action." During the first week of the conflict, he demolished the Spanish fleet in Manila Bay through seven hours of unimpeded target practice. Once the war ended, McKinley pledged "to educate the Filipinos, and to uplift and civilize and Christianize them." But after centuries of Spanish rule, the majority of islanders—already Christians—were eager to create their own nation.

20–5
William McKinley, "Decision on the Philippines" (1900)

The Filipino rebels, like the Cubans, at first welcomed American troops and fought with them against Spain. But when the Spanish-American War ended and they perceived that American troops were not preparing to leave, the rebels, led by Emilio Aguinaldo, turned against their former allies and attacked the American base of operations in Manila in February 1899. Predicting a brief skirmish, American commanders seriously underestimated the population's capacity to endure great suffering for the sake of independence.

U.S. troops had provoked this conflict in various ways. Military leaders, the majority veterans of the Indian Wars, commonly described the natives as "gu-gus" and reported themselves, as one said, as "just itching to get at the niggers." While awaiting action, American soldiers repeatedly insulted or physically abused civilians, raped Filipino women, and otherwise whipped up resentment.

The resulting conflict took the form of modern guerrilla warfare, with brutalities on both sides. By the time the fighting slowed down in 1902, 4,300 American lives had been lost, and one of every five Filipinos had died in battle or from starvation or disease. On some of the Philippine islands, intermittent fighting lasted until 1935.

The conquest of the Philippines, which remained a U.S. territory until 1946, evoked for its defenders the vision of empire. Once again, Josiah Strong proclaimed judgment over an era. His famous treatise *Expansion* (1900) roundly defended American overseas involvements by carefully distinguishing between freedom and independence. People could achieve freedom, he argued, only under the rule of law. And because white Americans had proven themselves superior in the realm of government, they could best bring "freedom" to nonwhite peoples by setting aside the ideal of national independence for a period of enforced guidance. Many began to wonder, however, whether the United States could become an empire without sacrificing its democratic spirit, and to ask whether the subjugated people were really so fortunate under the rule of the United States.

CRITICS OF EMPIRE

No mass movement formed to forestall U.S. expansion, but distinguished figures like Mark Twain, Andrew Carnegie, William Jennings Bryan, and Harvard philosopher William James voiced their opposition strongly. Organized protest to military action, especially against the widely reported atrocities in the Philippines, owed much to the Anti-Imperialist League, which was founded by a small group of prominent Bostonians. In historic Faneuil Hall, which had witnessed the birth of both the American Revolution and the antislavery movement, a mass meeting was convened in June 1898 to protest the "insane and wicked ambition which is driving the nation to ruin." Within a few months, the league reported 25,000 members. Most supported American economic expansion but advocated free trade rather than political domination as the means to reach this goal.

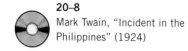

20–8

Mark Twain, "Incident in the Philippines" (1924)

CHRONOLOGY

1867	Grange founded.
	Secretary of State Seward negotiates the purchase of Alaska.
1874	Tompkins Square Riot.
	Granger laws begin to regulate railroad shipping rates.
1877	Rutherford B. Hayes elected president.
	Great Uprising of 1877.
1879	Henry George publishes *Progress and Poverty.*
1881	President James A. Garfield assassinated; Chester A. Arthur becomes president.
1883	Pendleton Act passed.
1884	Grover Cleveland elected president.
1887	Interstate Commerce Act creates the Interstate Commerce Commission.
1888	Edward Bellamy publishes *Looking Backward.*
	National Colored Farmers' Alliance and Cooperative Union formed.
	Benjamin Harrison elected president.
1889	National Farmers' Alliance and Industrial Union formed.
1890	Sherman Silver Purchase Act.
	McKinley tariff enacted.
	National American Woman Suffrage Association formed.
1891	National Women's Alliance formed.
	Populist (People's) Party formed.
1892	Coeur d'Alene miners' strike.

	Homestead strike.
	Ida B. Wells begins crusade against lynching.
1893	Western Federation of Miners formed.
	Financial panic and depression.
	World's Columbian Exhibition opens in Chicago.
1894	"Coxey's Army" marches on Washington, D.C.
	Pullman strike and boycott.
1896	*Plessy* v. *Ferguson* upholds segregation.
	William McKinley defeats William Jennings Bryan for president.
	Dingley tariff again raises import duties to an all-time high.
1897	Eugene V. Debs helps found Social Democratic Party.
1898	Hawai'i is annexed.
	Spanish-American War begins.
	Anti-Imperialist League formed.
	Cumming v. *Richmond County Board of Education* sanctions segregated education.
1899	Secretary of State John Hay announces Open Door policy.
	Guerrilla war begins in the Philippines.
	Gold Standard Act.
1900	Josiah Strong publishes *Expansion.*

A few outspoken antiimperialists, such as former Illinois governor John Peter Altgeld, openly toasted Filipino rebels as heroes. Morrison Swift, leader of the Coxey's Army contingent from Massachusetts, formed a Filipino Liberation Society and sent antiwar materials to American troops. Others, such as Samuel Gompers, a league vice president, felt no sympathy for conquered peoples but simply wanted to prevent colonized nonwhites from immigrating into the United States and "inundating" American labor.

Military leaders and staunch imperialists did not distinguish between racist and nonracist antiimperialists. They called all dissenters "unhung traitors" and demanded their arrest. Newspaper editors accused universities of harboring antiwar professors, although college students as a group were enthusiastic supporters of the war.

Most Americans put aside their doubts and welcomed the new era of imperialism. Untouched by the private tragedies of dead or wounded American soldiers and the mass destruction of civilian society in the Philippines, the vast majority could approve Theodore Roosevelt's defense of armed conflict: "No triumph of peace is quite so great as the supreme triumphs of war."

Conclusion

The conflicts marking the last quarter of the nineteenth century that pitted farmers, workers, and the proprietors of small businesses against powerful outside interests had offered Americans an important moment of democratic promise. By the end of the century, however, the rural and working-class campaigns to retain a large degree of self-government in their communities had been defeated, their organizations destroyed, their autonomy eroded. The rise of a national governing class and its counterpart, the large bureaucratic state, established new rules of behavior, new sources of prestige, and new rewards for the most successful citizens.

But the nation would pay a steep price, in the next era, for the failure of democratic reform. Regional antagonisms, nativist movements against the foreign-born, and above all deepening racial tensions blighted American society. As the new century opened, progressive reformers moved to correct flaws in government while accepting the framework of a corporate society and its overseas empire.

Summary

Toward a National Governing Class In the last three decades of the nineteenth century, the expansion and growth of the economy caused a similar trend in all levels of government. The modern apparatus of departments, cabinets, and agencies arose in the federal government. Legislatures controlled political power and patronage flourished as machine politics became prevalent. In response, reformers promoted civil service and improving public services.

Farmers and Workers Organize Their Communities Facing hard times and a loss of status and power, farmers and workers formed organizations both to provide services and protest against conditions. In both cases, the railroads were a major target. The Great Strike of 1877 was a peak of labor unrest. Women played important roles in farm and labor movements. They also founded other organizations. The Populist movement united farmers and workers in a short-lived reform and third-party movement.

The Crisis of the 1890s A severe, long depression caused high unemployment and hardship. Strikes, often violent, broke out across the nation. At the same time, religious leaders developed the social gospel doctrine to promote social reform that aided the poor.

Politics of Reform, Politics of Order The economic crisis of the 1890s weakened the two-party system. The Populists mounted a third-party threat but were co-opted by the Democrats. The Republicans won the 1896 election. During this period, nativism and racism arose. The institution of Jim Crow led to violence against African Americans and, in the South, reform dissipated into racism.

"Imperialism of Righteousness" Many Americans believed the economic problems of the 1890s showed the need for the United States to expand. In part, this belief was supported by ideas that the American civilization and the white race were superior to other cultures and peoples. Religious evangelism was one aspect of overseas expansion, but many in government and business desired an overseas empire. The United States acquired overseas territories through war and annexation.

The Spanish-American War Support for the Cuban independence movement and yellow journalism helped precipitate the Spanish-American War. The short conflict established the United States as an imperialist nation, but expansion aroused strong opposition from many Americans.

REVIEW QUESTIONS

1. Discuss some of the problems accompanying the expansion of government during the late nineteenth century. What role did political parties play in this process? Explain how a prominent reformer such as James Garfield might become a leading "machine" politician?

2. What were the major causes and consequences of the Populist movement of the 1880s and 1890s? Why did the election of 1896 prove so important for the future of American politics?

3. Discuss the role of women in both the Grange and the People's Party. What were their specific goals?

4. Discuss the causes and consequences of the financial crisis of the 1890s. How did various reformers and politicians respond to the event? What kinds of programs did they offer to restore the economy or reduce poverty?

5. How did the exclusion of African Americans affect the outcome of Populism? Explain the rise of Jim Crow legislation in the South, and discuss its impact on the status of African Americans.

6. Describe American foreign policy during the 1890s. Why did the United States intervene in Cuba and the Philippines? What were some of the leading arguments for and against overseas expansion?

KEY TERMS

Coxey's Army (p. 540)

Dingley Tariff of 1897 (p. 545)

Farmers' Alliance (p. 536)

Free silver (p. 544)

Grandfather clauses (p. 546)

Grange (p. 535)

Granger laws (p. 536)

Great Uprising (p. 537)

Interstate Commerce Commission
  (ICC) (p. 533)

Jim Crow laws (p. 546)

National American Woman Suffrage
  Association (p. 538)

Nativism (p. 546)

Pendleton Civil Service Reform Act
  (p. 535)

Plessy v. Ferguson (p. 546)

Poll taxes (p. 547)

Populist movement (p. 535)

Protective association (p. 540)

Segregation (p. 546)

Sherman Silver Purchase Act (p. 544)

Solid South (p. 543)

Southern Farmers' Alliance (p. 536)

Woman's Christian Temperance
  Union (WCTU) (p. 538)

RECOMMENDED READING

Ruth Bordin, *Woman and Temperance: The Quest for Power and Liberty, 1873–1900*
(1981). Relates the history of the WCTU to other campaigns for women's
emancipation in the late nineteenth century and highlights the leadership
of Frances E. Willard. Bordin demonstrates the central position temperance occupied in the political struggles of the era.

Matthew Freye Jacobson, *Barbarian Virtues: The United Sates Encounters Foreign Peoples at Home and Abroad, 1876–1917* (2000). Links the histories of immigration and empire building to examine public discussions about foreign
people, especially their "fitness" for self-government. Jacobson casts the
search for markets as backdrop for cultural history.

Michael Kazin, *The Populist Persuasion: An American History* (1995; rev. ed., 1998).
A fresh interpretation of Populist-style movements through the nineteenth
and twentieth centuries that suggests such movements can be either
"right" or "left" depending on circumstances.

Walter LaFeber, *The New Empire: An Interpretation of American Expansion,
1860–1898* (1963, 1998). The best overview of U.S. imperial involvement
in the late nineteenth century. LaFeber shows how overseas commitments
grew out of the economic expansionist assumptions of American leaders
and expanded continuously, if often chaotically, with the opportunities
presented by the crises experienced by the older imperial powers.

Leon F. Litwack, *Trouble in Mind: Black Southerners in the Age of Jim Crow* (1998).
An expansive social history of the first generation of African Americans
born in freedom and surviving a period of extraordinary violent and repressive race relations in the South. Litwack examines the retrenchment
of their political and civil rights but emphasizes their resourcefulness and
resistance.

Nell Irvin Painter, *Standing at Armageddon: The United States, 1877–1919* (1987).
Presents a broad overview of racial and industrial conflicts and the political movements that formed in their wake. Painter attempts to show how
this period proved decisive to the future history of the United States.

Emily S. Rosenberg, *Spreading the American Dream: American Economic and Cultural Expansion, 1890–1945* (1982). Insightfully examines the significance of expansionist ideology. Rosenberg studies the cultural and social roots of American foreign policy.

Elizabeth Sanders, *Roots of Reform: Farmers, Workers, and the American State, 1877–1917* (1999). A painstaking reconstruction of the legislative history of congressional bills with emphasis on the lobbying of dirt farmers as well as their search for allies. Sanders, a political scientist, shines new light on familiar conflicts between debtors and creditors and the political processes of the Gilded Age.

David O. Stowell, *Streets, Railroads, and the Great Strike of 1877* (1999). Examines in close detail the uprising of 1877 in Buffalo, Albany, and Syracuse, New York, casting the strike simultaneously as a struggle between workers and the railroad corporations and an attempt by the community to protest against usurpation of streets by the trains. Stowell emphasizes the importance of the urban setting of this strike and provides ample data on the physical injuries inflicted by trains on local residents.

William Appleman Williams, *Empire as a Way of Life: An Essay on the Causes and Character of America's Present Predicament* (1982). A lucid general exploration of American views of empire. Williams shows that Americans allowed the idea of empire and, more generally, economic expansion, to dominate their concept of democracy, especially in the last half of the nineteenth century.

The women, trudging stoutly along under great difficulties, were able to complete their march only when troops of cavalry from Fort Meyers were rushed into Washington . . . No inauguration has ever produced such scenes . . .
—Washington Post, *March 4, 1913*

THE JUNGLE

UPTON SINCLAIR

The great woman suffrage parade leaves Capitol Hill and heads for the White House, March 3, 1913. Dramatic tactics and careful organizing like those that marked this parade helped secure reform in the Progressive Era. The head of a suffrage parade at Washington D.C. oil over a photograph, 1913, (Granger Collection 4E 1028.04).

VOTES FOR WOMEN

21

URBAN AMERICA AND THE PROGRESSIVE ERA

1900–1917

WHAT ROLE did women play in the development of the progressive movement?

WHY DID prohibitionists focus on alcohol as the preeminent social evil?

WHAT APPROACHES did labor activists take to union formation?

WHY WAS birth control such a controversial issue at the turn of the twentieth century?

WHAT ROLE did Theodore Roosevelt envision the federal government playing in the national economy?

AMERICAN COMMUNITIES

The Henry Street Settlement House: Women Settlement House Workers Create a Community of Reform

A SHY AND FRIGHTENED YOUNG GIRL APPEARED IN THE DOORWAY OF A weekly home-nursing class for women on Manhattan's Lower East Side. The teacher beckoned her to come forward. Tugging on the teacher's skirt, the girl pleaded in broken English for the teacher to come home with her. "Mother," "baby," "blood," she kept repeating. The teacher gathered up the sheets that were part of the interrupted lesson in bed making. The two hurried through narrow, garbage-strewn, foul-smelling streets and then groped their way up a pitch-dark, rickety staircase. They reached a cramped, two-room apartment, home to an immigrant family of seven and several boarders. There, in a vermin-infested bed, encrusted with dried blood, lay a mother and her newborn baby. The mother had been abandoned by a doctor because she could not afford his fee.

The teacher, Lillian Wald, was a twenty-five-year-old nurse at New York Hospital. Years later she recalled this scene as her baptism by fire and the turning point in her life. Born in 1867, Wald had enjoyed a comfortable upbringing in a middle-class German Jewish family in Rochester. Despite her parents' objections, she had moved to New York City to become a professional nurse. Resentful of the disdainful treatment nurses received from doctors and horrified by the inhumane conditions at a juvenile asylum she worked in, Wald was determined to find a way of caring for the sick in their neighborhoods and homes. With nursing school classmate Mary Brewster, Wald rented a fifth-floor walk-up apartment on the Lower East Side and established a visiting nurse service. The two provided professional care in the home to hundreds of families for a nominal fee of 10 to 25 cents. They also offered each family they visited information on basic health care, sanitation, and disease prevention. In 1895, philanthropist Jacob Schiff generously donated a red brick Georgian house on Henry Street as a new base of operation.

The Henry Street Settlement stood in the center of perhaps the most overcrowded neighborhood in the world, New York's Lower East Side. Roughly 500,000 people were packed into an area only as large as a midsized Kansas farm. Population density was about 500 per acre, roughly four times the figure for the rest of New York City and far more concentrated than even the worst slums of London or Calcutta. A single city block might have as many as 3,000 residents. Home for most Lower East Siders was a small tenement apartment that might include paying boarders squeezed in alongside the immediate family. Residents were mostly recent immigrants from southern and eastern Europe: Jews, Italians, Germans, Greeks, Hungarians, Slavs. Men, women, and

children toiled in the garment shops, small factories, retail stores, breweries, and warehouses to be found on nearly every street. An Irish-dominated machine controlled local political affairs.

The Henry Street Settlement became a model for a new kind of reform community composed essentially of college-educated women who encouraged and supported one another in a wide variety of humanitarian, civic, political, and cultural activities. Settlement house living arrangements closely resembled those in the dormitories of such new women's colleges as Smith, Wellesley, and Vassar. Like these colleges, the settlement house was an "experiment," but one designed, in settlement house pioneer Jane Addams's words, "to aid in the solution of the social and industrial problems which are engendered by the modern conditions of urban life." Unlike earlier moral reformers who tried to impose their ideas from outside, settlement house residents lived in poor communities and worked for immediate improvements in the health and welfare of those communities. Yet, as Addams and others repeatedly stressed, the college-educated women were beneficiaries as well. The settlement house allowed them to preserve a collegial spirit, satisfy the desire for service, and apply their academic training.

New York City

With its combined moral and social appeal, the settlement house movement attracted many educated young women and grew rapidly. There were six settlement houses in the United States in 1891, some 74 in 1897, more than 200 by 1900, and more than 400 by 1910. Few women made settlement work a career. The average stay was less than five years. Roughly half of those who worked in the movement eventually married. Those who did make a career of settlement house work, however, typically chose not to marry, and most lived together with female companions. As the movement flourished, settlement house residents called attention to the plight of the poor and fostered respect for different cultural heritages in countless articles and lectures. Leaders of the movement, including Jane Addams, Lillian Wald, and Florence Kelley, emerged as influential political figures during the progressive era.

Wald attracted a dedicated group of nurses, educators, and reformers to live at the Henry Street Settlement. By 1909 Henry Street had more than forty residents, supported by the donations of well-to-do New Yorkers. Wald and her allies convinced the New York Board of Health to assign a nurse to every public school in the city. They lobbied the Board of Education to create the first school lunch programs. They persuaded the city to set up municipal milk stations to ensure the purity of milk. Henry Street also pioneered tuberculosis treatment and prevention. Its leaders became powerful advocates for playground construction, improved street cleaning, and tougher housing inspection. The settlement's Neighborhood Playhouse became an internationally acclaimed center for innovative theater, music, and dance.

As settlement house workers expanded their influence from local neighborhoods to larger political and social circles, they became, in the phrase of one historian, "spearheads for reform."

Lillian Wald became a national figure—an outspoken advocate of child labor legislation and woman suffrage and a vigorous opponent of American involvement in World War I. She offered Henry Street as a meeting place to the National Negro Conference in 1909, out of which emerged the National Association for the Advancement of Colored People. It was no cliché for Wald to say, as she did on many occasions, "The whole world is my neighborhood."

THE CURRENTS OF PROGRESSIVISM

Between the 1890s and World War I, a large and diverse number of Americans claimed the political label "progressive." Progressivism is best understood as a varied collection of reform communities, often fleeting, uniting citizens in a host of political, professional, and religious organizations, some of which were national in scope.

As a political movement, progressivism flowered in the soil of several key issues: ending political corruption, bringing more businesslike methods to governing, and offering a more compassionate legislative response to the excesses of industrialism. As a national movement, progressivism reached its peak in 1912, when the four major presidential candidates all ran on some version of a progressive platform.

Three basic attitudes underlay the various crusades and movements that emerged in response to the fears gnawing at large segments of the population. The first was anger over the excesses of industrial capitalism and urban growth. At the same time, progressives shared an essential optimism about the ability of citizens to improve social and economic conditions. They were reformers, not revolutionaries. Second, progressives emphasized social cohesion and common bonds as a way of understanding how modern society and economics actually worked. They largely rejected the ideal of individualism that had informed nineteenth-century economic and political theory. For progressives, poverty and success hinged on more than simply individual character; the economy was more than merely a sum of individual calculations. Progressives thus opposed **social Darwinism**, with its claim that any effort to improve social conditions would prove fruitless because society is like a jungle in which only the "fittest" survive. Third, progressives believed in the need for citizens to intervene actively, both politically and morally, to improve social conditions. They pushed for a stronger government role in regulating the economy and solving the nation's social problems.

Progressive rhetoric and methods drew on two distinct sources of inspiration. One was evangelical Protestantism, which emphasized both the capacity and the duty of Christians to purge the world of poverty, inequality, and economic greed. A second strain of progressive thought looked to natural and social scientists to develop rational measures for improving the human condition, believing that experts trained in statistical analysis and engineering could make government and industry more efficient. Progressivism thus offered an uneasy combination of social justice and social control, a tension that would characterize American reform for the rest of the twentieth century.

WHAT ROLE did women play in the development of the progressive movement?

21-12
Herbert Croly, *Progressive Democracy* (1914)

21-8
Walker Percy, "Birmingham under the Commission Plan" (1911)

21-5
James H. Patten, Chairman of the National Legislative Committee of the American Purity Federation, Testimony Before Congress (1910)

Social Darwinism   The application of Charles Darwin's theory of biological evolution to society, holding that the fittest and wealthiest survive, the weak and the poor perish, and government action is unable to alter this "natural" process.

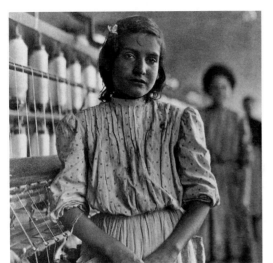

Photographer Lewis Hine, a pioneer of social documentary photography, made this evocative 1908 portrait of "Mamie," a typical young spinner working at a cotton mill in Lancaster, South Carolina. The National Child Labor Committee hired Hine to help document, publicize, and curb the widespread employment of children in industrial occupations.

Lewis Hine (American, 1874–1940), A Carolina Spinner, 1908. Gelatin silver print, 4 3/4 ¥ 7 in. Milwaukee Art Museum, Gift of the Sheldon M. Barnett Family. (M1973.83)

Progressive era   An era in the United States (roughly between 1900 and 1917) in which important movements challenged traditional relationships and attitudes.

The young Jane Addams, founder of the Hull House settlement in south Chicago, and a leading voice for a variety of Progressive Era reform campaigns inspired thousands of educated, middle-class American women to serve the needs of the urban poor.

Jane Addams Memorial Collection (JAMC neg.21), The University Library, University of Illinois at Chicago

WOMEN SPEARHEAD REFORM

In the 1890s the settlement house movement had begun to provide an alternative to traditional concepts of private charity and humanitarian reform. Settlement workers found they could not transform their neighborhoods without confronting a host of broad social questions: chronic poverty, overcrowded tenement houses, child labor, industrial accidents, and public health.

Jane Addams founded one of the first settlement houses, Hull House, in Chicago in 1889 after years of struggling to find work and a social identity equal to her talents. Hull House was located in a run-down slum area of Chicago. It had a day nursery, a dispensary for medicines and medical advice, a boardinghouse, an art gallery, and a music school. Addams often spoke of the "subjective necessity" of settlement houses. By this she meant that they gave young, educated women a way to satisfy their powerful desire to connect with the real world.

Social reformer Florence Kelley helped direct the support of the settlement house movement behind groundbreaking state and federal labor legislation. In 1893, she wrote a report detailing the dismal conditions in sweatshops and the effects of long hours on the women and children who worked in them. This report became the basis for landmark legislation in Illinois that limited women to an eight-hour workday, barred children under fourteen from working, and abolished tenement labor. Moving to Henry Street Settlement in 1898, Kelley served as general secretary of the new National Consumers' League. With Lillian Wald she established the New York Child Labor Committee and pushed for the creation of the U.S. Children's Bureau, established in 1912.

Kelley, Addams, Wald, and their circle consciously used their power as women to reshape politics in the **progressive era**. Electoral politics and the state were historically male preserves, but female social progressives turned their gender into an advantage. They built upon the tradition of female moral reform, where women had long operated outside male-dominated political institutions to agitate and organize.

THE URBAN MACHINE

By the turn of the century Democratic Party machines, usually dominated by first- and second-generation Irish, controlled the political life of most large American cities. The keys to machine strength were disciplined organization and the delivery of essential services to both immigrant communities and business elites. Recent immigrants in particular faced frequent unemployment, sickness, and discrimination. In exchange for votes, machine politicians offered their constituents a variety of services. These included municipal jobs in the police and fire departments, work at city construction sites, intervention with legal problems, and food and coal during hard times.

For those who did business with the city—construction companies, road builders, realtors—staying on the machine's good side was simply another business expense. In exchange for valuable franchises and city contracts, businessmen routinely bribed machine politicians and contributed liberally to their campaign funds. George Washington Plunkitt, a stalwart of New York's Tammany Hall machine, good-naturedly defended what he called "honest graft": making money from inside information on public improvements. "It's just like lookin' ahead in Wall Street or in the coffee or cotton market."

Organized prostitution and gambling, patronized largely by visitors to the city, could flourish only when "protected" by politicians who shared in the profits. Many machine figures began as saloonkeepers, and liquor dealers and beer brewers provided important financial support for "the organization." Vaudeville and burlesque theater, boxing, horse racing, and professional baseball were other urban enterprises with economic and political links to machines.

On New York City's Lower East Side, where the Henry Street Settlement was located, Timothy D. "Big Tim" Sullivan embodied the popular machine style.

21-6
Jane Addams, *Twenty Years at Hull House* (1910)

OVERVIEW

CURRENTS OF PROGRESSIVISM

	Key Figures	Issues	Institutions/Achievements
Local Communities	Jane Addams, Lillian Wald, Florence Kelley, Frederic C. Howe, Samuel Jones	■ Improving health, education, welfare in urban immigrant neighborhoods ■ Child labor, eight-hour day ■ Celebrating immigrant cultures ■ Reforming urban politics ■ Municipal ownership/regulation of utilities	■ Hull House Settlement ■ Henry Street Settlement ■ National Consumers League ■ New York Child Labor Committee ■ Bureau of Municipal Research
State	Robert M. LaFollette, Hiram Johnson, Al Smith	■ Limiting power of railroads, other corporations ■ Improving civil service ■ Direct democracy ■ Applying academic scholarship to human needs	■ "Wisconsin Idea" ■ State Worker's Compensation ■ Unemployment Insurance ■ Public utility regulation
	James K. Vardaman,	■ Disfranchisement of African Americans	■ Legalized segregation
National	Hoke Smith, Theodore Roosevelt, Woodrow Wilson	■ Trustbusting ■ Conservation and Western development ■ National regulation of corporate and financial excesses ■ National regulation of corporate and financial excesses ■ Reform of national banking	■ Reclamation Bureau (1902) ■ U.S. Forest Service (1905) ■ Food and Drug Administration (1906) ■ Meat Inspection Act (1906) ■ Hepburn Act–ICC (1906) ■ Graduated Income Tax (1913) ■ Federal Reserve Act (1913) ■ Clayton Antitrust Act (1914) ■ Federal Trade Commission (1914)
Intellectual/ Cultural	Jacob Riis	■ Muckraking	■ *How the Other Half Lives* (1890)
	Lincoln Steffens, Ida Tarbell, Upton Sinclair, S. S. McClure		■ *Shame of the Cities* (1902) ■ *History of Standard Oil* (1904) ■ *The Jungle* (1906) ■ *McClure's Magazine*
	John Dewey Louis Brandeis Edwin A. Ross	■ Education reform ■ Sociological jurisprudence ■ Empowering "ethical elite"	■ *Democracy and Education* (1916) ■ *Muller* v. *Oregon* (1908) ■ *Social Control* (1901)

21-9
Helen M. Todd, "Getting Out the Vote" (1911)

19-10
William T. Riordon, from *Plunkitt of Tammany Hall* (1905)

19-11
John Spargo, from *The Bitter Cry of Children* (1906)

Critics charged that Sullivan controlled the city's gambling and made money from prostitution. But Big Tim, who had risen from desperate poverty, remained enormously popular with his constituents until his death in 1913. Sullivan, whose district included the largest number of immigrants and transients in the city, provided shoe giveaways and free Christmas dinners to thousands every winter. To help pay for these and other charitable activities, he informally taxed the saloons, theaters, and restaurants in the district. Sullivan also made a fortune through his investments in Vaudeville and the early movie business.

State legislatures, controlled by Republican rural and small-town elements, proved a formidable check on what city-based machines could accomplish. Reform campaigns that publicized excessive graft and corruption sometimes led voters to throw machine-backed mayors and aldermen out of office. And there were never enough patronage jobs for all the people clamoring for appointments. In the early twentieth century, to expand their base of support, political machines in the Northeast began concentrating more on passing welfare legislation beneficial to working-class and immigrant constituencies. In New York, for example, Tammany Hall figures such as Robert Wagner, Al Smith, and Big Tim Sullivan worked with middle-class progressive groups to pass child labor laws, factory safety regulations, worker's compensation plans, and other efforts to make government more responsive to social needs. Urban machines also began to champion cultural pluralism, opposing **prohibition** and immigration restrictions and defending the contributions made by new ethnic groups in the cities.

POLITICAL PROGRESSIVES AND URBAN REFORM

Political progressivism originated in the cities. It was both a challenge to the power of machine politics and a response to deteriorating urban conditions. City governments, especially in the Northeast and industrial Midwest, seemed hardly capable of providing the basic services needed to sustain large populations. For example, an impure water supply left Pittsburgh with one of the world's highest rates of death from typhoid, dysentery, and cholera. Most New York City neighborhoods rarely enjoyed street cleaning, and playgrounds were nonexistent.

Reformers placed much of the blame for urban ills on the machines and looked for ways to restructure city government. Reformers revised city charters in favor of stronger mayoral power and expanded use of appointed administrators and career civil servants.

Business and professional elites became the biggest boosters of structural reforms in urban government. In the summer of 1900 a hurricane in the Gulf of Mexico unleashed a tidal wave on Galveston, Texas. To cope with this disaster, leading businessmen convinced the state legislature to replace the mayor-council government with a small board of commissioners. Each commissioner was elected at large, and each was responsible for a different city department. Under this plan voters could more easily identify and hold accountable those responsible for city services. The city commission, enjoying both policy-making and administrative powers, proved very effective in rebuilding Galveston. By 1917 nearly 500 cities, including Houston, Oakland, Kansas City, Denver, and Buffalo, had adopted the commission form of government. Another approach, the city manager plan, gained popularity in small and midsized cities. In this system, a city council appointed a professional, nonpartisan city manager to handle the day-to-day operations of the community.

Progressive politicians who focused on the human problems of the industrial city championed a different kind of reform, one based on changing policies rather than the political structure. In Cleveland, wealthy businessman Thomas L. Johnson

---

QUICK REVIEW

Municipal Reform

◆ Urban reformers sought to break alliances between city bosses and business leaders.

◆ Urban reformers developed the concept of the city commission and the city manager.

◆ Business groups often promoted these reforms.

Prohibition   A ban on the production, sale, and consumption of liquor, achieved temporarily through state laws and the Eighteenth Amendment.

served as mayor from 1901 to 1909. He emphasized both efficiency and social welfare. His popular program included lower streetcar fares, public baths, milk and meat inspection, and an expanded park and playground system.

PROGRESSIVISM IN THE STATEHOUSE: WEST AND SOUTH

Their motives and achievements were mixed, but progressive politicians became a powerful force in many state capitals. In Wisconsin, Republican dissident Robert M. La Follette forged a coalition of angry farmers, small businessmen, and workers with his fiery attacks on railroads and other large corporations. Leader of the progressive faction of the state Republicans, "Fighting Bob" won three terms as governor (1900–1906) and then served as a U.S. senator until his death in 1925. As governor he pushed through tougher corporate tax rates, a direct primary, an improved civil service code, and a railroad commission designed to regulate freight charges. La Follette used faculty experts at the University of Wisconsin to help research and write his bills. Other states began copying the "Wisconsin Idea"—the application of academic scholarship and theory to the needs of the people.

In practice, La Follette's railroad commission accomplished far less than progressive rhetoric claimed. Ordinary consumers did not see lower passenger fares or reduced food prices. And as commissioners began to realize, the national reach of the railroads limited the effectiveness of state regulation. Although La Follette championed a more open political system, he also enrolled state employees in a tight political machine of his own. The La Follette family would dominate Wisconsin politics for forty years.

Western progressives displayed the greatest enthusiasm for institutional political reform. In the early 1900s, Oregon voters approved a series of constitutional amendments designed to strengthen direct democracy. The two most important were the *initiative*, which allowed a direct vote on specific measures put on the state ballot by petition, and the *referendum*, which allowed voters to decide on bills referred to them by the legislature. Other reforms included the *direct primary*, which allowed voters to cross party lines, and the *recall*, which gave voters the right to remove elected officials by popular vote. Widely copied throughout the West, all these measures intentionally weakened political parties.

Southern progressives supported the push toward a fully segregated public sphere. Between 1900 and 1910 Southern states strengthened "Jim Crow" laws requiring separation of races in restaurants, streetcars, beaches, and theaters. Schools were separate but hardly equal. A 1916 Bureau of Education study found that per capita expenditures for education in Southern states averaged $10.32 a year for white children and $2.89 for black children. And African American teachers received far lower salaries than their white counterparts. Black taxpayers, in effect, subsidized improved schools for white students, even as they saw their own children's educational opportunities deteriorate. The legacy of Southern progressivism was, thus, closely linked to the strengthening of the legal and institutional guarantees of white supremacy.

NEW JOURNALISM: MUCKRAKING

Changes in journalism helped fuel a new reform consciousness by drawing the attention of millions to urban poverty, political corruption, the plight of industrial workers, and immoral business practices. As early as 1890, journalist Jacob Riis had shocked the nation with his landmark book *How the Other Half Lives,* a portrait of New York City's poor. A Danish immigrant who arrived in New York City in 1871, Riis became a newspaper reporter, covering the police beat and learning

---

IMAGE KEY

for pages 560–561

a. Cover, featuring a factory, of "The Jungle" by Upton Sinclair.

b. A photo of a women's suffrage parade in Washington D.C. in 1913.

c. Suffragette Dorothy Newell has "Votes for Women" written on her back.

d. Bull Moose Party campaign paraphernalia.

e. The Flanner House Baby Clinic, about 1918.

f. Publicity poster for 1913 pageant organized by John Reed and other Greenwich Village radicals supporting the striking silk workers in Paterson, New Jersey.

g. Detail of photo of Women's suffrage parade in Washington, D.C. in 1913.

h. American cartoon showing President Theodore Roosevelt slaying those trusts he considered "bad" for the public interest while restraining those whose business practices he considered "good" for the country.

Initiative Procedure by which citizens can introduce a subject for legislation, usually through a petition signed by a specific number of voters.

Referendum Submission of a law, proposed or already in effect, to a direct popular vote for approval or rejection.

Recall The process of removing an official from office by popular vote, usually after using petitions to call for such a vote.

Muckraking Journalism exposing economic, social, and political evils, so named by Theodore Roosevelt for its "raking the muck" of American society.

This picture of Bohemian immigrant cigar makers at work in a New York City tenement first appeared in Jacob Riis's *How the Other Half Lives* (1890), a pathbreaking work of "exposure journalism." Apartments like these, owned and rented out by cigar manufacturers, served as both living quarters and workshops, leading to filthy and unhealthy conditions. Note how the entire family works together to roll as many cigars as possible.

Bohemian Cigar Makers at Work in Their Tenement, ca. 1890. Museum of the City of New York, The Jacob A. Riis Collection, (#147.90.13.1.150)

18-11
Lincoln Steffens, from *The Shame of the Cities* (1904)

■ ■ ■ ■ ■ ■ ■ ■ ■ ■ ■ ■ ■ ■
WHY DID prohibitionists
focus on alcohol as the preeminent
social evil?
■ ■ ■ ■ ■ ■ ■ ■ ■ ■ ■ ■ ■ ■

about the city's desperate underside. Riis's book included a remarkable series of photographs he had taken in tenements, lodging houses, sweatshops, and saloons, which had a powerful impact on a whole generation of urban reformers.

Within a few years, magazine journalists had turned to uncovering the seamier side of American life. The key innovator was S. S. McClure, a young Midwestern editor who in 1893 started America's first large-circulation magazine, *McClure's*. Charging only a dime for his monthly, McClure effectively combined popular fiction with articles on science, technology, travel, and recent history. He attracted a new readership among the urban middle class.

In 1902 McClure began hiring talented reporters to write detailed accounts of the nation's social problems. Lincoln Steffens's series *The Shame of the Cities* (1902) revealed the widespread graft at the center of American urban politics. He showed how big-city bosses routinely worked hand in glove with businessmen seeking lucrative municipal contracts for gas, water, electricity, and mass transit. Ida Tarbell, in her *History of the Standard Oil Company* (1904), thoroughly documented how John D. Rockefeller ruthlessly squeezed out competitors with unfair business practices.

McClure's and other magazines discovered that "exposure journalism" paid off handsomely in terms of increased circulation. A series such as Steffens's fueled reform campaigns that swept individual communities. Between 1902 and 1908, magazines were full of articles exposing insurance scandals, patent medicine frauds, and stock market swindles. Upton Sinclair's 1906 novel *The Jungle,* a socialist tract set among Chicago packinghouse workers, exposed the filthy sanitation and abysmal working conditions in the stockyards and the meatpacking industry. In an effort to boost sales, Sinclair's publisher devoted an entire issue of a monthly magazine it owned, *World's Work*, to articles and photographs that substantiated Sinclair's devastating portrait.

SOCIAL CONTROL AND ITS LIMITS

Many middle- and upper-class Protestant progressives feared that immigrants and large cities threatened the stability of American democracy. They worried that alien cultural practices were disrupting what they viewed as traditional American morality. Viewing themselves as part of what sociologist Edward Ross called the "ethical elite," progressives often believed they had a mission to frame laws and regulations for the social control of immigrants, industrial workers, and African Americans. This was the moralistic and frequently xenophobic side of progressivism, and it provided a powerful source of support for the regulation of drinking, prostitution, leisure activities, and schooling. Organizations devoted to social control constituted other versions of reform communities. These attempts at moral reform met with mixed success.

THE PROHIBITION MOVEMENT

During the last two decades of the nineteenth century, the Woman's Christian Temperance Union had grown into a powerful mass organization. The WCTU appealed especially to women angered by men who used alcohol and then abused their wives and children. But local WCTU chapters put their energy into non-temperance activities as well, including homeless shelters, Sunday schools, prison reform, child nurseries, and woman suffrage. By 1911 the WCTU, with a quarter million members, was the largest women's organization in American history.

Other temperance groups had a narrower focus. The Anti-Saloon League, founded in 1893, began by organizing local-option campaigns in which rural counties and small towns banned liquor within their geographical limits. It drew much of its financial support from local businessmen, who saw a link between closing a community's saloons and increasing the productivity of workers. The league was a one-issue pressure group that played effectively on antiurban and antiimmigrant prejudice.

The battle to ban alcohol revealed deep ethnic and cultural divides within America's urban communities. Opponents of alcohol were generally "pietists," who viewed the world from a position of moral absolutism. These included native-born, middle-class Protestants associated with evangelical churches along with some old-stock Protestant immigrant denominations. Opponents of prohibition were generally "ritualists" with less arbitrary notions of personal morality. These were largely new-stock, working-class Catholic and Jewish immigrants, along with some Protestants, such as German Lutherans.

THE SOCIAL EVIL

Many of the same reformers who battled the saloon and drinking also engaged in efforts to eradicate prostitution. Crusades against "the social evil" had appeared at intervals throughout the nineteenth century, but they reached a new level of intensity between 1895 and 1920.

Between 1908 and 1914 exposés of the "white slave traffic" became a national sensation. Dozens of books, articles, and motion pictures alleged an international conspiracy to seduce and sell girls into prostitution. Most of these materials exaggerated the practices they attacked. They also made foreigners, especially Jews and southern Europeans, scapegoats for the sexual anxieties of native-born whites. In 1910 Congress passed legislation that permitted the deportation of foreign-born prostitutes or any foreigner convicted of procuring or employing them. That same year, the Mann Act made it a federal offense to transport women across state lines for "immoral purposes."

The progressive bent for defining social problems through statistics was nowhere more evident than in these reports. Vice commission investigators combed red-light districts, tenement houses, hotels, and dance halls, drawing up detailed lists of places where prostitution took place. They interviewed prostitutes, pimps, and customers. These reports agreed that commercialized sex was a business run by and for the profit and pleasure of men. They also documented the dangers of venereal disease to the larger community. The highly publicized vice reports were effective in forcing police crackdowns in urban red-light districts.

For wage-earning women, prostitution was a rational choice in a world of limited opportunities. Maimie Pinzer, a prostitute, summed up her feelings in a letter to a wealthy female reformer: "I don't propose to get up at 6:30 to be at work at 8 and work in a close, stuffy room with people I despise, until dark, for $6 or $7 a week! When I could, just by phoning, spend an afternoon with some congenial person and in the end have more than a week's work could pay me." The antivice crusades succeeded in closing down many urban red-light districts and larger brothels, but these were replaced by the streetwalker and call girl, who were more vulnerable to harassment and control by policemen and pimps.

THE REDEMPTION OF LEISURE

For large numbers of working-class adults and children, leisure meant time and money spent at vaudeville and burlesque theaters, amusement parks, dance halls, and motion picture houses. For many cultural traditionalists, the flood of new urban commercial amusements posed a grave threat: "Commercialized leisure" must be controlled by the community, if it is to become an agency of civilization rather than the reverse," warned Cleveland progressive Frederic C. Howe in 1914.

By 1908 movies had become the most popular form of cheap entertainment in America. One survey estimated that 11,500 movie theaters attracted 5 million patrons each day. For 5 or 10 cents, "nickelodeon" theaters offered programs that might include a slapstick comedy, a western, a travelogue, and a melodrama.

Movies, **by John Sloan**, 1913, the most talented artist among the so-called Ashcan realist school of painting. Active in socialist and bohemian circles, Sloan served as art editor for *The Masses* magazine for several years. His work celebrated the vitality and diversity of urban working-class life and leisure, including the new commercial culture represented by the motion picture.

John Sloan, *Movies*, 1913. Oil painting. The Toledo Museum of Art

Early movies were most popular in the tenement and immigrant districts of big cities, and with children. As the films themselves became more sophisticated and as "movie palaces" began to replace cheap storefront theaters, the new medium attracted a large middle-class clientele as well.

Progressive reformers seized on the new medium as an alternative to the older entertainment traditions, such as concert saloons and burlesque theater, that had been closely allied with machine politics and the vice economy. In 1909, New York City movie producers and exhibitors joined with the reform-minded People's Institute to establish the voluntary National Board of Censorship (NBC). Movie entrepreneurs, most of whom were themselves immigrants, sought to shed the stigma of the slums, attract more middle-class patronage, and increase profits. A revolving group of civic activists reviewed new movies, passing them, suggesting changes, or condemning them. Local censoring committees all over the nation subscribed to the board's weekly bulletin. They aimed at achieving what John Collier of the NBC called "the redemption of leisure." By 1914 the NBC was reviewing 95 percent of the nation's film output.

WORKING-CLASS COMMUNITIES AND PROTEST

The Industrial Revolution, which had begun transforming American life and labor in the nineteenth century, reached maturity in the early twentieth. In 1900, out of a total labor force of 28.5 million, 16 million people worked at industrial occupations and 11 million on farms. By 1920, in a labor force of nearly 42 million, almost 29 million were in industry, but farm labor had declined to 10.4 million. The world of the industrial worker included large manufacturing towns in New England; barren mining settlements in the West; primitive lumber and turpentine camps in the South; steelmaking and coal-mining cities in Pennsylvania and Ohio; and densely packed immigrant ghettos from New York to San Francisco, where workers toiled in garment trade sweatshops.

All these industrial workers shared the need to sell their labor for wages in order to survive. At the same time, differences in skill, ethnicity, and race proved powerful barriers to efforts at organizing trade unions that could bargain for improved wages and working conditions. So, too, did the economic and political power of the large corporations that dominated much of American industry. These years saw many labor struggles that created effective trade unions or laid the groundwork for others. Industrial workers also became a force in local and national politics, adding a chorus of insistent voices to the calls for social justice.

NEW IMMIGRANTS FROM TWO HEMISPHERES

On the eve of World War I, close to 60 percent of the industrial labor force was foreign-born. In the nineteenth century, much of the overseas migration had come from the industrial districts of northern and western Europe. English, Welsh, and German artisans had brought with them skills critical for emerging industries such as steelmaking and coal mining. Unlike their predecessors, nearly all the new Italian, Polish, Hungarian, Jewish, and Greek immigrants lacked industrial skills. They thus entered the bottom ranks of factories, mines, mills, and sweatshops.

WHAT APPROACHES did labor activists take to union formation?

Immigration to the United States (1901–1920)

Total: 14,532,000		Percent of Total (90)
Italy	3,157,000	22
Austria-Hungary	3,047,000	21
Russia and Poland	2,524,000	17
Canada	922,000	6
Great Britain	867,000	6
Scandinavia	709,000	5
Ireland	487,000	3
Germany	486,000	3
France and Low Countries (Belgium, Netherlands, Switzerland.)	361,000	2
Mexico	268,000	2
West Indies	231,000	2
Japan	213,000	2
China	41,000	*
Australia and New Zealand	23,000	*

*Less than 1% of total.

Source: U.S. Bureau of the Census, *Historical Statistics of the United States from Colonial Times to 1970* (Washington, DC), 1975.

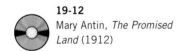
19-12
Mary Antin, *The Promised Land* (1912)

These new immigrants had been driven from their European farms and towns by several forces, including the undermining of subsistence farming by commercial agriculture; a falling death rate that brought a shortage of land; and religious and political persecution. American corporations also sent agents to recruit cheap labor. Except for Jewish immigrants, a majority of whom fled virulent anti-Semitism in Russia and Russian Poland, most newcomers planned on earning a stake and then returning home.

The decision to migrate usually occurred through social networks—people linked by kinship, personal acquaintance, and work experience. These "chains," extending from places of origin to specific destinations in the United States, helped migrants cope with the considerable risks entailed by the long and difficult journey. A study conducted by the U.S. Immigration Commission in 1909 found that about 60 percent of the new immigrants had their passage arranged by immigrants already in America.

The low-paid, backbreaking work in basic industry became nearly the exclusive preserve of the new immigrants. In 1907, of the 14,359 common laborers employed at Pittsburgh's U.S. Steel mills, 11,694 were eastern Europeans. For twelve-hour days and seven-day weeks, two-thirds of these workers made less than $12.50 a week, one-third less than $10.00. This was far less than the $15.00 that the Pittsburgh Associated Charities had estimated as the minimum for providing necessities for a family of five. Small wonder that the new immigration was disproportionately male. One-third of the immigrant steelworkers were single. Workers with families generally supplemented their incomes by taking in single men as boarders.

Between 1898 and 1907 more than 80,000 Japanese entered the United States. The vast majority were young men working as contract laborers in the West.

American law prevented Japanese immigrants (the *Issei*) from obtaining American citizenship, because they were not white. Most Japanese settled near Los Angeles, where they established small communities centered around fishing, truck farming, and the flower and nursery business. In 1920 Japanese farmers produced 10 percent of the dollar volume of California agriculture on 1 percent of the farm acreage.

Mexican immigration also grew in these years, providing a critical source of labor for the West's farms, railroads, and mines. Economic and political crises spurred tens of thousands of Mexico's rural and urban poor to emigrate north. Large numbers of seasonal agricultural workers regularly came up from Mexico to work in the expanding sugar beet industry and then returned. But between 1900 and 1914, the number of people of Mexican descent living and working in the United States tripled, from roughly 100,000 to 300,000.

URBAN GHETTOS

By 1920, immigrants and their children constituted almost 60 percent of the population of cities over 100,000. The sheer size and dynamism of these cities made the immigrant experience more complex than in smaller cities and more isolated communities. Workers in the urban garment trades toiled for low wages and suffered layoffs, unemployment, and poor health. But conditions in the small, labor-intensive shops of the clothing industry differed significantly from those in the large-scale, capital-intensive industries like steel.

New York City had become the center of both Jewish immigration and America's huge ready-to-wear clothing industry. The city's Jewish population was 1.4 million in 1915, almost 30 percent of its inhabitants. In small factories, lofts, and tenement apartments some 200,000 people, most of them Jews, some of them Italians, worked in the clothing trades. Most of the industry operated on the grueling piece-rate, or task, system, in which manufacturers and subcontractors paid individuals or teams of workers to complete a certain quota of labor within a specific time.

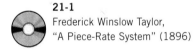

21-1
Frederick Winslow Taylor,
"A Piece-Rate System" (1896)

The garment industry was highly seasonal. A typical workweek was sixty hours, with seventy common during busy season. But there were long stretches of unemployment in slack times. Even skilled cutters, all men, earned an average of only $16 per week. Unskilled workers, nearly all of them young single women, made only $6 or $7 a week.

In November 1909 two New York garment manufacturers responded to strikes by unskilled women workers by hiring thugs and prostitutes to beat up pickets. The strikers won the support of the Women's Trade Union League, a group of sympathetic female reformers that included Lillian Wald, Mary Dreier, and prominent society figures. At a dramatic mass meeting in Cooper Union Hall, Clara Lemlich, a teenage working girl speaking in Yiddish, made an emotional plea for a general strike. She called for everyone in the crowd to take an old Jewish oath: "If I turn traitor to the cause I now pledge, may this hand wither from the arm I now raise." The Uprising of the 20,000, as it became known, swept through the city's garment district.

The strikers demanded union recognition, better wages, and safer and more sanitary conditions. Hundreds of them were arrested, and many were beaten by police. After three cold months on the picket line, the strikers returned to work without union recognition. But the International Ladies Garment Workers Union (ILGWU), founded in 1900, did gain strength and negotiated contracts with some of the city's shirtwaist makers. The strike was an important breakthrough in the drive to organize unskilled workers into industrial unions.

QUICK REVIEW

Triangle Shirtwaist Fire

- 1911: fire kills 146 workers.
- Managers had locked the exits.
- Tragedy led to the enactment of new industrial safety laws.

New York City Police set up this makeshift morgue to help identify victims of the disastrous Triangle Shirtwaist Company fire, March 25, 1911. Unable to open the locked doors of the sweatshop and desperate to escape from smoke and flames, many of the 146 who died had leaped eight stories to their death.

UPI/CORBIS

On March 25, 1911, the issues raised by the strike took on new urgency when a fire raced through three floors of the Triangle Shirtwaist Company. As the flames spread, workers found themselves trapped by exit doors that had been locked from the outside. Fire escapes were nonexistent. Within half an hour, 146 people, mostly young Jewish women, had been killed by smoke or had leaped to their death. In the bitter aftermath, women progressives led by Florence Kelley and Frances Perkins of the National Consumers' League joined with Tammany Hall leaders Al Smith, Robert Wagner, and Big Tim Sullivan to create a New York State Factory Investigation Commission. Under Perkins's vigorous leadership, the commission conducted an unprecedented round of public hearings and on-site inspections, leading to a series of state laws that dramatically improved safety conditions and limited the hours for working women and children.

THE AFL: "UNIONS, PURE AND SIMPLE"

Following the depression of the 1890s, the American Federation of Labor (AFL) emerged as the strongest and most stable organization of workers. Samuel Gompers's strategy of recruiting skilled labor into unions organized by craft had paid off. Union membership climbed from under 500,000 in 1897 to 1.7 million by 1904. The national unions—the United Mine Workers of America, the Brotherhood of Carpenters and Joiners, the International Association of Machinists—represented workers of specific occupations in collective bargaining. Trade autonomy and exclusive jurisdiction were the ruling principles within the AFL.

But the strength of craft organization also gave rise to weakness. In 1905 Gompers told a union gathering in Minneapolis that "caucasians" would not "let their standard of living be destroyed by negroes, Chinamen, Japs, or any others." Each trade looked mainly to the welfare of its own. Many explicitly barred women and African Americans from membership. There were some important exceptions. The United Mine Workers of America (UMWA) followed a more inclusive policy, recruiting both skilled underground pitmen and the unskilled aboveground workers. The UMWA even tried to recruit strikebreakers brought in by coal operators. With 260,000 members in 1904, the UMWA became the largest AFL affiliate.

AFL unions had a difficult time holding on to their gains. Economic slumps, technological changes, and aggressive counterattacks by employer organizations could be devastating. Trade associations using management-controlled efficiency drives fought union efforts to regulate output and shop practices. The National Association of Manufacturers (NAM), a group of smaller industrialists founded in 1903, launched an "open shop" campaign to eradicate unions altogether. "Open shop" was simply a new name for a workplace where unions were not allowed.

Unfriendly judicial decisions also hurt organizing efforts. In 1906 a federal judge issued a permanent injunction against an iron molders strike at the Allis Chalmers Company of Milwaukee. In the so-called Danbury Hatters' case (*Loewe v. Lawler,* 1908), a federal court ruled that secondary boycotts, aimed by strikers at other companies doing business with their employer were illegal. Not until the 1930s would unions be able to count on legal support for collective bargaining and the right to strike.

THE IWW: "ONE BIG UNION"

Some workers developed more radical visions of labor organizing. In company towns, where a single large corporation was dominant, miners suffered from low wages, poor food, and primitive sanitation, as well as injuries and death from frequent cave-ins and explosions. In response to the brutal realities of labor organizing in the West, in 1905, leaders of the Western Federation of Miners, the Socialist Party, and various radical groups gathered in Chicago to found the Industrial Workers of the World (IWW). The IWW charter proclaimed bluntly, "The working class and the employing class have nothing in common. . . . Between these two classes a struggle must go on until the workers of the world unite as a class, take possession of the earth and the machinery of production, and abolish the wage system."

William D. "Big Bill" Haywood, an imposing, one-eyed, hard-rock miner, emerged as the most influential and flamboyant spokesman for the IWW, or **Wobblies**, as they were called. Haywood, a charismatic speaker and effective organizer, regularly denounced the AFL for its conservative emphasis on organizing skilled workers by trade. The Wobblies concentrated their efforts on miners, lumberjacks, sailors, "harvest stiffs," and other casual laborers. Openly contemptuous of bourgeois respectability, the IWW stressed the power of collective direct action on the job—strikes and, occasionally, sabotage.

The IWW briefly became a force among Eastern industrial workers, tapping the rage and growing militance of the immigrants and unskilled. In 1909, an IWW–led steel strike at McKees Rocks, Pennsylvania, challenged the power of U.S. Steel. In the 1912 "Bread and Roses" strike in Lawrence, Massachusetts, IWW organizers turned a spontaneous walkout of textile workers into a successful struggle for union recognition.

These battles gained the IWW a great deal of sympathy from radical intellectuals, along with public scorn from the AFL and employers' groups. The IWW failed to establish permanent organizations in the Eastern cities, but it remained a force in the lumber camps, mines, and wheat fields of the West. In spite of its militant rhetoric, the IWW concerned itself with practical gains. "The final aim is revolution," said one Wobbly organizer, "but for the present let's see if we can get a bed to sleep in, water enough to take a bath in and decent food to eat." But when the United States entered World War I, the Justice Department used the IWW's anticapitalist rhetoric and antiwar stance to crush it.

Wobblies   Popular name for the members of the Industrial Workers of the World (IWW).

WOMEN'S MOVEMENTS AND BLACK AWAKENING

THE NEW WOMAN

The settlement house movement discussed in the opening of this chapter was just one of the new avenues of opportunity that opened to progressive era women. A steady proliferation of women's organizations attracted growing numbers of educated, middle-class women in the early twentieth century. With more men working in offices, more children attending school, and family size declining, the middle-class home was emptier. At the same time, more middle-class women were graduating from high school and college.

The women's club movement combined an earlier focus on self-improvement and intellectual pursuits with newer benevolent efforts on behalf of working women and children. The Buffalo Union, for example, sponsored art lectures for housewives and classes in typing, stenography, and bookkeeping for

WHY WAS birth control such a controversial issue at the turn of the twentieth century?

young working women. It also maintained a library, set up a "noon rest" downtown where women could eat lunch, and ran a school for training domestics. In Chicago the Women's Club became a powerful ally for reformers. For many middle-class women the club movement provided a new kind of female-centered community.

Other women's associations made even more explicit efforts to bridge class lines between middle-class homemakers and working-class women. The National Consumers' League (NCL), started in 1898 by Maud Nathan and Josephine Lowell, sponsored a "white label" campaign in which manufacturers who met safety and sanitary standards could put NCL labels on their food and clothing. Under the dynamic leadership of Florence Kelley, the NCL took an even more aggressive stance by publicizing labor abuses in department stores and lobbying for maximum-hour and minimum-wage laws in state legislatures. In its efforts to protect home and housewife, worker and consumer, the NCL embodied the ideal of "social housekeeping."

BIRTH CONTROL

The phrase "birth control," coined by Margaret Sanger around 1913, described her campaign to provide contraceptive information and devices for women. Sanger had seen her own mother die at age forty-nine after bearing eleven children. In 1910, Sanger was a thirty-year-old nurse and housewife living with her husband and three children in a New York City suburb. Excited by a socialist lecture she had attended, she convinced her husband to move to the city, where she threw herself into the bohemian milieu. She became an organizer for the IWW, and in 1912 she wrote a series of articles on female sexuality for a socialist newspaper.

When postal officials confiscated the paper for violating obscenity laws, Sanger left for Europe to learn more about contraception. She returned to New York determined to challenge the obscenity statutes with her own magazine, the *Woman Rebel*. Sanger's journal celebrated female autonomy, including the right to sexual expression and control over one's body. When she distributed her pamphlet *Family Limitation,* postal inspectors confiscated copies and she found herself facing forty-five years in prison. In October 1914 she fled to Europe again.

An older generation of feminists had advocated "voluntary motherhood," or the right to say no to a husband's sexual demands. The new birth control advocates embraced contraception as a way of advancing sexual freedom for middle-class women as well as responding to the misery of those working-class women who bore numerous children while living in poverty. Sanger returned to the United States in October 1915. After the government dropped the obscenity charges, she embarked on a national speaking tour. In 1916 she again defied the law by opening a birth control clinic in a working-class neighborhood in Brooklyn and offering birth control information without a physician present. Arrested and jailed, she gained more publicity for her crusade. Within a few years, birth control leagues and clinics could be found in every major city and most large towns in the country.

RACISM AND ACCOMMODATION

African Americans endured a deeply racist popular culture that made hateful stereotypes of black people a normal feature of political debate and everyday life. White Southern politicians and writers claimed that African Americans had undergone a natural "reversion to savagery" upon the end of slavery. In Northern

21-4
Platform Adopted by the
National Negro Committee
(1909)

cities "coon songs," based on gross caricatures of black life, were extremely popular in theaters and as sheet music. Like the antebellum minstrel shows, these songs reduced African Americans to creatures of pure appetite for food, sex, alcohol, and violence.

In this political and cultural climate, Booker T. Washington won recognition as the most influential black leader of the day. Born a slave in 1856, Washington was educated at Hampton Institute in Virginia, one of the first freedmen's schools devoted to industrial education. In 1881 he founded Tuskegee Institute, a black school in Alabama devoted to industrial and moral education. He became the leading spokesman for racial accommodation, urging blacks to focus on economic improvement and self-reliance, as opposed to political and civil rights. His widely read autobiography, *Up from Slavery* (1901), stands as a classic narrative of an American self-made man. Written with a shrewd eye toward cementing his support among white Americans, it stressed the importance of learning values such as frugality, cleanliness, and personal morality. But Washington also gained a large following among African Americans, especially those who aspired to business success. Publicly he insisted that "agitation of questions of social equality is the extremest folly." But privately Washington also spent money and worked behind the scenes trying to halt disfranchisement and segregation.

RACIAL JUSTICE, THE NAACP, BLACK WOMEN'S ACTIVISM

Washington's focus on economic self-help remained deeply influential in African American communities long after his death in 1915. But alternative black voices challenged his racial philosophy while he lived. In the early 1900s, scholar and activist W. E. B. Du Bois created a significant alternative to Washington's leadership. A product of the black middle class, Du Bois had been educated at Fisk University and Harvard, where in 1895 he became the first African American to receive a Ph.D. Through essays on black history, culture, education, and politics, Du Bois explored the concept of "double consciousness." Black people, he argued, would always feel the tension between an African heritage and their desire to assimilate as Americans.

Du Bois criticized Booker T. Washington's philosophy for its acceptance of "the alleged inferiority of the Negro." The black community, he argued, must fight for the right to vote, for civic equality, and for higher education for the "talented tenth" of their youth. In 1905 Du Bois and editor William Monroe Trotter brought together a group of educated black men to oppose Washington's conciliatory views. Discrimination they encountered in Buffalo, New York, prompted the men to move their meeting to Niagara Falls, Ontario. The **Niagara movement** protested legal segregation, the exclusion of blacks from labor unions, and the curtailment of voting and other civil rights.

The Niagara movement failed to generate much change. But in 1909 many of its members, led by Du Bois, attended a National Negro Conference held at the Henry Street Settlement in New York. A new, interracial organization emerged from this conference, the **National Association for the Advancement of Colored People (NAACP)**. Du Bois was the only black officer of the original NAACP.

The disfranchisement of black voters in the South severely curtailed African American political influence. In response,

Niagara movement African American group organized in 1905 to promote racial integration, civil and political rights, and equal access to economic opportunity.

National Association for the Advancement of Colored People Interracial organization co-founded by W. E. B. DuBois in 1910 dedicated to restoring African American political and social rights.

17-11
W.E.B. Du Bois, from "Of Mr. Booker T. Washington and Others" (1903)

In July 1905, a group of African American leaders—including W. E. B. Du Bois (second from right, middle row)—met in Niagara Falls, Ontario, to protest legal segregation and the denial of civil rights to the nation's black population.

Photographs and Print Division, Schomburg Center for Research in Black Culture, The New York Public Library, Astor, Lenox and Tilden Foundations.

WHAT ROLE

did Theodore Roosevelt envision the federal government playing in the national economy?

18-9
Booker T. Washington, Atlanta Exposition Address (1895)

21-7
Theodore Roosevelt, from *The New Nationalism* (1910)

Sherman Antitrust Act   The first federal antitrust measure, passed in 1890; sought to promote economic competition by prohibiting business combinations in restraint of trade or commerce.

African American women created new strategies to challenge white supremacy and improve life in their communities. As Sallie Mial, a North Carolina Baptist home missionary, told her male brethren, "We have a peculiar work to do. We can go where you cannot afford to go." Founded in 1900, the Women's Convention of the National Baptist Convention, the largest black denomination in the United States, offered African American women a new public space to pursue reform work and "racial uplift." They organized settlement houses and built playgrounds; they created day-care facilities and kindergartens; they campaigned for women's suffrage, temperance, and advances in public health.

National Progressivism

Theodore Roosevelt and Presidential Activism

The assassination of William McKinley in 1901 made forty-two-year-old Theodore Roosevelt the youngest man to ever hold the office of president. Born to a wealthy New York family in 1858, Roosevelt overcame a sickly childhood through strenuous physical exercise and rugged outdoor living. After graduating from Harvard he immediately threw himself into a career in the rough and tumble of New York politics. He won election to the state assembly, ran an unsuccessful campaign for mayor of New York, served as president of the New York City Board of Police Commissioners, and went to Washington as assistant secretary of the navy. During the Spanish-American War, he won national fame as leader of the Rough Rider regiment in Cuba. Upon his return, he was elected governor of New York and then in 1900 vice president. Roosevelt viewed the presidency as a "bully pulpit"—a platform from which he could exhort Americans to reform their society—and he aimed to make the most of it.

Roosevelt was a uniquely colorful figure, a shrewd publicist, and a creative politician. He preached the virtues of "the strenuous life," and he believed that educated and wealthy Americans had a special responsibility to serve, guide, and inspire those less fortunate. In style, Roosevelt made key contributions to national progressivism. He knew how to inspire and guide public opinion. He stimulated discussion and aroused curiosity like no one before him. In 1902 Roosevelt demonstrated his unique style of activism when he personally intervened in a bitter strike by anthracite coal miners. Using public calls for conciliation, a series of White House bargaining sessions, and private pressure on the mine owners, Roosevelt secured a settlement that won better pay and working conditions for the miners, but without recognition of their union. Roosevelt also pushed for efficient government as the solution to social problems. Unlike most nineteenth-century Republicans, who had largely ignored economic and social inequalities, Roosevelt frankly acknowledged them. Administrative agencies run by experts, he believed, could find rational solutions that could satisfy everyone.

Trustbusting and Regulation

One of the first issues Roosevelt faced was growing public concern with the rapid business consolidations taking place in the American economy. In 1902 he directed the Justice Department to begin a series of prosecutions under the **Sherman Antitrust Act**. The first target was the Northern Securities Company, a huge merger of transcontinental railroads brought about by financier J. P. Morgan. The deal would have created a giant holding company controlling nearly all the long-distance rail lines from Chicago to California. The Justice Department fought the case all the way through a hearing before the Supreme Court. In *Northern Securities* v. *United States* (1904), the Court held that the stock transactions constituted an illegal combination in restraint of interstate commerce.

This case established Roosevelt's reputation as a "trustbuster." During his two terms, the Justice Department filed forty-three cases under the Sherman Antitrust Act to restrain or dissolve business monopolies. Roosevelt viewed these suits as necessary to publicize the issue and assert the federal government's ultimate authority over big business. But he did not really believe in the need to break up large corporations. Unlike many progressives, who were nostalgic for smaller companies and freer competition, Roosevelt accepted centralization as a fact of modern economic life and considered government regulation the best way to deal with big business.

After easily defeating Democrat Alton B. Parker in the 1904 election, Roosevelt felt more secure in pushing for regulatory legislation. In 1906 Roosevelt responded to public pressure for greater government intervention and, overcoming objections from a conservative Congress, signed three important measures into law. The **Hepburn Act** strengthened the Interstate Commerce Commission (ICC), established in 1887 as the first independent regulatory agency, by authorizing it to set maximum railroad rates and inspect financial records. The Pure **Food and Drug Act** established the Food and Drug Administration (FDA), which tested and approved drugs before they went on the market. The Meat Inspection Act (passed with help from the shocking publicity surrounding Upton Sinclair's muckraking novel *The Jungle*) empowered the Department of Agriculture to inspect and label meat products.

But regulatory legislation found advocates among American big business as well. Large meatpackers such as Swift and Armour strongly supported stricter federal regulation as a way to drive out smaller companies that could not meet tougher standards. The new laws also helped American packers compete more profitably in the European export market by giving their meat the official seal of federal inspectors.

As a naturalist and outdoorsman, Theodore Roosevelt also believed in the need for government regulation of the natural environment. He worried about the destruction of forests, prairies, streams, and the wilderness. In 1905 he created the U.S. Forest Service and named conservationist Gifford Pinchot to head it. Pinchot recruited a force of forest rangers to manage the reserves. By 1909 total timber and forest reserves had increased from 45 to 195 million acres, and more than 80 million acres of mineral lands had been withdrawn from public sale.

REPUBLICAN SPLIT

By the end of his second term, Roosevelt had moved beyond the idea of regulation to push for the most far-reaching federal economic and social programs ever proposed. He saw the central problem as "how to exercise . . . responsible control over the business use of vast wealth."

In 1908, Roosevelt kept his promise to retire after a second term. He chose Secretary of War William Howard Taft as his successor. Taft easily defeated Democrat William Jennings Bryan in the 1908 election. During Taft's presidency, the gulf between "insurgent" progressives and the "stand pat" wing split the Republican Party wide open. To some degree, the battles were as much over style as substance. Compared with Roosevelt, the reflective and judicious Taft brought a much more restrained concept of the presidency to the White House. He supported some progressive measures, including the constitutional amendment legalizing a graduated income tax (ratified in 1913), safety codes for mines and railroads, and the creation of a federal Children's Bureau (1912). But in a series of bitter political fights involving tariff, antitrust, and conservation policies, Taft alienated Roosevelt and many other progressives.

Hepburn Act   Act that strengthened the Interstate Commerce Commission (ICC) by authorizing it to set maximum railroad rates and inspect financial records.

Food and Drug Act   Act that established the Food and Drug Administration (FDA), which tested and approved drugs before they went on the market.

MAP EXPLORATION

To explore an interactive version of this map, go to
http://www.prenhall.com/faraghertlc/map21.1

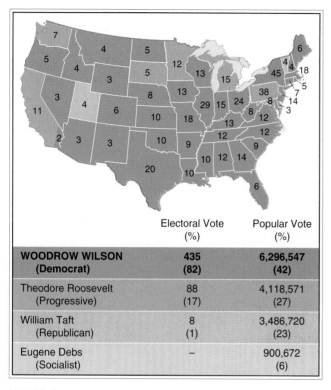

	Electoral Vote (%)	Popular Vote (%)
WOODROW WILSON (Democrat)	**435 (82)**	**6,296,547 (42)**
Theodore Roosevelt (Progressive)	88 (17)	4,118,571 (27)
William Taft (Republican)	8 (1)	3,486,720 (23)
Eugene Debs (Socialist)	–	900,672 (6)

MAP 21-1

The Election of 1912   The split within the Republican Party allowed Woodrow Wilson to become only the second Democrat since the Civil War to be elected president. Eugene Debs's vote was the highest ever polled by a Socialist candidate.

WHAT CAUSED the split in the Republican Party?

QUICK REVIEW

Democratic Victory in 1912

♦ Republicans split between Taft and Roosevelt.

♦ Democrats put themselves forward as the "true progressives."

♦ Wilson won with only 42 percent of the popular vote.

21-10
Louis Brandeis, *Other People's Money and How the Bankers Use It* (1913)

New Freedom   Woodrow Wilson's 1912 program for limited government intervention in the economy to restore competition by curtailing the restrictive influences of trusts and protective tariffs, thereby providing opportunities for individual achievement.

After returning from an African safari and a triumphant European tour in 1910, Roosevelt threw himself back into national politics. He directly challenged Taft for the Republican Party leadership. In a dozen bitter state presidential primaries (the first ever held), Taft and Roosevelt fought for the nomination. Although Roosevelt won most of these contests, the old guard still controlled the national convention and renominated Taft in June 1912. Roosevelt's supporters stormed out, and in August the new Progressive Party nominated Roosevelt and Hiram Johnson of California as its presidential ticket. The platform called for woman suffrage, the eight-hour day, prohibition of child labor, minimum-wage standards for working women, and stricter regulation of large corporations.

THE ELECTION OF 1912: A FOUR-WAY RACE

With the Republicans so badly divided, the Democrats sensed a chance for their first presidential victory in twenty years. They chose Governor Woodrow Wilson of New Jersey as their candidate. Although not nearly as well known nationally as Taft and Roosevelt, Wilson had built a strong reputation as a reformer. The son of a Virginia Presbyterian minister, Wilson spent most of his early career in academia. He studied law at the University of Virginia and then earned a Ph.D. in political science from Johns Hopkins. After teaching history and political science at several schools, he became president of Princeton University in 1902. In 1910, he won election as New Jersey's governor, running against the state Democratic machine. He won the Democratic nomination for president with the support of many of the party's progressives, including William Jennings Bryan.

Wilson declared himself and the Democratic Party to be the true progressives. Crafted largely by progressive lawyer Louis Brandeis, Wilson's platform was far more ambiguous than Roosevelt's. The **New Freedom** emphasized restoring conditions of free competition and equality of economic opportunity. Wilson did favor a variety of progressive reforms for workers, farmers, and consumers. But in sounding older, nineteenth-century Democratic themes of states' rights and small government, Wilson argued against allowing the federal government to become as large and paternalistic as Roosevelt advocated.

Socialist party nominee Eugene V. Debs offered the fourth and most radical choice to voters. The Socialists had more than doubled their membership since 1908, to more than 100,000. On election days Socialist strength was far greater than that, as the party's candidates attracted increasing numbers of voters. By 1912 more than a thousand Socialists held elective office in thirty-three states and 160 cities. Geographically, Socialist strength had shifted to the trans-Mississippi South and West.

Debs and the Socialists also took credit for pushing both Roosevelt and Wilson farther toward the left. Both the Democratic and Progressive Party platforms contained proposals that had been considered extremely radical only ten years earlier.

In the end, the divisions in the Republican Party gave the election to Wilson. He won easily, polling 6.3 million votes to Roosevelt's 4.1 million. Taft came in third with 3.5 million. Eugene Debs won 900,000 votes, 6 percent of the total, for the strongest Socialist showing in American history. Even though he won with only 42 percent of the popular vote, Wilson swept the electoral college with 435 votes to Roosevelt's 88 and Taft's 8, giving him the largest electoral majority up to that time. In several respects, the election of 1912 was the first "modern" presidential race. It featured the first direct primaries, challenges to traditional party loyalties, an issue-oriented campaign, and a high degree of interest group activity.

WOODROW WILSON'S FIRST TERM

As president, Wilson followed Roosevelt's lead in expanding the activist dimensions of the office. He became more responsive to pressure for a greater federal role in regulating business and the economy. This increase in direct lobbying—from hundreds of local and national reform groups, Washington-based organizations, and the new Progressive Party—was itself a new and defining feature of the era's political life. With the help of a Democratic-controlled Congress, Wilson pushed through a significant battery of reform proposals.

The **Underwood-Simmons Act** of 1913 substantially reduced tariff duties on a variety of raw materials and manufactured goods, including wool, sugar, agricultural machinery, shoes, iron, and steel. Taking advantage of the newly ratified **Sixteenth Amendment**, which gave Congress the power to levy taxes on income, it also imposed the first graduated tax (up to 6 percent) on personal incomes. The **Federal Reserve Act** that same year restructured the nation's banking and currency system. It created twelve Federal Reserve Banks, regulated by a central board in Washington. Member banks were required to keep a portion of their cash reserves in the Federal Reserve Bank of their district. By giving central direction to banking and monetary policy, the Federal Reserve Board diminished the power of large private banks.

Wilson also supported the **Clayton Antitrust Act** of 1914, which replaced the old Sherman Act of 1890 as the nation's basic antitrust law. The Clayton Act reflected the growing political clout of the American Federation of Labor. It exempted unions from being construed as illegal combinations in restraint of trade, and it forbade federal courts from issuing injunctions against strikers. But Wilson adopted the view that permanent federal regulation was necessary for checking the abuses of big business. The **Federal Trade Commission (FTC)**, established in 1914, sought to give the federal government the same sort of regulatory control over corporations that the ICC had over railroads.

On social issues, Wilson proved more cautious in his first two years. His initial failure to support federal child labor legislation and rural credits to farmers angered many progressives. A Southerner, Wilson also sanctioned the spread of racial segregation in federal offices. As the reelection campaign of 1916 approached, Wilson worried about defections from the labor and social justice wings of his party. He proceeded to support a rural credits act providing government capital to federal farm banks, as well as federal aid to agricultural extension programs in schools. He also came out in favor of child labor reform and a worker's compensation bill for federal employees. But by 1916 the dark cloud of war in Europe had already begun to cast its long shadow over progressive reform.

This political cartoon, drawn by Charles Jay Budd, appeared on the cover of *Harper's Weekly*, September 28, 1912. It employed the imagery of autumn county fairs to depict voters as unhappy with their three choices for president.

Theodore Roosevelt Collection, Harvard College Library

21-3
Eugene V. Debs, "The Outlook for Socialism in the United States" (1900)

21-11
Woodrow Wilson, from *The New Freedom* (1913)

Underwood-Simmons Act of 1913
Reform law that lowered tariff rates and levied the first regular federal income tax.

Sixteenth Amendment of 1913
Authorized a federal income tax.

Federal Reserve Act   The 1913 law that revised banking and currency by extending limited government regulation through the creation of the Federal Reserve System.

Clayton Antitrust Act of 1914   Replaced the old Sherman Act of 1890 as the nation's basic antitrust law. It exempted unions from being construed as illegal combinations in restraint of trade, and it forbade federal courts from issuing injunctions against strikers.

Federal Trade Commission (FTC)
Government agency established in 1914 to provide regulatory oversight of business activity.

CHRONOLOGY

1889 Jane Addams founds Hull House in Chicago.

1890 Jacob Riis publishes *How the Other Half Lives.*

1895 Booker T. Washington addresses Cotton States Exposition in Atlanta, emphasizing an accommodationist philosophy.

Lillian Wald establishes Henry Street Settlement in New York.

1898 Florence Kelley becomes general secretary of the new National Consumers' League.

1900 Robert M. La Follette elected governor of Wisconsin.

1901 Theodore Roosevelt succeeds the assassinated William McKinley as president.

1904 Lincoln Steffens publishes *The Shame of the Cities.*

1905 President Roosevelt creates U.S. Forest Service and names Gifford Pinchot head.

Industrial Workers of the World is founded in Chicago.

1906 Upton Sinclair's *The Jungle* exposes conditions in the meatpacking industry.

Congress passes Pure Food and Drug Act and Meat Inspection Act and establishes Food and Drug Administration.

1908 In *Muller* v. *Oregon* the Supreme Court upholds a state law limiting maximum hours for working women.

1909 Uprising of 20,000 garment workers in New York City's garment industries helps organize unskilled workers into unions.

National Association for the Advancement of Colored People (NAACP) is founded.

1911 Triangle Shirtwaist Company fire kills 146 garment workers in New York City.

Socialist critic Max Eastman begins publishing *The Masses.*

1912 Democrat Woodrow Wilson wins presidency, defeating Republican William H. Taft, Progressive Theodore Roosevelt, and Socialist Eugene V. Debs.

Bread and Roses strike involves 25,000 textile workers in Lawrence, Massachusetts.

Margaret Sanger begins writing and speaking in support of birth control for women.

1913 Sixteenth Amendment, legalizing a graduated income tax, is ratified.

1914 Clayton Antitrust Act exempts unions from being construed as illegal combinations in restraint of trade.

Federal Trade Commission is established.

Ludlow Massacre occurs.

1916 National Park Service is established.

CONCLUSION

The American political and social landscape was significantly altered by progressivism, but these shifts reflected the tensions and ambiguities of progressivism itself. Nearly every new election law had the effect of excluding some people from voting while including others. For African Americans, progressivism largely meant disfranchisement from voting altogether. Direct primary laws eliminated some of the most blatant abuses of big-city machines, but in cities and states dominated by one party, the majority party's primary effectively decided the general election. Stricter election laws made it more difficult for third parties to get on the ballot. Voting itself steadily declined in these years.

Over all, party voting became a less important form of political participation. Interest group activity, congressional and statehouse lobbying, and direct appeals to public opinion gained currency as ways of influencing government. Business groups such as the National Association of Manufacturers and individual trade associations were among the most active groups pressing their demands on government. Political action often shifted from legislatures to the new administrative agencies and commissions created to deal with social and economic problems. Popular magazines and journals grew significantly in both number and circulation, becoming more influential in shaping and appealing to national public opinion.

Social progressives and their allies could point to significant improvements in the everyday lives of ordinary Americans. On the state level, real advances had been made through a range of social legislation covering working conditions, child labor, minimum wages, and worker compensation. Social progressives, too, had discovered the power of organizing into extraparty lobbying groups such as the National Consumers' League and the National American Woman Suffrage Association. Yet the tensions between fighting for social justice and the urge toward social control remained unresolved. The emphasis on efficiency, uplift, and rational administration often collided with humane impulses to aid the poor, the immigrant, the slum dweller. The large majority of African Americans, blue-collar workers, and urban poor remained untouched by federal assistance programs.

Progressives had tried to confront the new realities of urban and industrial society. What had begun as a discrete collection of local and state struggles had by 1912 come to reshape state and national politics. Politics itself had been transformed by the calls for social justice. Federal and state power would now play a more decisive role than ever in shaping work, play, and social life in local communities.

SUMMARY

The Currents of Progressivism Progressives launched a comprehensive reform campaign. Women acted as spearheads of reforms that touched all levels of government and focused on problems in cities. Reformers used the press to pursue their programs.

Social Control and Its Limits Fears of moral decline led some reformers to seek social control of immigrants, workers, and African Americans. Their efforts met with mixed results.

Working-Class Communities and Protest Immigrants from Europe, North America, and Asia flooded into the United States creating crowded urban communities in large cities. Deplorable working conditions in the garment trades led to unions and strikes, but it took a tragic fire for the New York state government to institute legal reform. During this period, two national unions emerged.

Women's Movements and Black Awakening Women and African Americans actively pursued a reform agenda. Women's organizations took up numerous causes and sought to cross class lines. A major issue was birth control. African Americans responded to legal segregation in two distinct ways: accommodation and activism.

National Progressivism The progressive movement reached the national level after Theodore Roosevelt became president. Roosevelt championed government regulation to achieve reform and became involved in areas such as business and conservation of the natural environment. His successor William Howard Taft was more restrained in his reform efforts. The election of 1912 became a referendum on reform agenda. Wilson won the election and began implementing much of his program.

REVIEW QUESTIONS

1. Discuss the tensions within progressivism between the ideals of social justice and the urge for social control. What concrete achievements are associated with each wing of the movement? What were the driving forces behind them?

2. Describe the different manifestations of progressivism at the local, state, and national levels. To what extent did progressives redefine the role of the state in American politics?

3. What gains were made by working-class communities in the progressive era? What barriers did they face?

4. How did the era's new immigration reshape America's cities and workplaces? What connections can you draw between the new immigrant experience and progressive era politics?

5. Analyze the progressive era from the perspective of African Americans. What political and social developments were most crucial, and what legacies did they leave?

6. Evaluate the lasting impact of progressive reform. How do the goals, methods, and language of progressives still find voice in contemporary America?

KEY TERMS

Clayton Antitrust Act (p. 581)
Federal Reserve Act (p. 581)
Federal Trade Commission (FTC) (p. 581)
Food and Drug Act (p. 579)
Hepburn Act (p. 579)
Initiative (p. 567)
Muckraking (p. 567)
National Association for the Advancement of Colored People (p. 577)
New Freedom (p. 580)

Niagara movement (p. 577)
Progressive era (p. 564)
Prohibition (p. 566)
Recall (p. 567)
Referendum (p. 567)
Sherman Antitrust Act (p. 578)
Sixteenth Amendment (p. 581)
Social Darwinism (p. 563)
Underwood-Simmons Act (p. 581)
Wobblies (p. 575)

RECOMMENDED READING

Robert M. Crunden, *Ministers of Reform: The Progressives' Achievement in American Civilization, 1889–1920* (1982). Emphasizes the moral and religious traditions of middle-class Protestants as the core of the progressive ethos.

Alan Dawley, *Struggles for Justice: Social Responsibility and the Liberal State* (1991). Offers an important interpretation of progressivism that focuses on how the working class and women pushed the state toward a more activist role in confronting social problems.

Susan A. Glenn, *Daughters of the Shtetl: Life and Labor in the Immigrant Generation* (1990). A sensitive analysis of the experiences of immigrant Jewish women in the garment trades.

Dewey Grantham, *Southern Progressivism: The Reconciliation of Progress and Tradition* (1982). Examines the contradictions within the Southern progressive tradition.

Morton Keller, *Regulating a New Society: Public Policy and Social Change in America, 1900–1930* (1994). A comprehensive study of public policymaking on local and national levels in early twentieth-century America.

Arthur Link and Richard L. McCormick, *Progressivism* (1983). The best overview of progressivism and electoral politics.

Daniel T. Rodgers, *Atlantic Crossings: Social Politics in a Progressive Age* (1998). A magisterial work of comparative history focusing on the transnational conversations that deeply influenced American progressive thinkers and reformers.

Elizabeth Sanders, *Roots of Reform: Farmers, Workers, and the American State, 1877–1917* (1999). Arguing for the centrality of agrarian movements in shaping progressive era reform, Sanders explores the irony of how these efforts led to an increasingly bureaucratic state.

Kathryn Kish Sklar, *Florence Kelley and the Nation's Work* (1995). The first installment in a two-volume biography, this book brilliantly brings Florence Kelley alive within the rich context of late nineteenth-century women's political culture.

Christine Stansell, *American Moderns: Bohemian New York and the Creation of a New Century* (2000). Vividly written account that places radical politics and "New Women" at the center of the shaping of modernism.

On the other hand, if there is little enthusiasm, the people everywhere are taking the war as a grim necessity, feeling that they have been forced into it by events beyond their control . . .

—Ray Stannard Baker, June 17, 1917

Female workers build a vehicle in an engineering shop in 1917.

22

WORLD WAR I
1914–1920

HOW DID Theodore Roosevelt use force as component of U.S. foreign policy?

WHY DID most Americans oppose U.S. involvement in World War I in 1914?

HOW DID the federal government try to change public opinion about U.S. involvement in World War I?

WHAT WERE the domestic effects in the United States of World War I?

WHAT STEPS did the federal government take to suppress the antiwar movement?

WHAT WERE the most important elements of Woodrow Wilson's Fourteen Points?

AMERICAN COMMUNITIES
Vigilante Justice in Bisbee, Arizona

EARLY IN THE MORNING OF JULY 12, 1917, 2,000 ARMED VIGILANTES swept through Bisbee, Arizona, acting on behalf of the Phelps-Dodge mining company and Bisbee's leading businessmen to break a bitter strike that had crippled Bisbee's booming copper industry. The vigilantes seized miners in their homes, on the street, and in restaurants and stores. Any miner who wasn't working or willing to work was herded into Bisbee's downtown plaza, where two machine guns commanded the scene. From the Plaza more than 2,000 were marched to the local baseball park. There mine managers gave them a last chance to return to work. Hundreds accepted and were released. The remaining 1,400 were forced at gunpoint onto a freight train, which took them 173 miles east to Columbus, New Mexico, where they were dumped in the desert.

The Bisbee deportation occurred against a complex backdrop. America had just entered World War I, corporations were seeking higher profits, and labor militancy was on the rise. Bisbee was only one of many American communities to suffer vigilantism during the war. Any number of offenses—not displaying a flag, failing to buy war bonds, criticizing the draft, alleged spying, any apparently "disloyal" behavior—could trigger vigilante action. In Western communities like Bisbee, vigilantes used the superpatriotic mood to settle scores with labor organizers and radicals.

Arizona was the leading producer of copper in the United States. With a population of 8,000, Bisbee lay in the heart of the state's richest mining district. The giant Phelps-Dodge Company dominated Bisbee's political and social life. It owned the town's hospital, department store, newspaper, library, and largest hotel. With the introduction of new technology and open pit mining after 1900, unskilled laborers—most of them Slavic, Italian, Czech, and Mexican immigrants—had increasingly replaced skilled American and English-born miners in Bisbee's work force.

America's entry into the war pushed the price of copper to an all-time high, prompting Phelps-Dodge to increase production. Miners viewed the increased demand for labor as an opportunity to flex their own muscle and improve wages and working conditions. Two rival union locals, one affiliated with the American Federation of Labor (AFL), the other with the more radical Industrial Workers of the World (IWW), or "Wobblies," sought to organize Bisbee's workers. On June 26, 1917, Bisbee's Wobblies went on strike. They demanded better mine safety, an end to discrimination against union workers, and a substantial pay increase. The IWW, making special efforts to attract lower paid, foreign-born workers to their cause, even hired two Mexican organizers. Although the IWW had only 300 or 400 members in Bisbee, more than half the town's 4,700 miners supported the strike.

The walkout was peaceful, but Walter Douglas, district manager for Phelps-Dodge, was unmoved. "There will be no compromise," he declared, "because you cannot compromise with a rattlesnake." Douglas, Cochise County Sheriff Harry Wheeler, and Bisbee's leading businessmen met secretly to plan the July 12 deportation. The approximately 2,000 men they deputized to carry it out were members of Bisbee's Citizens' Protective League and the Workers Loyalty League. These vigilantes included company officials, small businessmen, professionals, and antiunion workers. Local telephone and telegraph offices agreed to isolate Bisbee by censoring outgoing messages. The El Paso and Southwestern Railroad, a subsidiary of Phelps-Dodge, provided the waiting boxcars.

The participants in this illegal conspiracy defended themselves by exaggerating the threat of organized labor. They also appealed to patriotism and played on racial fears. The IWW opposed American involvement in the war, making it vulnerable to charges of disloyalty. A proclamation, posted in Bisbee the day of the deportation, claimed, "There is no labor trouble—we are sure of that—but a direct attempt to embarrass and injure the government of the United States." Sheriff Wheeler told a visiting journalist he worried that Mexicans "would take advantage of the disturbed conditions of the strike and start an uprising, destroying the mines and murdering American women and children."

An army census of the deportees, who had found temporary refuge at an army camp in Columbus, New Mexico, offered quite a different picture. Of the 1,400 men, 520 owned property in Bisbee. Nearly 500 had already registered for the draft, and more than 200 had purchased Liberty Bonds. More than 400 were married with children; only 400 were members of the IWW. Eighty percent were immigrants, including nearly 400 Mexicans. A presidential mediation committee concluded that "conditions in Bisbee were in fact peaceful and free from manifestations of disorder or violence." The deported miners nonetheless found it difficult to shake the accusations that their strike was anti-American and foreign inspired.

At their camp, the miners organized their own police force and elected an executive committee to seek relief. In a letter to President Wilson, they claimed "Common American citizens here are now convinced that they have no constitutional rights." They promised to return to digging copper if the federal government operated the nation's mines and smelters. IWW leader William D. "Big Bill" Haywood threatened a general strike of metal miners and harvest workers if the government did not return the deportees to their homes. The presidential mediation committee criticized the mine companies and declared the deportation illegal, but it also denied that the federal government had any jurisdiction in the matter. Arizona's attorney general refused to offer protection for a return to Bisbee.

Bisbee

In September, the men began gradually to drift away from Columbus. Only a few ever returned to Bisbee. The events convinced President Wilson that the IWW was a subversive organization and a threat to national security. The Justice Department began planning an all-out legal assault that would soon cripple the Wobblies. But Wilson could not ignore protests against the Bisbee outrage from such prominent and patriotic Americans as Samuel Gompers, head of the American Federation of Labor. To demonstrate his administration's commitment to harmonious industrial relations, the president appointed a special commission to investigate and mediate wartime labor conflicts. But Arizona's mines would remain union free until the New Deal era of the 1930s.

America's entry into the war created a national sense of purpose and an unprecedented mobilization of resources. Unifying the country and winning the war now took precedence over progressive reforms. The war also aroused powerful political emotions and provided an excuse for some citizens to try to cleanse their communities of anyone who did not conform. In a 1918 speech, Arizona State Senator Fred Sutter hailed the benefits of vigilante justice. "And what are the results in Bisbee since the deportation?" he asked. "They are, sir, a practically 100 percent American camp; a foreigner to get a job there today had to give a pretty good account of himself. The mines are today producing more copper than ever before and we are a quiet, peaceful, law-abiding community and will continue so, so long as the IWWs or other enemies of the government let us alone."

Becoming a World Power

Roosevelt: The Big Stick

Like many of his class and background, Theodore Roosevelt took for granted the superiority of Protestant Anglo-American culture and the goal of spreading its values and influence. He believed that to maintain and increase its economic and political stature, America must be militarily strong. In 1900 Roosevelt summarized his activist views, declaring, "I have always been fond of the West African proverb, 'Speak softly and carry a big stick, you will go far.'"

Roosevelt brought the "big stick" approach to several disputes in the Caribbean region. Since the 1880s, several British, French, and American companies had pursued various plans for building a canal across the Isthmus of Panama, thereby connecting the Atlantic and Pacific Oceans. Roosevelt tried to negotiate a leasing agreement with Colombia, of which Panama was a province. But when the Colombian Senate rejected a final American offer in the fall of 1903, Roosevelt invented a new strategy. A combination of native forces and foreign promoters associated with the canal project plotted a revolt against Colombia. Roosevelt kept in touch with at least one leader of the revolt, Philippe Bunau-Varilla, an engineer and agent for the New Panama Canal Company, and the president let him know that U.S. warships were steaming toward Panama.

On November 3, 1903, just as the USS *Nashville* arrived in Colón harbor, the province of Panama declared itself independent of Colombia. The United States immediately recognized the new Republic of Panama. Less than two weeks later, Bunau-Varilla, serving as a minister from Panama, signed a treaty granting the United States full sovereignty in perpetuity over a ten-mile-wide canal zone. America guaranteed Panama's independence and agreed to pay it $10 million initially and an additional $250,000 a year for the canal zone. Years after the canal was completed, the U.S. Senate voted another $25 million to Colombia as compensation.

The Panama Canal was a triumph of modern engineering and gave the United States a tremendous strategic and commercial advantage in the Western Hemisphere. It took eight years to build and cost hundreds of poorly paid manual workers their lives. Several earlier attempts to build a canal in the region had

HOW DID Theodore Roosevelt use force as a component of U.S. foreign policy?

IMAGE KEY
for pages 586–587

a. British Prime Minister Lloyd George, French Prime Minister George Clemenceau, and U.S. President Woodrow Wilson in Versailles, France in 1919.

b. Women war workers working in an engineering shop, 1917.

c. The *New York Times*: the sinking of the *Lusitania* in 1915.

d. A British World War I biplane being shot down.

e. A 1905 cartoon from *Judge* magazine.

f. President Woodrow Wilson reading his war message to Congress, April, 1917.

g. An American World War I Liberty Loan poster.

h. Women draft protesters at New York's City Hall June 1917.

i. A portrait of Woodrow Wilson (1856–1924).

failed, but with better equipment and a vigorous campaign against disease, the United States succeeded. In 1914, after $720 million in construction costs, the first merchant ships sailed through the canal.

"The inevitable effect of our building the Canal," wrote Secretary of State Elihu Root in 1905, "must be to require us to police the surrounding premises." Roosevelt agreed. He was especially concerned that European powers might step in if America did not. In 1903 Great Britain, Germany, and Italy had imposed a blockade on Venezuela in a dispute over debt payments owed to private investors. To prevent armed intervention by the Europeans, Roosevelt in 1904 proclaimed what became known as the **Roosevelt Corollary** to the **Monroe Doctrine**. "Chronic wrongdoing, or an impotence which results in a general loosening of the ties of civilized society," the statement read, justified "the exercise of an international police power" anywhere in the hemisphere. Roosevelt invoked the corollary to justify U.S. intervention in the region, beginning with the Dominican Republic in 1905. He and later presidents cited the corollary to justify armed intervention in the internal affairs of Cuba, Haiti, Nicaragua, and Mexico.

With the outbreak of the Russo-Japanese War in 1904, Roosevelt worried about the future of the **Open Door** policy in Asia. In 1899, in a series of diplomatic notes, Secretary of State John Hay had won approval for the so-called Open Door approach, giving all nations equal access to trading and development rights in China. A total victory by Russia or Japan could upset the balance of power in East Asia and threaten American business enterprises there. He became especially concerned after the Japanese scored a series of military victories over Russia and began to loom as a dominant power in East Asia.

Roosevelt mediated a settlement of the Russo-Japanese War at Portsmouth, New Hampshire, in 1905 (for which he was awarded the 1906 Nobel Peace Prize). In this settlement, Japan won recognition of its dominant position in Korea and consolidated its economic control over Manchuria. Yet repeated incidents of anti-Japanese racism in California kept American-Japanese relations strained.

Roosevelt built up American naval strength in the Pacific, and in 1908 he sent battleships to visit Japan in a muscle-flexing display of sea power. In that same year, the two burgeoning Pacific powers reached a reconciliation. The Root-Takahira Agreement affirmed the "existing status quo" in Asia, mutual respect for territorial possessions in the Pacific, and the Open Door trade policy in China.

WILSON: MORALISM AND REALISM IN MEXICO

Right after he took office in 1913, President Wilson had to face international crises of a scope and complexity unprecedented in U.S. history. Wilson had no experience in diplomacy, but he brought to foreign affairs a set of fundamental principles that combined a moralist's faith in American democracy with a realist's understanding of the power of international commerce. He believed that American economic expansion, accompanied by democratic principles and Christianity, was a civilizing force in the world.

Wilson, like most corporate and political leaders of the day, emphasized foreign investments and industrial exports as the keys to the nation's prosperity. He believed that the United States, with its superior industrial efficiency, could achieve supremacy in world commerce if artificial barriers to free trade were removed. He championed and extended the Open Door principles of John Hay, advocating strong diplomatic and military measures "for making ourselves supreme in the world from an economic point of view." Wilson often couched his vision of a dynamic, expansive American capitalism in terms of a moral crusade. Yet he quickly found that the complex realities of power politics could interfere with moral vision.

Roosevelt Corollary   President Theodore Roosevelt's policy asserting U.S. authority to intervene in the affairs of Latin American nations; an expansion of the Monroe Doctrine.

Monroe Doctrine   In December 1823, Monroe declared to Congress that Americans "are henceforth not to be considered as subjects for future colonization by any European power."

Open Door   American policy of seeking equal trade and investment opportunities in foreign nations or regions.

Wilson's policies toward Mexico, which foreshadowed the problems he would encounter in World War I, best illustrate his difficulties. The 1911 Mexican Revolution had overthrown the brutally corrupt dictatorship of Porfirio Díaz, and popular leader Francisco Madero had won wide support by promising democracy and economic reform for millions of landless peasants. U.S. businessmen, however, were nervous about the future of their investments, which totaled over $1 billion, an amount greater than Mexico's own investment and more than all other foreign investment in that country combined. Wilson at first gave his blessing to the revolutionary movement, but right before he took office, he was stunned by the ousting and murder of Madero by his chief lieutenant, General Victoriano Huerta. Other nations, including Great Britain and Japan, recognized the Huerta regime, but Wilson refused. He announced that the United States would support only governments that rested on the rule of law. An armed faction opposed to Huerta, known as the Constitutionalists and led by Venustiano Carranza, emerged in Northern Mexico. Both sides rejected an effort by Wilson to broker a compromise between them. Carranza, an ardent nationalist, pressed for the right to buy U.S. arms, which he won in 1914. Wilson also isolated Huerta diplomatically by persuading the British to withdraw their support in exchange for American guarantees of English property interests in Mexico.

But Huerta stubbornly remained in power. In April 1914 Wilson used a minor insult to U.S. sailors in Tampico as an excuse to invade. American naval forces bombarded and then occupied Veracruz, the main port through which Huerta received arms shipments. Wilson accepted the offer of the ABC Powers—Argentina, Brazil, and Chile—to mediate the dispute. Huerta rejected a plan for him to step aside in favor of a provisional government. But then in August, Carranza managed to overthrow Huerta. Playing to nationalist sentiment, Carranza too denounced Wilson for his intervention.

As war loomed in Europe, Mexico's revolutionary politics continued to frustrate Wilson. For a brief period Wilson threw his support behind Francisco "Pancho" Villa, Carranza's former ally who now led a rebel army of his own in northen Mexico.

Mexican revolutionary leaders and sometime allies Francisco "Pancho" Villa (center) and Emiliano Zapata (right) are shown at the National Palace in Mexico City, ca. 1916. Zapata's army operated out of a base in the Southern agricultural state of Morelos, while Villa's army controlled large portions of Mexico's north. In 1914 Villa captured the imagination of American reformers, journalists, and moviemakers with his military exploits against the oppressive Huerta regime. But in 1916, after several border clashes between his forces and U.S. military units, President Wilson dispatched a punitive expedition in pursuit of Villa.

Culver Pictures, Inc. (PE0151CP007023)

Militarism   The tendency to see military might as the most important and best tool for the expansion of a nation's power and prestige.

Imperialism   The policy and practice of exploiting nations and peoples for the benefit of an imperial power either directly through military occupation and colonial rule or indirectly through economic domination of resources and markets.

WHY DID most Americans oppose U.S. involvement in World War I in 1914?

22–1
The Great War

Allies   In World War I, Britain, France, Russia, and other belligerent nations fighting against the Central Powers but not including the United States.

But Carranza's forces dealt Villa a major setback in April 1915. In October, its attention focused on the war in Europe, the Wilson administration recognized Carranza as Mexico's de facto president. Meanwhile Pancho Villa, feeling betrayed, turned on the United States and tried to provoke a crisis that might draw Washington into war with Mexico. In 1916, Villa led several raids in Mexico and across the border into the United States that killed a few dozen Americans. The man once viewed by Wilson as a fighter for democracy was now dismissed as a dangerous bandit.

In March 1916, enraged by Villa's defiance, Wilson dispatched General John J. Pershing and an army that eventually numbered 15,000 to capture him. For a year, Pershing's troops chased Villa in vain, penetrating 300 miles into Mexico. The invasion made Villa a symbol of national resistance in Mexico. Skirmishes between American forces and Carranza's army brought the two nations to the brink of war again in June 1916. Wilson prepared a message to Congress asking permission for American troops to occupy all of Northern Mexico, but he never delivered it. There was fierce opposition to war with Mexico throughout the country. Perhaps more important, mounting tensions with Germany caused Wilson to hesitate. He told an aide that "Germany is anxious to have us at war with Mexico, so that our minds and our energies will be taken off the great war across the sea." Wilson thus accepted negotiations by a face-saving international commission.

Wilson's attempt to guide the course of Mexico's revolution and protect U.S. interests left a bitter legacy of suspicion and distrust in Mexico. It also suggested the limits of a foreign policy tied to a moral vision rooted in the idea of American exceptionalism. **Militarism** and **imperialism**, Wilson had believed, were hallmarks of the old European way. American liberal values—rooted in capitalist development, democracy, and free trade—were the wave of the future. Wilson declared that he had no desire to interfere with Mexican sovereignty. But in both cases that is exactly what he did. The United States, he argued, must actively use its enormous moral and material power to create the new order. That principle would soon engage America in Europe's bloodiest war and its most momentous revolution.

THE GREAT WAR

THE GUNS OF AUGUST

Only a complex and fragile system of alliances had kept the European powers at peace with each other since 1871. Two great competing camps had evolved by 1907: the Triple Alliance (also known as the Central Powers), which included Germany, Austria-Hungary, and Italy; and the Triple Entente (also known as the **Allies**), which included Great Britain, France, and Russia. At the heart of this division was the competition between Great Britain, long the world's dominant colonial and commercial power, and Germany, which had powerful aspirations for an empire of its own.

The alliance system managed to keep small conflicts from escalating into larger ones for most of the late nineteenth and early twentieth centuries. But its inclusiveness was also its weakness: the alliance system threatened to entangle many nations in any war that did erupt. On June 28, 1914, Archduke Franz Ferdinand, heir to the throne of the unstable Austro-Hungarian Empire, was assassinated in Sarajevo, Bosnia. The archduke's killer was a Serbian nationalist who believed the Austro-Hungarian province of Bosnia ought to be annexed to neighboring Serbia. Germany pushed Austria-Hungary to retaliate against Serbia, and the Serbians in turn asked Russia for help.

By early August both sides had exchanged declarations of war and begun mobilizing their forces. Germany invaded Belgium and prepared to move across the French border. But after the German armies were stopped at the River Marne in September, the war settled into a long, bloody stalemate. New and grimly efficient weapons, such as the machine gun and the tank, and the horrors of trench warfare meant unprecedented casualties for all involved. Centered in Northern France, the fighting killed 5 million people over the next two and a half years.

AMERICAN NEUTRALITY

The outbreak of war in Europe shocked Americans. President Wilson issued a formal proclamation of neutrality and urged citizens to be "impartial in thought as well as in action."

Both sides bombarded the United States with vigorous propaganda campaigns. The British effectively exploited their bonds of language and heritage with Americans. Reports of looting, raping, and the killing of innocent civilians by German troops circulated widely in the press. Many of these atrocity stories were exaggerated. German propagandists blamed the war on Russian expansionism and France's desire to avenge its defeat by Germany in 1870–1871. It is difficult to measure the impact of war propaganda on American public opinion. As a whole, though, it highlighted the terrible human costs of the war and, thus, strengthened the conviction that America should stay out of it.

Economic ties between the United States and the Allies were perhaps the greatest barrier to true neutrality. Early in the war Britain imposed a blockade on all shipping to Germany. The United States, as a neutral country, might have insisted on the right of nonbelligerents to trade with both sides, as required by international law. But in practice, although Wilson protested the blockade, he wanted to avoid antagonizing Britain and disrupting trade between the United States and the Allies. Trade with Germany all but ended while trade with the Allies increased dramatically. As war orders poured in from Britain and France, the value of American trade with the Allies shot up from $824 million in 1914 to $3.2 billion in 1916. Increased trade with the Allies helped produce a great economic boom at home, and the United States became neutral in name only.

PREPAREDNESS AND PEACE

In February 1915, Germany declared the waters around the British Isles to be a war zone, a policy that it would enforce with unrestricted submarine warfare. All enemy shipping, despite the requirements of international law to the contrary, would be subject to surprise submarine attack. Neutral powers were warned that the problems of identification at sea put their ships at risk.

On May 7, 1915, a German U-boat sank the British liner *Lusitania* off the coast of Ireland. Among the 1,198 people who died were 128 American citizens. The *Lusitania* was in fact secretly carrying war materials, and passengers had been warned about a possible attack. Wilson nevertheless denounced the sinking as illegal and inhuman, and the American press loudly condemned the act as barbaric. An angry exchange of diplomatic notes led Secretary of State William Jennings Bryan to resign in protest against a policy he thought too warlike.

Tensions heated up again in March 1916 when a German U-boat torpedoed the *Sussex*, an unarmed French passenger ship, injuring four Americans. President Wilson threatened to break off diplomatic relations with Germany unless it abandoned its methods of submarine warfare. Germany promised that all vessels would be visited prior to attack, but this crisis prompted Wilson to begin preparing for war. The National Security League, active in large Eastern cities and bankrolled by conservative banking and commercial interests, helped push for a

QUICK REVIEW

The Outbreak of War

- June 28, 1914: Archduke Franz Ferdinand assassinated.
- July 28, 1914: Austria declares war on Serbia with German support.
- Chain reaction draws all European powers into the war.

QUICK REVIEW

Anglo-American Ties

- 1915: United States gave tacit support to British naval blockade of Germany.
- May 1915: German submarine sank the *Lusitania*.
- Americans demanded a tough stand against Germany but did not want to be drawn into the war.

The New York Times printed a special Extra edition announcing that a German submarine had torpedoed the British passenger liner *Lusitania* on May 7, 1915, off the Irish coast. The ship's manifest later revealed that the *Lusitania* carried a shipment of arms along with its passengers. The 1,198 lives lost included 128 Americans, and the incident helped push the United States toward "preparedness" for war.

©Bettmann/CORBIS (PG3064A)

22–2
Boy Scouts of America, from "Boy Scouts Support the War Effort" (1917)

bigger army and navy and, most important, a system of universal military training. In June 1916, Congress passed the National Defense Act, which more than doubled the size of the regular army. In August, Congress passed a bill that dramatically increased spending for new battleships, cruisers, and destroyers.

Not all Americans supported these preparations for battle, and opposition to military buildup found expression in scores of American communities. As early as August 29, 1914, 1,500 women clad in black had marched down New York's Fifth Avenue in the Woman's Peace Parade. Out of this gathering evolved the American Union against Militarism, which lobbied against the **preparedness** campaign and against intervention in Mexico. Antiwar feeling was especially strong in the South and Midwest. A group of thirty to fifty House Democrats, led by majority leader Claude Kitchin of North Carolina, stubbornly opposed Wilson's military buildup.

A large reservoir of popular antiwar sentiment flowed through the culture in various ways. Movie director Thomas Ince won a huge audience for his 1916 film *Civilization*, which depicted Christ returning to reveal the horrors of war to world leaders. Two of the most popular songs of 1915 were "Don't Take My Darling Boy Away" and "I Didn't Raise My Boy to Be a Soldier."

Wilson acknowledged the active opposition to involvement in the war by adopting the winning slogan "He Kept Us Out of War" in the 1916 presidential campaign. He made a point of appealing to progressives of all kinds, stressing his support for the eight-hour day and his administration's efforts on behalf of farmers. The war-induced prosperity no doubt helped him to defeat conservative Republican Charles Evans Hughes in a very close election. But Wilson knew that the peace was as fragile as his victory.

SAFE FOR DEMOCRACY

By the end of January 1917, Germany's leaders had decided against a negotiated peace settlement, placing their hopes instead in a final decisive offensive against the Allies. On February 1, 1917, with the aim of breaking the British blockade, Germany declared unlimited submarine warfare, with no warnings, knowing that it

Preparedness Military buildup in preparation for possible U.S. participation in World War I.

might bring America into the conflict. In effect, German leaders were gambling that they could destroy the ability of the Allies to fight before the United States would be able to effectively mobilize manpower and resources.

Wilson was indignant and disappointed. Germany had made it impossible for him to preserve his twin goals of U.S. neutrality and freedom of the seas. He broke off diplomatic relations with Germany and called on Congress to approve the arming of U.S. merchant ships. On March 1, the White House shocked the country when it made public a recently intercepted coded message, sent by German foreign secretary Arthur Zimmermann to the German ambassador in Mexico. The Zimmermann note proposed that an alliance be made between Germany and Mexico if the United States entered the war. Zimmermann suggested that Mexico take up arms against the United States and receive in return the "lost territory in New Mexico, Texas, and Arizona." The specter of a German-Mexican alliance helped turn the tide of public opinion in the Southwest, where opposition to U.S. involvement in the war had been strong.

Revelation of the Zimmermann note stiffened Wilson's resolve. He issued an executive order in mid-March authorizing the arming of all merchant ships and allowing them to shoot at submarines. In that month, German U-boats sank seven U.S. merchant ships, leaving a heavy death toll. Anti-German feeling increased, and thousands took part in prowar demonstrations in New York, Boston, Philadelphia, and other cities. Wilson finally called a special session of Congress to ask for a declaration of war.

On April 2, 1917, on a rainy night before a packed and very quiet assembly, Wilson made his case. He reviewed the escalation of submarine warfare and said that neutrality was no longer feasible or desirable. But the conflict was not merely about U.S. shipping rights, Wilson argued. He employed highly idealistic language to make the case for war, reflecting his deeply held belief that America had a special mission as mankind's most enlightened and advanced nation: "The world must be made safe for democracy. Its peace must be planted upon the tested foundations of political liberty."

Wilson's eloquent speech won over the Congress, most of the press, and even his bitterest political critics, such as Theodore Roosevelt. On April 6, President Wilson signed the declaration of war. All that remained was to win over the American public.

AMERICAN MOBILIZATION

SELLING THE WAR

Just a week after signing the war declaration, Wilson created the **Committee on Public Information (CPI)** to organize public opinion. It was dominated by its civilian chairman, the journalist and reformer George Creel. Creel quickly transformed the CPI from its original function as coordinator of government news into a sophisticated and aggressive agency for promoting the war. To sell the war, Creel raised the art of public relations to new heights. He enlisted more than 150,000 people to work on a score of CPI committees. They produced more than 100 million pieces of literature—pamphlets, articles, books—that explained the causes and meaning of the war. The CPI also created posters, slides, newspaper advertising, and films to promote the war. It called upon movie stars such as Charlie Chaplin, Mary Pickford, and Douglas Fairbanks to help sell war bonds at huge rallies. Famous journalists like the muckraker Ida Tarbell and well-known artists like Charles Dana Gibson were recruited. Across the nation, a volunteer army of 75,000 "Four Minute Men" gave brief patriotic speeches before stage and movie shows.

HOW DID the federal government try to change public opinion about U.S. involvement in World War I?

Committee on Public Information (CPI) Government agency during World War I that sought to shape public opinion in support of the war effort through newspapers, pamphlets, speeches, films, and other media.

Halt the Hun. This 1918 Liberty Loan poster used anti-German sentiment to encourage the purchase of war bonds. Its depiction of an American soldier as the protector of an innocent mother and child implied that the Germans were guilty of unspeakable war crimes.

Howard Chandler Christy, *Hold the Hun! Fight or Buy Bonds*, poster, 1917. Museum of the City of New York, gift of John Campbell. The Granger Collection (4E695.09)

22–6
Newton B. Baker, "The Treatment of German-Americans" (1918)

QUICK REVIEW

African American Soldiers

◆ 200,000 African Americans served in France.

◆ One in five saw combat.

◆ African American combat units served with distinction in the French army.

The CPI led an aggressively negative campaign against all things German. Posters and advertisements depicted the Germans as Huns, bestial monsters outside the civilized world. German music and literature, indeed the German language itself, were suspect, and were banished from the concert halls, schools, and libraries of many communities. The CPI also urged ethnic Americans to abandon their Old World ties, to become "unhyphenated Americans."

"YOU'RE IN THE ARMY NOW"

Traditionally, the United States had relied on volunteer forces organized at the state level. But volunteer rates after April 6 were less than they had been for the Civil War or the Spanish-American War, reflecting the softness of prowar sentiment. The administration, thus, introduced the **Selective Service Act**, which provided for the registration and classification for military service of all men between ages twenty-one and thirty-five. To prevent the widespread opposition to the draft that had occurred during the Civil War, the new draft had no unpopular provision allowing draftees to buy their way out of service by paying for a substitute.

On June 5, 1917, nearly 10 million men registered for the draft. There was scattered organized resistance, but overall, registration records offered evidence of national support. A supplemental registration in August 1918 extended the age limits to eighteen and forty-five. Of the 2.8 million men eventually called up for service, about 340,000, or 12 percent, failed to show up. Another 2 million Americans volunteered for the various armed services.

The vast polyglot army posed unprecedented challenges of organization and control. But progressive elements within the administration also saw opportunities for pressing reform measures involving education, alcohol, and sex. Army psychologists gave the new Stanford-Binet intelligence test to all recruits and were shocked to find illiteracy rates as high as 25 percent. The low test scores among recent immigrants and rural African Americans undoubtedly reflected the cultural biases embedded in the tests.

African Americans were organized into totally segregated units, barred entirely from the marines and the Coast Guard, and largely relegated to working as cooks, laundrymen, stevedores, and the like in the army and navy. Thousands of black soldiers endured humiliating, sometimes violent treatment, particularly from Southern white officers. African American servicemen faced hostility from white civilians as well, North and South, often being denied service in restaurants and admission to theaters near training camps.

More than 200,000 African Americans eventually served in France, but only about one in five saw combat, as opposed to two out of three white soldiers. Black combat units served with distinction in various divisions of the French army. The all-black 369th U.S. Infantry, for example, saw the first and longest service of any American regiment deployed in a foreign army, serving in the trenches for 191 days. The French government awarded the Croix de Guerre to the entire regiment, and 171 officers and enlisted men were cited individually for exceptional bravery in action. African American soldiers by and large enjoyed a friendly reception from French civilians as well. The contrast with their treatment at home would remain a sore point with these troops upon their return to the United States.

African American troops advance toward the sound of gunfire in northern France, 1918. Nearly 400,000 black men served in World War I, but due to the racist beliefs held by most military and political leaders, only 42,000 went into combat. "Many of the white field officers," wrote black Lieutenant Howard H. Long, "seemed far more concerned with reminding their Negro subordinates that they were Negroes than they were in having an effective unit that would perform well in combat."

Brown Brothers (F149)

AMERICANS IN BATTLE

Shipping tonnage lost each month to submarine warfare had been reduced to 200,000; the flow of weapons, supplies, and troops continued. No American soldiers were lost on the way to Europe.

President Wilson appointed General John J. Pershing, recently returned from pursuing Pancho Villa in Mexico, as commander of the American Expeditionary Force (AEF). Pershing insisted that the AEF maintain its own identity, distinct from that of the French and British armies. He was also reluctant to send American troops into battle before they had received at least six months' training. The AEF's combat role would be brief but intense: not until early 1918 did AEF units reach the front in large numbers; eight months later the war was over.

In the early spring of 1918 the Germans launched a major offensive that brought them within fifty miles of Paris. In early June about 70,000 AEF soldiers helped the French stop the Germans in the battles of Château-Thierry and Belleau Wood. In July, Allied forces led by Marshal Ferdinand Foch of France, began a counteroffensive designed to defeat Germany once and for all. American reinforcements began flooding the ports of Liverpool in England and Brest and Saint-Nazaire in France. The "doughboys" (a nickname for soldiers dating back to Civil War–era recruits who joined the army for the money) streamed in at a rate of over 250,000 a month. By September, General Pershing had more than a million Americans in his army.

In late September 1918, the AEF took over the southern part of a 200-mile front in the Meuse-Argonne offensive. In seven weeks of fighting, most through terrible mud and rain, U.S. soldiers used more ammunition than the entire Union army had in the four years of the Civil War. The Germans, exhausted and badly outnumbered, began to fall back and look for a cease-fire. On November 11, 1918, the war ended with the signing of an armistice.

The massive influx of American troops and supplies no doubt hastened the end of the war. About two-thirds of the U.S. soldiers saw at least some fighting, but even they managed to avoid the horrors of the sustained trench warfare that had marked the earlier years of the war. For most Americans at the front, the war experience was a mixture of fear, exhaustion, and fatigue. Their time in France would

22–4
American Troops in the Trenches (1918)

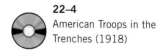

Selective Service Act   The law establishing the military draft for World War I.

MAP EXPLORATION

To explore an interactive version of this map, go to **http://www.prenhall.com/faraghertlc/map22.1**

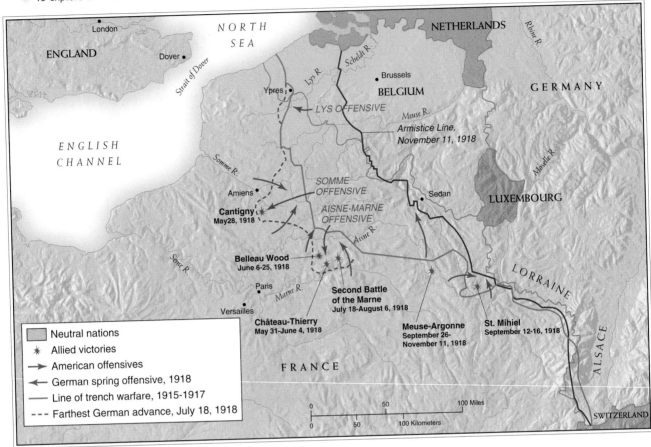

MAP 22-1
The Western Front, 1918   American units saw their first substantial action in late May, helping to stop the German offensive at the Battle of Cantigny. By September, more than 1 million American troops were fighting in a counter offensive campaign at St. Mihiel, the largest single American engagement of the war.

HOW DID the entrance of the United States help turn the tide of World War I?

22–5
Eugene Kennedy,
A "Doughboy" Describes
the Fighting Front (1918)

23–1
J. Grimke, "Address of Welcome
to the Men Who Have Returned
from the Battlefront" (1919)

WHAT WERE the domestic
effects of World War I in the
United States?

remain a decisive moment in their lives. In all, more than 52,000 Americans died in battle. Another 60,000 died from influenza and pneumonia, half of these while still in training camp. More than 200,000 Americans were wounded in the war. These figures, awful as they were, paled against the estimated casualties (killed and wounded) suffered by the European nations: 9 million for Russia, more than 6 million for Germany, nearly 5 million for France, and over 2 million each for Great Britain and Italy.

OVER HERE

ORGANIZING THE ECONOMY

In the summer of 1917 President Wilson established the **War Industries Board (WIB)** as a clearinghouse for industrial mobilization to support the war effort. Led by the successful Wall Street speculator Bernard M. Baruch, the WIB proved a major innovation in expanding the regulatory power of the federal government.

The WIB had to balance price controls against war profits. Only by ensuring a fair rate of return on investment could it encourage stepped-up production.

The WIB eventually handled 3,000 contracts worth $14.5 billion with various businesses. Standardization of goods brought large savings and streamlined production. Baruch continually negotiated with business leaders, describing the system as "voluntary cooperation with the big stick in the cupboard." At first Elbert Gary of U.S. Steel refused to accept the government's price for steel and Henry Ford balked at limiting private car production, but when Baruch warned that he would instruct the military to take over their plants, both industrialists backed down.

In August 1917, Congress passed the Food and Fuel Act, authorizing the president to regulate the production and distribution of the food and fuel necessary for the war effort. To lead the Food Administration (FA), Wilson appointed Herbert Hoover, a millionaire engineer who had already won fame for directing a program of war relief for Belgium. He became one of the best known figures of the war administration. Hoover imposed price controls on certain agricultural commodities, such as sugar, pork, and wheat. These were purchased by the government and then sold to the public through licensed dealers. The FA also raised the purchase price of grain so that farmers would increase production. But Hoover stopped short of imposing mandatory food rationing, preferring to rely on persuasion, high prices, and voluntary controls.

Hoover's success, like George Creel's at the CPI, depended on motivating hundreds of thousands of volunteers in thousands of American communities. The FA coordinated the work of local committees that distributed posters and leaflets urging people to save food, recycle scraps, and substitute for scarce produce. Hoover exhorted Americans to "go back to simple food, simple clothes, simple pleasures." He urged them to grow their own vegetables. These efforts resulted in a sharp cutback in the consumption of sugar and wheat as well as a boost in the supply of livestock. The resultant increase in food exports helped sustain the Allied war effort.

The enormous cost of fighting the war, about $33 billion, required unprecedented large expenditures for the federal government. The tax structure shifted dramatically as a result. Taxes on incomes and profits replaced excise and customs levies as the major source of revenue. The minimum income subject to the graduated federal income tax, in effect only since 1913, was lowered to $1,000 from $3,000, increasing the number of Americans who paid income tax from 437,000 in 1916 to 4,425,000 in 1918. Tax rates were as steep as 70 percent in the highest brackets.

The bulk of war financing came from government borrowing, especially in the form of the popular **Liberty Bonds** sold to the American public. Bond drives became highly organized patriotic campaigns that ultimately raised a total of $23 billion for the war effort. The administration also used the new Federal Reserve Banks to expand the money supply, making borrowing easier. The federal debt jumped from $1 billion in 1915 to $20 billion in 1920.

THE BUSINESS OF WAR

Over all, the war meant expansion and high profits for American business. Between 1916 and 1918, Ford Motor Company increased its work force from 32,000 to 48,000, General Motors from 10,000 to 50,000. Total capital expenditure in U.S. manufacturing jumped from $600 million in 1915 to $2.5 billion in 1918. Corporate profits as a whole nearly tripled between 1914 and 1919, and many large businesses did much better than that. Expanded farm acreage and increased investment in farm machinery led to a jump of 20–30 percent in overall farm production.

War Industries Board (WIB) The federal agency that reorganized industry for maximum efficiency and productivity during World War I.

Liberty Bonds Interest-bearing certificates sold by the U.S. government to finance the American World War I effort.

The most important and long-lasting economic legacy of the war was the organizational shift toward corporatism in American business. Never before had business and the federal government cooperated so closely. Under war administrators like Baruch and Hoover, entire industries (such as radio manufacturing) and economic sectors (such as agriculture and energy) were organized, regulated, and subsidized. War agencies used both public and private power—legal authority and voluntarism—to hammer out and enforce agreements. Here was the genesis of the modern bureaucratic state.

LABOR AND THE WAR

The expansion of the wartime economy often meant severe disruptions and discomfort for America's workers. Overcrowding, rapid work force turnover, and high inflation rates were typical in war-boom communities. In Bridgeport, Connecticut, a center for small-arms manufacturing, the population grew by 50,000 in less than a year. In 1917 the number of families grew by 12,000, but available housing stock increased by only 6,000 units. Chronic congestion became common in many cities.

That same economic expansion, combined with army mobilization and a decline in immigration from Europe, caused a growing wartime labor shortage, so that working people generally enjoyed higher wages and a better standard of living. Trade unions, especially those affiliated with the American Federation of Labor (AFL), enjoyed a sharp rise in membership.

Organized labor's power and prestige, though by no means equal to business's or government's, clearly grew during the war. Samuel Gompers, president of the AFL, pledged the AFL's patriotic support for the war effort, and in April 1918 President Wilson appointed him to the National War Labor Board (NWLB). During 1917 the nation had seen thousands of strikes involving more than a million workers. Wages were usually at issue, reflecting workers' concerns with spiraling inflation and higher prices. The NWLB, co-chaired by labor attorney Frank Walsh and former president William H. Taft, acted as a kind of supreme court for labor, arbitrating disputes and working to prevent disruptions in production. The great majority of these interventions resulted in improved wages and reduced hours of work.

Most important, the NWLB supported the right of workers to organize unions and furthered the acceptance of the eight-hour day for war workers—central aims of the labor movement. It also backed time-and-a-half pay for overtime, as well as the principle of equal pay for women workers. AFL unions gained more than a million new members during the war, and overall union membership rose from 2.7 million in 1914 to more than 5 million by 1920.

If the war boosted the fortunes of the AFL, it also spelled the end for more radical elements of the U.S. labor movement. The Industrial Workers of the World (IWW), unlike the AFL, had concentrated on organizing unskilled workers into all-inclusive industrial unions. The Wobblies denounced capitalism as an unreformable system based on exploitation, and they opposed U.S. entry into the war. IWW leaders advised their members to refuse induction for "the capitalists' war." In September 1917, the Wilson administration responded to appeals from Western business leaders for a crackdown on the Wobblies. Justice Department agents, acting under the broad authority of the recently passed **Espionage Act**, swooped down on IWW offices in more than sixty towns and cities, arresting more than 300 people and confiscating files. The mass trials and convictions that followed broke the back of America's radical labor movement and marked the beginning of a powerful wave of political repression.

Espionage Act Law whose vague prohibition against obstructing the nation's war effort was used to crush dissent and criticism during World War I.

WOMEN AT WORK

For many of the 8 million women already in the labor force, the war meant a chance to switch from low-paying jobs, such as domestic service, to higher paying industrial employment. About a million women workers joined the labor force for the first time. Of the estimated 9.4 million workers directly engaged in war work, some 2.25 million were women. Of these, 1.25 million worked in manufacturing. Female munitions plant workers, train engineers, drill press operators, streetcar conductors, and mail carriers became a common sight around the country.

In response to the widened range of female employment, the Labor Department created the Women in Industry Service (WIS). Directed by Mary Van Kleeck, the service advised employers on using female labor and formulated general standards for the treatment of women workers. The WIS represented the first attempt by the federal government to take a practical stand on improving working conditions for women. Its standards included the eight-hour day, equal pay for equal work, a minimum wage, the prohibition of night work, and the provision of rest periods, meal breaks, and restroom facilities. These standards had no legal force, however, and WIS inspectors found that employers often flouted them. Women also suffered discrimination over pay. Government surveys found that women's average earnings were roughly half of men's in the same industries.

At war's end, women lost nearly all their defense-related jobs. By 1920, more women who worked outside the home did so in white-collar occupations—as telephone operators, secretaries, and clerks, for example—than in manufacturing or domestic service. The new awareness of women's work led Congress to create the Women's Bureau in the Labor Department, which continued the WIS wartime program of education and investigation through the postwar years.

Women workers at the Midvale Steel and Ordinance Company in Pennsylvania, 1918. Wartime labor shortages created new opportunities for over 1 million women to take high-wage manufacturing jobs like these. The opening proved temporary, however, and with the war's end nearly all these women lost their jobs. By 1920 the number of women employed in manufacturing was lower than it had been in 1910.

National Archives and Records Administration (1-SC-31731)

WOMAN SUFFRAGE

The presence of so many new women wageworkers, combined with the highly visible volunteer work of millions of middle-class women, helped finally to secure the vote for women. These women played a key role in the success of the Food Administration, and the Women's Committee of the Council of National Defense included a variety of women's organizations.

Until World War I, the fight for woman suffrage had been waged largely within individual states. Western states and territories had led the way. Ethnocultural divisions between Catholics and Protestants hindered suffrage efforts in the East. The close identification in the East between the suffrage and prohibition movements led many Catholic immigrants and German Lutherans to oppose the vote for women because they feared it would lead to prohibition.

The U.S. entry into the war provided a unique opportunity for suffrage groups to shift their strategy to a national campaign for a constitutional amendment granting the vote to women. Under the leadership of Carrie Chapman Catt, the National American Woman Suffrage Association (NAWSA) threw its support behind the war effort and doubled its membership to 2 million. Catt gambled that a strong show of patriotism would help clinch the century-old fight to win the vote for women. The NAWSA pursued a moderate policy of lobbying Congress for a constitutional amendment and calling for state referendums on woman suffrage.

A young Quaker activist, Alice Paul, injected new energy and more radical tactics into the movement. Dissatisfied with the NAWSA's conservative strategy of quiet lobbying and orderly demonstrations, Paul joined forces with Western women voters to form the National Woman's Party. Borrowing from English suffragists, this party pursued a more aggressive and dramatic strategy of agitation. Paul and her supporters picketed the White House, publicly burned President Wilson's speeches, and condemned the president and the Democrats for failing to produce an amendment. Although some in the NAWSA objected to these tactics, Paul's radical approach helped make the NAWSA position—passage of the

QUICK REVIEW

Votes for Women

◆ Woman suffrage movement began in the mid-nineteenth century.

◆ Early twentieth-century leaders adopted activist tactics.

◆ Nineteenth Amendment ratified in 1920.

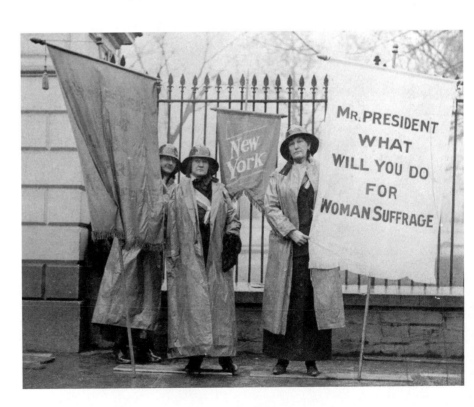

Members of the National Woman's Party (NWP) picketed President Wilson at the White House in 1917. Their militant action in the midst of the war crisis aroused both anger and sympathy. The NWP campaign helped push the president and the Congress to accept woman suffrage as a "war measure."

Library of Congress

MAP EXPLORATION

To explore an interactive version of this map, go to **http://www.prenhall.com/faraghertlc/map22.2**

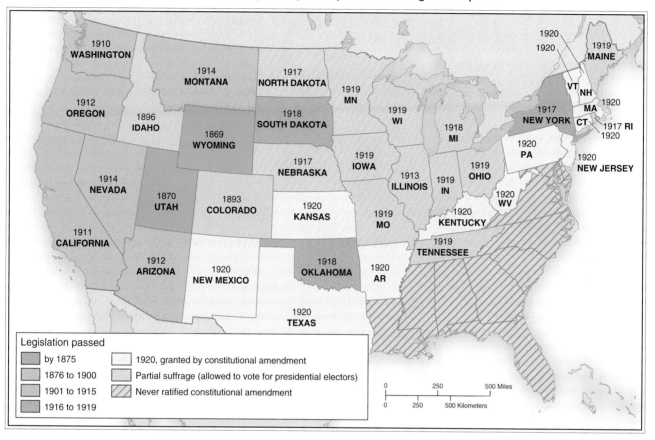

MAP 22-2

Woman Suffrage by State, 1869–1919   Dates for the enactment of woman suffrage in the individual states. Years before ratification of the Nineteenth Amendment in 1920, a number of Western states had legislated full or partial voting rights for women. In 1917 Montana suffragist Jeannette Rankin became the first woman elected to Congress.

Barbara G. Shortridge, *Atlas of American Women* (New York: Macmillan, 1987)

WHAT WERE the reasons behind the regional differences in support of woman suffrage?

woman suffrage amendment as a "war measure"—more acceptable to Wilson. In 1917 the president urged Congress to pass a woman suffrage amendment as "vital to the winning of the war." The House did so in January 1918 and a more reluctant Senate approved it in June 1919. Another year of hard work was spent convincing the state legislatures. In August 1920, Tennessee gave the final vote needed to ratify the Nineteenth Amendment to the Constitution, finally making woman suffrage legal nationwide.

PROHIBITION

Another reform effort closely associated with women's groups triumphed at the same time. The movement to eliminate alcohol from American life had attracted many Americans, especially women, since before the Civil War. Temperance advocates saw drinking as the source of many of the worst problems faced by the working class, including family violence, unemployment, and poverty. By the early twentieth century the Woman's Christian Temperance Union, with a quarter-million members, had become the single largest women's organization in American history.

The moral fervor that accompanied America's entry into the war provided a crucial boost to the cause. With so many breweries bearing German names, the movement benefited as well from the strong anti-German feeling of the war years. Outlawing beer and whiskey would also help conserve precious grain, prohibitionists argued.

In 1917, a coalition of progressives and rural fundamentalists in Congress pushed through a constitutional amendment providing for a national ban on alcoholic drinks. The Eighteenth Amendment was ratified by the states in January 1919 and became the law of the land one year later. Although Prohibition would create a host of problems in the postwar years, especially as a stimulus for the growth of organized crime, many Americans, particularly native Protestants, considered it a worthy moral reform.

REPRESSION AND REACTION

MUZZLING DISSENT: THE ESPIONAGE AND SEDITION ACTS

WHAT STEPS

did the federal government take
to suppress the antiwar movement?

The Espionage Act of June 1917 became the government's key tool for the suppression of antiwar sentiment. It set severe penalties (up to twenty years' imprisonment and a $10,000 fine) for anyone found guilty of aiding the enemy, obstructing recruitment, or causing insubordination in the armed forces. The act also empowered the postmaster general to exclude from the mails any newspapers or magazines he thought treasonous. Within a year the mailing rights of forty-five newpapers had been revoked.

To enforce the Espionage Act, the government had to increase its overall police and surveillance machinery. Civilian intelligence was coordinated by the newly created Bureau of Investigation in the Justice Department. This agency was reorganized after the war as the Federal Bureau of Investigation (FBI). In May 1918 the **Sedition Act**, an amendment to the Espionage Act, outlawed "any disloyal, profane, scurrilous, or abusive language intended to cause contempt, scorn, contumely, or disrepute" to the government, Constitution, or flag.

These acts became a convenient vehicle for striking out at socialists, pacifists, radical labor activists, and others who resisted the patriotic tide. The most celebrated prosecution came in June 1918 when federal agents arrested Eugene V. Debs in Canton, Ohio, after he gave a speech defending antiwar protesters. Debs served thirty-two months in federal prison before being pardoned by President Warren G. Harding on Christmas Day 1921.

The Supreme Court upheld the constitutionality of the acts in several 1919 decisions. In *Debs* v. *United States*, the Court affirmed the guilt of Eugene V. Debs for his antiwar speech in Canton, even though he had not explicitly urged violation of the draft laws. In *Abrams* v. *United States*, the Court upheld Sedition Act convictions of four Russian immigrants who had printed pamphlets denouncing American military intervention in the Russian Revolution.

THE GREAT MIGRATION AND RACIAL TENSIONS

Economic opportunity brought on by war prosperity triggered a massive migration of rural black Southerners to Northern cities. From 1914 to 1920, somewhere between 300,000 and 500,000 African Americans left the rural South for the North. Chicago's black population increased by 65,000, or 150 percent; Detroit's by 35,000, or 600 percent. Acute labor shortages led Northern factory managers to recruit black migrants to the expanding industrial centers. The Pennsylvania Railroad alone drew 10,000 black workers from Florida and south Georgia. Black workers

Sedition Act Broad law restricting criticism of America's involvement in World War I or its government, flag, military, taxes, or officials.

This Southern African American family is shown arriving in Chicago around 1910. Black migrants to Northern cities often faced overcrowding, inferior housing, and a high death rate from disease. But the chance to earn daily wages of $6 to $8 (the equivalent of a week's wages in much of the South), as well as the desire to escape persistent racial violence, kept the migrants coming.

Stock Montage, Inc./Historical Pictures Collection

eagerly left low-paying jobs as field hands and domestic servants for the chance at relatively high-paying work in meatpacking plants, shipyards, and steel mills.

Kinship and community networks were crucial in shaping what came to be called the **Great Migration**. They spread news about job openings, urban residential districts, and boardinghouses in Northern cities. Black clubs, churches, and fraternal lodges in Southern communities frequently sponsored the migration of their members, as well as return trips to the South. Single African American women often made the trip first because they could more easily obtain steady work as maids, cooks, and laundresses. Relatively few African American men actually secured high-paying skilled jobs in industry or manufacturing. Most had to settle for work as construction laborers, teamsters, janitors, porters, or other low-paying jobs.

The persistence of lynching and other racial violence in the South no doubt contributed to the Great Migration, but racial violence was not limited to the South. On July 2, 1917, in East St. Louis, Illinois, a ferocious mob of whites attacked African Americans, killing at least 200. Before this riot, some of the city's manufacturers had been steadily recruiting black labor as a way to keep local union demands down. In Chicago, on July 27, 1919, antiblack rioting broke out on a Lake Michigan beach. For two weeks white gangs hunted African Americans in the streets and burned hundreds out of their homes. Twenty-three African Americans and fifteen whites died, and more than 500 were injured.

In both East St. Louis and Chicago, local authorities held African Americans responsible for the violence. President Wilson refused requests for federal intervention or investigation.

Black disillusionment about the war grew quickly. So did a newly militant spirit. A heightened sense of race consciousness and activism was evident among black veterans

22–3
Letters from the Great Migration (1917)

Great Migration The mass movement of African Americans from the rural South to the urban North, spurred especially by new job opportunities during World War I and the 1920s.

and the growing black communities of Northern cities. Taking the lead in the fight against bigotry and injustice, the NAACP held a national conference on lynching in 1919. It pledged to defend persecuted African Americans, publicize the horrors of lynch law, and seek federal legislation against "Judge Lynch." By 1919 membership in the NAACP had reached 60,000 and the circulation of its journal exceeded half a million.

LABOR STRIFE

The relative labor peace of 1917 and 1918 dissolved after the armistice. More than 4 million American workers were involved in some 3,600 strikes in 1919 alone. This unprecedented strike wave had several causes. Most of the modest wartime wage gains were wiped out by spiraling inflation and high prices for food, fuel, and housing. With the end of government controls on industry, many employers withdrew their recognition of unions. Difficult working conditions, such as the twelve-hour day in steel mills, were still routine in some industries.

Several of the postwar strikes received widespread national attention. They seemed to be more than simple economic conflicts, and they provoked deep fears about the larger social order. In February 1919, a strike in the shipyards of Seattle, Washington, over wages escalated into a general citywide strike involving 60,000 workers. The local press and Mayor Ole Hanson denounced the strikers as revolutionaries. Hanson effectively ended the strike by requesting federal troops to occupy the city.

In September, Boston policemen went out on strike when the police commissioner rejected a citizens' commission study that recommended a pay raise. Massachusetts governor Calvin Coolidge called in the National Guard to restore order and won a national reputation by crushing the strike. The entire police force was fired.

The biggest strike took place in the steel industry, involving some 350,000 steelworkers. Centered in several Midwestern cities, this epic struggle lasted from September 1919 to January 1920. The major demands were union recognition, the eight-hour day, and wage increases. The steel companies used black strikebreakers and armed guards to keep the mills running. Elbert Gary, president of U.S. Steel, directed a sophisticated propaganda campaign that branded the strikers as revolutionaries. Public opinion turned against the strike and condoned the use of

The Great Migration: Black Population Growth in Selected Northern Cities, 1910–1920

| City | 1910 | | 1920 | | |
	Number	Percent	Number	Percent	Percent Increase
New York	91,709	1.9	152,467	2.7	66.3
Chicago	44,103	2.0	109,458	4.1	148.2
Philadelphia	84,459	5.5	134,229	7.4	58.9
Detroit	5,741	1.2	40,838	4.1	611.3
St. Louis	43,960	6.4	69,854	9.0	58.9
Cleveland	8,448	1.5	34,451	4.3	307.8
Pittsburgh	25,623	4.8	37,725	6.4	47.2
Cincinnati	19,739	5.4	30,079	7.5	53.2

Source: U.S. Department of Commerce.

state and federal troops to break it. The failed steel strike proved to be the era's most bitter and devastating defeat for organized labor.

An Uneasy Peace

The Fourteen Points

President Wilson arrived in Paris with the United States delegation in January 1919. He brought with him a plan for peace that he had outlined a year earlier in a speech to Congress on U.S. war aims. The Fourteen Points, as they were called, had originally served wartime purposes: to appeal to antiwar factions in Austria-Hungary and Germany, to convince Russia to stay in the war, and to help sustain Allied morale. As a blueprint for peace, they contained three main elements. First, Wilson offered a series of specific proposals for setting postwar boundaries in Europe and creating new countries out of the collapsed Austro-Hungarian and Ottoman Empires. Second, Wilson listed general principles for governing international conduct, including freedom of the seas, free trade, open covenants instead of secret treaties, reduced armaments, and mediation for competing colonial claims. Third, and most important, Wilson called for a **League of Nations** to help implement these principles and resolve future disputes.

WHAT WERE the most important elements of Woodrow Wilson's Fourteen Points?

League of Nations   International organization created by the Versailles Treaty after World War I to ensure world stability.

Woodrow Wilson, Georges Clemenceau, and David Lloyd George are among the central figures depicted in John Christen Johansen's *Signing of the Treaty of Versailles*. But all the gathered statesmen appear dwarfed by their surroundings.

John Christen Johansen, *Signing of the Treaty of Versailles*, 1919. National Portrait Gallery, Smithsonian Institution, Washington, D.C./Art Resource, New York (S0022240)

QUICK REVIEW

Wilson's Fourteen Points

◆ Wilson articulated U.S. war aims in his Fourteen Points.

◆ The Allies did not explicitly support Wilson's program.

◆ Domestic political failures undermined Wilson's position at the Paris Peace Conference.

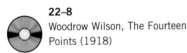

22–8
Woodrow Wilson, The Fourteen Points (1918)

Central Powers Germany and its World War I allies in Austria, Italy, Turkey, and Bulgaria.

Self-determination The right of a people or a nation to decide · on its own political allegiance or form of government without external influence.

Bolsheviks Members of the Communist movement in Russia that established the Soviet government after the 1917 Russian Revolution.

The most controversial element, both at home and abroad, would prove to be the League of Nations, whose covenant called for collective security as the ultimate method of keeping the peace. In the United States, Wilson's critics focused on this provision as an unacceptable surrender of the nation's sovereignty and independence in foreign affairs.

WILSON IN PARIS

Despite Wilson's devotion to "open covenants," much of the negotiating at Versailles was in fact done in secret among the Big Four: Great Britain, France, the United States and Italy. The ideal of self-determination found limited expression. The independent states of Austria, Hungary, Poland, Yugoslavia, and Czechoslovakia were carved out of the homelands of the beaten **Central Powers**. But the Allies resisted Wilson's call for independence for the colonies of the defeated nations. A compromise mandate system of protectorates gave the French and British control of parts of the old German and Turkish empires in Africa and West Asia. Japan won control of former German colonies in China. Among those trying, but failing, to influence the treaty negotiations were the sixty-odd delegates to the first Pan African Congress, held in Paris at the same time as the peace talks. The group included Americans W. E. B. Du Bois and William Monroe Trotter as well as representatives from Africa and the West Indies. All were disappointed with the failure of the peace conference to grant **self-determination** to thousands of Africans living in former German colonies.

Another disappointment for Wilson came with the issue of war guilt. He had strongly opposed the extraction of harsh economic reparations from the Central Powers, but the French and British, with their awful war losses fresh in mind, insisted on making Germany pay. The final treaty contained a clause attributing the war to "the aggression of Germany," and a commission later set German war reparations at $33 billion. Bitter resentment in Germany over the punitive treaty helped sow the seeds for the Nazi rise to power in the 1930s.

Hovering over the proceedings was the specter of the Russian Revolution. The repressive and corrupt regime of Czar Nicholas II had been overthrown in March 1917 by a coalition of forces demanding change. The new provisional government, headed by Alexander Kerensky, vowed to keep Russia in the fight against Germany. But the war had taken a terrible toll on Russian soldiers and civilians and had become very unpopular. The radical **Bolsheviks**, led by V. I. Lenin, gained a large following by promising "peace, land, and bread," and they began plotting to seize power. The Bolsheviks followed the teachings of German revolutionary Karl Marx, emphasizing the inevitability of class struggle and the replacement of capitalism by communism. In November 1917 the Bolsheviks took control of the Russian government.

The final treaty was signed on June 28, 1919, in the Hall of Mirrors at the Versailles palace. The Germans had no choice but to accept its harsh terms. President Wilson had been disappointed by the secret deals and the endless compromising of his ideals, no doubt underestimating the stubborn reality of power politics in the wake of Europe's most devastating war. He had nonetheless won a commitment to the League of Nations, the centerpiece of his plan, and he was confident that the American people would accept the treaty. The tougher fight would be with the Senate, where a two-thirds vote was needed for ratification.

THE TREATY FIGHT

Preoccupied with peace conference politics in Paris, Wilson had neglected politics at home. His troubles had actually started earlier. Republicans had captured both the House and the Senate in the 1918 elections. Wilson had then made a tactical error by including no prominent Republicans in the U.S. peace delegation. He therefore faced a variety of tough opponents to the treaty he brought home.

Wilson's most extreme enemies in the Senate were a group of about sixteen "**irreconcilables**," opposed to a treaty in any form. Some were isolationist progressives, who opposed the League of Nations as steadfastly as they opposed American entry into the war. Others were racist xenophobes.

The less dogmatic but more influential opponents were led by Republican Henry Cabot Lodge of Massachusetts, powerful majority leader of the Senate. They had strong reservations about the League of Nations, especially the provisions for collective security in the event of a member nation's being attacked. Lodge argued that this provision impinged on congressional authority to declare war and placed unacceptable restraints on the nation's ability to pursue an independent foreign policy. Lodge proposed a series of amendments that would have weakened the League. But Wilson refused to compromise, motivated in part by the long-standing hatred he and Lodge felt toward each other.

In September, Wilson set out on a speaking tour across the country to drum up support for the League and the treaty. The crowds were large and responsive, but they did not change any votes in the Senate. The strain took its toll. On September 25, after speaking in Pueblo, Colorado, the sixty-three-year-old Wilson collapsed from exhaustion. His doctor canceled the rest of the trip. A week later, back in Washington, the president suffered a stroke that left him partially paralyzed. In November, Lodge brought the treaty out of committee for a vote, having appended to it fourteen reservations—that is, recommended changes. A bedridden Wilson stubbornly refused to compromise and instructed Democrats to vote against the Lodge version of the treaty. On November 19, Democrats joined with the "irreconcilables" to defeat the amended treaty, 39 to 55.

Wilson refused to budge. In January, he urged Democrats to either stand by the original treaty or vote it down. The 1920 election, he warned, would be "a great and solemn referendum" on the whole issue. In the final vote, on March 19, 1920, twenty-one Democrats broke with the president and voted for the Lodge version, giving it a majority of 49 to 35. But this was seven votes short of the two-thirds needed for ratification. As a result, the United States never signed the **Versailles Treaty**, nor did it join the League of Nations. The absence of the United States weakened the League and made it more difficult for the organization to realize Wilson's dream of a peaceful community of nations.

THE RED SCARE

The revolutionary changes taking place in Russia became an important backdrop for domestic politics. In the United States it became common to blame socialism, the IWW, and trade unionism in general on foreign radicals and alien ideologies. The accusation of Bolshevism became a powerful weapon for turning public opinion against strikers and political dissenters of all kinds.

In fact, by 1919 the American radicals were already weakened and badly split. The Socialist Party had around 40,000 members. Two small Communist Parties, made up largely of immigrants, had a total of perhaps 70,000. In June 1919 simultaneous bombings in eight cities killed two people and damaged the residence of Attorney General A. Mitchell Palmer. With public alarm growing, state and federal officials began a coordinated campaign to root out subversives and their alleged Russian connections.

Palmer used the broad authority of the 1918 Alien Act, which enabled the government to deport any immigrant found to be a member of a revolutionary

Irreconcilables   Group of U.S. senators adamantly opposed to ratification of the Treaty of Versailles after World War I.

Versailles Treaty   The treaty ending World War I and creating the League of Nations.

organization prior to or after coming to the United States. In a series of raids in late 1919, Justice Department agents in eleven cities arrested and roughed up several hundred members of the IWW and the Union of Russian Workers. Little evidence of revolutionary intent was found, but 249 people were deported, including prominent anarchists Emma Goldman and Alexander Berkman. In early 1920, some 6,000 people in thirty-three cities, including many U.S. citizens and noncommunists, were arrested and herded into prisons and bullpens. Again, no evidence of a grand plot was found, but another 600 aliens were deported. The Palmer raids had a ripple effect around the nation, encouraging other repressive measures against radicals.

A report prepared by a group of distinguished lawyers questioned the legality of the attorney general's tactics. Palmer's popularity had waned by the spring of 1920, when it became clear that his predictions of revolutionary uprisings were wildly exaggerated. But the **Red Scare** left an ugly legacy: wholesale violations of constitutional rights, deportations of hundreds of innocent people, fuel for the fires of nativism and intolerance. Business groups, such as the National Association of Manufacturers, found "Red-baiting" to be an effective tool in postwar efforts to keep unions out of their factories. Indeed, the government-sanctioned Red Scare reemerged later in the century as a powerful political force.

THE ELECTION OF 1920

Woodrow Wilson had wanted the 1920 election to be a "solemn referendum" on the League of Nations and his conduct of the war. Ill and exhausted, Wilson did not run for reelection. A badly divided Democratic Party compromised on Governor James M. Cox of Ohio as its candidate. A proven vote-getter, Cox distanced himself from Wilson's policies, which had come under withering attack from many quarters.

The Republicans nominated Senator Warren G. Harding of Ohio. A political hack, the handsome and genial Harding had virtually no qualifications to be president, except that he looked like one. Harding's campaign was vague and ambiguous about the Versailles Treaty and almost everything else. "America's present need," he said, "is not heroics but healing; not nostrums but normalcy; not revolution but restoration."

The notion of a "return to normalcy" proved very attractive to voters exhausted by the war, inflation, big government, and social dislocation. Harding won the greatest landslide in history to that date, carrying every state outside the South and taking the popular vote by 16 million to 9 million. Republicans retained their majorities in the House and Senate as well. Socialist Eugene V. Debs, still a powerful symbol of the dream of radical social change, managed to poll 900,000 votes from jail. But the overall vote repudiated Wilson and the progressive movement. Americans seemed eager to pull back from moralism in public and international controversies. Yet many of the economic, social, and cultural changes wrought by the war would accelerate during the 1920s. In truth, there could never be a "return to normalcy."

CONCLUSION

Compared to the casualties and social upheavals endured by the European powers, the Great War's impact on American life might appear slight, yet the war created economic, social, and political dislocations that helped reshape American life long after Armistice Day. Republican administrations invoked the wartime partnership between government and industry to justify an aggressive peacetime policy fostering cooperation between the state and business. Wartime production needs contributed to what economists later called "the second industrial revolution." Patriotic fervor and the exaggerated specter of Bolshevism were used to

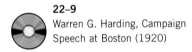
22–9
Warren G. Harding, Campaign Speech at Boston (1920)

22–7
An Official Report

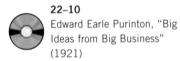
22–10
Edward Earle Purinton, "Big Ideas from Big Business" (1921)

Red Scare Post–World War I public hysteria over Bolshevik influence in the United States directed against labor activism, radical dissenters, and some ethnic groups.

CHRONOLOGY

1903 United States obtains Panama Canal rights.

1905 President Theodore Roosevelt mediates peace treaty between Japan and Russia at Portsmouth Conference.

1908 Root-Takahira Agreement with Japan affirms status quo in Asia and Open Door policy in China.

1911 Mexican Revolution begins.

1914 U.S. forces invade Mexico.

Panama Canal opens.

World War I begins in Europe.

President Woodrow Wilson issues proclamation of neutrality.

1915 Germany declares war zone around Great Britain.

German U-boat sinks *Lusitania*.

1916 Pancho Villa raids New Mexico, is pursued by General Pershing.

Wilson is reelected.

National Defense Act establishes preparedness program.

1917 February: Germany resumes unrestricted submarine warfare.

March: Zimmermann Note, suggesting a German-Mexican alliance, shocks Americans.

April: United States declares war on the Central Powers.

May: Selective Service Act is passed.

June: Espionage Act is passed.

November: Bolshevik Revolution begins in Russia.

1918 January: Wilson unveils Fourteen Points.

May: Sedition Act is passed.

June: U.S. troops begin to see action in France.

November: Armistice ends war.

1919 January: Eighteenth Amendment (Prohibition) is ratified.

Wilson serves as chief U.S. negotiator at Paris Peace Conference.

June: Versailles Treaty is signed in Paris.

July: Race riot breaks out in Chicago.

Steel strike begins in several Midwestern cities.

November: Palmer raids begin.

1920 March: Senate finally votes down Versailles Treaty and League of Nations.

August: Nineteenth Amendment (woman suffrage) is ratified.

November: Warren G. Harding is elected president.

---

repress radicalism, organized labor, feminism, and the entire legacy of progressive reform. The wartime measure of national prohibition evolved into perhaps the most contentious social issue of peacetime. Sophisticated use of sales techniques, psychology, and propaganda during the war helped define the newly powerful advertising and public relations industries of the 1920s. The growing visibility of immigrants and African Americans, especially in the nation's cities, provoked a xenophobic and racist backlash in the politics of the 1920s. More than anything else, the desire for "normalcy" reflected the deep anxieties evoked by America's wartime experience.

SUMMARY

Becoming a World Power Theodore Roosevelt's aggressive foreign policy made the United States a world power. He used force and diplomacy to pursue his goals. Woodrow Wilson tried to blend morality and realism in foreign policy but experienced difficulties in dealing with the Mexican Revolution.

The Great War When World War I erupted, the United States adopted a policy of neutrality that proved impossible to maintain. Despite strong opposition, Wilson launched a preparedness program in 1916. German actions in 1917 led Wilson to declare war on that nation and its allies.

American Mobilization The United States was unprepared for war and the government was uncertain about the public's willingness to fight. The Committee on Public Information mobilized popular support for the war and opposition faded. The greatest challenge was raising, training, and deploying military forces. African Americans experienced racism from American military figures but received much better treatment from the French. By 1918, American forces joined the fighting in France. Eight months later, the war ended, thanks in part to American involvement.

Over Here During World War I, industry, fuel, and food were all regulated by government committees. War bond drives financed much of the war costs. Labor also faced regulations but won many rights. The radical labor movement, however, was decimated. Another major aspect was the entry of women in the workplace and their wartime service helped secure passage of woman suffrage. Moral reform achieved their goal of Prohibition.

Repression and Reaction As the government tried to unify public opinion behind the war, it cracked down on dissenters and radicals, especially in the wake of the Russian Revolution. Tensions also arose over the African American migration to Northern cities. The war's end ushered in a brief period of militant labor activities that largely failed.

An Uneasy Peace Wilson went to the Versailles conference with a comprehensive plan for peace but was unable to implement much of his program. The treaty dealt harshly with Germany. Wilson also faced resistance at home and Congress did not approve the treaty. The Russian Revolution produced a Red Scare in the United States. Seeking less turmoil and a break from two decades of change, the American people elected Harding as president.

REVIEW QUESTIONS

1. What central issues drew the United States deeper into international politics in the early years of the century? How did American presidents justify a more expansive role? What diplomatic and military policies did they exploit for these ends?

2. Compare the arguments for and against American participation in the Great War. Which Americans were most likely to support entry? Which were more likely to oppose it?

3. How did mobilizing for war change the economy and its relationship to government? Which of these changes, if any, spilled over to the postwar years?

4. How did the war affect political life in the United States? What techniques were used to stifle dissent? What was the war's political legacy?

5. To what extent was the war an extension of progressivism?

6. Analyze the impact of the war on American workers. How did the conflict affect the lives of African Americans and women?

7. What principles guided Woodrow Wilson's Fourteen Points? How would you explain the United States's failure to ratify the Treaty of Versailles?

KEY TERMS

Allies (p. 592)

Bolsheviks (p. 608)

Central Powers (p. 608)

Committee on Public Information (CPI) (p. 595)

Espionage Act (p. 600)

Great Migration (p. 605)

Imperialism (p. 592)

Irreconcilables (p. 609)

League of Nations (p. 607)

Liberty Bonds (p. 599)

Militarism (p. 592)

Monroe Doctrine (p. 590)

Open Door (p. 590)

Preparedness (p. 594)

Red Scare (p. 610)

Roosevelt Corollary (p. 590)

Sedition Act (p. 604)

Selective Service Act (p. 596)

Self-determination (p. 608)

Versailles Treaty (p. 609)

War Industries Board (WIB) (p. 598)

RECOMMENDED READING

Marc Allen Eisner, *From Warfare State to Welfare State: World War I, Compensatory State Building, and the Limits of the Modern Order* (2000). Demonstrates how, to compensate for the limited capacities of the state to wage total war, policymakers incorporated business organizations and structures into the network of committees coordinating the war effort.

Kathleen Kennedy, *Disloyal Mothers and Scurrilous Citizens: Women and Subversion During World War I* (1999). Analyzes the federal government's campaign against antiwar women activists and their refusal to adhere to accepted notions of "patriotic motherhood."

Thomas J. Knock, *To End All Wars: Woodrow Wilson and the Quest for a New World Order* (1992). A persuasive analysis of Wilson's internationalism, its links to his domestic policies, and his design for the League of Nations.

Walter LaFeber, *The American Age* (1989). A fine survey of the history of U.S. foreign policy that includes an analysis of the pre–World War I era.

Paul L. Murphy, *World War I and the Origin of Civil Liberties* (1979). A good overview of the various civil liberties issues raised by the war and government efforts to suppress dissent.

Ronald Schaffer, *America in the Great War: The Rise of the War Welfare State* (1991). Excellent material on how the war transformed the relationship between business and government and spurred improved conditions for industrial workers.

Joe William Trotter Jr., ed., *The Great Migration in Historical Perspective* (1991). An excellent collection of essays examining the Great Migration, with special attention to issues of class and gender within the African American community.

Neil A. Wynn, *From Progressivism to Prosperity: World War I and American Society* (1986). An illuminating account of the social impact of the war on American life. Effectively connects the war experience with both progressive era trends and postwar developments in the 1920s.

Susan Zeiger, *In Uncle Sam's Service: Women Workers with the American Expeditionary Force, 1917–1919* (1999). The first in-depth study of American women's experiences with the armed forces overseas.

Robert H. Zieger, *America's Great War: World War I and the American Experience* (2000). The best new one-volume synthesis on how the war transformed the United States and its role in the world.

Happy times were here again.
— *Upton Sinclair, from* The Flivver King

Toward a Modern America: The 1920's. "More than a car. FORD. A National Institution" poster, 1923.

HOW DID the widespread use of automobiles change American society in the 1920s?

WHAT ROLE did new communication technologies play in the development of mass culture?

The soup for men who eat to win!

WHAT VALUES and beliefs did Harding and Coolidge share?

WHAT EXPLAINS the resurgence of the Ku Klux Klan in the 1920s?

WHAT WERE the most important issues in the election of 1928?

AMERICAN COMMUNITIES

The Movie Audience and Hollywood: Mass Culture Creates a New National Community

INSIDE MIDTOWN MANHATTAN'S MAGNIFICENT NEW ROXY THEATER, a sellout crowd eagerly settled in for opening night. Outside, thousands of fans cheered wildly at the arrival of movie stars such as Charlie Chaplin, Gloria Swanson, and Harold Lloyd. A squadron of smartly uniformed ushers guided patrons under a five-story-tall rotunda to some 6,200 velvet-covered seats. The audience marveled at the huge gold and rose-colored murals, classical statuary, plush carpeting, and Gothic-style windows. It was easy to believe newspaper reports that the theater had cost $10 million to build. Suddenly, light flooded the orchestra pit and 110 musicians began playing "The Star Spangled Banner." A troupe of 100 performers took the stage, dancing ballet numbers and singing old Southern melodies such as "My Old Kentucky Home" and "Swanee River." Congratulatory telegrams from President Calvin Coolidge and other dignitaries flashed on the screen. Finally, the evening's feature presentation, The Love of Sunya, starring Gloria Swanson, began. Samuel L. "Roxy" Rothapfel, the theater's designer, had realized his grand dream—to build "the cathedral of the motion picture."

When Roxy's opened in March 1927, nearly 60 million Americans "worshiped" each week at movie theaters across the nation. The "movie palaces" of the 1920s were designed to transport patrons to exotic places and different times. As film pioneer Marcus Loew put it, "We sell tickets to theaters, not movies." Every large community boasted at least one opulent movie theater. Houston's Majestic was built to represent an ancient Italian garden; it had a ceiling made to look like an open sky, complete with stars and cloud formations. The Tivoli in Chicago featured opulent French Renaissance decor; Grauman's Egyptian in Los Angeles re-created the look of a pharaoh's tomb; and Albuquerque's Kimo drew inspiration from Navajo art and religion.

The remarkable popularity of motion pictures, and later radio, forged a new kind of community. A huge national audience regularly went to the movies, and the same entertainment could be enjoyed virtually anywhere in the country by just about everyone. Movies emerged as the most popular form in the new mass culture, with an appeal that extended far beyond the films themselves, or even the theaters. Americans embraced the cult of celebrity, voraciously consuming fan magazines, gossip columns, and news of the stars. By the 1920s, the production center for this dream world was Hollywood, California, a suburb of Los Angeles that had barely existed in 1890.

Motion picture companies found Hollywood an alluring alternative to the east coast cities where they had been born. Its reliably sunny and dry climate was ideal for year-round filming. Its unique surroundings offered a perfect variety of scenic locations—mountains, desert, ocean—and downtown Los Angeles was only an hour away. Land was cheap and plentiful. And because Los Angeles was the leading nonunion, open-shop city in the country, so was labor. By the early 1920s Hollywood produced more than 80 percent of the nation's motion pictures and was assuming mythical status. The isolation of the town, its great distance from the Eastern cities, its lack of traditional sources of culture and learning—all contributed to movie folk looking at life in a self-consciously "Hollywood" way.

With its feel of a modern frontier boomtown, Hollywood was a new kind of American community. It lured the young and cosmopolitan with the promise of upward mobility and a new way of life. Most of the top studio executives were Jewish immigrants from eastern and central Europe. In contrast to most Americans, who hailed from rural areas or small towns, more than half of Hollywood's writers, directors, editors, and actors were born in cities of over 100,000. Two-thirds of its performers were under thirty-five, and three-fourths of its actresses were under twenty-five. More than 90 percent of its writers (women made up one-third to one-half of this key group) had attended college or worked in journalism. The movies this atypical community created evoked the pleasures of leisure, consumption, and personal freedom, redefining the nation's cultural values in the 1920s.

Movie stars dominated Hollywood. Charlie Chaplin, Mary Pickford, Rudolph Valentino, Gloria Swanson, and Douglas Fairbanks became popular idols as much for their highly publicized private lives as for their roles on screen. Many accumulated great wealth, becoming the nation's experts on how to live well. Movie folk built luxurious mansions in a variety of architectural styles and outfitted them with swimming pools, tennis courts, golf courses, and lavish gardens.

Visitors often noted that Hollywood had no museums, art galleries, live theater, or other traditional institutions of high culture. How would the town's wealthy movie elite spend their time and money? By 1916 Charlie Chaplin, a working-class immigrant from the London slums, was earning $10,000 a week for the comedies that made his most famous face in the world. He recalled trying to figure out what to do with his new wealth. "The money I earned was legendary, a symbol in figures, for I had never actually seen it. I therefore had to do something to prove I had it. So I procured a secretary, a valet, a car, a chauffeur."

Hollywood

Ordinary Americans found it easy to identify with movie stars despite their wealth and status. Unlike industrialists or politicians, stars had no social authority over large groups of employees or voters. They, too, had to answer to a boss, and most had risen from humble beginnings. But above all, Hollywood, like the movies it churned out, represented for millions of Americans

new possibilities: freedom, material success, upward mobility, and the chance to remake one's very identity. By the end of the decade the Hollywood "dream factory" had helped forge a national community whose collective aspirations and desires were increasingly defined by those possibilities, even if relatively few Americans realized them during the 1920s.

POSTWAR PROSPERITY AND ITS PRICE

THE SECOND INDUSTRIAL REVOLUTION

The prosperity of the 1920s rested on what historians have called the "second industrial revolution" in American manufacturing, in which technological innovations made it possible to increase industrial output without expanding the labor force. Electricity replaced steam as the main power source for industry in these years, making possible the replacement of older machinery with more efficient and flexible electric machinery.

Much of the newer, automatic machinery could be operated by unskilled and semiskilled workers, and it boosted the overall efficiency of American industry. Thus, in 1929 the average worker in manufacturing produced roughly three-quarters more per hour than he or she had in 1919. The machine industry itself employed more workers than any other manufacturing sector—some 1.1 million in 1929—supplying not only a growing home market but 35 percent of the world market as well.

During the late nineteenth century, heavy industries such as machine tools, railroads, iron, and steel had pioneered mass-production techniques. These industries manufactured what economists call producer-durable goods. In the 1920s, modern mass-production techniques were increasingly applied as well to newer consumer-durable goods such as automobiles, radios, washing machines, and telephones. With more efficient management, greater mechanization, intensive product research, and ingenious sales and advertising methods, the consumer-based industries helped to nearly double industrial production in the 1920s.

THE MODERN CORPORATION

In the late nineteenth century, individual entrepreneurs such as John D. Rockefeller in oil and Andrew Carnegie in steel had provided a model for success. They maintained both corporate control (ownership) and business leadership (management) in their enterprises. In the 1920s, a managerial revolution increasingly divorced ownership of corporate stock from the everyday control of businesses. The new corporate ideal was to be found in men such as Alfred P. Sloan of General Motors and Owen D. Young of the Radio Corporation of America.

During the 1920s, the most successful corporations were those that led in three key areas: the integration of production and distribution, product diversification, and the expansion of

HOW DID the widespread use of automobiles change American society in the 1920s?

Stock Market Prices, 1921–1932
Common stock prices rose steeply during the 1920s. Although only about 4 million Americans owned stocks during the period, "stock watching" became something of a national sport.

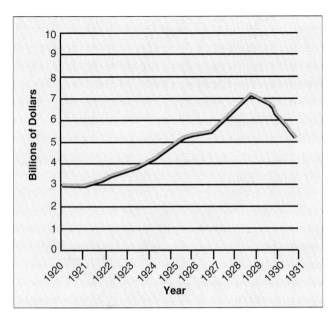

Consumer Debt, 1920–1931
The expansion of consumer borrowing was a key component of the era's prosperity. These figures do not include mortgages or money borrowed to purchase stocks. They reveal the great increase in "installment buying" for such consumer durable goods as automobiles and household appliances.

industrial research. Until the end of World War I, for example, the chemical manufacturer Du Pont had specialized in explosives such as gunpowder. After the war, Du Pont moved aggressively into the consumer market with a diverse array of products. Similarly, the great electrical manufacturers—General Electric and Westinghouse—which had previously concentrated on lighting and power equipment, now diversified into household appliances like radios, washing machines, and refrigerators. The chemical and electrical industries also led the way in industrial research, hiring personnel to develop new products and test their commercial viability.

By 1929 the 200 largest corporations owned nearly half the nation's corporate wealth—that is, physical plant, stock, and property. Half the total industrial income—revenue from sales of goods—was concentrated in 100 corporations. Oligopoly—the control of a market by a few large producers—became the norm. Four companies packed almost three-quarters of all American meat. Another four rolled nine out of every ten cigarettes. National chain grocery stores, clothing shops, and pharmacies began squeezing out local neighborhood businesses. One grocery chain alone, the Great Atlantic and Pacific Tea Company (A&P), accounted for 10 percent of all retail food sales in America.

A growing class of salaried executives, plant managers, and engineers formed a new elite who made corporate policy without themselves having a controlling interest in the companies they worked for. They stressed scientific management and the latest theories of behavioral psychology in their effort to make their workplaces more productive, stable, and profitable.

WELFARE CAPITALISM

The wartime gains made by organized labor and the active sympathy shown to trade unions by government agencies such as the National War Labor Board troubled most corporate leaders. To challenge the power and appeal of trade unions and collective bargaining, large employers aggressively promoted a variety of new programs designed to improve worker well-being and morale. These schemes, collectively known as **welfare capitalism**, became a key part of corporate strategy in the 1920s.

One approach was to encourage workers to acquire property through stock-purchase plans or, less frequently, home ownership plans. Other programs offered workers insurance policies covering accidents, illness, old age, and death. Many plant managers and personnel departments consciously worked to improve safety conditions, provide medical services, and establish sports and recreation programs for workers. But welfare capitalism could not solve the most chronic problems faced by industrial workers: seasonal unemployment, low wages, long hours, and unhealthy factory conditions.

Large corporations also mounted an effective antiunion campaign in the early 1920s called "the American plan," a name meant to associate unionism with foreign and un-American ideas. Backed by powerful business lobbies such as the National Association of Manufacturers and the Chamber of Commerce, campaign leaders called for the **open shop**, in which no employee would be compelled to join a union. If a union existed, nonmembers would still get whatever wages and rights the union had won—a policy that put organizers at a disadvantage in signing up new members.

Welfare capitalism A paternalistic system of labor relations emphasizing management responsibility for employee well-being.

Open shop Factory of business employing workers whether or not they are union members; in practice, such a business usually refuses to hire union members and follows antiunion policies.

The A&P grocery chain expanded from 400 stores in 1912 to more than 15,000 by the end of the 1920s, making it a familiar sight in communities across America. A&P advertisements, like this one from 1927, emphasized cleanliness, order, and the availability of name brand goods at discount prices.

From *Ladies Home Journal.* A&P Food Stores LTD

IMAGE KEY

for pages 614–615

a. Silent film star Gertrude Olmstead wears a ruffled flapper dress with a striped hat in 1925.

b. "More than a car. FORD: A National Institution" poster, 1923.

c. A clarinet like those used during "the Jazz Age" of the 1920s.

d. An old football symbolizes the exuberance of the times.

e. Men are shown piecing together automobiles on an assembly line in the Rouge plant of the Ford Motor Company.

f. Campbell's Tomato Soup advertisement.

g. The price of stocks through the 1920s and early 1930s.

h. Women dressed in the white robes and hoods of the Ku Klux Klan in 1924.

The open shop undercut the gains won in a union shop, where new employees had to join an existing union, or a closed shop, where employers agreed to hire only union members. As alternatives, large employers such as U.S. Steel and International Harvester began setting up company unions. Their intent was to substitute largely symbolic employee representation in management conferences for the more confrontational process of collective bargaining.

These management strategies contributed to a sharp decline in the ranks of organized labor. Total union membership dropped from about 5 million in 1920 to 3.5 million in 1926. A large proportion of the remaining union members were concentrated in the skilled crafts of the building and printing trades. A conservative and timid union leadership was also responsible for the trend. The federal government, which had provided limited wartime support for unions, now reverted to a more probusiness posture. The Supreme Court in particular was unsympathetic toward unions, consistently upholding the use of injunctions to prevent strikes, picketing, and other union activities.

THE AUTO AGE

In their classic community study *Middletown* (1929), sociologists Robert and Helen Lynd noted the dramatic impact of the car on the social life of Muncie, Indiana. "Why on earth do you need to study what's changing this country?" asked one lifelong Muncie resident in 1924. "I can tell you what's happening in just four letters: A-U-T-O!" This remark hardly seems much of an exaggeration today. No other single development could match the impact of the postwar automobile explosion on the way Americans worked, lived, and played. The auto industry offered the clearest example of the rise to prominence of consumer durables. During the

Finished automobiles roll off the moving assembly line at the Ford Motor Company, Highland Park, Michigan, ca. 1920. During the 1920s Henry Ford achieved the status of folk hero, as his name became synonymous with the techniques of mass production. Ford cultivated a public image of himself as the heroic genius of the auto industry, greatly exaggerating his personal achievements.

Brown Brothers

1920s, America made approximately 85 percent of all the world's passenger cars. By 1929 the motor vehicle industry was the most productive in the United States in terms of value, producing some 4.8 million cars that year.

This extraordinary new industry had mushroomed in less than a generation. Its great pioneer, Henry Ford, had shown how the use of a continuous assembly line could drastically reduce the number of worker hours required to produce a single vehicle. In 1914, at his sprawling new Highland Park assembly plant just outside Detroit, Ford's system finished one car every ninety minutes. By 1925, cars were rolling off his assembly line at the rate of one every ten seconds.

In 1914 Ford startled American industry by inaugurating a new wage scale: $5 for an eight-hour day. This was roughly double the going pay rate for industrial labor, along with a shorter workday as well. But in defying the conventional economic wisdom of the day, Ford acted less out of benevolence than out of shrewdness. He understood that workers were consumers as well as producers, and the new wage scale helped boost sales of Ford cars. It also reduced the high turnover rate in his labor force and increased worker efficiency. Ford's mass-production system and economies of scale permitted him to progressively reduce the price of his cars, bringing them within the reach of millions of Americans. The famous Model T, thoroughly standardized and available only in black, cost just under $300 in 1924—about three months' wages for the best-paid factory workers.

The auto industry provided a large market for makers of steel, rubber, glass, and petroleum products. It stimulated public spending for good roads and extended the housing boom to new suburbs. Showrooms, repair shops, and gas stations appeared in thousands of communities. New small enterprises, from motels to billboard advertising to roadside diners, sprang up as motorists took to the highway. The rapid development of Florida and California, in particular, was partly a response to the growing influence of the automobile.

For some the car merely reinforced old social patterns, making it easier for them to get to church on Sunday, for example, or visit neighbors. Others used their cars to go to new places, shop in nearby cities, or take vacations. The automobile made leisure, in the sense of getting away from the routines of work and school, a more regular part of everyday life. It undoubtedly also changed the courtship practices of America's youth. Young people took advantage of the car to gain privacy and distance from their parents. "What on earth do you want me to do?" complained one "Middletown" high school girl to her anxious father. "Just sit around home all evening?" Many had their first sexual experiences in a car.

Cars also promoted urban and suburban growth. The federal census for 1920 was the first in American history in which the proportion of the population who lived in urban places (those with 2,500 or more people) exceeded the proportion of the population living in rural areas. More revealing of urban growth was the steady increase in the number of big cities. In 1910 there were sixty cities with more than 100,000 inhabitants; in 1920 there were sixty-eight; and by 1930 there were ninety-two. During the 1920s New York grew by 20 percent to nearly 7 million, whereas Detroit, home of the auto industry, doubled its population, to nearly 2 million.

EXCEPTIONS: AGRICULTURE, AILING INDUSTRIES

Amid prosperity and progress, there were large pockets of the country that lagged behind. Advances in real income and improvements in the standard of living for workers and farmers were uneven at best. During the 1920s, one-quarter of all American workers were employed in agriculture, yet the farm sector failed to share in the general prosperity. The years 1914–1919 had been a kind of golden age for the nation's farmers. But with the war's end, American farmers began to suffer from a chronic worldwide surplus of such farm staples as cotton, hogs, and corn.

Prices began to drop sharply in 1920. Cotton, which sold at 37 ¢ a pound in mid-1920, fell to 14 ¢ by year's end. By 1921 net farm income was down more than half from the year before. Land values also dropped, wiping out billions in capital investment. Behind these aggregate statistics were hundreds of thousands of individual human tragedies on the nation's 6 million farms.

In the South, farmers' dependency on "King Cotton" deepened, as the region lagged farther behind the rest of the nation in both agricultural diversity and standard of living. Cotton acreage expanded as large and heavily mechanized farms opened up new land in Oklahoma, west Texas, and the Mississippi-Yazoo delta. But in most of the South, from North Carolina to east Texas, small one- and two-mule cotton farms, most under 50 acres, still dominated the countryside. While editors, state officials, and reformers preached the need for greater variety of crops, Southern farmers actually raised less corn and livestock by the end of the decade. With few large urban centers and inadequate transportation, even those Southern farmers who had access to capital found it extremely difficult to find reliable markets for vegetables, fruit, poultry, or dairy products. The average Southern farm had land and buildings worth $3,525; for Northern farms, the figure was $11,029. The number of white tenant farmers increased by 200,000 during the 1920s, while black tenantry declined slightly as a result of the Great Migration. Some 700,000 Southern farmers, roughly half white and half black, still labored as sharecroppers. Modern conveniences such as electricity, indoor plumbing, automobiles, and phonographs remained far beyond the reach of the great majority of Southern farmers. Widespread rural poverty, poor diet, little access to capital— the world of Southern agriculture had changed very little since the days of Populist revolt in the 1890s.

Large sectors of American industry also failed to share in the decade's general prosperity. As oil and natural gas gained in importance, America's coal mines became a less important source of energy. Economic hardship was widespread in many mining communities dependent on coal, particularly in Appalachia and the Southern Midwest. And those miners who did work earned lower hourly wages.

The number of miles of railroad track actually decreased after 1920 as automobiles and trucks began to displace trains. In textiles, the women's fashions of the 1920s generally required less material than had earlier fashions, and competition from synthetic fibers such as rayon depressed demand for cotton textiles. To improve profit margins, textile manufacturers in New England and other parts of the Northeast began a long-range shift of operations to the South, where nonunion shops and substandard wages became the rule. Older New England manufacturing centers such as Lawrence, Lowell, and Fall River, Massachusetts, and Nashua and Manchester,

Until 1924 Henry Ford had disdained national advertising for his cars. But as General Motors gained a competitive edge by making yearly changes in style and technology, Ford was forced to pay more attention to advertising. This ad was directed at "Mrs. Consumer," combining appeals to both female independence and motherly duties.

Ford Motor Company

Cancel distance & conquer weather

23-2
The Sahara of the Bozart
(1920)

WHAT ROLE did new communication technologies play in the development of mass culture?

23-4
Advertisements (1925, 1927)

New Hampshire were hard hit by this shift. Southern mills increased their work force from 220,000 to 257,000 between 1923 and 1933. By 1933 they employed nearly 70 percent of the workers in the industry. Southern mills generally operated night and day, used the newest labor-saving machinery, and cut back on the wage gains of the World War I years.

THE NEW MASS CULTURE

ADVERTISING MODERNITY

A thriving advertising industry both reflected and encouraged the growing importance of consumer goods in American life. Previously, advertising had been confined mostly to staid newspapers and magazines and offered little more than basic product information. The successful efforts of the government's Committee on Public Information, set up to "sell" World War I to Americans, suggested that new techniques using modern communication media could convince people to buy a wide range of goods and services. As a profession, advertising reached a higher level of respectability, sophistication, and economic power in American life during the 1920s.

Advertisers began focusing on the needs, desires, and anxieties of the consumer rather than on the qualities of the product. Ad agencies and their clients invested extraordinary amounts of time, energy, and money trying to discover and, to some extent, shape people's beliefs. One of the more spectacular examples of advertising effectiveness involved an old product, Listerine, which had been marketed as a general antiseptic for years by Lambert Pharmaceutical Company. A new ad campaign touting Listerine as a cure for halitosis—a scientific-sounding term for bad breath—boosted Lambert's profits from $100,000 in 1922 to more than $4 million in 1927.

Above all, advertising celebrated consumption itself as a positive good. In this sense the new advertising ethic was a therapeutic one, promising that products would contribute to the buyer's physical, psychic, or emotional well-being. Well-financed ad campaigns were especially crucial for marketing newer consumer goods such as cars, electrical appliances, and personal hygiene products. Total advertising volume in all media—newspapers, magazines, radio, billboards—jumped from $1.4 billion in 1919 to $3 billion in 1929.

RADIO BROADCASTING

In the fall of 1920, Westinghouse executive Harry P. Davis noticed that amateur broadcasts from the garage of an employee had attracted attention in the local Pittsburgh press. A department store advertised radio sets capable of picking up these "wireless concerts." Davis converted this amateur station to a stronger one at the Westinghouse main plant. Beginning with the presidential election returns that November, station KDKA offered regular nightly broadcasts that were probably heard by only a few hundred people. Radio broadcasting, begun as a service for selling cheap radio sets left over from World War I, would soon sweep the nation.

Before KDKA, wireless technology had been of interest only to the military, the telephone industry, and a few thousand "ham" (amateur) operators who enjoyed communicating with each other. The "radio mania" of the early 1920s was a response to the new possibilities offered by broadcasting. By 1923 nearly 600 stations had been licensed by the Department of Commerce, and about 600,000 Americans had bought radios. Early programs included live popular music, the playing of phonograph records, talks by college professors, church services, and news and weather reports. For millions of Americans, especially in rural areas and small towns, radio provided a new and exciting link to the larger national community of consumption.

Who would pay for radio programs? By the end of the decade commercial (or "toll") broadcasting emerged as the answer. The dominant corporations in the industry—General Electric, Westinghouse, Radio Corporation of America (RCA), and American Telephone and Telegraph (AT&T)—settled on the idea that advertisers would foot the bill for radio. Sponsors advertised directly or indirectly to the mass audience through such shows as the *Eveready Hour*, the *Ipana Troubadors*, and the *Taystee Loafers*.

Radio broadcasting created a national community of listeners, just as motion pictures created one of viewers. NBC and CBS led the way in creating popular radio programs that relied heavily on older cultural forms. The variety show, hosted by vaudeville comedians, became network radio's first important format. Radio's first truly national hit, The *Amos 'n' Andy Show* (1928), was a direct descendant of nineteenth-century "blackface" minstrel entertainment. Radio did more than any previous medium to publicize and commercialize previously isolated forms of American music such as country and western, blues, and jazz. Broadcasts of baseball and college football games proved especially popular. By 1930, some 600 stations were broadcasting to more than 12 million homes with radios, or roughly 40 percent of American families. By that time all the elements that characterize the present American system of broadcasting—regular daily programming paid for and produced by commercial advertisers, national networks carrying shows across the nation, and mass ownership of receiver sets in American homes—were in place.

MOVIE-MADE AMERICA

The early movie industry, centered in New York and a few other big cities, had made moviegoing a regular habit for millions of Americans, especially immigrants and the working class. They flocked to cheap, storefront theaters, called nickelodeons, to watch short westerns, slapstick comedies, melodramas, and travelogues. With the shift of the industry westward to Hollywood, movies entered a new phase of business expansion.

Large studios such as Paramount, Fox, Metro-Goldwyn-Mayer (MGM), Universal, and Warner Brothers dominated the business with longer and more expensively produced movies—feature films. These companies were founded and controlled by immigrants from Europe, all of whom had a talent for discovering and exploiting changes in popular tastes. Adolph Zukor, the Hungarian-born head of Paramount, had been a furrier in New York City. Warsaw-born Samuel Goldwyn, a founder of MGM, had been a glove salesman. William Fox, of Fox Pictures, began as a garment cutter in Brooklyn. Most of the immigrant moguls had started in the business by buying or managing small movie theaters before beginning to produce films.

Each studio combined the three functions of production, distribution, and exhibition, and each controlled hundreds of movie theaters around the country. The era of silent films ended when Warner Brothers scored a huge hit in 1927 with *The Jazz Singer*, starring Al Jolson, which successfully introduced sound.

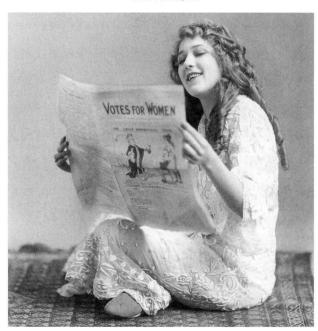

Mary Pickford, one of the most popular movie stars of the 1910s and 1920s, is shown here reading a feminist newspaper in a publicity photo, ca. 1917. Pickford frequently portrayed young women struggling for economic freedom from men. She wrote weekly columns for women in which she backed suffrage and urged her female readers to be more self-sufficient. Pickford embodied the new mass-media-based "celebrity" of the 1920s.

Culver Pictures, Inc.

New genres—musicals, gangster films, and screwball comedies—soon became popular. The higher costs associated with "talkies" also increased the studios' reliance on Wall Street investors and banks for working capital.

At the heart of Hollywood's success was the star system and the accompanying cult of celebrity. Stars became vital to the fantasy lives of millions of fans. For many in the audience, there was only a vague line separating the on-screen and off-screen adventures of the stars. Studio publicity, fan magazines, and gossip columns reinforced this ambiguity. Young Americans in particular looked to movies to learn how to dress, wear their hair, talk, or kiss.

A NEW MORALITY?

Movie stars, radio personalities, sports heroes, and popular musicians became the elite figures in a new culture of celebrity defined by the mass media. They were the model for achievement in the new age. Great events and abstract issues were made real through movie close-ups, radio interviews, and tabloid photos.

One of the most enduring images of the "Roaring Twenties" is the flapper. She was usually portrayed on screen, in novels, and in the press as a young, sexually aggressive woman with bobbed hair, rouged cheeks, and short skirt. She loved to dance to jazz music, enjoyed smoking cigarettes, and drank bootleg liquor in cabarets and dance halls. She could also be competitive, assertive, and a good pal.

Was the flapper a genuine representative of the 1920s? Did she embody the "new morality" that was so widely discussed and chronicled in the media of the day? The flapper certainly did exist, but she was neither as new nor as widespread a phenomenon as the image would suggest. The delight in sensuality, personal pleasure, and rhythmically complex dance and music had long been key elements of subcultures on the fringes of middle-class society: bohemian enclaves, communities of political radicals, African American ghettos, working-class dance halls. In the 1920s, these activities became normative for a growing number of white middle-class Americans, including women. Jazz, sexual experimentation, heavy makeup, and cigarette smoking spread to college campuses.

Several sources, most of them rooted in earlier years, can be found for the increased sexual openness of the 1920s. New psychological and social theories like those of Havelock Ellis, Ellen Key, and Sigmund Freud stressed the central role of sexuality in human experience, maintaining that sex is a positive, healthy impulse that, if repressed, could damage mental and emotional health. The pioneering efforts of Margaret Sanger in educating women about birth control had begun before World War I (see Chapter 21).

Advertisers routinely used sex appeal to sell products. Tabloid newspapers exploited sex with "cheesecake" photos, but they also provided features giving advice on sex hygiene and venereal disease. And movies, of course, featured powerful sex symbols such as Rudolph Valentino, Gloria Swanson, John Gilbert, and Clara Bow. Movies also taught young people an etiquette of sex. One typical eighteen-year-old college student wrote in the motion picture diary she kept for a sociological study: "These passionate pictures stir such longings, desires, and urges as I never expected any person to possess. Just the way the passionate lover held his sweetheart suggests so many beautiful and intimate relations, which even my reenacting a scene does not satisfy any more."

This 1925 *Judge* cartoon, "Sheik with Sheba," drawn by John Held Jr., offered one view of contemporary culture. The flashy new automobile, the hip flask with illegal liquor, the cigarettes, and the stylish "new woman" were all part of the "Roaring Twenties" image.

The Granger Collection (4E746.21)

Sociological surveys also suggested that genuine changes in sexual behavior began in the prewar years among both married and single women. Katherine Bement Davis's pioneering study of 2,200 middle-class women, carried out in 1918 and published in 1929, revealed that most used contraceptives and described sexual relations in positive terms. Women born after the turn of the century were twice as likely to have had premarital sex as those born before 1900. The critical change took place in the generation that came of age in the late teens and early twenties. By the 1920s, male and female "morals" were becoming more alike.

23–5
Family Planning 1926

THE STATE, THE ECONOMY, AND BUSINESS

HARDING AND COOLIDGE

Handsome, genial, and well-spoken, Warren Harding may have looked the part of a president—but acting like one was another matter. Harding was a product of small-town Marion, Ohio, and the machine politics in his native state. Republican Party officials had made a point of keeping Senator Harding, a compromise choice, as removed from the public eye as possible in the 1920 election. They correctly saw that active campaigning could only hurt their candidate by exposing his shallowness and intellectual weakness. Harding understood his own limitations. He sadly told one visitor to the White House shortly after taking office, "I knew that this job would be too much for me."

Harding surrounded himself with a close circle of friends, the "Ohio gang," delegating to them a great deal of administrative power. The president often conducted business as if he were in the relaxed, convivial, and masculine confines of a small-town saloon.

Soon after Harding's death in 1923, a series of congressional investigations revealed a deep pattern of corruption. Attorney General Harry M. Daugherty had received bribes from violators of the Prohibition statutes. He had also failed to investigate graft in the Veterans Bureau, where Charles R. Forbes had pocketed a large chunk of the $250 million spent on hospitals and supplies. The worst affair was the Teapot Dome scandal involving Interior Secretary Albert Fall. Fall received hundreds of thousands of dollars in payoffs when he secretly leased navy oil reserves in Teapot Dome, Wyoming, and Elk Hills, California, to two private oil developers. He eventually became the first cabinet officer ever to go to jail.

But the Harding administration's legacy was not all scandal. Andrew Mellon, an influential Pittsburgh banker, served as secretary of the treasury under all three Republican presidents of the 1920s. One of the richest men in America, and a leading investor in the Aluminum Corporation of America and Gulf Oil, Mellon believed government ought to be run on the same conservative principles as a corporation. His tax program sharply cut taxes for both higher income brackets and for businesses. By 1926, a person with an income of a million a year paid less than a third of the income tax he or she had paid in 1921. Over all, Mellon's policies succeeded in rolling back much of the progressive taxation associated with Woodrow Wilson.

When Calvin Coolidge succeeded to the presidency, he seemed to most people the temperamental opposite of Harding. Born and raised in rural Vermont, elected governor of Massachusetts, and coming to national prominence only through the 1919 Boston police strike (see Chapter 22), "Silent Cal" was the quintessential New England Yankee. Taciturn, genteel, and completely honest, Coolidge believed in the least amount of government possible. He spent only four hours a day at the office. He was in awe of wealthy men such as Andrew Mellon, and he thought them best suited to make society's key decisions.

WHAT VALUES and beliefs did Harding and Coolidge share?

QUICK REVIEW

The Teapot Dome Scandal

♦ Corruption and scandals plagued the Harding administration.

♦ Albert Fall, the secretary of the interior, leased petroleum reserves in exchange for cash.

♦ As a result of his part in the Teapot Dome scandal, Fall went to prison.

Coolidge easily won election on his own in 1924. He benefited from the general prosperity and the contrast he provided with the disgraced Harding. Coolidge defeated little-known Democrat John W. Davis.

In his full term, Coolidge showed most interest in reducing federal spending, lowering taxes, and blocking congressional initiatives. He saw his primary function as clearing the way for American businessmen. They, after all, were the agents of the era's unprecedented prosperity.

HERBERT HOOVER AND THE "ASSOCIATIVE STATE"

The most influential figure of the Republican new era was Herbert Hoover, who as secretary of commerce dominated the cabinets of Harding and Coolidge before becoming president himself in 1929. A successful engineer, administrator, and politician, Hoover effectively embodied the belief that enlightened business, encouraged and informed by the government, would act in the public interest. In the modern industrial age, Hoover believed, the government needed only to advise private citizens' groups about what national or international polices to pursue.

Unlike an earlier generation of Republicans, Hoover wanted not just to create a favorable climate for business but also to actively assist the business community. He spoke of creating an "associative state," in which the government would encourage voluntary cooperation among corporations, consumers, workers, farmers, and small businessmen. This became the central occupation of the Department of Commerce under Hoover's leadership. Under Hoover, the Bureau of Standards became one of the nation's leading research centers, setting engineering standards for key American industries such as machine tools and automobiles. The bureau also helped standardize the styles, sizes, and designs of many consumer products such as canned goods and refrigerators.

Hoover actively encouraged the creation and expansion of national trade associations. By 1929 there were about 2,000 of them. To some this practice violated the spirit of antitrust laws, but in the 1920s the Justice Department's Antitrust Division took a very lax view of its responsibility. In addition, the Supreme Court consistently upheld the legality of trade associations. Hoover also had a strong influence on presidential appointments to regulatory commissions; most of these went to men who had worked for the very firms the commissions had been designed to supervise. Regulatory commissions thus benefited from the technical expertise brought by industry leaders, but they in turn tended to remain uncritical of the industries they oversaw.

The government thus provided an ideal climate for the concentration of corporate wealth and power. The trend toward large corporate trusts and holding companies had been well under way since the late nineteenth century, but it accelerated in the 1920s. By 1929, the 200 largest American corporations owned almost half the total corporate wealth and about a fifth of the total national wealth.

COMMERCE AND FOREIGN POLICY

Throughout the 1920s, Republican leaders pursued policies designed to expand American economic activity abroad. The focus was on friendly nations and investments that would help foreign citizens buy American goods. Toward this end, Republican leaders urged close cooperation between bankers and the government as a strategy for expanding American investment and economic influence abroad. For Hoover and other policymakers, American business abroad was simply rugged individualism at work around the globe.

American oil, autos, farm machinery, and electrical equipment supplied a growing world market. Much of this expansion took place through the establishment of branch plants overseas by American companies. America's overall direct investment abroad increased from $3.8 billion in 1919 to $7.5 billion in 1929.

The strategy of maximum freedom for private enterprise, backed by limited government advice and assistance, significantly boosted the power and profits of American overseas investors. But in Central and Latin America, in particular, aggressive U.S. investment also fostered chronically underdeveloped economies, dependent on a few staple crops (sugar, coffee, cocoa, bananas) grown for export. U.S. economic dominance in the hemisphere also hampered the growth of democratic politics by favoring autocratic, military regimes that could be counted on to protect U.S. investments.

RESISTANCE TO MODERNITY

PROHIBITION

The Eighteenth Amendment, banning the manufacture, sale, and transportation of alcoholic beverages, took effect in January 1920. Prohibition was the culmination of a long campaign that associated drinking with the degradation of working-class family life and the worst evils of urban politics. Supporters, a coalition of women's temperance groups, middle-class progressives, and rural Protestants, hailed the new law as "a noble experiment." But it became clear rather quickly that enforcing the new law would be extremely difficult. The **Volstead Act** of 1919 established a federal Prohibition Bureau to enforce the Eighteenth Amendment, yet the bureau was severely understaffed, with only about 1,500 agents to police the entire country.

The public demand for alcohol, especially in the big cities, led to widespread lawbreaking. Illegal stills and breweries, as well as liquor smuggled in from Canada, supplied the needs of those Americans who continued to drink. Nearly every town and city had at least one "speakeasy," where people could drink and enjoy music and other entertainment. Local law enforcement personnel, especially in the cities, were easily bribed to overlook these illegal establishments. By the early 1920s many Eastern states no longer made even a token effort at enforcing the law.

Prohibition gave an enormous boost to violent organized crime. The pattern of organized crime in the 1920s closely resembled the larger trends in American business: smaller operations gave way to larger and more complex combinations. Successful organized crime figures, like Chicago's Al "Scarface" Capone, became celebrities in their own right and received heavy coverage in the mass media.

Organized crime, based on its huge profits from liquor, also made significant inroads into legitimate businesses, labor unions, and city government. By the time Congress and the states ratified the Twenty-first Amendment in 1933, repealing Prohibition, organized crime was a permanent feature of American life.

IMMIGRATION RESTRICTION

Sentiment for restricting immigration, growing since the late nineteenth century, reached its peak immediately after World War I. Antiimmigrant feeling reflected major shifts in both the size and makeup of the immigrant stream. The "new immigrants" were mostly Catholic and Jewish, and they were darker skinned than the "old immigrants." To many Americans they seemed more exotic, more foreign, and less willing and able to assimilate the nation's political and cultural values. They were also relatively poorer, more physically isolated in the nation's cities, and less politically strong than earlier immigrants. In the 1890s, the anti-Catholic American Protective Association called for a curb on immigration, and by exploiting

WHAT EXPLAINS the resurgence of the Ku Klux Klan in the 1920s?

Volstead Act The 1920 law defining the liquor forbidden under the Eighteenth Amendment and giving enforcement responsibilities to the Prohibition Bureau of the Department of the Treasury.

Annual Immigration to the United States, 1860–1930

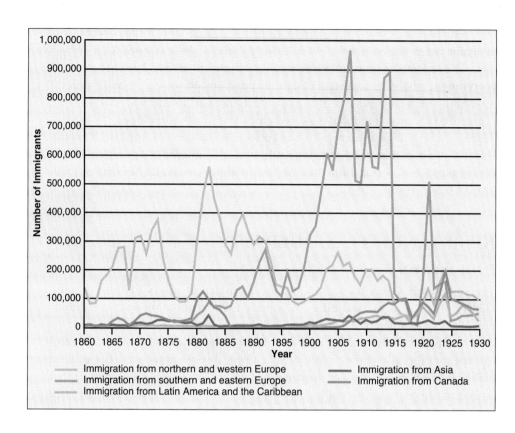

Immigration from northern and western Europe
Immigration from southern and eastern Europe
Immigration from Latin America and the Caribbean
Immigration from Asia
Immigration from Canada

23–3
National Origins Quota Act, 1924

Immigration Act   1921 act setting a maximum of 357,000 new immigrants each year.

the economic depression of that decade it reached a membership of 2.5 million. In 1894 a group of prominent Harvard graduates, including Henry Cabot Lodge and John Fiske, founded the Immigration Restriction League, providing an influential forum for the fears of the nation's elite. The league used newer scientific arguments, based on a flawed application of Darwinian evolutionary theory and genetics, to support its call for immigration restriction.

Theories of scientific racism, which had become more popular in the early 1900s, reinforced antiimmigrant bias. Eugenicists, who enjoyed considerable vogue in these years, held that heredity determined almost all of a person's capacities and that genetic inferiority predisposed people to crime and poverty. Such pseudoscientific thinking sought to explain historical and social development solely as a function of "racial" differences.

Against this background, the war and its aftermath provided the final push for immigration restriction. The postwar depression coincided with the resumption of massive immigration, bringing much hostile comment on the relationship between rising unemployment and the new influx of foreigners. Sensational press coverage of organized crime figures, many of them Italian or Jewish, also played a part.

In 1921 Congress passed the **Immigration Act**, setting a maximum of 357,000 new immigrants each year. Quotas limited annual immigration from any European country to 3 percent of the number of its natives counted in the 1910 U.S. census. But restrictionists complained that the new law still allowed too many southern and eastern Europeans in. The Johnson-Reed Immigration Act of 1924 revised the quotas to 2 percent of the number of foreign-born counted for each nationality in the census for 1890, when far fewer southern or eastern Europeans were present in the United States. The maximum total allowed each year was also cut, to 164,000. The quota laws did not apply to Canada, Mexico, or any other nation in the Western Hemisphere. The immigration restriction laws reversed earlier practices and became a permanent feature of national policy.

THE KU KLUX KLAN

If immigration restriction was resurgent nativism's most significant legislative expression, a revived Ku Klux Klan (KKK) was its most effective mass movement. The original Klan had been formed in the 1870s. The new Klan, born in Stone Mountain, Georgia, in 1915, was inspired by D. W. Griffith's racist spectacle *The Birth of a Nation*, a film released in that year depicting the original KKK as a heroic organization. The new Klan patterned itself on the secret rituals and antiblack hostility of its predecessor.

When Hiram W. Evans, a dentist from Dallas, became imperial wizard of the Klan in 1922, he hired professional fundraisers and publicists and directed an effective recruiting scheme that paid a commission to sponsors of new members. The Klan advocated "100 percent Americanism" and "the faithful maintenance of White Supremacy." It staunchly supported Prohibition, and it attacked birth control and Darwinism.

By 1924 the new Klan counted more than 3 million members across the country. Its slogan, "Native, White, Protestant Supremacy," proved especially attractive in the Midwest and South, including many cities. Klansmen boycotted businesses, threatened families, and sometimes resorted to violence—public whippings, arson, and lynching—against their chosen enemies. The Klan's targets sometimes included white Protestants accused of sexual promiscuity, blasphemy, or drunkenness, but most victims were African Americans, Catholics, and Jews. Support for Prohibition enforcement probably united Klansmen more than any single issue.

The Klan had a strong presence among delegates to the 1924 Democratic National Convention. The Klan began to fade in 1925 when its Indiana leader,

Women members of the Ku Klux Klan in New Castle, Indiana, August 1, 1923. The revived Klan was a powerful presence in scores of American communities during the early 1920s, especially among native-born white Protestants who feared cultural and political change. In addition to preaching "100 percent Americanism," local Klan chapters also served as a social function for members and their families.

Ball State University Libraries, Archives & Special Collections, W.A. Swift Photo Collection

Grand Dragon David C. Stephenson, became involved in a sordid personal affair. Stephenson had picked up a young secretary at a party, got her drunk on bootleg liquor, and then assaulted her on a train. After the woman took poison and died, Stephenson was convicted of manslaughter. With one of its most famous leaders disgraced and in jail, the new Klan began to lose members and influence.

PROMISES POSTPONED

FEMINISM IN TRANSITION

WHAT WERE the most important issues in the election of 1928?

The achievement of the suffrage removed the central issue that had given cohesion to the disparate forces of female reform activism. In addition, female activists of all persuasions found themselves swimming against a national tide of hostility to political idealism. During the 1920s, the women's movement split into two main wings over a fundamental disagreement about female identity. Should activists stress women's differences from men—their vulnerability and the double burden of work and family—and continue to press for protective legislation, such as laws that limited the length of the workweek for women? Or should they emphasize the ways that women were like men—sharing similar aspirations—and push for full legal and civil equality?

In 1920, the National American Woman Suffrage Association reorganized itself as the **League of Women Voters**. The league represented the historical mainstream of the suffrage movement, those who believed that the vote for women would bring a nurturing sensibility and a reform vision to American politics. Most league members continued working in a variety of reform organizations, and the league itself concentrated on educating the new female electorate, encouraging women to run for office, and supporting laws for the protection of women and children.

A newer, smaller, and more militant group was the National Woman's Party (NWP), founded in 1916 by militant suffragist Alice Paul. The NWP argued that women were still subordinate to men. It opposed protective legislation for women, claiming that such laws reinforced sex stereotyping and prevented women from competing with men in many fields. Largely representing the interests of professional and business women, the NWP focused on passage of a brief Equal Rights Amendment (ERA) to the Constitution, introduced in Congress in 1923: "Men and women shall have equal rights throughout the United States and every place subject to its jurisdiction."

Many of the older generation of women reformers opposed the ERA as elitist, arguing that far more women benefited from protective laws than were injured by them. ERA supporters countered that maximum hours laws or laws prohibiting women from night work prevented women from getting many lucrative jobs. But most women's groups opposed the ERA. These included the League of Women Voters, the National Consumers' League, and the Women's Trade Union League. ERA supporters generally stressed individualism, competition, and the abstract language of "equality" and "rights." They dreamed of a labor market that might be one in which women might have the widest opportunity. Anti-ERA forces looked at the labor market as it was, insisting it was more important to protect women from existing exploitation. The NWP campaign failed to get the ERA passed by Congress, but the debates it sparked would be echoed during the feminist movement of the 1970s.

A small number of professional women made real gains in the fields of real estate, banking, and journalism. The press regularly announced new "firsts" for women, such as Amelia Earhart's 1928 airplane flight across the Atlantic. As business expanded, a greater percentage of working women were employed in white-collar

League of Women Voters League formed in 1920 advocating for women's rights, among them the right for women to serve on juries and equal pay laws.

positions, as opposed to manufacturing and domestic service, but men still dominated in the higher paid and managerial white-collar occupations.

The most significant, if limited, victory for feminist reformers was the 1921 **Sheppard-Towner Act**, which established the first federally funded health care program, providing matching funds for states to set up prenatal and child health care centers. These centers also provided public health nurses for house calls. Although hailed as a genuine reform breakthrough, especially for women in rural and isolated communities, the act aroused much opposition. The NWP disliked it for its assumption that all women were mothers. Birth control advocates such as Margaret Sanger complained that contraception was not part of the program. The American Medical Association (AMA) objected to government-sponsored health care and to nurses who functioned outside the supervision of physicians. By 1929, largely as a result of intense AMA lobbying, Congress cut off funds for the program.

MEXICAN IMMIGRATION

The 1920s brought a dramatic influx of Mexicans to the United States. Mexican immigration, which was not included in the immigration laws of 1921 and 1924, had picked up substantially after the outbreak of the Mexican Revolution in 1911, when political instability and economic hardships provided incentives to cross the border to *El Norte*. According to the U.S. Immigration Service, an estimated 459,000 Mexicans entered the United States between 1921 and 1930, more than double the number for the previous decade. The official count no doubt underrepresented the true numbers of immigrants from Mexico. Many Mexicans shunned the main border crossings at El Paso, Texas; Nogales, Arizona; and Calexico, California, and, thus, avoided paying the $8 head tax and $10 visa fee.

The primary pull was the tremendous agricultural expansion occurring in the American Southwest. Irrigation and large-scale agribusiness had begun transforming California's Imperial and San Joaquin Valleys from arid desert into lucrative fruit and vegetable fields. Cotton pickers were needed in the vast plantations of Lower Rio Grande Valley in Texas and the Salt River Valley in Arizona. The sugar beet fields of Michigan, Minnesota, and Colorado also attracted many Mexican farm workers. American industry had also begun recruiting Mexican workers, first to fill wartime needs and later to fill the gap left by the decline in European immigration.

The new Mexican immigration appeared more permanent than previous waves—that is, more and more newcomers stayed. By 1930, San Antonio's Mexican community accounted for roughly 80,000 people out of a total population of a quarter million. Around 100,000 Mexicans lived in Los Angeles. Substantial Mexican communities also flourished in Midwestern cities. Many of the immigrants alternated between agricultural and factory jobs, depending on the seasonal availability of work. Mexican women often worked in the fields alongside their husbands. They also had jobs as domestics and seamstresses or took in laundry and boarders.

Racism and local patterns of residential segregation confined most Mexicans to barrios. Housing conditions were generally poor, particularly for recent arrivals, who were forced to live in rude shacks without running water or electricity. Disease and infant mortality rates were much higher than average,

Sheppard-Towner Act The first federal social welfare law, passed in 1921, providing federal funds for infant and maternity care.

Mexican Immigration to the United States in the 1920s Many Mexican migrants avoided official border crossing stations so they would not have to pay visa fees. Thus these official figures probably underestimated the true size of the decade's Mexican migration. As the economy contracted with the onset of the Great Depression, immigration from Mexico dropped off sharply.

Mexican workers gathered outside a San Antonio labor bureau in 1924. These employment agencies contracted Mexicans to work for Texas farmers, railroads, and construction companies. Note the three Anglo men in front (wearing suits and ties), who probably owned and operated this agency. During the 1920s, San Antonio's Mexican population doubled from roughly 40,000 to over 80,000, making it the second largest colonia in *El Norte* after Los Angeles.

Goldbeck Collection, Harry Ransom Humanities Research Center, University of Texas at Austin. Photo by Summerville (46ND)

and most Mexicans worked at low-paying, unskilled jobs and received inadequate health care. Legal restrictions passed by states and cities made it difficult for Mexicans to enter teaching, legal, and other professions. Mexicans were routinely banned from local public works projects as well. Many felt a deep ambivalence about applying for American citizenship. Loyalty to the Old Country was strong, and many cherished dreams of returning to live out their days in Mexico.

Ugly racist campaigns against Mexicans were common in the 1920s, especially when "cheap Mexican labor" was blamed for local unemployment or hard times. Stereotypes of Mexicans as "greasers" or "wetbacks" were prevalent in newspapers and movies of the day. Nativist efforts to limit Mexican immigration were thwarted by the lobbying of powerful agribusiness interests.

Mutual aid societies—*mutualistas*—became key social and political institutions in the Mexican communities of the Southwest and Midwest. They provided death benefits and widows' pensions for members and also served as centers of resistance to civil rights violations and discrimination. In 1928, the Federation of Mexican Workers Unions formed in response to a large farm labor strike in the Imperial Valley of California. A group of middle-class Mexican professionals in Texas organized the League of United Latin American Citizens (LULAC) in 1929. The founding of these organizations marked only the beginnings of a long struggle to bring economic, social, and racial equality to Mexican Americans.

The "New Negro"

The Great Migration spurred by World War I showed no signs of letting up during the 1920s, and African American communities in Northern cities grew rapidly. New York City's Harlem began attracting middle-class African Americans in the prewar years. After the war, heavy black migration from the South and the Caribbean encouraged real estate speculators and landlords to remake Harlem as an exclusively black neighborhood.

Harlem emerged as the demographic and cultural capital of black America, but its appeal transcended national borders as mass migration from the Caribbean helped reshape the community. Between 1900 and 1930 some 300,000 West Indians emigrated to the United States, roughly half of whom settled in New York City. By the late 1920s about one-quarter of Harlem's population had been born in Jamaica, Barbados, Trinidad, the Bahamas, and other parts of the Caribbean. Some of the leading cultural, business, and political figures of the era—poet Claude McKay, newspaper publisher P. M. H. Savory, labor organizer Hubert Harrison, black nationalist Marcus Garvey—had roots in the West Indies. Most black Caribbean migrants came from societies where class differences mattered more than racial ones, and many refused to accept racial bigotry without protest. A large number also carried with them entrepreneurial experience that contributed to their success in running small businesses. Intraracial tensions and

QUICK REVIEW

Harlem

◆ Harlem attacted middle-class African Americans in the prewar years.

◆ After the war, black people from the South and the Caribbean arrived in large numbers.

◆ Harlem became the political and intellectual center of African American culture.

 # MAP EXPLORATION

To explore an interactive version of this map, go to **http://www.prenhall.com/faraghertlc/map23.1**

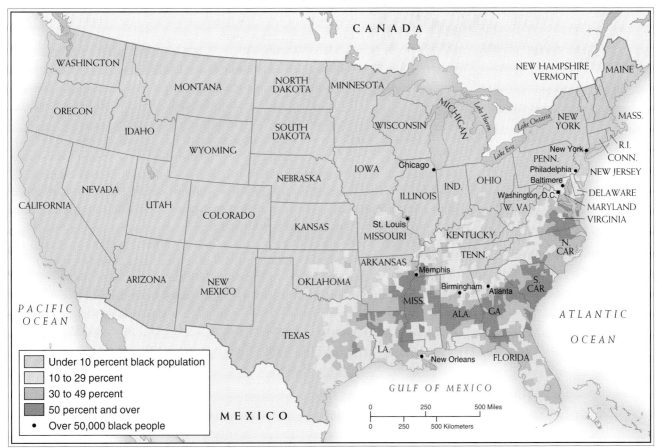

MAP 23-1

Black Population, 1920   Although the Great Migration had drawn hundreds of thousands of African Americans to the urban North, the Southern states of the former Confederacy still remained the center of the African American population in 1920.

WHY WERE African Americans drawn to Northern cities?

A **1925 pensive** portrait of Langston Hughes, one of the leading literary voices of the Harlem Renaissance. Winold Reiss's work suggested Hughes's determination to create poetry out of the everyday life experiences of Harlem's burgeoning African American population.

Winold Reiss, *Portrait of Langston Hughes* (1902–1967, Poet) © 1925. National Portrait Gallery, Washington, D.C., Art Resource, NY (S0041021)

Harlem Renaissance   A new African American cultural awareness that flourished in literature, art, and music in the 1920s.

resentment between American-born blacks and an increasingly visible West Indian population was one reflection of Harlem's transformation into a hemispheric center for black people.

The demand for housing in this restricted geographical area led to skyrocketing rents, but most Harlemites held low-wage jobs. This combination produced extremely overcrowded apartments, unsanitary conditions, and the rapid deterioration of housing stock. Disease and death rates were abnormally high. Yet Harlem also boasted a large middle-class population and supported a wide array of churches, theaters, newspapers and journals, and black-owned businesses. It became a magnet for African American intellectuals, artists, musicians, and writers from all over the world.

Harlem became the political and intellectual center for what writer Alain Locke called the "New Negro." Locke was referring to a new spirit in the work of black writers and intellectuals, an optimistic faith that encouraged African Americans to develop and celebrate their distinctive culture, firmly rooted in the history, folk culture, and experiences of African American people. This faith was the common denominator uniting the disparate figures associated with the **Harlem Renaissance**. The assertion of cultural independence resonated in the poetry of Langston Hughes and Claude McKay, the novels of Zora Neale Hurston and Jessie Fauset, the essays of Countee Cullen and James Weldon Johnson, the acting of Paul Robeson, and the blues singing of Bessie Smith.

The newly militant spirit that black veterans had brought home from World War I matured and found a variety of expressions in the Harlem of the 1920s. New leaders and movements began to appear alongside established organizations like the National Association for the Advancement of Colored People. A. Philip Randolph began a long career as a labor leader, socialist, and civil rights activist in these years. Harlem was also headquarters to Marcus Garvey's Universal Negro Improvement Association. Garvey created a mass movement that stressed black economic self-determination and unity among the black communities of the United States, the Caribbean, and Africa. His newspaper, *Negro World*, spoke to black communities around the world, urging black businesses to trade among themselves.

Garvey's best-publicized project was the Black Star Line, a black-owned and -operated fleet of ships that would link people of African descent around the world. But insufficient capital and serious financial mismanagement resulted in the spectacular failure of the enterprise. In 1923, Garvey was found guilty of mail fraud in his fundraising efforts; he later went to jail and was subsequently deported to England. Despite the disgrace, Harlem's largest newspaper, the *Amsterdam News*, explained Garvey's continuing appeal to African Americans: "In a world where black is despised, he taught them that black is beautiful. He taught them to admire and praise black things and black people."

Harlem in the 1920s also became a popular tourist attraction for "slumming" whites. Nightclubs like the Cotton Club were often controlled by white organized crime figures. They featured bootleg liquor, floor shows, and the best jazz bands of the day, led by Duke Ellington, Fletcher Henderson, Cab Calloway, and Louis Armstrong. Yet these clubs were rigidly segregated. Black dancers, singers, and musicians provided the entertainment, but no African Americans were allowed in the audience. Chronicled in novels and newspapers, Harlem became a potent symbol to white America of the ultimate good time. For the vast majority of Harlem residents, the day-to-day reality was depressingly different.

THE ELECTION OF 1928

The 1928 campaign featured two politicians who represented profoundly different sides of American life. Al Smith, the Democratic nominee for president, was a pure product of New York City's Lower East Side. Smith came from a background that included Irish, German, and Italian ancestry, and he was raised as a Roman Catholic. He rose through the political ranks of New York's Tammany Hall machine. A personable man with a deep sympathy for poor and working-class people, Smith served four terms as governor of New York, pushing through an array of laws reforming factory conditions, housing, and welfare programs.

Herbert Hoover easily won the Republican nomination after Calvin Coolidge announced he would not run for reelection. Hoover epitomized the successful and forward-looking American. An engineer and self-made millionaire, he offered a unique combination of experience in humanitarian war relief, administrative efficiency, and probusiness policies. Hoover was one of the best known men in America and promised to continue the Republican control of national politics.

Smith himself quickly became the central issue of the campaign. His sharp New York accent, jarring to many Americans who heard it over the radio, marked him clearly as a man of the city. So did his brown derby and fashionable suits, as well as his promise to work for the repeal of Prohibition. As the first Roman Catholic nominee of a major party, Smith also drew a torrent of anti-Catholic bigotry, especially in the South and Midwest.

Hoover polled 21 million votes to Smith's 15 million, and swept the electoral college 444 to 87, including New York State. Even the Solid South, reliably Democratic since the Civil War, gave five states to Hoover—a clear reflection of the ethnocultural split in the party. Yet the election offered important clues to the future of the Democrats. Smith ran better in the big cities of the North and East than any other Democrat in modern times. He outpolled Hoover in the aggregate vote of the nation's twelve largest cities and carried six of them, thus pointing the way to the Democrats' future dominance with urban, Northeastern, and ethnic voters.

MAP EXPLORATION

To explore an interactive version of this map, go to
http://www.prenhall.com/faraghertlc/map23.2

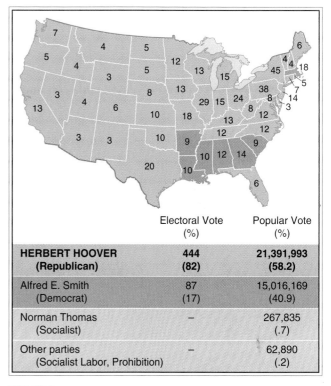

	Electoral Vote (%)	Popular Vote (%)
HERBERT HOOVER (Republican)	**444 (82)**	**21,391,993 (58.2)**
Alfred E. Smith (Democrat)	87 (17)	15,016,169 (40.9)
Norman Thomas (Socialist)	–	267,835 (.7)
Other parties (Socialist Labor, Prohibition)	–	62,890 (.2)

MAP 23-2

The Election of 1928   Although Al Smith managed to carry the nation's twelve largest cities, Herbert Hoover's victory in 1928 was one of the largest popular and electoral landslides in the nation's history.

WHAT VALUES did Hoover claim to stand for in the election of 1928?

CONCLUSION

America's big cities, if not dominant politically, now defined the nation's cultural and economic life as never before. The mass media brought cosmopolitan entertainments and values to the remotest small communities. New consumer durable goods associated with mass-production techniques—automobiles, radios, telephones, household appliances—were manufactured largely in cities. The advertising and public relations companies that sang their praises were also distinctly urban enterprises. Even with the curtailing of European immigration, big cities attracted a kaleidoscopic variety of migrants: white people from small towns and farms, African Americans from the rural South, Mexicans from across the border, intellectuals and professionals looking to make their mark.

Many Americans, of course, remained deeply suspicious of postwar cultural and economic trends. Yet the partisans of Prohibition, members of the Ku Klux Klan, and religious fundamentalists usually found themselves on the defensive against what they viewed as alien cultural and economic forces centered in the metropolis. Large sectors of the population did not share in the era's prosperity, but the large numbers who did—or at least had a taste of good times—ensured Republican political dominance throughout the decade. Thus, America in the 1920s balanced dizzying change in the cultural and economic realms with conservative politics.

CHRONOLOGY

1920   Prohibition takes effect.

Warren G. Harding is elected president.

Station KDKA in Pittsburgh goes on the air.

Census reports that urban population is greater than rural population for the first time.

1921   First immigration quotas are established by Congress.

Sheppard-Towner Act establishes first federally funded health care program.

1922   Washington conference produces Five-Power Treaty, scaling down navies.

1923   Equal Rights Amendment is first introduced in Congress.

Harding dies in office; Calvin Coolidge becomes president.

1924   Ku Klux Klan is at height of its influence.

Dawes Plan for war reparations stabilizes European economies.

Johnson-Reed Immigration Act tightens quotas established in 1921.

1925   Scopes trial pits religious fundamentalism against modernity.

F. Scott Fitzgerald publishes *The Great Gatsby*.

1926   National Broadcasting Company establishes first national radio network.

1927   McNary-Haugen Farm Relief bill finally passed by Congress but is vetoed by President Coolidge as unwarranted federal interference in the economy.

Warner Brothers produces *The Jazz Singer*, the first feature-length motion picture with sound.

Charles Lindbergh makes first solo flight across the Atlantic Ocean.

1928   Kellogg-Briand Pact renounces war.

Herbert Hoover defeats Al Smith for the presidency.

1929   Robert and Helen Lynd publish their classic community study *Middletown*.

SUMMARY

Postwar Prosperity and its Price The twenties ushered in the second industrial revolution that stimulated a boom in several industries. At the same time, the modern corporation changed how business was organized and worked. Prosperity fostered the corporate idea of welfare capitalism while unions declined. The epitome of the new age was the automobile that influenced where people lived, their daily life, and their leisure activities, among many other things. Despite the appearance of prosperity, several sectors of the economy experienced significant declines.

The New Mass Culture New media transformed American culture in the 1920s. Popular entertainment and advertising encouraged the culture of consumption and the idea of celebrity. The media promoted a new morality that celebrated sensuality and personal pleasure.

The State, the Economy, and Business The Republican presidents promoted a business-government partnership that stressed business profits. Despite abuses and scandals, the nation experienced general prosperity. U. S. foreign policy aimed to promote business expansion overseas.

Resistance to Modernity Not all Americans embraced modern changes. Especially outside big cities, resistance to modern trends and longing for the past were evident in several movements, including Prohibition, immigration restriction, and the Ku Klux Klan.

Promises Postponed Prosperity did not lead to advances in status and rights for several groups. Though winning the right to vote, women faced strong barriers to achieving other political, social, and economic gains but did make some progress. Mexican immigration increased and although immigrants faced racism, they built strong communities. African Americans also emerged from the war with mixed feelings. They developed a strong movement based on race pride and consciousness that led to a rich cultural flowering. The opposing forces evident in the 1920s came to a head in the 1928 election that was won by Herbert Hoover.

REVIEW QUESTIONS

1. Describe the impact of the "second industrial revolution" on American business, workers, and consumers. Which technological and economic changes had the biggest impact on American society?

2. Analyze the uneven distribution of the 1920s' economic prosperity. Which Americans gained the most, and which were largely left out?

3. How did an expanding mass culture change the contours of everyday life in the decade following World War I? What role did new technologies of mass communication play in shaping these changes? What connections can you draw between the "culture of consumption" then and today?

4. What were the key policies and goals articulated by Republican political leaders of the 1920s? How did they apply these to both domestic and foreign affairs?

5. How did some Americans resist the rapid changes taking place in the post–World War I world? What cultural and political strategies did they employ?

6. Discuss the 1928 election as a mirror of the divisions in American society.

KEY TERMS

Harlem Renaissance (p. 634)

Immigration Act (p. 628)

League of Women Voters (p. 630)

Open shop (p. 618)

Sheppard-Towner Act (p. 631)

Volstead Act (p. 627)

Welfare capitalism (p. 618)

RECOMMENDED READING

Nancy F. Cott, *The Grounding of American Feminism* (1987). Includes a sophisticated analysis of the debates among feminists during the 1920s.

Lynn Dumenil, *The Modern Temper: America in the 1920s* (1995). An excellent synthesis of recent scholarship, which emphasizes the ambivalence that many Americans felt toward the emergence of modern society.

James J. Flink, *The Car Culture* (1975). The best single volume on the history of the automobile and how it changed American life.

David J. Goldberg, *Discontented America: The United States in the 1920s* (1999). Focuses on Americans' continuing discomfort with racial, ethnic, religious, and class difference during the decade.

Ellis W. Hawley, *The Great War and the Search for Modern Order* (1979). An influential study of the relations between the state and business and the growth of mass consumer society.

Desmond King, *Making Americans: Immigration, Race, and the Origins of Diverse Democracy* (2000). Fine analysis of the shift of U.S. immigration policies in the 1920s, with special attention to the influence of eugenics, and the long-term consequences of the new restrictive legislation.

Nancy Maclean, *Behind the Mask of Chivalry: The Making of the Second Ku Klux Klan* (1994). An excellent case study of the KKK in Athens, Georgia, with important insights on the Klan's relationship to issues involving gender and class difference.

Roland Marchand, *Advertising the American Dream: Making Way for Modernity, 1920–1940* (1985). A superb, beautifully illustrated account of the rise of the modern advertising industry.

Emily S. Rosenberg, *Spreading the American Dream* (1982). A fine study of American economic and cultural expansion around the world from 1890 to 1945.

Susan Smulyan, *Selling Radio: The Commercialization of American Broadcasting, 1920–1934* (1994). The best analysis of the rise of commercial radio broadcasting in the 1920s.

Advertising and the Modern Woman

DURING the 1920s, for the first time in American history, consumer demand was the chief impetus to economic growth. As a direct consequence, the 1920s witnessed the emergence of advertising as a major industry. Most of the ads from this period promoted benefits that had little to do with product. Why? The simplest explanation is that the ad agency and the manufacturer believed that youth and feminine beauty would sell. By the late twenties, advertisements for all sorts of products touted the "modern young woman" as the arbiter of taste and beauty. In so doing, the advertisers signaled a deep shift in American culture. Which specific feminine characteristics are promoted in the advertisements shown here?

The image of a young, attractive woman in this Lucky Strike ad from the 1920s is much more prominent than the product she is promoting. How does the ad make the connection between cigarettes and femminine beauty? What is the underying message of the command to "reach for a Lucky—instead of a sweet?"

The Creoles of Louisiana one of the purest French and Spanish blood and their charm is the charm of courtly France and of patrician Spain.
A distinguishing mark of their aristocratic ancestry is their wonderful hair, thick, dark, lustrous and beautiful.

The Wonder of Creole Hair

CREOLE charm has been as much admired in aristocratic European circles as in America. Empress Josephine, wife of Napoleon, was a Creole. Queen Hortense of Holland and Prince Eugene, Viceroy of Italy, were Creoles. The glorious Creole hair has always been especially admired. The hair is a special pride and care of the Creoles and for generations La Creole Hair Dressing has been favorite among them. It preserves the youthful color and beauty of the hair even through advanced years.

La Creole Ends Gray Hair

La Creole not alone prevents gray hair. La Creole *treatment* will bring back to its youthful color and beauty, hair that has become gray, gray-streaked, or faded. La Creole contains no dyes. It promotes the youthfully vigorous healthy condition of hair and scalp which nature intended. Its effect on the hair is gradual but certain. Two to five weeks treatment is required to bring back any shade—lightest brown to deepest black—whatever the natural color was. After that an occasional application will preserve the vigorous healthy color permanently.

Good taste and good breeding approve the use of La Creole and there is no reason for making any secret of its use, though it can never be detected.

La Creole must not be confused with dyes—it can not give a dyed look and there is nothing to stain the scalp or to wash or rub off. It makes the hair soft, wavy, lustrous and beautiful. Eliminates dandruff.

Absolutely guaranteed to bring back the hair's color or money refunded.

Send coupon for booklet "La Creole—Hair Beautiful." Shows style of hair dressing best suited to each type of face.

At Drug Stores and Toilet Counters, Price $1.00
If your Dealer can't supply you, send his name and address. We will see that you are supplied.

VAN VLEET-MANSFIELD LABORATORIES
132 Tenth Street, Memphis, Tenn.

Van Vleet-Mansfield Laboratories
132 Tenth St., Memphis, Tenn.

Please send booklet "La Creole—Hair Beautiful," teaching the hair dress most becoming to each individual.

Name ....
Address ....
City .... State ....

▲

Virtually all ads during this period, except those aimed explicitly at African Americans, avoided any ethnic or racial references. "La Creole" ads are exceptions. The product name itself referred to a specific Community of people in Louisiana, descendants of French settlers. But the term was also used to refer to individuals of mixed racial background. How does the "La Creole" ad deal with this? What does that suggest for how you might interpret the other ads?

This ad for a line of hair products created and manufactured by Madame C.J. Walker, one of the first African-American millionaires. The ad promises "fascinating beauty" to users of its product.
▼

You, too, may be a fascinating beauty

PERHAPS YOU ENVY the girl with irresistible beauty, whose skin is flawless and velvety, whose hair has a beautiful silky sheen, the girl who receives glances of undoubted admiration.

You need not envy her. Create new beauty for yourself by using Madam C. J. Walker's famous beauty preparations.

When Madam Walker and her associates started to develop her beauty preparations, which are now used all over the world, they perfected their toiletries step by step.

Each preparation was beyond the point of experiment before it was followed by another. Each preparation's wide use and high merit were always *proved*. Today they are unsurpassed.

Try these products and you won't have reason to envy another girl her lovely hair and her charming complexion.

You can obtain any of these marvelous preparations at your nearest druggist or from a Madam C. J. Walker agent (there's one near you) or write the company direct at Indianapolis.

Madam C. J. WALKER'S Beauty Preparations

COMPLEXION AND TOILET SOAP—A preservative of beauty—mild and safe for the most tender skin. Perfumed delightfully. 20 cents per large bar.

VEGETABLE OIL ANTISEPTIC SOAP—A popular-priced household soap of purest vegetable oils. Lathers well in hardest water, removes grease and dirt, yet will not harm a baby's skin. A bargain at 10 cents a bar.

SUPERFINE FACE POWDER (Brown)—Clinging, velvety smooth, invisible and admirably perfumed. Imparts an olive tint to fair complexions and harmonizes bewitchingly with darker skins. Obtainable in rose-flesh and white. 50 cents per sealed box.

GLOSSINE—Oils and softens dry, brittle hair. Imparts a rich, healthy lustre. Indispensable for bobbed hair and unsurpassed in the opinion of social leaders and well-groomed gentlemen. 35 cents per long-lasting box.

THESE ARE BUT FOUR OF EIGHTEEN MADAM C. J. WALKER BEAUTY PREPARATIONS—AS FINE AS MONEY CAN BUY

I remembered seeing the people passing on their way to California . . . It hurt me to see the people in their rickety old cars, their clothes in tatters, escaping from the drought and the dust bowls.
—Carlotta Silvas Martin, January 1936

Hands in their pockets, hungry men stand numbly in one of New York City's breadlines. Said one observer: "The wretched men, many without overcoats or decent shoes, usually began to line up soon after six o'clock—in good weather or bad, rain or snow.

24

THE GREAT DEPRESSION AND THE NEW DEAL

1929–1940

WHAT CAUSED the stock market crash of 1929?

WHAT DID FDR hope to accomplish in his first hundred days in office?

WHAT GROUPS formed the New Deal coalition?

WHAT WERE conditions like in the Dust Bowl in the 1930s?

YEARS OF DUST

RESETTLEMENT ADMINISTRATION
Rescues Victims
Restores Land to Proper Use

WHAT ROLE did the federal government play in the arts during the 1930s?

WHAT EFFECT did the New Deal have on the lives and economic prospects of minorities?

AMERICAN COMMUNITIES
Sit-Down Strike at Flint:
Automobile Workers Organize a New Union

IN THE GLOOMY EVENING OF FEBRUARY 11, 1937, 400 TIRED, UNSHAVEN, but very happy strikers marched out of the sprawling automobile factory known as Fisher Body Number 1. Most carried American flags and small bundles of clothing. A makeshift banner on top of the plant announced "Victory Is Ours." A wildly cheering parade line of a thousand supporters greeted the strikers at the gates. Shouting with joy, honking horns, and singing songs, the celebrants marched to two other factories to greet other emerging strikers. After forty-four days, the great Flint sit-down strike was over.

Flint, Michigan, was the heart of production for General Motors, the largest corporation in the world. In 1936 GM's net profits had reached $285 million, and its total assets were $1.5 billion. Originally a center for lumbering and then carriage making, Flint had boomed with the auto industry during the 1920s. Thousands of migrants streamed into the city, attracted by assembly-line jobs averaging about $30 a week. By 1930 Flint's population had grown to about 150,000 people, 80 percent of whom depended on work at General Motors. A severe housing shortage made living conditions difficult. Tar-paper shacks, tents, even railroad cars were the only shelter available for many. Parts of the city resembled a mining camp.

The Great Depression hit Flint very hard. Employment at GM fell from a 1929 high of 56,000 to fewer than 17,000 in 1932. As late as 1938 close to half the city's families were receiving some kind of emergency relief. By that time, as in thousands of other American communities, Flint's private and county relief agencies had been overwhelmed by the needs of the unemployed and their families. Two new national agencies based in Washington, D.C., the Federal Emergency Relief Administration and the Works Progress Administration, had replaced local sources of aid during the economic crisis.

The United Automobile Workers (UAW) came to Flint in 1936 seeking to organize GM workers into one industrial union. The previous year, Congress had passed the National Labor Relations Act (also known as the Wagner Act), which made union organizing easier by guaranteeing the right of workers to join unions and to bargain collectively. The act established the National Labor Relations Board to oversee union elections and prohibit illegal antiunion activities by employers. But the obstacles to labor organizing were still enormous. Unemployment was high, and GM had maintained a vigorous antiunion policy for years. By the fall of 1936, the UAW had signed up only a thousand members. The key moment came with the seizure of two Flint GM plants by a few hundred auto workers on December 30, 1936. The idea was to stay in the factories until strikers could achieve a collective bargaining agreement with General Motors. "We don't aim to keep the plants or try to run them,"

explained one sit-downer to a reporter, "but we want to see that nobody takes our jobs. We don't think we're breaking the law, or at least we don't think we're doing anything really bad."

The sit-down strike was a new and daring tactic that gained popularity among American industrial workers during the 1930s. In 1936 there were forty-eight sit-downs involving nearly 90,000 workers, and in 1937 some 400,000 workers participated in 477 sit-down strikes. Sit-downs expressed the militant exuberance of the rank and file. As one union song of the day put it:

When they tie the can to a union man,
Sit down! Sit down!
When they give him the sack they'll take him back,
Sit down! Sit down!
When the speed up comes, just twiddle your thumbs,
Sit down! Sit down!
When the boss won't talk don't take a walk,
Sit down! Sit down!

The Flint strikers carefully organized themselves into what one historian called "the sit-down community." Each plant elected a strike committee and appointed its own police chief and sanitary engineer. Strikers were divided into "families" of fifteen, each with a captain. No alcohol was allowed, and strikers were careful not to destroy company property. Committees were organized for every conceivable purpose: food, recreation, sanitation, education, and contact with the outside. Sit-downers formed glee clubs and small orchestras to entertain themselves. Using loudspeakers, they broadcast concerts and speeches to their supporters outside the gates. A Women's Emergency Brigade—the strikers' wives, mothers, and daughters—provided crucial support preparing food and maintaining militant picket lines.

As the sit-down strike continued through January 1937, support in Flint and around the nation grew. Over-all production in the GM empire dropped from 53,000 vehicles per week to 1,500. Reporters and union supporters flocked to the plants. On January 11, in the so-called Battle of Running Bulls, strikers and their supporters clashed violently with Flint police and private GM guards. Michigan governor Frank Murphy, sympathetic to the strikers, brought in the National Guard to protect them. He refused to enforce an injunction obtained by GM to evict the strikers.

In the face of determined unity by the sit-downers, GM gave in and recognized the UAW as the exclusive bargaining agent in all sixty of its factories. The strike was perhaps the most important in American labor history, sparking a huge growth in union membership in the automobile and other mass-production industries. Rose Pesotta, a textile union organizer, described the

Flint

wild victory celebration in Flint's overflowing Pengelly Building: "People sang and joked and laughed and cried, deliriously joyful. Victory meant a freedom they had never known before. No longer would they be afraid to join unions."

Out of the tight-knit, temporary community of the sit-down strike emerged a looser yet more permanent kind of community: a powerful, nationwide trade union of automobile workers. The UAW struggled successfully to win recognition and collective bargaining rights from other carmakers, such as Chrysler and Ford. The national UAW, like other new unions in the mass-production

industries, was composed of locals around the country. The permanent community of unionized auto workers won significant improvements in wages, working conditions, and benefits. Locals also became influential in the political and social lives of their larger communities—industrial cities such as Flint, Detroit, and Toledo. Nationally, organized labor became a crucial component of the New Deal political coalition and a key power broker in the Democratic Party. The new reality of a national community of organized labor would alter the national political and economic landscape for decades to come.

HARD TIMES

THE CRASH

Only about 4 million Americans out of a total population of 120 million owned any stocks when the tumbling of prices on the New York Stock Exchange ended the speculative mania of the 1920s. Many of these stock buyers had been lured into the market through easy-credit, margin accounts. These allowed investors to purchase stocks by making a small down payment (as low as 10 percent), borrowing the rest from a broker, and using the shares as collateral, or security, on the loan.

Although often portrayed as a one- or two-day catastrophe, the Wall Street crash of 1929 was in reality a steep downward slide. The bull market peaked in early September, and prices drifted downward. On October 23 the Dow Jones industrials lost 21 points in one hour, and many large investors concluded the boom was over. The boom itself rested on expectations of continually rising prices; once those expectations began to melt, the market had to decline. On Monday, October 28, the Dow lost 38 points, or 13 percent of its value. On October 29, "Black Tuesday," the bottom seemed to fall out. Over 16 million shares, more than double the previous record, were traded as panic selling took hold. For many stocks no buyers were available at any price.

The situation worsened. The market's fragile foundation of credit, based on margin debt, quickly crumbled. Many investors with margin accounts had no choice but to sell when stock values fell. Since the shares themselves represented the security for their loans, more money had to be put up to cover the loans when prices declined. By mid-November about $30 billion in the market price of stocks had been wiped out. Half the value of the stocks listed in the *New York Times* index was lost in ten weeks.

The nation's political and economic leaders downplayed the impact of Wall Street's woes. "The fundamental business of the country," President Herbert Hoover told Americans in late October, "is on a sound and prosperous basis." Secretary of the Treasury Andrew Mellon spoke for many in the financial world when he described the benefits of the slump: "It will purge the rottenness out of the system." At the end of 1929 hardly anyone was predicting that a depression would follow the stock market crash.

UNDERLYING WEAKNESSES

It would be oversimple to say that the stock market crash "caused" the **Great Depression**. But like a person who catches a chill, the economy after the crash became less resistant to existing sources of infection. The resulting sickness revealed

WHAT CAUSED the stock market crash of 1929?

IMAGE KEY

for pages 642–643

a. The National Recovery Agency seal with an eagle holding a cog in one talon and lightning bolts in the other over the slogan "We Do Our Part."

b. The Civilian Conservation Corps' emblem.

c. Hungry men stand in a bread line in New York City.

d. A Works Progress Administration poster, depicting a farmer and a miner shaking hands.

e. An old fashioned box radio in a wooden cabinet.

f. Anxious citizens crowd along Wall Street sidewalks while automobiles edge down the street on Black Tuesday, October 29, 1929.

g. Gov. Franklin D. Roosevelt shakes hands with a poor mine worker during a campaign trip.

h. Ben Shahn's 1936 poster for the Resettlement Adminstration.

i. Isaac Soyer's "Employment Agency," oil on canvas.

Stockbrokers, their customers, and employees of the New York Stock Exchange gather nervously on Wall Street during the stock market crash of 1929. October 29 was the worst single day in the 112-year history of the exchange, as panic selling caused many stocks to lose half their value.

Brown Brothers (010634-1)

Great Depression The nation's worst economic crisis, extending through the 1930s, producing unprecedented bank failures, unemployment, and industrial and agricultural collapse.

underlying economic weaknesses left over from the previous decade. First, workers and consumers by and large received too small a share of the enormous increases in labor productivity.

Better machinery and more efficient industrial organization had increased labor productivity enormously, but wages and salaries had not risen nearly as much. In effect, the automobile of American capitalism had one foot pressed to the accelerator of production and another on the brake of consumption. Between 1923 and 1929 manufacturing output per worker-hour increased by 32 percent. Wages during the same period rose only 8 percent, or one-quarter the rise in productivity. Moreover, the rise in productivity itself had encouraged overproduction in many industries. The farm sector had never been able to regain its prosperity of the World War I years. Farmers suffered under a triple burden of declining prices for their crops, a drop in exports, and large debts incurred by wartime expansion (see Chapter 23).

The most important weakness in the economy was the extremely unequal distribution of income and wealth. In 1929, the top 0.1 percent of American families (24,000 families) had an aggregate income equal to that of the bottom 42 percent

Distribution of Total Family Income Among Various Segments of the Population, 1929–1944 (in Percentages)

Year	Poorest Fifth	Second Poorest Fifth	Middle Fifth	Second Wealthiest Fifth	Wealthiest Fifth	Wealthiest 5 Percent
1929	12.5		13.8	19.3	54.4	30.0
1935–1936	4.1	9.2	14.1	20.9	51.7	26.5
1941	4.1	9.5	15.3	22.3	48.8	24.0
1944	4.9	10.9	16.2	22.2	45.8	20.7

Source: Adapted from U.S. Bureau of the Census, *Historical Statistics of the United States, Colonial Times to 1970*, Bicentennial ed. (Washington, D.C.: U.S. Government Printing Office, 1975), p. 301.

(11.5 million families). The top 5 percent of American families received 30 percent of the nation's income; the bottom 60 percent got only 26 percent. Nearly 80 percent of the nation's families (21.5 million households) had no savings; the top 0.1 percent held 34 percent of all savings.

The stock market crash undermined the confidence, investment, and spending of businesses and the well-to-do. Manufacturers decreased their production and began laying off workers, and layoffs brought further declines in consumer spending and another round of production cutbacks. A spurt of consumer spending might have checked this downward spiral, but consumers had less to spend as industries laid off workers and reduced work hours. With a shrinking market for products, businesses were hesitant to expand. A large proportion of the nation's banking funds were tied to the speculative bubble of Wall Street stock buying. Many banks began to fail as anxious depositors withdrew their funds, which were uninsured. Thousands of families lost their savings to these failures. An 86 percent plunge in agricultural prices between 1929 and 1933, compared to a decline in agricultural production of only 6 percent, brought suffering to America's farmers.

MASS UNEMPLOYMENT

At a time when unemployment insurance did not exist and public relief was completely inadequate, the loss of a job could mean economic catastrophe for workers and their families. Massive unemployment across America became the most powerful sign of a deepening depression. By 1933, 12.6 million workers—over one-quarter of the labor force—were without jobs. Other sources put the figure that year above 16 million, or nearly one out of every three workers. None of these statistics tells us how long people were unemployed or how many Americans found only part-time work.

What did it mean to be unemployed and without hope in the early 1930s? Figures give us only an outline of the grim reality. Many Americans, raised believing that they were responsible for their own fate, blamed themselves for their failure to find work. Contemporary journalists and social workers noted the

Unemployment, 1929–1945

In 1939, despite six years of New Deal programs, unemployment still hovered around 18 percent of the work force. Only the onset of World War II ended the unemployment crisis.

Source: U.S. Bureau of the Census, *Historical Statistics of the United States, Colonial Times to 1970*, Bicentennial ed. (Washington, DC: U.S. Government Printing Office, 1975), p. 135.

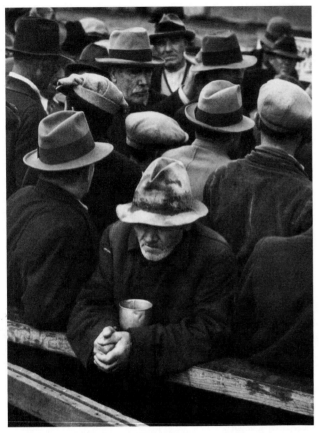

Dorothea Lange captured the lonely despair of unemployment in *White Angel Bread Line, San Francisco*, 1933. During the 1920s Lange had specialized in taking portraits of wealthy families, but by 1932 she could no longer stand the contradiction between her portrait business and "what was going on in the street." She said of this photograph: "There are moments such as these when time stands still and all you can do is hold your breath and hope it will wait for you."

Dorothea Lange, *White Angel Bread Line, San Francisco*, 1933. Copyright, the Dorothea Lange Collection, The Oakland Museum of California, City of Oakland. Gift of Paul S. Taylor

common feelings of shame and guilt expressed by the unemployed. Even those who did not blame themselves struggled with feelings of inadequacy, uselessness, and despair. One unemployed Houston woman told a relief caseworker, "I'm just no good, I guess. I've given up ever amounting to anything. It's no use."

Joblessness proved especially difficult for men between the ages of thirty-five and fifty-five, the period in their lives when family responsibilities were heaviest. Nathan Ackerman, a psychiatrist who went to Pennsylvania to observe the impact of prolonged unemployment on coal miners, found an enormous sense of "internal distress":

> They gave each other solace. They were loath to go home because they were indicted, as if it were their fault for being unemployed. . . . The women punished the men for not bringing home the bacon, by withholding themselves sexually . . . . These men suffered from depression.

Women found it easier to hold onto jobs, since their labor was cheaper. Female clerks, secretaries, maids, and waitresses earned much less than male factory workers, but their jobs were more likely to survive hard times. Unemployment upset the psychological balance in many families by undermining the traditional authority of the male breadwinner. Men responded in a variety of ways: some withdrew emotionally; others became angry or took to drinking. A few committed suicide. One Chicago social worker, writing about unemployment in 1934, summed up the strains she found in families: "Fathers feel they have lost their prestige in the home; there is much nagging, mothers nag at the fathers, parents nag at the children. Children of working age who earn meager salaries find it hard to turn over all their earnings and deny themselves even the greatest necessities and as a result leave home."

Pressures on those lucky enough to have a job increased as well. Anna Novak, a Chicago meatpacker, recalled the degrading harassment at the hands of foremen: "You could get along swell if you let the boss slap you on the behind and feel you up." Fear of unemployment and a deep desire for security marked the Depression generation. "I mean there's a conditioning here by the Depression," a sanitation worker told an interviewer many years later. "I'm what I call a security cat. I don't dare switch [jobs]. 'Cause I got too much whiskers on it, seniority."

HOOVER'S FAILURE

The enormity of the Great Depression overwhelmed traditional—and meager—sources of relief. In most communities across America these sources were a patchwork of private agencies and local government units, such as towns, cities, or counties. They simply lacked the money, resources, and staff to deal with the worsening situation. One West Virginia coal-mining county with 1,500 unemployed miners had only $9,000 to meet relief needs for that year. Unemployed transients, attracted by warm weather, posed a special problem for communities in California and Florida. By the end of 1931, Los Angeles had 70,000 nonresident jobless and homeless men; new arrivals numbered about 1,200 a day.

Isaac Soyer's *Employment Agency*, a 1937 oil painting, offered one of the decade's most sensitive efforts at depicting the anxiety and sense of isolation felt by millions of Depression-era job hunters.

Isaac Soyer, *Employment Agency*, 1937. Oil on canvas, 34" × 45", (87 × 114.3 cm). Whitney Museum of American Art, New York

There was great irony, even tragedy, in President Hoover's failure to respond to human suffering. He had administered large-scale humanitarian efforts during World War I with great efficiency, yet he failed to face the facts of the Depression. He resisted the growing calls from Congress and local communities for a greater federal role in relief efforts or public works projects. He worried, as he told Congress after vetoing one measure, about injuring "the initiative and enterprise of the American people." The President's Emergency Committee for Unemployment, established in 1930, and its successor, the President's Organization for Unemployment Relief (POUR), created in 1931, did little more than encourage local groups to raise money to help the unemployed.

Hoover's plan for recovery centered on restoring business confidence. His administration's most important institutional response to the Depression was the Reconstruction Finance Corporation (RFC), established in early 1932. The RFC was designed to make government credit available to ailing banks, railroads, insurance companies, and other businesses, thereby stimulating economic activity. The key assumption here was that the credit problem was one of supply (for businesses) rather than demand (from consumers). The RFC managed to save numerous banks and other businesses from going under, but its approach did not hasten recovery.

PROTEST AND THE ELECTION OF 1932

By 1932, the desperate mood of many Americans was finding expression in direct, sometimes violent protests that were widely covered in the press. On March 7, Communist organizers led a march of several thousand Detroit auto workers and unemployed to the Ford River Rouge factory in nearby Dearborn. When the demonstrators refused orders to turn back, Ford-controlled police fired tear gas and bullets, killing four and seriously wounding fifty others. Some 40,000 people attended a tense funeral service a few days later. Desperate farmers in Iowa organized the Farmers' Holiday Association, aimed at

QUICK REVIEW

The 1932 Election

- Republicans renominated Hoover.
- The Democratic platform differed little from the Republican platform.
- Franklin D. Roosevelt's victory was a repudiation of Hoover.

MAP EXPLORATION

To explore an interactive version of this map, go to
http://www.prenhall.com/faraghertlc/map24.1

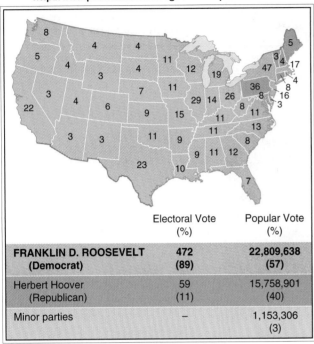

	Electoral Vote (%)	Popular Vote (%)
FRANKLIN D. ROOSEVELT (Democrat)	**472 (89)**	**22,809,638 (57)**
Herbert Hoover (Republican)	59 (11)	15,758,901 (40)
Minor parties	–	1,153,306 (3)

MAP 24-1

The Election of 1932 Democrats owed their overwhelming victory in 1932 to the popular identification of the Depression with the Hoover administration. Roosevelt's popular vote was about the same as Hoover's in 1928, and FDR's electoral college margin was even greater.

DID THE ELECTION of 1932 represent a repudiation of Hoover or an affirmation of Roosevelt?

WHAT DID FDR hope to accomplish in his first hundred days in office?

Bonus Army Unemployed veterans of World War I gathering in Washington in 1932 demanding payment of service bonuses not due until 1945.

New deal The economic and political policies of the Roosevelt administration in the 1930s.

raising prices by refusing to sell produce. In August, some 1,500 farmers turned back cargo trucks outside Sioux City, Iowa, and made a point by dumping milk and other perishables into ditches.

That spring the **Bonus Army** began descending on Washington, D.C. to demand the cash bonuses that Congress had promised in 1924 to every veteran of World War I. By summer around 20,000 veterans and their families were camped out all over the capital city. Their lobbying convinced the House to pass a bill for immediate payment, but the Senate rejected the bill and most of the veterans left. At the end of July, U.S. Army troops led by Chief of Staff General Douglas MacArthur forcibly evicted the remaining 2,000 veterans from their encampment. The spectacle of these unarmed and unemployed men, the heroes of 1918, being driven off by bayonets and bullets provided the most disturbing evidence yet of the failure of Hoover's administration.

In 1932, Democrats nominated Franklin D. Roosevelt (FDR), governor of New York, as their candidate. Roosevelt's acceptance speech stressed the need for reconstructing the nation's economy. "I pledge you, I pledge myself," he said, "to a **new deal** for the American people." But his plans for recovery were vague at best. Hoover bitterly condemned Roosevelt's ideas as a "radical departure" from the American way of life. But with the Depression growing worse every day, probably any Democrat would have defeated Hoover. Roosevelt carried forty-two states, taking the electoral college 472 to 59 and the popular vote by about 23 million to 16 million.

FDR AND THE FIRST NEW DEAL

FDR THE MAN

No president of this century had a greater impact on American life and politics than Franklin Delano Roosevelt. He was born in 1882 in Dutchess County, New York, where he grew up an only child, secure and confident, on his family's vast estate. Franklin's father, James, had made a fortune through railroad investments, but he was already in his fifties when Franklin was born, and it was his mother, Sara Delano, who was the dominant figure in his childhood. Roosevelt's education at Groton, Harvard, and Columbia Law School reinforced the aristocratic values of his family.

In 1905, Franklin married his distant cousin, Anna Eleanor Roosevelt, niece of President Theodore Roosevelt. Eleanor would later emerge as an influential adviser and political force on her own. Franklin turned to politics as a career early on. He was elected as a Democrat to the New York State Senate in 1910, served as assistant navy secretary from 1913 to 1920, and was nominated for vice president by the Democrats in the losing 1920 campaign.

In the summer of 1921 Roosevelt was stricken with polio at his summer home. He was never to walk again without support. The disease strengthened his relationship with Eleanor, who encouraged him not only to fight his handicap but also to continue his political career. His patience and determination in fighting the illness transformed him. The wealthy aristocrat, for whom everything had come relatively easy, now personally understood the meaning of struggle and hardship. "Once I spent two years lying in bed trying to move my big toe," he recalled. "After that anything else seems easy."

Elected governor of New York in 1928, Roosevelt served two terms and won a national reputation for reform. As governor, his achievements included instituting unemployment insurance, strengthening child labor laws, providing tax relief for farmers, and providing pensions for the old. As the Depression hit the state, he slowly increased public works and set up a Temporary Emergency Relief Administration. With his eye on the White House, he began assembling a group of key advisers, the "brains trust," who would follow him to Washington. The "brain trusters" shared a faith in the power of experts to set the economy right and a basic belief in government–business cooperation. They rejected the old progressive dream of re-creating an ideal society of small producers. Structural economic reform, they argued, must accept the modern reality of large corporate enterprise based on mass production and distribution.

RESTORING CONFIDENCE

In the first days of his administration Roosevelt conveyed a sense of optimism and activism that helped restore the badly shaken confidence of the nation. "First of all," he told Americans in his Inaugural Address on March 4, 1933, "let me assert my firm belief that the only thing we have to fear is fear itself." The very next day he issued an executive order calling for a four-day "bank holiday" to shore up the country's ailing financial system. Contemporary investigations had revealed a disquieting pattern of stock manipulation, illegal loans to bank officials, and tax evasion that helped erode public confidence in the banking system. Between election day and the inauguration, the banking system had come alarmingly close to shutting down altogether due to widespread bank failures and the hoarding of currency.

Roosevelt, therefore, called for a special session of Congress to deal with the banking crisis as well as with unemployment aid and farm relief. On March 12 he broadcast his first "**fireside chat**" to explain the steps he had taken to meet the financial emergency. These radio broadcasts became a standard part of Roosevelt's political technique, and they proved enormously successful. They communicated a genuine sense of compassion from the White House.

Congress immediately passed the **Emergency Banking Act**, which gave the president broad discretionary powers over all banking transactions and foreign exchange. It authorized healthy banks to reopen only under licenses from the Treasury Department and provided for greater federal authority in managing the affairs of failed banks. By the middle of March about half the country's banks, holding about 90 percent of the nation's deposits, were open for business again. Banks began to attract new deposits from people who had been holding back their money. The bank crisis had passed.

THE HUNDRED DAYS

From March to June of 1933—the "Hundred Days"—FDR pushed through Congress an extraordinary number of acts designed to combat various aspects of the Depression. What came to be called the New Deal was no unified program to end the Depression, but

Fireside chat Speeches broadcast nationally over the radio in which President Franklin D. Roosevelt explained complex issues and programs in plain language, as though his listeners were gathered around the fireside with him.

Emergency Banking Act 1933 act which gave the president broad discretionary powers over all banking transactions and foreign exchange.

This *New Yorker* magazine cover depicted an ebullient Franklin D. Roosevelt riding to his 1933 inauguration in the company of a glum Herbert Hoover. This drawing typified many mass media images of the day contrasting the different moods and temperaments of the new president and the defeated incumbent.

By Peter Arno, March 4, 1933. Franklin D. Roosevelt Library (CT65-521)

rather an improvised series of reform and relief measures, some of which seemed to contradict each other. Roosevelt responded to pressures from Congress, from business, and from organized labor, but he also used his own considerable influence over public opinion to get his way.

Five measures were particularly important and innovative. The Civilian Conservation Corps (CCC), established in March 1933 as an unemployment relief effort, provided work for jobless young men in protecting and conserving the nation's natural resources. Road construction, reforestation, flood control, and national park improvements were some of the major projects performed in work camps across the country. CCC workers received room and board and $30 each month, up to $25 of which had to be sent home to dependents. By the time the program was phased out in 1942, more than 2.5 million youths had worked in some 1,500 CCC camps.

In May, Congress authorized $500 million for the Federal Emergency Relief Administration (FERA). Half the money went as direct relief to the states; the rest was distributed on the basis of a dollar of federal aid for every three dollars of state and local funds spent for relief. This system of outright federal grants differed significantly from Hoover's approach, which provided only for loans. Establishment of work relief projects, however, was left to state and local governments. To direct the FERA Roosevelt turned to Harry Hopkins, an experienced reformer from the world of New York social work. A brilliant administrator with a special commitment to ending discrimination in relief work, Hopkins became the New Deal's most influential figure in relief policies and one of Roosevelt's most trusted advisers.

The Agricultural Adjustment Administration (AAA) was set up to provide immediate relief to the nation's farmers. The AAA established parity prices for basic farm commodities based on the purchasing power that farmers had enjoyed during the prosperous years of 1909 to 1914. That period now became the benchmark for setting the prices of farm commodities. The AAA also incorporated the

OVERVIEW
KEY LEGISLATION OF THE FIRST NEW DEAL ("HUNDRED DAYS," MARCH 9–JUNE 16, 1933)

Legislation	Purpose
Emergency Banking Relief Act	Enlarged federal authority over private banks.
	Government loans to private banks.
Civilian Conservation Corps	Unemployment relief.
	Conservation of natural resources.
Federal Emergency Relief Administration	Direct federal money for relief, funneled through state and local governments.
Agricultural Adjustment Administration	Federal farm aid based on parity pricing and subsidy.
Tennessee Valley Authority	Economic development and cheap electricity for Tennessee Valley.
National Industrial Recovery Act	Self-regulating industrial codes to revive economic activity.
Public Works Administration	Federal public works projects to increase employment and consumer spending.

principle of subsidy, whereby farmers received benefit payments in return for reducing acreage or otherwise cutting production where surpluses existed. The funds for these payments were to be raised from new taxes on food processing.

The AAA raised total farm income and was especially successful in pushing up the prices of wheat, cotton, and corn. But it had some troubling side effects as well. Landlords often failed to share their AAA payments with tenant farmers, and they frequently used benefits to buy tractors and other equipment that displaced sharecroppers. Many Americans were disturbed, too, by the sight of surplus crops, livestock, and milk being destroyed while millions went hungry.

The Southern Tenant Farmers Union (STFU), founded in 1934, emerged as an important voice of protest against AAA policies. The STFU (over half of whose members were black) succeeded in drawing national attention to the plight of sharecroppers and tenant farmers, but it failed to influence national farm policy.

The **Tennessee Valley Authority (TVA)** proved to be one of the most unique and controversial projects of the New Deal era. The TVA, an independent public corporation, built dams and power plants, produced cheap fertilizer for farmers, and, most significantly, brought cheap electricity for the first time to thousands of people in six Southern states. Denounced by some as a dangerous step toward socialism, the TVA stood for decades as a model of how careful government planning could dramatically improve the social and economic welfare of an underdeveloped region.

On the very last of the Hundred Days, Congress passed the **National Industrial Recovery Act**, the closest attempt yet at a systematic plan for economic recovery. In theory, each industry would be self-governed by a code hammered out by representatives of business, labor, and the consuming public. Once approved by the NRA in Washington, the codes would have the force of law. In practice, almost all the NRA codes were written by the largest firms in any given industry; labor and consumers got short shrift. The sheer administrative complexities involved with code writing and compliance made a great many people unhappy with the NRA's operation.

The Public Works Administration (PWA), led by Secretary of the Interior Harold Ickes, authorized $3.3 billion for the construction of roads, public buildings, and other projects. The idea was to provide jobs and, thus, stimulate the economy through increased consumer spending. Eventually the PWA spent over $4.2 billion building roads, schools, post offices, bridges, courthouses, and other public buildings around the country. In thousands of communities today, these structures remain the most tangible reminders of the New Deal era.

Tennessee Valley Authority (TVA)
Federal regional planning agency established to promote conservation, produce electric power, and encourage economic development in seven Southern states.

National Industrial Recovery Act
1933 act which was meant to be a systematic plan for economic recovery.

QUICK REVIEW

The National Recovery Administration (NRA)

◆ Sought to halt the slide in prices, wages, and employment.

◆ Tended to help business, often at the expense of labor.

◆ Declared unconstitutional in 1935.

LEFT TURN AND THE SECOND NEW DEAL

ROOSEVELT'S CRITICS

Criticism of the New Deal came from the right and the left. On the right, pro-Republican newspapers and the American Liberty League, a group of conservative businessmen organized in 1934, denounced Roosevelt and his advisors. Dominated by wealthy executives of Du Pont and General Motors, the league attracted support from a group of conservative Democrats, including Al Smith, the former presidential candidate, who declared the New Deal's laws "socialistic." The league supported anti–New Dealers for Congress, but in the 1934 election Democrats built up their majorities from 310 to 319 in the House and from 60 to 69 in the Senate—an unusually strong showing for the incumbent party in a midterm election.

Some of Roosevelt's staunchest early supporters turned critical. Father Charles E. Coughlin, a Catholic priest in suburban Detroit, attracted a huge national radio

WHAT GROUPS formed the New Deal coalition?

audience of 40 million listeners with passionate sermons attacking Wall Street, international bankers, and "plutocratic capitalism." Coughlin at first supported Roosevelt and the New Deal, and he tried to build a close personal relationship with the president. But by 1934 the ambitious Coughlin, frustrated by his limited influence on the administration, began attacking FDR. Roosevelt was a tool of special interests, he charged, who wanted dictatorial powers.

More troublesome for Roosevelt and his allies were the vocal and popular movements on the left. In California, well-known novelist and socialist Upton Sinclair entered the 1934 Democratic primary for governor. He proposed a $50 a month pension for all poor people over age sixty. Sinclair shocked local and national Democrats by winning the primary easily. He lost a close general election only because the Republican candidate received heavy financial and tactical support from wealthy Hollywood studio executives and frightened regular Democrats.

Huey Long, Louisiana's flamboyant backcountry orator, posed the greatest potential threat to Roosevelt's leadership. Long had captured Louisiana's governorship in 1928 by attacking the state's entrenched oil industry and calling for a radical redistribution of wealth. In office, he significantly improved public education, roads, medical care, and other public services, winning the loyalty of the state's poor farmers and industrial workers. Elected to the U.S. Senate in 1930, Long came to Washington with national ambitions. He at first supported Roosevelt, but in 1934 he began denouncing the New Deal as a failure and organized the Share Our Wealth Society. Long promised that limiting the size of large fortunes would mean a homestead worth $5,000 and a $2,500 annual income for everyone. Although Long's economics were fuzzy at best, he undoubtedly touched a deep nerve with his "Every Man a King" slogan. The Democratic National Committee was shocked when a secret poll in the summer of 1935 revealed that Long might attract 3 or 4 million votes. Only his assassination that September by a disgruntled political enemy prevented Long's third-party candidacy, which might have proved disastrous for FDR.

A newly militant labor movement also loomed as a force to be reckoned with. Section 7a of the National Industrial Recovery Act required that workers be allowed to bargain collectively with employers, through representatives of their own choosing. Though this provision of the NIRA was not enforced, it did help raise expectations and spark union organizing. Almost 1.5 million workers took part in some 1,800 strikes in 1934. But employers resisted unionization nearly everywhere, often with violence and the help of local and state police.

THE SECOND HUNDRED DAYS

The popularity of leaders like Sinclair, Townsend, and Long suggested Roosevelt might be losing electoral support among workers, farmers, the aged, and the unemployed. In early 1935, Roosevelt and his closest advisors responded by turning left and concentrating on a new program of social reform. What came to be called the "Second Hundred Days" marked the high point of progressive lawmaking in the New Deal.

In April the administration pushed through the Emergency Relief Appropriation Act, which allocated $5 billion for large-scale public works programs for the jobless. The major responsible agency here was the Works Progress Administration (WPA), led by Harry Hopkins. Over the next seven years Hopkins oversaw the employment of more than 8 million Americans on a vast array of construction projects: roads, bridges, dams, airports, and sewers. Among the most innovative WPA programs were community service projects that employed thousands of jobless artists, musicians, actors, and writers.

The landmark **Social Security Act of 1935** provided for old-age pensions and unemployment insurance. A payroll tax on workers and their employers created

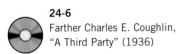

24-6
Farther Charles E. Coughlin, "A Third Party" (1936)

24-4
Share The Wealth

Social Security Act of 1935
Act establishing federal old-age pensions and unemployment insurance.

OVERVIEW

KEY LEGISLATION OF THE SECOND NEW DEAL (1935–1938)

Legislation	Purpose
Emergency Relief Appropriations Act (1935) (includes Works Progress Administration)	Large-scale public works program for the jobless.
Social Security Act (1935)	Federal old-age pensions and unemployment insurance.
National Labor Relations Act (1935)	Federal guarantee of right to organize trade unions and collective bargaining.
Resettlement Administration (1935)	Relocation of poor rural families.
	Reforestation and soil erosion projects.
National Housing Act (1937)	Federal funding for public housing and slum clearance.
Fair Labor Standards Act (1938)	Federal minimum wage and maximum hours.

a fund from which retirees received monthly pensions after age sixty-five. The unemployment compensation plan established a minimum weekly payment and a minimum number of weeks during which those who lost jobs could collect. The original law failed to cover domestics and farm workers, many of whom were Latinos and African Americans. It also made no provisions for casual laborers or public employees. And to collect unemployment, one had to have first lost a job. But the law, which has since been amended many times, established the crucial principle of federal responsibility for America's most vulnerable citizens.

Another 1935 law, the **National Labor Relations Act** (often called the Wagner Act for its chief sponsor, Democratic senator Robert F. Wagner of New York), guaranteed the right of American workers to join or form independent labor unions and bargain collectively for improved wages, benefits, and working conditions. The National Labor Relations Board would conduct secret-ballot elections in shops and factories to determine which union, if any, workers desired as their sole bargaining agent. The law also defined and prohibited unfair labor practices by employers, including firing workers for union activity.

Finally, the Resettlement Administration (RA) produced one of the most utopian New Deal programs, one designed to create new kinds of model communities. The RA helped destitute farm families relocate to more productive areas. It granted loans for purchasing land and equipment, and it directed reforestation and soil erosion projects, particularly in the hard-hit Southwest. Due to lack of funds and poor administration, however, only about 1 percent of the projected 500,000 families were actually moved.

LABOR'S UPSURGE: RISE OF THE CIO

In 1932 the American labor movement was nearly dead. Yet by 1942, unions claimed more than 10.5 million members, nearly a third of the total nonagricultural work force. This remarkable turnaround was one of the key events of the Depression era. The growth in the size and power of the labor movement permanently changed the work lives and economic status of millions, as well as the national and local political landscapes.

QUICK REVIEW

The Social Security Act

* Provided unemployment compensation, old-age pensions, and aid for dependent mothers and children and the blind.
* The law excluded more than a fourth of all workers.
* Funded by a payroll tax.

National Labor Relations Act
Act establishing Federal guarantee of right to organize trade unions and collective bargaining.

Philip Evergood, *American Tragedy* (1937). A classic example of the social realism characteristic of much Depression-era art, this painting depicts the police violence against strikers at the Republic Steel Mill. Evergood was one of many artists who found work in the Federal Art Project painting murals in public buildings.

Philip Evergood, *American Tragedy*, 1937. Oil on canvas, 29" × 39". Private Collection, Terry Dintenfass Gallery. Photo by Philip Evergood

At the core of this growth was a series of dramatic successes in the organization of workers in large-scale, mass-production industries, such as those producing automobiles, steel, rubber, electrical goods, and textiles. Workers in these fields had largely been ignored by the conservative, craft-conscious unions that dominated the American Federation of Labor. At the 1935 AFL convention, a group of more militant union officials led by John L. Lewis (of the United Mine Workers) and Sidney Hillman (of the Amalgamated Clothing Workers) formed the Committee for Industrial Organization (CIO). They emphasized the need for opening the new unions to all, regardless of a worker's level of skill. And they differed from nearly all old-line AFL unions by calling for the inclusion of black and women workers. In 1938 CIO unions withdrew from the AFL and reorganized themselves as the **Congress of Industrial Organizations**.

The gruff son of a Welsh miner, Lewis was articulate, ruthless, and very ambitious. He saw the new legal protection given by the Wagner Act as a historic opportunity. But despite the act—whose constitutionality was unclear until 1937—Lewis knew that establishing permanent unions in the mass-production industries would be a bruising battle. He committed the substantial resources of the United Mine Workers to a series of organizing drives, focusing first on the steel and auto industries. Many CIO organizers were Communists or radicals of other persuasions, and their dedication, commitment, and willingness to work within disciplined organizations proved invaluable in the often dangerous task of creating industrial unions.

Militant rank-and-file unionists were often ahead of Lewis and other CIO leaders. After the dramatic breakthrough in the Flint sit-down strike at General Motors, membership in CIO unions grew rapidly. In eight months, membership in the United Automobile Workers alone soared from 88,000 to 400,000. CIO victories in the steel, rubber, and electrical industries followed, but often at a very high cost. One bloody example of the perils of union organizing was the 1937 Memorial Day Massacre in Chicago. In a field near the struck Republic Steel Mill in South Chicago, police fired into a crowd of union supporters, killing ten workers and wounding scores more.

Overall, the success of the CIO's organizing drives was remarkable. For the first time ever, the labor movement had gained a permanent place in the nation's

Congress of Industrial Organizations An alliance of industrial unions that spurred the 1930s organizational drive among the mass-production industries.

mass-production industries. Organized labor took its place as a key power broker in Roosevelt's New Deal and the national Democratic Party. Frances Perkins, FDR's secretary of labor and the nation's first woman cabinet member, captured the close relationship between the new unionism and the New Deal: "Programs long thought of as merely labor welfare, such as shorter hours, higher wages, and a voice in the terms of conditions of work, are really essential economic factors for recovery."

THE NEW DEAL COALITION AT HIGH TIDE

Did the American public support Roosevelt and his New Deal policies? Both major political parties looked forward to the 1936 elections as a national referendum, and the campaign itself was an exciting and hard-fought contest. Very few political observers predicted its lopsided result.

Republicans nominated Governor Alfred M. Landon of Kansas, an easygoing, colorless man with little personal magnetism, who emphasized a nostalgic appeal to traditional American values. His campaign served as a lightning rod for all those, including many conservative Democrats, who were dissatisfied with Roosevelt and the direction he had taken.

Roosevelt attacked the "economic royalists" who denied that government "could do anything to protect the citizen in his right to work and his right to live." At the same time, FDR was careful to distance himself from radicalism. "It was this administration," he declared, "which saved the system of private profit and free enterprise after it had been dragged to the brink of ruin." As Roosevelt's campaign crossed the country, his advisors were heartened by huge and enthusiastic crowds, especially in large cities like Chicago and Pittsburgh. Still, the vast majority of the nation's newspapers endorsed Landon. And a widely touted "scientific" poll by the *Literary Digest* forecast a Republican victory in November.

On Election day Roosevelt carried every state but Maine and Vermont, polling 61 percent of the popular vote. The *Literary Digest*, it turned out, had drawn the sample for its poll from people whose addresses were listed in telephone directories and car registration records, thus omitting the poorer Americans who had no telephones or cars—and who supported Roosevelt. In 1936 the Democrats drew millions of new voters into the political process and at the same time forged a new coalition of voters who would dominate national politics for two generations.

This "**New Deal coalition**," as it came to be known, included traditional-minded white Southern Democrats, big-city political machines, industrial workers of all races, trade unionists, and many Depression-hit farmers. Roosevelt was especially popular among first- and second-generation Catholics and Jews, and the New Deal drew enthusiastic support from millions in the ethnic working class who had never bothered with politics. As one Slovak worker in Chicago's stockyards put it, "Our people did not know anything about the government until the Depression years. In my neighborhood, I don't remember anyone voting." The severity of the Great Depression had overwhelmed the ethnically based support networks—mutual benefit societies, immigrant banks, and religious charities—that had traditionally helped so many to survive hard times. Working-class voters in large cities like New York, Chicago, Detroit, and Philadelphia increasingly took credit for putting and keeping Democrats in power locally and nationally—and their attitudes toward politics changed. The federal government no longer seemed so remote or irrelevant to their lives. Popular federal programs like Social Security, the WPA, and Home Owners Loan Corporation mortgages changed the consciousness of a generation of the ethnic working class. In exchange for their votes, they now looked to the state—especially the federal government—for relief, protection, and help in achieving the American dream.

New Deal coalition Coalition that included traditional-minded white Southern Democrats, big-city political machines, industrial workers of all races, trade unionists, and many Depression-hit farmers.

THE NEW DEAL AND THE WEST

THE DUST BOWL

The southern Great Plains had suffered several drought years in the early 1930s. Such dry spells occurred regularly in roughly twenty-year cycles. But this time the parched earth became swept up in violent dust storms. Black blizzards of dust a mile and a half high rolled across the landscape, darkening the sky and whipping the earth into great drifts of dust that settled over hundreds of miles. Dust storms made it difficult for humans and livestock to breathe and destroyed crops and trees over vast areas. The hardest hit regions were western Kansas, eastern Colorado, western Oklahoma, the Texas Panhandle, and eastern New Mexico. It was the calamity in this southern part of the Great Plains that prompted a Denver journalist to coin the phrase "Dust Bowl." Dust storms turned day into night, terrifying those caught in them. "Dust pneumonia" and other respiratory infections afflicted thousands, and many travelers found themselves stranded in automobiles and trains unable to move. The dust storms were largely the consequence of years of stripping the landscape of its natural vegetation. During World War I, wheat fetched record-high prices on the world market, and for the next twenty years Great Plains farmers had turned the region into a vast wheat factory. With native grasses destroyed for the sake of wheat growing, there was nothing left to prevent soil erosion. Dust storms blew away tens of millions of acres of rich topsoil, and thousands of farm families left the region. Those who stayed suffered deep economic and psychological losses from the calamity.

The Department of Agriculture, under Secretary Henry A. Wallace, sought to change farming practices to relieve the distress. The Soil Conservation Service (SCS) conducted research into controlling wind and water erosion, set up demonstration projects, and offered technical assistance, supplies, and equipment to farmers engaged in conservation work on farms and ranches. The SCS pumped additional federal funds into the Great Plains and created a new rural organization, the soil conservation district, which administered conservation regulations locally.

By 1940 the acreage subject to blowing in the Dust Bowl area of the southern Plains had been reduced from roughly 50 million acres to less than 4 million acres. In the face of the Dust Bowl disaster, New Deal farm policies had restricted market forces in agriculture.

While large landowners and ranchers reaped sizable benefits from AAA subsidies and other New Deal programs, tenant farmers and sharecroppers received very little. In the cotton lands of Texas, Oklahoma, Missouri, and Arkansas, thousands of tenant and sharecropper families were forced off the land. They became part of a stream of roughly 300,000 people, disparagingly called "Okies," who migrated to California in the 1930s. Most Okies could find work only as poorly paid agricultural laborers in the fertile San Joaquin and Imperial Valley districts. There they faced discrimination and scorn as "poor white trash" while they struggled to create communities amid the squalor of migrant labor camps. Only with the outbreak of World War II and the pressing demand for labor were migrants able to significantly improve their situation.

Mexican farm laborers faced stiff competition from Dust Bowl refugees. Southwestern communities, responding to racial

WHAT WERE conditions like in the Dust Bowl in the 1930s?

Years of Dust. This 1936 poster by the artist and photographer Ben Shahn served to publicize the work of the Resettlement Administration, which offered aid to destitute farm families hit hard by the Dust Bowl. Shahn's stark imagery here was typical of the documentary aesthetic associated with Depression-era art and photography.

The Granger Collection (4EBU96)

hostility from unemployed whites and looking for ways to reduce their welfare burden, campaigned to deport Mexicans and Mexican Americans.

WATER POLICY

The New Deal ushered in an era of large-scale water projects designed to provide irrigation and cheap power and to prevent floods. The long-range impact of these undertakings on Western life was enormous. The key government agency in this realm was the Bureau of Reclamation of the Department of the Interior, established under the National Reclamation Act of 1902. Until the late 1920s the bureau's efforts had been of little consequence, providing irrigation for only a very small portion of land. But its fortunes changed when its focus shifted to building huge multipurpose dams designed to control entire river systems.

The first of these projects was the Boulder Dam (later renamed the Hoover Dam). The dam, actually begun during the Hoover administration, was designed to harness the Colorado River, wildest and most isolated of the major Western rivers. Its planned benefits included flood prevention, the irrigation of California's Imperial Valley, the supplying of domestic water for southern California, and the generation of cheap electricity for Los Angeles and southern Arizona. Hoover, however, had opposed the public power aspect of the project, arguing that the government ought not to compete with private utility companies. Roosevelt's support for government-sponsored power projects was a significant factor in his winning the political backing of the West in 1932 and subsequent election years.

The success of Boulder Dam transformed the Bureau of Reclamation into a major federal agency with huge resources at its disposal. In 1938 it completed the All-American Canal—an 80-mile channel connecting the Colorado River to the Imperial Valley, with a 130-mile branch to the Coachella Valley. More than a million acres of desert land were opened up to the cultivation of citrus fruits, melons, vegetables, and cotton. Irrigation districts receiving water promised to repay, without interest, the cost of the canal over a forty-year period. This interest-free loan was in effect a huge government subsidy to the private growers who benefited from the canal.

The largest power and irrigation project of all was the Grand Coulee Dam, northwest of Spokane, Washington. Completed in 1941, it was designed to convert the power of the Columbia River into cheap electricity and to irrigate previously uncultivated land, thereby stimulating the economic development of the Pacific Northwest. The construction of Grand Coulee employed tens of thousands of workers and pumped millions of dollars into the region's badly depressed economy. Grand Coulee provided the cheapest electricity in the United States and helped attract new manufacturing to a region previously dependent on the export of raw materials, such as lumber and metals.

The Grand Coulee and smaller dams nearby reduced the Columbia River, long a potent symbol of the Western wilderness, to a string of lakes. Spawning salmon could no

QUICK REVIEW

The SCS

◆ Soil Conservation Service created in response to soil erosion in the Dust Bowl

◆ SCS energetically enforced new agricultural practices.

◆ 1940: Affected area had been reduced from 50 million acres to 4 million acres.

 MAP EXPLORATION
To explore an interactive version of this map, go to
http://www.prenhall.com/faraghertlc/map24.2

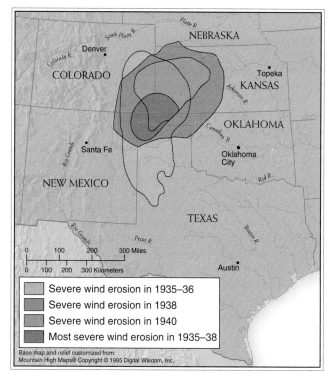

Severe wind erosion in 1935–36
Severe wind erosion in 1938
Severe wind erosion in 1940
Most severe wind erosion in 1935–38

Base map and relief customized from:
Mountain High Maps® Copyright © 1995 Digital Wisdom, Inc.

MAP 24-2

The Dust Bowl, 1935–1940 This map shows the extent of the Dust Bowl in the southern Great Plains. Federal programs designed to improve soil conservation, water management, and farming practices could not prevent a mass exodus of hundreds of thousands out of the Great Plains.

WHAT WERE the reasons for this ecological disaster?

longer run the river above the dam. In California, the federal guarantee of river water made a relative handful of large farmers fabulously wealthy. But tens of thousands of farm workers, mostly of Mexican descent, labored in the newly fertile fields for very low wages, and their health suffered from contact with pesticides. The Colorado River, no longer emptying into the Pacific, began to build up salt deposits, making its water increasingly unfit for drinking or irrigation. Water pollution in the form of high salinity continues to plague the 2,000-mile river to this day.

DEPRESSION-ERA CULTURE

A NEW DEAL FOR THE ARTS

The Depression hit America's writers, artists, and teachers just as hard as blue-collar workers. In 1935, the WPA allocated $300 million for the unemployed in these fields. Over the next four years, Federal Project No. 1, an umbrella agency covering writing, theater, music, and the visual arts, proved to be one of the most innovative and successful New Deal programs. "Federal One," as it was called, offered work to desperate artists and intellectuals, enriched the cultural lives of millions, and left a substantial legacy of artistic and cultural production.

The Federal Writers Project (FWP) employed 5,000 writers on a variety of programs. Most notably, it produced a popular series of state and city guidebooks, each combining history, folklore, and tourism. The 150-volume "Life in America" series included valuable oral histories of former slaves, studies of ethnic and Indian cultures, and pioneering collections of American songs and folk tales. Work on the Writers Project helped many American writers to survive, hone their craft, and go on to great achievement and prominence. These included Ralph Ellison, Richard Wright, Margaret Walker, John Cheever, Saul Bellow, and Zora Neale Hurston. Novelist Anzia Yezierska recalled a strong spirit of camaraderie among the writers: "Each morning I walked to the Project as light-hearted as if I were going to a party."

The Federal Theater Project reached as many as 30 million Americans with its productions. Tickets were cheap, and a variety of dramatic forms were made available. Among its most successful productions were the "Living Newspaper" plays based on contemporary controversies and current events.

The Federal Music Project, under Nikolai Sokoloff of the Cleveland Symphony Orchestra, employed 15,000 musicians and financed hundreds of thousands of low-priced public concerts by touring orchestras. The Composers' Forum Laboratory supported new works by American composers such as Aaron Copland and William Schuman.

Among the painters who received government assistance through the FAP were Willem de Kooning, Jackson Pollock, and Louise Nevelson. The FAP employed painters and sculptors to teach studio skills and art history in schools, churches, and settlement houses. It also commissioned artists to paint hundreds of murals on the walls of post offices, meeting halls, courthouses, and other government buildings.

THE DOCUMENTARY IMPULSE

During the 1930s an enormous number of artists, novelists, journalists, photographers, and filmmakers tried to document the devastation wrought by the Depression in American communities. They also depicted people's struggles to cope with and reverse hard times.

■ ■ ■ ■ ■ ■ ■ ■ ■ ■

WHAT ROLE did the federal government play in the arts during the 1930s?

■ ■ ■ ■ ■ ■ ■ ■ ■ ■

QUICK REVIEW

The FWP

♦ Federal Writers Project employed 5,000 writers.

♦ Produced a series of state and city guidebooks.

♦ The FWP helped many notable American writers survive the Depression.

The Joad family prepares to leave the Dust Bowl in Oklahoma for a new life in California in this still-photo from the movie *The Grapes of Wrath* (1940). Director John Ford's adaptation of John Steinbeck's novel reflected the influence of the "documentary impulse" in Hollywood films and other forms of Depression-era popular culture.

The Museum of Modern Art/Film Stills Archive

The "documentary impulse" became a prominent style in 1930s cultural expression. The most direct and influential expression of the documentary style was the photograph. In 1935 Roy Stryker, chief of the Historical Section of the Resettlement Administration (later part of the Farm Security Administration), gathered a remarkable group of photographers to help document the work of the agency. These photographers, including Dorothea Lange, Walker Evans, Arthur Rothstein, Russell Lee, Ben Shahn, and Marion Post Wolcott, left us the single most significant visual record of the Great Depression.

That double vision, combining a frank portrayal of pain and suffering with a faith in the possibility of overcoming disaster, could be found in many other cultural works of the period. John Steinbeck's *Grapes of Wrath* (1939) sympathetically portrayed the hardships of Oklahoma Dust Bowl migrants on their way to California. "We ain't gonna die out," Ma Joad asserts near the end of the book. "People is goin' on—changin' a little, maybe, but goin' right on." A similar, if more personal, ending could be found in Margaret Mitchell's 1936 bestseller *Gone with the Wind.* Although this romantic novel was set in the Civil War–era South, many Americans identified with Scarlett O'Hara's determination to overcome the disaster of war.

WAITING FOR LEFTY

For some, the capitalist system itself, with its enormous disparities of private wealth amid desperate poverty, was the culprit responsible for the Great Depression. Relatively few Americans became communists or socialists in the 1930s (at its height, the Communist Party of the United States had perhaps 100,000 members), and many of these remained active for only a brief time. Yet Marxist analysis, with its emphasis on class conflict and the failures of capitalism, had a wide influence on the era's thought and writing.

Some writers joined the Communist Party believing it to be the best hope for political revolution. They saw in the Soviet Union an alternative to an American system that appeared mired in exploitation, racial inequality, and human misery.

Communist writers, like the novelist Michael Gold and the poet Meridel LeSueur, sought to radicalize art and literature, and they celebrated collective struggle over individual achievement.

A more common pattern for intellectuals, especially when they were young, was brief flirtation with communism. Many African American writers, attracted by the Communist Party's militant opposition to lynching, job discrimination, and segregation, briefly joined the party or found their first supportive audiences there. These included Richard Wright, Ralph Ellison, and Langston Hughes. Many playwrights and actors associated with New York's influential Group Theater were part of the Communist Party orbit in those years. One production of the group, Clifford Odets's *Waiting for Lefty* (1935), depicted a union organizing drive among taxi drivers. At the play's climax, the audience was invited to join the actors in shouting "Strike!" A commercial and political success, it offered perhaps the most celebrated example of radical, politically engaged art.

Left-wing influence reached its height after 1935 during the "Popular Front" period. Alarmed by the rise of fascism in Europe, communists around the world followed the Soviet line of uniting with liberals and all other antifascists. Communists became strong supporters of Roosevelt's New Deal, and their influence was especially strong within the various WPA arts projects. Some 3,200 Americans volunteered for the Communist Party–organized Abraham Lincoln Brigade, which fought in the Spanish Civil War on the republican side against the fascists led by Francisco Franco.

FILM AND RADIO IN THE 1930S

Several film genres proved enormously popular during the 1930s. Gangster films did very well in the early Depression years. They depicted violent criminals brought to justice by society—but along the way they gave audiences a vicarious exposure to the pleasures of wealth, power, and lawbreaking. Social disorder was treated comically in Marx Brothers films. Mae West's popular comedies made people laugh by subverting expectations about sex roles. West was an independent woman, not afraid of pleasure. When Cary Grant asked her, "Haven't you ever met a man who could make you happy?" she replied, "Sure, lots of times."

Movie musicals offered audiences extravagant song-and-dance spectacles, as in Busby Berkeley's *Gold Diggers of 1933* and *42nd Street* (1933). "Screwball comedies" featured sophisticated, fast-paced humor and usually paired popular male and female stars: Clark Gable and Claudette Colbert in *It Happened One Night* (1934), Katharine Hepburn and Cary Grant in *Bringing Up Baby* (1938). A few movies, notably from the Warner Brothers studio, tried to offer a more "socially conscious" view of Depression-era life. By and large, however, Hollywood avoided confronting controversial social or political issues.

The Depression helped radio expand as an influx of talent arrived from the weakened worlds of vaudeville, ethnic theater, and the recording industry. The well-financed networks offered an attractive outlet to advertisers seeking a national audience. Radio programming achieved a regularity and professionalism absent in the 1920s, making it much easier for a listener to identify a show with its sponsor.

Much of network radio was based on older cultural forms. The variety show, hosted by comedians and singers and based on the old vaudeville format, was the first important style. It featured stars like Eddie Cantor, Ed Wynn, Kate Smith, and Al Jolson, who constantly plugged the sponsor's product. The use of a studio audience re-created the human interaction so necessary in vaudeville. The popular comedy show *Amos 'n' Andy* adapted the minstrel "blackface" tradition to the new medium. White comedians Freeman Gosden and Charles Correll used only their two voices to invent a world of stereotyped African Americans for their millions of listeners.

The spectacular growth of the daytime serial, or soap opera, dominated radio drama. Aimed mainly at women working in the home, "soaps" revolved around strong, warm female characters who provided advice and strength to weak, indecisive friends and relatives. Thrillers such as *Inner Sanctum* and *The Shadow* emphasized crime and suspense. These shows made great use of music and sound effects to sharpen their impact.

THE LIMITS OF REFORM

COURT PACKING

In May 1935, in *Schecter* v. *United States,* the Supreme Court found the National Recovery Administration unconstitutional in its entirety. Its ruling in *Butler* v. *United States,* in early 1936, invalidated the Agricultural Adjustment Administration. The Court was composed mostly of Republican appointees, six of whom were over seventy. Roosevelt looked for a way to get more friendly judges on the high court.

In February 1937, FDR asked Congress for legislation that would expand the Supreme Court from nine to a maximum of fifteen justices. The president would be empowered to make a new appointment whenever an incumbent judge failed to retire upon reaching age seventy. Roosevelt argued that age prevented justices from keeping up with their workload, but few people believed this logic. Newspapers almost unanimously denounced FDR's "court-packing bill."

Even more damaging was the determined opposition from a coalition of conservatives and outraged New Dealers in the Congress, such as Democratic senator Burton K. Wheeler of Montana. As the battle dragged on through the spring and summer, FDR's claims weakened. Conservative justice Willis Van Devanter announced plans to retire, giving Roosevelt the chance to make his first Court appointment.

More important, the Court upheld the constitutionality of some key laws from the second New Deal, including the Social Security Act and the National Labor Relations Act. At the end of August, FDR backed off from his plan and accepted a compromise bill that reformed lower court procedures but left the Supreme Court untouched. FDR lost the battle for his judiciary proposal, but he may have won the war for a more responsive Court. Still, the political price was very high. The Court fight badly weakened Roosevelt's relations with Congress. Many more conservative Democrats now felt free to oppose further New Deal measures.

THE WOMEN'S NETWORK

The Great Depression and the New Deal brought some significant changes for women in American economics and politics. Most women continued to perform unpaid domestic labor within their homes, work that was not covered by the Social Security Act. A growing minority, however, also worked for wages and salaries outside the home. By 1940, 25.1 percent of the work force was female, but sexual stereotyping still routinely forced women into low-paying and low-status jobs.

The New Deal brought a measurable, if temporary, increase in women's political influence. For those women associated with social reform, the New Deal opened up possibilities to effect change. A "women's network," linked by personal friendships and professional connections, made its presence felt in national politics and government. Most of the women in this network had long been active in movements promoting suffrage, labor law reform, and welfare programs.

WHAT EFFECT did the New Deal have on the lives and economic prospects of minorities?

Eleanor Roosevelt on a campaign tour with her husband in Nebraska, 1935. Long active in women's organizations and Democratic Party circles, she used political activity both to maintain her independence and make herself a valuable ally to FDR. "The attitude of women toward change in society," she argued, "is going to determine to a great extent our future in this country."

UPI/CORBIS (UP11)

Eleanor Roosevelt became a powerful political figure in her own right, actively using her prominence as First Lady to fight for the liberal causes she believed in. She revolutionized the role of the political wife by taking a position involving no institutional duties and turning it into a base for independent action. Privately, she enjoyed great influence with her husband. She was a strong supporter of protective labor legislation for women, and her overall outlook owed much to the social reform tradition of the women's movement.

One of her first public acts as First Lady was to convene a White House Conference on the Emergency Needs of Women in November 1933. She helped Ellen Woodward, head of women's projects in the Federal Emergency Relief Administration, find jobs for 100,000 women, ranging from nursery school teaching to sewing. Roosevelt worked vigorously for antilynching legislation, compulsory health insurance, and child labor reform, and she fought racial discrimination in New Deal relief programs. She saw herself as the guardian of "human values" within the administration, a buffer between Depression victims and government bureaucracy. She frequently testified before legislative committees, lobbied her husband privately and the Congress publicly, and wrote a widely syndicated newspaper column.

New Deal agencies opened up spaces for scores of women in the federal bureaucracy. In addition, the social work profession, which remained roughly two-thirds female in the 1930s, grew enormously in response to the massive relief and welfare programs. Yet despite the best efforts of the "women's network," women never constituted more than 19 percent of those employed by work relief programs, even though they made up 37 percent of the unemployed. In sum, although the 1930s saw no radical challenges to existing male and female roles, working-class women and professional women held their own and managed to make some gains.

QUICK REVIEW

Impact of the New Deal on Women

◆ Women received a smaller percentage of jobs created by New Deal programs than men.

◆ Increase in the minimum wage brought greater improvements to women than to men.

◆ Women gained political influence under the New Deal.

A NEW DEAL FOR MINORITIES?

"The Negro was born in Depression," recalled Clifford Burke. "It only became official when it hit the white man." The old saying among black workers that they were "last hired, first fired" was never more true than during times of high unemployment. With jobs made scarce by the Depression, even traditional "Negro occupations"—domestic service, cooking, janitorial work, elevator operating—were coveted. One white clerk in Florida expressed a widely held view among white Southerners when he defended a lynch mob attack on a store with black employees: "A nigger hasn't got no right to have a job when there are white men who can do the work and are out of work."

The Roosevelt administration made little overt effort to combat racism and segregation. FDR was especially worried about offending the powerful Southern Democratic congressmen who were a key element in his political coalition. And local administration of many federal programs meant that most early New Deal programs routinely accepted discrimination. The CCC established separate camps for African Americans. The NRA labor codes tolerated lower wages for black workers doing the same jobs as white workers. African Americans could not get jobs with the TVA. Finally, the Social Security Act excluded domestics and casual laborers—workers whose ranks were disproportionately African Americans—from old-age insurance.

Yet some limited gains were made. President Roosevelt issued an executive order in 1935 banning discrimination in WPA projects. In the cities, the WPA, paying minimum wages of $12 a week, enabled thousands of African Americans to survive. Between 15 and 20 percent of all WPA employees were black people, although African Americans made up less than 10 percent of the nation's population. The Public Works Administration, under Harold Ickes, constructed a number of integrated housing complexes and employed more than its fair share of black workers in construction.

Hard times were especially trying for Mexican Americans as well. As the Great Depression drastically reduced the demand for their labor, they faced massive layoffs, deepening poverty, and deportation. During the 1930s over 400,000 Mexican nationals and their children returned to Mexico, often coerced by local officials unwilling to provide them with relief but happy to offer train fare to border towns. Many native-born Americans argued that deporting Mexicans could reduce unemployment for U.S. citizens. But these claims reflected deep racial prejudice inflamed by the economic crisis.

The New Deal record for minorities was mixed at best. African Americans, especially in the cities, benefited from New Deal relief and work programs, though this assistance was not colorblind. Black industrial workers made inroads into labor unions affiliated with the CIO. The New Deal made no explicit attempt to attack the deeply rooted patterns of racism and discrimination in American life. The deteriorating economic and political conditions faced by Mexicans and Mexican Americans resulted in a mass reverse exodus. Yet by 1936, for the first time ever, a majority of black voters had switched their political allegiance to the Democrats—concrete evidence that they supported the directions taken by FDR's New Deal.

THE ROOSEVELT RECESSION

The nation's economy had improved significantly by 1937. Unemployment had declined to "only" 14 percent (9 million people), farm prices had improved to 1930 levels, and industrial production was slightly higher than the 1929 mark. Roosevelt, uneasy about the federal deficit, which had grown to more than $4 billion, called for large reductions in federal spending, particularly in WPA and farm programs. Federal Reserve System officials, worried about inflation, tightened credit policies.

The retrenchment brought about a steep recession. The stock market collapsed in August 1937, and industrial output and farm prices plummeted. By March

1938 Fair Labor Standards Act
Act that established the first federal minimum wage (25 ¢ an hour) and set a maximum work week of forty-four hours for all employees engaged in interstate commerce.

1938, the jobless rate hovered around 20 percent. As conditions worsened, Roosevelt began to blame the "new depression" on a "strike of capital," claiming businessmen had refused to invest because they wanted to hurt his prestige. In truth, the administration's own severe spending cutbacks were more responsible for the decline.

The blunt reality was that even after five years the New Deal had not brought about economic recovery. Throughout 1937 and 1938 the administration drifted. Roosevelt received conflicting advice on the economy. Some advisers, suspicious of the reluctance of business to make new investments, urged a massive antitrust campaign against monopolies. Others urged a return to the strategy of "priming the economic pump" with more federal spending. Emergency spending bills in the spring of 1938 pumped new life into the WPA and the PWA, but Republican gains in the 1938 congressional elections made it harder than ever to get new reform measures through.

There were a couple of important exceptions. The **1938 Fair Labor Standards Act** established the first federal minimum wage (25 ¢ an hour) and set a maximum work week of forty-four hours for all employees engaged in interstate commerce. The National Housing Act of 1937, also known as the Wagner-Steagall Act, funded public housing construction and slum clearance and provided rent subsidies for low-income families. But by and large, by 1938 the reform whirlwind of the New Deal was over.

Conclusion

Far from being the radical program its conservative critics charged, the New Deal did little to alter fundamental property relations or the distribution of wealth. But the New Deal profoundly changed many areas of American

---

CHRONOLOGY

1929	Stock market crash.
1930	Democrats regain control of the House of Representatives.
1932	Reconstruction Finance Corporation established to make government credit available.
	Bonus Army marches on Washington.
	Franklin D. Roosevelt elected president.
1933	Roughly 13 million workers unemployed.
	The "hundred days" legislation of the First New Deal.
	Twenty-first Amendment repeals Prohibition (Eighteenth Amendment).
1934	Indian Reorganization Act repeals Dawes Severalty Act and reasserts the status of Indian tribes as semisovereign nations.
	Growing popularity of Father Charles E. Coughlin and Huey Long, critics of Roosevelt.
1935	Second New Deal.
	Committee for Industrial Organization (CIO) established.
	Dust storms turn the southern Great Plains into the Dust Bowl.
	Boulder Dam completed.
1936	Roosevelt defeats Alfred M. Landon in reelection landslide.
	Sit-down strike begins at General Motors plants in Flint, Michigan.
1937	General Motors recognizes United Automobile Workers.
	Roosevelt's "Court-packing" plan causes controversy.
	Memorial Day Massacre in Chicago demonstrates the perils of union organizing.
	"Roosevelt recession" begins.
1938	CIO unions withdraw from the American Federation of Labor to form the Congress of Industrial Organizations.
	Fair Labor Standards Act establishes the first federal minimum wage.

life. Over all, it radically increased the role of the federal government in American lives and communities. Western and Southern communities in particular were transformed. Relief programs and the Social Security system established at least the framework for a welfare state. The federal government guaranteed the right of workers to join trade unions, and it set standards for minimum wages and maximum hours. In politics, the New Deal established the Democrats as the majority party. Some version of the Roosevelt New Deal coalition would dominate the nation's political life for another three decades.

The New Deal's efforts to end racial and gender discrimination were modest at best. Some of the more ambitious programs, such as subsidizing the arts or building model communities, enjoyed only brief success. Other reform proposals, such as national health insurance, never got off the ground. Conservative counterpressures, especially after 1937, limited what could be changed.

Still, the New Deal did more than strengthen the presence of the national government in people's lives. It also fed expectations that the federal presence would intensify. With the coming of World War II, the direct role of national government in shaping American communities would expand beyond the dreams of even the most ardent New Dealer.

SUMMARY

Hard Times The stock market crash triggered the Great Depression though underlying economic weaknesses caused the downturn. The sharp decline led to mass unemployment that caused great stress and strains on American society and families. Hoover's attempts to deal with the Depression proved ineffective and led to a protest by veterans. The election of 1932 pitted Hoover against the reform-minded Franklin Delano Roosevelt who won a landslide victory.

FDR and First New Deal Upon becoming president, Franklin D. Roosevelt sought to bolster confidence both through his words and his actions. In the first hundred days of his term, Roosevelt pushed through several reform programs addressing various economic and societal problems.

Left Turn and the Second New Deal Faced with critics on the right and left, Roosevelt responded with the second New Deal that addressed several remaining issues. Labor responded to the Depression by developing the CIO and increasing union membership in large-scale mass production industries. The 1936 election was a referendum on the New Deal as Roosevelt won by a stunning landslide.

The New Deal and the West The New Deal in the West focused on environmental concerns. These programs aimed at addressing problems that arose from poor weather conditions, the state of the land, and water resources in order to improve agriculture and conserve the environment.

Depression-Era Culture American culture was profoundly affected by the Depression. Government sponsorship revived the arts and also stimulated the documenting of the state of the nation and its people. The movies and radio experienced golden ages as they sought to entertain the American people.

The Limits of Reform Frustrated with their decisions, Roosevelt tried to change the number of Supreme Court judges and experienced failure. The New Deal provided women with a temporary increase in women's political influence. Hardest hit by the Depression, minorities received some help from the New Deal, but their experience was mixed. By the late 1930s, the New Deal had not ended the Depression as the 1937 recession showed.

REVIEW QUESTIONS

1. What were the underlying causes of the Great Depression? What consequences did it have for ordinary Americans, and how did the Hoover administration attempt to deal with the crisis?

2. Analyze the key elements of Franklin D. Roosevelt's first New Deal program. To what degree did these succeed in getting the economy back on track and in providing relief to suffering Americans?

3. How did the so-called Second New Deal differ from the first? What political pressures did Roosevelt face that contributed to the new policies?

4. How did the New Deal reshape Western communities and politics? What specific programs had the greatest impact in the region? How are these changes still visible today?

5. Evaluate the impact of the labor movement and radicalism on the 1930s. How did they influence American political and cultural life?

6. To what extent were the grim realities of Depression reflected in popular culture? To what degree were they absent?

7. Discuss the long- and short-range effects of the New Deal on American political and economic life. What were its key successes and failures? What legacies of New Deal–era policies and political struggles can you find in contemporary America?

KEY TERMS

Bonus Army (p. 650)

Congress of Industrial Organizations (p. 656)

Emergency Banking Act (p. 651)

1938 Fair Labor Standards Act (p. 666)

Fireside chat (p. 651)

Great Depression (p. 645)

National Industrial Recovery Act (p. 653)

National Labor Relations Act (p. 655)

New Deal (p. 650)

New Deal coalition (p. 657)

Social Security Act of 1935 (p. 654)

Tennessee Valley Authority (TVA) (p. 653)

RECOMMENDED READING

Anthony J. Badger, *The New Deal: The Depression Years, 1933–1940* (1989). Very useful overview that emphasizes the limited nature of New Deal reforms.

Alan Brinkley, *The End of Reform: New Deal Liberalism in Recession and War* (1995). A sophisticated analysis of the political and economic limits faced by New Deal reformers from 1937 through World War II.

Lizabeth Cohen, *Making a New Deal: Industrial Workers in Chicago, 1919–1939* (1990). A brilliant study that demonstrates the transformation of immigrant and African American workers into key actors in the creation of the CIO and in New Deal politics and illuminates the complex relationship between ethnic cultures and mass culture.

Michael Denning, *The Cultural Front: The Laboring of American Culture in the Twentieth Century* (1997). A provocative reinterpretation of 1930s culture, emphasizing the impact of the Popular Front and its lasting influence on American modernism and mass culture.

Ronald Edsforth, *The New Deal: America's Response to the Great Depression* (2000). A concise political history of the 1930s, offering an excellent synthesis of the massive secondary literature.

David M. Kennedy, *Freedom From Fear: The American People in Depression and War* (1999). An absorbing, magisterial narrative account of the U.S. experience in depression and war.

Richard Lowitt, *The New Deal and the West* (1984). A comprehensive study of the New Deal's impact in the West, with special attention to water policy and agriculture.

Robert S. McElvaine, *The Great Depression: America, 1929–1941* (1984). The best one-volume overview of the Great Depression. It is especially strong on the origins and early years of the worst economic calamity in American history.

Lois Scharf, *To Work and to Wed* (1980). Examines female employment and feminism during the Great Depression.

Harvard Sitkoff, *A New Deal for Blacks* (1978). Focuses on the narrow gains made by African Americans from New Deal measures, as well as the racism that pervaded most government programs.

The event was not spectacular, no fuses burned, no lights flashed. But to us it meant that release of atomic energy on a large scale would be only a matter of time.

—*Enrico Fermi, from* The First Reactor

WAR GARDENS FOR VICTORY

GROW VITAMINS AT YOUR KITCHEN DOOR

Enter VICTORY GARDEN CONTEST

REGISTER 404 S. 8th ST. MAY 1–15

CONSUMER INTEREST DIVISION, MINNEAPOLIS DEFENSE COUNCIL • A WAR CHEST AGENCY

On June 6, 1944, American, British, and Canadian forces seized a beachhead in German-occupied France. The landings began the final phase of World War II in Europe, which ended eleven months later with German surrender to the U.S., Britain, the Soviet Union, and their allies.

25

WORLD WAR II
1941–1945

WHAT STEPS did Roosevelt take in the late 1930s to prepare the United States for war?

WHAT WERE the economic consequences of the war for the United States?

WHAT LED to the internment of Japanese Americans?

WHAT ROLE did women play in the armed forces during World War II?

WHAT WERE the main elements of the Allied war strategy?

HOW DID Truman explain his decision to use the atomic bomb against the Japanese?

AMERICAN COMMUNITIES
Los Alamos, New Mexico

On Monday, July 16, 1945, at 5:29:45 a.m., Mountain War Time, the first atomic bomb exploded in a brilliant flash visible in three states. Within just seven minutes, a huge, multicolored, bell-shaped cloud soared 38,000 feet into the atmosphere and threw back a blanket of smoke and soot to the earth below. The heat generated by the blast was four times the temperature at the center of the sun, and the light produced rivaled that of nearly twenty suns. Even ten miles away people felt a strong surge of heat. The giant fireball ripped a crater a half-mile wide in the ground, fusing the desert sand into glass. The shock wave blew out windows in houses more than 200 miles away. The blast killed every living creature—squirrels, rabbits, snakes, plants, and insects—within a mile and the smells of death lingered for nearly a month.

Very early that morning, Ruby Wilkening had driven to a nearby mountain ridge, where she joined several other women waiting for the blast. Wilkening worried about her husband, a physicist, who was already at the test site. No one knew exactly what to expect, not even the scientists who developed the bomb.

The Wilkenings were part of a unique community of scientists who had been marshaled for war. President Franklin D. Roosevelt, convinced by Albert Einstein and other physicists that the Nazis might successfully develop an atomic bomb, had inaugurated a small nuclear research program in 1939. Soon after the United States entered World War II, the president released resources to create the Manhattan Project and placed it under the direction of the Army Corps of Engineers. By December 1942 a team headed by Italian-born Nobel Prize–winner Enrico Fermi had produced the first chain reaction in uranium under the University of Chicago's football stadium. Now the mission was to build a new, formidable weapon of war, the atomic bomb.

The government moved the key researchers and their families to Los Alamos, New Mexico, a remote and sparsely populated region of soaring peaks, ancient Indian ruins, modern Pueblos, and villages occupied by the descendants of the earliest Spanish settlers. The scientists and their families arrived in March 1943. They occupied a former boys' preparatory school until new houses could be built. Some families doubled up in rugged log cabins or nearby ranches. Telephone service to the outside world was poor, and the mountain roads were so rough that changing flat tires became a tiresome but familiar routine. Construction of new quarters proceeded slowly, causing nasty disputes between the "long-hairs" (scientists) and the "plumbers" (army engineers) in charge of the grounds. Despite the chaos, outstanding American and European scientists eagerly signed up. Most were young, with an average age of twenty-seven, and quite a few were recently married. Many couples began their families at Los Alamos, producing

a total of nearly a thousand babies between 1943 and 1949.

The scientists and their families formed an exceptionally close-knit community, united by the need for secrecy and their shared antagonism toward their army guardians. The military atmosphere was oppressive. Homes and laboratories were cordoned off by barbed wire and guarded by military police. Everything, from linens to food packages, was stamped "Government Issue." The scientists were followed by security personnel whenever they left Los Alamos. Several scientists were reprimanded for discussing their work at home, although many of their wives worked forty-eight hours a week in the Technical Area. All outgoing mail was censored. Well-known scientists commonly worked under aliases—Fermi became "Eugene Farmer"—and code names were used for such terms as atom, bomb, and uranium fission. The birth certificates of babies born at Los Alamos listed their place of birth simply as rural Sandoval County, and children registered without surnames at nearby public schools. Even automobile accidents went unreported, and newspapers carried no wedding announcements or obituaries. Only a group thoroughly committed to the war effort could accept such restrictions on personal liberty.

A profound urgency motivated the research team, which included refugees from Nazi Germany and Fascist Italy and a large proportion of Jews. The director of the project, California physicist J. Robert Oppenheimer, promoted a scientific élan that offset the military style of commanding general Leslie Groves. Just thirty-eight, slightly built, and deeply emotional, "Oppie" personified the idealism that helped the community of scientists overcome whatever moral reservations they held about placing such a potentially ominous weapon in the hands of the government.

In the Technical Area of Los Alamos, Oppenheimer directed research from an office with a desk, long tables, and blackboard along the walls in a typical two-story army building. At seven o'clock each workday morning, the siren dubbed "Oppie's Whistle" called the other scientists to their laboratories to wrestle with the theoretical and practical problems of building an atomic device. Once a week Oppenheimer called together the heads of the various technical divisions to discuss their work in round-table conferences. From May to November 1944, after the bomb had been designed, the key issue was testing it. Many scientists feared a test might fail, scattering the precious plutonium at the bomb's core and discrediting the entire project. Finally, with plutonium production increasing, the Los Alamos team agreed to test "the gadget" at a site 160 miles away.

The unprecedented scientific mobilization at Los Alamos mirrored changes occurring throughout American society as the nation rallied behind the war effort. Sixteen million men and women left home for military service and nearly as many moved to

Los Alamos

take advantage of wartime jobs. Several states in the South and Southwest experienced huge surges in population. California alone grew by 2 million people, a large proportion from Mexico. Many broad social changes with roots in earlier times—the economic expansion of the West, the erosion of farm tenancy among black people in the South and white people in Appalachia, and

the increasing employment of married women—accelerated during the war. The United States, initially reluctant to enter the war, emerged from it the world's leading superpower and free from the weight of the Great Depression. The events of the war eroded old communities, created new ones like Los Alamos, and transformed nearly all aspects of American society.

The Coming of World War II

The worldwide Great Depression further undermined a political order that had been shaky since World War I. Production declined by nearly 40 percent, international trade dropped by as much as two-thirds, unemployment rose, and political unrest spread across Europe and Asia. Demagogues played upon nationalist hatreds, fueled by old resentments and current despair, and offered solutions in the form of territorial expansion by military conquest.

Preoccupied with restoring the domestic economy, President Franklin D. Roosevelt had no specific plan to deal with growing conflict elsewhere in the world. Moreover, the majority of Americans strongly opposed foreign entanglements. But as debate over diplomatic policy heated up, terrifying events overseas pulled the nation steadily toward war.

The Shadows of War

War spread first across Asia. Militarist-imperialist leaders in Japan, which suffered economically from loss of trade during the 1930s, determined to make their nation the richest in the world. The Japanese army seized control of Manchuria in 1931 and in 1932 installed a puppet government there. When reprimanded by the League of Nations, Japan simply withdrew from the organization. In 1937 Japan provoked full-scale war with an invasion of northern China. When it seized control of the capital city of Nanking, Japan's army murdered as many as 300,000 Chinese men, women, and children and destroyed much of the city. Within the year Japan controlled all but China's western interior and threatened all Asia and the Pacific.

Meanwhile, the rise of authoritarian nationalism in Italy and Germany cast a dark shadow over Europe. The economic hardships brought on by the Great Depression—and, in Germany, resentment over the harsh terms of the Treaty of Versailles, which ended World War I—fueled the rise of demagogic mass movements. Glorifying war as a test of national virility, the Italian Fascist dictator Benito Mussolini, who had seized power in 1922, declared, "We have buried the putrid corpse of liberty." In Germany, the National Socialists (Nazis), led by Adolf Hitler, combined militaristic rhetoric with a racist doctrine of Aryan (Nordic) supremacy that claimed biological superiority for the blond-haired and blue-eyed peoples of northern Europe and classified nonwhites, including Jews, as "degenerate races."

Hitler, who became chancellor of Germany in January 1933 with the backing of major industrialists and about a third of the electorate, prepared for war. With his brown-shirted storm troopers ruling the streets, he quickly destroyed opposition parties and effectively made himself dictator of the strongest nation in central Europe. Renouncing the disarmament provisions of the Versailles treaty, he began to rebuild Germany's armed forces.

WHAT STEPS did Roosevelt take in the late 1930s to prepare the United States for war?

25–1
Albert Einstein, Letter to President Roosevelt (1939)

IMAGE KEY

for pages 670–671

a. A cloth patch with a yellow Star of David that all Jews had to wear under the Nazi regime.

b. A Victory Garden contest poster.

c. All POWs had to carry identification (ID) tags with them at all times. These two came from the Oflag XVIIA and Stelag VI/A camps in Germany.

d. American soldiers landing on the coast of France at Normandy on June 6, 1944; D-Day.

e. Unusually addressed letters to Winston Churchill.

f. The mushroom cloud produced by the explosion of an atomic bomb.

g. The Pearl Harbor attack, December 7, 1941.

h. Japanese-Americans were forced into internment camps during the war.

i. New recruits to the Women's Army Corps (WAC) during World War II.

j. The D-Day invasion of the beaches of Normandy, France, June 6, 1944.

Blitzkrieg German war tactic in World War II ("lightning war") involving the concentration of air and armored firepower to punch and exploit holes in opposing defensive lines.

The prospect of war grew as both Mussolini and Hitler began to act on their imperial visions. In 1935 Italy invaded Ethiopia and formally claimed the impoverished African kingdom as a colony. In 1936 Hitler sent 35,000 troops to occupy the Rhineland, a region demilitarized by the Versailles Treaty. When the Spanish Civil War broke out later that year, Italy and Germany both supported the fascist insurrection of General Francisco Franco and then, in November, drew up a formal alliance to become the Rome-Berlin Axis. Hitler was now nearly ready to put into operation his plan to secure *Lebensraum*—living space for Germany's growing population—through further territorial expansion.

After annexing his native Austria, Hitler turned his attention to Czechoslovakia, a country that both Britain and France were pledged by treaty to assist. War seemed imminent. But Britain and France surprised Hitler by agreeing, at a conference in Munich the last week of September 1938, to allow Germany to annex the Sudetenland, a part of Czechoslovakia bordering Germany. In return, Hitler pledged to stop his territorial advance. Less than six months later, in March 1939, Hitler seized the rest of Czechoslovakia.

By this time, much of the world was aware of the horror of Hitler's regime, especially its virulent racist doctrines. After 1935, when Hitler published the notorious Nuremberg Laws denying civil rights to Jews, the campaign against them became steadily more vicious. On the night of November 9, 1938, Nazi storm troopers rounded up Jews, beating them mercilessly and murdering an untold number. They smashed windows in Jewish shops, hospitals, and orphanages and burned synagogues to the ground. This attack came to be known as *Kristallnacht*, "the Night of Broken Glass." The Nazi government soon expropriated Jewish property and excluded Jews from all but the most menial forms of employment. Pressured by Hitler, Hungary and Italy also enacted laws against Jews.

ROOSEVELT READIES FOR WAR

While Americans looked on anxiously, the twists and turns of world events prompted President Franklin D. Roosevelt to ready the nation for war. In October 1937 he had called for international cooperation to "quarantine the aggressors." But a poll of Congress revealed that a two-thirds majority opposed economic sanctions, calling any such plan a "back door to war." Forced to draw back, Roosevelt nevertheless won from Congress $1 billion in appropriations to enlarge the navy.

Everything changed on September 1, 1939, when Hitler invaded Poland. Committed by treaty to defend Poland against unprovoked attack, Great Britain and France issued a joint declaration of war against Germany two days later. After the fall of Warsaw at the end of the month, the fighting slowed to a near halt. Even along their border, French and German troops did not exchange fire. From the east, however, the invasion continued. Just two weeks before Hitler overran Poland, the Soviet Union had stunned the world by signing a nonaggression pact with its former enemy. The Red Army now entered Poland, and the two great powers proceeded to split the hapless nation between them. Soviet forces then headed north, invading Finland on November 30. The European war had begun.

Calculating that the United States would stay out of the war, Hitler began a crushing offensive against Western Europe in April 1940. Using the technique of *Blitzkrieg* (lightning war)—massed, fast-moving columns of tanks supported by air power—that had overwhelmed Poland, Nazi troops moved first against Germany's northern neighbors. After taking Denmark and Norway, the Nazi armored divisions swept over Holland, Belgium, and Luxembourg and sent more than 338,000 British troops into retreat across the English Channel from Dunkerque. Hitler's army, joined by the Italians, easily conquered France in June 1940. Hitler now turned toward England. In the Battle of Britain, Nazi bombers pounded population and industrial centers while U-boats cut off incoming supplies.

Even with Great Britain under attack, opinion polls indicated Americans' determination to stay out of the war. But most Americans, like Roosevelt himself, believed that the security of the United States depended on both a strong defense and the defeat of Germany. Invoking the **Neutrality Act of 1939**, which permitted the sale of arms to Britain, France, and China, the president clarified his position: "all aid to the Allies short of war." In May 1940 he began to transfer surplus U.S. planes and equipment to the Allies. In September the president secured the first peacetime military draft in American history, the Selective Service Act of 1940, which sent 1.4 million men to army training camps by July 1941.

President Roosevelt could not yet admit the inevitability of U.S. involvement—especially during an election year. His popularity had dropped with the "Roosevelt recession" that began in 1937, raising doubts that he could win what would be an unprecedented third term. In his campaign he promised voters not to "send your boys to any foreign wars." Roosevelt and his vice presidential candidate Henry Wallace won by a margin of 5 million popular votes over the Republican dark-horse candidate, Wendell L. Willkie of Indiana.

Roosevelt now moved more aggressively to aid the Allies in their struggle with the **Axis powers**. He proposed a bill that would allow the president to sell, exchange, or lease arms to any country whose defense appeared vital to U.S. security. Passed by Congress in March 1941, the **Lend-Lease Act** made Great Britain the first beneficiary of massive aid. After Congress authorized the merchant marine to sail fully armed while conveying lend-lease supplies directly to Britain, a formal declaration of war was only a matter of time.

In August 1941 Roosevelt met secretly at sea off Newfoundland with British prime minister Winston Churchill to map military strategy and declare common goals for the postwar world. Known as the **Atlantic Charter**, their proclamation specified the right of all peoples to live in freedom from fear, want, and tyranny.

PEARL HARBOR

Throughout 1940 and much of 1941 the United States focused on events in Europe, but the war in Asia went on. Roosevelt, anticipating danger to American interests in the Pacific, had directed the transfer of the Pacific Fleet from bases in California to Pearl Harbor, on the island of Oahu, Hawai'i, in May 1940. On September 27 Japan formally joined Germany and Italy as the Asian partner of the Axis alliance.

The United States and Japan each played for time. Roosevelt wanted to save his resources to fight against Germany, while Japan's leaders gambled that America's preoccupation with Europe might allow them to conquer all of Southeast Asia, including the French colonies in Indochina (Vietnam, Cambodia, and Laos) and the British possessions of Burma and India. When Japan occupied Indochina in July 1941, however, Roosevelt responded by freezing Japanese assets in the United States and cutting off its oil supplies.

Confrontation with Japan now looked likely. U.S. intelligence had broken the Japanese diplomatic code, and the president knew that Japan was preparing for war against the Western powers. Roosevelt's advisers expected an attack somewhere in the Pacific and by the end of November placed all American forces there on high alert.

Early Sunday morning, December 7, 1941, Japanese carriers launched an attack on Pearl Harbor that caught American forces completely off guard. Within

25–3
Franklin D. Roosevelt, The Four Freedoms (1941)

25–4
Franklin Delano Roosevelt, Annual Message to Congress (1941)

Neutrality Act of 1939 Permitted the sale of arms to Britain, France, and China.

Axis powers The opponents of the United States and its allies in World War II.

Lend-Lease Act An arrangement for the transfer of war supplies, including food, machinery, and services to nations whose defense was considered vital to the defense of the United States in Word War II.

Atlantic Charter Statement of common principles and war aims developed by President Franklin Roosevelt and British Prime Minister Winston Churchill at a meeting in August 1941.

two hours, Japanese pilots had destroyed nearly 200 American planes and badly damaged the fleet; more than 2,400 Americans were killed and nearly 1,200 wounded. On the same day, Japan struck U.S. bases on the Philippines, Guam, and Wake Island.

On December 8, declaring the attack on Pearl Harbor a day that "will live in infamy," Roosevelt asked Congress for a declaration of war against Japan. With only one dissenting vote—by pacifist Jeannette Rankin of Montana, who had voted against U.S. entry into World War I in 1917—Congress acceded. The United States had not yet declared war on Japan's European allies, but Hitler made that unnecessary when he asked the *Reichstag* on December 11 to support war against the "half Judaized, and the other half Negrified" American nation. Mussolini joined him in the declaration, and the United States on the same day recognized that a state of war existed with Germany and Italy. World War II now began for Americans.

Japanese attack planes devastated the U.S. fleet stationed on the Hawai'ian island of Oahu. Before December 7, 1941, few Americans had heard of Pearl Harbor, but the "sneak" attack became a symbol of Japanese treachery and the necessity for U.S. revenge.

National Archives and Records Administration

On the day after the attack on Pearl Harbor, President Franklin D. Roosevelt addressed a joint session of Congress and asked for an immediate declaration of war against Japan. The resolution passed with one dissenting vote, and the United States entered World War II.

AP/Wide World Photos

ARSENAL OF DEMOCRACY

L ate in 1940 President Roosevelt called upon all Americans to make the nation a "great arsenal of democracy." During the next three years, the economic machinery that had failed during the 1930s was swiftly retooled for military purposes, with dramatic results. The Great Depression suddenly ended.

MOBILIZING FOR WAR

A few days after the United States declared war on Germany, Congress passed the **War Powers Act**, which established a precedent for executive authority that would endure long after the war's end. The president gained the power to reorganize the federal government and create new agencies; to establish programs censoring all news and information and abridging civil liberties; to seize property owned by foreigners; and even to award government contracts without competitive bidding.

Roosevelt promptly created special wartime agencies. At the top of his agenda was a massive reorientation and management of the economy, and an alphabet soup of new agencies arose to fill any gaps in production.

In June 1942 the president created the Office of War Information (OWI) to coordinate information from the multiplying federal agencies and to engage the press, radio, and film industry in an informational campaign—in short, to sell the war to the American people.

The federal government also sponsored various measures to prevent subversion of the war effort. The Federal Bureau of Investigation (FBI) was kept busy, its appropriation rising from $6 million to $16 million in just two years. The attorney general authorized wiretapping in cases of espionage or sabotage, but the FBI used it extensively—and illegally—in domestic surveillance. The Joint Chiefs of Staff created the Office of Strategic Services (OSS) to assess the enemy's military strength, to gather intelligence information, and to oversee espionage activities. Its head, Colonel William Donovan, envisioned the OSS as an "adjunct to military strategy" and engaged leading social scientists to plot psychological warfare against the enemy.

WHAT WERE the economic consequences of the war for the United States?

War Powers Act   Gave the U.S. president the power to reorganize the federal government and create new agencies; to establish programs censoring news, information, and abridging civil liberties; to seize foreign-owned property; and award government contracts without bidding.

Effects of War Spending, 1940–1945

Wartime spending had a multiplier effect on the U.S. economy. Government contracts with industry rapidly increased the gross national product, and the sharp upswing in production utilized all available workers and sharply reduced unemployment.

Robert L. Heilbroner, *The Economic Transformation of America* (New York: Harcourt, Brace, 1977), p. 205.

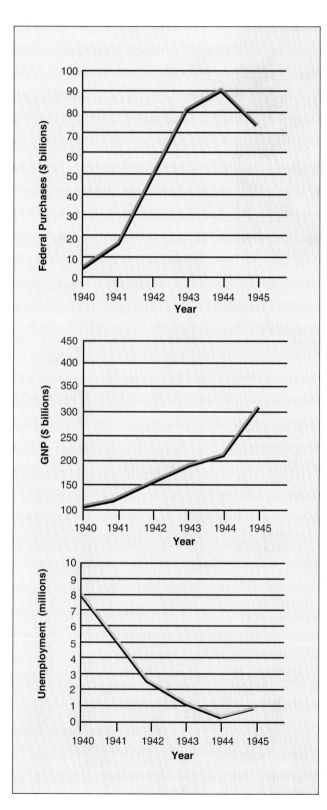

It cost about $250 million a day to fight the war, and the federal government spent twice as much during the war as during its entire prior history. The federal budget grew to ten times what it had been during the New Deal. The exception to this pattern of expansion was the New Deal itself. As President Roosevelt announced in 1942, "Dr. New Deal" had been replaced by "Dr. Win the War." One by one, New Deal agencies vanished.

ECONOMIC CONVERSION

The decisive factor for victory, even more than military prowess and superior strategy, would be, many observers agreed, the ability of the United States to outproduce its enemies. The country enjoyed many advantages to meet this challenge: a large industrial base, abundant natural resources (largely free from interference by the war), and a civilian population large enough to permit it to increase both its labor force and its armed forces. The war would lift the United States out of the Great Depression and create the biggest economic boom in the history of any nation. But first the entire civilian economy had to be both expanded and transformed for the production of arms and other military supplies.

By the summer of 1941 the federal government was pouring vast amounts into defense production. Six months after the attack on Pearl Harbor its allocations topped $100 billion for equipment and supplies, which exceeded what American firms had produced in any previous war. Facing war orders too large to fill, American industries were now primed for all-out production.

With better equipment and more motivation, American workers proved twice as productive as the Germans, five times as productive as the Japanese. No wonder the actual volume of industrial output expanded at the fastest rate in American history. Military production alone grew from 2 percent of the 1939 total gross national product to 40 percent of the 1943 total. "Something is happening," announced *Time* magazine, "that Adolf Hitler does not understand . . . it is the miracle of production."

Defense production transformed entire regions. The impact was strongest in the West—the major staging area for the war in the Pacific—where the federal government spent nearly $40 billion for military and industrial expansion. California secured 10 percent of all federal funds, and by 1944 Los Angeles had become the nation's second largest manufacturing center, only slightly behind Detroit. The South also benefited from 60 of the army's 100 new camps. Its textile factories hummed: the army alone required nearly 520 million pairs of socks and 230 million pairs of pants. The economic boom lifted entire populations out of sharecropping and tenancy into well-paid industrial jobs in the cities and pumped unprecedented profits into Southern business. Across the country the rural population decreased by almost 20 percent.

Despite a "Food for Freedom" program, American farmers could not keep up with the rising international demand or even the domestic market for milk, potatoes, fruits, and sugar. The Department of Agriculture reached its goals only in areas such as livestock production thanks to skyrocketing wholesale prices for meat. The war also speeded the development of large-scale, mechanized production of crops, including the first widespread use of chemical fertilizers and pesticides. By 1945 farm income had doubled, but thousands of small farms had disappeared, never to return.

NEW WORKERS

The wartime economy brought an unprecedented number of new workers into the labor force. The *bracero* program, negotiated by United States and Mexico in 1942, opened to Mexicans short-term employment in trades previously closed to them, such as shipbuilding on the Pacific coast. Sioux and Navajos were hired in large numbers to help build military depots and military training centers. African Americans found new opportunities in industry; the number of black workers rose from 2,900,000 to 3,800,000.

The war most dramatically altered the wage-earning patterns of women. The female labor force grew by over 50 percent, reaching 19.5 million in 1945. The rate of growth proved especially high for white women over the age of thirty-five, and for the first time married women became the majority of female wage earners. The employment rate changed comparatively little for African American women; fully 90 percent had been in the labor force in 1940. However, many black women left domestic service for higher paying jobs in manufacturing.

Neither government nor industry expected women to stay in their jobs when the war ended. Recruitment campaigns targeted "Mrs. Stay-at-Home" yet underscored the temporary aspect of her wartime service. "Rosie the Riveter" appeared in posters and advertisements as the model female citizen, but only "for the duration." In Washington, D.C., women bus drivers were given badges to wear on their uniforms that read: "I am taking the place of a man who went to war."

Compared to the Great Depression, when married women were barred from many jobs, World War II opened up new fields. The number of women automobile workers, for example, jumped from 29,000 to 200,000, that of women electrical workers from 100,000 to 374,000. Polled near the end of the war, the overwhelming majority—75 percent—of women workers expressed a desire to keep working, preferably at the same jobs.

Facing a shortage of workers and increased production demands, the War Manpower Commission and the Office of War Information conducted a campaign to recruit women into the labor force. Women were encouraged to "take a job for your husband/son/brother" and to "keep the world safe for your children." Higher wages also enticed many women to take jobs in factories producing aircraft, ships, and ordnance. This photograph shows women working on the assembly line at Douglas Aircraft's plant in Long Beach, California, in 1944.

The Granger Collection (4E887.35)

QUICK REVIEW

Rosie the Riveter

◆ Demand for labor drew women into the workplace.

◆ Companies opened positions for women in nontraditional jobs.

◆ Most women were forced to leave industrial jobs after the war.

The major advances proved short-lived. As early as 1943 some industries began planning to lay off women as war production wound down. With jobs reserved for returning veterans, women in industry saw their numbers diminish rapidly; as many as 4 million lost their jobs between 1944 and 1946.

WARTIME STRIKES

Although 17 million new jobs were created during the war, the economic gains were not evenly distributed. Wages increased by as much as 50 percent, but never as fast as profits or prices. This widely reported disparity produced one of the most turbulent periods in American labor history.

Labor strife began even before U.S. involvement in World War II. Only two weeks after the 1940 election, workers struck at the Vultee aircraft plant in Los Angeles. After the attorney general denounced the strikers as unpatriotic and the FBI began to harass participants, workers throughout the city walked off their jobs in sympathy with the aircraft workers.

More workers went on strike in 1941, before the United States entered the war, than in any previous year except 1919. Rising production orders and tightening labor markets made strikes feasible: jobs were plentiful, and business leaders, anticipating hefty profits, had reason to settle quickly. This climate prompted a militant union drive at Ford Motor Company's enormous River Rouge plant, and the United Auto Workers (UAW) emerged as one of the most powerful labor organizations in the world.

Once the United States entered the war, the major unions dutifully agreed to no-strike pledges for its duration. The National War Labor Board, with representatives from business and labor, encouraged employers to allow unions in their plants, and unions secured contracts that included automatic dues checkoff, high wages, and new fringe benefits such as pension plans. Total union membership increased from 10.5 million to 14.7 million, with the women's share alone rising from 11 to 23 percent.

Unions also enrolled 1,250,000 African Americans, twice the prewar number, but many white workers resisted this change. "Hate strikes" broke out in plants across the country when African Americans were hired or promoted to jobs customarily held by white workers. For example, at a U.S. Rubber Company factory in Detroit, more than half the workers walked out in 1943 when African American women began to operate the machinery. Such strikes usually ended quickly because black workers refused to back down.

Rank-and-file union members staged other illegal "wildcat" strikes. The most dramatic, a walkout of more than a half-million coal miners in 1943 led by the rambunctious John L. Lewis, withstood the attacks of the government and the press. Roosevelt repeatedly ordered the mines seized, only to find, as Lewis retorted, that coal could not be mined with bayonets. The Democratic majority in Congress passed the first federal antistrike bill, giving the president power to penalize strikers, even to draft them. And yet the strikes grew in size and number, reaching a level greater than in any other four-year period in American history.

THE HOME FRONT

WHAT LED to the

internment of Japanese Americans?

Most Americans thoroughly appreciated the burst of prosperity brought on by wartime production, but they also experienced food rationing, long workdays, and separation from loved ones. Alongside national unity ran deep conflicts on the home front. Racial and ethnic hostilities flared repeatedly and on several occasions erupted in violence.

FAMILIES IN WARTIME

Despite the uncertainties of wartime, or perhaps because of them, men and women rushed into marriage. The surge in personal income caused by the wartime economic boom meant that many young couples could afford to set up their own households—something their counterparts in the 1930s had not been able to do. As one social scientist remarked at the time, "Economic conditions were ripe for a rush to the altar." For other couples, the prospect of separation provided the incentive. The U.S. Census Bureau estimated that between 1940 and 1943 at least a million more people married than would have been expected had there been no war. The marriage rate skyrocketed, peaking in 1946, but by 1946 the number of divorces also set records.

Housing shortages were acute, and rents were high. So scarce were apartments that taxi drivers became, for an extra fee, up-to-the-minute guides to vacancies. Able to set their own terms, landlords frequently discriminated against families with children and even more so against racial minorities.

Supplying a household was scarcely less difficult. Although retailers extended their store hours into the evenings and weekends, shopping had to be squeezed in between long hours on the job. Extra planning was necessary for purchasing government-rationed staples such as meat, cheese, sugar, milk, coffee, gasoline, and even shoes. Many women found it nearly impossible to manage both a demanding job and a household. This dual responsibility contributed to high turnover and absentee rates in factories.

The care of small children became a major problem. Wartime employment or military service often separated husbands and wives, leaving children in the hands of only one parent. But even when families stayed together, both adults often worked long hours, sometimes on different shifts. Although the War Manpower Commission estimated that as many as 2 million children needed some form of child care, federally funded day-care centers served less than 10 percent of defense workers' children.

Juvenile delinquency rose during the war. With employers often relaxing minimum age requirements for employment, many teenagers quit school for the high wages of factory jobs. In 1944 the U.S. Office of Education and the Children's Bureau inaugurated a back-to-school campaign. Local school boards appealed to employers to hire only older workers, and toward the end of the war the student dropout rate began to decline.

Public health improved greatly during the war. Forced to cut back on expenditures for medical care during the Great Depression, many Americans now spent large portions of their wartime paychecks on doctors, dentists, and prescription drugs. But even more important were the benefits provided to the more than 16 million men inducted into the armed forces and their dependents. Nationally, incidences of such communicable diseases as typhoid fever, tuberculosis, and diphtheria dropped considerably, the infant death rate fell by more than a third, and life expectancy increased by three years. The death rate in 1942, excluding battle deaths, was the lowest in the nation's history.

THE INTERNMENT OF JAPANESE AMERICANS

After the attack on Pearl Harbor, many Americans feared an invasion of the mainland and suspected Japanese Americans of secret loyalty to an enemy government. On December 8, 1941, the federal government froze the financial assets of those born in Japan, known as **Issei**, who had been barred from U.S. citizenship. Although a State Department intelligence report certified their loyalty, Japanese Americans—two-thirds of whom were American-born citizens—became the only ethnic group singled out for legal sanctions.

Issei   The first generation of Japanese to come to America starting in the late1800s.

Byron Takashi Tsuzuki, *Forced Removal, Act II*, 1944. This Japanese American artist illustrates the forced relocation of Japanese Americans from their homes to one of ten inland camps in 1942. About 110,000 Japanese Americans were interned during World War II, some for up to four years. Beginning in January 1945, they were allowed to return to the Pacific coast.

Byron Takashi Tsuzuki, *Forced Removal, Act II*, 1944. Japanese American National Museum, Collection of August and MASKO (Kitty) Nakagawa

QUICK REVIEW

Internment

◆ December 8, 1941: Financial assets of Issei frozen.

◆ February 19, 1942: Civil rights of Japanese Americans suspended and 112,000 people relocated to internment camps.

◆ 1944: Supreme Court upheld constitutionality of relocation.

25–6
Japanese Relocation Order, February 19, 1942

Charges of sedition masked long-standing racial prejudices. The press began to use the word "Jap" in headlines, while political cartoonists employed blatant racial stereotypes. Popular songs appeared with titles like "You're a Sap, Mister Jap, to Make a Yankee Cranky." "The very fact that no sabotage has taken place to date," an army report suggested, with twisted logic, "is a disturbing and confirming indication that action will be taken."

On February 19, 1942, President Roosevelt signed Executive Order 9066, suspending the civil rights of Japanese Americans and authorizing the exclusion of more than 112,000 men, women, and children from designated military areas, mainly in California, but also in Oregon, Washington, and Southern Arizona.

During the spring of 1942, Japanese American families received one week's notice to close up their businesses and homes before being transported to one of the ten internment camps managed by the War Relocation Authority. The guarded camps were located as far away as Arkansas, although the majority had been set up in isolated and arid districts of Utah, Colorado, Idaho, Arizona,

Wyoming, and California. Karl G. Yoneda described his quarters at Manzanar in northern California:

> There were no lights, stoves, or window panes. My two cousins and I, together with seven others, were crowded into a 25 × 30 foot room. We slept on army cots with our clothes on. The next morning we discovered that there were no toilets or washrooms. . . . We saw GIs manning machine guns in the watchtowers. The barbed wire fence which surrounded the camp was visible against the background of the snow-covered Sierra mountain range. "So this is the American-style concentration camp," someone remarked.

By August, virtually every West Coast resident who had at least one Japanese grandparent had been interned.

The Japanese American Citizens League charged that "racial animosity" rather than military necessity had dictated the internment policy. Despite the protest of the American Civil Liberties Union and several church groups against the abridgment of the civil rights of Japanese Americans, the Supreme Court in *Korematsu* v. *United States* (1944) upheld the constitutionality of relocation on grounds of national security. By this time a program of gradual release was in place, although the last center, at Tule Lake, California, did not close until March 1946. In protest, nearly 6,000 Japanese Americans renounced their U.S. citizenship. Japanese Americans had lost homes and businesses valued at $500 million in what many historians judge as being the worst violation of American civil liberties during the war. Not until 1988 did the U.S. Congress vote reparations of $20,000 and a public apology to each of the 60,000 surviving victims.

CIVIL RIGHTS AND RACE RIOTS

Throughout the war, African American activists conducted a "Double V" campaign, mobilizing not only for Allied victory, but also for their own rights as citizens. "The army is about to take me to fight for democracy," one Detroit resident said, "but I would as leave fight for democracy right here." Black militants demanded, at a minimum, fair housing and equal employment opportunities. President Roosevelt responded in a lukewarm fashion, supporting advances in civil rights that would not, in his opinion, disrupt the war effort.

25–5
A. Philip Randolph, "Why Should We March?" (1942)

Before the United States entered the war, A. Philip Randolph, president of both the Brotherhood of Sleeping Car Porters and the National Negro Congress, had organized the March on Washington Movement. Eager to stop the movement, President Roosevelt met with Randolph, who proposed an executive order "making it mandatory that Negroes be permitted to work." Randolph reviewed several drafts before approving the text that became, on June 25, 1941, Executive Order 8802, banning discrimination in defense industries and government. Randolph called off the march but did not disband his all-black March on Washington organization. He remained determined to "shake up white America."

Other civil rights organizations formed during wartime to fight both discrimination and Jim Crow practices, including segregation in the U.S. armed forces. The interracial Congress of Racial Equality (CORE), formed by pacifists in 1942, staged sit-ins at Chicago, Detroit, and Denver restaurants that refused to serve African Americans. Meanwhile, membership in the National Association for the Advancement of Colored People (NAACP), which took a strong stand against discrimination in the military, grew from 50,000 in 1940 to 450,000 in 1946.

This painting is by Horace Pippin, a self-taught African American artist who began painting as therapy for an injury suffered while serving with the U.S. Army's 369th Colored Infantry Regiment during World War I. It is one of a series drawn during World War II illustrating the contradiction between the principles of liberty and justice, for which Americans were fighting abroad, and the reality of race prejudice at home.

Horace Pippin (1888–1946), *Mr. Prejudice*, 1943. Oil on canvas, 18"× 14". Philadelphia Museum of Art, Gift of Dr. and Mrs. Matthew T. Moore. Photo by Graydon Wood (1984–108–1)

The struggle for equality took shape within local communities. In February 1942, when twenty black families attempted to move into new federally funded apartments adjacent to a Polish American community in Detroit, a mob of 700 white protesters halted the moving vans and burned a cross on the project's grounds. The police overlooked the white rioters but arrested black youths. Finally, two months later, 1,000 state troopers supervised the move of these families into the Sojourner Truth Homes, named after the famous abolitionist and former slave.

Racial violence reached its wartime peak during the summer of 1943, when 274 conflicts broke out in nearly fifty cities. In Detroit, where the black population had grown by more than a third since the beginning of the war, twenty-five blacks and nine whites were killed and more than 700 were injured. The poet Langston Hughes, who supported U.S. involvement in the war, wrote:

> *Looky here, America*
> *What you done done—*
> *Let things drift*
> *Until the riots come*
>
> *Yet you say we're fighting*
> *For democracy.*
> *Then why don't democracy*
> *Include me?*
>
> *I ask you this question*
> *Cause I want to know*
> *How long I got to fight*
> *BOTH HITLER—AND JIM CROW.*

ZOOT-SUIT RIOTS

On the night of June 4, 1943, sailors poured into nearly 200 cars and taxis to drive through the streets of East Los Angeles in search of Mexican Americans dressed in zoot suits. The sailors assaulted their victims at random, even chasing one youth into a movie theater and stripping him of his clothes while the audience cheered. Riots broke out and continued for five days.

Two communities had collided, with tragic results. The sailors had only recently been uprooted from their hometowns and regrouped under the strict discipline of boot camp. Now stationed in southern California while awaiting departure overseas, they came face-to-face with Mexican American teenagers wearing long-draped coats, pegged pants, pocket watches with oversized chains, and big floppy hats. To the sailors, the zoot suit was not just a flamboyant fashion. Unlike the uniform the young sailors wore, the zoot suit signaled a lack of patriotism.

The zoot-suiters, however, represented less than 10 percent of their community's youth. More than 300,000 Mexican Americans were serving in the armed forces (a number representing a greater proportion of their draft-age population than other Americans), and they served in the most hazardous branches, the paratrooper and marine corps. Many others were employed in war industries in Los Angeles, which had become home to the largest community of Mexican Americans in the nation. For the first time Mexican Americans were finding well-paying jobs, and, like African Americans, they expected their government to protect them from discrimination.

In Los Angeles, military and civilian authorities eventually contained the zoot-suit riots by ruling several sections of the city off limits to military personnel.

25–7
Sterling A. Brown, "Out of Their Mouths" (1942)

The Los Angeles City Council passed legislation making the wearing of a zoot suit in public a criminal offense. Many Mexican Americans expressed concern about their personal safety; some feared that, after the government rounded up the Japanese, they would be the next group sent to internment camps.

POPULAR CULTURE AND "THE GOOD WAR"

Global events shaped the lives of American civilians but appeared to touch them only indirectly in their everyday activities. Food shortages, long hours in the factories, and even fears for loved ones abroad did not take away all the pleasures of full employment and prosperity. With money in their pockets, Americans spent freely at vacation resorts, country clubs, race tracks, nightclubs, dance halls, and movie theaters. Sales of books skyrocketed, and spectator sports attracted huge audiences.

Hollywood artists meanwhile threw themselves into a perpetual round of fundraising and morale-boosting public events. Movie stars called on fans to buy war bonds and to support the troops. Combat films such as *Action in the North Atlantic* made heroes of ordinary Americans under fire, depicting GIs of different races and ethnicities discovering their common humanity. Movies with antifascist themes, such as *Tender Comrade*, promoted friendship among Russians and Americans, while films like *Since You Went Away* portrayed the loyalty and resilience of families with servicemen stationed overseas.

Never to see a single battle, safeguarded by two oceans, many Americans nevertheless experienced the war years as the most intense of their entire lives. Popular music, Hollywood movies, radio programs, and advertisements—all screened by the Office of War Information—encouraged a sense of personal involvement in a collective effort to preserve democracy at home and to save the world from fascism. No one was excluded, no action considered insignificant. Even casual conversation came under the purview of the government, which warned that "Loose Lips Sink Ships."

25–2
Charles Lindbergh, Radio Address (1941)

MEN AND WOMEN IN UNIFORM

During World War I, American soldiers served for a relatively brief period and in small numbers. A quarter-century later, World War II mobilized 16.4 million Americans into the armed forces. Although only 34 percent of men who served in the army saw combat—the majority during the final year of the war—the experience had a powerful impact on nearly everyone.

WHAT ROLE did women play in the armed forces during World War II?

CREATING THE ARMED FORCES

Before the European war broke out in 1939, the majority of the 200,000 men in the U.S. armed forces were employed as military police, engaging in such tasks as patrolling the Mexican border or occupying colonial possessions, such as the Philippines. Neither the army nor the navy was prepared for the scale of combat World War II entailed. Only the U.S. Marine Corps, which had been planning since the 1920s to wrest control of the western Pacific from Japan, was poised to fight.

On October 16, 1940, National Registration Day, all men between the ages of twenty-one and thirty-six were legally obligated to register for military service. After the United States entered the war, the draft age was lowered to eighteen, and local boards were instructed to choose first from the youngest.

One-third of the men examined by the Selective Service were rejected. Surprising numbers were refused induction because they were physically unfit for military service. For the first time, men were screened for "neuropsychiatric disorders or emotional problems." At a time when only one American in four graduated from high school, induction centers turned away many conscripts because they were functionally illiterate. But those who passed the screening tests joined the best educated army in history: nearly half of white draftees had graduated from high school and 10 percent had attended college.

The officer corps, whose top-ranking members were from the Command and General Staff School at Fort Leavenworth, tended to be highly professional, politically conservative, and personally autocratic. General Douglas MacArthur, supreme commander in the Pacific theater, was said to admire the discipline of the German army and to disparage political democracy. General Dwight D. Eisenhower, however, supreme commander of the Allied forces in Europe, projected a new and contrasting spirit. Distrusted by MacArthur and many of the older brass, Eisenhower appeared to his troops a model of leadership.

The democratic rhetoric of the war contributed to this transformation. A shortage of officers during World War I had prompted a huge expansion of the Reserve Officer Training Corps, but its drilling and discipline alone could not create good officers, and it was still insufficient to meet the demand for trained officers. Racing to make up for the deficiency, Army Chief of Staff George Marshall opened schools for officer candidates. In 1942, in seventeen-week training periods, these schools produced more than 54,000 platoon leaders. Closer in sensibility to the civilian population, these new officers were the kind of leaders Eisenhower sought.

Most GIs (short for "government issue"), who were the vast majority of draftees, had limited contact with officers at the higher levels and instead forged bonds with their company commanders and men within their own combat units. "Everyone wants someone to look up to when he's scared," one GI explained. Most of all, soldiers depended on the solidarity of the group and the loyalty of their buddies to pull through the war.

WOMEN ENTER THE MILITARY

With the approach of World War II, Massachusetts Republican congresswoman Edith Nourse Rogers proposed legislation for the formation of a women's corps. The army instead drafted its own bill, which both Rogers and Eleanor Roosevelt supported, creating in May 1942 the Women's Army Auxiliary Corps (WAAC), later changed to Women's Army Corps (WAC). In 1942–1943 other bills established a women's division of the navy (WAVES), the Women's Airforce Service Pilots, and the Marine Corps Women's Reserve.

Although barred from combat, women were not necessarily protected from danger. Nurses accompanied the troops into combat in Africa, Italy, and France, treated men under fire, and dug and lived in their own foxholes. More than 1,000 women flew planes, although not in combat missions.

The WACS and WAVES were both subject to hostile commentary and bad publicity. The overwhelming majority of soliders believed that most WACS were prostitutes, and the War Department itself, fearing "immorality" among women in the armed forces, closely monitored their conduct and established much stricter rules for women than for men. The U.S. Marine Corps even used intelligence officers to ferret out suspected lesbians or women who showed "homosexual tendencies" (as opposed to homosexual acts), both causes for dishonorable discharge.

OLD PRACTICES AND NEW HORIZONS

The Selective Service Act, in response to the demands of African American leaders, specified that "there shall be no discrimination against any person on account of race or color." The draft brought hundreds of thousands of young black men into the army, and African Americans enlisted at a rate 60 percent above their

New recruits to the Women's Army Corps (WAC) pick up their clothing "issue" (allotment). These volunteers served in many capacities, from nursing men in combat to performing clerical and communications duties "stateside" (within the United States). Approximately 140,000 women served in the WACS during World War II.

National Archives and Records Administration

proportion of the general population. By 1944 black soliders represented 10 percent of the army's troops, and overall approximately 1 million African Americans served in the armed forces during World War II. The army, however, channeled black recruits into segregated, poorly equipped units, which were commanded by white officers. Secretary of War Henry Stimson refused to challenge this policy, saying that the army could not operate effectively as "a sociological laboratory." The majority served in the Signal, Engineer, and Quartermaster Corps, mainly in construction or stevedore work. Only toward the end of the war, when the shortage of infantry neared a crisis, were African Americans permitted to rise to combat status. The all-black 761st Tank Battalion, the first African American unit in combat, won a Medal of Honor after 183 days in action. And despite the very small number of African Americans admitted to the Air Force, the 99th Pursuit Squadron earned high marks in action against the feared German air force, the Luftwaffe. Even the Marine Corps and the Coast Guard agreed to end their historic exclusion of African Americans, although they recruited and promoted only a small number.

The ordinary black soldier, sailor, or marine experienced few benefits from the late-in-the-war gains of a few. They encountered discrimination everywhere, from the army canteen to the religious chapels. Even the blood banks kept blood segregated by race (although a black physician, Dr. Charles Drew, had invented the process for storing plasma).

The army also grouped Japanese Americans into segregated units, sending most to fight far from the Pacific theater. Better educated than the average soldier, many **Nisei** soldiers who knew Japanese served state-side as interpreters and translators. When the army decided to create a Nisei regiment, more than 10,000 volunteers stepped forward, only one in five of whom was accepted. The Nisei 442nd fought heroically in Italy and France and became the most decorated regiment in the war.

Despite segregation, the armed forces ultimately pulled Americans of all varieties out of their communities. Many Jews and other second-generation European immigrants, for example, described their stint in the military as an "Americanizing" experience. Many Indian peoples left reservations for the first time, approximately

Nisei U.S. citizens born of immigrant Japanese parents.

25,000 serving in the armed forces. Many Navajo "code talkers," for example, who used a special code based on their native language to transmit information among military units, learned English in special classes established by the marines. For many African Americans, military service provided a bridge to postwar civil rights agitation.

Many homosexuals also discovered a wider world. Despite a policy barring them from military service, most slipped through mass screening at induction centers. Moreover, the emotional pressures of wartime, especially the fear of death, encouraged close friendships, and homosexuals in the military often found more room than in civilian life to express their sexual orientation openly. In army canteens, for example, men often danced with one another, whereas in civilian settings they would have been subject to ridicule or even arrest for such activity.

Most soldiers looked back at the war, with all its dangers and discomforts, as the greatest experience they would ever know. As the *New Republic* predicted in 1943, they met fellow Americans from every part of the country and recognized for the first time in their lives "the bigness and wholeness of the United States."

THE MEDICAL CORPS

The chance of being killed in combat was surprisingly small, estimated at less than 1 in 50, but the risk of injury was much higher. By the time the war ended, the army reported 949,000 casualties, including 175,000 who had been killed in action. Although the European Theater produced the greatest number of casualties, the Pacific held grave dangers in addition to artillery fire. For the soliders fighting in hot, humid jungles, malaria, typhus, diarrhea, or dengue fever posed the most common threat to their lives.

The prolonged stress of combat also took a toll in the form of "battle fatigue." Despite the rigorous screening of recruits, more than 1 million soldiers suffered at one time or another from debilitating psychiatric symptoms, and the number of men discharged for neuropsychiatric reasons was 2.5 times greater than in previous wars. The cause, psychiatrists concluded, was not individual weakness, but long stints in the front lines. In France, for example, where soldiers spent up to 200 days in the field without a break from fighting, thousands cracked, occasionally inflicting wounds on themselves in order to be sent home. In 1944 the army concluded that eight months in combat was the maximum and instituted, when replacements were available, a rotation system to relieve exhausted soldiers.

To care for sick and wounded soldiers, the army depended on a variety of medical personnel. Soldiers received first-aid training as part of basic training, and they went into battle equipped with bandages to treat minor wounds. For the most part, however, they relied on the talents of trained physicians and medics. The Army Medical Corps sent doctors to the front lines. Working in make-shift tent hospitals, these physicians advanced surgical techniques and, with the use of new "wonder" drugs such as penicillin, saved the lives of many wounded soldiers. Of the soldiers who underwent emergency surgery on the field, more than 85 percent survived. Overall, less than 4 percent of all soldiers who received medical care died as a result of their injuries. Much of the success in treatment came from the use of blood plasma, which reduced the often lethal effect of shock from severe bleeding. By 1945, the American Red Cross Blood Bank, which was formed four years earlier, had collected more than 13 million units of blood from volunteers, converted most of it into dried plasma, and made it readily available throughout the European Theater.

A Red Cross medical officer treats one of the U.S. Army's "walking wounded" during World War II, using a medicine chest as a surgical table.

Getty Images Inc.–Hulton Archive Photos.

Grateful for the care of skilled surgeons, many soldiers nevertheless named medics the true heroes of the battlefront. Between thirty to forty medics were attached to each infantry battalion, and they were responsible for emergency first aid and for transporting the wounded to the aid station and if necessary on to the field hospital. Many medics were recruited from the approximately 35,000 conscientious objectors, who were defined by the Selective Service as a person "who, by reason of religious training and belief, is conscientiously opposed to participation in war in any form."

In the military hospitals, American nurses supplied the bulk of care to recovering soldiers. Before World War II, the Army Nurse Corps, created in 1901, was scarcely a military organization, with recruits earning neither military pay nor rank. To overcome the short supply of nurses, Congress extended military rank to nurses in 1944, although only for the duration and for six months after the war ended. In 1945 Congress came close to passing a bill to draft nurses. Like medics, army nurses went first to training centers in the United States, learning how to dig foxholes and dodge bullets before being sent overseas. By 1945, approximately 56,000 women, including 500 African American women, were on active duty in the Army Nurse Corps, staffing medical facilities in every theater of the war.

THE WORLD AT WAR

During the first year of declared war, the Allies remained on the defensive. Hitler's forces held the European continent and pounded England with aerial bombardments while driving deep into Russia and across northern Africa to take the Suez Canal. The situation in the Pacific was scarcely better. Just two hours after the attack on Pearl Harbor, Japanese planes struck the main U.S. base in the Philippines and demolished half the air force commanded by General Douglas MacArthur. Within a short time, MacArthur was forced to withdraw his troops to the Bataan Peninsula, admitting that Japan had practically seized the Pacific.

But the Allies enjoyed several important advantages: vast natural resources and a skilled work force with sufficient reserves to accelerate the production of weapons and ammunitions; the determination of millions of antifascists throughout Europe and Asia; and the capacity of the Soviet Union to endure immense losses. Slowly at first, but then with quickening speed, these advantages made themselves felt.

WHAT WERE the main elements of the Allied war strategy?

SOVIETS HALT NAZI DRIVE

The weapons and tactics of World War II were radically different from those of World War I. Unlike World War I, which was fought by immobile armies kept in trenches by bursts of machine-gun fire, World War II was a war of offensive maneuvers punctuated by surprise attacks. Its chief weapons were tanks and airplanes, combining mobility and concentrated firepower. Also of major importance were artillery and explosives, which according to some estimates accounted for over 30 percent of the casualties. Major improvements in communication systems, mainly two-way radio transmission and radiotelephony that permitted commanders to stay in contact with division leaders, also played a decisive role from the beginning of the war.

Early on, Hitler had used these methods to seize the advantage, purposefully creating terror among the stricken populations of Western Europe. In the summer of 1941, he turned his attention to the east, hoping to invade and conquer the Soviet Union before the United States entered the war. But he had to delay the invasion in order to support Mussolini, whose weak army had been pushed back in North Africa and Greece. The attack on Russia did not come until June 22, six weeks later than planned and too late to achieve its goals before the brutal Russian winter began.

The burden of the war now fell on the Soviet Union. From June to September, Hitler's forces overran the Red Army, killing or capturing nearly 3 million soldiers and leaving thousands to die from exposure or starvation. But Nazi commanders did not count on civilian resistance. The Soviets rallied, cutting German supply lines and sending every available resource to Soviet troops concentrated just outside Moscow. After furious fighting and the onset of severe winter weather, the Red Army launched a massive counterattack, catching the freezing German troops off guard. For the first time, the Nazi war machine suffered a major setback.

Turning strategically away from Moscow, during the summer of 1942 German troops headed toward the Crimea and the rich oil fields of the Caucasus. Still set on conquering the Soviet Union and turning its vast resources to his own use, Hitler decided to attack Stalingrad, a major industrial city on the Volga River. The Soviets suffered more casualties during the following battles than Americans did during the entire war. But intense house-to-house and street fighting and a massive Soviet counteroffensive took an even greater toll on the Nazi fighting machine. By February 1943, the German Sixth Army had met defeat, overpowered by Soviet troops and weapons. More than 100,000 German soldiers surrendered.

Already in retreat but plotting one last desperate attempt to halt the Red Army, the Germans threw most of their remaining armored vehicles into action at Kursk, in the Ukraine, in July 1943. The clash quickly developed into the greatest land battle in history. More than 2 million troops and 6,000 tanks went into action. After another stunning defeat, the Germans had decisively lost the initiative. Their only option was to delay the advance of the Red Army against their homeland.

Meanwhile, the Soviet Union had begun to recover from its early losses, even as tens of millions of its own people remained homeless and near starvation. Assisted by the U.S. Lend-Lease program, by 1942 the Soviets were outproducing Germany in many types of weapons and other supplies. Nazi officers and German civilians alike began to doubt that Hitler could win the war. The Soviet victories had turned the tide of the war.

THE ALLIED OFFENSIVE

In the spring of 1942, Germany, Italy, and Japan commanded a territory extending from France to the Pacific Ocean. They controlled central Europe and a large section of the Soviet Union as well as considerable parts of China and the southwestern Pacific. But their momentum was flagging. American shipbuilding outpaced the punishment Nazi submarines inflicted on Allied shipping, and sub-sinking destroyers greatly reduced the submarines' threat. The United States far outstripped Germany in the production of landing craft and amphibious vehicles, two of the most important innovations of the war. Also outnumbered by the Allies, the German air force was limited to defensive action. On land, the United States and Great Britain had the trucks and jeeps to field fully mobile armies, while German troops marched in and out of Russia with packhorses.

Still, German forces represented a mighty opponent on the European continent. Fighting the Nazis almost alone, the Soviets repeatedly appealed for the creation of a Second Front, an Allied offensive against Germany from the west. The Allies focused instead on securing North Africa and then on an invasion of Italy, hoping to move from there into central Europe.

On the night of October 23–24, 1942, near El Alamein in the desert of western Egypt, the British Eighth Army halted a major offensive by the German Afrika Korps, headed by General Erwin Rommel, the famed "Desert Fox." Although suffering heavy losses—approximately 13,000 men and more than 500 tanks—British forces destroyed the Italian North African Army and much of Germany's Afrika

QUICK REVIEW

The Beginning of the End

◆ Allies gained footholds in North Africa.

◆ Allies took control of much of Italy.

◆ June 6, 1944: D-Day invasion of Normandy launched.

Korps. Americans entered the war in Europe as part of **Operation Torch**, the landing of British and American troops on the coast of Morocco and Algeria in November 1942, the largest amphibious military landing to that date. The Allies then

Operation Torch   The Allied invasion of Axis-held North Africa in 1942.

MAP EXPLORATION

To explore an interactive version of this map, go to **http://www.prenhall.com/faraghertlc/map25.1**

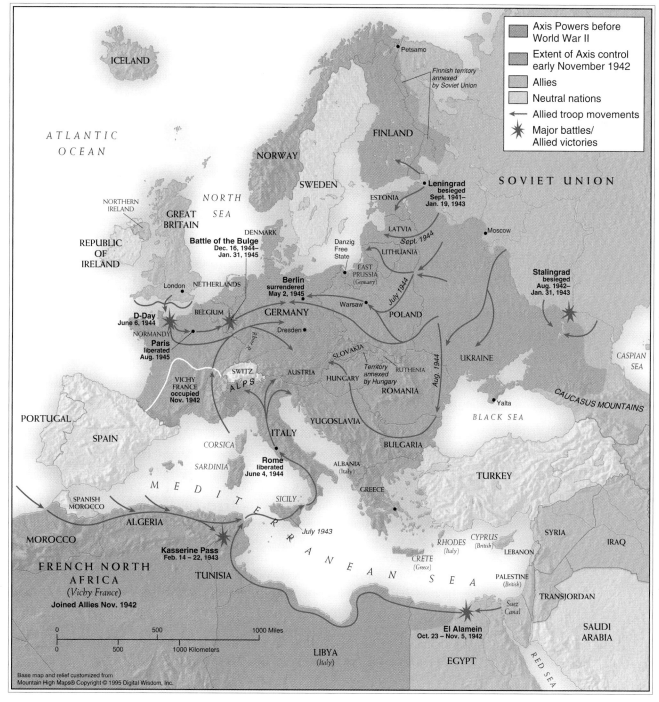

MAP 25-1

The War in Europe   The Allies remained on the defensive during the first years of the war, but by 1943 the British and Americans, with an almost endless supply of resources, had turned the tide.

WHAT WERE the key turning points of the war in Europe?

The D-Day landing, June 6, 1944, marked the greatest amphibious maneuver in military history. Troop ships ferried Allied soldiers from England to Normandy beaches. Within a month, nearly 1 million men had assembled in France, ready to retake western and central Europe from German forces.

Photo by Robert Capa. CORBIS

fought their way along the coast, entering Tunis in triumph six months later. With the surrender of a quarter-million Germans and Italians in Tunisia in May 1943, the Allies controlled North Africa and had a secure position in the Mediterranean.

During the North African campaign, the Allies announced that they would accept nothing less than the unconditional surrender of their enemies. In January 1943, Roosevelt and Churchill had met in Casablanca in Morocco and ruled out any possibility of negotiation with the Axis powers. Roosevelt's supporters hailed the policy as a clear statement of goals, a promise to the world that the scourge of fascism would be completely banished. Stalin, who did not attend the meeting, criticized the policy, fearing that it would only increase the enemy's determination to fight to the end. Other critics similarly charged that the demand for total capitulation would serve to prolong the war and lengthen the casualty list.

Allied aerial bombing further increased pressure on Germany. Many U.S. leaders believed that in the B-17 Flying Fortress, the air force possessed the ultimate weapon, "the mightiest bomber ever built." The U.S. Army Air Corps described this bomber as a "humane" weapon, capable of hitting specific military targets and sparing the lives of civilians. But when weather or darkness required pilots to depend on radar for sightings, they couldn't distinguish clearly between factories and schools or between military barracks and private homes, and bombs might fall within a range of nearly two miles from the intended target. American pilots preferred to bomb during daylight hours, while the British bombed during the night. Bombing missions over the Rhineland and the Ruhr successfully took out many German factories, but the Germans responded by relocating their plants, often dispersing light industry to the countryside.

Determined to break German resistance, the Royal Air Force redirected its main attack away from military sites to cities, including fuel dumps and public transportation. Hamburg was practically leveled. Between 60,000 and 100,000 people were killed, and 300,000 buildings were destroyed. Sixty other cities were hit hard, leaving 20 percent of Germany's total residential area in ruins. The very worst air raid of the war—650,000 incendiary bombs dropped on the city of Dresden, destroying 8 square miles and killing 135,000 civilians—had no military value.

THE ALLIED INVASION OF EUROPE

During the summer of 1943, the Allies began to advance on southern Italy. On July 10, British and American troops stormed Sicily from two directions and conquered the island in mid-August. King Vittorio Emmanuel dismissed Mussolini, calling him "the most despised man in Italy," and Italians, by now disgusted with the Fascist government, celebrated in the streets. Italy surrendered to the Allies on September 8, and Allied troops landed on the southern Italian peninsula. But Hitler sent new divisions into Italy, occupied the northern peninsula, and effectively stalled the Allied campaign. When the European war ended, the German and Allied armies were still battling on Italy's rugged terrain.

Elsewhere in occupied Europe, armed uprisings against the Nazis spread. The brutalized inhabitants of Warsaw's Jewish ghetto repeatedly rose up against their tormentors during the winter and spring of 1943. Realizing that they could not hope to defeat superior forces, they finally sealed off their quarter, executed collaborators, and fought invaders, street by street and house by house. Scattered revolts followed in the Nazi labor camps, where military prisoners of war and civilians were being worked to death on starvation rations.

Partisans were active in many sections of Europe, from Norway to Greece and from Poland to France. Untrained and unarmed by any military standard, organized groups of men, women, and children risked their lives to distribute antifascist propaganda, taking action against rich and powerful Nazi collaborators.

Meanwhile, Stalin continued to push for a second front. Stalled in Italy, the Allies prepared in early 1944 for **Operation Overlord**, a campaign to retake the Continent with a decisive counterattack through France. American and British forces began by filling the southern half of England with military camps. All leaves were canceled.

The Allied invasion finally began on **D-Day**, June 6, 1944. Under steady German fire the Allied fleet brought to the shores of Normandy more than 175,000 troops and more than 20,000 vehicles—an accomplishment unimaginable in any previous war. Although the Germans had responded slowly, anticipating an Allied strike at Calais instead of Normandy, at Omaha Beach they had prepared their defense almost perfectly. Wave after wave of Allied landings met machine-gun and mortar fire, and the tides filled with corpses and those pretending to be dead. Some 2,500 troops died, many before they could fire a shot. Nevertheless, in the next six weeks, nearly 1 million more Allied soldiers came ashore, broke out of Normandy, and prepared to march inland.

As the fighting continued, all eyes turned to Paris, the premier city of Europe. Allied bombers pounded factories producing German munitions on the outskirts of the French capital. As dispirited German soldiers retreated, many now hoping only to survive, the French Resistance unfurled the French flag at impromptu demonstrations on Bastille Day, July 14. On August 10, railway workers staged one of the first successful strikes against Nazi occupiers, and three days later the Paris police defected to the Resistance, which proclaimed in leaflets that "the hour of liberation has come." General Charles de Gaulle, accompanied by Allied troops, arrived in Paris on August 25 to become president of the reestablished French Republic.

One occupied European nation after another now swiftly fell to the Allied armies, but the Allied troops had only reached a resting place between bloody battles.

THE HIGH COST OF EUROPEAN VICTORY

In September 1944 Allied commanders searched for a strategy to end the war quickly. Missing a spectacular chance to move through largely undefended territory and on to Berlin, they turned north instead, intending to open the Nether-

Operation Overlord United States and British invasion of France in June 1944 during World War II.

D-Day June 6, 1944, the day of the first paratroop drops and amphibious landings on the coast of Normandy, France, in the first stage of Operation Overlord during World War II.

lands for Allied armies on their way to Germany's industrial heartland. Faulty intelligence reports overlooked a well-armed German division at Arnhem, Holland, waiting to cut Allied paratroopers to pieces. By the end of the battle, the Germans had captured 6,000 Americans.

In a final, desperate effort to reverse the Allied momentum, Hitler directed his last reserves, a quarter-million men, at Allied lines in the Belgian forest of the Ardennes. In what is known as the **Battle of the Bulge**, the Germans took the Allies by surprise, driving them back 50 miles before they were stopped. This last effort exhausted the German capacity for counterattack. After Christmas Day 1944, the Germans fell back, retreating into their own territory.

The end was now in sight. In March 1945 the Allies rolled across the Rhine and took the Ruhr Valley with its precious industrial resources. The defense of Germany, now hopeless, had fallen into the hands of young teenagers and elderly men. By the time of the German surrender, May 8, Hitler had committed suicide in a Berlin bunker and high Nazi officials were planning their escape routes. The casualties of the Allied European campaign had been enormous, if still small compared to those of the **Eastern Front**: more than 200,000 killed and almost 800,000 wounded, missing, or dead in nonbattle accidents and unrelated illness.

THE WAR IN ASIA AND THE PACIFIC

The war that had begun with Pearl Harbor rapidly escalated into scattered fighting across a region of the world far larger than all of Europe, stretching from Southeast Asia to the Aleutian Islands. Japan followed up its early advantage by cutting the supply routes between Burma and China, crushing the British navy, and seizing the Philippines, Hong Kong, Wake Island, British Malaya, and Thailand. Although China offically joined the Allies on December 9, 1941, and General Stillwell arrived in March as commander of the China-Burma-India theater, the military mission there remained on the defensive. Meanwhile, after tenacious fighting on the Bataan Peninsula and on the island of Corregidor, the U.S. troops not captured or killed retreated to Australia.

At first, nationalist and anticolonial sentiment played into Japanese hands. Japan succeeded with only 200,000 men because so few inhabitants of the imperial colonies of Britain and France would fight to defend them. Japan installed puppet "independent" governments in Burma and the Philippines, but the new Japanese empire proved terrifyingly cruel. Nationalists from Indochina to the Philippines turned against the Japanese, establishing guerrilla armies that cut Japanese supply lines and prepared the way for Allied victory.

Six months after the disaster at Pearl Harbor, the United States began to regain naval superiority in the central Pacific and halt Japanese expansion. In an aircraft carrier duel with spectacular aerial battles during the Battle of the Coral Sea on May 7 and 8, the United States blocked a Japanese threat to Australia. A month later, the Japanese fleet converged on Midway Island, which was strategically vital to American communications and the defense of Hawai'i. American strategists, however, thanks to specialists who had broken Japanese codes, knew when and where the Japanese planned to attack. The two carrier fleets, separated by hundreds of miles, clashed at the Battle of Midway on June 4. American planes sank four of Japan's vital aircraft carriers and destroyed hundreds of planes, ending Japan's offensive threat to Hawai'i and the west coast of the United States.

Battle of the Bulge German offensive in December, 1944 that penetrated deep into Belgium (creating a "bulge"). Allied forces, while outnumbered, attacked from the north and south. By January, 1945, the German forces were destroyed or routed, but not without some 77,000 Allied casualities.

Eastern Front The area of military operations in World War II located east of Germany in eastern Europe and the Soviet Union.

MAP EXPLORATION

To explore an interactive version of this map, go to **http://www.prenhall.com/faraghertlc/map25.2**

MAP 25-2

War in the Pacific   Across an ocean battlefield utterly unlike the European theater, Allies battled Japanese troops near their homeland.

HOW DID strategies in the Pacific differ from those in Europe?

But the war for the Pacific was far from over. By pulling back their offensive perimeter, the Japanese concentrated their remaining forces. Their commanders calculated that bitter fighting, with high casualties on both sides, would wear down the American troops. The U.S. command, divided between General Douglas MacArthur in the southwest Pacific and Admiral Chester Nimitz in the central Pacific, needed to develop a counterstrategy to strangle the Japanese import-based economy and to retake strategic islands closer to the homeland.

The Allies launched their counteroffensive campaign on the Solomon Islands and Papua, near New Guinea. American and Australian ground forces fought together through the jungles of Papua, while the marines prepared to attack the Japanese stronghold of Guadalcanal.

For the next two years, the U.S. Navy and Marine Corps, in a strategy known as "**island hopping**," pushed to capture a series of important atolls from their well-armed Japanese defenders and open a path to Japan. The first of these assaults, which cost more than 1,000 marines their lives, was on Tarawa, in November 1943, in the Gilbert Islands. In subsequent battles in 1944, American forces occupied Guam, Saipan, and Tinian in the Marianas Islands, within air range of the Japanese home islands. In another decisive naval engagement, the Battle of the Philippine Sea, fought in June 1944, the Japanese fleet suffered a crippling loss.

In October 1944, General MacArthur led a force of 250,000 to retake the Philippines. In a bid to defend the islands, practically all that remained of the Japanese navy threw itself at the American invaders in the Battle of Leyte Gulf, the largest naval battle in history. The Japanese lost eighteen ships, leaving the United States in control of the Pacific. The ground fighting in the Philippines, meanwhile, cost 100,000 Filipino civilians their lives and left Manila devastated.

The struggle for the island of Okinawa, 350 miles southwest of the home islands of Japan, proved even more bloody. The invasion of the island, which began on Easter Sunday, April 1, 1945, was the largest amphibious operation mounted by Americans in the Pacific war. It was met by waves of Japanese *kamikaze* ("divine wind") pilots flying suicide missions in planes with a 500-pound bomb and only enough fuel for a one-way flight. On the ground, U.S. troops used flamethrowers, each with three hundred gallons of napalm, against the dug-in Japanese. More Americans died or were wounded here than at Normandy. By the end of June, the fighting had killed more than 200,000 people.

Attacks on mainland Japan began to take their toll. U.S. submarines drastically reduced the ability of ships to reach Japan with supplies. Since the taking of Guam, American bombers had been able to reach Tokyo and other Japanese cities, with devastating results. Massive fire bombings burned thousands of civilians alive in their mostly wood or bamboo homes and apartments and left hundreds of thousands homeless.

Japan could not hold out forever. Without a navy or air force, the government could not transport the oil, tin, rubber, and grain needed to maintain its soldiers. Great Britain and particularly the United States, however, pressed for quick unconditional surrender. They had special reasons to hurry. Earlier they had sought a commitment from the Soviet Union to invade Japan, but now they looked beyond the war, determined to prevent the Red Army from taking any territories held by the Japanese. These calculations and the anticipation that an invasion would be extremely bloody set the stage for the use of a secret weapon that American scientists had been preparing: the atomic bomb.

THE LAST STAGES OF WAR

From the attack on Pearl Harbor until mid-1943, President Roosevelt and his advisers had focused on military strategy rather than on plans for peace. But once the defeat of Nazi Germany appeared in sight, high government officials began to reconsider their diplomatic objectives. Roosevelt wanted to both crush the Axis powers and establish a system of collective security to prevent another world war. He knew he could not succeed without the cooperation of the other key leaders, Stalin and Churchill.

Island hopping The Pacific campaigns of 1944 that were the American naval versions of the Blitzkrieg.

HOW DID Truman explain his decision to use the atomic bomb against the Japanese?

During 1944 and 1945, the "Big Three" met to hammer out the shape of the postwar world. Although none of these nations expected to reach a final agreement, neither did they anticipate how quickly they would be confronted with momentous global events. It soon became clear that the only thing holding the Allies together was the mission of destroying the Axis.

THE HOLOCAUST

Not until the last stages of the war did Americans learn the extent of Hitler's atrocities. As part of his "final solution to the Jewish question," Hitler had ordered the systematic extermination of not only Jews, but also Gypsies, other "inferior races," homosexuals, and anyone deemed an enemy of the Reich. Beginning in 1933, and accelerating after 1941, the Nazis murdered millions of people from Germany and the European nations they conquered.

During the war the U.S. government released little information on what came to be known as the **Holocaust**. Although liberal magazines such as the *Nation* and small committees of intellectuals tried to call attention to what was happening in German concentration camps, major news media like the *New York Times* and *Time* magazine treated reports of the camps and killings as minor news items. As late as 1943, only 43 percent of Americans polled believed that Hitler was systematically murdering European Jews.

Roosevelt and his advisers maintained that the liberation of European Jews depended primarily on a speedy and total Allied victory. When American Jews pleaded for a military strike against the rail lines leading to the notorious extermination camp in Auschwitz, Poland, the War Department replied that Allied armed forces would not be employed "for the purpose of rescuing victims of enemy oppression unless such rescues are the direct result of military operations conducted with the objective of defeating the armed forces of the enemy." In short, the government viewed civilian rescue as a diversion of precious resources.

Allied troops discovered the death camps when they invaded Germany and liberated Poland. When Eisenhower and General George S. Patton visited the Ohrdruf

Holocaust   The systematic murder of millions of European Jews and others deemed undesirable by Nazi Germany.

Belsen Camp: The *Compound for Women*, painted by American artist Leslie Cole, depicts Belsen as the Allied troops found it when they invaded Germany in 1945.

Leslie Cole, *Belsen Camp: The Compound for Women.* Imperial War Museum, London concentration camp in April 1945, they found barracks crowded with corpses and crematories still reeking of burned flesh. "I want every American unit not actually in the front lines to see this place," Eisenhower declared. "We are told that the American soldier does not know what he is fighting for. Now, at least, he will know what he is fighting against." At Buchenwald in the first three months of 1944, more than 14,000 prisoners were murdered. In all, the Holocaust claimed the lives of as many as 6 million Jews, 250,000 Gypsies, and 60,000 homosexuals, among others.

THE YALTA CONFERENCE

In early February 1945, Roosevelt held his last meeting with Churchill and Stalin at Yalta, a Crimean resort on the Black Sea. Although diplomats avoided the touchy phrase "spheres of influence," it was clear that this principle guided all negotiations. Neither the United States nor Great Britain did more than object to the Soviet Union's plan to retain the Baltic states and part of Poland as a buffer zone to protect it against any future German aggression. In return, Britain planned to reclaim its empire in Asia, and the United States hoped to hold several Pacific islands in order to monitor any military resurgence in Japan. The delegates also negotiated the terms of membership in the United Nations, which had been outlined at a meeting several months earlier.

The biggest and most controversial item on the agenda at Yalta was the Soviet entry into the Pacific war, which Roosevelt believed necessary for a timely Allied victory. After driving a hard bargain involving rights to territory in China, Stalin agreed to declare war against Japan within two or three months of Germany's surrender.

The death of Franklin Roosevelt of a stroke on April 12, 1945, cast a dark shadow over all hopes for long-term, peaceful solutions to global problems. Stung by a Republican congressional comeback in 1942, Roosevelt had rebounded in 1944 to win an unprecedented fourth term as president. In an overwhelming electoral college victory (432 to 99), he had defeated Republican New York governor Thomas E. Dewey. Loyal Democrats continued to link their hopes for peace to Roosevelt's leadership, but the president did not live to witness the surrender of Germany on May 8, 1945. And now, as new and still greater challenges were appearing, the nation's great pragmatic idealist was gone.

THE ATOMIC BOMB

Roosevelt's death made cooperation among the Allied nations much more difficult. His successor, Harry Truman, who had been a Kansas City machine politician, a Missouri judge, and a U.S. senator, lacked diplomatic experience as well as Roosevelt's personal finesse. As a result, negotiations at the Potsdam Conference, held just outside Berlin from July 17 to August 2, 1945, lacked the spirited cooperation characteristic of the wartime meetings of Allied leaders that Roosevelt had attended. The American, British, and Soviet delegations had a huge agenda, including reparations, the future of Germany, and the status of other Axis powers such as Italy. Although they divided sharply over most issues, they held fast to the demand of Japan's unconditional surrender.

It was during the Potsdam meetings that Truman first learned about the successful testing of an atomic bomb in New Mexico. Until this time, the United States had been pushing the Soviet Union to enter the Pacific war as a means to avoid a costly U.S. land invasion. But after Secretary of War Stimson received a cable reading "Babies satisfactorily born," U.S. diplomats concluded that Soviet assistance was no longer needed to bring the war to an end.

On August 3, 1945, Japan wired its refusal to surrender. Three days later, the Army Air Force B-29 bomber *Enola Gay* dropped the bomb that destroyed the

Yalta Conference Meeting of U.S. President Franklin Roosevelt, British Prime Minister Winston Churchill, and Soviet Premier Joseph Stalin held in February 1945 to plan the final stages of World War II and postwar arrangements.

Japanese city of Hiroshima. An estimated 40,000 people died instantly; in the following weeks 100,000 more died from radiation poisoning or burns; by 1950 the death toll reached 200,000.

An editorialist wrote in the Japanese *Nippon Times*, "This is not war, this is not even murder; this is pure nihilism . . . a crime against God which strikes at the very basis of moral existence." In the United States, several leading religious publications echoed this view. The *Christian Century* interpreted the use of the bomb as a "moral earthquake" that made the long-denounced use of poison gas by Germany in World War I utterly insignificant by comparison.

Most Americans learned about the atomic bomb for the first time on August 7, when the news media reported the destruction and death it had wrought in Hiroshima. But concerns about the implications of this new weapon were soon overwhelmed by an outpouring of relief when Japan surrendered on August 14 after a second bomb destroyed Nagasaki, killing another 70,000 people.

The Allied insistence on unconditional surrender and the decision to use the atomic bomb against Japan remain two of the most controversial aspects of the war. Although Truman stated in his memoirs, written much later, that he gave the order with the expectation of saving "a half a million American lives" in ground combat, no such official estimate exists. An intelligence document of April 30, 1946, states, "The dropping of the bomb was the pretext seized upon by all leaders as the reason for ending the war, but . . . [even if the bomb had not been used] the Japanese would have capitulated upon the entry of Russia into the war." There is no question, however, that the use of nuclear force did strengthen the U.S. diplomatic mission. It certainly intimidated the Soviet Union, which would soon regain its status as a major enemy of the United States. Truman and his advisers in the State Department knew that their atomic monopoly could not last, but they hoped that in the meantime the United States could play the leading role in building the postwar world.

An atomic bomb's explosion and resulting mushroom cloud, similar to the blasts of Hiroshima and Nagasaki.

Corbis.

CONCLUSION

The new tactics and weapons of the Second World War made warfare incomparably more deadly than before to both military and civilian populations. Between 40 and 50 million people died in World War II—four times the number in World War I—and half the casualties were women and children. More than 405,000 Americans died, and more than 670,000 were wounded. Although slight compared to the casualties suffered by other Allied nations—more than 20 million Soviets died during the war—the human cost of World War II for Americans was second only to that of the Civil War.

Coming at the end of two decades of resolutions to avoid military entanglements, the war pushed the nation's leaders to the center of global politics and into risky military and political alliances that would not outlive the war. The United States emerged the strongest nation in the world, but in a world where the prospects for lasting peace appeared increasingly remote.

If World War II raised the nation's international commitments to a new height, its impact on ordinary Americans was not so easy to gauge. Many new communities formed as Americans migrated in mass numbers to new regions that were booming as a result of the wartime economy. Enjoying a rare moment of full employment, many workers new to well-paying industrial jobs anticipated further advances against discrimination. Exuberant at the Allies' victory over fascism and the return of the troops, the majority were optimistic as they looked ahead.

CHRONOLOGY

1931 September: Japan occupies Manchuria.

1933 March: Adolf Hitler seizes power.

May: Japan quits League of Nations.

1935 October: Italy invades Ethiopia.

1935– 1937 Neutrality Acts authorize the president to block the sale of munitions to belligerent nations.

1937 August: Japan invades China.

October: Franklin D. Roosevelt calls for international cooperation against aggression.

1938 March: Germany annexes Austria.

September: Munich Agreement lets Germany annex Sudetenland of Czechoslovakia.

November: *Kristallnacht*, Nazis attack Jews and destroy Jewish property.

1939 March: Germany annexes remainder of Czechoslovakia.

August: Germany and the Soviet Union sign nonaggression pact.

September: Germany invades Poland; World War II begins.

November: Soviet Union invades Finland.

1940 April–June: Germany's *Bliztkrieg* sweeps over Western Europe.

September: Germany, Italy, and Japan— the Axis powers—conclude a military alliance.

First peacetime military draft in American history.

November: Roosevelt is elected to an unprecedented third term.

1941 March: Lend-Lease Act extends aid to Great Britain.

May: German troops secure the Balkans.

Philip Randolph plans March on Washington movement for July.

June: Germany invades Soviet Union.

Fair Employment Practices Committee formed.

August: United States and Great Britain agree to the Atlantic Charter.

December: Japanese attack Pearl Harbor; United States enters the war.

1942 January: War mobilization begins.

February: Executive order mandates internment of Japanese Americans.

May–June: Battles of Coral Sea and Midway give the United States naval superiority in the Pacific.

August: Manhattan Project begins.

November: United States stages amphibious landing in North Africa; Operation Torch begins.

1943 January: Casablanca Conference announces unconditional surrender policy.

February: Soviet victory over Germans at Stalingrad.

April–May: Coal miners strike.

May: German Afrika Korps troops surrender in Tunis.

July: Allied invasion of Italy.

Summer: Race riots break out in nearly fifty cities.

1944 June–August: Operation Overlord and liberation of Paris.

November: Roosevelt elected to fourth term.

1945 February: Yalta Conference renews American-Soviet alliance.

February–June: United States captures Iwo Jima and Okinawa in Pacific.

April: Roosevelt dies in office; Harry Truman becomes president.

May: Germany surrenders.

July–August: Potsdam Conference.

August: United States drops atomic bombs on Hiroshima and Nagasaki; Japan surrenders.

SUMMARY

The Coming of World War II War broke out first in Asia in the early thirties and later spread to Africa and Europe. Japan, Italy, and Germany were the aggressors. After the conflict expanded to include Russia, France, and Great Britain, Roosevelt launched a preparedness campaign. The Japanese attack on Pearl Harbor brought the United States into the Second World War.

Arsenal of Democracy The government comprehensively mobilized the nation for war. The New Deal focus quickly switched to a win-the-war effort based on reorienting the economy to military production. The economic conversion ended the Great Depression. Increased production fueled profits and job opportunities, especially for minorities and women. Growing labor unrest before the United States entered the conflict ceased and unions began admitting African Americans.

The Home Front The war drastically altered life in the United States. Families faced new strains and pressures. Japanese Americans suffered the worst discrimination, but African Americans seeking a victory at war and for their rights also experienced mixed results, as did Mexican Americans. Popular culture promoted the "good war" to Americans of all ages.

Men and Women in Uniform The military was unprepared for combat when war broke out. The draft organized the male population for military service. The process of building the military transformed the officer corps and facilitated the forging of bonds among military personnel while "Americanizing" immigrant groups. Women joined the military and played important roles. Despite racism, the same was true of minorities. Great emphasis was placed on building a medical corps to handle casualties.

The World at War The war was fought on several fronts. Until 1942, the Allies were on the defensive. A variety of successes changed the tide of the conflict. In Europe, the war was fought in the air and on the ground, with the Soviets bearing most of the ground war burden. English and American forces approached Europe from two directions, first through North Africa and Italy and then across France. During this period, air strikes on Germany also occurred. The war in the Pacific involved naval battles and island-hopping invasions. When the war ended in Europe, all resources were trained on Japan. Air strikes took a heavy toll on the Japanese.

The Last Stages of War By 1945, the war was coming to a close. Americans learned about the extent of the Holocaust, though not until the concentration camps were liberated was the full horror known. At the Yalta Conference, Roosevelt, Stalin, and Churchill negotiated terms to end the war and plan for the peace. Roosevelt's death thrust Harry Truman into the presidency. One of his first decisions was to drop the atomic bomb on Japan, ending World War II.

REVIEW QUESTIONS

1. Describe the response of Americans to the rise of nationalism in Japan, Italy, and Germany during the 1930s. How did President Franklin D. Roosevelt ready the nation for war?

2. What role did the federal government play in gearing up the economy for wartime production?

3. How did the war affect the lives of American women?

4. Discuss the causes and consequences of the Japanese American internment program.

5. Describe the role of popular culture in promoting the war effort at home.

6. How did military service affect the lives of those who served in World War II?

7. What were the main points of Allied military strategy in both Europe and Asia?

8. How successful were diplomatic efforts in ending the war and in establishing the terms of peace?

KEY TERMS

Atlantic Charter (p. 675)
Axis powers (p. 675)
Battle of the Bulge (p. 694)
Blitzkrieg (p. 674)
D-Day (p. 693)
Eastern Front (p. 694)
Holocaust (p. 697)
Island hopping (p. 696)

Issei (p. 681)
Lend-Lease Act (p. 675)
Neutrality Act of 1939 (p. 675)
Nisei (p. 687)
Operation Overlord (p. 693)
Operation Torch (p. 691)
War Powers Act (p. 677)
Yalta Conference (p. 698)

RECOMMENDED READING

Stephen E. Ambrose, *D-Day, June 6, 1944: The Climactic Battle of World War II* (1994). A vivid and extremely readable, moment-by-moment reconstruction of the preparation and battle, relying heavily upon the oral histories of American veterans.

Philip D. Beidler, *The Good War's Greatest Hits: World War II and American Remembering* (1998). Examines the popular culture produced about World War II, such as movies, photographs, cartoons, and books, to show how these sources created a lasting image of World War II as the "good war."

Amy Bentley, *Eating for Victory: Food Rationing and the Politics of Domesticity* (1998). Brings together several areas of scholarship, including the social history of food and women's history, and provides a fascinating overview of rationing programs and Victory Gardens during World War II.

Allan Berube, *Coming Out under Fire: The History of Gay Men and Women in World War Two* (1991). A study of government policy toward homosexuals during the war and the formation of a gay community. Berube offers many insights into the new opportunities offered homosexuals through travel and varied companionship and of the effects of sanctions against them.

Paul Boyer, *By the Bomb's Early Light: American Thought and Culture at the Dawn of the Atomic Age* (1985). An analysis of the intellectual and cultural assumptions in relation to atomic weaponry. Boyer examines the development of a political logic, on the part of President Harry Truman and others, that made use of atomic weapons against the Japanese inevitable.

Wayne S. Cole, *Roosevelt and the Isolationists, 1932–45* (1983). Shows the president and his critics sparring over foreign policy issues. Cole analyzes the complexities of liberal–conservative divisions over war and offers insights into the logic of conservatives who feared the growth of a permanent bureaucratic, militarized state.

Richard M. Dalfiume, *Desegregation of the U.S. Armed Forces: Fighting on Two Fronts, 1939–1953* (1969). Analyzes wartime race relations in the military. By examining the official mechanisms to end discrimination and the remaining patterns of racism in the armed forces, Dalfiume reveals how changing attitudes from the top ran up against old assumptions among enlisted men and women.

Roger Daniels, *Concentration Camps USA: Japanese Americans and World War II* (1981). Perhaps the best account of Japanese American internment. Daniels details the government programs, the experiences of detention and camp life, and the many long-term consequences of lost liberty.

Sherna Berger Gluck, *Rosie the Riveter Revisited: Women, the War, and Social Change* (1987). An oral history–based study of women workers during World War II. Gluck's interviewees reveal the diversity of experiences and attitudes of women workers as well as their common feelings of accomplishment.

Laura Hein and Mark Selden, eds., *Living With the Bomb: American and Japanese Cultural Conflict in the Nuclear Age* (1997). Essays dealing with the ambiguous legacy of the atomic bomb in both the United States and Japan. Reviews the "official story" of the bomb as the symbol of U.S. triumph in the "Good War" in light of the growing number of dissenting voices and the impact of both views on memorials and museum exhibits.

John W. Jeffries, *Wartime America: The World War II Homefront* (1996). Provides a useful synthesis of scholarship and assesses the major differences in the interpretations of leading historians.

Gerald F. Linderman, *The World within War: America's Combat Experience in World War II* (1997). Emphasizes the less glamorous aspects of war, mainly the strains placed on the combat soldiers on the front lines. Linderman examines in especially close detail the grim experiences of army infantrymen and the marine riflemen who fought in the Pacific campaign and provides a nuanced analysis of their complex responses to the horror of war.

Katrina R. Mason, *Children of Los Alamos: An Oral History of the Town Where the Atomic Age Began* (1995). Recollections of those who spent their childhood in Los Alamos. They describe their affection for the geographical setting as well as sense of safety growing up in a community so well protected. They also comment on the ethnic diversity of those who populated the town and the pride they took in their parents' contribution to building the bomb and ending the war.

Neil R. McMillan, ed., *Remaking Dixie: The Impact of World War II on the American South* (1997). A collection of essays on the impact of World War II on the South that pay special attention to the experiences of African Americans and women. Several authors question the degree to which Southern society was transformed by wartime mobilization.

Robert J. Moskin, *Mr. Truman's War: The Final Victories of World War II and the Birth of the Postwar World* (1996). A lively history of the final stages of World War II, including the surrender of Germany and the emergence of postwar foreign policy. Moskin provides an assessment of the impact of the war on social and economic conditions in the United States.

William M. Tuttle Jr., *"Daddy's Gone to War": The Second World War in the Lives of America's Children* (1993). Draws from 2,500 letters that the author solicited from men and women in their fifties and sixties about their wartime childhood memories.

David S. Wyman, *The Abandonment of the Jews: America and the Holocaust, 1941–1945* (1984). A detailed examination of U.S. immigration policy and response to Hitler's program of genocide. Wyman shows both the indifference of the Roosevelt administration to appeals for Allied protection of Jews and the inclinations of leading American Jewish organizations to stress the formation of a future Jewish state instead of the protection of European Jewry.

To my mind we are in a situation no less dangerous than the one we were facing in 1939, and it is of the greatest importance that we realize it. We must realize . . . that democracy will not be saved by ideals alone.

—Edward Teller

As international tensions rose with the onset of the Cold War, Americans wondered how to prepare for a possible nuclear war. Many families stocked extra food and water and bought a battery-powered radio, but few actually installed backyard bomb shelters like the one being tested by this family in a Long Island suburb not far from Levittown.

26

THE COLD WAR

1945–1952

WHAT STEPS did the allies take to promote growth in the postwar global economy?

HOW DID the Truman Doctrine shape U.S. postwar foreign policy?

HOW DID the "Fair Deal" differ from the "New Deal"?

WHAT CONTRIBUTED to the rise of McCarthyism?

WHAT WERE the most important demographic trends in the 1950s?

WHAT ISSUES were at the center of the election of 1952?

AMERICAN COMMUNITIES
University of Washington, Seattle: Students and Faculty Face the Cold War

IN MAY 1948, A PHILOSOPHY PROFESSOR AT THE UNIVERSITY OF *Washington in Seattle answered a knock on his office door. Two state legislators, members of the state's Committee on Un-American Activities, entered. "Our information," they charged, "puts you in the center of a Communist conspiracy."*

The accused professor, Melvin Rader, had never been a Communist. A self-described liberal, Rader drew fire because he had joined several organizations supported by Communists. During the 1930s, in response to the rise of Nazism and fascism, Rader had become a prominent political activist in his community. At one point he served as president of the University of Washington Teacher's Union, which had formed during the upsurge of labor organizing during the New Deal. When invited to join the Communist Party, Rader bluntly refused. "The experience of teaching social philosophy had clarified my concepts of freedom and democracy," he later explained. "I was an American in search of a way— but it was not the Communist way."

Despite this disavowal, Rader was caught up in a Red Scare that curtailed free speech and political activity on campuses throughout the United States. At some universities, such as Yale, the Federal Bureau of Investigation (FBI) set up camp with the consent of the college administration, spying on students and faculty, screening the credentials of job or scholarship applicants, and seeking to entice students to report on their friends or roommates. The University of Washington administration turned down the recommendation of the Physics Department to hire J. Robert Oppenheimer because the famed atomic scientist had become a vocal opponent of the arms race and the proliferation of nuclear weapons.

Although one state legislator claimed that "not less than 150 members" of the University of Washington faculty were subversives, the state's Committee on Un-American Activities turned up just six members of the Communist Party. These six were brought up before the university's Faculty Committee on Tenure and Academic Freedom, charged with violations ranging from neglect of duty to failing to inform the university administration of their party membership. Three were ultimately dismissed, while the other three were placed on probation.

What had provoked this paranoia? Instead of peace in the wake of World War II, a pattern of cold war—icy relations— prevailed between the United States and the Soviet Union. Uneasy allies during World War II, the two superpowers now viewed each other as arch-enemies, and nearly all other nations lined up with one or the other of them. Within the United States, the Cold War demanded pledges of absolute loyalty from citizens

in every institution, from the university to trade unions and from the mass media to government itself.

If not for the outbreak of the Cold War, this era would have marked one of the most fruitful in the history of higher education. The Servicemen's Readjustment Act, popularly known as the G.I. Bill of Rights, passed by Congress in 1944, offered stipends covering tuition and living expenses to veterans attending vocational schools or college. By the 1947–1948 academic year, the federal government was subsidizing nearly half of all male college students. Between 1945 and 1950, 2.3 million students benefited from the G.I. Bill, at a cost of more than $10 billion.

At the University of Washington the student population in 1946 had grown by 50 percent over its prewar peak of 10,000, and veterans represented fully two-thirds of the student body. A quickly expanded faculty taught into the evening to use classroom space efficiently. Meanwhile, the state legislature pumped in funds for the construction of new buildings, including dormitories and prefabricated units for married students. According to many observers, a feeling of community flourished among these war-weary undergraduates. Often the first in their families to attend college, they joined fellow students in campaigns to improve the campus. Married, often fathers of young children, they expected university administrators to treat them as adults. They wanted less supervision of undergraduate social life, more affordable housing, and better cultural opportunities than had previously been the case. On some campuses, film societies and student-run cooperatives vied with fraternities and sororities as centers of undergraduate social activity.

The Cold War put a damper on these community-building efforts. FBI director J. Edgar Hoover testified that the college campuses were centers of "red propaganda," full of teachers "tearing down respect for agencies of government, belittling tradition and moral custom and . . . creating doubts in the validity of the American way of life." Due to Communistic teachers and "Communist-line textbooks," a senator lamented, thousands of parents sent "their sons and daughters to college as good Americans," only to see them return home "four years later as wild-eyed radicals."

Although these extravagant charges were never substantiated, several states, including Washington, enacted or revived loyalty-security programs, obligating all state employees to swear in writing their loyalty to the United States and to disclaim membership in any subversive organization. Nationwide, approximately 200 faculty members were dismissed outright and many others were denied tenure. Thousands of students simply left school, dropped

Seattle

out of organizations, or changed friends after "visits" from FBI agents or interviews with administrators. The main effect on campus was the restraint of free speech generally and fear of criticizing U.S. racial, military, or diplomatic policies in particular.

This gloomy mood reversed the wave of optimism that had swept through America only a few years earlier. V-J Day, marking

victory over Japan, had erupted into a two-day national holiday of wild celebrations, complete with ticker-tape parades, spontaneous dancing, and kisses for returned GIs who, living in the richest and most powerful nation in the world, finally seemed to have gained the peace for which they had fought and sacrificed. But peace proved fragile and elusive.

GLOBAL INSECURITIES AT WAR'S END

The war that had engulfed the world from 1939 to 1945 created an international interdependence that no country could ignore. The legendary African American folk singer Leadbelly (Huddie Ledbetter) added a fresh lyric to an old spiritual melody: "We're in the same boat, brother. . . . And if you shake one end you're going to rock the other." Never before, not even at the end of World War I, had hopes been so strong for a genuine "community of nations."

FINANCING THE FUTURE

In 1941 Henry Luce, publisher of *Time, Life,* and *Fortune* magazines, had forecast the dawn of "the American Century." Americans must, he wrote, "accept wholeheartedly our duty and our opportunity as the most powerful and vital nation in the world and in consequence to assert upon the world the full impact of our influence, for such means as we see fit." Indeed, immediately after the bombing of Hiroshima, President Truman pronounced the United States "the most powerful nation in the world—the most powerful nation, perhaps, in all history."

Americans had good reason to be confident about their prospects for setting the terms of reconstruction. Unlike Great Britain and France, the United States had not only escaped the ravages of the war but had also actually prospered. By June 1945, the capital assets of manufacturing had increased 65 percent over prewar levels and were equal in value to approximately half the entire world's goods and services.

Yet many Americans recognized that it was the massive government spending associated with wartime industry, rather than New Deal programs, that had ended the nightmare of the 1930s. A great question loomed: What would happen when wartime production slowed and millions of troops returned home?

"We need markets—big markets—in which to buy and sell," answered Assistant Secretary of State for Economic Affairs Will Clayton. Just to maintain the current level of growth, the United States needed an estimated $14 billion in exports—an unprecedented amount. Many business leaders even looked to the Soviet Union as a potential trading partner. With this prospect vanishing, eastern European markets threatened, and large chunks of former colonial territories closed off, U.S. business and government leaders became determined to integrate Western Europe and Asia into a liberal international economy open to American trade and investment.

During the final stages of the war, President Roosevelt's advisors laid plans to establish U.S. primacy in the postwar global economy. In July 1944 representatives from forty-four Allied nations met at Bretton Woods, New Hampshire, and established the **International Bank for Reconstruction and Development (World Bank)** and the **International Monetary Fund (IMF)** to help rebuild war-torn Europe and to assist the nations of Asia, Latin America, and Africa. By stabilizing exchange rates to permit the expansion of international trade, the IMF would deter currency conflicts and trade

WHAT STEPS did the allies take to promote growth in the postwar global economy?

International Bank for Reconstruction and Development (World Bank) Designed to revive postwar international trade, it drew on the resources of member nations to make economic development loans to governments for such projects as new dams or agricultural modernization.

International Monetary Fund (IMF) International organization established in 1945 to assist nations in maintaining stable currencies.

IMAGE KEY

for pages 704–705

a. A man reading "The Mirror" newspaper with a headline about actress Lucille Ball.
b. A photo of parents and their three children in a home-based fallout shelter. "The Cold War at Home and Abroad, 1946–1952."
c. The North Atlantic Treaty Organization (NATO) treaty with signatures and seal.
d. A fallout shelter sign directing the populace to safety during a nuclear attack.
e. Civilians atop the bombed out ruins of buildings watching American C-54 cargo planes fly overhead during the Allied airlift to bring food and supplies to besieged citizens of Soviet-controlled Berlin.
f. American President Harry Truman shakes hands with supporters from a train car during a rally in the 1948 presidential campaign.
g. Senator Joseph McCarthy points to Oregon on an organizational map implying Communist Party organizations in the United States.
h. An unidentified model displays a kitchen interior circa 1950s.
i. Soldiers in the Korean conflict endured frigid conditions in winter and blistering summers.

wars—two maladies of the 1930s that were largely responsible for the political instability and national rivalries leading to World War II. As the principal supplier of funds for the IMF and the World Bank—more than $7 billion to each—the United States, in essence, could unilaterally shape the world economy by determining the allocation of loans.

The Soviet Union participated in the Bretton Woods conference but refused to ratify the agreements that, in essence, allowed the United States to rebuild the world economy along capitalist lines. By spurning both the World Bank and the IMF, the Soviet Union cut off the possibility of aid to its own people as well as to its Eastern European client states and, equally important, isolated itself economically.

THE DIVISION OF EUROPE

The Atlantic Charter of 1941 committed the Allies to recognize the right of all nations to self-determination and to renounce all claims to new territories as the spoils of war. The Allied leaders themselves, however, violated the charter's main points before the war had ended by dividing occupied Europe into spheres of influence (see Chapter 25).

As long as Franklin Roosevelt remained alive, this strategy had seemed reconcilable with world peace. The president had balanced his own international idealism with his belief that the United States was entitled to extraordinary influence in Latin America and the Philippines and that other great powers might have similar privileges or responsibilities elsewhere. Roosevelt also recognized the diplomatic consequences of the brutal ground war that had been fought largely on Soviet territory: the Soviet Union's unnegotiable demand for territorial security along its European border.

From the early days of the war, the USSR was intent on reestablishing its 1941 borders, and by the time of the Potsdam Conference in July 1945 the Soviets had not only regained but had also extended their territory. Much of Eastern Europe, including a large portion of Poland and the little Baltic nations, was now under its control as client states.

When the Allies turned to plan the future of Germany, they agreed to dismember Germany and eventually decided to divide the conquered nation into four occupation zones, each governed by one of the Allied nations. But the Allies could not agree on long-term plans. Having borne the brunt of German aggression, France and the USSR both opposed reunification. The latter, in addition, demanded heavy reparations along with a limit on postwar reindustrialization. Roosevelt appeared to agree with the Soviets, but American business leaders, envisioning a new center for U.S. commerce, shared Winston Churchill's hope of rebuilding Germany into a powerful counterforce against the Soviet Union and a strong market for U.S. and British goods.

After the war, continuing disagreements about the future Germany darkened hopes for cooperation between the Soviet Union and the United States. By July 1946, Americans had begun to withhold reparations from their zone and to institute a program of amnesty for former Nazis. Then, in December, the Americans and British merged their zones and extended an invitation to France and the USSR to join. Although France accepted the offer, the Soviets, fearing a resurgence of united Germany, held out.

The United States and the Soviet Union were now at loggerheads. Twice in the twentieth century, Germany had invaded Russia, and the USSR now interpreted these U.S. moves toward consolidation of Germany an act of supreme hostility. For its part, the United States envisioned a united Germany as a bulwark against Soviet expansion.

THE UNITED NATIONS AND HOPES FOR COLLECTIVE SECURITY

The dream of postwar international cooperation had been seeded earlier by President Roosevelt. In late summer and fall 1944 at the Dumbarton Oaks Conference in Washington, D.C., and again in April 1945 in San Francisco, the Allies worked to shape the United Nations as an international agency that would arbitrate disputes among members as well as impede aggressors, by military force if necessary.

The terms of membership, however, limited the UN's ability to mediate disputes. Although all member nations enjoyed representation in the General Assembly, only five members (the United States, Great Britain, the Soviet Union, France, and Nationalist China) served permanently on the Security Council, which had the "primary responsibility for the maintenance of international peace and security," and each enjoyed absolute veto power over the decisions of the other members.

The UN achieved its greatest success with its humanitarian programs. Its relief agency provided the war-torn countries of Europe and Asia with billions of dollars for medical supplies, food, and clothing. The UN also dedicated itself to protecting human rights, and its high standards of human dignity owed much to the lobbying of Eleanor Roosevelt, one of the first delegates from the United States.

On other issues, however, the UN operated strictly along lines dictated by the **Cold War**. The Western nations allied with the United States held the balance of power and maintained their position by controlling the admission of new member nations. They successfully excluded Communist China, for example. Moreover, the polarization between East and West made negotiated settlements virtually impossible.

Cold War The political and economic confrontation between the Soviet Union and the United States that dominated world affairs from 1946 to 1989.

THE POLICY OF CONTAINMENT

In March 1946, in a speech delivered in Fulton, Missouri, Winston Churchill spoke to the new reality. With President Harry Truman at his side, the former British prime minister declared that "an iron curtain has descended across the [European] continent." He called directly upon the United States, standing "at this time at the pinnacle of world power," to recognize its "awe-inspiring accountability to the future" and to act assertively to turn back Soviet expansion.

Although Truman responded cautiously to Churchill's pronouncement, he and his administration ultimately decided to meet the challenge. Within a short time, they were wholeheartedly committed to securing U.S. leadership in the world and, equally important, preventing communism from spreading further. As a doctrine uniting military, economic, and diplomatic strategies, the "containment" of communism also fostered an ideological opposition, an "us"-versus-"them" theme that divided the world into "freedom" and "slavery," "democracy" and "autocracy," and "tolerance" and "coercive force." The **Truman Doctrine** laid down the first plank in a global campaign against communism.

HOW DID the Truman Doctrine shape U.S. postwar foreign policy?

26–4
Containment (1947)

THE TRUMAN DOCTRINE

Many Americans believed that Franklin D. Roosevelt, had he lived, would have been able to stem the tide of tensions between the Soviet Union and the United States. His successor sorely lacked FDR's talent for diplomacy. More comfortable with machine politicians than with polished New Dealers, the new president liked to talk tough and act defiantly. Just ten days after he took office, Truman complained that U.S.–Soviet negotiations had been a "one-way street." He vowed to "baby" them no longer.

A perceived crisis in the Mediterranean prompted President Truman to show his colors. On February 21, 1947, amid a civil war in Greece, Great Britain informed

Truman Doctrine Doctrine pronounced in President Harry Truman's statement in 1947 that the United States should assist other nations that were facing external pressure or internal revolution.

26–5
Harry S Truman, The Truman Doctrine (1947)

26–1
George F. Kennan, "Long Telegram" (1946)

26–3
George Marshall, The Marshall Plan (1947)

Marshall Plan Secretary of State George C. Marshall's European Recovery Plan of June 5, 1947, committing the United States to help in the rebuilding of post–World War II Europe.

the U.S. State Department that it could no longer afford to prop up the anti-Communist government there and announced its intention to withdraw all aid. Without U.S. intervention, Truman concluded, Greece, Turkey, and perhaps the entire oil-rich Middle East would fall under Soviet control.

On March 12, 1947, the president made his argument before Congress. Never mentioning the Soviet Union by name, he appealed for all-out resistance to a "certain ideology" wherever it appeared in the world. The preservation of peace and the freedom of all Americans depended, the president insisted, on containing communism.

Congress approved a $400 million appropriation in aid for Greece and Turkey, which helped the monarchy and right-wing military crush the rebel movement. Truman's victory buoyed his popularity for the upcoming 1948 election. It also helped to generate popular support for a campaign against communism, both at home and abroad.

The significance of what became known as the Truman Doctrine far outlasted the events in the Mediterranean: the United States had declared its right to intervene to save other nations from communism. As early as February 1946, foreign-policy adviser George F. Kennan had sent an 8,000-word "long telegram" to the State Department insisting that Soviet fanaticism made cooperation impossible. The USSR intended to extend its realm not by military means alone, he explained, but by "subversion" within "free" nations. It was now the responsibility of the United States, Truman insisted, to safeguard the "Free World" by diplomatic, economic, and, if necessary, military means. He had, in sum, fused anti-Communism and internationalism into an aggressive foreign policy.

THE MARSHALL PLAN

The Truman Doctrine complemented the European Recovery Program, commonly known as the **Marshall Plan**. Introduced in a commencement speech at Harvard University on June 5, 1947, by secretary of state and former army chief of staff George C. Marshall, the plan sought to reduce "hunger, poverty, desperation, and chaos" and to restore "the confidence of the European people in the economic future of their own countries and of Europe as a whole." Indirectly, the Marshall plan aimed to turn back both socialist and Communist electoral bids for power in northern and Western Europe.

Considered by many historians the most successful postwar U.S. diplomatic venture, the Marshall Plan, in effect brought recipients of aid into a bilateral agreement with the United States. In addition, the Western European nations, seventeen in all, ratified the General Agreement on Tariffs and Trade (GATT), which reduced commercial barriers among member nations and opened all to U.S. trade and investment. The plan was costly to Americans, in its initial year taking 12 percent of the federal budget, but effective. Industrial production in the European nations covered by the plan rose by 200 percent between 1947 and 1952. Although deflationary programs cut wages and increased unemployment, profits soared and the standard of living improved.

The Marshall Plan drove a deeper wedge between the United States and the Soviet Union. Although invited to participate, Stalin denounced the plan for what it was, an American scheme to rebuild Germany and to incorporate it into an anti-Soviet bloc. The president readily acknowledged that the Marshall Plan and the Truman Doctrine were "two halves of the same walnut."

THE BERLIN CRISIS AND THE FORMATION OF NATO

As Stalin recognized, the Marshall Plan also sought to rebuild and integrate the western zones of Germany into a unified region compatible with U.S. political and economic interests. Within a year of its introduction, the United States and

MAP EXPLORATION

To explore an interactive version of this map, go to **http://www.prenhall.com/faraghertlc/map26.1**

MAP 26-1
Divided Europe   During the cold war, Europe was divided into opposing military alliances, the North American Treaty Organization (NATO) and the Warsaw Pact (Communist bloc).

WHICH COUNTRIES were aligned with the United States, and which with the Soviet Union?

Britain moved closer to this goal by introducing a common currency in the western zones. Stalin reacted to this challenge on June 24, 1948, by halting all traffic to West Berlin, formally controlled by the Western allies but situated deep within the Soviet-occupied zone.

The **Berlin blockade** created both a crisis and an opportunity for the Truman administration to test its mettle. With help from the Royal Air Force, the United States began an around-the-clock airlift of historic proportions—Operation Vittles—that delivered nearly 2 million tons of supplies to West Berliners. The Soviet Union finally lifted the blockade in May 1949, clearing the way for the Western powers

Berlin blockade   Three-hundred-day Soviet blockade of land access to United States, British, and French occupation zones in Berlin, 1948–1949.

North Atlantic Treaty Organization (NATO) Organization of ten European countries, Canada, and the United States who together formed a mutual defense pact in April 1949.

to merge their occupation zones into a single nation, the Federal Republic of West Germany. The USSR countered by establishing the German Democratic Republic in their sector.

The Berlin Crisis made a U.S.-led military alliance against the USSR attractive to Western European nations. In April 1949 ten European nations, Canada, and the United States formed the **North Atlantic Treaty Organization (NATO)**, a mutual defense pact in which "an armed attack against one or more of them . . . shall be considered an attack against them all." NATO complemented the Marshall Plan, strengthening economic ties among the member nations by, according to one analyst, keeping "the Russians out, the Americans in, and the Germans down." It also deepened divisions between Eastern and Western Europe, making a permanent military mobilization on both sides almost inevitable.

Congress approved $1.3 billion in military aid, which involved the creation of U.S. Army bases and the deployment of American troops abroad. Critics, such as isolationist senator Robert A. Taft, warned that the United States could not afford to

OVERVIEW

MAJOR COLD WAR POLICIES

Policy	Date	Provisions
Truman Doctrine	1947	Pledged the United States to the containment of communism in Europe and elsewhere. The doctrine was the foundation of Truman's foreign policy. It impelled the United States to support any nation whose stability was threatened by communism or the Soviet Union.
Federal Employees Loyalty Program and Security Program	1947	Established by Executive Order 9835, this barred Communists and fascists from federal employment and outlined procedures for investigating current and prospective federal employees.
Marshall Plan	1947	U.S. program to aid war-torn Europe, also known as the European Recovery Program. The Marshall Plan was a cornerstone in the U.S. use of economic policy to contain communism.
National Security Act	1947	Established Department of Defense (to coordinate the three armed services), the National Security Council (to advise the president on security issues), and the Central Intelligence Agency (to gather and evaluate intelligence data).
Smith-Mundt Act	1948	Launched an overseas campaign of anti-Communist propaganda.
North Atlantic Treaty Organization (NATO)	1948	A military alliance of twelve nations formed to deter possible aggression of the Soviet Union against Western Europe.
NSC-68	1950	National Security Council Paper calling for an expanded and aggressive U.S. defense policy, including greater military spending and higher taxes.
Internal Security Act (also known as the McCarran Act and the Subversive Activities Control Act)	1950	Legislation providing for the registration of all Communist and totalitarian groups and authorizing the arrest of suspect persons during a national emergency.
Psychological Strategy Board	1951	Created to coordinate anti-Communist propaganda campaigns.
Immigration and Nationality Act (also known as McCarran-Walter Immigration Act)	1952	Reaffirmed the national origins quota system but tightened immigration controls, barring homosexuals and people considered subversive from entering the United States.

police all Europe without sidetracking domestic policies and undercutting the UN, but opinion polls revealed strong support for Truman's tough line against the Soviets.

Between 1947 and 1949, the Truman administration had defined the policies that would shape the Cold War for decades to come. The Truman Doctrine explained the ideological basis of containment; the Marshall Plan put into place its economic underpinnings in Western Europe; and NATO created the mechanisms for military enforcement. When NATO extended membership to a rearmed West Germany in May 1955, the Soviet Union responded by creating a counterpart, the Warsaw Pact, including East Germany.

ATOMIC DIPLOMACY

The policy of containment depended on the ability of the United States to back up its commitments through military means, and Truman invested his faith in the U.S. monopoly of atomic weapons. The United States began to build atomic stockpiles and to conduct tests on the Bikini Islands in the Pacific. By 1950, as a scientific adviser subsequently observed, the United States "had a stockpile capable of somewhat more than reproducing World War II in a single day."

Despite warnings to the contrary by leading scientists, U.S. military analysts estimated it would take the Soviet Union three to ten years to produce an atomic bomb. In August 1949, the Soviet Union proved them wrong by testing its own atomic bomb. "There is only one thing worse than one nation having the atomic bomb," Nobel prize-winning scientist Harold C. Urey said, "that's two nations having it."

Within a few years, both the United States and the Soviet Union had tested hydrogen bombs a thousand times more powerful than the weapons dropped on Hiroshima and Nagasaki in 1945. Both proceeded to stockpile bombs attached to missiles, inaugurating the fateful nuclear arms race that scientists had feared since 1945.

The United States and the Soviet Union were now firmly locked into the Cold War. The nuclear arms race imperiled their futures, diverted their economies, and fostered fears of impending doom. Prospects for global peace had dissipated, and despite the Allied victory in World War II, the world had again divided into hostile camps.

COLD WAR LIBERALISM

Truman's aggressive, gutsy personality suited the confrontational mood of the Cold War. He linked the Soviet threat in Europe to the need for a strong presidency. Pressed to establish his own political identity, "Give 'em Hell Harry" successfully portrayed himself as a fierce fighter against all challengers, yet loyal to Roosevelt's legacy.

HOW DID the "Fair Deal" differ from the "New Deal"?

"TO ERR IS TRUMAN"

Within a year of assuming office, Harry Truman rated lower in public approval than any other twentieth-century president except Roosevelt's own predecessor, Herbert Hoover, who had been blamed for the Great Depression. The responsibilities of reestablishing peacetime conditions seemed to overwhelm the new president's administration. "To err is Truman," critics jeered.

In handling the enormous task of reconverting the economy to peacetime production, Truman appeared both inept and mean-spirited. The president faced millions of restless would-be consumers tired of rationing and eager to spend their wartime savings on shiny cars, new furniture, choice cuts of meat, and colorful clothing. The demand for consumer items rapidly outran supply, fueling inflation and creating a huge black market. When Congress proposed extending wartime price controls, Truman vetoed the bill and prices skyrocketed.

Council of Economic Advisors
Board of three professional economists established in 1946 to advise the president on economic policy.

In 1945 and 1946, the country appeared ready to explode. While homemakers protested rising prices by boycotting neighborhood stores, industrial workers struck in unprecedented numbers. Employers, fearing a rapid decline to Depression-level profits, determined to slash wages or at least hold them steady; workers wanted a bigger cut of the huge war profits they had heard about. The spectacle of nearly 4.6 million workers on picket lines alarmed the new president. In May 1946, Truman proposed to draft strikers into the army who refused to return to work under a presidential order. The usually conservative Senate killed this plan.

Congress defeated most of Truman's proposals to revive the New Deal. One week after Japan's surrender, the president introduced a twenty-one-point program that included greater unemployment compensation, higher minimum wages, and housing assistance. Later he added proposals for national health insurance and atomic energy legislation. Congress turned back the bulk of these bills, passing the Employment Act of 1946 only after substantial modification. The act created a new executive body, the **Council of Economic Advisors**, which would confer with the president and formulate policies for maintaining employment, production, and purchasing power. But the measure did not include funding mechanisms to guarantee full employment, thus falling far short of the bill's intent.

Republicans, sensing victory in the upcoming off-year elections, asked the voters, "Had enough?" Apparently the voters had. They gave Republicans majorities in both houses of Congress and in the state capitols. And in a symbolic repudiation of Roosevelt, they passed an amendment to the Constitution establishing a two-term limit for the presidency.

Police and strikers confront each other in Los Angeles during one of many postwar strikes in 1946. Employers wanted to cut wages, and workers refused to give up the higher living standard achieved during the war.

AP/Wide World Photos

The Republicans, dominant in Congress for the first time since 1931, prepared a counteroffensive against the New Deal, beginning with an attack on organized labor. Unions had by this time reached a peak in size and prestige, with membership topping 15 million and encompassing nearly 40 percent of all wage earners. Concluding that labor had gone too far, the Republican-dominated Eightieth Congress aimed to outlaw many practices approved by the Wagner Act of 1935 (see Chapter 24).

The Labor-Management Relations Act of 1947, better known as **Taft-Hartley Act**, brought to an end the closed shop, the secondary boycott, and the use of union dues for political activities. It also mandated an eighty-day cooling-off period in the case of strikes affecting national safety or health. Taft-Hartley furthermore required all union officials to swear under oath that they were not Communists— a Cold War mandate that abridged freedoms ordinarily guaranteed by the First Amendment. Unions that refused to cooperate were denied the services of the National Labor Relations Board, which arbitrated strikes and issued credentials to unions.

Truman regained some support from organized labor when he vetoed the Taft-Hartley Act, saying it would "conflict with important principles of our democratic society." Congress, however, overrode his veto, and Truman himself went on to invoke the act against strikers.

THE 1948 ELECTION

Harry Truman had considered some of Roosevelt's advisors to be "crackpots and the lunatic fringe." By 1946 Truman had forced out the remaining social planners who had staffed the Washington bureaus for over a decade, including one of the best-loved New Dealers, Secretary of Interior Harold Ickes. Truman also fired the secretary of commerce, Henry Wallace, for advocating a more conciliatory policy toward the Soviet Union.

However, Wallace would not retreat and made plans to run against Truman for president. He pledged to expand New Deal programs by moving boldly to establish full employment, racial equality, and stronger labor unions. He also promised peace with the Soviet Union. As the 1948 election neared, Wallace appeared a viable candidate on the new Progressive Party ticket until Truman accused him of being a tool of communists.

Meanwhile, Truman repositioned himself to discredit congressional Republicans. He proposed programs calling for federal funds for education and new housing and a national program of medical insurance that he knew the Republicans would oppose, and he called Congress back for a fruitless special session in 1948. He then hammered away at the Republican controlled "do-nothing Congress" to good effect in his reelection campaign.

To cut Wallace's lead on civil rights, Truman issued executive orders in July 1948 desegregating the armed forces and banning discrimination in the federal civil service. In response, some 300 Southern delegates bolted from the Democratic National Convention and formed a States' Rights (**Dixiecrat**) ticket, headed by Governor J. Strom Thurmond of South Carolina, known for his segregationist views. With the South as good as lost, and popular New York governor Thomas E. Dewey heading the Republican ticket, Truman appeared hopelessly far from victory.

Yet as the election neared, Truman campaigned vigorously and managed to revive the New Deal coalition. Fear of the Republicans won back the bulk of organized labor, while the recognition of the new State of Israel in May 1948 helped prevent

Taft-Hartley Act Federal legislation of 1947 that substantially limited the tools available to labor unions in labor-management disputes.

Dixiecrat States' Rights Democrat.

QUICK REVIEW

Truman's 1948 Presidential Campaign

- Truman campaigned from the back of a train.
- Truman tied Dewey to inflation, housing shortages, and fears about Social Security.
- Dewey's failure to campaign aggressively may have cost him the election.

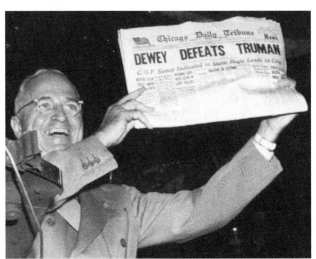

Harry Truman holds up a copy of the *Chicago Tribune* with headlines confidently and mistakenly predicting the victory of his opponent, Thomas E. Dewey.
UPI/CORBIS (U885941B)

MAP EXPLORATION
To explore an interactive version of this map, go to
http://www.prenhall.com/faraghertlc/map26.2

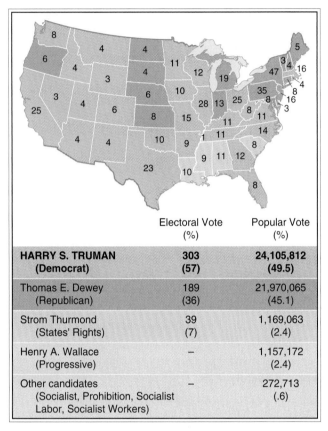

	Electoral Vote (%)	Popular Vote (%)
HARRY S. TRUMAN (Democrat)	**303 (57)**	**24,105,812 (49.5)**
Thomas E. Dewey (Republican)	189 (36)	21,970,065 (45.1)
Strom Thurmond (States' Rights)	39 (7)	1,169,063 (2.4)
Henry A. Wallace (Progressive)	–	1,157,172 (2.4)
Other candidates (Socialist, Prohibition, Socialist Labor, Socialist Workers)	–	272,713 (.6)

MAP 26-2
The Election of 1948 An initially unpopular candidate, Truman made a whistle-stop tour of the country by train to win 49.5 percent of the popular vote to Dewey's 45.1 percent.

WHY WAS Truman relatively unpopular at the beginning of the 1948 campaign?

the defection of many liberal Jewish voters from Democratic ranks. The success of the Berlin airlift also buoyed the president's popularity. By election time, Truman had deprived Henry Wallace of nearly all his liberal support. Meanwhile, Dewey, who had run a hard-hitting campaign against Roosevelt in 1944, expected to coast to victory.

Truman won the popular vote by a margin of 5 percent and trounced Dewey 303 to 189 in the electoral college. Moreover, Democrats again had majorities in both houses of Congress. But, as it turned out, Truman had hit the highest point of his popularity and was about to begin a steady slide downhill.

THE FAIR DEAL

"Every segment of our population and every individual has a right," Truman announced in January 1949, "to expect from our Government a fair deal." The return of Democratic congressional majorities, he hoped, would enable him to translate campaign promises into concrete legislative achievements and expand the New Deal. But a powerful bloc of conservative Southern Democrats and Midwestern Republicans turned back his domestic agenda.

Truman broke no new ground. Congress passed a National Housing Act in 1949, promoting federally funded construction of low-income housing. It also raised the minimum wage from 40 to 75 cents per hour and expanded the Social Security program to cover an additional 10 million people. Otherwise, Truman made little headway. He and congressional liberals introduced a variety of bills to weaken Southern segregationism: a federal antilynching law; outlawing the poll tax; prohibiting discrimination in interstate transportation. These measures were all defeated by Southern-led filibusters. Proposals to create a national health insurance plan, provide federal aid for education, and repeal or modify Taft-Hartley remained bottled up in committees.

Truman managed best by laying out the basic principles of Cold War liberalism. Toning down the rhetoric of economic equality espoused by the visionary wing of the Roosevelt coalition, his Fair Deal exalted economic growth—not the reapportionment of wealth or political power—as the proper mechanism for ensuring social harmony and national welfare. His administration insisted, therefore, on an ambitious program of expanded foreign trade, while relying on the federal government to encourage high levels of productivity at home. Equally important, Truman further tempered liberalism by making anti-communism a key element in both foreign policy and the domestic agenda.

THE COLD WAR AT HOME

WHAT CONTRIBUTED to the rise of McCarthyism?

"Communists . . . are everywhere—in factories, offices, butcher shops, on street corners, in private businesses," Attorney General J. Howard McGrath warned in 1949: "At this very moment [they are] busy at work—undermining your government, plotting to destroy the liberties of every citizen, and feverishly trying in whatever way they can, to aid the Soviet Union."

Republican senator Joseph R. McCarthy even claimed to have in his personal possession a list of communists serving secretly in government agencies. By this time, the Communist Party, U.S.A., which had formed in 1919, was steadily losing ground.

Nevertheless, during the earliest days of the Cold War, anti-communism already occupied center stage in domestic politics. Thus, FBI director J. Edgar Hoover characteristically warned Americans not to be complacent in the face of low numbers of Communists because "for every party member there are ten others ready, willing, and able to do the Party's work" in infiltrating and corrupting "various spheres of American life."

The federal government, with the help of the media, would lead the campaign, finding in the threat of communism a rationale for the massive reordering of its operation and the quieting of the voices of dissent. In this far-reaching quest for security, Americans moved toward a greater concentration of power in government, and, while promising to lead the "free world," allowed many of their own rights to be circumscribed.

THE NATIONAL SECURITY ACT OF 1947

The imperative of national security destroyed old-fashioned isolation, forcing the United States into international alliances such as NATO and into the role of world leader. "If we falter in our leadership," Truman warned, "we may endanger the peace of the world—and we shall surely endanger the welfare of this nation." Such a responsibility required a massive amount of resources. Truman went on, therefore, to argue successfully that national security demanded a substantial increase in the size of the federal government, including both military forces and surveillance agencies. Security measures were required to keep the nation in a steady state of preparedness, readily justified during wartime, now extended into the very uneasy peacetime.

The National Security Act of 1947, passed by Congress in July, established the Department of Defense and the **National Security Council (NSC)** to administer and coordinate defense policies and to advise the president. The Department of Defense replaced the War Department and united the armed forces—the army, navy, and air force—under the jurisdiction of a single secretary with cabinet-level status. The act also created the National Security Resources Board (NSRB) to coordinate plans throughout the government "in the event of war" and, for the first time in American history, to maintain a program of military preparedness in peacetime.

The Department of Defense, together with the NSRB, became the principal sponsor of scientific research during the first ten years of the Cold War. It was commonly recognized at the time that World War II had been "a physicists' war," leading to the creation of the ultimate weapon, the atom bomb, as well as major advances in military technology in areas of navigation and detection systems, strategic targeting, and communication. Many scientists anticipated that, at the end of the war, the special relationship between science and government would continue under the auspices of a new federal agency that would channel funds mainly to universities for basic research under civilian control.

The National Security Act added to this system of defense in 1947 by establishing the **Central Intelligence Agency (CIA).** With roots in the wartime Office of Strategic Services, the CIA now became a permanent operation devoted to collecting political, military, and economic information for security purposes throughout the world. Although information about the CIA was classified—that is, secret from both Congress and the public—historians have estimated that the agency soon dwarfed the State Department in number of employees and size of budget.

QUICK REVIEW

National Security Act of 1947

- Established Department of Defense, the National Security Council, and the National Security Resources Board (NSRB).
- Department of Defense and the NSRB became principal sponsors of scientific research.
- National security spending required a substantial increase in the size of the defense budget.

National Security Council (NSC)
The formal policymaking body for national defense and foreign relations, created in 1947 and consisting of the president, the secretary of defense, the secretary of state, and others appointed by the president.

Central Intelligence Agency (CIA)
Agency established in 1947 that coordinates the gathering and evaluation of military and economic information on other nations.

The national security state required a huge work force. Before World War II, approximately 900,000 civilians worked for the federal government, with about 10 percent engaged in security work; by the beginning of the Cold War, nearly 4 million people were on the government's payroll, with 75 percent working in national security agencies.

National security took up increasingly large portions of the nation's resources and required an enormous increase in the size of the defense budget. By the end of Truman's second term, defense allocations accounted for 10 percent of the gross national product, directly or indirectly employed hundreds of thousands of well-paid workers, and subsidized some of the nation's most profitable corporations. This vast financial outlay created the rationale for permanent, large-scale military spending as a basic stimulus to economic growth.

THE LOYALTY-SECURITY PROGRAM

National security also required increased surveillance at home. Within two weeks of proclaiming the Truman Doctrine, the president signed Executive Order 9835 on March 21, 1947, and thereby established a loyalty program for all federal employees. The new Federal Employees Loyalty and Security Program, directed at members of the Communist Party—as well as fascists and anyone guilty of "sympathetic association" with either—in effect established a political test for federal employment. Later amendments added "homosexuals" as potential security risks on the grounds that they might succumb to blackmail by enemy agents.

Many state and municipal governments enacted loyalty programs and required public employees, including teachers at all levels, to sign loyalty oaths. In all, some 6.6 million people underwent loyalty and security checks. An estimated 500 government workers were fired and perhaps as many as 6,000 more chose to resign.

Attorney General Clark aided this effort by publishing a list of hundreds of potentially subversive organizations selected by criteria so vague that any views "hostile or inimical to the American form of government" could make an organization liable for investigation and prosecution. There was, moreover, no right of appeal. The attorney general's list effectively outlawed many political and social organizations, indirectly stigmatizing hundreds of thousands of individuals who had done nothing illegal. Fraternal and social institutions, especially popular among aging European immigrants of various nationalities, were among the largest organizations destroyed. The state of New York, for example, legally dismantled the International Workers' Order, which had provided insurance to nearly 200,000 immigrants and their families. Only a handful of organizations had the funds to challenge the listing legally; most simply closed their doors.

In 1950 Congress overrode the president's veto to pass a bill that Truman called "the greatest danger to freedom of press, speech, and assembly since the Sedition Act of 1798." The Internal Security (McCarran) Act required Communist organizations to register with the Subversive Activities Control Board and authorized the arrest of suspect persons during a national emergency. The Immigration and Nationality Act, also sponsored by Republican senator Pat McCarran of Nevada and adopted in 1952, again over Truman's veto, barred people deemed "subversive" or "homosexual" from becoming citizens or even from visiting the United States. It also empowered the attorney general to deport immigrants who were members of Communist organizations, even if they had become citizens. Challenged repeatedly on constitutional grounds, the Subversive Activities Control Board remained in place until 1973, when it was terminated.

THE RED SCARE IN HOLLYWOOD

Anti-Communist Democratic representative Martin Dies of Texas, who had chaired a congressional committee on "un-American activities" since 1938, told reporters at a press conference in Hollywood in 1944:

> Hollywood is the greatest source of revenue in this nation for the Communists and other subversive groups. . . . Two elements stand out in . . . the making of pictures which extoll foreign ideology— propaganda for a cause which seeks to spread its ideas to our people[,] and the "leftist" or radical screenwriters.

A few years later, Dies's successor, J. Parnell Thomas of New Jersey, directed the committee to investigate supposed Communist infiltration of the movie industry.

Renamed and made a permanent standing committee in 1945, the **House Un-American Activities Committee (HUAC)** had the power to subpoena witnesses and compel them to answer all questions or face contempt of Congress charges. In well-publicized hearings held in Hollywood in October 1947, the mother of actress Ginger Rogers defended her daughter by saying that she had been duped into appearing in the pro-Soviet wartime film *Tender Comrade* (1943) and "had been forced" to read the subversive line "Share and share alike, that's democracy." HUAC encouraged testimony by "friendly witnesses," including Ronald Reagan and Gary Cooper. The committee intimidated many others who feared the loss of their careers into naming former friends and co-workers in order to be cleared for future work in Hollywood.

A small but prominent minority refused to cooperate with HUAC. By claiming the freedoms of speech and association guaranteed by the First and Sixth Amendments to the Constitution, they became known as "unfriendly witnesses." A handful served prison sentences for contempt of Congress.

Hollywood studios refused to employ any writer, director, or actor who refused to cooperate with HUAC. The resulting blacklist remained in effect until the 1960s and limited the production of films dealing directly with social or political issues. Meanwhile, the privately published *Red Channels: The Report of Communist Influence in Radio and Television* (1950) persuaded advertisers to cancel their accounts with many programs considered friendly to the Soviet Union, the United Nations, or liberal causes.

SPY CASES

In August 1948, Whittaker Chambers, a *Time* magazine editor, appeared before HUAC to name Alger Hiss as a fellow Communist in the Washington underground during the 1930s. Hiss, then president of the prestigious Carnegie Endowment for International Peace and former member of FDR's State Department, denied the charges and sued his accuser for slander. A federal grand jury in January 1950 convicted Hiss of perjury (for denying he knew Chambers), and he received a five-year prison term. Hiss was released two years later, still proclaiming his innocence.

Many Democrats, including Truman himself, at first dismissed the allegations against Hiss—conveniently publicized at the start of the 1948 election campaign—as a red herring, a Republican maneuver to gain votes. Nevertheless, the highly publicized allegations against Hiss proved detrimental to Democrats, suggesting that both FDR and Truman had allowed Communists to infiltrate the federal government.

The most dramatic spy case of the era involved Julius Rosenberg, former government engineer, and his wife, Ethel, who were accused of stealing and plotting to convey atomic secrets to Soviet agents during World War II. The government's

26–6
Ronald Reagan, Testimony Before the House Un-American Activities Committee (1947)

House Un-American Activities Committee (HUAC)   Originally intended to ferret out pro-Fascists, it later investigated "un-American propaganda" that attacked constitutional government.

McCarthyism Anti-Communist attitudes and actions associated with Senator Joe McCarthy in the early 1950s, including smear tactics and innuendo.

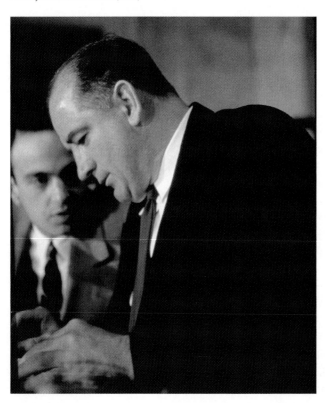

26–7
Joseph R. McCarthy, from Speech Delivered to the Women's Club of Wheeling, West Virginia (1950)

The tables turned on Senator Joseph McCarthy (1908–1957) after he instigated an investigation of the U.S. Army for harboring Communists. A congressional committee then investigated McCarthy for attempting to make the army grant special privileges to his staff aide, Private David Schine. During the televised hearings, Senator McCarthy—shown here with his staff assistant Roy Cohn—discredited himself. In December 1954, the Senate voted to censure him.
Photo by Hank Walker. TimePix (3701)

case against the Rosenbergs rested on the testimony of their supposed accomplices, some of them secretly coached by the FBI. Although the Rosenbergs maintained their innocence to the end, in March 1951 a jury found them guilty of conspiring to commit espionage. The American press showed them no sympathy, but around the world the Rosenbergs were defended by citizens' committees and their convictions protested in large-scale demonstrations. Scientist Albert Einstein, the pope, and the president of France, among many prominent figures, all pleaded for clemency. Julius and Ethel Rosenberg died in the electric chair on June 19, 1953.

McCarthyism

In a sensational Lincoln Day speech to the Republican Women's Club of Wheeling, West Virginia, on February 9, 1950, Republican senator Joseph R. McCarthy of Wisconsin announced that the United States had been sold out by the "traitorous actions of those who have been treated so well by the nation." These "bright young men who have been born with silver spoons in their mouths"—such as Secretary of State Dean Acheson, whom McCarthy called a "pompous diplomat in striped pants, with a phony English accent"—were part of a conspiracy, he charged, of more than 200 Communists working in the State Department.

McCarthy refused to reveal names, however, and a few days later, after a drinking bout, he told persistent reporters: "I'm not going to tell you anything. I just want you to know I've got a pailful [of dirt] . . . and I'm going to use it where it does the most good." Although investigations uncovered not a single Communist in the State Department, McCarthy launched a flamboyant offensive against New Deal Democrats and the Truman administration for failing to defend the nation's security. His name provided the label for the entire campaign to silence critics of the Cold War: **McCarthyism**.

Behind the blitz of publicity, the previously obscure junior senator from Wisconsin had struck a chord. Communism seemed to many Americans to be much more than a military threat—indeed, nothing less than a demonic force capable of undermining basic values. It compelled patriots to proclaim themselves ready for atomic warfare: "Better Dead Than Red." McCarthy also had help from organizations such as the American Legion and the Chamber of Commerce, and prominent religious leaders and union leaders.

Civil rights organizations faced the severest persecution since the 1920s. The Civil Rights Congress and the Negro Youth Council, for instance, were destroyed after frequent charges of Communist influence. W. E. B. Du Bois, the renowned African American historian, and famed concert singer (and former All-American football hero) Paul Robeson had public appearances canceled and their right to travel abroad abridged.

In attacks on women's organizations and homosexual groups, meanwhile, anti-Communist rhetoric cloaked deep fears about changing sexual mores. Aided by FBI reports, the federal government fired up to sixty homosexuals per month in the early 1950s. Dishonorable discharges from the U.S. armed forces for homosexuality, an administrative procedure without appeal, also increased dramatically. Noted historian Arthur Schlesinger Jr. suggested that critics of Cold War policies were not "real" men or, perhaps, "real" women either.

Joseph McCarthy and his fellow Red-hunters eventually burned themselves out. During televised congressional hearings in 1954, not only did McCarthy fail to prove wild charges of Communist infiltration of the army, but in the glare of the television cameras he appeared deranged. Cowed for years, the Senate finally condemned him for "conduct unbecoming a member."

26–9
Senator Joseph McCarthy's telegram to President Truman following the "Wheeling [W.Va.] Speech," February 11, 1950

COLD WAR CULTURE

As the Truman Doctrine clearly specified, the Cold War did not necessarily depend on military confrontation; nor was it defined exclusively by a quest for economic supremacy. The Cold War embodied the struggle of one "way of life" against another. It was, in short, a contest of values. The president therefore pledged the United States to "contain" communism from spreading beyond the parameters of the Soviet Union and its client states and simultaneously called for fortifications at home. If Americans were to rebuild the world based on their own values, they must rededicate themselves to the defense of their birthright: freedom and democracy.

WHAT WERE the most important demographic trends in the 1950s?

AN ANXIOUS MOOD

"We have about 50 percent of the world's wealth," George Kennan noted in 1948, "but only 3.6 percent of its population." Very large pockets of poverty remained, and not all Americans benefited from the postwar abundance. Nonetheless, millions of Americans achieved middle-class status, often through new programs subsidized by the federal government.

Prosperity did not dispel an anxious mood, fueled in part by the reality and the rhetoric of the Cold War. Many Americans also feared an economic backslide. If war production had ended the hardships of the Great Depression, how would the economy fare in peacetime? No one could say. Above all, peace itself seemed precarious.

Anxieties intensified by the Cold War surfaced as major themes in popular culture. One of the most acclaimed Hollywood films of the era, the winner of nine Academy Awards, *The Best Years of Our Lives* (1946), followed the stories of three returning veterans as they tried to readjust to civilian life. The former soldiers found that the dreams of reunion with family and loved ones that had sustained them through years of fighting now seemed hollow. In some cases, their wives and children had become so self-reliant that the men had no clear function to perform in the household; in other cases, the prospect for employment appeared dim.

The genre of *film noir* (French for "black") deepened this mood into an aesthetic. Movies like *Out of the Past, Detour,* and *They Live by Night* featured stories of ruthless fate and betrayal. Their protagonists were usually strangers or loners falsely accused of crimes or trapped into committing them. The high-contrast lighting of these black and white films accentuated the difficulty of distinguishing friend from foe.

Plays and novels also described alienation and anxiety in vivid terms. Playwright Arthur Miller in *Death of a Salesman* (1949) sketched an exacting portrait of self-destructive individualism. Willy Loman, the play's hero, is obsessively devoted to his career in sales but is nevertheless a miserable failure. Worse, he has trained his sons to excel in personal presentation and style—the very methods prescribed by standard American success manuals—making them both shallow and materialistic. J. D. Salinger's widely praised novel *Catcher in the Rye* (1951) explored the mental anguish of a teenage boy estranged from the crass materialism of his parents.

Hollywood studios played directly into the mounting fears, releasing by 1954 more than forty films with titles such as *I Married a Communist* (1950) and *The Red Menace* (1949) that sensationalized the Communist threat. The television industry sponsored the dramatic series *The Hunter,* featuring the adventures of an American businessman fighting Communist agents throughout the Free World. Few of these films or programs were popular, however.

THE FAMILY AS BULWARK

Postwar prosperity helped to strengthen the ideal of domesticity, although many Americans interpreted their rush toward marriage and parenthood, as one writer put it, as a "defense—an impregnable bulwark" against the anxieties of the era.

Young couples were marrying younger and producing more children than at any other time in the past century. The U.S. Census Bureau predicted that the "baby boom" would be temporary. To everyone's surprise, the birthrate continued to grow at a record pace, peaking at over 118 per 1,000 women in 1957.

The new families who enjoyed postwar prosperity inaugurated a spending spree of trailblazing proportions. "The year 1946," *Life* magazine proclaimed, "finds the U.S. on the threshold of marvels, ranging from runless stockings and shineless serge suits to jet-propelled airplanes that will flash across the country in just a little less than the speed of sound." By the time Harry Truman left office two-thirds of all American households claimed at least one television set.

These two trends—the baby boom and high rates of consumer spending—encouraged a major change in the middle-class family. Having worked during World War II, often in occupations traditionally closed to them, many women wished to continue in full-time employment. Reconversion to peacetime production forced the majority from their factory positions, but most women quickly returned, taking jobs at a faster rate than men and providing half the total growth of the labor force. By 1952, 2 million more wives worked than during the war. Gone, however, were the high-paying unionized jobs in manufacturing. Instead, most women found minimum-wage jobs in the expanding service sector: clerical work, health care and education, and restaurant, hotel, and retail services. Older women whose children were grown might work because they had come to value a job for its own sake. Younger women often worked for reasons of "economic necessity"—that is, to maintain a middle-class standard of living that now required more than one income. Indeed, mothers of young children were the most likely to be employed.

Even though most women sought employment primarily to support their families, they ran up against popular opinion and expert advice urging them to return to their homes. Public opinion registered resounding disapproval—by 86 percent of those surveyed—of a married woman's working if jobs were scarce and her husband could support her. Commentators appealed for a return to an imaginary "traditional" family, where men alone were breadwinners and women stayed happily at home.

This campaign began on a shrill note. Ferdinand Lundberg and Marynia Farnham, in their best-selling *Modern Woman: The Lost Sex* (1947), attributed the "super-jittery age in which we live" to women's abandonment of the home to pursue careers. To counter this trend, they proposed federally funded psychotherapy to readjust women to their housewifely roles and cash subsidies to encourage them to bear more children.

Articles in popular magazines, television shows, and high-profile experts chimed in with similar messages. Talcott Parsons, the distinguished Harvard sociologist, delineated the parameters of the "democratic" family: husbands served as breadwinners while wives—"the emotional hub of the family"—

27–3
Ladies Home Journal,
"Young Mother" (1956)

U.S. Birth Rate, 1930–1980
The bulge of the "baby boom," a leading demographic factor in the postwar economy, stands out for this fifty-year period.

This model is displaying the ideal kitchen of the 1950s. The "American way of life," defined as a high standard of living, was one of the tangible fruits of U.S. victory in World War II.
CORBIS (GNGN10375)

stayed home to care for their families. In the first edition of *Baby and Child Care* (1946), the child-rearing advice manual that soon outsold the Bible, Benjamin Spock similarly advised women to devote themselves full time, if financially possible, to their maternal responsibilities.

Patterns of women's higher education reflected this conservative trend. Having made slight gains during World War II when college-age men were serving in the armed forces or working in war industries, women lost ground after the **GI Bill** created a huge upsurge in male enrollment. Women represented 40 percent of all college graduates in 1940 but only 25 percent a decade later.

With a growing number of middle-class women working to help support their families, these Cold War policies and prescriptions worked at cross-purposes. As early as 1947, *Life* magazine registered concern in a thirteen-page feature, "American Woman's Dilemma." How could women comfortably take part in a world beyond the home and at the same time heed the advice of FBI director J. Edgar Hoover, who exhorted the nation's women to fight "the twin enemies of freedom—crime and communism" by fulfilling their singular role as "homemakers and mothers"?

MILITARY-INDUSTRIAL COMMUNITIES IN THE WEST

All regions of the United States felt the impact of the Cold War but perhaps none so directly as the Trans-Mississippi West. Defense spending during World War II had stimulated the Western economy and encouraged a mass migration of people eager to find employment in wartime industry. Following the war, many cities successfully converted to peacetime production; Los Angeles, for example, attracted one-eighth of all new business in the nation during the late 1940s. However, the Cold War, by reviving defense funding, provided the most important boost to the Western economy. The Department of Defense and private corporations and subcontractors generated billions of dollars for research and development of military equipment of various kinds.

The federal government poured so much defense money—nearly 10 percent of the entire military budget—into California that the state's rate of economic growth between 1949 and 1952 outpaced that of the nation as a whole,

QUICK REVIEW

Working Wives

- 1952: More wives worked than during the war but held lower paying jobs.
- Many women worked to maintain a middle-class standard of living.
- Working women faced criticism by advocates of return to "traditional" family.

GI Bill Legislation in June 1944 that eased the return of veterans into American society by providing educational and employment benefits.

with nearly 40 percent coming from the manufacture of aircraft alone. Ten years later, it was estimated that one-third of all workers in Los Angeles were employed by defense industries, particularly aerospace, and that their absolute number was far greater than during the peak of production in World War II. The concentration of defense workers was even greater in the suburbs of Los Angeles. Orange County, for example, grew quickly during the Cold War to become a major producer of communication equipment. The San Francisco Bay Area also benefited economically from defense spending, and cities such as Sunnyvale, Mountain View, and San Jose began their ascendance as home to the nation's budding high-technology industry.

The Cold War also pumped new life into communities that had grown up during World War II. Hanford, Washington, and Los Alamos, New Mexico, both centers of the Manhattan Project, employed a greater number of people in the construction of the Cold War nuclear arsenal than in the development of the atom bomb that brought an end to World War II. Los Alamos grew from its rural origins at such a fast pace that thirty years later its population density was one of the highest in the state, second only to the metropolitan region of Albuquerque. The community lost little of its secretive quality, with entry restricted to mainly well-paid workers and residents who could neither own land or homes within its boundaries. Meanwhile, the federal government continued to place its distinctive stamp on the architecture, with institutional and purely functional aesthetics governing the design of concrete structures with hospital-green interiors.

New communities accompanied the growth of the U.S. military bases and training camps in the Western states. Many of these installations, as well as hospitals and supply depots, not only survived but also expanded during the transition from the actual warfare of World War II to the virtual warfare of the Cold War. Between 1950 and 1953 approximately twenty Western bases were reopened. California became at least a temporary home to more military personnel than any other state, but Texas was not far behind. The availability of public lands with areas of sparse population made Western states especially attractive to military planners commissioned to design dangerous and secretive installations such as the White Sands Missile Range in the New Mexican desert.

ZEAL FOR DEMOCRACY

World War II revitalized patriotism by rallying Americans to define themselves and their institutions against Nazi and fascist forces abroad. Pledging allegiance to the flag, for example, gained new symbolic meaning as school children were directed to avoid saluting, a gesture now perceived as disturbingly similar to the militaristic Nazi hand-raising, and were instead told to hold their right hand steadily over their heart.

Following the massive V-J Day celebrations that marked the end of World War II, Americans began to retreat from public displays of patriotism but were soon chastized for their "national apathy" by organizations like the Freedoms Foundation of Valley Forge, which aimed to mobilize a "vast articulate, creative army of ministers, teachers, professional people, students, men and women from the farm and factory" to defend "the American Way." Soon, other new groups, such as the American Heritage Foundation, founded in 1947, joined such stalwarts as the American Legion, the Chamber of Commerce, and local business and veterans groups in this endeavor.

In 1948, Attorney General Tom Clark, with the support of President Truman, funding from private donors, and planning by the American Heritage Foundation, put on track the "Freedom Train." Carrying documents illustrating basic

26–2
Kenneth MacFarland, "The Unfinished Work" (1946)

American rights and liberties, such as the Bill of Rights and the Constitution, the Freedom Train traveled to various cities across the United States where local citizens got aboard to view various patriotic displays at the average rate of 8,500 people per day. The popular songwriter Irving Berlin memorialized the Freedom Train, lyrically assuring the expectant viewers who endured long lines that inside "you'll find a precious freight."

Patriotic messages also permeated public education. According to guidelines set down by the Truman administration, teachers were to "strengthen national security through education," specifically designing their lesson plans to illustrate the superiority of the American democratic system over Soviet communism. In 1947 the federal Office of Education launched the "Zeal for Democracy" program for implementation by school boards nationwide. The program veered toward propaganda, announcing its intention to "promote and strengthen democratic thinking and practice, just as the schools of totalitarian states have so effectively promoted the ideals of their respective cultures." Meanwhile, as part of a separate program in civil defense, school children were taught to "duck" under their desks and "cover" their heads to protect themselves in the event of a surprise nuclear attack by the Soviets.

There were voices of protest to these Cold War programs. The black poet Langston Hughes, for example, expressed his skepticism in verse, writing that he hoped the Freedom Train would carry no Jim Crow car. A fearless minority of scholars protested infringements on their academic freedom by refusing to sign loyalty oaths and by writing books pointing out the potential dangers of aggressively nationalistic foreign and domestic policies. But the chilling atmosphere made many individuals reluctant to express contrary opinions or ideas.

END OF THE DEMOCRATIC ERA

Cold War tensions festered in Europe and pushed the United States and Soviet Union to the brink of armed conflict. With so much happening in Europe, neither superpower would have predicted that events in Asia would soon transform their political and ideological competition into a war threatening to destroy the world. Yet, in 1949, Communists in China seized power in the most heavily populated nation in the world. Then, a few months later, in June 1950, Communists threatened to take over all of Korea. The precarious balance of power was seemingly shifting.

WHAT ISSUES were at the center of the election of 1952?

THE "LOSS" OF CHINA

At the close of World War II, the United States acted deliberately to secure Japan firmly in its realm. General Douglas MacArthur directed an interim government in a modest reconstruction program that included land reform, the creation of independent trade unions, the abolition of contract marriages, the granting of woman suffrage, sweeping demilitarization, and, eventually, a constitutional democracy that barred Communists from all posts. American leaders worked to rebuild the nation's economy along capitalist lines and integrate Japan, like West Germany, into an anti-Soviet bloc. Japan also housed huge U.S. military bases, thus placing U.S. troops and weapons strategically close to the Soviet Union's Asian rim.

The situation in China could not be handled as easily. After years of civil war, the pro–Western Nationalist government of Jiang Jeishi (Chiang Kai-shek) collapsed. Since World War II, the United States had been sending aid to the unpopular government while warning Jiang that without major reforms the Nationalists were heading for defeat. Moreover, they tried to convince him to accept a coalition government. After refusing to intervene on their behalf, the United States watched as Jiang's troops were finally forced to surrender to the Communists, led by Mao Zedong, who enjoyed the support of the Chinese countryside, where 85 percent of the population lived. Surrendering to Mao the entire China mainland, the defeated Nationalist government withdrew to the island of Formosa (Taiwan). On October 1, 1949, the People's Republic of China (PRC) was formally established.

MAP EXPLORATION

To explore an interactive version of this map, go to **http://www.prenhall.com/faraghertlc/map26.3**

MAP 26-3

The Korean War   The intensity of battles underscored the strategic importance of Korea in the cold war.

HOW DID the United States military campaign in Korea reflect Truman's doctrine of containment?

The news of China's "fall" to communism created an uproar in the United States. The Asia First wing of the Republican Party, which envisioned the Far East rather than Europe as the prime site of U.S. trade and investment, blamed the Truman administration for the "loss" of China.

THE KOREAN WAR

At the end of World War II, the Allies had divided the small peninsula of Korea, ceded by Japan, at the 38th parallel. Although all parties hoped to reunite the nation under its own government, the line between North and South instead hardened. The United States backed the unpopular government of Syngman Rhee (the Republic of Korea), and the Soviet Union sponsored a rival government in North Korea under Kim Il Sung.

On June 25, 1950, the U.S. State Department received a cablegram reporting a military attack on South Korea by the Communist-controlled North. "If we are tough enough now," President Truman pledged, "if we stand up to them like we did in Greece three years ago, they won't take any next steps." The Soviet Union, on the other hand, regarded the invasion as Kim Il Sung's affair. Despite Soviet disclaimers, Truman sought approval from the UN Security Council to send troops into South Korea. Because of the absence of the Soviet delegate, who could have vetoed the decision, the Security Council agreed. Two-thirds of Americans polled approved the president's decision to send troops under the command of General Douglas MacArthur.

Korean War   Pacific war started on June 25, 1950, when North Korea, helped by Soviet equipment and Chinese training, attacked South Korea.

American soldiers fought in Korea under the command of General Douglas MacArthur until President Truman named General Matthew Ridgway as his replacement in April 1951. Nearly 1.8 million Americans served in Korea.

National Archives and Records Administration

Military events at first seemed to justify the president's decision. Seoul, the capital of South Korea, had fallen to North Korean troops within weeks of the invasion, and Communist forces continued to push south until they had taken most of the peninsula. The situation appeared grim until Truman authorized MacArthur to carry out an amphibious landing at Inchon, which he did on September 15, 1950. With tactical brilliance and good fortune, the general orchestrated a military campaign that halted the Communist drive. By October, UN troops had retaken South Korea.

Basking in victory, the Truman administration could not resist the temptation to expand its war aims. Hoping to prove that Democrats were not "soft" on communism, the president and his advisors decided to roll back the Communists beyond the 38th parallel. Until this point, China had not actively been involved in the war, but it now warned that any attempt to cross the dividing line would be interpreted as a threat to its own national security. Truman flew to Wake Island in the Pacific on October 15 for a conference with MacArthur, who assured the president of a speedy victory.

MacArthur had sorely miscalculated. Chinese troops massed just above the UN offensive line, at the Yalu River. Suddenly, and without any air support, the Chinese attacked in human waves. MacArthur's force was all but crushed. The Chinese drove the UN troops back into South Korea, where they regrouped along the 38th parallel. By summer 1951 a stalemate had been reached very near the old border. Negotiations for a settlement went on for the next eighteen months amid heavy fighting.

MacArthur tried without success to convince Truman to prepare for a new invasion of Communist territory. Encouraged by strong support at home, he continued to provoke the president by speaking out against official policy, calling for bombing of supply lines in China and a naval blockade of the Chinese coast—actions certain to lead to a Chinese-American war. Finally, on April 10, 1951, Truman dismissed MacArthur for insubordination and other unauthorized activities.

THE PRICE OF NATIONAL SECURITY

By instituting a peacetime draft in 1948 and then ordering American troops into Korea, Truman had bypassed congressional authority. Truman carefully referred to the military deployment not as a U.S. war but as a UN-sanctioned "police action."

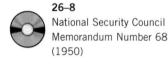

26–8
National Security Council Memorandum Number 68 (1950)

The president derived his authority from **National Security Council Paper 68 (NSC-68)**, a paper released to him by the National Security Council in April 1950. NSC-68 pledged the United States not only to drive back Communist influence wherever it appeared but also to "foster the seeds of destruction within the Soviet Union."

Initially reluctant, Truman fulfilled the prescriptions of NSC-68 after the outbreak of the Korean War and agreed to its mandate for a rapid and permanent military buildup. By the time the conflict subsided, the defense budget had quadrupled, and the U.S. Army had grown to 3.6 million, or six times its size at the beginning of the conflict. At the same time, the federal government accelerated the development of both conventional and nonconventional weapons. In the first instance, it began to stockpile nuclear bombs and weapons, including the first hydrogen, or H-bomb, which was tested in November 1952.

The Korean War also provided the rationale for the expansion of anti-Communist propaganda. At the end of World War II President Truman had taken steps to transform the Office of War Information into a peacetime program that operated on a much smaller budget. But by 1948 Congress was ready to pass with bipartisan support the Smith-Mundt Act, designed "to promote the better understanding of the United States among the peoples of the world and to strengthen

National Security Council Paper 68 (NSC-68) Policy statement that committed the United States to a military approach to the Cold War.

cooperative international relations." Within a year, Congress doubled the budget for such programming, granting $3 million to revive the Voice of America, the short-wave international radio program that had been established in 1942. The new legislation also funded the development of film, print media, cultural exchange programs, and exhibitions, and it created a foundation to promote anti-Communist propaganda throughout the world.

The outcome of the Korean War did nothing to improve the case for rolling back communism. Negotiations and fighting proceeded in tandem until the summer of 1953, when a settlement was reached in which both North Korea and South Korea occupied almost the same territory as when the war began. Approximately 54,000 Americans died in Korea; the North Koreans and Chinese lost well over 2 million people. The UN troops had employed both "carpet bombing" (an intense, destructive attack on a given area) and napalm (jellied gasoline bombs), destroying most of the housing and food supplies in both Koreas. True to the pattern of modern warfare, which emerged during World War II, the majority of civilians killed were women and children. Nearly 1 million Koreans were left homeless.

For the United States, the Korean War enlarged the geographical range of the Cold War to include East Asia. The war also lined up the People's Republic of China and the United States as unwavering enemies for the next twenty years and heightened the U.S. commitment to Southeast Asia. Moreover, the Korean War did much to establish an ominous tradition of "unwinnable" conflicts that left many Americans skeptical of official policy.

In retrospect many Americans recognized that Truman, in fighting communism in Korea, had pledged the United States to defend a corrupt government and a brutal dictator. Decades later the Korean War inspired the dark comedy *M*A*S*H*, adapted for television from the film written by Hollywood screenwriter Ring Lardner Jr., an "unfriendly witness" before HUAC, who was jailed during the Korean War for contempt of Congress. As late as 1990, members of Congress were still debating the terms of a Korean War memorial. "It ended on a sad note for Americans," one historian has concluded, "and the war and its memories drifted off into a void."

THE ELECTION OF 1952

There was only one burning issue during the election campaign of 1952: the Korean War. Truman's popularity had wavered continually since he took office in 1945, but it sank to an all-time low in the early 1950s shortly after he dismissed MacArthur as commander of the UN troops in Korea. Congress received thousands of letters and telegrams calling for Truman's impeachment. "Oust President Truman" bumper stickers could be seen. MacArthur, meanwhile, returned home a hero, welcomed by more than 7 million fans in New York City alone.

Popular dissatisfaction with Truman increased. Newspapers reported that several agencies had been dealing in 5 percent kickbacks for government contracts. Business and organized labor complained about the price and wage freezes imposed during the Korean War. A late 1951 Gallup poll showed the president's approval rating at 23 percent. In March 1952, Truman announced he would not run for reelection, a decision rare for a president eligible for another term.

In accepting political defeat and disgrace, Truman turned to the popular but uncharismatic governor of Illinois, Adlai E. Stevenson Jr. Admired for his honesty and intelligence, Stevenson offered no solutions to the conflict in Korea, the accelerating arms race, or the cold war generally. Accepting the Democratic nomination, he candidly admitted that "the ordeal of the twentieth century is far from over," a prospect displeasing to voters aching for peace.

QUICK REVIEW

The Election of 1952

◆ Korean War the most important issue of the campaign.

◆ Truman's approval rating sank to 23%, leading to his decision not to run for a second term.

◆ Eisenhower positioned himself as a "modern Republican."

CHRONOLOGY

1941 Henry Luce forecasts the dawn of "the American Century."

1944 GI Bill of Rights benefits World War II veterans.

International Monetary Fund and World Bank founded.

1945 Franklin D. Roosevelt dies in office; Harry S Truman becomes president.

United Nations charter signed.

World War II ends.

Strike wave begins.

Truman proposes program of economic reforms.

1946 Employment Act creates Council of Economic Advisors.

Churchill's Iron Curtain speech.

Atomic Energy Act establishes Atomic Energy Commission.

Republicans win control of Congress.

Benjamin Spock publishes *Baby and Child Care.*

1947 Americans for Democratic Action founded.

Truman Doctrine announced; Congress appropriates $400 million in aid for Greece and Turkey.

Federal Employees Loyalty and Security Program established and attorney general's list of subversive organizations authorized.

Marshall Plan announced.

Taft-Hartley Act restricts union activities.

National Security Act establishes Department of Defense, the National Security Council, and the Central Intelligence Agency.

House Un-American Activities Committee hearings in Hollywood.

1948 Smith-Mundt Act passed by Congress.

Ferdinand Lundberg and Marynia Farnham publish *Modern Woman: The Lost Sex.*

State of Israel founded.

Berlin blockade begins.

Henry Wallace nominated for president on Progressive Party ticket.

Truman announces peacetime draft and desegregates U.S. armed forces and civil service.

Truman wins election; Democrats sweep both houses of Congress.

1949 Truman announces Fair Deal.

North Atlantic Treaty Organization (NATO) created.

Communists, led by Mao Zedong, take power in China.

Berlin blockade ends.

Soviet Union explodes atomic bomb.

1950 Alger Hiss convicted of perjury.

Senator Joseph McCarthy begins anti-Communist crusade.

Soviet Union and the People's Republic of China sign an alliance.

Adoption of NSC-68 consolidates presidential war powers.

Korean War begins.

Internal Security (McCarran) Act requires registration of Communist organizations and arrest of Communists during national emergencies.

1951 Truman dismisses General Douglas MacArthur.

Psychological Strategy Board created.

Armistice talks begin in Korea.

1952 Immigration and Nationality Act retains quota system, lifts ban on immigration of Asian and Pacific peoples but bans "subversives" and homosexuals.

United States explodes first hydrogen bomb.

Dwight D. Eisenhower wins presidency; Richard Nixon becomes vice president.

1953 Julius and Ethel Rosenberg executed for atomic espionage.

Armistice ends fighting in Korea.

1954 Army-McCarthy hearings end.

1955 Warsaw Pact created.

The Republicans made the most of the Democrats' dilemma. Without proposing any sweeping answers of their own, they pointed to all the obvious shortcomings of their opponents. Their campaign strategy, known as "$K_1 C_2$"—Korea, Communism, and Corruption—took steady aim at the Truman administration, and when opinion polls showed that Dwight Eisenhower possessed an "unprecedented" 64 percent approval rating, they found in "Ike" the perfect candidate to head the ticket.

Eisenhower styled himself the representative of "modern Republicanism." He wisely avoided the negative impressions made by the unsuccessful 1948 Republican candidate, Thomas Dewey, who had seemed as aggressive as Truman on foreign policy and simultaneously eager to overturn the New Deal domestic legislation. Eisenhower knew better: voters wanted peace and a limited welfare state. He referred to New Deal reforms as "a solid floor that keeps all of us from falling into the pit of disaster." And athough he did not go into specifics, he promised to end the Korean War with "an early and honorable" peace. Whenever he was tempted to address questions of finance or the economy, his advisors warned him: "The chief reason that people want to vote for you is because they think you have more ability to keep us out of another war."

Meanwhile, Eisenhower's vice presidential candidate, Richard Nixon, waged a relentless and defamatory attack on Stevenson, calling him "Adlai the Appeaser." Senator Joseph McCarthy chimed in, proclaiming that with club in hand he might be able to make "a good American" of Stevenson. A month before the election, McCarthy went on network television with his requisite "exhibits" and "documents," this time purportedly showing that the Democratic presidential candidate had promoted communism at home and abroad. These outrageous charges kept the Stevenson campaign off balance.

The Republican campaign was itself not entirely free of scandal: Nixon had been caught accepting personal gifts from wealthy benefactors. Pleading his case on national television, he described his wife Pat's "good Republican cloth coat" and their modest style of living. He then contritely admitted that he had indeed accepted one gift, a puppy named Checkers that his daughters loved and that he refused to give back. "The Poor Richard Show," as critics called the event, defused the scandal without answering the most important charges.

Richard Nixon used the new medium of television to convince American voters that he had not established an illegal slush fund in his campaign for the vice presidency in 1952. Viewers responded enthusiastically to his melodramatic delivery and swamped the Republican campaign headquarters with telegrams endorsing his candidacy.

Checkers speech, September 24, 1952. AP/Wide World Photos

Unaffected by the scandal, Eisenhower continued to enchant the voters as a peace candidate. Ten days before the election he dramatically announced, "I shall go to Korea" to settle the war. Eisenhower received 55 percent of the vote and carried thirty-nine states, in part because he brought out an unusually large number of voters in normally Democratic areas. He won the popular vote in much of the South and in the Northern cities of New York, Chicago, Boston, and Cleveland. Riding his coattails, the Republicans regained narrow control of Congress. The New Deal coalition of ethnic and black voters, labor, Northern liberals, and Southern conservatives no longer commanded a majority.

Conclusion

The election of Dwight Eisenhower helped diminish the intensity of the dour mood of an impending Cold War without actually bringing a halt to the conflict. "The Eisenhower Movement," wrote journalist Walter Lippmann, was a "mission in American politics" to restore a sense of community among the American people. In a larger sense, many of the issues of the immediate post–World War II years seemed to have been settled, or put off for a distant future. The international boundaries of communism were frozen with the Chinese Revolution, the Berlin Crisis, and then the Korean War. Meanwhile, at home Cold War defense spending had become a permanent part of the national budget, an undeniable drain on tax revenues, but an important element in the government contribution to economic prosperity. If the nuclear arms race remained a cause for anxiety, joined by more personal worries about the changing patterns of family life, a sense of relative security nevertheless spread. Prospects for world peace had dimmed, but the worst nightmares of the 1940s had eased as well.

Summary

Global Insecurities at War's End The end of World War Two did not end global insecurities. The United States emerged as the world's greatest power, but the future remained uncertain. The alliance with the Soviet Union showed strains, but hope remained for collective security under the United Nations.

The Policy of Containment The growing split between the Soviet Union and the United States led President Truman to develop a policy of containment to block communist expansion. A cornerstone of Truman's doctrine was providing financial aid to nations fighting communism and economic aid to rebuild Europe. A crisis over Berlin led to the creation of NATO, a political alliance, to block Soviet expansion in Europe.

Cold War Liberalism Truman was unable to enlarge the New Deal, but he did maintain a strong federal government. Truman faced strong opposition in Congress and his popularity dropped. Still Truman won reelection in 1948 and proclaimed his "Fair Deal," though foreign affairs soon occupied most of his attention.

The Cold War at Home Often under the call for national security, the fear of communism spread throughout the nation in the late forties and early fifties. The government aided by the media led the anti-Communist crusade that profoundly affected many individuals and the American public. The Red Scare fostered loyalty programs for federal government employees, congressional investigations into Hollywood that led to blacklists, and highly publicized spy trials of government officials and scientists. The peak was reached when Senator Joseph McCarthy launched his anti-Communist campaign. His failure diffused the fears of many Americans.

Cold War Culture The growing cold war abroad and the Red Scare at home created anxiety and fear among many Americans, as did fears of a declining economy. These emotions found expression in popular culture, especially movies. Strengthened by prosperity, family life supplied needed security and stability for many Americans. The increasing rates of child birth and consumer spending led many women to work though staying home was promoted by numerous sources. Defense spending most affected the West, especially California where older and newer communities arose as part of the growing military–industrial partnership. At the same time, patriotism surged and was evident in the "Zeal for Democracy" campaign and the stress on the American way of life, though some protested against the uneven application of democracy.

End of the Democratic Era Events in Asia in the late 1940s and early fifties heightened cold war tensions. The communist victory in China and the Korean War led to a steep decline in Truman's popularity. Running as a peace candidate, Dwight D. Eisenhower won the 1952 presidential election.

REVIEW QUESTIONS

1. Discuss the origins of the Cold War and the sources of growing tensions between the United States and the Soviet Union at the close of World War II.

2. Describe the basic elements of President Harry Truman's policy of containment. How did the threat of atomic warfare affect this policy?

3. Compare the presidencies of Franklin D. Roosevelt and Harry S Truman, both Democrats.

4. Describe the impact of McCarthyism on American political life. How did the anti-Communist campaigns affect the media? What were the sources of Senator Joseph McCarthy's popularity? What brought about his downfall?

5. How did the Cold War affect American culture?

6. Discuss the role of the United States in Korea in the decade after World War II. How did the Korean War affect the 1952 presidential election?

7. Why did Dwight D. Eisenhower win the 1952 presidential election?

KEY TERMS

RECOMMENDED READING

Mark S. Byrnes, *The Truman Years, 1945–1953* (2000). A concise history of the
Truman administration and its role at the moment when the United States
became the dominant economic power in the world. Byrnes covers this
transformation with particular attention to the way the president helped
shape a view of the world that presented the United States and the Soviet
Union as permanent enemies in a struggle for domination. Includes a set
of twenty-one key documents and a detailed chronology of events.

Warren I. Cohen, *America in the Age of Soviet Power, 1945–1991* (1993). A highly
readable volume in the "Cambridge History of American Foreign Relations" series, this study examines the origins of the Cold War in policies
ending World War II, including the breakup of the colonial empires, and
concludes with the collapse of communism in the Soviet Union in 1991.

Kevin J. Fernlund, ed., *The Cold War American West, 1945–1989* (1998). Ten
essays illustrating the impact of the Cold War on the region of the United
States that housed the bulk of military bases, airfields, nucelar testing
grounds, and toxic waste dumps. Presenting a variety of interpretations,
the contributors ask a common question: Was the West transformed or
deformed by the policies of the growing national security state?

John Fousek, *To Lead the Free World: American Nationalism and the Cultural Roots
of the Cold War* (2000). Examines the "public culture" of the Cold War
through an innovative study of various responses to the official doctrines
and declarations of the Truman administration. Fousek pays special
attention to the publications of major civil rights organizations and the
two largest labor unions of the period and argues that "a broad public
consensus" supported Truman's nationalistic foreign policy.

Richard M. Fried, *The Russians Are Coming! The Russians Are Coming!: Pageantry and Patriotism in Cold-War America* (1998). Examines, through vivid example, the creation of the fear of communism and its translation into patriotic zeal. Fried takes as his thesis that rallying the public to "fight" the Cold War required as much organization and energy as mobilizing Americans to defend the home front during World War II.

Margot A. Henriksen, *Dr. Strangelove's America: Society and Culture in the Atomic Age* (1997). Argues in a lively fashion that the atomic bomb played the "central, defining role" in American culture and society from 1945 into the early 1980s. Henriksen culls evidence from a wide range of sources, including novels, movies, TV programs, and rock 'n' roll songs.

George Lipsitz, *A Rainbow at Midnight: Labor and Culture in the 1940s* (1994). A vivid account of economic and cultural hopes, uneasiness, and disappointments after World War II. Lipsitz shows how struggles for economic democracy were defeated and how popular culture—for example, country and western music and rock 'n' roll, as well as stock car racing and the roller derby—arose in blue-collar communities.

Elaine Tyler May, *Homeward Bound: American Families in the Cold War Era* (1988). A lively account of the effects on family life and women's roles of the national mood of "containment." May argues that government policy became part of a popular culture that solidified the Cold War era's "feminine mystique."

David G. McCullough, *Truman* (1992). A heroic rendition of Truman's personal life and political career. Through personal correspondence and other documents, McCullough details Truman's view of himself and the generally favorable view of him held by supporters of Cold War liberalism.

Patrick McGilligan and Paul Buhle, *Tender Comrades: A Backstory of the Hollywood Blacklist* (1997). A collection of interviews with thirty-five victims of the Hollywood Blacklist, including some of the most important writers, directors, and film stars. The collection is especially valuable for its detailing of film production during the years of World War II and afterward, including the creation of *film noir*.

Joanne Meyerowitz, ed., *Not June Cleaver: Women and Gender in Postwar America, 1945–1960* (1994). A collection of essays that refute the common stereotype of women as homebound during the postwar era.

Stanley Weintraub, *MacArthur's War: Korea and the Undoing of an American Hero* (2000). Tells the story of the downfall of the commander of U.S. forces in the Far East, who was "senior to everyone but God" in the military services. The author additionally offers a detailed description of the horror and ruin accompanying the brutal ground war in Korea.

We were trapped. And I thought, Okay,
so I'm going to die here, in school . . .
Even the adults, the school officials, were panicked,
feeling like there was no protection . . .
[A] gentleman, who I believed to be the police chief,
said . . . "I'll get them out." And we were taken
to the basement of this place.

— *Melba Patillo Beals, from*
Voices of Freedom

MISSILE EQUIPMENT
MARIEL PORT FACILITY
4 NOVEMBER 1962

4 MISSILE TRANSPORTERS

OXIDIZER TR

OXIDIZER TRAILE

WE INSIST!
MAX ROACH'S – FREEDOM NOW SUITE
8002

FEATURING ABBEY LINCOLN
COLEMAN HAWKINS, OLATUNJI   CANDID

Elvis Presley swivels onto his toes
while singing into a microphone
on stage with his band.

27

AMERICA AT MIDCENTURY
1952–1963

WHAT GOALS did Eisenhower have for his administration?

WHY DID the youth market expand so rapidly at midcentury?

WHAT PLACE did television have in mid-twentieth-century American culture?

ON WHAT grounds did the United States intervene in Central America?

HOW DID Kennedy respond to the Cuban Revolution?

AMERICAN COMMUNITIES
Popular Music in Memphis

THE NINETEEN-YEAR-OLD SINGER WAS PEERING NERVOUSLY OUT OVER the large crowd. He knew that people had come to Overton Park's outdoor amphitheater that hot, sticky July day in 1954 to hear the headliner, country music star Slim Whitman. Sun Records, a local Memphis label, had just released the teenager's first record, and it had begun to receive some airplay on local radio. But the singer and his two bandmates had never played in a setting even remotely as large as this one. And their music defied categories: it wasn't black and it wasn't white; it wasn't pop and it wasn't country. But when the singer launched into his version of a black blues song called "That's All Right," the crowd went wild. "I came offstage," the singer later recalled, "and my manager told me that they was hollering because I was wiggling my legs. I went back out for an encore, and I did a little more, and the more I did, the wilder they went." Elvis Presley had arrived.

Elvis combined a hard-driving, rhythmic approach to blues and country music with a riveting performance style, inventing the new music known as rock 'n' roll. An unprecedented cultural phenomenon, rock 'n' roll was a music made largely for and by teenagers. In communities all over America, rock 'n' roll brought teens together around jukeboxes, at sock hops, in cars, and at private parties. It demonstrated the enormous consumer power of American teens. Rock 'n' roll also embodied a postwar trend accelerating the integration of white and black music. This cultural integration prefigured the social and political integration won by the civil rights movement.

Located halfway between St. Louis and New Orleans on the Mississippi River, Memphis had become a thriving commercial city by the 1850s, with an economy centered on the lucrative cotton trade of the surrounding delta region. It grew rapidly in the post–Civil War years, attracting a polyglot population of white businessmen and planters, poor rural white and black people, and German and Irish immigrants. By the early twentieth century Memphis also boasted a remarkable diversity of popular theater and music, including a large opera house, numerous brass bands, vaudeville and burlesque, minstrel shows, jug bands, and blues clubs.

Like most other American cities, Memphis enjoyed healthy growth during World War II, with lumber mills, furniture factories, and chemical manufacturing supplementing the cotton market as sources of jobs and prosperity. And like the rest of the South, Memphis was a legally segregated city; white and black residents lived, went to school, and worked apart. Class differences among white people were important as well. Like thousands of other poor rural white people in these years, Elvis Presley had moved from Mississippi to Memphis in 1949, where his father found work in a munitions plant. The Presleys were poor enough to qualify for

an apartment in Lauderdale Courts, a Memphis public housing project. To James Conaway, who grew up in an all-white, middle-class East Memphis neighborhood, people like the Presleys were "white trash." Negroes, he recalled, were "not necessarily below the rank of a country boy like Elvis, but of another universe, and yet there was more affection for them than for some whites."

Gloria Wade-Gayles, who lived in the all-black Foote Homes housing project, vividly remembered that her family and neighbors "had no illusion about their lack of power, but they believed in their strength." For them, strength grew from total immersion in a black community that included ministers, teachers, insurance men, morticians, barbers, and entertainers. "Surviving meant being black, and being black meant believing in our humanity, and retaining it, in a world that denied we had it in the first place."

Yet in the cultural realm, class and racial barriers could be challenged. Elvis Presley grew up a dreamy, shy boy, who turned to music for emotional release and spiritual expression. He soaked up the wide range of music styles available in Memphis. The Assembly of God Church his family attended featured a renowned hundred-voice choir. Elvis and his friends went to marathon all-night "gospel singings" at Ellis Auditorium, where they enjoyed the tight harmonies and emotional style of white gospel quartets.

Elvis also drew from the sounds he heard on Beale Street, the main black thoroughfare of Memphis and one of the nation's most influential centers of African American music. In the postwar years, local black rhythm and blues artists like B. B. King, Junior Parker, and Muddy Waters attracted legions of black and white fans with their emotional power and exciting showmanship. At the Handy Theater on Beale Street, the teenaged Elvis Presley, like thousands of other white young people, heard black performers at the "Midnight Rambles"—late shows for white people only. Elvis himself performed along with black contestants in amateur shows at Beale Street's Palace Theater. Nat D. Williams, a prominent black Memphis disc jockey and music promoter, recalled how black audiences responded to Elvis's unique style. "He had a way of singing the blues that was distinctive. He could sing 'em not necessarily like a Negro, but he didn't sing 'em altogether like a typical white musician. . . . Always he had that certain humanness about him that Negroes like to put in their songs."

The expansion of the broadcasting and recording industries in the postwar years also contributed to the weakening of racial barriers in the musical realm. Two Memphis radio stations featured the hard-driving rhythm and blues music that was beginning to attract a strong following among young white listeners. These Memphis stations also featured spirituals by African American artists such as Mahalia Jackson and Clara Ward.

Elvis himself understood his debt to black music and black performers. "The colored folks," he told an interviewer in 1956, "been singing and playing it just like I'm doing now, man, for more years than I know. They played it like that in the shanties and in their juke joints and nobody paid it no mind until I goosed it up. I got it from them."

Dissatisfied with the cloying pop music of the day, white teenagers across the nation were increasingly turning to the rhythmic drive and emotional intensity of black rhythm and blues. They quickly adopted rock 'n' roll (the term had long been an African American slang expression for dancing and sexual intercourse) as their music. But it was more than just music: it was also an attitude, a celebration of being young, and a sense of having something that adult authority could not understand or control.

When Sun Records sold Presley's contract to RCA Records in 1956, Elvis became an international star. Records like "Heartbreak Hotel," "Don't Be Cruel," and "Jailhouse Rock" shot to the top of the charts and blurred the old boundaries between pop, country, and rhythm and blues. By helping to accustom white teenagers to the style and sound of black artists, Elvis helped establish rock 'n' roll as an interracial phenomenon. Institutional racism would continue to plague the music business—many black artists were routinely cheated out of royalties and severely underpaid—but the music of postwar Memphis at least pointed the way toward the exciting cultural possibilities that could emerge from breaking down the barriers of race. It also gave postwar American teenagers a newfound sense of community.

AMERICAN SOCIETY AT MIDCENTURY

THE EISENHOWER PRESIDENCY

Dwight D. Eisenhower's landslide election victory in 1952 set the stage for the first full two-term Republican presidency since that of Ulysses S. Grant. During his eight-year administration, intellectuals and liberals found it easy to satirize and attack Eisenhower (Ike) for his blandness, his frequent verbal gaffes, his vagueness, and his often contradictory pronouncements. But for Eisenhower, politics demanded conciliation and compromise more than devotion to principle and truth. "The public loves Ike," observed one journalist in 1959. "The less he does the more they love him. That, probably, is the secret. Here is a man who doesn't rock the boat."

In practice, this meant that Eisenhower wanted to run government in a businesslike manner while letting the states and corporate interests guide domestic policy and the economy. Eisenhower appointed nine businessmen to his first Cabinet. Former General Motors (GM) chief Charles Wilson served as secretary of defense and epitomized the administration's economic views with his famous aphorism "What's good for General Motors' business is good for America." In his appointments to the Federal Trade Commission, the Federal Communications Commission, and the Federal Power Commission, Eisenhower favored men congenial to the corporate interests they were charged with regulating. Eisenhower also secured passage in 1953 of the Submerged Lands Act, which transferred $40 billion worth of disputed offshore oil lands from the federal government to the Gulf states. This ensured a greater role for the states and private companies in the oil business and accelerated a trend toward the destruction of the natural environment.

At the same time, Eisenhower accepted the New Deal legacy of greater federal responsibility for social welfare. He rejected calls from conservative Republicans to dismantle the Social Security system. His administration agreed to a modest expansion of Social Security and unemployment insurance and small increases in the minimum wage. Ike also created the Department of Health, Education, and Welfare, appointing Oveta Culp Hobby as the second woman to hold a cabinet post. In agriculture Eisenhower continued the policy of parity payments designed to sustain farm prices. Between 1952 and 1960 federal spending on agriculture jumped from about $1 billion to $7 billion.

WHAT GOALS did Eisenhower have for his administration?

Presidential contender Dwight D. Eisenhower hosts a group of Republican National Committee women at his campaign headquarters in 1952. Ike's status as America's biggest war hero, along with his genial public persona, made him an extremely popular candidate with voters across party lines.

© Bettmann/CORBIS (BE036973)

IMAGE KEY

for pages 736–737

After the Korean War ended in 1953, and again in 1958, when the unemployment rate reached 7.5 percent, the economy went into a recession. The administration refused to cut taxes or increase spending to stimulate growth. Eisenhower feared starting an inflationary spiral more than he worried about unemployment or poverty. By the time he left office, Eisenhower could proudly point out that real wages for an average family had risen 20 percent during his term. Combined with low inflation and steady, if modest, growth, the Eisenhower years meant greater prosperity for most Americans.

SUBSIDIZING PROSPERITY

During the Eisenhower years the federal government played a crucial role in subsidizing programs that helped millions of Americans achieve middle-class status. The Federal Housing Administration (FHA), established in 1934, put the full faith and credit of the federal government behind residential mortgages and attracted new private capital into home building. A typical FHA mortgage required less than 10 percent for a down payment and spread low-interest monthly payments over thirty years.

Yet FHA policies also had long-range drawbacks. FHA insurance went overwhelmingly to new residential developments, usually on the fringes of urban areas, hastening the decline of older, inner-city neighborhoods. It was FHA policy to favor the construction of single-family projects while discouraging multiunit housing, to refuse loans for the repair of older structures and rental units, and to require for any loan guarantee an "unbiased professional estimate" rating the property, the prospective borrower, and the neighborhood. In practice, these estimates resulted in blatant discrimination against communities that were racially mixed. The FHA's Underwriting Manual bluntly warned: "If a neighborhood is to retain stability, it is necessary that properties shall continue to be occupied by the same social and racial classes." FHA policies in effect inscribed the racial and income segregation of suburbia in public policy.

The revolution in American life wrought by the 1944 Servicemen's Readjustment Act, known as the GI Bill of Rights, extended beyond its impact on higher education (see Chapter 26). In addition to educational grants, the act provided returning veterans with low-interest mortgages and business loans, thus subsidizing the growth of the suburbs as well as the postwar expansion of higher education. Through 1956, nearly 10 million veterans received tuition and training benefits under the act. Veteran's Administration–insured loans totaled more than $50 billion by 1962, providing assistance to millions of former GIs who started businesses.

The **Federal Highway Act of 1956** gave another key boost to postwar growth, especially in the suburbs. By 1972 the program had become the single largest public works program in American history; 41,000 miles of highway were built at a cost of $76 billion. Federal subsidy of the interstate highway system stimulated both the automobile industry and suburb building, but it also accelerated the decline of American mass transit and older cities. By 1970, the nation possessed the world's best roads and one of its worst public transportation systems.

The shadow of the cold war prompted the federal government to take new initiatives in aid for education. After the Soviet Union launched its first Sputnik satellite in the fall of 1957, American officials worried that the country might be lagging behind the Soviets in training scientists and engineers. The **National Defense Education Act (NDEA)** of 1958 allocated $280 million in grants for state universities to upgrade their science facilities. The NDEA also created $300 million in low-interest loans for college students, who had to repay only half the amount if they went on to teach in elementary or secondary school after graduation. In addition, the NDEA provided fellowship support for graduate students planning to go into college and university teaching. The NDEA represented a new consensus on the importance of high-quality education to the national interest.

SUBURBAN LIFE

The suburban boom strengthened the domestic ideal of the nuclear family as the model for American life. Suburban domesticity was usually presented as women's only path to happiness and fulfillment. This cultural image often masked a stifling existence defined by housework, child care, and boredom. In the late 1950s,

Federal Highway Act of 1956 Measure that provided federal funding to build a nationwide system of interstate and defense highways.

National Defense Education Act (NDEA) 1958 act that allocated $280 million in grants for state universities to upgrade their science facilities, created $300 million in low-interest loans for college students, and provided fellowship support for graduate students planning to go into college and university teaching.

QUICK REVIEW

Growth of Higher Education

- 1950: 2.6 million students enrolled in college.
- 1960: 3.2 million students enrolled in college.
- 1970: 7.5 million students enrolled in college.

This photo, which appeared in a 1950 issue of *Life* magazine, posed a family of pioneer suburbanites in front of their Levittown, New York, home. The prefabricated house was built in 1948.

Bernard Hoffman/*Life Magazine*/© 1950 TimePix (Set #31949)

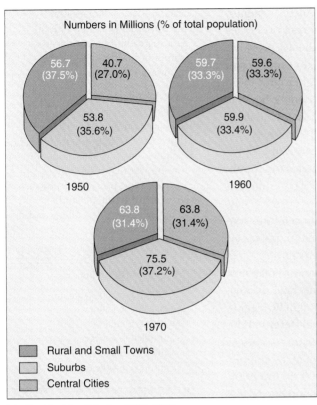

Numbers in Millions (% of total population)

56.7 (37.5%) 40.7 (27.0%) 53.8 (35.6%)

1950

59.7 (33.3%) 59.6 (33.3%) 59.9 (33.4%)

1960

63.8 (31.4%) 63.8 (31.4%) 75.5 (37.2%)

1970

■ Rural and Small Towns
□ Suburbs
□ Central Cities

The Growth of the Suburbs, 1950–1970
Suburban growth, at the expense of older inner cities, was one of the key social trends in the twenty-five years following World War II. By 1970, more Americans lived in suburbs than in either inner cities or rural areas.

Source: Adapted from U.S. Bureau of the Census, *Current Censuses, 1930–1970* (Washington, DC: U.S. Government Printing Office, 1975).

29-2
The Feminist Mystique (1963)

Betty Friedan, a wife, mother, and journalist, began a systematic survey of her Smith College classmates. She found "a strange discrepancy between the reality of our lives as women and the image to which we were trying to conform." Friedan expanded her research and in 1963 published *The Feminine Mystique*, a landmark book that articulated the frustrations of suburban women and helped to launch a revived feminist movement.

Contemporary journalists, novelists, and social scientists contributed to the popular image of suburban life as essentially dull, conformist, and peopled exclusively by the educated middle class, yet many new suburbs had a distinctively blue-collar cast. Milpitas, California, for example, grew up around a Ford auto plant about fifty miles outside San Jose. Its residents were blue-collar assembly-line workers and their families, rather than salaried, college-educated, white-collar employees. Self-segregation and zoning ordinances gave some new suburbs distinctively Italian, Jewish, or Irish ethnic identities, similar to older urban neighborhoods. For millions of new suburbanites, architectural and psychological conformity was an acceptable price to pay for the comforts of home ownership, a small plot of land, and a sense of security and status.

ORGANIZED LABOR AND THE AFL-CIO

By the mid-1950s American trade unions reached a historic high point in their penetration of the labor market, reflecting the enormous gains made during the organizing drives in core mass-production industries during the New Deal and World War II. Whereas only one in eight nonagricultural workers were union members on the eve of the Great Depression, twenty-five years later the figure stood at one in three. Union influence in political life, especially within the Democratic Party, had also increased. Yet the Republican sweep to power in 1952 meant that for the first time in a generation organized labor was without an ally in the White House. New leaders in the nation's two major labor organizations, the American Federation of Labor (dominated by old-line construction and craft unions) and the Congress of Industrial Organizations (centered around unions in mass-production industry) now pushed for a merger of the two rival groups as a way to protect and build on the movement's recent gains.

George Meany, the gruff, cigar-chomping head of the AFL, seemed the epitome of the modern labor boss. Originally a plumber, he had worked his way through the AFL bureaucracy and had played a leading role on the National War Labor Board during World War II. An outspoken anti-Communist, Meany had pushed the AFL closer to the Democratic Party, and he took pride in never having been on a strike or a picket line. Unions, he believed, must focus on improving the economic well-being of their members. Meany's counterpart in the CIO was Walter Reuther, originally a tool-and-die maker in the auto shops of Detroit. Reuther had come to prominence as a leader of the United Automobile Workers during the tumultuous organizing drives of the 1930s and 1940s. Although he had moved away from his early socialist leanings, Reuther believed strongly that American unions ought to stand for something beyond the bread-and-butter needs of their members. His support of a broader social vision, including racial equality, aggressive union organizing, and expansion of the welfare state, reflected the more militant tradition of CIO unions. Despite their differences, both Meany and Reuther believed a merger of their two organizations offered the best strategy for the labor movement. In 1955 the newly combined AFL-CIO brought some 12.5 million union members under one banner, with Meany as president and Reuther as director of the Industrial Union Department.

The merger marked the apex of trade union membership, and after 1955 its share of the labor market began a slow and steady decline. To be sure, union membership helped bring the trappings of middle-class prosperity to millions of workers and their families: home ownership, higher education for children, travel, and comfortable retirement. But the AFL-CIO showed little commitment to bringing unorganized workers into the fold. Scandals involving union corruption and racketeering hurt the labor movement's public image. In 1957 the AFL-CIO expelled its largest single affiliate, the International Brotherhood of Teamsters, because of its close ties to organized crime. In 1959, after highly publicized hearings into union corruption, Congress passed the **Landrum-Griffin Act**, which widened government control over union affairs and further restricted union use of picketing and secondary boycotts during strikes.

THE EXPANSION OF HIGHER EDUCATION

American higher education experienced rapid growth after the war. The number of students enrolled in colleges and universities climbed from 2.6 million in 1950 to 3.2 million in 1960. It then more than doubled—to 7.5 million—by 1970, as the baby boom generation came of age.

Several factors contributed to this explosion. A variety of new federal programs, including the GI Bill and the National Defense Education Act, helped subsidize college education for millions of new students. Government spending on research and development in universities, especially for defense-related projects, promoted a postwar shift to graduate education and faculty research and away from traditional undergraduate teaching.

Colleges and universities by and large accepted the values of postwar corporate culture. By the mid-1950s, 20 percent of all college graduates majored in business or other commercial fields. The college degree became a requirement for a whole range of expanding white-collar occupations in banking, insurance, real estate, advertising and marketing, and other corporate enterprises. Universities themselves were increasingly run like businesses, with administrators adopting the language of input-output, cost effectiveness, and quality control.

YOUTH CULTURE

THE YOUTH MARKET

The term "teenager," describing someone between thirteen and nineteen, entered standard usage only at the end of World War II. Birthrates had accelerated gradually during the late 1930s and more rapidly during the war years. The children born in those years had by the late 1950s come of age in a society that, compared with that of their parents and the rest of the world, was uniquely affluent. Together, the demographic growth of teens and the postwar economic expansion created a burgeoning youth market. In 1959, *Life* summarized the new power of the youth market. "Counting only what is spent to satisfy their special teenage demands," the magazine reported, "the youngsters and their parents will shell out about $10 billion this year, a billion more than the total sales of GM."

The increasing uniformity of public school education also contributed to the public recognition of the special status of teenagers. In 1900, about one of

Landrum-Griffin Act 1959 act that widened government control over union affairs and further restricted union use of picketing and secondary boycotts during strikes.

WHY DID the youth market expand so rapidly at midcentury?

every eight teenagers was in school; by the 1950s, the figure was six out of eight. Psychologists wrote guidebooks for parents, two prominent examples being Dorothy Baruch's *How to Live with Your Teenager* (1953) and Paul Landis's *Understanding Teenagers* (1955). Traditional sources of adult authority and socialization—the marketplace, schools, child-rearing manuals, the mass media—all reinforced the notion of teenagers as a special community, united by age, rank, and status.

"HAIL! HAIL! ROCK 'N' ROLL!"

In the recording industry, small independent record labels led the way in aggressively recording African American rhythm and blues artists. Atlantic Records, in New York, developed the most influential galaxy of artists, including Ray Charles, Ruth Brown, the Drifters, Joe Turner, LaVerne Baker, and the Clovers. Chess, in Chicago, had the blues-based, singer-songwriter-guitarists Chuck Berry and Bo Diddley, and the "doo-wop" group the Moonglows. In New Orleans, Imperial had the veteran pianist-singer Fats Domino, while Specialty unleashed the outrageous Little Richard on the world. On radio, over jukeboxes, and in record stores, all of these African American artists "crossed over," adding millions of white teenagers to their solid base of black fans.

The older, more established record companies, such as RCA, Decca, MGM, and Capitol, had largely ignored black music. Their response to the new trend was to offer slick, toned-down "cover" versions by white pop singers of rhythm and blues originals. While African American artists began to enjoy newfound mass acceptance, there were limits to how closely white kids could identify with black performers. Also, because of the superior promotional power of the major companies and the institutional racism in the music business, white cover versions almost always outsold the black originals.

The stage was thus set for the arrival of white rock 'n' roll artists who could exploit the new sounds and styles. Elvis Presley burst upon the national scene and created as big a cultural convulsion as anyone in this century. With his carefully pomaded hair, flashy outfits, and sexy sneer, Elvis was a big hit with young female fans and a nightmare for their parents. Elvis reinvented American popular music. As a symbol of rebellious youth and the embodiment of youthful sexuality, Elvis revitalized American popular culture.

This photo of Elvis Presley singing at a 1956 state fair in Memphis captured his dramatic stage presence. Performing with only a trio, his sound was spare but hard driving. Both the music and Presley's stage moves owed a great deal to African American rhythm and blues artists.

Getty Images, Inc. (C422)

ALMOST GROWN

Teenage consumers remade the landscape of popular music into their own turf. The dollar value of annual record sales nearly tripled between 1954 and 1959, from $213 million to $603 million. New magazines aimed exclusively at teens flourished. Paradoxically, behavior patterns among white middle-class teenagers in the 1950s and early 1960s exhibited a new kind of youth orientation and at the same time a more pronounced identification with adults.

Postwar affluence multiplied the number of two-car families, making it easier for sixteen-year-olds to win driving privileges formerly reserved for eighteen-year-olds. Girls began dating, wearing brassieres and nylon stockings, and using cosmetics at an earlier age than before—twelve or thirteen rather than fifteen or sixteen. Several factors contributed to this trend, including a continuing decline in the age of menarche (first menstruation), the sharp drop in the age of marriage after World War II, and the precocious social climate of junior high schools (institutions that became widespread only after 1945). By the late 1950s, eighteen had become the most common age at which American females married.

Many observers of the emerging youth culture were disturbed by an apparent decline in parental control over teens. A psychiatrist writing in the *New York Times* described rock 'n' roll as "a cannibalistic and tribalistic kind of a music" and "a communicable disease." Many clergymen and church leaders declared it "the devil's music." Much of the opposition to rock 'n' roll, particularly in the South, played on long-standing racist fears that white females might be attracted to black music and black performers. The undercurrent beneath all this opposition was a deep anxiety over the more open expression of sexual feelings by both performers and audiences.

Paralleling the rise of rock 'n' roll was a growing concern with an alleged increase in juvenile delinquency. Gang fights, drug and alcohol abuse, car theft, and sexual offenses received the most attention. The U.S. Senate established a special subcommittee on juvenile delinquency. Highly publicized hearings in 1955 and 1956 convinced much of the public that youthful criminals were terrorizing the country. Although crime statistics do suggest an increase in juvenile crime during the 1950s, particularly in the suburbs, the public perception of the severity of the problem was surely exaggerated.

MASS CULTURE AND ITS DISCONTENTS

TELEVISION: TUBE OF PLENTY

No mass medium ever achieved such power and popularity as rapidly as television. The three main television networks—NBC, CBS, ABC—grew directly from radio organizations. Nearly all TV stations were affiliated with one or more of the networks; only a handful of independent stations could be found around the country.

The television business, like radio, was based on the selling of time to advertisers who wanted to reach the mass audiences tuning into shows. Radio had offered entire shows produced by and for single sponsors, usually advertisers who wanted a close identification between their product and a star. Sponsors now bought scattered time slots for spot advertisements rather than bankrolling an entire show.

Ad agencies switched their creative energy to producing slick thirty-second commercials rather than entertainment programs. A shift from broadcasting live shows to filming them opened up lucrative opportunities for reruns and foreign export. The total net revenue of the TV networks and their affiliated stations in 1947 was about $2 million; by 1957 it was nearly $1 billion.

WHAT PLACE did television have in mid-twentieth-century American culture?

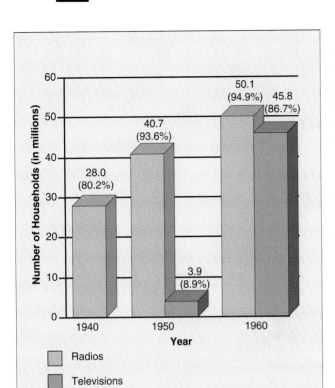

Radio and Television Ownership, 1940–1960

By 1960 nearly 90 percent of American households owned at least one television set, as TV replaced radio as the nation's dominant mass medium of entertainment. Radio ownership rose as well, but Americans increasingly listened to radio as an accompaniment to other activities, such as driving.

Set largely among urban ethnic families, early shows like *I Remember Mama, The Goldbergs, The Life of Riley, Life with Luigi,* and *The Honeymooners* often featured working-class families struggling with the dilemmas posed by a consumer society. By the late 1950s all the urban ethnic comedy shows were off the air. A new breed of situation comedies presented nonethnic white, affluent, and insular suburban middle-class families. Shows like *Father Knows Best, Leave It to Beaver, The Adventures of Ozzie and Harriet,* and *The Donna Reed Show* epitomized the ideal suburban American family of the day. Their plots focused on genial crises, usually brought on by children's mischief and resolved by kindly fathers. In retrospect, what is most striking about these shows is what is absent—politics, social issues, cities, white ethnic groups, African Americans, and Latinos were virtually unrepresented.

TELEVISION AND POLITICS

As in Hollywood, the Cold War chill severely restricted the range of political discussion on television. An important exception was Edward R. Murrow's *See It Now* on CBS—but that show was off the air by 1955. Television news did not come into its own until 1963, with the beginning of half-hour nightly network newscasts. Only then did television's extraordinary power to rivet the nation's attention during a crisis become clear.

Still, some of the ways that TV would alter the nation's political life emerged in the 1950s. Television made Democratic senator Estes Kefauver of Tennessee a national political figure through live coverage of his 1951 Senate investigation into organized crime. It also contributed to the political downfall of Senator Joseph McCarthy in 1954 by showing his cruel bullying tactics during Senate hearings into alleged subversive Communist influence in the army. The 1952 election also brought the first use of TV political advertising for presidential candidates. Ever since then, television image-making has been the single most important element in American electoral politics.

CULTURE CRITICS

The urge to denounce the mass media for degrading the quality of American life tended to unite radical and conservative critics. Thus, Marxist writer Dwight Macdonald sounded an old conservative warning when he described "a tepid, flaccid Middlebrow Culture that threatens to engulf everything in its spreading ooze."

Critics of mass culture argued that the audiences for the mass media were atomized, anonymous, and detached. These critics undoubtedly overestimated the power of the media. They ignored the preponderance of research suggesting that most people watched and responded to mass media in family, peer group, and other social settings. The critics also missed the genuine vitality and creative brilliance to be found within mass culture: African American music; the films of Nicholas Ray, Elia Kazan, and Howard Hawks; the experimental television of Ernie Kovacs; the satire of *Mad* magazine.

Some of the sharpest dissents from the cultural conformity of the day came from a group of writers known collectively as the Beats. Led by the novelist Jack Kerouac and the poet Allen Ginsberg, the Beats shared a distrust of the American virtues of progress, power, and material gain. The Beat sensibility celebrated spontaneity, friendship, jazz, open sexuality, drug use, and the outcasts of American society. Kerouac, born and raised in a working-class French Canadian family in Lowell, Massachusetts, coined the term "beat" in 1948. It meant for him a "weariness with all the forms of the modern industrial state"—conformity, militarism, blind faith in technological progress. Kerouac's 1957 novel *On the Road*, chronicling the tumultuous adventures of Kerouac's circle of friends as they traveled by car back and forth across America, became the Beat manifesto.

Beat writers received a largely antagonistic, even virulent reception from the literary establishment. But millions of young Americans read their work and became intrigued by their alternative visions, which foreshadowed the mass youth rebellion and counterculture to come in the 1960s.

The Cold War Continued

The "New Look" in Foreign Affairs

Secretary of State John Foster Dulles gave shape to the "new look" in American foreign policy in the 1950s. Dulles had been involved in diplomatic affairs since World War I. He brought a strong sense of righteousness to his job, an almost missionary belief in America's responsibility to preserve the "free world" from godless, immoral communism.

Dulles articulated a more assertive policy toward the Communist threat by calling not simply for containment but also for a "rollback." The key would be greater reliance on America's nuclear superiority.

The limits of a policy based on nuclear strategy became painfully clear when American leaders faced tense situations that offered no clear way to intervene without provoking full-scale war. In the fall of 1956 Hungarians revolted against their Soviet-dominated Communist rulers, staging a general strike and taking over the streets and factories in Budapest and other cities. The United States opened its gates to thousands of Hungarian refugees, but despite urgent requests, it refused to intervene when Soviet tanks and troops crushed the revolt.

The death of Josef Stalin in 1953 and the worldwide condemnation of his crimes, revealed by his successor, Nikita Khrushchev, in 1956, gave Eisenhower fresh hope for a new spirit of peaceful coexistence between the two superpowers. Khrushchev made a twelve-day trip to America in 1959, a psychological thaw in the Cold War.

In early 1960 Khrushchev called for another summit in Paris, to discuss German reunification and nuclear disarmament. Eisenhower, meanwhile, planned his own friendship tour of the Soviet Union. But in May 1960 the Soviets shot down an American U-2 spy plane gathering intelligence on Soviet military installations. The summit collapsed when Eisenhower refused Khrushchev's demands for an apology and an end to the spy flights. The U-2 incident demonstrated the limits of personal diplomacy in resolving the deep structural rivalry between the superpowers.

Eisenhower often provided a moderate voice on issues of defense spending and missile development. The Soviet Union's dramatic launch of Sputnik, the first space-orbiting satellite, in October 1957 upset many Americans' precarious sense of security. In particular, this demonstration of Soviet technological prowess raised fears about Russian ability to deploy intercontinental ballistic missiles (ICBMs) against American cities. Critics attacked the Eisenhower administration for failure to keep up with the enemy. Senator Stuart Symington (Democrat from Missouri) bluntly warned that, "Unless our defense policies are promptly changed, the Soviets will move from superiority to supremacy." In addition to huge increases in defense spending, some urged a massive program to build "fallout shelters" for the entire population in case of nuclear attack.

ON WHAT grounds did the United States intervene in Central America?

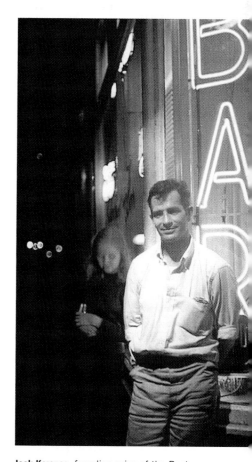

Jack Kerouac, founding voice of the Beat literary movement, in front of a neon-lit bar, ca. 1950. Kerouac's public readings, often to the accompaniment of live jazz music, created a performance atmosphere underlining the connections between his writing style and the rhythms and sensibility of contemporary jazz musicians.

Globe Photos, Inc. (YULSMAN)

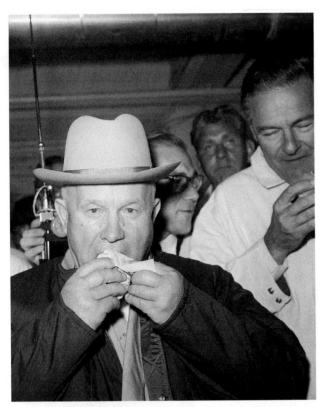

Soviet Premier Nikita Khrushchev enjoys a bite to eat during his tour of an Iowa farm in 1959. A colorful, earthy, and erratic man, Khrushchev loomed as the most visible human symbol of the USSR for Americans. On this trip he called for Soviet-American friendship, yet also boasted, "We will bury you."

© Bettmann/CORBIS (BE031798)

Eisenhower rejected these more radical responses. He knew from evidence provided by U-2 spy planes that the Soviet Union in fact trailed far behind the United States in ICBM development, but he kept this knowledge secret. Instead of panicking before Sputnik, he held to a doctrine of "sufficiency": maintaining enough military strength to survive any foreign attack and enough nuclear capability to deliver a massive counterattack. Yet, in Congress a bipartisan majority voted to increase the military budget by another $8 billion in 1958, thereby accelerating the arms race and expanding the defense sector of the economy.

COVERT ACTION

While the United States moderated its stance toward the Soviet Union and its Eastern European satellites, it hardened its policies in the third world. The need for anti-Communist tactics short of all-out military conflict pushed the Eisenhower administration to develop new means of fighting the Cold War. The premise rested on encouraging confusion or rivalry within the Communist sphere and on destabilizing or destroying anticapitalist movements around the world.

The Central Intelligence Agency, created in 1947, was perfectly designed for this task. For CIA director, Eisenhower named Allen Dulles, brother of the secretary of state and a former leader in the CIA's World War II precursor, the Office of Strategic Services. The CIA's mandate was to collect and analyze information, but it did much more under Dulles's command. Thousands of covert agents stationed all over the world carried out a wide range of political activities. Some agents arranged large, secret financial payments to friendly political parties or to foreign trade unions opposed to socialist policies.

INTERVENING AROUND THE WORLD

The Central Intelligence Agency produced a swift, major victory in Iran in 1953. The country's popular prime minister, Mohammed Mossadegh, had nationalized Britain's Anglo-Iranian Oil Company, and the State Department worried that this might set a precedent throughout the oil-rich Middle East. Kermit Roosevelt, CIA chief in Iran, organized and financed an opposition to Mossadegh within the Iranian army and on the streets of Teheran. This CIA-led movement forced Mossadegh out of office and replaced him with Riza Shah Pahlavi. The shah proved his loyalty to his American sponsors by renegotiating oil contracts so as to assure American companies 40 percent of Iran's oil concessions.

The most publicized CIA intervention of the Eisenhower years took place in Guatemala, where a fragile democracy had taken root in 1944. President Jácobo Arbenz Guzmán, elected in 1950, aggressively pursued land reform and encouraged the formation of trade unions. Arbenz also challenged the long-standing dominance of the American-based United Fruit Company by threatening to expropriate hundreds of thousands of acres that United Fruit was not cultivating. The company began intensive lobbying for U.S. intervention. United Fruit linked the land-reform program to the evils of international communism, and the CIA spent $7 million training antigovernment dissidents based in Honduras.

On June 14, 1954, a U.S.-sponsored military invasion began. Guatemalans appealed in vain to the United Nations for help. Meanwhile, President Eisenhower publicly denied any knowledge of CIA activities. The newly appointed military

QUICK REVIEW

U.S. Intervention Abroad

◆ U.S. policy shaped by Secretary of State John Foster Dulles.

◆ Eisenhower used the CIA to subvert democratically elected governments in Iran and Guatemala.

◆ The United States replaced France as the supporter of pro–Western Vietnamese in the south.

leader, Carlos Castillo Armas, was assassinated in 1957, and a decades-long civil war ensued between military factions and peasant guerrillas.

In Indochina, the United States provided France with massive military aid and CIA cooperation in its desperate struggle to maintain its colonial empire, fighting against the nationalist Vietminh movement led by Communist Ho Chi Minh. When Vietminh forces surrounded 25,000 French troops at Dien Bien Phu in March 1954, France pleaded with the United States to intervene directly. But Eisenhower, recalling the difficulties of the Korean conflict, rejected this call.

MAP EXPLORATION

To explore an interactive version of this map, go to **http://www.prenhall.com/faraghertlc/map27.1**

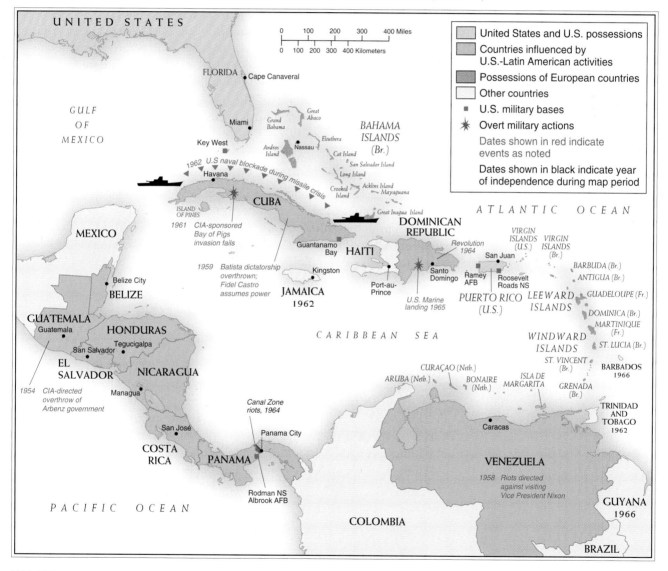

MAP 27-1

The U.S. in the Caribbean, 1948–1966   U.S. military intervention and economic presence grew steadily in the Caribbean following World War II. After 1960, opposition to the Cuban Revolution dominated U.S. Caribbean policies.

WHAT ARE the similarities and differences between American intervention in the Caribbean from 1948–1966 and intervention in this region earlier in the twentieth century?

28-1
Dwight D. Eisenhower,
Decision Not to Intervene
at Dien Bien Phu (1954)

At the same time, Eisenhower feared that the loss of one country to communism would inevitably lead to the loss of others. As he put it, "You have a row of dominoes set up, and you knock over the first one and what will happen to the last one is the certainty that it will go over quickly." According to this so-called domino theory, the "loss" of Vietnam would threaten other Southeast Asian nations, such as Laos, Thailand, the Philippines, and perhaps even India and Australia. After the French surrender at Dien Ben Phu, a conference in Geneva established a cease-fire and a temporary division of Vietnam along the 17th parallel into northern and southern sectors. The **Geneva Accord** called for reunification and national elections in 1956 but the United States, although it had attended the conference along with the Soviet Union and China, refused to sign the accord.

South Vietnamese leader Ngo Dinh Diem, a former Japanese collaborator and a Catholic in a country that was 90 percent Buddhist, quickly alienated many peasants with his corruption and repressive policies. Both Diem and Eisenhower refused to permit the 1956 elections stipulated in Geneva because they knew popular hero Ho Chi Minh would easily win. By 1959 Diem's harsh and unpopular government in Saigon faced a civil war; thousands of peasants had joined guerrilla forces determined to drive him out. Eisenhower's commitment of military advisers and economic aid to South Vietnam, based on Cold War assumptions, laid the foundation for the Vietnam War of the 1960s.

IKE'S WARNING: THE MILITARY–INDUSTRIAL COMPLEX

Throughout the 1950s small numbers of peace advocates in the United States had protested that the increasing reliance on nuclear weapons did not strengthen national security but rather threatened the entire planet with extinction. As he neared retirement, President Eisenhower came to share some of the protesters' anxiety and doubts about the arms race. He chose to devote his Farewell Address, delivered in January 1961, to warning the nation about the dangers of what he termed the "military–industrial complex." Its total influence, he cautioned, "economic, political, even spiritual—is felt in every city, every statehouse, every office of the federal government." The conjunction of a large military establishment and a large arms industry, Eisenhower noted, was new in American history. "The potential for the disastrous rise of misplaced power exists and will persist. We must never let the weight of this combination endanger our liberties or democratic processes."

The old soldier understood perhaps better than most the dangers of raw military force. Eisenhower's public posture of restraint and caution in foreign affairs accompanied an enormous expansion of American economic, diplomatic, and military strength. Yet the Eisenhower years also demonstrated the limits of power and intervention in a world that did not always conform to the simple dualistic assumptions of cold war ideology.

Geneva Accord Accord that called for reunification and national elections in Vietnam in 1956.

JOHN F. KENNEDY AND THE NEW FRONTIER

THE ELECTION OF 1960

■ ■ ■ ■ ■ ■ ■ ■ ■
HOW DID Kennedy respond
to the Cuban Revolution?
■ ■ ■ ■ ■ ■ ■ ■ ■

No one could have resembled Dwight Eisenhower less in personality, temperament, and public image than John Fitzgerald Kennedy (JFK). The handsome son of a prominent, wealthy Irish American diplomat, husband of a fashionable, trend-setting heiress, forty-two-year-old JFK embodied youth, excitement, and sophistication.

John F. Kennedy's political career began in Massachusetts, which elected him to the House in 1946 and then the Senate in 1952. Kennedy won the Democratic nomination for president after a bruising series of primaries in which he defeated party stalwarts Hubert Humphrey of Minnesota and Lyndon B. Johnson of Texas. Vice President Richard M. Nixon, the Republican nominee, was far better known than his younger opponent. The Kennedy campaign stressed its candidate's youth and his image as a war hero. During his World War II tour of duty in the Pacific, Kennedy had bravely rescued one of his crew after their PT boat had been sunk. Kennedy's supporters also pointed to his intellectual ability. JFK had won the Pulitzer Prize in 1957 for his book *Profiles in Courage*, which in fact had been written largely by his aides.

The election featured the first televised presidential debates. Nixon appeared nervous and the camera made him look unshaven. Kennedy, in contrast, benefited from a confident manner and telegenic good looks. Both candidates emphasized foreign policy. Nixon defended the Republican record and stressed his own maturity and experience. Kennedy hammered away at the alleged "missile gap" with the Soviet Union and promised more vigorous executive leadership.

Kennedy squeaked to victory in the closest election since 1884. He won by a little more than 100,000 votes out of nearly 69 million cast. Surrounding himself with prestigious Ivy League academics, Hollywood movie stars, and talented artists and writers, he imbued the presidency with an aura of celebrity. The new president's ringing inaugural address ("Ask not what your country can do for you—ask what you can do for your country") had special resonance for a whole generation of young Americans.

NEW FRONTIER LIBERALISM

Kennedy promised to revive the long-stalled liberal domestic agenda. His **New Frontier** advocated such liberal programs as a higher minimum wage, greater federal aid for education, increased Social Security benefits, medical care for the elderly, support for public housing, and various antipoverty measures. Yet the thin margin of his victory and the stubborn opposition of conservative Southern Democrats in Congress made it difficult to achieve these goals. Congress refused, for example, to enact the administration's attempt to extend Social Security and unemployment benefits to millions of uncovered workers.

Congress did approve a modest increase in the minimum wage (to $1.25 per hour), agreed to a less ambitious improvement in Social Security, and appropriated $5 billion for public housing. It also passed the Manpower Retraining Act, appropriating $435 million to train the unemployed. The Area Redevelopment Act provided federal funds for rural, depressed Appalachia. The Higher Education Act of 1963 offered aid to colleges for constructing buildings and upgrading libraries. One of the best publicized New Frontier programs was the Peace Corps, in which thousands of mostly young men and women traveled overseas for two-year stints in underdeveloped countries. As a force for change, the Peace Corps produced modest results, but it epitomized Kennedy's promise to provide opportunities for service for a new generation of idealistic young people.

Kennedy helped revive the issue of women's rights with his Presidential Commission on the Status of Women, led by Eleanor Roosevelt. One concrete legislative result, the **Equal Pay Act of 1963**, made it illegal for employers to pay men and women

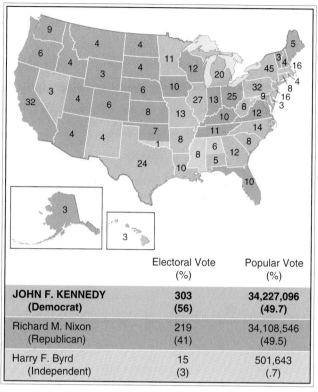

MAP EXPLORATION

To explore an interactive version of this map, go to
http://www.prenhall.com/faraghertlc/map27.2

	Electoral Vote (%)	Popular Vote (%)
JOHN F. KENNEDY (Democrat)	**303** **(56)**	**34,227,096** **(49.7)**
Richard M. Nixon (Republican)	219 (41)	34,108,546 (49.5)
Harry F. Byrd (Independent)	15 (3)	501,643 (.7)

MAP 27-2
The Election of 1960 Kennedy's popular vote margin over Nixon was only a little over 100,000, making this one of the closest elections in American history.

WHAT ROLE DID religion play in 1960 election?

29-1
John F. Kennedy, Inaugural Address (1961)

New Frontier John F. Kennedy's domestic and foreign policy initiatives, designed to reinvigorate sense of national purpose and energy.

Equal Pay Act of 1963 Act that made it illegal for employers to pay men and women different wages for the same job.

Presidential candidate John F. Kennedy smiles while listening to his opponent Richard M. Nixon during one of their televised debates in the 1960 election. Eighty-five million viewers watched at least one of the debates, which both reflected and increased the power of television in the electoral process.

AP/Wide World Photos

different wages for the same job. The work of the commission contributed to a new generation of women's rights activism.

Kennedy took a more aggressive stance on stimulating economic growth and creating new jobs than had Eisenhower. His administration pushed lower business taxes through Congress, even at the cost of a higher federal deficit. The Revenue Act of 1962 encouraged new investment and plant renovation by easing tax depreciation schedules for business. Kennedy also gained approval for lower U.S. tariffs as a way to increase foreign trade. To help keep inflation down, he intervened in the steel industry in 1961 and 1962, pressuring labor to keep its wage demands low and management to curb price increases.

Kennedy also increased the federal commitment to a wholly new realm of government spending: the space program. The **National Aeronautics and Space Administration (NASA)** had been established under Eisenhower in response to the Soviet success with Sputnik. In 1961, driven by the Cold War motivation of beating the Soviets to the moon and avoiding "another Sputnik," Kennedy won approval for a greatly expanded space program with the goal of landing an American on the moon by the end of the decade. In space, if not on earth, the New Frontier might actually be reached.

KENNEDY AND THE COLD WAR

During Kennedy's three years in office his approach to foreign policy shifted from aggressive containment to efforts at easing U.S.–Soviet tensions. Certainly when he first entered office, Kennedy and his chief aides considered it their main task to confront the Communist threat. To head the State Department Kennedy chose Dean Rusk, a conservative former assistant to Truman's secretary of state, Dean Acheson. Secretary of Defense Robert McNamara, a Republican and Ford Motor Company executive, was determined to streamline military procedures and weapons buying. Allen Dulles, Eisenhower's CIA director, remained at his post. These and other officials believed with Kennedy that Eisenhower had timidly accepted stalemate when the Cold War could have been won.

Between 1960 and 1962 defense appropriations increased by nearly a third, from $43 billion to $56 billion. JFK expanded Eisenhower's policy of covert operations, deploying the army's elite Special Forces as a supplement to CIA covert operations in counterinsurgency battles against third world guerrillas. The Special Forces reflected the president's desire as president to acquire greater flexibility, secrecy, and independence in the conduct of foreign policy.

The limits on the Special Forces and covert action became apparent in Southeast Asia. In Laos, where the United States had ignored the 1954 Geneva agreement and installed a friendly military regime, the CIA-backed government could not defeat Soviet-backed Pathet Lao guerrillas. The president had to arrange with the Soviets to neutralize Laos. In neighboring Vietnam, the situation proved more difficult. When Communist Vietcong guerrillas launched a civil war in South Vietnam against the U.S.–supported government in Saigon, Kennedy began sending hundreds of military advisers to support the rule of Ngo Dinh Diem. In May 1961, in response to North Vietnamese aid to the Vietcong, Kennedy ordered a covert action against Ho Chi Minh's government that included sabotage and intelligence gathering.

Kennedy's approach to Vietnam reflected an analysis of the situation in that country by two aides, General Maxwell Taylor and Walt Rostow, who saw it through

National Aeronautics and Space Administration (NASA) Federal agency created in 1958 to manage American space flights and exploration.

purely Cold War eyes, ignoring the inefficiency, corruption, and unpopularity of the Diem government. By 1963, with Diem's army unable to contain the Vietcong rebellion, Kennedy had sent nearly 16,000 support and combat troops to South Vietnam. By then, a wide spectrum of South Vietnamese society had joined the revolt against the hated Diem, including highly respected Buddhist monks and their students. Americans watched in horror as television news reports showed footage of Buddhists burning themselves to death on the streets of Saigon— the ultimate protest against Diem's repressive rule. The South Vietnamese army, bloated by U.S. aid and weakened by corruption, continued to disintegrate. In the fall of 1963, American military officers and CIA operatives stood aside with approval as a group of Vietnamese generals removed President Diem, killing him and his top advisers. It was the first of many coups that racked the South Vietnamese government over the next few years.

In Latin America, Kennedy looked for ways to forestall various revolutionary movements that were gaining ground. The erosion of peasant landholdings had accelerated rapidly after 1950. Millions of impoverished peasants were forced to relocate to already overcrowded cities. In 1961 Kennedy unveiled the **Alliance for Progress**, a ten-year, $100 billion plan to spur economic development in Latin America. Kennedy intended the program as a kind of Marshall Plan that would benefit the poor and middle classes of the continent. The alliance did help raise growth rates in Latin American economies, but the expansion in export crops and in consumption by the tiny upper class did little to aid the poor or encourage democracy. The United States hesitated to challenge the power of dictators and extreme conservatives who were staunch anti-Communist allies. Thus, the alliance soon degenerated into just another foreign aid program, incapable of generating genuine social change.

Astronaut John H. Glenn as he prepared for the first American manned space orbit of the earth. The space program of the early 1960s emphasized the technical training and courage of astronauts, consciously creating a set of public heroes as a way to ensure popular support and congressional funding.

NASA Headquarters

THE CUBAN REVOLUTION AND THE BAY OF PIGS

The direct impetus for the Alliance for Progress was the Cuban Revolution of 1959, which loomed over Latin America. The U.S. economic domination of Cuba that began with the Spanish American War (see Chapter 20) had continued through the 1950s. American-owned businesses controlled all of Cuba's oil production, 90 percent of its mines, and roughly half of its railroads and sugar and cattle industries. Havana, the island's capital, was an attractive tourist center for Americans, and U.S. crime syndicates shared control of the island's lucrative gambling, prostitution, and drug trade with dictator Fulgencio Batista. In the early 1950s, a peasant-based revolutionary movement, led by Fidel Castro, began gaining strength in the rural districts and mountains outside Havana.

On New Year's Day 1959, after years of guerrilla war, the rebels entered Havana and seized power amid great public rejoicing. Castro's land-reform program, involving the seizure of acreage from the tiny minority that controlled much of the fertile land, threatened to set an example for other Latin American countries. Although Castro had not joined the Cuban Communist Party, he turned to the Soviet Union after the United States withdrew economic aid. He began to sell sugar to the Soviets and soon nationalized American-owned oil companies and other enterprises. Eisenhower established an economic boycott of Cuba in 1960 and then severed diplomatic relations.

Kennedy inherited from Eisenhower plans for a U.S. invasion of Cuba, including the secret arming and training of Cuban exiles. The CIA drafted the invasion

Alliance for Progress   Program of economic aid to Latin America during the Kennedy administration.

plan, which was based on the assumption that a U.S.-led invasion would trigger a popular uprising of the Cuban people and bring down Castro. Kennedy went along with the plan, but at the last moment decided not to supply an Air Force cover for the operation. On April 17, 1961, a ragtag army of 1,400 counterrevolutionaries led by CIA operatives landed at the **Bay of Pigs**, on Cuba's south coast. Castro's efficient and loyal army easily subdued them.

The debacle revealed that the CIA, blinded by Cold War assumptions, had failed to understand the Cuban Revolution. There was no popular uprising against Castro. Instead, the invasion strengthened Castro's standing among the urban poor and peasants, already attracted by his programs of universal literacy and medical care. An embarrassed Kennedy reluctantly took the blame for the abortive invasion, and his administration was censured time and again by third world delegates to the United Nations. American liberals criticized Kennedy for plotting Castro's overthrow, while conservatives blamed him for not supporting the invasion. Despite the failure, Kennedy remained committed to getting rid of Castro and keeping up the economic boycott. The CIA continued to support anti-Castro operations and launched at least eight attempts to assassinate the Cuban leader.

THE MISSILE CRISIS

The aftermath of the Bay of Pigs led to the most serious confrontation of the Cold War: the **Cuban missile crisis** of October 1962. Frightened by U.S. belligerency, Castro asked Soviet premier Khrushchev for military help. Khrushchev responded in the summer of 1962 by shipping to Cuba a large amount of sophisticated weaponry, including intermediate-range nuclear missiles. In early October, U.S. reconnaissance planes found camouflaged missile silos dotting the island. Several Kennedy aides demanded an immediate bombing of Cuban bases, arguing that the missiles had decisively eroded the strategic global advantage the United States had previously enjoyed. Instead Kennedy went on national television on October 22. He announced the discovery of the missile sites, demanded the removal of all missiles, and ordered a strict naval blockade of all offensive military equipment shipped to Cuba. He also requested an emergency meeting of the UN Security Council and promised that any missiles launched from Cuba would bring "a full retaliatory response upon the Soviet Union." For a tense week, the American public wondered if nuclear Armageddon was imminent. Eyeball to eyeball, the two superpowers waited for each other to blink. On October 26 and 27 Khrushchev yielded, ordering twenty-five Soviet ships off their course to Cuba, thus avoiding a challenge to the American blockade. Khrushchev offered to remove all the missiles in return for a pledge from the United States not to invade Cuba. Khrushchev later added a demand for removal of American weapons from Turkey, as close to the Soviet Union as Cuba is to the United States. On November 20, after weeks of delicate negotiations, Kennedy publicly announced the withdrawal of Soviet missiles and bombers from Cuba. He also pledged to respect Cuban sovereignty and promised that U.S. forces would not invade the island.

The crisis had passed. The Soviets, determined not to be intimidated again, began the largest weapons buildup in their history. For his part Kennedy, perhaps chastened by this flirtation with nuclear disaster, made important gestures toward peaceful coexistence with the Soviets. In a June 1963 address at American University, Kennedy called for a rethinking of Cold War diplomacy. Shortly after, Washington and Moscow set up a "hot line"—a direct phone connection to permit instant communication during times of crisis. More substantial was the **Limited Nuclear Test-Ban Treaty**, signed in August 1963 by the United States, the Soviet Union, and Great Britain. The treaty prohibited above-ground, outer space, and under-

28-3
John F. Kennedy, Cuban Missile Address (1962)

Bay of Pigs Site in Cuba of an unsuccessful landing by fourteen hundred anti-Castro Cuban refugees in April 1961.

Cuban missile crisis Crisis between the Soviet Union and the United States over the placement of Soviet nuclear missiles in Cuba.

Limited Nuclear Test-Ban Treaty Treaty, signed by the United States, Britain, and the Soviet Union, outlawing nuclear testing in the atmosphere, in outer space, and under water.

Vice President Lyndon B. Johnson took the oath of office as president aboard *Air Force One* after the assassination of John F. Kennedy, November 22, 1963. Onlookers included the grief-stricken Jacqueline Kennedy (right) and Lady Bird Johnson (left). This haunting photo captured both the shock of Kennedy's assassination and the orderly succession of power that followed.

AP/Wide World Photos

water nuclear weapons tests. It eased international anxieties over radioactive fall-out. But underground testing continued to accelerate for years. The limited test ban was perhaps more symbolic than substantive, a psychological breakthrough in East–West relations after a particularly tense three years.

THE ASSASSINATION OF PRESIDENT KENNEDY

The assassination of John F. Kennedy in Dallas on November 22, 1963, sent the entire nation into shock and mourning. Tens of millions watched the televised spectacle of Kennedy's funeral, trying to make sense of the brutal murder. Although a special commission found the killing to be the work of a lone assassin, Lee Harvey Oswald, many Americans doubted this conclusion. Kennedy's death gave rise to a host of conspiracy theories, none of which seems provable. We will never know, of course, what Kennedy might have achieved in a second term. But in his 1,000 days as president, he demonstrated a capacity to change and grow in office. Having gone to the brink during the missile crisis, he managed to launch new initiatives toward peaceful coexistence. At the time of his death, relations between the United States and the Soviet Union were more amicable than at any other time since the end of World War II. Much of the domestic liberal agenda of the New Frontier would be finally implemented by Kennedy's successor, Lyndon B. Johnson, who dreamed of creating a **Great Society**.

29-3
Lyndon Johnson, The War on Poverty (1964)

CONCLUSION

America in 1963 still enjoyed the full flush of its postwar economic boom. To be sure, millions of Americans, particularly African Americans and Latinos, did not share in the good times, but millions of others had managed to achieve middle-class status since the early 1950s. An expanding economy, cheap energy, government subsidies, and a dominant position in the world marketplace had made the hallmarks of "the good life" available to more Americans than ever. The postwar "American dream" promised

Great Society   Theme of Lyndon Johnson's administration, focusing on poverty, education, and civil rights.

CHRONOLOGY

1950 David Riesman publishes *The Lonely Crowd*.

1952 Dwight D. Eisenhower is elected president.

1953 CIA installs Riza Shah Pahlavi as leader of Iran.

1954 Vietminh force French surrender at Dien Bien Phu.

CIA overthrows government of Jácobo Arbenz Guzmán in Guatemala.

United States explodes first hydrogen bomb.

1955 Jonas Salk pioneers vaccine for polio.

James Dean stars in the movie *Rebel Without a Cause*.

1956 Federal Highway Act authorizes Interstate Highway System.

Elvis Presley signs with RCA.

Eisenhower is reelected.

Allen Ginsberg publishes *Howl*.

1957 Soviet Union launches Sputnik, first space-orbiting satellite.

Jack Kerouac publishes *On the Road*.

1958 National Defense Education Act authorizes grants and loans to college students.

1959 Nikita Khrushchev visits the United States.

1960 Soviets shoot down U-2 spy plane.

John F. Kennedy is elected president.

Almost 90 percent of American homes have television.

1961 President Kennedy creates "Green Berets."

Bay of Pigs invasion of Cuba fails.

1962 Cuban missile crisis brings the world to the brink of a superpower confrontation.

1963 Report by the Presidential Commission on the Status of Women documents ongoing discrimination.

Betty Friedan publishes *The Feminine Mystique*.

Limited Nuclear Test-Ban Treaty is signed.

President Kennedy is assassinated.

---

home ownership, college education, secure employment at decent wages, affordable appliances, and the ability to travel—for one's children if not for one's self. The nation's public culture—its schools, mass media, politics, advertising—presented a powerful consensus based on the idea that the American dream was available to all who would work for it.

The presidential transition from the grandfatherly Dwight Eisenhower to the charismatic John F. Kennedy symbolized for many a generational shift as well. By 1963 young people had more influence than ever before in shaping the nation's political life, its media images, and its burgeoning consumer culture. Kennedy himself inspired millions of young Americans to pursue public service and to express their political idealism. But even by the time of Kennedy's death, the postwar consensus and the conditions that nurtured it were beginning to unravel.

SUMMARY

American Society at Midcentury The election of Dwight D. Eisenhower changed the tone of government as he sought a more conservative, corporate commonwealth. During his presidency, the federal government built on the growing prosperity to subsidize programs that helped Americans pursue higher education and buy homes, especially in new suburbs. The suburban boom strengthened domestic ideals but also provoked criticism for creating a dull, conformist lifestyle, among other things. During the fifties, labor unions reached a peak of membership and power. In part due to federal laws, higher education expanded greatly.

Youth Culture After World War II, increasing attention was directed at American youth. The rising birthrates in the late 1930s onward made young people a potent market. Teenagers gained a special status. They developed their own culture, especially rock 'n' roll music that drew heavily on black music and made black performers popular among white youth. Tensions arose over the status of teenagers and was partly reflected in an increase in juvenile delinquency.

Mass Culture and Its Discontents The rise of television contributed to the development of a mass culture that reflected many of the conformist tendencies of the postwar era. Criticism of mass culture came from the right and the left. The Beats offered strong dissent of conformity both in their writing and their lifestyles.

The Cold War Continued The waging of the Cold War changed when Eisenhower became president. He focused on relying more on America's nuclear superiority. Summit meetings between Eisenhower and Khruschev lessened tensions. Eisenhower's policy also employed covert action in several nations, as Eisenhower feared a domino effect of communism. When his term ended, Eisenhower left office warning against the growing military–industrial complex.

John F. Kennedy and the New Frontier The election of John F. Kennedy changed the direction of the nation. His New Frontier represented a return to liberal, activist politics but faced opposition from Congress. Still, Kennedy successfully implemented several social programs and energized the space program. In foreign policy, Kennedy generally followed the Cold War precepts of his predecessors. Though he tried to ease tensions with the Soviets, he confronted several crises. His assassination sent the nation into shock.

■ ▪ ■ ▪ ■ ▪ ■ ▪ ■ ▪ ■ ▪ ■ ▪ ■ ▪ ■ ▪ ■ ▪ ■ ▪ ■ ▪ ■ ■

REVIEW QUESTIONS

1. How did postwar economic prosperity change the lives of ordinary Americans? Which groups benefited most and which were largely excluded from "the affluent society"?

2. What role did federal programs play in expanding economic opportunities?

3. Analyze the origins of postwar youth culture. How was teenage life different in these years from previous eras? How did popular culture both reflect and distort the lives of American youth?

4. How did mass culture become even more central to American everyday life in the two decades following World War II? What problems did various cultural critics identify with this trend?

5. How did cold war politics and assumptions shape American foreign policy in these years? What were the key interventions the United States made in Europe and the third world?

6. Evaluate the domestic and international policies associated with John F. Kennedy and the New Frontier. What continuities with Eisenhower-era politics do you find in the Kennedy administration? How did JFK break with past practices?

KEY TERMS

Alliance for Progress (p. 753)

Bay of Pigs (p. 754)

Cuban missile crisis (p. 754)

Equal Pay Act of 1963 (p. 751)

Federal Highway Act of 1956 (p. 741)

Geneva Accord (p. 750)

Great Society (p. 755)

Landrum-Griffin Act (p. 743)

Limited Nuclear Test-Ban Treaty (p. 754)

New Frontier (p. 751)

National Aeronautics and Space Administration (NASA) (p. 752)

National Defense Education Act (NDEA) (p. 741)

RECOMMENDED READING

Roslyn Fraad Baxandall and Elizabeth Ewen, *Picture Windows: How the Suburbs Happened* (2000). The best new account of postwar suburbs, emphasizing the demand for affordable housing and making fine use of the voices of suburbanites.

Lawrence Freedman, *Kennedy's Wars: Berlin, Cuba, Laos, and Vietnam* (2000). A comprehensive new analysis of JFK's foreign policy, emphasizing the context of Cold War liberalism.

James B. Gilbert, *A Cycle of Outrage* (1986). An insightful examination of juvenile delinquency and its treatment by social scientists and the mass media during the 1950s.

Kenneth T. Jackson, *Crabgrass Frontier* (1985). The most comprehensive overview of the history of American suburbs. Jackson provides a broad historical context for understanding postwar suburbanization and offers an excellent analysis of the impact of government agencies such as the Federal Housing Administration.

David E. Kaiser, *American Tragedy: Kennedy, Johnson, and the Origins of the Vietnam War* (2000). The most detailed account yet of how the contradictions of Cold War thinking pushed policymakers in three administrations toward an unnecessary and unwinnable war.

Zachary Karabell, *Architects of Intervention: The United States, the Third World, and the Cold War, 1946–1962* (1999). A wide-ranging analysis of U.S. involvement in various third world countries, with special emphasis on the active role played by indiginous, non-American participants.

George Lipsitz, *Time Passages* (1990). An illuminating set of essays charting developments in American popular culture, especially strong analysis of music and early television.

Elaine Tyler May, *Homeward Bound: American Families in the Cold War* (1988). A thoughtful social history linking family life of the 1950s with the political shadow of the cold war.

Grace Palladino, *Teenagers: An American History* (1996). A lively and witty narrative account of the emergence of teenagers as a new social class.

James T. Patterson, *Grand Expectations: Postwar America, 1945–1974* (1996). A comprehensive overview of postwar life that centers on the "grand expectations" evoked by unprecedented prosperity.

Mark J. White, ed., *Kennedy: The New Frontier Revisited* (1998). Wide-ranging collection of recent essays that together offer a balanced view of Kennedy's presidency.

"We have discovered a new and powerful weapon–nonviolent resistance."

—*Martin Luther King, Jr., December 1956 address on Montgomery bus boycott*

The Black Panthers march in New York City.

THE CIVIL RIGHTS MOVEMENT
1945–1966

HOW DID World War II alter the expectations of African Americans?

WHAT ROLE did civil rights play in the election of 1960?

WHAT LED to the passage of the Civil Rights Act of 1964?

WHAT STEPS did Indian peoples take to expand and protect their rights in the decades after World War II?

1945   1966

AMERICAN COMMUNITIES

The Montgomery Bus Boycott: An African American Community Challenges Segregation

A STEADY STREAM OF CARS AND PEDESTRIANS JAMMED THE STREETS around the Holt Street Baptist Church in Montgomery, Alabama. By early evening a patient, orderly, and determined crowd of more than 5,000 African Americans had packed the church and spilled over onto the sidewalks. Loudspeakers had to be set up for the thousands who could not squeeze inside. After a brief prayer and a reading from Scripture, all attention focused on the twenty-six-year-old minister who was to address the gathering. "We are here this evening," he began slowly, "for serious business. We are here in a general sense because first and foremost we are American citizens, and we are determined to apply our citizenship to the fullness of its means."

Sensing the expectant mood of the crowd, the minister got down to specifics. Rosa Parks, a seamstress and well-known activist in Montgomery's African American community, had been taken from a bus, arrested, and put in jail for refusing to give up her seat to a white passenger on December 1, 1955. Composing roughly half the city's 100,000 people, Montgomery's black community had long endured the humiliation of a strictly segregated bus system. Drivers could order a whole row of black passengers to vacate their seats for one white person. And black people had to pay their fares at the front of the bus and then step back outside and reenter through the rear door. The day of the mass meeting, more than 30,000 African Americans had answered a hastily organized call to boycott the city's buses in protest of Mrs. Parks's arrest. As the minister quickened his cadence and drew shouts of encouragement, he seemed to gather strength and confidence from the crowd. "You know, my friends, there comes a time when people get tired of being trampled over by the iron feet of oppression. There comes a time, my friends, when people get tired of being flung across the abyss of humiliation, when they experience the bleakness of nagging despair."

Even before he concluded his speech, it was clear to all present that the bus boycott would continue for more than just a day. The minister laid out the key principles that would guide the boycott—nonviolence, Christian love, unity. In his brief but stirring address the minister created a powerful sense of communion. "If we are wrong, justice is a lie," he told the clapping and shouting throng. "And we are determined here in Montgomery to work and fight until justice runs down like water and righteousness like a mighty stream . . . Historians would look back at Montgomery," he noted, "and have to say: 'There lived a race of people, black people, fleecy locks and black complexion, of people who had the moral courage to stand up for their rights.' And thereby they injected a new meaning into the veins of history and of civilization."

The Reverend Dr. Martin Luther King Jr. made his way out of the church amid waves of applause and rows of hands reaching out to touch him. His prophetic speech catapulted him into leadership of the Montgomery bus boycott—but he had not started the movement. When Rosa Parks was arrested, local activists with deep roots in the black protest tradition galvanized the community with the idea of a boycott. Mrs. Parks herself had served for twelve years as secretary of the local NAACP chapter. She was a committed opponent of segregation and was thoroughly respected in the city's African American community. E. D. Nixon, president of the Alabama NAACP and head of the local Brotherhood of Sleeping Car Porters union, saw Mrs. Parks's arrest as the right case on which to make a stand. It was Nixon who brought Montgomery's black ministers together on December 5 to coordinate an extended boycott of city buses. They formed the Montgomery Improvement Association (MIA) and chose Dr. King as their leader. Significantly, Mrs. Parks's lawyer was Clifford Durr, a white liberal with a history of representing black clients. His politically active wife Virginia, for whom Mrs. Parks worked as a seamstress, had been a long-time crusader against the poll tax that prevented many blacks from voting. And two white ministers, Rev. Robert Graetz and Rev. Glenn Smiley, would offer important support to the MIA.

Montgomery

While Nixon organized black ministers, Jo Ann Robinson, an English teacher at Alabama State College, spread the word to the larger black community. Robinson led the Women's Political Council (WPC), an organization of black professional women founded in 1949. With her WPC allies, Robinson wrote, mimeographed, and distributed 50,000 copies of a leaflet telling the story of Mrs. Parks's arrest and urging all African Americans to stay off city buses on December 5. They did. Now the MIA faced the more difficult task of keeping the boycott going. Success depended on providing alternate transportation for the 30,000 to 40,000 maids, cooks, janitors, and other black working people who needed to get to work.

The MIA coordinated an elaborate system of car pools, using hundreds of private cars and volunteer drivers to provide as many as 20,000 rides each day. Many people walked. Local authorities, although shocked by the discipline and sense of purpose shown by Montgomery's African American community, refused to engage in serious negotiations. With the aid of the NAACP, the MIA brought suit in federal court against bus segregation in Montgomery. Police harassed boycotters with traffic tickets and arrests. White racists exploded bombs in the homes of Dr. King and E. D. Nixon. The days turned into weeks, then months, but still the boycott continued. All along, mass meetings in Montgomery's African American churches helped boost morale with singing, praying, and stories of individual sacrifice. One elderly woman, refusing all suggestions that she drop out of the boycott on account of her age, made a spontaneous remark that became a classic refrain of the movement: "My feets is tired, but my soul is rested."

The boycott reduced the bus company's revenues by two-thirds. In February 1956, city officials obtained indictments against King, Nixon, and 113 other boycotters under an old law forbidding hindrance to business without "just cause or legal excuse." A month later King went on trial. A growing contingent of newspaper reporters and TV crews from around the country watched as the judge found King guilty, fined him $1,000, and released him on bond pending appeal. But on June 4, a panel of three federal judges struck down Montgomery's bus segregation ordinances as unconstitutional. On November 13 the Supreme

Court affirmed the district court ruling. After eleven hard months and against all odds, the boycotters had won.

The struggle to end legal segregation took root in scores of Southern cities and towns. African American communities led these fights, developing a variety of tactics, leaders, and ideologies. With white allies, they engaged in direct-action protests such as boycotts, sit-ins, and mass civil disobedience as well as strategic legal battles in state and federal courts. The movement was not without its inner conflicts. Tensions between local movements and national civil rights organizations flared up regularly. Within African American communities, long-simmering distrust between the working classes and rural folk on the one hand and middle-class ministers, teachers, and business people on the other sometimes threatened to destroy political unity. There were generational conflicts between African American student activists and their elders. But overall, the civil rights movement created new social identities for African Americans and profoundly changed American society.

Origins of the Movement

Civil Rights after World War II

The boom in wartime production spurred a mass migration of nearly a million black Southerners to Northern cities. Although racial discrimination in housing and employment was by no means absent in Northern cities, greater economic opportunities and political freedom continued to attract rural African Americans after the war. Black people gained significant influence in local political machines in such cities as New York, Chicago, and Detroit. Within industrial unions such as the United Automobile Workers and the United Steel Workers, white and black workers learned the power of biracial unity in fighting for better wages and working conditions.

After World War II, civil rights issues returned to the national political stage for the first time since Reconstruction. Black voters had already begun to switch their allegiance from the Republicans to the Democrats during the New Deal. A series of symbolic and substantial acts by the Truman administration solidified that shift. In 1946 Truman created a President's Committee on Civil Rights. Its report, *To Secure These Rights* (1947), set out an ambitious program to end racial inequality. Recommendations included a permanent civil rights division in the Justice Department, voting rights protection, antilynching legislation, and a legal attack on segregated housing. Yet, although he publicly endorsed nearly all the proposals of the new committee, Truman introduced no legislation to make them law.

Truman and his advisers walked a political tightrope on civil rights. They understood that black voters in several key Northern states would be pivotal in the 1948 election. At the same time, they worried about the loyalty of white Southern Democrats adamantly opposed to changing the racial status quo. In July 1948, the president made his boldest move on behalf of civil rights, issuing an executive order barring segregation in the armed forces. When liberals forced the Democratic National Convention to adopt a strong civil rights plank that summer,

HOW DID World War II alter the expectations of African Americans?

Charlie Parker (alto sax) and Miles Davis (trumpet) with their group in 1947 at the Three Deuces Club in New York City. Parker and Davis were two creative leaders of the "bebop" movement of the 1940s. Working in Northern cities, boppers reshaped jazz music and created a distinct language and style that was widely imitated by young people. They challenged older stereotypes of African American musicians by insisting that they be treated as serious artists.

Frank Driggs Collection

QUICK REVIEW

The Postwar NAACP

◆ During the war, membership increased from 50,000 to 500,000.

◆ Used courts to attack segregation.

◆ Lack of federal enforcement of court decisions undermined effectiveness.

Congress of Racial Equality (CORE) Civil rights group formed in 1942 and committed to nonviolent civil disobedience.

a group of outraged Southerners walked out and nominated Governor Strom Thurmond of South Carolina for president on a States' Rights ticket. Thurmond carried four Southern states in the election. But with the help of over 70 percent of the Northern black vote, Truman barely managed to defeat Republican Thomas E. Dewey in November. The deep split over race issues would continue to rack the national Democratic Party for a generation.

During the war, membership in the National Association for the Advancement of Colored People had mushroomed from 50,000 to 500,000. Working- and middle-class urban black people provided the backbone of this new membership. The NAACP conducted voter registration drives and lobbied against discrimination in housing and employment. Its Legal Defense and Education Fund, vigorously led by special counsel Thurgood Marshall, mounted several significant legal challenges to segregation laws. In *Morgan* v. *Virginia* (1946), the Supreme Court declared that segregation on interstate buses was an undue burden on interstate commerce. Other Supreme Court decisions struck down all-white election primaries, racially restrictive housing covenants, and the exclusion of blacks from law and graduate schools.

The NAACP's legal work demonstrated the potential for using federal courts in attacking segregation. Courts were one place where black people, using the constitutional language of rights, could make forceful arguments that could not be voiced in Congress or at political conventions. But federal enforcement of court decisions was often lacking. In 1947 a group of black and white activists tested compliance with the *Morgan* decision by traveling on a bus through the Upper South. This "Freedom Ride" was cosponsored by the Christian pacifist Fellowship of Reconciliation (FOR) and its recent offshoot, the **Congress of Racial Equality (CORE)**, which was devoted to interracial, nonviolent direct action. In North Carolina, several riders were arrested and sentenced to thirty days on a chain gang for refusing to leave the bus.

Two symbolic "firsts" raised black expectations and inspired pride. In 1947 Jackie Robinson broke the color barrier in major league baseball, winning rookie-of-the-year honors with the Brooklyn Dodgers. Robinson's courage in the face of racial epithets from fans and players paved the way for the black ballplayers who soon followed him to the big leagues. In 1950 United Nations diplomat Ralph Bunche won the Nobel Peace Prize for arranging the 1948 Arab-Israeli truce. Bunche, however, later declined an appointment as undersecretary of state because he did not want to subject his family to the humiliating segregation laws of Washington, D.C.

Cultural change could have political implications as well. Although black musicians had pioneered the development of swing and, earlier, jazz, white bandleaders and musicians had reaped most of the recognition and money from the public. Artists such as Charlie Parker, Dizzy Gillespie, Thelonius Monk, Bud Powell, and Miles Davis revolted against the standard big-band format of swing, preferring small groups and competitive jam sessions to express their musical visions. The new music, dubbed "bebop" by critics and fans, demanded a much more sophisticated knowledge of harmony and melody and featured more complex rhythms and extended improvisation than previous jazz styles. Serious about both their music and the way it was presented, these black artists refused to cater to white expectations of grinning, easygoing black performers.

THE SEGREGATED SOUTH

The 1896 Supreme Court ruling in *Plessy* v. *Ferguson* had sanctioned the principle of "separate but equal" facilities in Southern life. In practice, segregation meant separate but unequal. A tight web of state and local ordinances enforced strict separation of the races in schools, restaurants, hotels, movie theaters, libraries, restrooms, hospitals, even cemeteries, and the facilities for black people were consistently inferior to those for whites. There were no black policemen in the Deep South and only a handful of black lawyers. "A white man," one scholar observed, "can steal from or maltreat a Negro in almost any way without fear of reprisal, because the Negro cannot claim the protection of the police or courts."

In the late 1940s only about 10 percent of eligible Southern black people voted, most of these in urban areas. A combination of legal and extralegal measures kept all but the most determined black people disfranchised. Poll taxes, all-white primaries, and discriminatory registration procedures reinforced the belief that voting was "the white man's business." African Americans who insisted on exercising their right to vote, especially in remote rural areas, faced physical violence—beatings, shootings, lynchings.

Outsiders often noted that despite Jim Crow laws (see Chapter 20) contact between blacks and whites was ironically close. The mass of black Southerners worked on white-owned plantations and in white households. One black preacher neatly summarized the nation's regional differences this way: "In the South, they don't care how close you get as long as you don't get too big; in the North, they don't care how big you get as long as you don't get too close." The South's racial code forced African Americans to accept, at least outwardly, social conventions that reinforced their low standing with whites. A black person did not shake hands with a white person, or enter a white home through the front door, or address a white person except formally.

BROWN V. BOARD OF EDUCATION

Since the late 1930s, the NAACP had chipped away at the legal foundations of segregation. Rather than making a frontal assault on the *Plessy* separate-but-equal rule, civil rights attorneys launched a series of suits seeking complete equality in segregated facilities. The aim of this strategy was to make segregation so prohibitively expensive that the South would be forced to dismantle it. In the 1939 case *Missouri* v. *ex.rel. Gaines*, the Supreme Court ruled that the University of Missouri law school must either admit African Americans or build another fully equal law school for them. NAACP lawyers pushed their arguments further, asserting that equality could not be measured simply by money or physical plant. In *McLaurin* v. *Oklahoma State Regents* (1950), the Court agreed with Thurgood Marshall's argument that regulations forcing a black law student to sit, eat, and study in areas apart from white students inevitably created a "badge of inferiority."

By 1951, Marshall had begun coordinating the NAACP's legal resources for a direct attack on the separate-but-equal doctrine. The goal was to overturn *Plessy* and the constitutionality of segregation

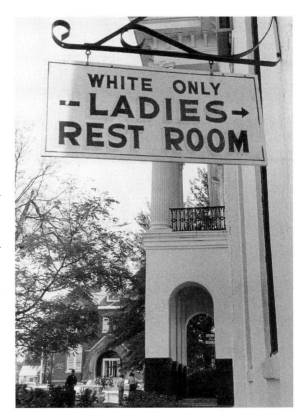

Signs designating "White" and "Colored" restrooms, waiting rooms, entrances, benches, and even water fountains were a common sight in the segregated South. They were a constant reminder that legal separation of the races in public spaces was the law of the land.

(a) Photo by Dan McCoy. Black Star; (b) Segregation trailways. CORBIS

27–2
Brown v. Board of Education
(1954)

IMAGE KEY

for pages 760–761

a. Martin Luther King, Jr. and Malcolm X.

b. Black Panthers in trademark berets marching in New York City, July 22, 1968.

c. Official program for the March on Washington for "jobs and freedom," August 28, 1963.

d. A poster for the National Association for the Advancement of Colored People (NAACP) features ballplayer Larry Doby, workers, children, and students.

e. The album cover for *Cotton Club Days, Volume 2* by Duke Ellington, featuring a photo of the jazz bandleader.

f. Elizabeth Eckford is heckled by white students while integrating Central High School in Little Rock, Arkansas in 1957.

g. Young black men carrying signs bearing slogans In Tallahassee, Florida in March, 1964.

h. A Native American man standing guard during the American Indian Movement's 1973 occupation of the reservation town at Wounded Knee, South Dakota.

Brown v. Board of Education
Supreme Court decision in 1954 that declared that "separate but equal" schools for children of different races violated the Constitution.

Southern Manifesto A document signed by 101 members of Congress from Southern states in 1956 that argued that the Supreme Court's decision in *Brown* v. *Board of Education of Topeka* itself contradicted the Constitution.

itself. For a test case, Marshall combined five lawsuits challenging segregation in public schools. The Supreme Court heard initial arguments on the cases, grouped together as ***Brown v. Board of Education***, in December 1952.

In his argument before the Court, Thurgood Marshall tried to establish that separate facilities, by definition, denied black people their full rights as American citizens. He used evidence from psychologists and sociologists demonstrating that black children educated in segregated schools developed a negative self-image and low self-esteem. Chief Justice Earl Warren, eager for a unanimous decision, patiently worked at convincing two holdouts.

On May 17, 1954, Warren read the Court's unanimous decision aloud. "Does segregation of children in public schools solely on the basis of race . . . deprive the children of the minority group of equal educational opportunities?" The chief justice paused. "We believe that it does." Warren made a point of citing several of the psychological studies of segregation's effects. He ended by directly addressing the constitutional issue. Segregation deprived the plaintiffs of the equal protection of the laws guaranteed by the Fourteenth Amendment. "We conclude that in the field of public education the doctrine of 'separate but equal' has no place. Separate educational facilities are inherently unequal." "Any language in *Plessy* v. *Ferguson* contrary to this finding is rejected."

African Americans and their liberal allies around the country hailed the decision and the legal genius of Thurgood Marshall. But the issue of enforcement soon dampened this enthusiasm. To gain a unanimous decision, Warren had had to agree to let the Court delay for one year its ruling on how to implement desegregation. This second *Brown* ruling, handed down in May 1955, assigned responsibility for desegregation plans to local school boards. The Court left it to federal district judges to monitor compliance, requiring only that desegregation proceed "with all deliberate speed." Thus, although the Court had made a momentous and clear constitutional ruling, the need for compromise dictated gradual enforcement by unspecified means.

CRISIS IN LITTLE ROCK

Resistance to *Brown* took many forms. Most affected states passed laws transferring authority for pupil assignment to local school boards. This prevented the NAACP from bringing statewide suits against segregated school systems. Counties and towns created layers of administrative delays designed to stop implementation of *Brown*. Some school boards transferred public school property to new, all-white private "academies." State legislatures in Virginia, Alabama, Mississippi, and Georgia, resurrecting pre–Civil War doctrines, passed resolutions declaring their right to "interpose" themselves between the people and the federal government and to "nullify" federal laws. In 1956, 101 congressmen from the former Confederate states signed the **Southern Manifesto**, urging their states to refuse compliance with desegregation. President Dwight Eisenhower declined to publicly endorse *Brown*, contributing to the spirit of Southern resistance. Privately, the president opposed the *Brown* decision.

In Little Rock, Arkansas, the tense controversy over school integration became a test case of state versus federal power. A federal court ordered public schools to begin desegregation in September 1957, and the local school board made plans to comply. But Governor Orval Faubus, facing a tough reelection fight, decided to make a campaign issue out of defying the court order. He dispatched Arkansas National Guard troops to Central High School to prevent nine black students from entering. For three weeks, armed troops stood guard at the school. Screaming crowds, encouraged by Faubus, menaced the black students, beat up two black reporters, and chanted "Two, four, six, eight, we ain't going to integrate." Moderate whites, such as *Arkansas Gazette* editor Harry Ashmore, opposed Faubus, fearing that his controversial tactics would make it harder to attract new businesses and investment capital to the city.

At first, President Eisenhower tried to intervene quietly, gaining Faubus's assurance that he would protect the nine black children. But when Faubus suddenly withdrew his troops, leaving the black students at the mercy of the white mob, Eisenhower had to move. On September 24 he placed the Arkansas National Guard under federal control and ordered a thousand paratroopers of the 101st Airborne Division to Little Rock. The nine black students arrived in a U.S. Army car. With fixed bayonets, the soldiers protected the students as they finally integrated Central High School in Little Rock. Eisenhower, the veteran military commander, justified his actions on the basis of upholding federal authority and enforcing the law. He also defended his intervention as crucial to national prestige abroad, noting the propaganda victory Faubus had handed to the Soviet bloc. "Our enemies," the President argued, "are gloating over this incident and using it everywhere to misrepresent our whole nation." But he made no endorsement of desegregation. Unfazed, Governor Faubus kept Little Rock high schools closed during the 1958–1959 academic year to prevent what he called "violence and disorder."

 MAP EXPLORATION

To explore an interactive version of this map, go to **http://www.prenhall.com/faraghertlc/map28.1**

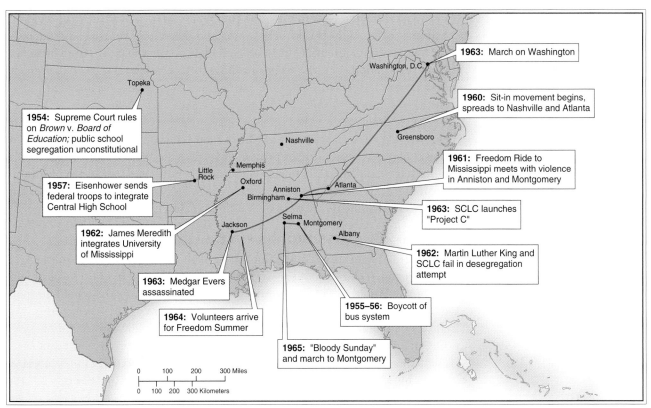

MAP 28-1

Map of the Civil Rights Movement   Key battlegrounds in the struggle for racial justice in communities across the South.

HOW DID the *Brown* decision pave the way for subsequent events?

WHAT ROLE did civil

rights play in the election of 1960?

QUICK REVIEW

The Southern Christian Leadership Conference

- 1957: Martin Luther King founded Southern Christian Leadership Conference.
- Called on people to embrace nonviolent protest.
- Used the Southern black church as a leading institution in the fight for civil rights.

No Easy Road to Freedom, 1957–1962

Martin Luther King and the SCLC

The 381-day Montgomery bus boycott made Martin Luther King a prominent national figure. King himself was an extraordinary and complex man. Born in 1929 in Atlanta, he enjoyed a middle-class upbringing as the son of a prominent Baptist minister. As a graduate student, he was drawn to the social Christianity of American theologian Walter Rauschenbusch, who insisted on connecting religious faith with struggles for social justice. Above all, King admired Mohandas Gandhi, a lawyer turned ascetic who had led a successful nonviolent resistance movement against British colonial rule in India.

A unique blend of traditional African American folk preacher and erudite intellectual, King used his passion and intelligence to help transform a community's pain into a powerful moral force for change. He recognized the need to exploit the momentum of the Montgomery movement. In early 1957, with the help of Bayard Rustin of the War Resister's League and other aides, he brought together nearly 100 black ministers to found the **Southern Christian Leadership Conference (SCLC)**. The clergymen elected King president and his close friend, the Reverend Ralph Abernathy, treasurer. The SCLC called upon black people "to understand that nonviolence is not a symbol of weakness or cowardice, but as Jesus demonstrated, nonviolent resistance transforms weakness into strength and breeds courage in the face of danger."

But King and other black leaders believed white Southerners could be divided roughly into three groups: a tiny minority—often with legal training, social connections, and money—who might be counted on to help overthrow segregation; extreme segregationists who were willing and able to use violence and terror in defense of white supremacy; and a broad middle group who favored and benefited from segregation, but who were unwilling to take personal risks to prevent its destruction. In the battles to come, civil rights leaders made this nuanced view of the white South a central part of their larger political strategy.

Previously, the struggle for racial equality had been dominated by a Northern elite focusing on legal action. The SCLC now envisioned the Southern black church, preaching massive nonviolent protest, as leading the fight. But the organization failed to generate the kind of mass, direct-action movement that had made history in Montgomery. Instead, the next great spark to light the fire of protest came from what seemed at the time a most unlikely source: black college students.

Sit-Ins: Greensboro, Nashville, Atlanta

On Monday, February 1, 1960, four black freshmen from North Carolina Agricultural and Technical College in Greensboro sat down at the whites-only lunch counter in Woolworth's. They were refused service. Although they could buy pencils or toothpaste, black people were not allowed to eat in Woolworth's. But the four students stayed at the counter until closing time. Word of their actions spread quickly, and the next day they returned with over two dozen supporters. On the third day, students occupied sixty-three of the sixty-six lunch counter seats. By Thursday they had been joined by three white students from the Women's College of the University of North Carolina in Greensboro. Scores of sympathizers overflowed Woolworth's and started a sit-in down the street in S. H. Kress. On Friday hundreds of black students and a few whites jammed the lunch counters.

City officials, looking to end the protest, offered to negotiate in exchange for an end to demonstrations. But white business leaders and politicians proved unwill-

Southern Christian Leadership Conference (SCLC) Black civil rights organization founded in 1957 by Martin Luther King Jr. and other clergy.

ing to change the racial status quo, and the sit-ins resumed on April 1. In response to the April 21 arrest of forty-five students for trespassing, an outraged African American community organized an economic boycott of targeted stores. With the boycott cutting deeply into merchants' profits, Greensboro's leaders reluctantly gave in. On July 25, 1960, the first African American ate a meal at Woolworth's.

During the next eighteen months 70,000 people—most of them black students, a few of them white allies—participated in sit-ins against segregation in dozens of communities. More than 3,000 were arrested. African Americans had discovered a new form of direct-action protest, dignified and powerful, which white people could not ignore. The sit-in movement also transformed participants' self-image, empowering them psychologically and emotionally.

In Nashville, the Reverend James Lawson, a Northern-born black minister, had led workshops in nonviolent resistance since 1958. Lawson gathered around him a group of deeply committed black students from Nashville colleges who wanted to end segregation through Christian idealism and Gandhian principles. In the spring of 1960 more than 150 Nashville students were arrested in disciplined sit-ins aimed at desegregating downtown lunch counters, and Lawson found himself expelled from the divinity school at Vanderbilt. The Nashville group developed rules of conduct that became a model for protesters elsewhere: "Don't strike back or curse if abused. . . . Show yourself courteous and friendly at all times. . . . Report all serious incidents to your leader in a polite manner. Remember love and nonviolence."

The second day of the sit-in at the Greensboro, North Carolina, Woolworth lunch counter, February 2, 1960. From left: Joseph McNeil, Franklin McCain, Billy Smith, and Clarence Henderson. The Greensboro protest sparked a wave of sit-ins across the South, mostly by college students, demanding an end to segregation in restaurants and other public places.

Photo by John G. Moebes, *Greensboro News & Record*

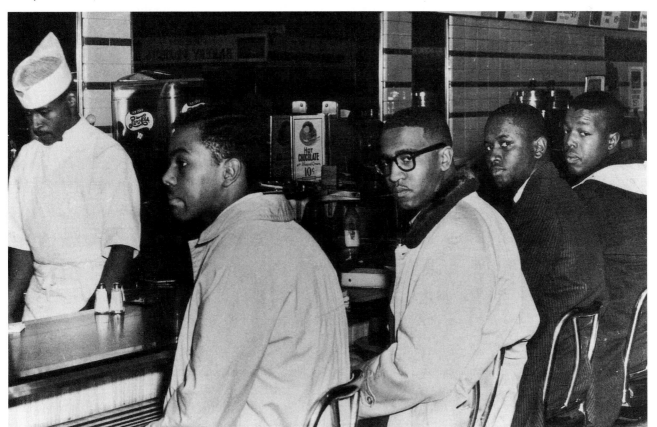

The most ambitious sit-in campaign developed in Atlanta, the South's largest and richest city, home to the region's most powerful and prestigious black community. Led by Julian Bond and Lonnie King, the students formed the Committee on an Appeal for Human Rights. Over the summer they planned a fall campaign of large-scale sit-ins at major Atlanta department stores and a boycott of downtown merchants. Their slogan became "Close out your charge account with segregation, open up your account with freedom." In October 1960 Martin Luther King and thirty-six students were arrested when they sat down in the all-white Magnolia Room restaurant in Rich's Department Store. The campaign stretched on for months, and hundreds of protesters went to jail. The city's business leaders finally relented in September 1961, and desegregation came to Atlanta.

SNCC AND THE "BELOVED COMMUNITY"

The sit-in movement pumped new energy into the civil rights cause, creating a new generation of activists and leaders. Mass arrests, beatings, and vilification in the Southern white press only strengthened the resolve of those in the movement. Students also had to deal with the fears of their families, many of whom had made great sacrifices to send them off to college.

The new student militancy also caused discord within black communities. The authority of local African American elites had traditionally depended on their influence and cooperation with the white establishment. Student calls for freedom disturbed many community leaders worried about upsetting traditional patronage networks. The president of Southern University in Baton Rouge, the largest black college in the nation, suspended eighteen sit-in leaders in 1960 and forced the entire student body of 5,000 to reapply to the college so that agitators could be screened out.

An April 1960 conference of 120 black student activists in Raleigh, North Carolina, underlined the generational and radical aspects of the new movement. The meeting had been called by Ella Baker, executive director of the SCLC. For years Baker had played an important behind-the-scenes role in the civil rights cause, serving as a community organizer and field secretary for the NAACP before heading the staff of the SCLC. She understood the psychological importance of the students' remaining independent of adult control and encouraged the trend toward group-centered leadership among the students. With Baker's encouragement, the conference voted to establish a new group, the **Student Nonviolent Coordinating Committee (SNCC)**.

SNCC's emphasis was on fighting segregation through direct confrontation, mass action, and civil disobedience. SNCC fieldworkers initiated and supported local, community-based activity. Three-quarters of the first fieldworkers were less than twenty-two years old. Leadership was vested in a nonhierarchical Coordinating Committee, but local groups were free to determine their own direction. SNCC people distrusted bureaucracy and structure; they stressed spontaneity and improvisation. Over the next few years SNCC was at the forefront of nearly every major civil rights battle.

THE ELECTION OF 1960 AND CIVIL RIGHTS

The issue of race relations was kept from center stage during the very close presidential campaign of 1960. As vice president, Richard Nixon had been a leading Republican voice for stronger civil rights legislation. In contrast, Democratic nominee Senator John F. Kennedy had played virtually no role in the congressional battles over civil rights during the 1950s. But during the campaign, their roles reversed. Kennedy praised the sit-in movement as part of a revival of national reform spirit. He declared, "It is in the American tradition to stand up for one's

27–4
Student Nonviolent Coordinating Committee, Statement of Purpose (1960)

28–2
Charles Sherrod, Student Nonviolent Coordinating Committee Memorandum (1961)

Student Nonviolent Coordinating Committee (SNCC) Black civil rights organization founded in 1960 that drew heavily on younger activists and college students.

rights—even if the new way is to sit down." While the Republican platform contained a strong civil rights plank, Nixon, eager to court white Southern voters, minimized his own identification with the movement. In October, when Martin Luther King Jr. was jailed after leading a demonstration in Atlanta, Kennedy telephoned King's wife, Coretta Scott King, to reassure her and express his personal support. Kennedy's brother Robert telephoned the judge in the case and angrily warned him that he had violated King's civil rights and endangered the national Democratic ticket. The judge released King soon afterward.

News of this intervention did not gain wide attention in the white South, much to the relief of the Kennedys. The race was tight, and they knew they could not afford to alienate traditional white Southern Democrats. But the campaign effectively played up the story among black voters all over the country. Kennedy won 70 percent of the black vote, which helped put him over the top in such critical states as Illinois, Texas, Michigan, and Pennsylvania and secure his narrow victory over Nixon. Many civil rights activists optimistically looked forward to a new president who would have to acknowledge his political debt to the black vote.

But the very closeness of his victory constrained Kennedy on the race question. Democrats had lost ground in the House and Senate, and Kennedy had to worry about alienating conservative Southern Democrats who chaired key congressional committees. Passage of major civil rights legislation would be virtually impossible. The new president told leaders such as Roy Wilkins of the NAACP that a strategy of "minimum legislation, maximum executive action" offered the best road to change. The president did appoint some forty African Americans to high federal positions, including Thurgood Marshall to the federal appellate court. He established a Committee on Equal Employment Opportunity, chaired by Vice President Lyndon B. Johnson, to fight discrimination in the federal civil service and in corporations that received government contracts.

Most significantly, the Kennedy administration sought to invigorate the Civil Rights Division of the Justice Department. Robert Kennedy, the new attorney general, began assembling a staff of brilliant and committed attorneys, headed by Washington lawyer Burke Marshall. Kennedy encouraged them to get out of Washington and get into the field wherever racial troubles arose. In early 1961, when Louisiana school officials balked at a school desegregation order, Robert Kennedy warned them that he would ask the federal court to hold them in contempt. When Burke Marshall started court proceedings, the state officials gave in. But the new, more aggressive mood at Justice could not solve the central political dilemma: how to move forward on civil rights without alienating Southern Democrats. Pressure from the newly energized Southern civil rights movement soon revealed the true difficulty of that problem.

FREEDOM RIDES

In the spring of 1961 James Farmer, national director of CORE, announced plans for an interracial Freedom Ride through the South. The goal was to test compliance with court orders banning segregation in interstate travel and terminal accommodations. CORE had just recently made Farmer its leader in an effort to revitalize the organization. He designed the Freedom Ride to induce a crisis, in the spirit of the sit-ins. "Our intention," Farmer declared, "was to provoke the Southern authorities into arresting us and thereby prod the Justice Department into enforcing the law of the land." CORE informed the Justice Department and the Federal Bureau of Investigation of its plans but received no reply.

On May 4 seven blacks and six whites split into two interracial groups and left Washington on public buses bound for Alabama and Mississippi. At first the two

A Freedom Riders' bus burns after being firebombed in Anniston, Alabama, May 14, 1961. After setting the bus afire, whites attacked the passengers fleeing the smoke and flames. Violent scenes like this one received extensive publicity in the mass media and helped compel the Justice Department to enforce court rulings banning segregation on interstate bus lines.

UPI/CORBIS (U12 79611 < 25)

buses encountered only isolated harassment and violence as they headed south. But when one bus entered Anniston, Alabama, on May 14, an angry mob surrounded it, smashing windows and slashing tires. Six miles out of town, the tires went flat. A firebomb tossed through a window forced the passengers out. The mob then beat the Freedom Riders with blackjacks, iron bars, and clubs, and the bus burst into flames. A caravan of cars organized by the Birmingham office of the SCLC rescued the wounded. Another mob attacked the second bus in Anniston, leaving one Freedom Rider close to death and permanently brain-damaged.

In Birmingham, a mob of forty white people waited on the loading platform and attacked the bus that managed to get out of Anniston. Although police had been warned to expect trouble, they did nothing to stop the mob from beating the Freedom Riders with pipes and fists, nor did they make any arrests. FBI agents observed and took notes but did nothing. The remaining Freedom Riders decided to travel as a single group on the next lap, from Birmingham to Montgomery, but no bus would take them. Stranded and frightened, they reluctantly boarded a special flight to New Orleans arranged by the Justice Department. On May 17 the CORE-sponsored Freedom Ride disbanded.

But that was not the end of the Freedom Rides. SNCC leaders in Atlanta and Nashville assembled a fresh group of volunteers to continue the trip. On May 20, twenty-one Freedom Riders left Birmingham for Montgomery. The bus station in the Alabama capital was eerily quiet and deserted as they pulled in. But when the passengers left the bus a mob of several hundred whites rushed them, yelling "Get those niggers!" and clubbing people to the ground. As John Lewis, veteran of the Nashville sit-in movement, lay in a pool of blood, a policeman handed him a state court injunction forbidding interracial travel in Alabama. The mob indiscriminately beat journalists and clubbed John Siegenthaler, a Justice Department attorney sent to observe the scene.

The mob violence and the indifference of Alabama officials made the Freedom Ride page-one news around the country and throughout the world. The Kennedy administration, preparing for the president's first summit meeting with Soviet premier Nikita Khrushchev, saw the situation as a threat to its international prestige. The attorney general called for a cooling-off period, but Martin Luther

King Jr., James Farmer, and the SNCC leaders announced that the Freedom Ride would continue. When Robert Kennedy warned that the racial turmoil would embarrass the president in his meeting with Khrushchev, Ralph Abernathy of the SCLC replied, "Doesn't the attorney general know that we've been embarrassed all our lives?"

A bandaged but spirited group of twenty-seven Freedom Riders prepared to leave Montgomery for Jackson, Mississippi, on May 24. To avoid further violence Robert Kennedy arranged a compromise through Mississippi senator James Eastland. In exchange for a guarantee of safe passage through Mississippi, the federal government promised not to interfere with the arrest of the Freedom Riders in Jackson. This Freedom Ride and several that followed thus escaped violence. But more than 300 people were arrested that summer. Sticking to a policy of "jail, no bail," Freedom Riders clogged the prison, where they endured beatings and intimidation by prison guards that went largely unreported in the press. Their jail experiences turned most of them into committed core leaders of the student movement.

The Justice Department eventually petitioned the Interstate Commerce Commission to issue clear rules prohibiting segregation on interstate carriers. By creating a crisis, the Freedom Rides had forced the Kennedy administration to act. The Freedom Rides exposed the ugly face of Southern racism to the world. At the same time, they reinforced white resistance to desegregation. The jailings and brutality experienced by Freedom Riders made clear to the civil rights community the limits of moral suasion alone for effecting change.

THE ALBANY MOVEMENT: THE LIMITS OF PROTEST

Where the federal government chose not to enforce the constitutional rights of black people, segregationist forces tenaciously held their ground, especially in the more remote areas of the Deep South. In Albany, a small city in southwest Georgia, activists from SNCC, the NAACP, and other local groups formed a coalition known as **the Albany movement**. Starting in October 1961 and continuing for more than a year, thousands of Albany's black citizens marched, sat in, and boycotted as part of a citywide campaign to integrate public facilities and win voting rights. More than a thousand people spent time in jail. In December, the arrival of Martin Luther King Jr. and the SCLC transformed Albany into a national symbol of the struggle.

But the gains at Albany proved minimal. Albany police chief Laurie Pritchett shrewdly deprived the movement of the kind of national sympathy won by the Freedom Riders. Pritchett filled the jails with black demonstrators, kept their mistreatment to a minimum, and prevented white mobs from running wild. "We met 'nonviolence' with 'nonviolence,'" he boasted.

By late 1962 the Albany movement had collapsed, and Pritchett proudly declared the city "as segregated as ever." One activist summed up the losing campaign: "We ran out of people before he ran out of jails." Albany showed that mass protest without violent white reaction and direct federal intervention could not end Jim Crow.

In the fall of 1962 James Meredith, an air force veteran, tried to register as the first black student at the University of Mississippi. Governor Ross Barnett defied a federal court order and personally blocked Meredith's path at the admissions office. When Barnett refused to assure Robert Kennedy that Meredith would be protected, the attorney general dispatched 500 federal marshals to the campus. Over the radio, Barnett encouraged resistance to the "oppressive power of the United States," and an angry mob of several thousand white people, many of them

The Albany movement Coalition formed in 1961 in Albany, a small city in southwest Georgia, of activists from SNCC, the NAACP, and other local groups.

armed, laid siege to the campus on September 30. A night of violence left 2 people dead and 160 marshals wounded, 28 from gunfire. President Kennedy ordered 5,000 army troops onto the campus to stop the riot. A federal guard remained to protect Meredith, who graduated the following summer.

THE MOVEMENT AT HIGH TIDE, 1963–1965

BIRMINGHAM

WHAT LED to the passage of the Civil Rights Act of 1964?

At the end of 1962, Martin Luther King Jr. and his SCLC allies decided to launch a new campaign against segregation in Birmingham, Alabama. After the failure in Albany, King and his aides looked for a way to shore up his leadership and inject new momentum into the freedom struggle.

Working closely with local civil rights groups led by the longtime Birmingham activist Rev. Fred Shuttlesworth, the SCLC carefully planned its campaign. The strategy was to fill the city jails with protesters, boycott downtown department stores, and enrage Public Safety Commissioner Eugene "Bull" Connor. In April, King arrived with a manifesto demanding an end to racist hiring practices and segregated public accommodations and the creation of a biracial committee to oversee desegregation. Connor's police began jailing hundreds of demonstrators, including King himself, who defied a state court injunction against further protests.

Held in solitary confinement for several days, King managed to write a response to a group of Birmingham clergy who had deplored the protests. King's *Letter from Birmingham Jail* was soon widely reprinted and circulated as a pamphlet. It set out the key moral issues at stake and scoffed at those who claimed the campaign was illegal and ill timed. King wrote:

> We know through painful experience that freedom is never
> voluntarily given by the oppressor; it must be demanded by the
> oppressed. . . . For years now I have heard the word "Wait!" It rings
> in the ear of every Negro with a piercing familiarity. This "Wait" has
> almost always meant "Never."

After King's release on bail, the campaign intensified. In early May, Bull Connor's forces began using high-powered water cannons, billy clubs, and snarling police dogs to break up demonstrations. Millions of Americans reacted with horror to the violent scenes from Birmingham shown on national television. Many younger black people, especially from the city's poor and working-class districts, began to fight back, hurling bottles and bricks at police. On May 10, mediators from the Justice Department negotiated an uneasy truce. The SCLC agreed to an immediate end to the protests. In exchange, businesses would desegregate and begin hiring African Americans over the next three months, and a biracial city committee would oversee desegregation of public facilities.

King claimed the events in Birmingham represented "the most magnificent victory for justice we've ever seen in the Deep South." But whites such as Bull Connor and Governor George Wallace denounced the agreement. When bombs rocked SCLC headquarters and the home of King's brother, a Birmingham minister, enraged blacks took to the streets and pelted police and firefighters with stones and bottles. President Kennedy ordered 3,000 army troops into the city and prepared to nationalize the Alabama National Guard. The violence receded, and white business people and politicians began to carry out the agreed-upon pact. But in September a bomb killed four black girls in a Birmingham Baptist church, reminding the city and the world that racial harmony was still a long way off.

The civil rights community now drew support from millions of Americans, black and white, who were inspired by the protesters and repelled by the face of Southern bigotry. At the same time, Birmingham changed the nature of black protest. The black unemployed and working poor who joined in the struggle brought a different perspective from that of the students, professionals, and members of the religious middle class who had dominated the movement before Birmingham. They cared less about the philosophy of nonviolence and more about immediate gains in employment and housing and an end to police brutality. "Freedom now!" they cried.

JFK AND THE MARCH ON WASHINGTON

The growth of black activism and white support convinced President Kennedy the moment had come to press for sweeping civil rights legislation. In June 1963, Alabama governor George Wallace threatened to personally block the admission of two black students to the state university. Only the deployment of National Guard troops, placed under federal control by the president, ensured the students' safety and their peaceful admission into the University of Alabama.

It was a defining moment for Kennedy. On June 11 the president went on national television and offered his personal endorsement of the civil rights activism. "Today we are committed to a worldwide struggle to promote and protect the rights of all who wish to be free. And when Americans are sent to Vietnam or West Berlin, we do not ask for whites only. . . . Are we to say to the rest of the world, and much more importantly, to each other, that this is a land of the free except for Negroes?" Reviewing the racial situation, Kennedy told his audience that "We face . . . a moral crisis as a country and a people. . . . It is a time to act in the Congress, in your state and local legislative body, and, above all, in all our daily lives." The next week Kennedy asked Congress for a broad law that would ensure voting rights, outlaw segregation in public facilities, and bolster federal authority to deny funds for discriminatory programs.

Movement leaders lauded the president's initiative, yet they understood that racial hatred still haunted the nation. Only a few hours after Kennedy's television speech, a gunman murdered Medgar Evers, leader of the Mississippi NAACP, outside his home in Jackson, Mississippi. To pressure Congress and demonstrate the urgency of their cause, a broad coalition of civil rights groups planned a massive, nonviolent March on Washington.

The Kennedy administration originally opposed the march, fearing it would jeopardize support for the president's civil rights bill in Congress. But as plans for the rally solidified, Kennedy reluctantly gave his approval. Leaders from the SCLC, the NAACP, SNCC, the Urban League, and CORE—the leading organizations in the civil rights community—put aside their tactical differences to forge a broad consensus for the event. John Lewis, the young head of SNCC, who had endured numerous brutal assaults, planned a speech that denounced the Kennedys as hypocrites. Randolph, the acknowledged elder statesman of the movement, convinced Lewis at the last moment to tone down his remarks. "We've come this far," he implored. "For the sake of unity, change it."

On August 28, 1963, more than a quarter of a million people, including 50,000 whites, gathered at the Lincoln Memorial to

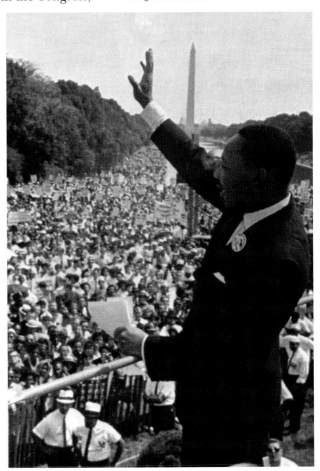

The Reverend Dr. Martin Luther King Jr. acknowledging the huge throng at the historic March on Washington for "jobs and freedom," August 28, 1963. The size of the crowd, the stirring oratory and song, and the live network television coverage produced one of the most memorable political events in the nation's history.

George Ballis/Take Stock

28–5
John Lewis, Address at the
March on Washington (1963)

rally for "jobs and freedom." Americans from all walks of life joined the largest political assembly in the nation's history until then. At the end of a long, exhilarating day of speeches and freedom songs, Martin Luther King Jr. stirred the crowd with his dream for America:

> I have a dream today that one day this nation will rise up and live out the true meaning of its creed: "We hold these truths to be self-evident—that all men are created equal." . . . When we allow freedom to ring, when we let it ring from every village and every hamlet, from every state and every city, we will be able to speed up that day when all of God's children—black men and white men, Jews and Gentiles, Protestants and Catholics—will be able to join hands and sing in the words of the old Negro spiritual, "Free at last! Free at last! Thank God Almighty, we are free at last!"

LBJ AND THE CIVIL RIGHTS ACT OF 1964

An extraordinary demonstration of interracial unity, the March on Washington stood as the high-water mark in the struggle for civil rights. But the assassination of John F. Kennedy on November 22, 1963, in Dallas threw an ominous cloud over the whole nation and the civil rights movement in particular. In the Deep South, many ardent segregationists welcomed the president's death because of his support for civil rights.

Lyndon Baines Johnson (LBJ), Kennedy's successor, had never been much of a friend to civil rights. Johnson had built a career as one of the shrewdest and most powerful Democrats in Congress. Throughout the 1950s he had worked to obstruct the passage and enforcement of civil rights laws—though as vice president he had ably chaired Kennedy's working group on equal employment. Civil rights activists looked upon Johnson warily as he took over the Oval Office.

As president, Johnson realized that he faced a new political reality, one created by the civil rights movement. Eager to unite the Democratic Party and prove himself as a national leader, he seized on civil rights as a golden political opportunity. Throughout the early months of 1964, the new president let it be known publicly and privately that he would brook no compromise on civil rights.

Johnson exploited all his skills as a political insider. He cajoled, flattered, and threatened key members of the House and Senate. Working with the president, the fifteen-year-old Leadership Conference on Civil Rights coordinated a sophisticated lobbying effort in Congress. The House passed the bill in February by a 290–130 vote. The more difficult fight would be in the Senate, where a Southern filibuster promised to block the bill or weaken it. But by June, Johnson's persistence had paid off and the Southern filibuster had collapsed.

On July 2, 1964, Johnson signed the **Civil Rights Act of 1964**. Every major provision had survived intact. This landmark law represented the most significant civil rights legislation since Reconstruction. It prohibited discrimination in most places of public accommodation; outlawed discrimination in employment on the basis of race, color, religion, sex, or national origin; outlawed bias in federally assisted programs; authorized the Justice Department to institute suits to desegregate public schools and other facilities; created the Equal Employment Opportunity Commission; and provided technical and financial aid to communities desegregating their schools.

MISSISSIPPI FREEDOM SUMMER

While President Johnson and his liberal allies won the congressional battle for the new civil rights bill, activists in Mississippi mounted a far more radical and dangerous campaign than any yet attempted in the South. In the spring of 1964, a coalition of

---

QUICK REVIEW

Johnson and Civil Rights

◆ Johnson had worked to obstruct civil rights legislation in the 1950s.

◆ Saw civil rights for African Americans as a way of uniting the Democratic Party.

◆ Applied personal political skills to passage of Civil Rights Act of 1964.

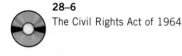

28–6
The Civil Rights Act of 1964

Civil Rights Act of 1964 Federal legislation that outlawed discrimination in public accommodations and employment on the basis of race, skin color, sex, religion, or national origin.

workers led by SNCC launched the **Freedom Summer** project, an ambitious effort to register black voters and directly challenge the iron rule of segregation. Mississippi stood as the toughest test for the civil rights movement, racially and economically. It was the poorest, most backward state in the nation, and had remained largely untouched by the freedom struggle. African Americans constituted 42 percent of the state's population, but fewer than 5 percent could register to vote. Median black family income was under $1,500 a year, roughly one-third that of white families. A small white planter elite controlled most of the state's wealth, and a long tradition of terror against black people had maintained the racial caste system.

Bob Moses of SNCC and Dave Dennis of CORE planned Freedom Summer as a way of opening up this closed society to the glare of national publicity. The

Freedom Summer Voter registration effort in rural Mississippi organized by black and white civil rights workers in 1964.

OVERVIEW

LANDMARK CIVIL RIGHTS LEGISLATION, SUPREME COURT DECISIONS, AND EXECUTIVE ORDERS

Year	Decision, Law, or Executive Order	Significance
1939	*Missouri v. ex.rel.Gaines*	Required University of Missouri Law School either to admit African Americans or build another fully equal law school.
1941	Executive Order 8802 (by President Roosevelt)	Banned racial discrimination in defense industry and government offices; established Fair Employment Practices Committee to investigate violations.
1946	*Morgan v. Virginia*	Ruled that segregation on interstate buses violated federal law and created an "undue burden" on interstate commerce.
1948	Executive Order 9981 (by President Truman)	Desegregated the U.S. armed forces.
1950	*McLaurin v. Oklahoma State Regents*	Ruled that forcing an African American student to sit, eat, and study in segregated facilities was unconstitutional because it inevitably created a "badge of inferiority."
1950	*Sweatt v. Painter*	Ruled that an inferior law school created by the University of Texas to serve African Americans violated their right to equal protection and ordered Herman Sweatt to be admitted to University of Texas Law School.
1954	*Brown v. Board of Education of Topeka I*	Declared "separate educational facilities are inherently unequal," thus overturning *Plessy v. Ferguson* (1896) and the "separate but equal" doctrine as it applied to public schools.
1955	*Brown v. Board of Education of Topeka II*	Ordered school desegregation to begin with "all deliberate speed," but offered no timetable.
1957	Civil Rights Act	Created Civil Rights Division within the Justice Department.
1964	Civil Rights Act	Prohibited discrimination in employment and most places of public accommodation on basis of race, color, religion, sex, or national origin; outlawed bias in federally assisted programs; created Equal Employment Opportunity Commission.
1965	Voting Rights Act	Authorized federal supervision of voter registration in states and counties where fewer than half of voting age residents were registered; outlawed literacy and other discriminatory tests in voter registration.

project recruited over 900 volunteers, mostly white college students, to aid in voter registration, teach in "freedom schools," and help build a "freedom party" as an alternative to Mississippi's all-white Democratic Party. Organizers expected violence, which was precisely why they wanted white volunteers. Dave Dennis later explained their reasoning: "The death of a white college student would bring on more attention to what was going on than for a black college student getting it."

The predictions of violence proved accurate. On June 21, while most project volunteers were still undergoing training in Ohio, three activists disappeared in Neshoba County, Mississippi, when they went to investigate the burning of a black church that was supposed to serve as a freedom school. Six weeks later, after a massive search belatedly ordered by President Johnson, FBI agents discovered the bodies of the three—white activists Michael Schwerner and Andrew Goodman, and a local black activist, James Chaney—buried in an earthen dam. Goodman and Schwerner had been shot once; Chaney had been severely beaten before being shot three times. Over the summer, at least three other civil rights workers died violently. Project workers suffered 1,000 arrests, 80 beatings, 35 shooting incidents, and 30 bombings in homes, churches, and schools.

Within the project, there were simmering problems. Black veterans of SNCC resented the affluent white volunteers, many of whom had not come to terms with their own racial prejudices. Sexual tensions between black male and white female volunteers also strained relations. A number of black and white women began to raise the issue of women's equality as a companion goal to racial equality. The day-to-day reality of violent reprisals, police harassment, and constant fear took a hard toll on everyone.

The project did manage to rivet national attention on Mississippi racism, and it got 60,000 black voters signed up to join the Mississippi Freedom Democratic Party (MFDP). In August 1964 the MFDP sent a slate of delegates to the Democratic National Convention looking to challenge the credentials of the all-white regular state delegation. Lyndon Johnson opposed the seating of the MFDP because he wanted to avoid a divisive floor fight. He was already concerned that Republicans might carry a number of Southern states in November. But MFDP leaders and sympathizers gave dramatic testimony before the convention, detailing the racism and brutality in Mississippi politics. "Is this America," asked Fannie Lou Hamer, "the land of the free and the home of the brave, where we are threatened daily because we want to live as decent human beings?" Led by vice presidential nominee Senator Hubert Humphrey, Johnson's forces offered a compromise that would have given the MFDP a token two seats on the floor. Bitter over what they saw as a betrayal, the MFDP delegates turned the offer down. Within SNCC, the defeat of the MFDP intensified African American disillusionment with the Democratic Party and the liberal establishment.

MALCOLM X AND BLACK CONSCIOUSNESS

Frustrated with the limits of nonviolent protest and electoral politics, younger activists within SNCC found themselves increasingly drawn to the militant rhetoric and vision of Malcolm X, who since 1950 had been the preeminent spokesman for the black nationalist religious sect, the **Nation of Islam (NOI).** Founded in Depression-era Detroit by Elijah Muhammad, the NOI, like the followers of black nationalist leader Marcus Garvey in the 1920s (see Chapter 23) aspired to create a self-reliant, highly disciplined, and proud community—a separate "nation" for black people. During the 1950s the NOI (also called Black Muslims) successfully organized in Northern black communities. It operated restaurants, retail stores, and schools as models for black economic self-sufficiency.

Nation of Islam (NOI) Religious movement among black Americans that emphasizes self-sufficiency, self-help, and separation from white society.

The man known as Malcolm X had been born Malcolm Little in 1925 and raised in Lansing, Michigan. His father, a preacher and a follower of Marcus Garvey, was killed in a racist attack by local whites. In his youth, Malcolm led a life of petty crime, eventually serving a seven-year prison term for burglary. While in jail he educated himself and converted to the Nation of Islam. He took the surname "X" to symbolize his original African family name, lost through slavery. Emerging from jail in 1952, he became a dynamic organizer, editor, and speaker for the Nation of Islam. He encouraged his audiences to take pride in their African heritage and to consider armed self-defense rather than relying solely on nonviolence.

Malcolm ridiculed the integrationist goals of the civil rights movement. Black Muslims, he told audiences, do not want "to integrate into this corrupt society, but to separate from it, to a land of our own, where we can reform ourselves, lift up our moral standards, and try to be godly." In his best-selling *Autobiography of Malcolm X* (1965), he admitted that his position was extremist. "The black race here in North America is in extremely bad condition. You show me a black man who isn't an extremist," he argued, "and I'll show you one who needs psychiatric attention."

In 1964, troubled by Elijah Muhammad's personal scandals (he faced paternity suits brought by two young female employees) and eager to find a more politically effective approach to improving conditions for blacks, Malcolm X broke with the Nation of Islam. He made a pilgrimage to Mecca, the Muslim holy city, where he met Islamic peoples of all colors and underwent a "radical alteration in my whole outlook about 'white' men." He returned to the United States as El-Hajj Malik El-Shabazz, abandoned his black separatist views, and founded the Organization of Afro-American Unity.

On February 21, 1965, Malcolm X was assassinated during a speech at Harlem's Audubon Ballroom. His assailants were members of a New Jersey branch of the NOI, possibly infiltrated by the FBI. "More than any other person," remarked black author Julius Lester, "Malcolm X was responsible for the new militancy that entered The Movement in 1965." SNCC leader John Lewis thought Malcolm had been the most effective voice "to articulate the aspirations, bitterness, and frustrations of the Negro people," forming "a living link between Africa and the civil rights movement in this country." As much as anyone, Malcolm X pointed the way to a new black consciousness that celebrated black history, black culture, the African heritage, and black self-sufficiency.

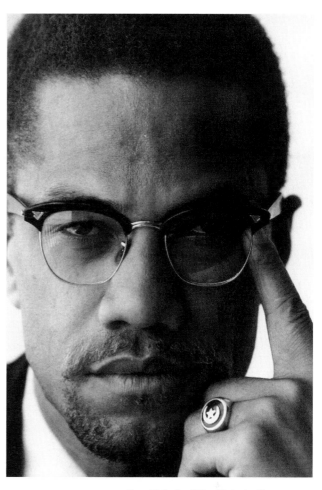

Born Malcolm Little, Malcolm X (1925–1965) took the name "X" as a symbol of the stolen identity of African slaves. He emerged in the early 1960s as the foremost advocate of racial unity and black nationalism. The Black Power movement, initiated in 1966 by SNCC members, was strongly influenced by Malcolm X.

Malcolm X in Egypt, 1964. Photo by John Launois. Black Star

SELMA AND THE VOTING RIGHTS ACT OF 1965

Lyndon Johnson won reelection in 1964 by a landslide, capturing 61 percent of the popular vote. Of the 6 million black people who voted in the election, 2 million more than in 1960, an overwhelming 94 percent cast their ballots for Johnson. With Democrats in firm control of both the Senate and the House, Johnson and his staff began drafting a tough voting rights bill in late 1964, partly with an eye toward countering Republican gains in the Deep South with newly registered black and Democratic voters. Martin Luther King and the SCLC shared this goal of passing a strong voting rights law that would provide Southern black people with direct federal protection of their right to vote.

28–8
Lyndon B. Johnson, Commencement Address at Howard University (1965)

Once again, movement leaders plotted to create a crisis that would arouse national indignation, pressure Congress, and force federal action. Selma, Alabama, because of its notorious record of preventing black voting, was selected as the target. Sensing that county sheriff Jim Clark might be another Bull Connor, King arrived in Selma in January 1965, just after accepting the Nobel Peace Prize in Oslo. King, the SCLC staff, and SNCC workers led daily marches on the Dallas County Courthouse, where hundreds of black citizens tried to get their names added to voter lists. By early February, Clark had imprisoned more than 3,000 protesters.

Despite the brutal beating of Reverend James Bevel, a key SCLC strategist, and the killing of Jimmy Lee Jackson, a young black demonstrator in nearby Marion, the SCLC failed to arouse the level of national indignation it sought. Consequently, in early March SCLC staffers called on black activists to march from Selma to Montgomery, where they planned to deliver a list of grievances to Governor Wallace. On Sunday, March 7, while King preached to his church in Atlanta, a group of 600 marchers crossed the Pettus Bridge on the Alabama River, on their way to Montgomery. A group of mounted, heavily armed county and state lawmen blocked their path and ordered them to turn back. When the marchers did not move, the lawmen attacked with billy clubs and tear gas, driving the protesters back over the bridge in a bloody rout. More than fifty marchers had to be treated in local hospitals.

MAP EXPLORATION

To explore an interactive version of this map, go to **http://www.prenhall.com/faraghertlc/map28.2**

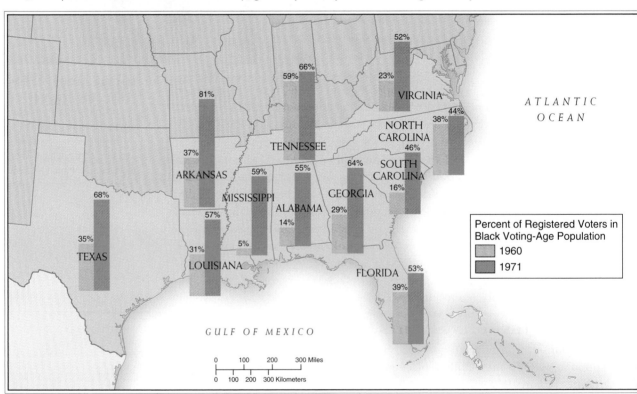

MAP 28-2

Impact of the Voting Rights Act of 1965 Voter registration among African Americans in the South increased significantly between 1960 and 1971.

IN WHICH states was the increase in registered African American voters particularly dramatic?

The dramatic "Bloody Sunday" attack received extensive coverage on network television, prompting a national uproar. Demands for federal intervention poured into the White House from all over the country. King issued a public call for civil rights supporters to come to Selma for a second march on Montgomery, but a federal court temporarily enjoined the SCLC from proceeding with the march. King found himself trapped. He reluctantly accepted a face-saving compromise: in return for a promise from Alabama authorities not to harm marchers, King would lead his followers across the Pettus Bridge, stop, pray briefly, and then turn back. This plan outraged the more militant SNCC activists and sharpened their distrust of King and the SCLC.

But just when it seemed the Selma movement might die, white racist violence revived it. A gang of white toughs attacked four white Unitarian ministers who had come to Selma to participate in the march. One of them, Rev. James J. Reeb of Boston, died of multiple skull fractures. His death brought new calls for federal action. On March 15, President Johnson delivered a televised address to a joint session of Congress to request passage of a voting rights bill. In a stirring speech, the president fused the political power of his office with the moral power of the movement. "Their cause must be our cause, too. Because it is not just Negroes, but really all of us who must overcome the crippling legacy of bigotry and injustice. And," he concluded firmly, invoking the movement's slogan, "we shall overcome." Johnson also prevailed upon federal judge Frank Johnson to issue a ruling allowing the march to proceed, and he warned Governor Wallace not to interfere.

On March 21 Martin Luther King led a group of more than 3,000 black and white marchers out of Selma on the road to Montgomery. Four days later they arrived at the Alabama statehouse. Their ranks had been swelled by more than 30,000 supporters, including hundreds of prominent politicians, entertainers, and black leaders.

In August 1965 President Johnson signed the **Voting Rights Act** into law. It authorized federal supervision of registration in states and counties where fewer than half of voting-age residents were registered. It also outlawed literacy and other discriminatory tests that had been used to prevent blacks from registering to vote. Between 1964 and 1968, black registrants in Mississippi leaped from 7 percent to 59 percent of the statewide black population; in Alabama, from 24 percent to 57 percent. In those years the number of Southern black voters grew from 1 million to 3.1 million. For the first time in their lives, black Southerners in hundreds of small towns and rural communities could enjoy full participation in American politics. Ten years after the Montgomery bus boycott, the civil rights movement had reached a peak of national influence and interracial unity.

> **Voting Rights Act** Legislation in 1965 that overturned a variety of practices by which states systematically denied voter registration to minorities.

FORGOTTEN MINORITIES, 1945–1965

The historic injustices of slavery, racism, and segregation gave a moral and political urgency to the black struggle for full citizenship rights, yet other minorities as well had long been denied their civil rights. After World War II, Latinos, Indian peoples, and Asian Americans began making their own halting efforts to improve their political, legal, and economic status. By the late 1960s, the success of the black civil rights movement had inspired these minority groups to adopt more militant strategies of their own.

WHAT STEPS did Indian peoples take to expand and protect their rights in the decades after World War II?

MEXICAN AMERICANS

The Mexican American community in the West and Southwest included both long-time U.S. citizens—who found white authorities nonetheless unwilling to recognize their rights—and noncitizen immigrants from Mexico. After World War II, several

Mexican American political organizations sought to secure equal rights and equal opportunity for their community by stressing its American identity. The most important of these groups were the League of United Latin American Citizens (LULAC), founded in Texas in 1928, and the G.I. Forum, founded in Texas in 1948 by Mexican American veterans of World War II. Both emphasized the learning of English, assimilation into American society, improved education, and the promotion of political power through voting. LULAC successfully pursued two important legal cases that anticipated *Brown* v. *Board of Education.* In *Mendez* v. *Westminster,* a 1947 California case, and in the 1948 *Delgado* case in Texas, the Supreme Court upheld lower court rulings that declared segregation of Mexican Americans unconstitutional. LULAC won another significant legal battle in the 1954 *Hernandez* decision, in which the Supreme Court ended the exclusion of Mexican Americans from Texas jury lists.

Mexican migration to the United States increased dramatically during and after World War II. The *bracero* program, a cooperative effort between the U.S. and Mexican governments, brought some 300,000 Mexicans to the United States during the war as temporary agricultural and railroad workers. American agribusiness came to depend on Mexicans as a key source of cheap farm labor, and the program continued after the war. Most braceros endured harsh work, poor food, and substandard housing in the camps in which they lived. Some migrated into the newly emerging barrio neighborhoods in cities such as San Antonio, Los Angeles, El Paso, and Denver. Many braceros and their children became American citizens, but most returned to Mexico. Another group of postwar Mexican immigrants were the *mojados,* or "wetbacks," so called because many swam across the Rio Grande River to enter the United States illegally.

In 1954, in an effort to curb the flow of undocumented immigrants from Mexico, the Eisenhower administration launched the massive "Operation Wetback." Over the next three years Immigration Service agents rounded up some 3.7 million allegedly illegal migrants and sent them back over the border. Immigration agents made lit-

Delegates to the 1948 National Convention of the League of United Latin American Citizens (LULAC) met in Kingsville, Texas. After World War II, LULAC grew to about 15,000 members active in 200 local councils, mostly in Texas and California.

Benson Latin American Collection

tle effort to distinguish the so-called illegals from braceros and Mexican American citizens. Many families were broken up, and thousands who had lived in the United States for a decade or more found themselves deported. Many deportees were denied basic civil liberties, such as due process, and suffered physical abuse and intimidation. Among Mexican Americans, Operation Wetback left a bitter legacy of deep mistrust and estrangement from Anglo culture and politics.

PUERTO RICANS

The United States took possession of the island of Puerto Rico in 1898, during the final stages of the Spanish-American War. The Jones Act of 1917 made the island an unincorporated territory of the United States and granted U.S. citizenship to all Puerto Ricans. Over the next several decades, Puerto Rico's economic base shifted from a diversified, subsistence-oriented agriculture to a single export crop—sugar. U.S. absentee owners dominated the sugar industry. Puerto Rico's sugar industry grew enormously profitable, but few island residents benefited from this expansion. By the 1930s, unemployment and poverty were widespread and the island was forced to import its foodstuffs.

Early Puerto Rican immigrants were forced to live in cramped, sparse conditions.

Bettman/Corbis.

Small communities of Puerto Rican migrants had begun to form in New York City during the 1920s. The largest was on the Upper East Side of Manhattan—*el barrio* in East Harlem. During the World War II, labor shortages led the federal government to sponsor the recruitment of Puerto Rican workers for industrial jobs in New Jersey, Philadelphia, and Chicago. But the "great migration" took place from 1945 to 1964.

The advent of direct air service between Puerto Rico and New York in 1945 made the city easily accessible. By 1970 there were about 800,000 Puerto Ricans in New York—more than 10 percent of the city's population. New Puerto Rican communities also took root in Connecticut, Massachusetts, New Jersey, and the Midwest.

The experience of Puerto Rican migrants both resembled and differed from that of other immigrant groups in significant ways. Like Mexican immigrants, Puerto Ricans were foreign in language, culture, and experience, yet unlike them they entered the United States as citizens. In New York, Puerto Ricans found themselves barred from most craft unions, excluded from certain neighborhoods, and forced to take jobs largely in the low-paying garment industry and service trades. Puerto Rican children were not well served by a public school system insensitive to language differences and too willing to track Spanish-speaking students into obsolete vocational programs.

By the early 1970s, Puerto Rican families were substantially poorer on average than the total population of the country, and they had the lowest median income of any Latino groups. The steep decline in manufacturing jobs and in the garment industry in New York during the 1960s and 1970s hit the Puerto Rican community especially hard. So did the city's fiscal crisis, which brought sharp cuts in funding for schools, health care, libraries, government jobs, and other public services traditionally available to immigrant groups. The structural shift in the U.S. economy away from manufacturing and toward service and high-technology jobs reinforced the Puerto Rican community's goal of improving educational opportunities for its members. The struggle to establish and improve bilingual education in schools became an important part of this effort.

INDIAN PEOPLES

The postwar years also brought significant changes in the status and lives of Indian peoples. Congress reversed the policies pursued under the New Deal, which had stressed Indian sovereignty and cultural independence. Responding to a variety

George Gillette (left foreground), chairman of the Fort Berthold Indian Council, wept as Secretary of Interior J. A. Krug signed a contract buying 155,000 acres of the tribe's best land in North Dakota for a reservoir project, May 20, 1948. "The members of the tribal council sign this contract with heavy hearts," Gillette said.
CORBIS

of pressure groups, including mining and other economic interests wishing to exploit the resources on Indian reservations, Congress adopted a policy known as "termination," designed to cancel Indian treaties and terminate sovereignty rights. In 1953, Congress passed House Concurrent Resolution 108, which allowed Congress to terminate a tribe as a political entity by passing legislation specific to that tribe. Supporters of termination had varied motives, but the policy added up to the return of enforced assimilation for solving the "Indian problem."

Between 1954 and 1962, Congress passed twelve termination bills covering more than sixty tribes, nearly all in the West. Even when tribes consented to their own termination, they discovered that dissolution brought unforeseen problems. For example, members of the Klamaths of Oregon and the Paiutes of Utah received large cash payments from the division of tribal assets. But after these one-time payments were spent, members had to take poorly paid, unskilled jobs to survive. Many Indian peoples became dependent on state social services and slipped into poverty and alcoholism.

Along with termination, the federal government gave greater emphasis to a relocation program aimed at speeding up assimilation. The Bureau of Indian Affairs encouraged reservation Indians to relocate to cities, where they were provided housing and jobs. For some, relocation meant assimilation, intermarriage with whites, and the loss of tribal identity. Others, homesick and unable to adjust to an alien culture and place, either returned to reservations or wound up on the margins of city life.

By the early 1960s, a new movement was emerging to defend Indian sovereignty. The National Congress of American Indians (NCAI) condemned termination, calling for a review of federal policies and a return to self-determination. The NCAI led a political and educational campaign that challenged the goal of assimilation and created a new awareness among white people that Indians had the right to remain Indians. When the termination policy ended in the early 1960s, it had affected only about 3 percent of federally recognized Indian peoples.

Taking their cue from the civil rights movement, Indian activists used the court system to reassert sovereign rights. Indian and white liberal lawyers, many with experience in civil rights cases, worked through the Native American Rights Fund, which became a powerful force in Western politics. A series of Supreme Court decisions, culminating in *United States* v. *Wheeler* (1978), reasserted the principle of "unique and limited" sovereignty. The Court recognized tribal independence except where limited by treaty or Congress.

The Indian population had been growing since the early years of the century, but most reservations had trouble making room for a new generation. Indians suffered increased rates of poverty, chronic unemployment, alcoholism, and poor health. The average Indian family in the early 1960s earned only one-third of the average family income in the United States. Those who remained in the cities usually became "ethnic Indians," identifying themselves more as Indians than as members of specific tribes. By the late 1960s, ethnic Indians had begun emphasizing civil rights over tribal rights, making common cause with African Americans and other minorities. The National Indian Youth Council (NIYC), founded in 1960, tried to unite the two causes of equality for individual Indians and special status for tribes. But the organization faced difficult contradictions between a common Indian identity, emphasizing Indians as a single ethnic group, and tribal identity, stressing the citizenship of Indians in separate nations.

QUICK REVIEW

Termination

- Cancellation of treaties and sovereignty rights under pressure from mining and other economic interests.
- 1954–1962: Termination bills passed covering sixty tribes.
- Termination contributed to poverty and social problems among Indian peoples.

ASIAN AMERICANS

The harsh relocation program of World War II devastated the Japanese American community on the west coast (see Chapter 25). But the war against Nazism also helped weaken older notions of white superiority and racism. During the war the state of California had aggressively enforced an alien land law by confiscating property declared illegally held by Japanese. In November 1946 a proposition supporting the law appeared on the state ballot. But, thanks in part to a campaign by the Japanese

CHRONOLOGY

1941 Executive Order 8802 forbids racial discrimination in defense industries and government.

1946 In *Morgan* v. *Virginia*, U.S. Supreme Court rules that segregation on interstate buses is unconstitutional.

President Harry Truman creates the Committee on Civil Rights.

1947 Jackie Robinson becomes the first African American on a major league baseball team.

1948 President Truman issues executive order desegregating the armed forces.

1954 In *Brown* v. *Board of Education,* Supreme Court rules segregated schools inherently unequal.

1955 Supreme Court rules that school desegregation must proceed "with all deliberate speed."

Montgomery bus boycott begins.

1956 Montgomery bus boycott ends in victory as the Supreme Court affirms a district court ruling that segregation on buses is unconstitutional.

1957 Southern Christian Leadership Conference (SCLC) is founded.

President Dwight Eisenhower sends in federal troops to protect African American students integrating Little Rock, Arkansas, high school.

1960 Sit-in movement begins as four college students sit at a lunch counter in Greensboro, North Carolina, and ask to be served.

Student Nonviolent Coordinating Committee (SNCC) founded.

1960 Board of Indian Commissioners is created.

Buffalo Bill, the King of the Border Men, sets off "Wild West" publishing craze.

1961 Freedom Rides begin.

1962 James Meredith integrates the University of Mississippi.

The Albany movement fails to end segregation in Albany, Georgia.

1963 SCLC initiates campaign to desegregate Birmingham, Alabama.

Medgar Evers, leader of the Mississippi NAACP, is assassinated.

March on Washington; Martin Luther King Jr. delivers his historic "I Have a Dream" speech.

1964 Mississippi Freedom Summer project brings students to Mississippi to teach and register voters.

President Johnson signs the Civil Rights Act of 1964.

Civil rights workers Michael Schwerner, James Chaney, and Andrew Goodman are found buried in Philadelphia, Mississippi.

Mississippi Freedom Democratic Party (MFDP) is denied seats at the 1964 Democratic Presidential Convention.

1965 SCLC and SNCC begin voter registration campaign in Selma, Alabama.

Malcolm X is assassinated.

Civil rights marchers walk from Selma to Montgomery.

Voting Rights Act of 1965 is signed into law.

American Citizens League (JACL) reminding voters of the wartime contributions of Nisei (second-generation Japanese Americans) soldiers, voters overwhelmingly rejected the referendum. Two years later the Supreme Court declared the law unconstitutional, calling it "nothing more than outright racial discrimination."

The 1952 Immigration and Nationality Act (see Chapter 26) removed the old ban against Japanese immigration, and also made Issei (first-generation Japanese Americans) eligible for naturalized citizenship. Japanese Americans, who lobbied hard for the new law, greeted it with elation. "It gave the Japanese equality with all other immigrants," said JACL leader Harry Takagi, "and that was the principle we had been struggling for from the very beginning." By 1965 some 46,000 immigrant Japanese, most of them elderly Issei, had taken their citizenship oaths.

In 1965 Congress passed a new Immigration and Nationality Act, abolishing the national-origins quotas and providing for the admission each year of 170,000 immigrants from the Eastern Hemisphere and 120,000 from the Western Hemisphere. The new law set a limit of 20,000 per country from the Eastern Hemisphere—these immigrants to be admitted on a first-come, first-served basis—and established preference categories for professional and highly skilled immigrants.

The 1965 act would have a profound effect on Asian American communities, opening the way for a new wave of immigration. In the twenty years following the act, the number of Asian Americans soared from 1 million to 5 million. Four times as many Asians settled in the United States in this period as in the entire previous history of the nation. This new wave also brought a strikingly different group of Asian immigrants to America. In 1960 the Asian American population was 52 percent Japanese, 27 percent Chinese, and 20 percent Filipino. In 1985, the composition was 21 percent Chinese, 21 percent Filipino, 15 percent Japanese, 12 percent Vietnamese, 11 percent Korean, 10 percent Asian Indian, 4 percent Laotian, and 3 percent Cambodian. These newcomers included significant numbers of highly educated professionals and city dwellers, a sharp contrast with the farmers and rural peoples of the past.

CONCLUSION

The mass movement for civil rights was arguably the most important domestic event of the twentieth century. The struggle that began in Montgomery, Alabama, in December 1955 ultimately transformed race relations in thousands of American communities. By the early 1960s this community-based movement had placed civil rights at the very center of national political life. It achieved its greatest successes by invoking the law of the land to destroy legal segregation and win individual freedom for African Americans. The Civil Rights Act of 1964 and the Voting Rights Act of 1965 testified to the power of an African American and white liberal coalition. Yet the persistence of racism, poverty, and ghetto slums challenged a central assumption of liberalism: that equal protection of constitutional rights would give all Americans equal opportunities in life. By the mid-1960s, many black people had begun to question the core values of liberalism, the benefits of alliance with whites, and the philosophy of nonviolence. At the same time, a conservative white backlash against the gains made by African Americans further weakened the liberal political consensus.

In challenging the persistence of widespread poverty and institutional racism, the civil rights movement called for deep structural changes in American life. By 1967, Martin Luther King Jr. was articulating a broad and radical vision linking the struggle against racial injustice to other defects in American society. "The black revolution," he argued, "is much more than a struggle for the rights of Negroes. It is forcing America to face all its interrelated flaws—racism, poverty, militarism, and materialism. It is exposing evils that are deeply rooted in the whole structure of our society." Curing these ills would prove far more difficult than ending legal segregation.

SUMMARY

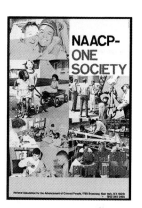

Origins of the Movement The migration of African Americans to Northern cities led to increased economic and political opportunities. Voting power and legal action by the NAACP led to increased civil rights. In the South, segregation prevailed. After World War II, the NAACP legal strategy culminated in the victory in *Brown* v. *Board of Education* that ended segregation in the schools. A crisis in Little Rock, Arkansas, forced President Eisenhower to use National Guard troops to integrate the schools there.

No Easy Road to Freedom, 1957–1962 African Americans used several nonviolent strategies to obtain civil rights, including boycotts, sit-ins, and freedom rides. A number of organizations emerged to pursue civil rights. Their campaigns often proved successful but met with strong resistance in the South.

The Movement at High Tide, 1963–1965 Between 1963 and 1965, civil rights activities reached new heights and registered important victories. The campaign in Birmingham, Alabama, met strong, violent resistance but resulted in several gains. The March on Washington attracted 250,000 people and after the assassination of John Kennedy led to passage of the Civil Rights Act. Direct action continued with the Mississippi Freedom Summer that suffered tragic violence. A different movement was founded by Malcom X who stressed militancy and black consciousness. In 1964, the Selma protests helped secure passage of the Voting Rights Act.

Forgotten Minorities, 1945–1965 The African American civil rights movement stimulated similar efforts by Mexican Americans, Puerto Ricans, Indian peoples, and Asian Americans. Each group pursued goals connected to their specific situation using a variety of strategies.

REVIEW QUESTIONS

1. What were the key legal and political antecedents to the civil rights struggle in the 1940s and early 1950s? What organizations played the most central role? Which tactics continued to be used, and which were abandoned?

2. How did African American communities challenge legal segregation in the South? Compare the strategies of key organizations, such as the NAACP, SNCC, SCLC, and CORE.

3. Discuss the varieties of white resistance to the civil rights movement. Which were most effective in slowing the drive for equality?

4. Analyze the civil rights movement's complex relationship with the national Democratic Party between 1948 and 1964. How was the party transformed by its association with the movement? What political gains and losses did that association entail?

5. What legal and institutional impact did the movement have on American life? How did it change American culture and politics? Where did it fail?

6. What relationship did the African Americans who struggled for civil rights have with other American minorities? How—if at all—did these minorities benefit? Did they build their own versions of the movement?

KEY TERMS

Brown v. *Board of Education* (p. 766)
Civil Rights Act of 1964 (p. 776)
Congress of Racial Equality (CORE) (p. 764)
Freedom Summer (p. 777)
Nation of Islam (NOI) (p. 778)
Southern Manifesto (p. 766)

Southern Christian Leadership Conference (SCLC) (p. 768)
Student Nonviolent Coordinating Committee (SNCC) (p. 770)
The Albany movement (p. 773)
Voting Rights Act (p. 781)

RECOMMENDED READING

Taylor Branch, *Parting the Waters: America in the King Years, 1954–1963* (1988); *Pillar of Fire: America in the King Years, 1963–1965* (1998). A deeply researched and monumental narrative history of the Southern civil rights movement organized around the life and influence of the Reverend Martin Luther King Jr.

Clayborne Carson, *In Struggle: SNCC and the Black Awakening of the 1960s* (1981). The most comprehensive history of the Student Nonviolent Coordinating Committee, arguably the most important civil rights organization. Carson stresses the evolution of SNCC's radicalism during the course of the decade.

William Chafe, *Civilities and Civil Rights: Greensboro, North Carolina, and the Black Struggle for Equality* (1980). Examines the community of Greensboro from 1945 to 1975. Chafe focuses on the "etiquette of civility" and its complex relationship with the promise of racial justice, along with black protest movements and relations between the city's black and white residents.

David Chappell, *Inside Agitators: White Southerners in the Civil Rights Movement* (1994). A thoughtful and sophisticated analysis of the varying roles played by white people in the movement.

Mary L. Dudziak, *Cold War Civil Rights: Race and the Image of American Democracy* (2000). Excellent analysis of the connections between the struggle for racial equality in America and the nation's contest with communism abroad.

Sara Evans, *Personal Politics: The Roots of Women's Liberation in the Civil Rights Movement and the New Left* (1979). A pathbreaking study showing the important connections between the struggle for black rights and the rebirth of feminism.

Aldon D. Morris, *The Origins of the Civil Rights Movement: Black Communities Organizing for Change* (1984). An important study combining history and social theory. Morris emphasizes the key role of ordinary black people, acting through their churches and other community organizations before 1960.

Howell Raines, *My Soul Is Rested: Movement Days in the Deep South Remembered* (1977). The best oral history of the civil rights movement, drawing from a wide range of participants and points of view. It is brilliantly edited by Raines, who covered the events as a journalist.

Jo Ann Gibson Robinson, *The Montgomery Bus Boycott and the Women Who Started It*, ed. David J. Garrow (1987). An important memoir by one of the key behind-the-scenes players in the Montgomery bus boycott. Robinson stresses the role of middle- and working-class black women in the struggle.

Robert Weisbrot, *Freedom Bound: A History of America's Civil Rights Movement* (1990). One of the best single-volume syntheses of the movement. Weisbrot is especially strong on the often turbulent relations between black activists and white liberals and the relationship between civil rights and broader currents of American reform.

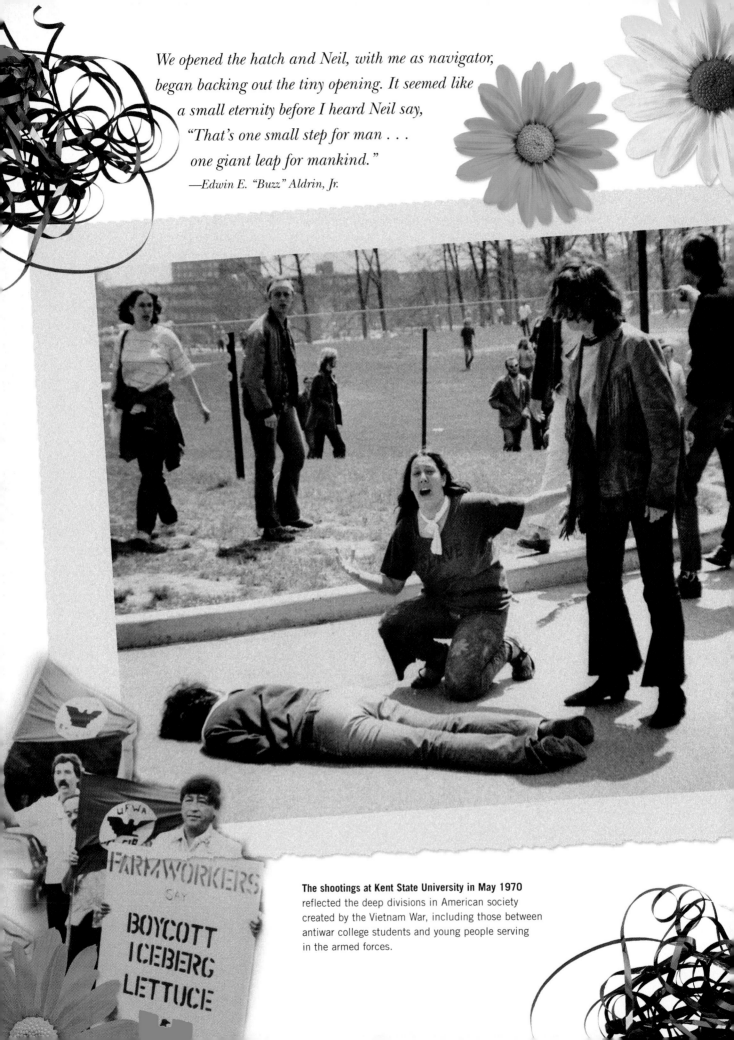

We opened the hatch and Neil, with me as navigator, began backing out the tiny opening. It seemed like a small eternity before I heard Neil say, "That's one small step for man . . . one giant leap for mankind."
—*Edwin E. "Buzz" Aldrin, Jr.*

The shootings at Kent State University in May 1970 reflected the deep divisions in American society created by the Vietnam War, including those between antiwar college students and young people serving in the armed forces.

BOYCOTT ICEBERG LETTUCE

29

War Abroad, War at Home
1965–1974

WHY DID Johnson escalate the war in Vietnam?

HOW DID campus protests shape national political debate?

WHAT WERE the goals of Johnson's Great Society?

WHAT DIVIDED the Democratic Party in 1968?

WHAT IS meant by the "politics of identity"?

HOW DID Nixon win the White House in 1968?

WHY WAS Nixon so secretive about his foreign policy?

AMERICAN COMMUNITIES
Uptown, Chicago, Illinois

DURING FREEDOM SUMMER OF 1964, WHILE TEAMS OF NORTHERN college students traveled south to join voter registration campaigns among African Americans, a small group moved to Chicago to help the city's poor people take control of their communities and to demand better city services. They targeted a neighborhood known as Uptown, a one-mile-square section five miles north of the Loop, the city center. The residents, many only recently transplanted from the poverty of the Appalachian South, lived in crowded tenements or in once elegant mansions now subdivided into tiny, run-down apartments. Four thousand people lived on just one street running four blocks, 20 percent of them on welfare. Chicago civic authorities had also selected this neighborhood for improvement. Designating it a Conservation Area under the terms of the Urban Renewal Act, they applied for federal funds in order to upgrade the housing for middle-income families and, in effect, to clear out the current residents. In contrast, the student organizers intended to mobilize the community "so as to demand an end to poverty and the construction of a decent social order."

With the assistance of the Packinghouse Workers union, the students formed Jobs or Income Now (JOIN), opened a storefront office, and invited local residents to work with them to halt the city's plans. They spent hours and hours listening to people, drawing out their ideas and helping them develop scores of additional programs. Confronting the bureaucracy of the welfare and unemployment compensation offices stood high on their list. They also campaigned against Mayor Richard Daley's policy of "police omnipresence" that had a fleet of squad cars and paddy wagons continually patrolling the neighborhood. To curb police harassment, they demanded the creation of civilian review boards. They also helped establish new social clubs, a food-buying cooperative, a community theater, and a health clinic. Within a few years, Uptown street kids had formed the Young Patriots organization, put out a community newspaper, Rising Up Angry, and staffed free breakfast programs.

Chicago JOIN was one of ten similar projects sponsored by Students for a Democratic Society (SDS). Impatient with the nation's chronic poverty and Cold War politics, twenty-nine students from nine universities had met in June 1960 to form a new kind of campus-based political organization. SDS soon caught the attention of liberal students, encouraging them, as part of the nation's largest college population to date, to make their voices heard. By its peak in 1968, SDS had 350 chapters and between 60,000 and 100,000 members. Its principle of participatory democracy—with its promise to give people control over the decisions affecting their lives—appealed to a wider following of more than a million students.

In June 1962, in Port Huron, Michigan, the founding members of SDS issued a declaration of principles, drafted mainly by graduate student Tom Hayden. "We are people . . . bred in at least modest comfort, housed now in universities," The Port Huron Statement opened, "looking uncomfortably to the world we inherit." The dire effects of poverty and social injustice, it continued, were not the only dismaying things about American society. A deeper ailment plagued American politics. Everyone, including middle-class students with few material wants, suffered from a sense of "loneliness, estrangement, and alienation." The Port Huron Statement defined SDS as a new kind of political movement that would bring people "out of isolation and into community." Through participatory democracy, not just the poor but also all Americans could overcome their feelings of "powerlessness [and hence] resignation before the enormity of events." As one organizer explained, programs like JOIN were attempts to create a poor people's movement as well as a means for students themselves to live an "authentic life" outside the constraints of middle-class society.

SDS began with a campaign to reform the university, especially to disentangle the financial ties between campus-based research programs and the military–industrial complex. Later it expanded to the nation's cities, sending small groups of students to live and organize in the poor communities of Boston, Louisville, Cleveland, and Newark as well as Chicago. Ultimately, few of these projects succeeded in mobilizing the poor to political action. Protests against local government did little to combat unemployment, and campaigns for better garbage collection or more playgrounds rarely evolved into lasting movements. Nevertheless, organizers did succeed in bringing many neighborhood residents "out of isolation and into community." By late 1967, SDS prepared to leave JOIN in the hands of the people it had organized, which was its goal from the beginning.

Initially, even Lyndon Baines Johnson promoted the ideal of civic participation. The Great Society, as the president called his domestic program, promised more than the abolition of poverty and racial inequality. In May 1964, at the University of Michigan, the president described his goal as a society "where every child can find knowledge to enrich his mind and to enlarge his talents," where "the city of man serves not only the needs of the body and the demands of commerce but the desire for beauty and the hunger for community."

By 1967 the Vietnam War had upset the domestic agendas of both SDS and the Johnson administration. If SDSers had once believed they could work with liberal Democrats to reduce poverty in the United States, they now interpreted social injustice at home as the inevitable consequence of dangerous and destructive foreign *policies pursued by liberals and conservatives alike. SDS threw its energies into the movement against the war in Vietnam. President Johnson, meanwhile, pursued a foreign policy that would swallow up the funding for his own plans for a war on poverty and would precipitate a very different war at home, Americans against Americans. As hawks and doves lined up on opposite sides, the Vietnam War created a huge and enduring rift. SDS member Richard Flacks had warned that the nation had to "choose*

between devoting its resources and energies to maintaining military superiority and international hegemony or rechanneling those resources and energies to meeting the desperate needs of its people." Ultimately, even President Johnson himself understood that the "bitch of a war" in Asia ruined "the woman I really loved—the Great Society." The dream of community did not vanish, but consensus appeared increasingly remote as the United States fought—and eventually lost—the longest war in its history.

Vietnam: America's Longest War

The Vietnam War had its roots in the Truman Doctrine and its goal of containing communism (see Chapter 26). After the defeat of the French by the Communist forces of Ho Chi Minh in 1954, Vietnam emerged as a major zone of Cold War contention. President John Kennedy called it "the cornerstone of the Free World in Southeast Asia, the keystone in the arch, the finger in the dike," a barrier to the spread of communism throughout the region and perhaps the world. President Lyndon Johnson sounded the same note at the beginning of his presidency. With American security at stake, he concluded, Americans had little choice but to fight.

Vietnam was not Valley Forge, however, and the United States ultimately paid a huge price for its determination to turn back communism in Indochina. More than 50,000 Americans died in an unwinnable overseas war that only deepened divisions at home.

Johnson's War

Although President Kennedy had greatly increased the number of military advisors in South Vietnam (see Chapter 27), it was his successor, Lyndon B. Johnson, who made the decision to engage the United States in a major war there. At first, Johnson simply hoped to stay the course in Vietnam. Facing a presidential election in November 1964, he knew that a major military setback would cripple his election campaign. But he was equally determined to avoid the fate of President Truman, who had bogged down politically after "losing" China to communism and producing a stalemate in Korea.

Throughout the winter and spring of 1964, as conditions grew steadily worse in South Vietnam, Johnson and his advisors quietly laid the groundwork for a sustained bombing campaign against North Vietnam. In early August, they found a pretext to set this plan in motion. After two U.S. destroyers in the Gulf of Tonkin, off the coast of North Vietnam, reported attacks by North Vietnamese patrol boats, Johnson retaliated by ordering air strikes against bases in North Vietnam.

Johnson now appealed to Congress to pass a resolution giving him the authority "to take all necessary measures" and "all necessary steps" to defend U.S. armed forces and to protect Southeast Asia "against aggression or subversion." This **Tonkin Gulf Resolution**, secretly drafted six weeks before the incident for which it was named, passed the Senate on August 7 with only two dissenting votes and moved unanimously through the House. It served, in Undersecretary of State Nicholas Katzenbach's words, as the "functional equivalent" of a declaration of war.

WHY DID Johnson escalate the war in Vietnam?

28-4
Students for a Democratic Society, The Port Huron Statement (1962)

Tonkin Gulf Resolution   Request to Congress from President Lyndon Johnson in response to North Vietnamese torpedo boat attacks in which he sought authorization for "all necessary measures" to protect American forces and stop further aggression.

28-7
The Tonkin Gulf Incident
(1964)

Ironically, Johnson had campaigned for the presidency with a call for restraint in Vietnam. This strategy helped him win a landslide victory over conservative Republican Barry Goldwater of Arizona. With the election behind him, Johnson faced a hard decision. The limited bombing raids against North Vietnam had failed to slow the movement of the Communist Vietcong forces across the border into the South. Meanwhile, the government in Saigon, the capital city of South Vietnam, appeared near collapse. Faced with the prospect of a Communist victory, the president chose to escalate U.S. involvement in Vietnam massively.

DEEPER INTO THE QUAGMIRE

In early February 1965, Johnson found a rationale to justify massive bombing of the North. The Vietcong had fired at the barracks of the U.S. Marine base at Pleiku in the central highlands of Vietnam, killing eight and wounding more than 100 Americans. Waving the list of casualties, the president rushed into an emergency meeting of the National Security Council to announce that the time had passed for keeping "our guns over the mantel and our shells in the cupboard." He ordered immediate reprisal bombing of North Vietnam and one week later, on February 13, authorized Operation Rolling Thunder, a campaign of gradually intensifying air attacks.

Once Rolling Thunder had begun, President Johnson found it increasingly difficult to speak frankly with the American public about his policies. Initially, he announced that only two battalions of marines were being assigned to Danang to defend the airfields where bombing runs began. But six week later, 50,000 U.S. troops were in Vietnam. By November 1965 the total topped 165,000, and more troops were on the way. But even after Johnson authorized a buildup to 431,000 troops in mid-1966, victory was still nowhere in sight.

The strategy pursued by the Johnson administration and implemented by General William Westmoreland—a war of attrition—was based on the premise that continued bombing would eventually exhaust North Vietnam's resources. Meanwhile, U.S. ground forces would defeat the Vietcong in South Vietnam, forcing its soldiers to defect and supporters to scatter, thereby restoring political stability to South Vietnam's pro-Western government. As Johnson once boasted, the strongest military power in the world surely could crush a Communist rebellion in a "pissant" country of peasants.

In practice, the United States wreaked havoc in South Vietnam, tearing apart its society and bringing ecological devastation to its land. Intending to locate and eradicate the support network of the Vietcong, U.S. ground troops conducted search-and-destroy missions throughout the countryside. They attacked villagers and their homes. Seeking to ferret out Vietcong sympathizers, U.S. troops turned at any one time as many as 4 million people—approximately one-quarter of the population of South Vietnam—into refugees. By late 1968, the United States had dropped more than 3 million tons of bombs on Vietnam and eventually delivered more than three times the tonnage dropped by the Allies on all fronts during World War II. Using herbicides to defoliate forests, the United States also conducted the most destructive chemical warfare in history.

Several advisors urged the president to inform the American people about his decisions on Vietnam, even to declare a state of national emergency. But Johnson feared he would lose

Refugees, Binh Dinh Province, 1967. The massive bombing and ground combat broke apart the farming communities of South Vietnam, creating huge numbers of civilian casualties and driving millions into quickly constructed refugee camps or already overcrowded cities. Approximately 25 percent of the South Vietnamese population fled their native villages, many never to return.

Photo by Philip Jones Griffiths. Magnum Photos, Inc.

momentum on domestic reform, including his antipoverty programs, if he drew attention to foreign policy. Seeking to avoid "undue excitement in the Congress and in domestic public opinion," he held to a course of intentional deceit.

THE CREDIBILITY GAP

Johnson's popularity had surged at the time of the Tonkin Gulf resolution, sky-rocketing in one day from 42 to 72 percent, according to a Louis Harris poll. But afterward it waned rapidly. The war dragged on. Every night network television news reported the soaring American body count, from 26 per week in 1965 to 180 in 1967. No president had worked so hard to control the news media, but by 1967 Johnson found himself badgered at press conferences by reporters who accused the president of creating a credibility gap.

Scenes of human suffering and devastation recorded by television cameras increasingly undermined the administration's moral justification of the war with claims that it was a necessary defense of freedom and democracy in South Vietnam. During the early 1960s, network news had either ignored Vietnam or had been patriotically supportive of U.S. policy. Beginning with a report on a ground operation against the South Vietnamese village of Cam Ne by Morley Safer for CBS News in August 1965, however, the tenor of news reporting changed. Although government officials described the operation as a strategic destruction of "fortified Vietcong bunkers," the *CBS Evening News* showed pictures of Marines setting fire to the thatched homes of civilians. After CBS aired Safer's report, President Johnson complained bitterly to the news director. But more critical commentary soon followed. By 1967, according to a noted media observer, "every subject tended to become Vietnam." Televised news reports now told of new varieties of American cluster bombs, which released up to 180,000 fiberglass shards, and showed the nightmarish effects of the defoliants used on forests in South Vietnam to uncover enemy strongholds.

Coverage of the war in the print media also became more skeptical of Johnson's policies. By 1967 independent news teams were probing the government's official claims. Harrison Salisbury, Pulitzer Prize–winning *New York Times* reporter, questioned the administration's claims that its bombing of the North precisely targeted military objectives, charging that U.S. planes had bombed the population center of Hanoi, capital of North Vietnam, and intentionally ravaged villages in the South. As American military deaths climbed at the rate of more than 800 per month during the first half of 1967, newspaper coverage of the war focused yet more intently on such disturbing events.

The most vocal congressional critic of Johnson's war policy was Democratic senator J. William Fulbright of Arkansas, who chaired the Senate Foreign Relations Committee and who had personally speeded the passage of the Tonkin Gulf resolution. A strong supporter of the Cold War, Fulbright had decided that the war in Vietnam was unwinnable and destructive to domestic reform. In *Arrogance of Power,* a book published in 1966 that became a national bestseller, he proposed a negotiated withdrawal from a neutralized Southeast Asia. Fulbright persuaded prominent Democrats in Congress, such as Frank Church, Mike Mansfield, and George McGovern, to put aside their personal loyalty to Johnson and oppose his conduct of the war. In 1967 the Congress passed a nonbinding resolution appealing to the United Nations to help negotiate an end to hostilities. Meanwhile, some of the nation's most trusted European allies called for restraint in Vietnam.

The impact of the war, which cost Americans $21 billion per year, was also felt at home. Johnson convinced Congress to levy a 10 percent surcharge on individual and corporate taxes. Later adjustments in the national budget tapped the Social Security fund, heretofore safe from interference. Inflation raced upward, fed by spending on

IMAGE KEY

for pages 790–791

a. Damaged cassette tape evocative of the Watergate scandal's secret Oval Office tapes.

b. Daisies represent the "Flower Power" mindset.

c. A weeping young woman kneels beside the body of a protester during the 1970 riots at Kent State University in Ohio.

d. Labor activist Caesar Chavez.

e. An antiwar peace button.

f. American soldiers atop captured Hill 875 near Dak To, Vietnam.

g. Antiwar protesters marching on the Pentagon and burning draft cards, October 1967.

h. A male student puts flowers in the guns of a row of soldiers during a protest at the Pentagon in Washington, D.C.

i. Crowds gather to hear Martin Luther King, Jr. speak.

j. President Nixon announces he will resign effective noon Friday during a broadcast from the Oval Office of the White House, in this August 8, 1974 file photo.

the war. Johnson replaced advisors who questioned his policy, but as casualties multiplied, more and more Americans began to question his handling of the war.

A GENERATION IN CONFLICT

HOW DID campus protests shape national political debate?

As the war in Vietnam escalated, Americans from all walks of life demanded an end to U.S. involvement. But between 1965 and 1971, its years of peak activity, it had a distinctly generational character. At the forefront were the baby boomers who were just coming of age.

This so-called sixties generation, the largest generation in American history, was also the best educated. By the late 1960s, nearly half of all young adults between the ages of 18 and 21 were enrolled in college. In 1965 there were 5 million college students; in 1973 the number had doubled to 10 million. Public universities made the largest gains; by 1970 eight had more than 30,000 students apiece. Although a small minority, groups of students began to combine protest against the war in Vietnam with a broader, penetrating critique of American society. Through music, dress, and even hairstyle, they expressed a deep estrangement from the values and aspirations of their parents' generation. As early as 1967, when opposition to the war had begun to swell, "flower children" were putting daisies in the rifle barrels of troops stationed to quash campus protests, providing a seemingly innocent counterpoint to the grim news of slaughter abroad.

These young people promoted a "culture of life" against the "culture of death" symbolized by the war. Campus organizations such as **Students for a Democratic Society (SDS)**, which had begun in the early 1960s in an attempt to build community, now turned against the government.

"THE TIMES THEY ARE A-CHANGIN'"

The first sign of a new kind of protest was the **free speech movement** at the University of California at Berkeley in 1964. That fall, civil rights activists returned to the 27,000-student campus from Freedom Summer in Mississippi. They soon began to picket Bay Area stores that practiced discrimination in hiring and to recruit other students to join them. When the university administration moved to prevent them from setting up information booths on campus, eighteen groups protested, including the arch-conservative Students for Goldwater, claiming that their right to free speech had been abridged. The administration responded by sending police to break up the protest rally and arrest participants. University president Clark Kerr met with students, agreed not to press charges, and seemed set to grant them a small space on campus for political activity. Then, under pressure from conservative regents, Kerr reversed himself and announced in November that the university planned to press new charges against the free speech movement's leaders. On December 2 a crowd of 7,000 gathered to protest this decision. Joining folk singer Joan Baez in singing "We Shall Overcome," a group of 1,000 people marched toward the university's administration building, where they planned to stage a sit-in until Kerr rescinded his order. The police arrested nearly 800 protestors in the largest mass arrest in California history.

Mario Savio, a Freedom Summer volunteer and philosophy student, explained that the free speech movement wanted more than just the right to conduct political activity on campus. He spoke for many students when he complained that the university had become a faceless bureaucratic machine rather than a community of learning.

Across the country college students began to demand a say in the structuring of their education. Brown University students, for example, demanded a revamp of the curriculum that would eliminate all required courses and make grades

Students for a Democratic Society (SDS) The leading student organization of the New Left of the early and mid-1960s.

Free speech movement Student movement at the University of California, Berkeley, formed in 1964 to protest limitations on political activities on campus.

optional. Students also protested campus rules that treated students as children instead of as adults. After a string of campus protests, most large universities, including the University of California, relinquished *in loco parentis* (in the place of parents) policies and allowed students to live off-campus and to set their own hours.

Across the bay in San Francisco, other young adults staked out a new form of community—a **counterculture**. In 1967, the "Summer of Love," the population of the Haight-Ashbury district swelled by 75,000 as youthful adventurers gathered for the most celebrated "be-in" of the era. They congregated in "the Haight" to listen to music, take drugs, and "be" with each other. "If you're going to San Francisco," a popular rock group sang, "be sure to wear some flowers in your hair . . . you're going to meet some gentle people there." In the fall, the majority returned to their own communities, often bringing with them a new lifestyle.

The generational rebellion took many forms, including a revolution in sexual behavior that triggered countless quarrels between parents and their maturing sons and daughters. During the 1960s more teenagers experienced premarital sex—by the decade's end three-quarters of all college seniors had engaged in sexual intercourse—and far more talked about it openly than in previous eras. "We've discarded the idea that the loss of virginity is related to degeneracy," one college student explained. Many heterosexual couples chose to live together outside marriage, a practice few parents condoned. A much smaller but significant number formed communes—approximately 4,000 by 1970—where members could share housekeeping and child care as well as sexual partners.

Mood-altering drugs played a large part in this counterculture. Harvard professor Timothy Leary urged young people to "turn on, tune in, drop out" and also advocated the mass production and distribution of LSD (lysergic acid diethylamide), which was not criminalized until 1968. Marijuana, illegal yet readily available, was often paired with rock music in a collective ritual of love and laughter. Singer Bob Dylan taunted adults with the lyrics of his hit single, "Everybody must get stoned."

Music played a large part in defining the counterculture. With the emergence of rock 'n' roll in the 1950s, popular music had begun to express a deliberate generational identity (see Chapter 27), a trend that gained momentum with the emergence of the British rock group The Beatles in 1964. Folk music, which had gained popularity on campuses in the early 1960s with the successful recordings of Peter, Paul, and Mary, Phil Ochs, and Judy Collins, as well as Joan Baez, continued to serve the voice of protest. Shortly after Freedom Summer, folk singer Bob Dylan issued a warning to parents:

Your sons and your daughters
are beyond your command
Your old road is
rapidly agin'.
Please get out of the new one
If you can't lend your hand

For the times they are a-changin'.

At a farm near Woodstock, New York, more than 400,000 people gathered in August 1969 for a three-day rock concert and to give witness to the ideals of the counterculture. Thousands took drugs while security officials and local police stood by.

The Woodstock Nation, as the counterculture was mythologized, did not actually represent the sentiments of most young Americans. But its attitudes and styles, especially its efforts to create a new community, did speak for the large minority seeking a peaceful alternative to the intensifying climate of war. "We used to think of ourselves as little clumps of weirdos," rock star Janis Joplin explained. "But now we're a whole new minority group." The slogan "Make Love, Not War" linked generational rebellion and opposition to the U.S. invasion of Vietnam.

The hippie counter culture emphasized peace and love.

Getty Images. Inc.–Taxi

Counterculture   Various alternatives to mainstream values and behaviors that became popular in the 1960s, including experimentation with psychedelic drugs, communal living, a return to the land, Asian religions, and experimental art.

FROM CAMPUS PROTEST TO MASS MOBILIZATION

Three weeks after the announcement of Operation Rolling Thunder in 1965, peace activists called for a day-long boycott of classes so that students and faculty might meet to discuss the war. At the University of Michigan in Ann Arbor, more than 3,000 students turned out for sessions held through the night because university administrators had bowed to the pressure of state legislators and had refused to cancel classes. During the following weeks, "teach-ins" spread across the United States and to Europe and Japan as well.

Students also began to protest against war-related research on their campuses. The expansion of higher education in the 1960s had depended largely on federally funded programs, including military research on counterinsurgency tactics and new chemical weapons. Student protesters demanded an end to these programs and, receiving no response from university administrators, turned to civil

MAP EXPLORATION

To explore an interactive version of this map, go to **http://www.prenhall.com/faraghertlc/map29.1**

MAP 29-1
Antiwar Protests on College and University Campuses, 1967–1969   Campus-based protests against the war in Vietnam, at first centered on the east coast and in California, spread to nearly every region of the country and around the world by the decade's end.

WHAT DIVISIONS in American society were exposed by the debate over Vietnam?

disobedience. In October 1967, the Dow Chemical Company, manufacturers of napalm, a form of jellied gasoline often used against civilians in Vietnam, sent job recruiters to the University of Wisconsin at Madison despite warnings that a group of students would try to prevent them from conducting interviews. A few hundred students staged a sit-in at the building where the recruitment interviews were scheduled, and 2,000 onlookers gathered outside. Ordered by university administrators to disperse the crowd, the city's police broke glass doors, dragged students through the debris, and clubbed those who refused to move. Suddenly the campus erupted. Students chanted *Sieg Heil* at the police, who attempted to disperse them with tear gas and mace. Undergraduate students and their teaching assistants boycotted classes for a week. During the next three years, the momentum grew, and demonstrations took place on campuses in every region of country.

Many student strikes and demonstrations merged opposition to the war with other campus and community issues. At Columbia University, students struck in 1968 against the administration's plans to build a new gymnasium in a city park used by residents of neighboring Harlem. In the Southwest, Mexican American students demonstrated against the use of funds for military projects that might otherwise be allocated to antipoverty and educational programs.

In April 1967, a day-long antiwar rally at the Sheep Meadow in Manhattan's Central Park drew more than 300,000 people. Meanwhile, 60,000 protesters turned out in San Francisco. By summer, Vietnam Veterans Against the War had begun to organize returning soldiers and sailors, encouraging them to cast off the medals and ribbons they had won in battle.

The steadily increasing size of antiwar demonstrations provoked conservatives and prowar Democrats to take a stronger stand in support of the war. Several newspaper and magazine editorialists called for the arrest of antiwar leaders on charges of treason. Secretary of State Dean Rusk, appearing on NBC's *Meet the Press,* expressed his concern that "authorities in Hanoi" might conclude, incorrectly, that the majority of Americans did not back their president and that "the net effect of these demonstrations will be to prolong the war, not to shorten it."

Many demonstrators themselves concluded that mass mobilizations alone had little impact on U.S. policy. Some sought to serve as moral witnesses. Despite a congressional act of 1965 providing for a five-year jail term and a $10,000 fine for destroying a draft card, nearly 200 young men destroyed their draft cards at the April Sheep Meadow demonstration and encouraged approximately a half-million more to resist the draft or refuse induction. Two Jesuit priests, Daniel and Philip Berrigan, raided the offices of the draft board in Catonsville, Maryland, in May 1968 and poured homemade napalm over records. Other activists determined to "bring the war home." An estimated 40,000 bombing incidents or bomb threats took place from January 1969 to April 1970; more than $21 million of property was damaged, and forty-three people were killed. Most of the perpetrators were never identified. Parallel wars were now being fought, one between two systems of government in Vietnam, another between the American government and masses of its citizens. Those Americans sent to Vietnam were caught in between.

TEENAGE SOLDIERS

Whereas the average age of the World War II soldier was twenty-six, the age of those who fought in Vietnam hovered around nineteen. Until late 1969 the Selective Service System—the draft—gave deferments to college students and to workers in selected occupations while recruiting hard in poor communities, advertising the armed forces as a provider of vocational training and social mobility. Working-class young men, disproportionately African American and Latino, signed up in

QUICK REVIEW

Opposition to the War

◆ Antiwar activists and students challenged the "Cold Warriors."

◆ In 1966 and 1967 antiwar activity intensified.

◆ Antiwar activists directed their anger against the Selective Service System.

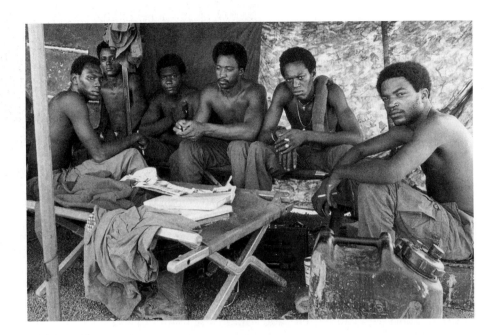

African American troops in Vietnam, 1970. Serving on the front lines in disproportionate numbers, many black soldiers echoed the growing racial militancy in the United States and increasingly chose to spend their off-duty time apart from white soldiers.

Mark Jury, *The Vietnam Photo Book*

large numbers under these inducements. They also bore the brunt of combat. Whereas college graduates constituted only 12 percent of all soldiers and 9 percent of those who were killed in combat, high school dropouts were the most likely to serve in Vietnam and by far the most likely to die there. These disparities created a rupture that would last well past the end of the war.

Yet the soldiers were not entirely isolated from the changes affecting their generation. GIs in significant numbers smoked marijuana, listened to rock music, and participated in the sexual revolution, but most condemned antiwar protest as the expressions of their privileged peers who did not have to fight. As the war dragged on, however, some soldiers began to show their frustration. By 1971 many GIs were putting peace symbols on their combat helmets, joining antiwar demonstrations, and staging their own events such as "Armed Farces Day." Sometimes entire companies refused to carry out duty assignments or even to enter battle. A smaller number took revenge by "fragging" reckless commanding officers with grenades meant for the enemy. Some African American soldiers complained about being asked to fight "a white man's war" and emblazoned their helmets with slogans like "No Gook Ever Called Me Nigger."

The nature of the war fed feelings of disaffection in the armed forces. U.S. troops entering South Vietnam expected a warm welcome from the people whose homeland they had been sent to defend. Instead, they encountered anti-American demonstrations and placards with slogans like "End Foreign Dominance of Our Country." Hostile Vietnamese civilians viewed the Americans as invaders. The enemy avoided open engagements in which the Americans could benefit from their superior arms and air power. Soldiers found themselves instead stumbling into booby traps as they chased an elusive guerrilla foe through deep, leech-infested swamps and dense jungles swarming with fire ants. They could never be sure who was friend and who was foe. Patently false U.S. government press releases that heralded glorious victories and extolled the gratitude of Vietnamese civilians deepened bitterness on the front lines.

Vietnam veterans returned to civilian life quietly and without fanfare, denied the glory earned by the combat veterans of previous wars. They reentered a society divided over the cause for which they had risked their lives. Tens of thousands suffered debilitating physical injuries. As many as 40 percent of them came back with drug dependencies or symptoms of post-traumatic stress disorder, haunted and depressed by troubling memories of atrocities. Moreover, finding and keeping a job proved to be particularly hard in the shrinking economy of the 1970s.

WARS ON POVERTY

During the early 1960s, the civil rights movement spurred a new awareness of and concern with poverty. What good was winning the right to sit at a lunch counter if one could not afford to buy a hamburger?

One of the most influential books of the times, Michael Harrington's *The Other America* (1962), added fuel to this fire. Harrington argued that one-fifth of the nation—as many as 40 to 50 million people—suffered from bad housing, malnutrition, poor medical care, and other deprivations of poverty. He documented the miseries of what he called the "invisible land of the other Americans," the rejects of society who simply did not exist for affluent suburbanites or the mass media.

These arguments motivated President Johnson to expand the antipoverty program that he had inherited from the Kennedy administration. "That's my kind of program," he told his advisers. "It will help people. I want you to move full speed ahead on it." Ironically, it was another kind of war that ultimately undercut his aspiration to wage "an unconditional **war on poverty**."

THE GREAT SOCIETY

In his State of the Union message in 1964, Johnson announced his plans to build a Great Society. Over the next two years, he used the political momentum of the civil rights movement and the overwhelming Democratic majorities in the House and Senate to push through the most ambitious reform program since the New Deal. In August 1964 the Economic Opportunity Act launched the War on Poverty. It established an **Office of Economic Opportunity (OEO)**, which coordinated a network of federal programs designed to increase opportunities in employment and education.

The programs had mixed results. The Job Corps provided vocational training mostly for urban black youth considered unemployable. Housed in dreary barrackslike camps far from home, trainees often found themselves learning factory skills that were already obsolete. The Neighborhood Youth Corps managed to provide work for about 2 million young people aged sixteen to twenty-one, but nearly all of these were low-paying, make-work jobs. Educational programs proved more successful. VISTA (Volunteers in Service to America) was a kind of domestic Peace Corps that brought several thousand idealistic volunteers into poor communities for social service work.

The most innovative and controversial element of the OEO was the Community Action Program (CAP). The program invited local communities to establish community action agencies (CAAs) to be funded through the OEO. The Economic Opportunity Act included language requiring these agencies to be "developed, conducted, and administered with the maximum feasible participation of residents of the areas and members of the groups served." In theory, as the SDS organizers had also believed, community action would empower the poor by giving them a direct say in mobilizing resources to attack poverty.

By 1966 the OEO was funding more than 1,000 CAAs, mostly in the black neighborhoods of big cities. The traditional powers in cities—mayors, business elites, and political machines—generally resisted institutional change. They looked at CAAs as merely another way to dispense services and patronage, with the federal government picking up the tab. A continual tug-of-war over who should control funding and decision making plagued the CAP in most cities, sparking intense

WHAT WERE the goals of Johnson's Great Society?

QUICK REVIEW

The Great Society
- Most ambitious reform program since the New Deal.
- Office of Economic Opportunity launched a War on Poverty.
- Programs had mixed results.

War on poverty   Set of programs introduced by Lyndon Johnson between 1963 and 1966 designed to break the cycle of poverty by providing funds for job training, community development, nutrition, and supplementary education.

Office of Economic Opportunity (OEO) Federal agency that coordinated many programs of the War on Poverty between 1964 and 1975.

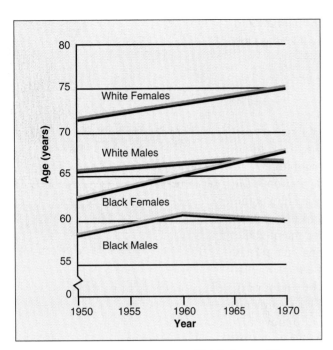

Comparative Figures on Life Expectancy at Birth by Race and Sex, 1950–1970
Shifting mortality statistics suggested that the increased longevity of females increasingly cut across race lines but did not diminish the difference between white people and black people as a whole.

Medicare   Basic medical insurance for the elderly, financed through the federal government; program created in 1965.

Percent of Population Below Poverty Level, by Race, 1959–1969
Note: The poverty threshold for a non-farm family of four was $3,743 in 1969 and $2,973 in 1959.

Congressional Quarterly, Civil Rights: A Progress Report, 1971, p. 46.

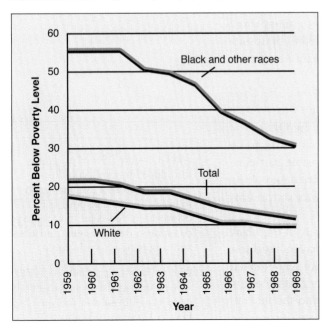

power struggles that helped cripple the antipoverty effort. Such was the case in Chicago, where Mayor Richard Daley demanded absolute control over the allocation of federal funds.

The most successful and popular offshoots of the CAAs were the so-called national-emphasis programs, designed in Washington and administered according to federal guidelines. The Legal Services Program, staffed by attorneys, helped millions of poor people in legal battles with housing authorities, welfare departments, police, and slumlords. Head Start and Follow Through reached more than 2 million poor children and significantly improved the long-range educational achievement of participants. Comprehensive Community Health Centers—one-stop clinics—provided basic medical services to poor patients who could not afford to see doctors. Upward Bound helped low-income teenagers develop the skills and confidence needed for college. Birth control programs dispensed contraceptive supplies and information to hundreds of thousands of poor women.

But the root cause of poverty lay in unequal income distribution. The Johnson administration never committed itself to the redistribution of income or wealth. Spending on social welfare jumped from 7.7 percent of the gross national product in 1960 to 16 percent in 1974. But roughly three-quarters of social welfare payments went to the nonpoor. The largest sums went to **Medicare**, established by Congress in 1965 to provide basic health care for the aged, and to expanded Social Security payments and unemployment compensation.

The War on Poverty, like the Great Society itself, became a forgotten dream. "More than five years after the passage of the Economic Opportunity Act," a 1970 study concluded, "the war on poverty has barely scratched the surface. Most poor people have had no contact with it, except perhaps to hear the promises of a better life to come." Having made the largest commitment to federal spending on social welfare since the New Deal, Johnson could take pride in the gains scored in the War on Poverty. At the same time, he had raised expectations higher than could be reached without a more drastic redistribution of economic and political power. Even in the short run, the president could not sustain the welfare programs and simultaneously fight a lengthy and expensive war abroad.

CRISIS IN THE CITIES

With funds for new construction limited during the Great Depression and World War II, and the postwar boom taking place in the suburbs, the housing stock in the cities diminished and deteriorated. The Federal Housing Administration had encouraged this trend by insuring loans to support the building of new homes in suburban areas (see Chapter 27). The federal government also encouraged "redlining," which left people in poor neighborhoods without access to building loans. In these areas, the supply of adequate housing declined sharply. Slumlords took advantage of this situation, collecting high rents while allowing their properties to deteriorate. City officials meanwhile appealed for federal funds under Title I of the 1949 Housing Act to upgrade housing. Designed as a program of civic revitalization, these urban renewal projects more often than not sliced apart poor neighborhoods with new highways, demolished them in favor of new office complexes, or, as in Chicago's Uptown, favored new developments for the middle class rather than the poor. In 1968 a federal survey showed that 80 percent of those residents who had been displaced under this program were nonwhite.

Urban employment opportunities declined along with the urban housing stock. The industries and corporations that had lured working men and women to the cities a century earlier either automated their plants, thus scaling back their work forces, or relocated to the suburbs or other regions, such as the South and Southwest, that promised lower corporate taxes and nonunion labor. Nationwide, military spending prompted by the escalation of the Vietnam War brought the unemployment rate down from 6 percent, where it was in 1960, to 4 percent in 1966, where it remained until the end of the decade. Black unemployment, however, was nearly twice that of white unemployment. In Northern cities, the proportion of the work force employed in the higher paying manufacturing jobs declined precipitously while the proportion working in minimum-wage service industries rose at a fast rate. In short, African Americans were losing good jobs and steadily falling farther behind whites.

Pollution, which had long plagued traffic-congested cities like Los Angeles and industrial cities like steel-producing Pittsburgh, became an increasingly pervasive urban problem. Cities like Phoenix that once had clean air began to issue smog alerts. Pointing to high levels of lead in the blood of urban children, scientists warned of the long-term threat of pollution to public health.

Despite deteriorating conditions, millions of Americans continued to move to the cities, mainly African Americans from the Deep South, white people from the Appalachian Mountains, and Latinos from Puerto Rico. By the mid-1960s, African Americans had become near majorities in the nation's decaying inner cities. The vast majority of these African Americans fled rural poverty only to find themselves earning minimum wages at best and living in miserable, racially segregated neighborhoods.

Demonstrators surround a police car after riots erupted in the Los Angeles suburb of Watts in 1965.

APWide World Photos

URBAN UPRISINGS

These deteriorating conditions brought urban pressures to the boiling point in the mid-1960s. In the "long, hot summers" of 1964 to 1968 the nation was rocked by more than 100 urban uprisings.

The first major uprising erupted in August 1965 in the Watts section of Los Angeles. Here, the male unemployment rate hovered around 30 percent. Watts lacked health-care facilities—the nearest hospital was twelve miles away—and in a city with little public transportation, fewer than one-fifth of its residents owned cars. It took only a minor arrest to set off the uprising, which quickly spread outward for fifty miles. Throwing rocks and bottles through store windows, participants reportedly shouted, "This is for Selma! This is for Birmingham!" and "Burn, baby, burn!" Nearly 50,000 people turned out, and 20,000 National Guard troops were sent in. After six days, 34 people lay dead, 900 were injured, and 4,000 more had been arrested. Los Angeles chief of police William H. Parker blamed civil rights workers, the mayor accused Communists, and both feigned ignorance when the media reported that white police assigned to "charcoal alley," their name for the Watts district, had for years referred to their nightsticks as "nigger knockers."

The following summer, large-scale uprisings occurred in San Francisco, Milwaukee, Dayton, and Cleveland. On July 12, 1967, in Newark, New Jersey, a city

28-10
Donald Wheeldin, "The Situation in Watts Today" (1967)

with severe housing shortages and the nation's highest black unemployment rate, the beating and arrest of a black taxi driver by a white police officer provoked a widespread protest. Five days of looting and burning of white-owned buildings ended with twenty-five people dead. One week later the Detroit "Great Rebellion" began. This time a vice squad of the Detroit police had raided a bar and arrested the after-hours patrons. Army tanks and paratroopers were brought in to quell the massive disturbance, which lasted a week and left 34 people dead and 7,000 under arrest.

The uprisings seemed at first to prompt badly needed reforms. After Watts, President Johnson set up a task force headed by Deputy Attorney General Ramsey Clark and allocated funds for a range of antipoverty programs. Several years later the Kerner Commission, headed by Governor Otto Kerner of Illinois, studied the riots and found that the participants in the uprisings were not the poorest or least educated members of their communities. They suffered instead from heightened expectations sparked by the civil rights movement and Johnson's promise of a Great Society, expectations that were not to be realized.

MAP EXPLORATION

To explore an interactive version of this map, go to **http://www.prenhall.com/faraghertlc/map29.2**

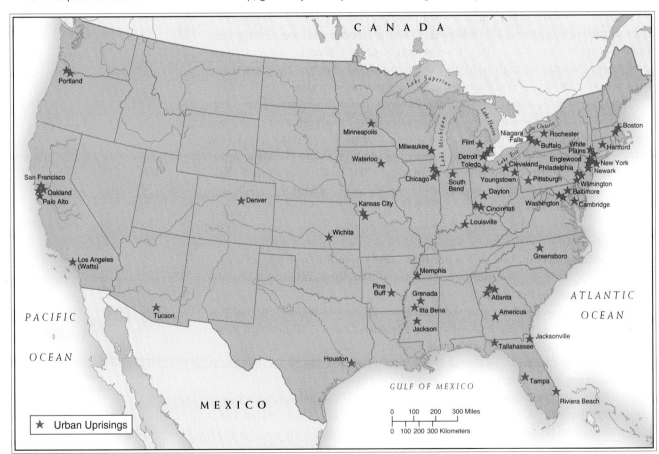

MAP 29-2

Urban Uprisings, 1965–1968   After World War II urban uprisings precipitated by racial conflict increased in African American communities. In Watts in 1965 and in Detroit and Newark in 1967, rioters struck out at symbols of white control of their communities, such as white-owned businesses and residential properties.

WHAT WERE the main factors behind urban unrest?

But Congress ignored the commission's warning that "our nation is moving toward two societies, one black, one white—separate and unequal." Moreover, the costs of the Vietnam War left little federal money for antipoverty programs. Senator William Fulbright noted, "Each war feeds on the other, and, although the President assures us that we have the resources to win both wars, in fact we are not winning either of them."

1968

The urban uprisings of the summer of 1967 marked the most drawn-out violence in the United States since the Civil War. But, rather than offering a respite, 1968 proved to be even more turbulent. The bloodiest and most destructive fighting of the Vietnam War resulted in a hopeless stalemate that soured most Americans on the conflict and undermined their faith in U.S. invincibility in world affairs. Disillusionment deepened in the spring when two of the most revered political leaders were struck down by assassins' bullets. Once again protesters and police clashed on the nation's campuses and city streets, and millions of Americans asked what was wrong with their country. Why was it so violent?

WHAT DIVIDED the Democratic Party in 1968?

THE TET OFFENSIVE

On January 30, 1968, the North Vietnamese and their Vietcong allies launched the Tet Offensive (named for the Vietnamese lunar new year holiday), stunning the U.S. military command in South Vietnam. The Vietcong managed to push into the major cities and provincial capitals of the South, as far as the courtyard of the U.S. embassy in Saigon. U.S. troops ultimately halted the offensive, suffering comparatively modest casualties of 1,600 dead and 8,000 wounded. The North Vietnamese and Vietcong suffered more than 40,000 deaths, about one-fifth of their total forces. Civilian casualties ran to the hundreds of thousands. As many as 1 million South Vietnamese became refugees, their villages totally ruined.

The Tet Offensive, despite the U.S. success in stopping it, shattered the credibility of American officials who had repeatedly claimed the enemy to be virtually beaten. Television and press coverage—including scenes of U.S. personnel shooting from the embassy windows in Saigon—dismayed the public. Americans saw the beautiful, ancient city of Hue devastated almost beyond recognition. Television newscasters began to warn parents: "The following scenes might not be suitable viewing for children."

The United States had chalked up a major military victory during the Tet Offensive but lost the war at home. For the first time, polls showed strong opposition to the war, 49 percent concluding that the entire operation in Vietnam was a mistake. Meanwhile, in Rome, Berlin, Paris, and London, students and others turned out in huge demonstrations to protest U.S. involvement in Vietnam. At home, sectors of the antiwar movement began to shift from resistance to open rebellion.

The Tet Offensive also opened a year of political drama at home. Congress resoundingly turned down a request for a general increase in troops issued by General Westmoreland. President Johnson, facing the 1968 election campaign, knew the odds were now against him. He watched as opinion polls showed his popularity plummet to an all-time low. After he squeaked to a narrow victory in the New Hampshire primary, Johnson decided to step down. On March 31 he announced he would not seek the Democratic Party's nomination. He also declared a bombing halt over North Vietnam and called Hanoi to peace talks, which began in Paris in May. Like Truman almost thirty years earlier, and despite his determination not to repeat that bit of history, Johnson had lost his presidency in Asia.

MAP EXPLORATION

To explore an interactive version of this map, go to **http://www.prenhall.com/faraghertlc/map29.3**

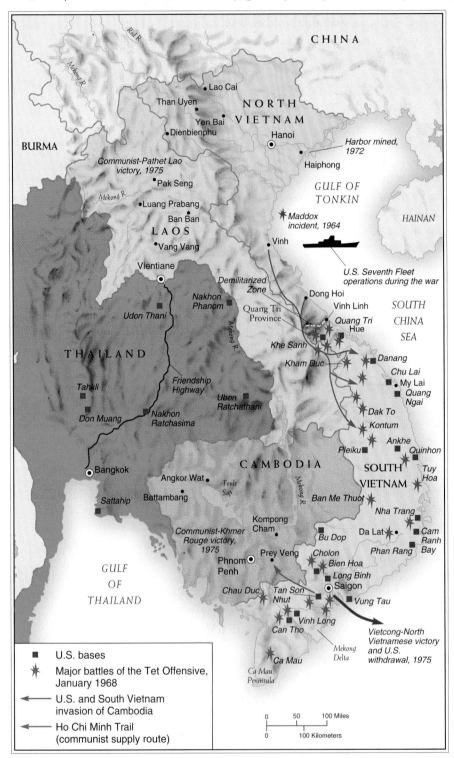

MAP 29-3

The Southeast Asian War The Indo-Chinese subcontinent, home to long-standing regional conflict, became the center of a prolonged war with the United States.

WHAT LED to the escalation of U.S. involvement in Vietnam?

KING, THE WAR, AND THE ASSASSINATION

By 1968 the civil rights leadership stood firmly in opposition to the war, and Martin Luther King Jr. had reached a turning point in his life. The Federal Bureau of Investigation had been harassing King, tapping his telephones and spreading malicious rumors about him. Despite the threat from the FBI (Bureau Chief J. Edgar Hoover had sworn to "destroy the burrhead"), King abandoned his customary caution in criticizing U.S. policy in Vietnam. In the fall of 1965, he began to connect domestic unrest with the war abroad, calling the U.S. government the "greatest purveyor of violence in the world today." As he became more militant in opposing the war, King lost the support of liberal Democrats who remained loyal to Johnson. King refused to compromise.

In the spring of 1968 King chose Memphis, Tennessee, home of striking sanitation workers, as the place to inaugurate a Poor People's Campaign for peace and justice. On April 4, 1968, as he stepped out on the balcony of his motel, King was shot and killed by a lone assassin, James Earl Ray.

Throughout the world crowds turned out to mourn King's death. Student Nonviolent Coordinating Committee leader Stokely Carmichael stormed, "When white America killed Dr. King, she declared war on us." Riots broke out in more than 100 cities. Chicago Mayor Richard Daley ordered his police to shoot to kill. In Washington, D.C., U.S. Army units set up machine guns outside the Capitol and the White House. By week's end, nearly 27,000 African Americans had been jailed.

THE DEMOCRATIC CAMPAIGN

The dramatic events of the first part of the year had a direct impact on the presidential campaign. For those liberals dissatisfied with Johnson's conduct of the war, and especially for African Americans suffering the loss of their greatest national leader, New York senator Robert F. Kennedy emerged as the candidate of choice. Kennedy enjoyed a strong record on civil rights, and, like King, he had begun to interpret the war as a mirror of injustice at home. Kennedy insisted during the Tet Offensive that "our nation must be told the truth about this war, in all its terrible reality." On this promise he began to build a campaign for the Democratic nomination.

"Martin Luther King," Robert Kennedy said when he heard the news of the assassination of the civil rights leader, "dedicated his life to love and to justice for his fellow human beings, and he died because of that effort." The funeral service for King was held in the Ebenezer Baptist Church in Atlanta on April 7, 1968.

Walk down West Hunter Street, Atlanta. © James L. Amos/CORBIS (JA 004098)

Ironically, Kennedy faced an opponent who agreed with him, Minnesota senator Eugene McCarthy. The race for the Democratic nomination positioned McCarthy, the witty philosopher, against Kennedy, the charismatic campaigner. McCarthy garnered support from liberal Democrats and white suburbanites. On college campuses his popularity with idealistic students was so great that his campaign became known as the "children's crusade." Kennedy reached out successfully to African Americans and Latinos and won all but the Oregon primary.

Kennedy appeared to be the Democratic Party's strongest candidate as June 4, the day of the California primary, dawned. But as the final tabulation of his victory came in just past midnight, Robert Kennedy was struck down by the bullet of an assassin, a Jordanian national named Sirhan Sirhan.

Vice President Hubert H. Humphrey, a longtime presidential hopeful, was now the sole Democrat with the credentials to succeed Johnson. But his reputation as a Cold War Democrat had become a liability. In the 1950s Humphrey had delivered stirring addresses for civil rights and antipoverty legislation, yet he also sponsored repressive Cold War measures and supported huge defense appropriations that diverted needed funds from domestic programs. He fully supported the Vietnam War and had publicly scorned peace activists as cowardly and un-American. Incongruously calling his campaign the "Politics of Joy," Humphrey simultaneously courted Democrats who grimly supported the war and the King-Kennedy wing, which was sickened by it.

Humphrey skillfully cultivated the Democratic power brokers. Without entering a single state primary, he lined up delegates loyal to city bosses, labor leaders, and conservative Southern Democrats. As the candidate least likely to rock the boat, he had secured his party's nomination well before delegates met in convention.

"THE WHOLE WORLD IS WATCHING!"

The events surrounding the Democratic Convention in Chicago, August 1968, demonstrated how deep the divisions within the United States had become. Antiwar activists had called for a massive demonstration at the delegates' hotel and at the convention center. The media focused, however, on the plans announced by the "Yippies," or Youth International Party, a largely imaginary organization of politicized hippies led by jokester and counterculture guru Abbie Hoffman. Yippies called for a Festival of Life, including a "nude-in" on Lake Michigan beaches and the release of a greased pig—Pigasus, the Yippie candidate for president. Still reeling from the riots following King's assassination, Chicago's Mayor Richard Daley refused to issue parade permits. According to later accounts, he sent hundreds of undercover police into the crowds to encourage rock throwing and generally to incite violence so that retaliation would appear necessary and reasonable.

Daley's strategy boomeranged when his officers staged what a presidential commission later termed a "police riot," randomly assaulting demonstrators, casual passersby, and television crews filming the events. For one of the few times in American history, the media appeared to join a protest against civil authorities. Angered by the embarrassing publicity, Daley sent his agents to raid McCarthy's campaign headquarters, where Democrats opposed to the war had gathered.

Inside the convention hall, a raging debate over a peace resolution underscored the depth of the division within the party over the war. Representative Wayne Hays of Ohio lashed out at those who substituted "beards for brains . . . [and] pot [for] patriotism." When the resolution failed, McCarthy delegates put on black armbands and followed folk singer Theodore Bikel in singing "We Shall Overcome." Later, as tear gas used against the demonstrators outside turned the amphitheater air acrid, delegates heard the beaming Humphrey praise Mayor

The "police riot" in Chicago, August 1968, during the Democratic National Convention capped a spring and summer of violence. Mayor Richard Daley had prepared his city for the anticipated protest against the war by assembling more than 20,000 law enforcement officials, including police, National Guard, and U.S. Army troops carrying flame throwers and bazookas. Television cameras and photographers recorded the massive clubbing and teargassing of demonstrators as well as bystanders and news reporters.

Photo by Jeffrey Blankfort. Jeroboam, Inc.

Daley and Johnson's conduct of the Vietnam War. When Senator Abraham Ribicoff of Connecticut addressed the convention and protested the "Gestapo tactics" of the police, television cameras focused on Mayor Daley saying, "You Jew son of a bitch . . . , go home!" The crowd outside chanted, "The whole world is watching! The whole world is watching!" Indeed, through satellite transmission, it was.

Protest and social strain spread worldwide. Across the United States the antiwar movement picked up steam. In Paris, students took over campuses and workers occupied factories. Young people scrawled on the walls such humorous and half-serious slogans as "Be Realistic, Demand the Impossible!" Similar protests against authority occurred in Eastern Europe. In Prague, Czechoslovakia, students wearing blue jeans and singing Beatles songs threw rocks at Soviet tanks. Meanwhile, demonstrations in Japan, Italy, Ireland, Germany, and England all brought young people into the streets to demand democratic reforms in their own countries and an end to the war in Vietnam.

THE POLITICS OF IDENTITY

The tragic events of 1968 brought whole sectors of the counterculture into political activism. With great media fanfare, gay liberation and women's liberation movements emerged in the late 1960s. By the early 1970s, young Latinos, Asian Americans, and Indian peoples had pressed their own claims. In different ways, these groups drew their own lessons from the nationalist movement that formed in the wake of Malcolm X's death—Black Power. Soon, "Brown Power," "Yellow Power," and "Red Power" became the slogans of movements constituted distinctly as new communities of protest.

BLACK POWER

Derived from a century-long tradition of black nationalism, the key tenets of **Black Power** were self-determination and self-sufficiency. National conferences of activists, held annually beginning in 1966, adopted separatist resolutions, including a plan to partition the United States into black and white nations. Black Power also promoted self-esteem by affirming the unique history and heritage of African peoples.

WHAT IS meant by the "politics of identity"?

Black Power Philosophy emerging after 1965 that real economic and political gains for African Americans could come only through self-help, self-determination, and organizing for direct political influence.

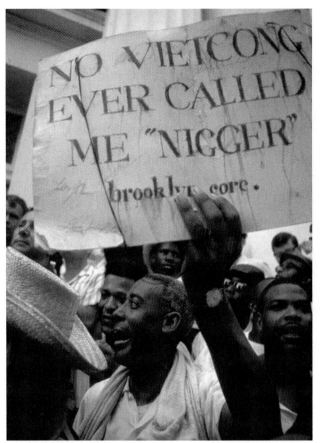

The war in Vietnam contributed to the growing racial militancy in the United States. African Americans served on the front lines in Vietnam in disproportionate numbers, and many came to view the conflict as a "white man's war."

James Meredith March through Mississippi. © 2001 Matt Herron c/o Mira.com.

28-9
Stokely Carmichael and Charles Hamilton, from *Black Power* (1967)

QUICK REVIEW

Black Panthers

◆ Founded in 1966 by Huey P. Newton and Bobby Seale.

◆ Adopted a strategy of armed self-defense, combined with community programs.

◆ Panthers faced raids, arrests, and prosecution.

Black Panther Political and social movement among black Americans, founded in Oakland, California, in 1966 that emphasized black economic and political power.

The movement's boldest expression was the **Black Panther** Party for Self-Defense, founded in Oakland, California, in 1966 by Huey P. Newton and Bobby Seale. Armed self-defense was the Panthers' strategy, and they adopted a paramilitary style—black leather jackets, shoes, black berets, and firearms—that infuriated local authorities. Monitoring local police, a practice Panthers termed "patrolling the pigs," was their major activity. In several communities, Panthers also ran free breakfast programs for schoolchildren, established medical clinics, and conducted educational classes. For a time the Panthers became folk heroes. Persecuted by local police and the FBI—there were more than thirty raids on Panther offices in eleven states during 1968 and 1969—the Panthers were arrested, prosecuted, and sentenced to long terms in jail that effectively destroyed the organization.

Black Power nevertheless continued to grow during the late 1960s and became a multifaceted movement. The Reverend Jesse Jackson, for example, rallied African Americans in Chicago to boycott the A&P supermarket chain until the firm hired 700 black workers. A dynamic speaker and skillful organizer, Jackson encouraged African Americans to support their own businesses and services. His program, Operation Breadbasket, strengthened community control. By 1970 it had spread beyond Chicago to fifteen other cities.

Cultural nationalism became the most enduring component of Black Power. In their popular book *Black Power* (1967), Stokely Carmichael and Charles V. Hamilton urged African Americans "to assert their own definitions, to reclaim their history, their culture; to create their own sense of community and togetherness." Thousands of college students responded by calling for more scholarships and for more classes on African American history and culture.

Meanwhile, trend setters put aside Western dress for African-style dashikis and hairdos, and black parents gave their children African names. Many well-known African Americans such as Imamu Amiri Baraka (formerly LeRoi Jones), Muhammad Ali (formerly Cassius Clay), and Kwame Touré (formerly Stokely Carmichael) rejected their "slave names." The African American holiday Kwanzaa began to replace Christmas as a seasonal family celebration. This deepening sense of racial pride and solidarity was summed up in the popular slogan "Black Is Beautiful."

SISTERHOOD IS POWERFUL

Like Black Power, the women's liberation movement especially attracted women who had been active in civil rights, SDS, and campus antiwar movements. These women resented the sexist attitudes and behaviors of their fellow male activists. Impatient with the legislative reforms promoted by NOW, and angered by the sexism of SNCC and SDS, these women proclaimed "Sisterhood Is Powerful." "Women are an oppressed class. Our oppression is total, affecting every facet of our lives," read the Redstocking Manifesto of 1969. "We are exploited as sex objects, breeders, domestic servants, and cheap labor."

The women's liberation movement developed a scathing critique of patriarchy—that is, the power of men to dominate all institutions, from the family to business to the military to the protest movements themselves. Patriarchy, they argued, was the prime cause of exploitation, racism, and war. Outraged and sometimes outrageous, radical feminists, as they called themselves, conducted "street theater" at the 1968 Miss America Beauty Pageant in Atlantic City, crowning a live sheep as queen and "throwing implements of female torture" (bras, girdles, curlers, and copies of the *Ladies' Home Journal*) into a "freedom trash can."

OVERVIEW

PROTEST MOVEMENTS OF THE 1960S

Year	Organization/Movement	Description
1962	Students for a Democratic Society (SDS)	Organization of college students that became the largest national organization of left-wing white students. Calling for "participatory democracy," SDS involved students in community-based campaigns against poverty and for citizens' control of neighborhoods. SDS played a prominent role in the campaign to end the war in Vietnam.
1964	Free Speech Movement	Formed at the University of California at Berkeley to protest the banning of on-campus political fund-raising. Decried the bureaucratic character of the "multiuniversity" and advocated an expansion of student rights.
1965	Anti-Vietnam War Movement	Advocated grass-roots opposition to U.S. involvement in Southeast Asia. By 1970 a national mobilization committee organized a demonstration of a half-million protesters in Washington, D.C.
1965	*La raza*	A movement of Chicano youth to advance the cultural and political self-determination of Mexican Americans. *La raza* included the Brown Berets, which addressed community issues, and regional civil rights groups such as the Crusade for Social Justice, formed in 1965.
1966	Black Power	Militant movement that emerged from the civil rights campaigns to advocate independent institutions for African Americans and pride in black culture and African heritage. The idea of Black Power, a term coined by Stokely Carmichael, inspired the formation of the paramilitary Black Panthers.
1968	American Indian Movement (AIM)	Organization formed to advance the self-determination of Indian peoples and challenge the authority of the Bureau of Indian Affairs. Its most effective tactic was occupation. In February, 1973, AIM insurgents protesting land and treaty violations occupied Wounded Knee, South Dakota, the location of an 1890 massacre, until the FBI and BIA agents drove them out.
1968	Women's Liberation	Movement of mainly young women that took shape following a protest at the Miss America Beauty Pageant. Impatient with the legislative reforms promoted by the National Organization for Women, founded in 1966, activists developed their own agenda shaped by the slogan "The Personal Is Political." Activities included the formation of "consciousness-raising" groups and the establishment of women's studies programs.
1968	Asian American Political Alliance (AAPA)	Formed at the University of California at Berkeley, the AAPA was one of the first pan-Asian political organizations to struggle against racial oppression. The AAPA encouraged Asian Americans to claim their own cultural identity and to protest the war against Asian peoples in Vietnam.
1969	Gay Liberation	Movement to protest discrimination against homosexuals and lesbians that emerged after the Stonewall Riots in New York City. Unlike earlier organizations such as the Mattachine Society, which focused on civil rights, Gay Liberationists sought to radically change American society and government, which they believed were corrupt.

The media focused on the audacious acts and brazen pronouncements of radical feminists, but the majority involved in the women's liberation movement were less flamboyant women who were simply trying to rise above the limitations imposed on them because of their sex. Most of their activism took place outside the limelight in consciousness-raising (CR) groups. CR groups, which multiplied by the thousands in the late 1960s and early 1970s, brought women together to discuss the relationship between public events and private lives, particularly between politics and sexuality. Here women shared their most intimate feelings toward men or other women and established the constituency for the movement's most important belief, expressed in the aphorism "The personal is political." Believing that no aspect of life lacked a political dimension, women in these groups explored the power dynamics of the institutions of family and marriage as well as the work force and government.

Participants in the women's liberation movement engaged in a wide range of activities. Some staged sit-ins at *Newsweek* to protest demeaning media depictions of women. Others established health clinics, day-care centers, rape crisis centers, and shelters for women fleeing abusive husbands or lovers. The women's liberation movement also had a significant educational impact. Feminist bookstores and publishing companies, such as the Feminist Press, reached out to eager readers. Scholarly books such as Kate Millett's *Sexual Politics* (1970) found a wide popular audience. By the early 1970s, campus activists were demanding women's studies programs and women's centers. Like black studies, women's studies programs included traditional academic goals, such as the generation of new scholarship but also encouraged personal change and self-esteem. Between 1970 and 1975, as many as 150 women's studies programs had been established. The movement continued to grow; by 1980 nearly 30,000 women's studies courses were offered at colleges and universities throughout the United States.

The women's liberation movement remained, however, a bastion of white middle-class women. The appeal to sisterhood did not unite women across race or class or even sexual orientation. Lesbians, who charged the early leaders of NOW with homophobia, found large pockets of "heterosexism" in the women's liberation movement and broke off to form their own organizations. Although some African American women were outraged at the posturing of Black Power leaders like Stokely Carmichael, who joked that "the only position for women in SNCC is prone," the majority remained wary of white women's appeals to sisterhood. African American women formed their own "womanist" movement to address their distinct cultural and political concerns. Similarly, by 1970 a Latina feminist movement had begun to address issues uniquely relevant to women of color in an Anglo-dominated society.

GAY LIBERATION

The gay community had been generations in the making but only gained visibility during World War II (see Chapter 25). By the mid-1950s, two pioneering homophile organizations, the Mattachine Society and the Daughters of Bilitis, were campaigning to reduce discrimination against homosexuals in employment, the armed forces, and all areas of social and cultural life. Other groups, such as the Society for Individual Rights, rooted themselves in New York's Greenwich Village, San Francisco's North Beach, and other centers of gay night life. But it was during the tumultuous 1960s that gay and lesbian movements encouraged many men and women to proclaim publicly their sexual identity: "Say It Loud, Gay Is Proud."

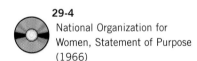

29-4
National Organization for Women, Statement of Purpose (1966)

29-5
The Gay Liberation Front, Come Out (1970)

The major event prompting gays to organize grew out of repeated police raids of gay bars and the harassment of their patrons. On Friday, June 27, 1969, New York police raided the Stonewall Inn, a well-known gay bar in Greenwich Village, and provoked an uprising of angry homosexuals that lasted the entire night. The next day, "Gay Power" graffiti appeared on buildings and sidewalks throughout the neighborhood. The Stonewall Riot, as it was called, sparked a new sense of collective identity among many gays and lesbians and touched off a new movement for both civil rights and liberation. Gay men and women in New York City formed the Gay Liberation Front (GLF), announcing themselves as "a revolutionary homosexual group of men and women formed with the realization that complete sexual liberation for all people cannot come about unless existing social institutions are abolished. We reject society's attempt to impose sexual roles and definitions of our nature. We are stepping outside these roles and simplistic myths. We are going to be who we are." The GLF also took a stand against the war in Vietnam and supported the Black Panthers. It quickly adopted the forms of public protest, such as street demonstrations and sit-ins, developed by the civil rights movement and given new direction by antiwar protesters.

Changes in public opinion and policies followed. As early as 1967 a group of Episcopal priests had urged church leaders to avoid taking a moral position against same-sex relationships. The San Francisco–based Council on Religion and Homosexuality established a network for clergy sympathetic to gay and lesbian parishioners. In 1973 the American Psychiatric Association, which since World War II had viewed homosexuality as a treatable mental illness, reclassified it as a normal sexual orientation. Meanwhile, there began a slow process of decriminalization of homosexual acts between consenting adults. In 1975 the U.S. Civil Service Commission ended its ban on the employment of homosexuals.

THE CHICANO REBELLION

By the mid-1960s young Mexican Americans adopted the slang term *Chicano*, in preference to Mexican American, to express a militant ethnic nationalism. Chicano militants demanded not only equality with white people, but also cultural and political self-determination. Tracing their roots to the heroic Aztecs, they identified *la raza* (the race or people) as the source of a common language, religion, and heritage.

Students played a large role in shaping the Chicano movement. In East Los Angeles, high school students staged "blowouts" or strikes to demand educational reform and a curricular emphasis on the history, literature, art, and language of Mexican Americans. Fifteen thousand students from five Los Angeles schools struck against poor educational facilities. The police conducted a mass arrest of protesters, and within a short time students in San Antonio and Denver were conducting their own blowouts, holding placards reading "Teachers, Sí, Bigots, No!" By 1969, on September 16, Mexican Independence Day, high school students throughout the Southwest skipped classes in the First National Chicano Boycott. Meanwhile, students organized to demand Mexican American studies on their campuses. In 1969, a group staged a sit-in at the administrative offices of the University of California at Berkeley, which one commentator called "the first important public appearance of something called Brown Power."

Chicano nationalism inspired a variety of regional political movements in the late 1960s. One of these, Rodolfo "Corky" Gonzales's Crusade for Justice, formed in 1965 to protest the failure of the Great Society's antipoverty programs. A former boxer and popular poet, Gonzales was especially well liked by barrio youth and college students. He led important campaigns for greater job opportunities and land reform throughout the Southwest well into the 1970s. In Colorado and New

Labor activist Cesar Chavez spearheaded the organization of Chicano agricultural workers into the United Farm Workers (UFW), the first successful union of migrant workers. In 1965, a strike of grape pickers in the fields around Delano, California, and a nationwide boycott of table grapes brought Chavez and the UFW into the media spotlight. Like Martin Luther King Jr., he advocated nonviolent methods for achieving justice and equality.

EPA Documercia (1927–1933) National Archives and Records Administration

Mexico, the *Alianza Federal de Mercedes,* formed in 1963 by Reies López Tijerina, fought to reclaim land fraudulently appropriated by white settlers. The Texas-based *La Raza Unida Party* (LRUP), meanwhile, increased Mexican American representation in local government and established social and cultural programs.

Mexican American activists, even those who won local office, soon discovered that economic power remained out of community hands. Stifled by poverty, ordinary Mexican Americans had less confidence in the political process, and many fell back into apathy after early hopes of great, sudden change. Despite these setbacks, a sense of collective identity had been forged among many Mexican Americans.

The Chicano movement found vivid expression in the performing and visual arts and in literature. *Teatro,* comprising film and drama, drew creatively on Mexican and Anglo cultural forms to explore the political dimensions of Mexican American society. *La Carpa de los Rasquachis (The Tent of the Underdogs),* appeared in 1974 as the first full-length Chicano play and was subsequently staged in many communities. One of the most popular and visible media was the mural, often based on the works of Mexican masters such as Diego Rivera. Chicano muralists painted an estimated 1,500 murals on public buildings throughout their communities, from the exteriors of retail shops to freeway overpasses, even to large drainage pipes. Artistic expression found its way into music and dance. The rock group *Los Lobos,* for example, dedicated their first recorded album to the United Farm Workers. One of the most important writers to capture the excitement of the Chicano movement was Oscar Zeta Acosta, whose *Revolt of the Cockroach,* published in 1973, renders into fiction some of the major events of the era.

RED POWER

The phrase "Red Power," attributed to Vine Deloria Jr., commonly expressed a growing sense of supratribal Indian identity. At the forefront of this movement was the **American Indian Movement (AIM)**, which was founded in 1968. Its members represented mainly urban Indian communities, and its leaders were young and militant. Like the Black Panthers and Brown Berets, AIM was initially organized to monitor law enforcement practices such as police harassment and brutality. It soon played a major role in building a network of urban Indian centers, churches,

American Indian Movement (AIM) Group of Native-American political activists who used confrontations with the federal government to publicize their case for Indian rights.

and philanthropic organizations and in establishing the "powwow circuit" that publicized news of protest activities across the country. Skillful in attracting attention from the news media, AIM quickly inspired a plethora of new publications and local chapters. Many young Indians turned to their elders to learn tribal ways, including traditional dress and spiritual practices.

The major catalyst of Red Power was the occupation of the deserted federal prison on Alcatraz Island in San Francisco Bay on November 20, 1969. A group of eighty-nine Indians, identifying themselves as "Indians of All Tribes," claimed the island according to the terms of an 1868 Sioux treaty that gave Indians rights to unused federal property on Indian land. The group demanded federal funds for a multifaceted cultural and educational center. For the next year and a half, an occupation force averaging around 100 and a stream of visitors from a large number of tribes celebrated the occupation. Although the protestors ultimately failed to achieve their specific goals, they had an enormous impact on the Indian community. With the occupation at Alcatraz, a participant testified, "we got back our worth, our pride, our dignity, our humanity." At the same time, the occupation fostered a new identity, a multitribal ethnicity —the American Indian.

The most dramatic series of events of the Red Power movement began in 1972, when Indian activists left the cities to return to their rural roots. In November, AIM staged an event known as the **Trail of Broken Treaties** that culminated in a week-long occupation of the Bureau of Indian Affairs in Washington, D.C. Emphasizing treaty violation rather than civil rights, AIM insurgents then moved to the Pine Ridge Reservation, the site of the 1890 massacre at Wounded Knee, South Dakota, where in the spring of 1973 they began a seige that lasted ten weeks. AIM activists demanded the removal of the leader of the Oglala Lakota, whom they believed to be a corrupt puppet of the Bureau of Indian Affairs, and the restoration of treaty rights. Dozens of FBI agents then invaded under shoot-to-kill orders, leaving two Indians dead and an unknown number of casualities on both sides.

Several tribes won in court, by legislation or by administrative fiat, small parts of what had earlier been taken from them. Despite these victories, tribal lands continued to suffer from industrial and government waste dumping and other commercial uses. On reservations and in urban areas with heavy Indian concentrations, alcohol abuse and ill health remained serious problems.

The 1960s also marked the beginning of an "Indian Renaissance" in literature. New books like Vine Deloria Jr.'s *Custer Died for Your Sins* (1969) and the classic *Black Elk Speaks* (1961), reprinted from the 1930s, reached millions of readers inside and outside Indian communities. A wide variety of Indian novelists, historians, and essayists, such as Pulitzer Prize–winning N. Scott Momaday and Leslie Silko, followed up these successes, and fiction and nonfiction works about Indian life and lore continued to attract a large audience.

THE ASIAN AMERICAN MOVEMENT

In 1968 students at the University of California at Berkeley founded the Asian American Political Alliance (AAPA), one of the first pan-Asian political organizations bringing together Chinese, Japanese, and Filipino American activists. Similar organizations soon appeared on campuses throughout California and spread quickly to the East Coast and Midwest.

These groups took a strong stand against the war in Vietnam, condemning it as a violation of the national sovereignty of the small Asian country. They also protested the racism directed against the peoples of Southeast Asia, particularly the practice common among American soldiers of referring to the enemy as "Gooks." This racist epithet, first used to denigrate Filipinos during the Spanish-American

Trail of Broken Treaties 1972 event staged by the American Indian Movement (AIM) that culminated in a week-long occupation of the Bureau of Indian Affairs in Washington, D.C.

Asian American became a vocal and visible community in the last half of the twentieth century.

Corbis

War, implied that Asians were something less than human and, therefore, proper targets for slaughter. In response, Asian American activists rallied behind the people of Vietnam and proclaimed racial solidarity with their "Asian brothers and sisters."

Between 1968 and 1973, major universities across the country introduced courses on Asian American studies, and a few, such as the City College of New York, set up interdisciplinary departments. Meanwhile, artists, writers, documentary filmmakers, oral historians, and anthropologists worked to recover the Asian American past. Maxine Hong Kingston's *Woman Warrior: A Memoir of a Girlhood among Ghosts* (1976) became a major bestseller.

Looking to the example of the Black Panthers, young Asian Americans also took their struggle into the community. In 1968, activists presented the San Francisco municipal government with a list of grievances about conditions in Chinatown, particularly the poor housing and medical facilities, and organized a protest march down the neighborhood's main street. They led a community-wide struggle to save San Francisco's International Hotel, a low-income residential facility mainly for Filipino and Chinese men, which was ultimately leveled for a new parking lot.

Community activists ranging from college students to neighborhood artists worked in a variety of campaigns to heighten public awareness. The Redress and Reparations Movement, initiated by Sansei (third-generation Japanese Americans), for example, encouraged students to ask their parents about their wartime experiences and prompted older civil rights organizations, such as the Japanese American Citizens League, to bring forward the issue of internment. At the same time, trade union organizers renewed labor organizing among new Asian workers, mainly in service industries, such as hotel and restaurant work, and in clothing manufacturing. Other campaigns reflected the growing diversity of the Asian population. Filipinos, the fastest growing group, organized to protest the destructive role of U.S.-backed Philippine dictator Ferdinand Marcos. Students from South Korea similarly denounced the repressive government in their homeland. Samoans sought to publicize the damage caused by nuclear testing in the Pacific Islands. Ultimately, however, in blurring intergroup differences, the Asian American movement failed to reach the growing populations of new immigrants, especially the numerous Southeast Asians fleeing their devastated homeland.

THE NIXON PRESIDENCY

HOW DID Nixon win the White House in 1968?

The sharp divisions among Americans in 1968, mainly due to President Johnson's policies in Vietnam, paved the way for the election of Richard Milhous Nixon. The new Republican president inherited not only an increasingly unpopular war but a nation riven by internal discord. Without specifying his plans, he promised a "just and honorable peace" in Southeast Asia and the restoration of law and order at home. Yet, once in office, Nixon puzzled both friends and foes. He ordered unprecedented illegal government action against private citizens while agreeing with Congress to enhance several welfare programs and improve environmental protection. He widened and intensified the war in Vietnam, yet made stunning moves toward détente with the People's Republic of China. An architect of the Cold War in the 1950s, Nixon became the first president to foresee its end. Nixon worked hard in the White House, centralizing authority and reigning defiantly as an "Imperial President"—until he brought himself down.

THE SOUTHERN STRATEGY

In 1968, Republican presidential contender Richard Nixon deftly built on voter hostility toward youthful protesters and the counterculture. He represented, he said, the "silent majority"—those Americans who worked, paid taxes, and did not demonstrate, picket, or protest loudly, "people who are not haters, people who love their country." Recovering from defeats in elections for the presidency in 1960 and the governorship of California in 1962, Nixon declared himself the one candidate who could restore law and order to the nation.

After signing the landmark Civil Rights Act of 1964, President Johnson said privately, "I think we just delivered the South to the Republicans for a long time to come." Republican strategists moved quickly to make this prediction come true. They also recognized the growing electoral importance of the Sunbelt, where populations grew with the rise of high-tech industries and retirement communities. A powerful conservatism dominated this region, home to many military bases, defense plants, and an increasingly influential Protestant evangelism. Nixon appealed directly to these voters by promising to appoint to federal courts judges who would undercut liberal interpretations of civil rights and be tough on crime.

Nixon selected as his running mate Maryland governor Spiro T. Agnew, known for his vitriolic oratory. Agnew treated dissent as near treason. The 1968 campaign underscored the antiliberal sentiment of the voting public. The most dramatic example was the relative success of Alabama governor George Wallace's third-party bid for the presidency. Wallace took state office in 1963 promising white Alabamans "Segregation now! Segregation tomorrow! Segregation forever!" In 1968 he waged a national campaign around a conservative hate list that included school busing, antiwar demonstrations, and urban uprisings. Winning only five Southern states, Wallace nevertheless captured 13.5 percent of the popular vote.

The Nixon-Agnew team squeaked to victory, capturing the popular vote by the slim margin of 43.4 percent to Humphrey and Maine senator Edmund Muskie's 42.7 percent but taking nearly all the West's electoral votes. Bitterly divided by the campaign, the Democrats would remain out of presidential contention for over two decades, except when the Republicans suffered scandal and disgrace. The Republicans in 1968 had paved the way for the conservative ascendancy.

NIXON'S WAR

Nixon promised to bring "peace with honor." Yet, despite this pledge, the Vietnam War raged for four more years before a peace settlement was reached.

Much of the responsibility for the prolonged conflict rested with Henry A. Kissinger. A dominating personality on the National Security Council, Kissinger insisted that the United States could not retain its global leadership by appearing weak to either allies or enemies. Brilliant and ruthless, Kissinger helped Nixon centralize foreign policymaking in the White House. Together, they overpowered those members of the State Department who had concluded that the majority of Americans no longer supported the war.

MAP EXPLORATION

To explore an interactive version of this map, go to
http://www.prenhall.com/faraghertlc/map29.4

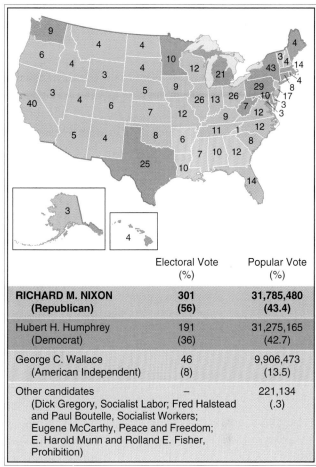

	Electoral Vote (%)	Popular Vote (%)
RICHARD M. NIXON (Republican)	**301 (56)**	**31,785,480 (43.4)**
Hubert H. Humphrey (Democrat)	191 (36)	31,275,165 (42.7)
George C. Wallace (American Independent)	46 (8)	9,906,473 (13.5)
Other candidates (Dick Gregory, Socialist Labor; Fred Halstead and Paul Boutelle, Socialist Workers; Eugene McCarthy, Peace and Freedom; E. Harold Munn and Rolland E. Fisher, Prohibition)	–	221,134 (.3)

MAP 29-4

The Election of 1968   Although the Republican Nixon-Agnew team won the popular vote by only a small margin, the Democrats lost in most of the Northern states that had voted Democratic since the days of FDR. Segregationist Governor George Wallace of Alabama polled more than 9 million votes.

WHAT WERE the most important factors in Nixon's victory in 1968?

28-11
Vietnamization (1969)

In public Nixon followed a policy of "Vietnamization." On May 14, 1969, he announced that the time was approaching "when the South Vietnamese . . . will be able to take over some of the fighting." During the next several months, he ordered the withdrawal of 60,000 U.S. troops. Hoping to placate public opinion, Nixon also intended to "demonstrate to Hanoi that we were serious in seeking a diplomatic settlement." In private, with Kissinger's guidance, Nixon mulled over the option of a "knockout blow" to the North Vietnamese.

On April 30, 1970, Nixon made one of the most controversial decisions of his presidency. Without seeking congressional approval, Nixon ordered U.S. troops to invade the tiny nation of Cambodia. Nixon had hoped in this way to end North Vietnamese infiltration into the south, but he had also decided to live up to what he privately called his "wild man" or "mad bomber" reputation. The enemy would be unable to anticipate the location or severity of the next U.S. strike, Nixon reasoned, and would thus feel compelled to negotiate.

Nixon could not have predicted the outpouring of protest that followed the invasion of Cambodia. The largest series of demonstrations and police-student confrontations in the nation's history took place on campuses and in city streets. At Kent State University in Ohio, twenty-eight National Guardsmen apparently panicked, shooting into an unarmed crowd of about 200 students, killing four and wounding nine. Ten days later, on May 14, at Jackson State University, a black school in Mississippi, state troopers entered a campus dormitory and began shooting wildly, killing two students and wounding twelve others. Demonstrations broke out on fifty campuses.

The nation was shocked. Thirty-seven college and university presidents signed a letter calling on the president to end the war. A few weeks later the Senate adopted a bipartisan resolution outlawing the use of funds for U.S. military operations in Cambodia, starting July 1, 1970. Although the House rejected the resolution, Nixon saw the writing on the wall. He had planned to negotiate a simultaneous withdrawal of North Vietnamese and U.S. troops, but he could no longer afford to hold out for this condition.

The president, still goaded by Kissinger, did not accept defeat easily. In February 1971 Nixon directed the South Vietnamese army to invade Laos and cut supply lines, but the demoralized invading force suffered a quick and humiliating defeat. Faced with enemy occupation of more and more territory during a major offensive in April 1972, Nixon ordered the mining of North Vietnamese harbors and directed B-52s to conduct massively destructive bombing missions in Cambodia and North Vietnam.

Nixon also sent Kissinger to Paris for secret negotiations with delegates from North Vietnam. They agreed to a cease-fire specifying the withdrawal of all U.S. troops and the return of all U.S. prisoners of war. Knowing these terms ensured defeat, South Vietnam's president refused to sign the agreement. On Christmas Day 1972, hoping for a better negotiating position, Nixon ordered one final wave of bomb attacks on North Vietnam's cities. To secure a halt to the bombing, the North Vietnamese offered to resume negotiations. But the terms of the Paris Peace Agreement, signed by North Vietnam and the United States in January 1973, differed little from the settlement Nixon could have procured in 1969, costing hundreds of thousands of deaths that might have been prevented. Beginning in March 1973, the withdrawal of U.S. troops left the outcome of the war a foregone conclusion. By December of that year only fifty American military personnel remained, and the government of South Vietnam had no future.

Public Opinion on the War in Vietnam
By 1969 Americans were sharply divided in their assessments of the progress of the war and peace negotiations. The American Institute of Public Opinion, founded in 1935 by George Gallup, charted a growing dissatisfaction with the war in Vietnam.

The Gallup Poll: Public Opinion, 1935–1974 (New York: Random House, 1974), p. 2189

In view of the developments since we entered the fighting in Vietnam, do you think the United States made a mistake sending troops to fight in Vietnam?

Yes	52%
No	39
No opinion	9°

Interviewing Date 1/22—28/1969, Survey #774-K, Question #6/Index #45

In April 1975 North Vietnamese troops took over Saigon, and the Communist-led Democratic Republic of Vietnam soon united the small nation. The war was finally over. It had cost the United States 58,000 lives and $150 billion. The country had not only failed to achieve its stated war goal but had also lost an important post in Southeast Asia. Equally important, the policy of containment introduced by President Truman had proved impossible to sustain.

While Nixon was maneuvering to bring about "peace with honor," the chilling crimes of war had already begun to haunt Americans. In 1971 the army court-martialed a young lieutenant, William L. Calley Jr. for the murder of "at least" twenty-two Vietnamese civilians during a 1968 search-and-destroy mission subsequently known as the **My Lai Massacre**. Calley's platoon had destroyed a village and slaughtered more than 350 unarmed South Vietnamese, raping and beating many of the women before killing them. "My Lai was not an isolated incident," one veteran attested, but "only a minor step beyond the standard official United States policy in Indochina." Commander of the platoon at My Lai, Calley was first sentenced to life imprisonment before being given a reduced term of ten years. The secretary of the army paroled Calley after he served three years under house arrest in his apartment.

"THE CHINA CARD"

Apart from Vietnam, Nixon's foreign policy defied the expectations of liberals and conservatives alike. Actually, he followed traditions of previous Republican moderates such as Herbert Hoover and Dwight Eisenhower, who had so effectively "proved" their anticommunism that they could conciliate international foes without undermining their popularity at home. Nixon added a new page, however—a policy of détente that replaced U.S.–Soviet bipolarity with multilateral relations. Nixon could cultivate relations with the People's Republic of China, a rising world power more rigidly Communist than the Soviet Union, to form an alliance against the Soviet Union. And he could easily persuade the Soviet Union to cooperate on trade agreements, thus limiting the two nations' ruthless competition to control governments in Asia, the Middle East, and Africa. Opponents of the Vietnam War accused Nixon of double dealing, while conservatives howled at any compromise with Communist governments. But Nixon persisted in his plans, anticipating an end to the Cold War on American terms.

Playing the "China card" was the most dramatic of the president's moves. Early in his political career Nixon had avidly supported the arch-conservative China lobby. But as president he considered the People's Republic of China too important to be isolated by the West and too obviously hostile to the Soviet Union to be discounted as a potential ally.

"Ping-pong diplomacy" began in April 1971, when the Chinese hosted a table tennis team from the United States. Henry Kissinger embarked on a secret mission a few months later. Finally, in February 1972, Richard and Pat Nixon flew to Beijing, where they were greeted by foreign minister Zhou Enlai and a band playing "The Star-Spangled Banner."

It was a momentous and surprising event, one that marked a new era in East–West diplomacy. Nixon claimed that he had succeeded in bridging "16,000

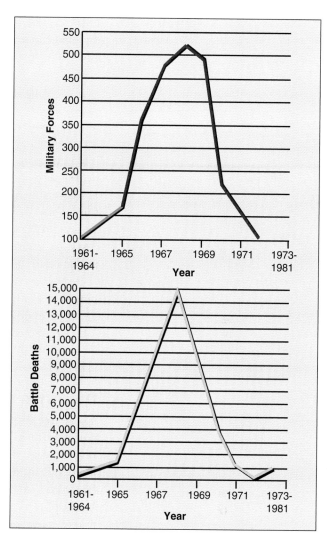

U.S. Military Forces in Vietnam and Casualties, 1961–1981
The United States government estimated battle deaths between 1969 and 1973 for South Vietnamese troops at 107,504 and North Vietnamese and Vietcong at more than a half-million. Although the United States suffered fewer deaths, the cost was enormous.

U.S. Department of Defense, *Selected Manpower Statistics*, annual, and unpublished data, beginning 1981, National Archives and Records Service, "Combat Area Casualty File" (3-330-80-3)

My Lai Massacre Killing of twenty-two Vietnamese civilians by U.S. forces during a 1968 search-and-destroy mission.

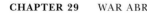
miles and twenty-two years of hostility." The president's move successfully increased diplomatic pressure on the Soviet Union but simultaneously weakened the Nationalist Chinese government in Taiwan, which now slipped into virtual diplomatic obscurity.

Next the president went to Moscow to negotiate with Soviet leader Leonid Brezhnev, who was anxious about U.S. involvement with China and eager for economic assistance. Declaring, "There must be room in this world for two great nations with different systems to live together and work together," Nixon offered to sell $1 billion of grain to the Soviets. Winning the favor of American wheat farmers, this deal simultaneously relieved U.S. trade deficits and crop surpluses. Afterward, the Soviet leader became visibly more cautious about supporting revolutions in the third world. Nixon also completed negotiations of the **Strategic Arms Limitation Treaty** (**SALT**, known later as SALT I). A limited measure, SALT I represented the first success at strategic arms control since the opening of the Cold War and a major public relations victory for the leaders of the two superpowers.

Nixon's last major diplomatic foray proved far less effective. The president sent Kissinger on a two-year mission of "shuttle diplomacy" to mediate Israeli-Arab disputes, to ensure the continued flow of oil, and to increase lucrative U.S. arms sales to Arab countries. The Egyptians and Israelis agreed to a cease-fire in their October 1973 Yom Kippur War, but little progress toward peace in the area was achieved.

DOMESTIC POLICY

Nixon deeply desired to restore order in American society. "We live in a deeply troubled and profoundly unsettled time," he noted. "Drugs, crime, campus revolts, racial discord, draft resistance—on every hand we find old standards violated, old values discarded." Despite his hostility to liberalism, however, Nixon had some surprises for conservatives. Determined to win reelection in 1972, he supported new Social Security benefits and subsidized housing for the poor and oversaw the creation of the **Environmental Protection Agency** and the Occupational Safety and Health Administration. Most notable was his support, under the guidance of Democratic adviser Daniel P. Moynihan, for the Family Assistance Plan, which proposed a minimal income for the poor in place of welfare benefits. Conservatives judged the plan too generous while liberals found it inadequate. Moreover, the plan was expensive. Bipartisan opposition ultimately killed the bill.

Nixon also embraced a policy of fiscal liberalism. Early in 1971 he accepted the idea of deficit spending. Later that year he ordered a first: he took the nation off the gold standard. Subsequently, the dollar's value would float on the world market rather than being tied to the value of gold. His ninety-day freeze on wages, rents, and prices, designed to halt the inflation caused by the massive spending on the Vietnam War, also closely resembled Democratic policies. Finally, Nixon's support of "black capitalism"—adjustments or quotas favoring minority contractors in construction projects—created an explosive precedent for "set-aside" programs later blamed on liberals.

Nixon lined up with conservatives, however, on most civil rights issues and thus enlarged Southern Republican constituencies. He accepted the principle of school integration but rejected the busing programs required to implement racial balance. His nominees to the Supreme Court were far more conservative than those appointed by Eisenhower. Warren E. Burger, who replaced Chief Justice Earl Warren, steered the Court away from the liberal direction it had taken since the 1950s.

Strategic Arms Limitation Treaty
Treaty signed in 1972 by the United States and the Soviet Union to slow the nuclear arms race.

Environmental Protection Agency
Federal agency created in 1970 to oversee environmental monitoring and cleanup programs.

One of the most newsworthy events of Nixon's administration was a distant result of President Kennedy's determination to outshine the Soviets in outer space (see Chapter 27). On July 21, 1969, the lunar module of Apollo 11 descended to the moon's Sea of Tranquility. As millions watched on television, astronauts Neil Armstrong and Buzz Aldrin stepped out to plant an American flag and to bear the message, "We came in peace for all mankind."

WATERGATE

At times Richard Nixon expressed his yearning for approval in strange ways. A few days after the bombing of Cambodia in May 1970, he wandered out of the White House alone at 5:00 in the morning to talk to antiwar demonstrators. He tried to engage them in small talk about football and pleaded, "I know that probably most of you think I'm an SOB, but I want you to know I understand just how you feel." According to H. R. Haldeman, one of Nixon's closest advisers, the student killings at Kent State deeply troubled the president.

Yet only a few months later Nixon ordered illegal wiretaps of news professionals. He also reaffirmed his support of Central Intelligence Agency (CIA) surveillance of U.S. citizens and organizations—a policy specifically forbidden by the CIA charter—and encouraged members of his administration to spy on Democrats planning for the 1972 election campaign. When news of these illegal activities surfaced, one of the most canny politicians in American history found himself the first president since Andrew Johnson to face the likelihood of impeachment proceedings.

FOREIGN POLICY AS CONSPIRACY

Nixon's conduct of foreign policy offered early clues into his political character. Although he had welcomed the publicity surrounding his historic moves toward détente with the Soviet Union and normalized relations with China, Nixon generally handled the nation's foreign affairs in surreptitious fashion. But as opposition to the Vietnam War mounted in Congress, he began to face hard questions about this practice. As early as 1970, Republicans as well as Democrats had condemned covert operations in foreign countries. In response, the president, the Department of State, and the CIA developed plans to tighten security even further. Nixon issued a tough mandate against all leaks of information by government personnel, news specialists, or politicians.

At the time, apart from the highly publicized tour to China, Nixon revealed little about his policy for other parts of the globe. Unknown to most Americans, he accelerated the delivery of arms supplies to foreign dictators, including the shah of Iran, Ferdinand Marcos of the Philippines, and the regime of Pieter William Botha in South Africa. His CIA assistants trained and aided SAVAK, the Iranian secret police force notorious for torturing political dissidents. They also stood behind the South African government in its effort to curtail the activities of the antiapartheid African National Congress. In Latin America, Nixon provided financial assistance and military aid to repressive regimes such as that of Anastasio Somoza of Nicaragua, notorious for its blatant corruption and repeated violations of human rights.

Still more controversial was Nixon's plan to overthrow the legally elected socialist government of Salvador Allende in Chile. With the assistance of nongovernment agencies, such as the AFL-CIO's American Institute for Free Labor

WHY WAS Nixon so secretive about his foreign policy?

Development, the CIA destabilized the regime by funding right-wing parties, launching demonstrations, and preparing the Chilean army for a coup. In September 1973, a military junta killed President Allende and captured, tortured, or murdered thousands of his supporters. Nixon and Kissinger warmly welcomed the new ruler, Augusto Pinochet, granting him financial assistance to restabilize the country.

Toward the end of Nixon's term, members of Congress who had been briefed on these policies began to break silence, and reports of clandestine operations flooded the media. Several former CIA agents issued anguished confessions of their activities in other countries. More troubling to Nixon, in spite of all his efforts the United States continued to lose ground as a superpower.

THE AGE OF DIRTY TRICKS

As Nixon approached the 1972 reelection campaign, he tightened his inner circle of White House staff who assisted him in withholding information from the public, discrediting critics, and engaging in assorted "dirty tricks." Circle members solicited illegal contributions for the campaign and laundered the money through Mexican bank accounts. They also formed a secret squad, "the plumbers," to halt the troublesome leaks of information. This team, headed by former CIA agent E. Howard Hunt and former FBI agent G. Gordon Liddy, assisted in conspiracy at the highest levels of government.

The first person on the squad's "hit list" was Daniel Ellsberg, a former researcher with the Department of Defense, who in 1971 had turned over to the press secret documents outlining the military history of American involvement in Vietnam. The so-called **Pentagon Papers** exposed the role of presidents and military leaders in deceiving the public and Congress about the conduct of the United States in Southeast Asia. Nixon sought to bar publication by the *New York Times*, but the Supreme Court ruled in favor of the newspaper on the basis of the First Amendment. Within weeks, a complete version of the Pentagon Papers became a bestselling book, and in 1972 the *New York Times* won a Pulitzer Prize for the series of articles. Frustrated in his attempt to suppress the report, Nixon directed the Department of Justice to prosecute Ellsberg on charges of conspiracy, espionage, and theft. Meanwhile, Hunt and Liddy, seeking to discredit Ellsberg, broke into the office of his former psychiatrist. They found nothing that would make their target less heroic in the eyes of an increasingly skeptical public, and by 1973 the charges against Ellsberg were dropped after the Nixon administration itself stood guilty of misconduct.

At the same time, Nixon ran a skillful negative campaign charging George McGovern, the liberal Democrat who had won his party's nomination on the first ballot, with supporting "abortion, acid [LSD], and amnesty" for those who had resisted the draft or deserted the armed forces. The Republicans also informed the news media that McGovern's running mate, Senator Thomas Eagleton, had once undergone electric shock therapy for depression, thus forcing his resignation from the Democratic team. Voter turnout fell to an all-time low, and McGovern lost every state but Massachusetts. (Later, when Nixon faced disgrace, bumper stickers appeared reading, "Don't Blame Me, I'm from Massachusetts.")

The Committee to Re-Elect the President (CREEP) enjoyed a huge war chest and spent a good portion on dirty tricks designed to divide the Democrats and discredit them in the eyes of the voting public. The most ambitious plan—wiretapping the Democratic National Committee headquarters—backfired.

On June 17, 1972, a security team had tripped up a group of intruders hired by CREEP to install listening devices in the Washington, D.C., Watergate apartment and office complex where the Democrats were headquartered. The police arrested

Pentagon Papers   Classified Defense Department documents on the history of the United States's involvement in Vietnam, prepared in 1968 and leaked to the press in 1971.

five men, who were later found guilty of conspiracy and burglary. Although Nixon disclaimed any knowledge of the plan, two *Washington Post* reporters, Bob Woodward and Carl Bernstein, followed a trail of evidence back to the nation's highest office.

Televised Senate hearings opened to public view more than a pattern of presidential wrongdoing: they showed an attempt to impede investigations of the **Watergate** case. Testifying before the committee, a former Nixon aide revealed the existence of secret tape recordings of conversations held in the Oval Office. After special prosecutor Archibald Cox refused to allow Nixon to claim executive privilege and withhold the tapes, the president ordered Cox fired. This "Saturday Night Massacre," as it came to be called, further tarnished Nixon's reputation and swelled curiosity about the tapes. On June 24, 1974, the Supreme Court voted unanimously that Nixon had to release the tapes to a new special prosecutor, Leon Jaworski.

THE FALL OF THE EXECUTIVE

Although incomplete, the Watergate tapes proved damning. They documented Nixon's ravings against his enemies, including anti-Semitic slurs, and his conniving efforts to harass private citizens through federal agencies. The tapes also proved that Nixon had not only known about plans to cover up the Watergate break-in but had also ordered it. The news media enjoyed a field day with the revelations. In July 1974, the House Judiciary Committee adopted three articles of impeachment, charging Nixon with obstructing justice.

Charges of executive criminality had clouded the Nixon administration since his vice president had resigned in disgrace. In 1972 Spiro Agnew had admitted accepting large kickbacks while serving as governor of Maryland. Pleading no contest to this and to charges of federal income tax evasion, Agnew had resigned from office in October 1973. Gerald Ford, a moderate Republican representative from Michigan, had replaced him and now stood in the wings while the president's drama unfolded.

Facing certain impeachment by the House of Representatives, Richard Nixon became, on August 9, 1974, the first U.S. president to resign from office.

30-1
House Judiciary Committee,
Conclusion on Impeachment
Resolution (1974)

CONCLUSION

The resignations of Richard Nixon and Spiro Agnew brought little to relieve the feeling of national exhaustion that attended the Vietnam War. U.S. troops had pulled out of Vietnam in 1973 and the war officially ended in 1975, but bitterness lingered over the unprecedented—and, for many, humiliating—defeat. Morover, confidence in the government's highest office was severely shaken. The passage of the War Powers Act in 1973, written to compel any future president to seek congressional approval for armed intervention abroad, dramatized both the widespread suspicion of presidential intentions and a yearning for peace. But the positive dream of community that had inspired Johnson, King, and a generaton of student activists could not be revived. No other vision took its place.

In 1968 seven prominent antiwar protesters had been brought to trial for allegedly conspiring to disrupt the Democratic National Convention in Chicago. Just a few years later, the majority of Americans had concluded that Presidents Johnson and Nixon had conspired to do far worse. They had intentionally deceived the public about the nature and fortunes of the war. This moral failure signaled a collapse at the center of the American political system. Since Dwight Eisenhower left office warning of the potential danger embedded in the "military–industrial complex," no president had survived the presidency with his honor intact.

Watergate   A complex scandal involving attempts to cover up illegal actions taken by administration officials and leading to the resignation of President Richard Nixon in 1974.

CHRONOLOGY

1964 President Lyndon Johnson calls for "an unconditional war on poverty" in his State of the Union Address.

Tonkin Gulf resolution.

The Economic Opportunity Act establishes the Office of Economic Opportunity.

Free speech movement gets under way at University of California at Berkeley.

Johnson defeats conservative Barry Goldwater for president.

1965 President Johnson authorizes Operation Rolling Thunder, the bombing of North Vietnam.

Teach-ins begin on college campuses.

First major march on Washington for peace is organized.

Watts uprising begins a wave of rebellions in black communities.

1966 J. William Fulbright publishes *The Arrogance of Power.*

Black Panther Party is formed.

National Organization for Women (NOW) is formed.

1967 Antiwar rally in New York City draws 300,000.

Vietnam Veterans against the War is formed.

Uprisings in Newark, Detroit, and other cities.

Hippie "Summer of Love."

1968 U.S. ground troops levels in Vietnam number 500,000.

Tet Offensive in Vietnam, followed by international protests against U.S. policies.

Martin Luther King Jr. is assassinated; riots break out in more than 100 cities.

Vietnam peace talks begin in Paris.

Robert Kennedy is assassinated.

Democratic National Convention, held in Chicago, nominates Hubert Humphrey; "police riot" against protesters.

Richard Nixon elected president.

American Indian Movement (AIM) founded.

1969 Woodstock music festival marks the high tide of the counterculture.

Stonewall Riot in Greenwich Village sparks the gay liberation movement.

Apollo 11 lands on the moon.

1970 U.S. incursion into Cambodia sparks campus demonstrations; students killed at Kent State and Jackson State universities.

Women's Strike for Equality marks the fiftieth anniversary of the woman suffrage amendment.

1971 Lieutenant William Calley Jr. court-martialed for My Lai Massacre.

New York Times starts publishing the Pentagon Papers.

1972 Nixon visits China and Soviet Union.

SALT I limits offensive intercontinental ballistic missiles.

Intruders attempting to "bug" Democratic headquarters in the Watergate complex are arrested.

Nixon is reelected in a landslide.

Nixon orders Christmas Day bombing of North Vietnam.

1973 Paris Peace Agreement ends war in Vietnam.

FBI seizes Indian occupants of Wounded Knee, South Dakota.

Watergate burglars tried; congressional hearings on Watergate.

CIA destabilizes elected Chilean government, which is overthrown.

Vice President Spiro T. Agnew resigns.

1974 House Judiciary Committee adopts articles of impeachment against Nixon.

Nixon resigns the presidency.

SUMMARY

Vietnam: America's Longest War Inheriting U. S. involvement in Vietnam, Lyndon Johnson expanded the American role to full-fledged war after the Tonkin Gulf Resolution. The U. S. strategy of attrition failed to break North Vietnam's resolve. The media eventually accused Johnson of creating a credibility gap between official reports on the war and its reality. Criticism soon spread to Congress and the war's continuation affected domestic policy.

A Generation in Conflict The sixties generation was the largest and best educated generation in American history. A minority of this generation began protesting the Vietnam War and other social ills. Many had taken part in civil rights demonstrations and they started protesting on college campuses, soon mobilizing large numbers of young people and others to take part in mass demonstrations. Conversely, large numbers of young men served as teenage soldiers in Vietnam experiencing frustration and alienation amid the horror of combat in tropical swamps and rain forests.

Wars on Poverty In 1964, Lyndon Johnson proclaimed his Great Society program that was designed to wage war on poverty. Programs were developed to improve opportunities in education and employment, empower communities, and increase social welfare. Part of the problem was the continuing decline of the cities. The deteriorating conditions helped precipitate a number of urban uprisings by African Americans.

1968 One of the most turbulent and influential years in American history was 1968. The Vietnam War experienced its most destructive fighting. Two major leaders were assassinated. The Democratic Convention in Chicago was accompanied by a full-scale riot. Lastly, student radical and antiwar protests erupted throughout Europe and in Japan.

The Politics of Identity In the late 1960s, numerous movements either intensified their efforts or emerged. Some African Americans embraced Black Power. The women's and gay liberation movements became powerful voices for their respective rights while Chicano nationalism and Red Power identified the Mexican American and Indian peoples movements. Asian Americans also became actively involved in rights movements.

The Nixon Presidency The conservative backlash to the liberal and radical movements of the 1960s helped Richard Nixon win the 1968 election. Nixon also campaigned on winning peace with honor, but his escalation of the conflict into Cambodia triggered a massive, national antiwar protest. At the same time, Nixon worked to normalize relations with China. Domestically, he supported both liberal and conservative programs.

Watergate The Nixon White House engaged in covert actions overseas and dirty tricks at home. His illegal actions during the 1972 presidential campaign eventually erupted into the Watergate scandal that led to convictions of several Nixon appointees and the resignation of the president.

REVIEW QUESTIONS

1. Discuss the events that led up to and contributed to U.S. involvement in Vietnam. How did U.S. involvement in the war affect domestic programs?

2. Discuss the reasons the protest movement against the Vietnam War started on college campuses. Describe how these movements were organized and how the opponents of the war differed from the supporters.

3. Discuss the programs sponsored by Johnson's plan for a Great Society. What was their impact on urban poverty in the late 1960s?

4. What was the impact of the assassinations of Martin Luther King Jr. and Robert Kennedy on the election of 1968? How were various communities affected?

5. How were the "politics of identity" movements different from earlier civil rights organizations? In what ways did the various movements resemble one another?

6. Why did Richard Nixon enjoy such a huge electoral victory in 1972? Discuss his foreign and domestic policies. What led to his sudden downfall?

KEY TERMS

American Indian Movement (AIM) (p. 814)
Black Panther (p. 810)
Black Power (p. 809)
Counterculture (p. 797)
Environmental Protection Agency (p. 820)
Free speech movement (p. 796)
Medicare (p. 802)
My Lai Massacre (p. 819)
Office of Economic Opportunity (OEO) (p. 801)

Pentagon Papers (p. 822)
Strategic Arms Limitation Treaty (SALT) (p. 820)
Students for a Democratic Society (SDS) (p. 796)
Tonkin Gulf Resolution (p. 793)
Trail of Broken Treaties (p. 815)
War on poverty (p. 801)
Watergate (p. 823)

RECOMMENDED READING

John A. Andrew III, *Lyndon Johnson and the Great Society* (1998). An assessment of the Great Society, with special emphasis on the two major issues of civil rights and poverty. Andrew discusses Johnson's aspirations and the obstacles that kept them out of reach.

Keith Beattie, *The Scar That Binds: American Culture and the Vietnam War* (1998). Examines memoirs, war novels and films, and the Vietnam Veterans Memorial in Washington, D.C., to discuss the cultural legacy of the war.

Alexander Bloom, ed., *Long Time Gone: Sixties America Then and Now* (2001). Ten essays covering various aspects of the social and political movements of the 1960s. The authors draw out the meaning of the "sixties" for today and dispel commonplace myths by providing accurate information and a sound context for interpretation.

Jane F. Gerhard, *Desiring Revolution: Second-Wave Feminism and the Rewriting of American Sexual Thought, 1920–1982* (2001). Discusses the background of the feminist side of the sexual revolution with special attention to popular versions of Freud's theories. Gerhard discusses disagreements among feminists on the meaning and experience of sexual liberation.

Michael H. Hunt, *Lyndon Johnson's War: America's Cold War Crusade in Vietnam, 1945–1968* (1996). Tracks Johnson's decisions to wage all-out war in Vietnam. Hunt interprets Johnson's actions as consistent with the Cold War foreign policy that had prevailed since the Truman administration and its pledge to "contain" communism.

Rebecca E. Klatch, *A Generation Divided: The New Left, the New Right, and the 1960s* (1999). Compares and contrasts the respective roles of Students for a Democratic Society and the conservative Young Americans for Freedom on college campuses. Klatch, a sociologist, presents lengthy oral interviews with former student activists in both camps.

Joan Morrison and Robert K. Morrison, eds., *From Camelot to Kent State: The Sixties Experience in the Words of Those Who Lived It* (2001). A collection of 59 oral histories with a range of people who lived through the 1960s. The volume includes stories of better known activists, such as Eldridge Cleaver and Abbie Hoffman, as well as those who were soldiers in Vietnam or student activists. This edition also contains many photographs.

Joseph Tilden Rhea, *Race Pride and the American Identity* (1997). Examines American Indians, Asian Americans, Latinos, and African Americans in their search for recognition. Rhea emphasizes the importance of political struggles and their impact on historical consciousness, including the establishment of historical sites and museums.

Ruth Rosen, *The World Split Open: How the Modern Women's Movement Changed America* (2000). Discusses the impact of women's liberation on American politics, business, and family life. Through extensive archival research and interviews, Rosen provides compelling evidence for the magnitude of change accompanying second-wave feminism.

Anthony Summers, *The Arrogance of Power: The Secret World of Richard Nixon* (2000). A popular biography of Nixon's life from his early political career in California through his presidency. Summers drew on more than a thousand interviews, including those with Nixon's psychotherapist, to portray the former president's erratic behavior and mental instability during as well as before the disastrous Watergate affair.

Marilyn B. Young, *The Vietnam Wars, 1945–1990* (1991). An excellent overview of the involvement of the French and the American military and diplomatic forces in Vietnam from the 1910s to 1975, and of the various movements against them. Young presents a thematic continuity that highlights the nationalism of the Vietnamese as ultimately more powerful than the troops and weaponry of their opponents.

Iconic Images of the Vietnam Era

PRESIDENTS HAVE their picture taken shaking hands with visitors countless times. Usually they are of interest only to the visitors. What do you think made the photograph of President Nixon with Elvis Presley of interest to so many? During the late 1960s and early 1970s violence at home and overseas was distressingly commonplace. What do you think made the photographs of Mary Vecchio and Kim Phuk so memorable?

Television famously brought the Vietnam War "into the living room." Nonetheless some of the most memorable images of the era were photographs. What is it about particular images that turn them into iconic representations of a moment of history? Pictured here are three such photographs. The first shows Richard Nixon and Elvis Presley in the Oval Office. Fifteen years earlier, Presley had scandalized the "older generation" with his uninhibited gyrations. Nixon, then and later, always campaigned for "family values." Next is a photograph of a student reacting to the killing of a classmate on May 4, 1970 at Kent State University in Ohio. The preceeding week Nixon had ordered U.S. troops into Cambodia to destroy North Vietnamese supply routes and command centers. Campuses across the country erupted and in Ohio, the governor called in the National Guard to quell the demonstrations at Kent State. Guard soldiers fired on the students, killing the young man shown this photograph. The third photograph shows the impact of an American napalm attack upon the children of a South Vietnamese village.

◄ **This is the single most requested item in the National Archives which contain, among other national treasures, originals of the Declaration of Independence, the Constitution, and the Bill of Rights.** President Nixon and Elvis Presley met at the singer's request. He had volunteered to work in the administration's anti-drug crusade. The president, looking for a way to reach out to young people, readily agreed. He appointed Presley a "deputy" in the anti-drug war. Presley was, at the time, addicted to a variety of uppers, downers, and other medications.

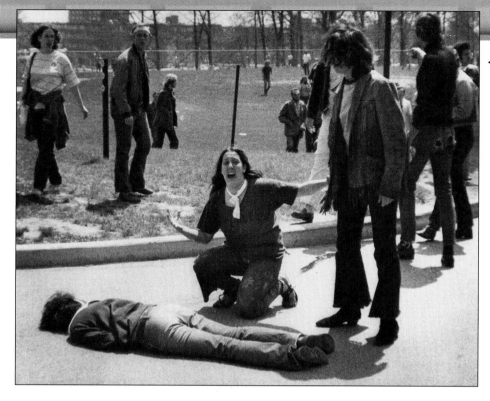

◄ **Mary Vecchio reacting to the death of fellow student Jeff Miller.** John Filo, a Kent State student and photographer for the yearbook, won a Pulitzer Prize for the picture. It appeared on the cover of *Newsweek* magazine with the caption "Nixon's Home Front."

© John Paul Filo/Getty Images - Hulton Archive

**This Pulitzer Prize-winning photo- ►
graph of 9-year-old Kim Phuc,** center, running after an aerial napalm attack on her village in 1972 was taken by Associated Press photographer Nick Ut (Cong Ut). Kim suffered burns over 65 percent of her body. She survived and is now a peace activist.

AP/Wide World Photos

"All the men are gone in our family," Mom was actually saying for the Khmer Rouge spies to hear. "They are only girls. Don't kill them. We are the only members left of the family " . . . We were lying to them about our identity. It was a horrible game.
—Celia Noup, *from* New Americas: An Oral History

Washington, D.C.: President and Mrs. Ronald Reagan
dance early January 21, 1981 at the Smithsonian
Museum of American History, the last stop on
a tour of inaugural balls. Mrs. Reagan wore
a one-shoulder white satin sheath gown
by James Galanos to the fetes.

30

THE CONSERVATIVE ASCENDANCY
1974–1987

WHAT EXPLAINS

the weakness of the U.S. economy

in the 1970s?

WHAT WERE the major social

and economic trends in America's cities

in the 1970s and 1980s?

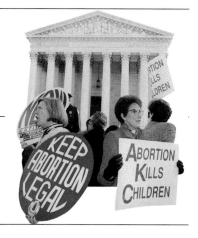

WHAT EXPLAINS

the rise of the New Right

in the 1980s?

HOW DID the Iran hostage crisis affect

the election of 1980?

WHAT ECONOMIC assumptions

underlay "Reagonomics"?

WHY DID the gap between rich

and poor grow in the 1980s?

HOW DID Reagan explain

and justify U.S. policy

in Central America?

AMERICAN COMMUNITIES

Grass-Roots Conservatism in Orange County, California

In 1962 Bee Gathright, a Brownie leader and mother of three young girls, listened to a neighbor's casual request. Would she allow the patio of her suburban Garden Grove home to be used for a meeting bringing together neighbors to hear a talk about liberalism and conservatism by a man from the nearby Knott's Berry Farm Freedom Center? Gathright agreed and found the meeting to be a revelation: "This is when I discovered that I was a conservative," she recalled three decades later. She soon arranged for the speaker to address a larger audience at the local public school. Gathright began to read widely in books and newspapers "because I began to hear that the Communists were going to bury us, were going to take over the world . . . I was afraid." She convinced her skeptical husband Neil, an aerospace engineer, to share her new-found activism. They attended study groups and soon joined the California Republican Assembly, a volunteer organization dedicated to electing conservatives to office. In 1964 the Gathrights' home served as a local headquarters for the presidential campaign of conservative Arizona Senator Barry Goldwater. After winning the Republican nomination Goldwater lost the election to President Lyndon Johnson in one of the biggest landslides in American electoral history. Most political commentators and analysts believed Goldwater's crushing defeat proved that "far Right" conservatism had little future in American politics.

Orange County in the 1960s and 1970s had thousands of "kitchen table" activists like the Gathrights, and they began a transformation of American conservatism and American politics that would culminate in the election of Ronald Reagan as president in 1980. Most of them were middle-class men and women, including large numbers of professionals and people with small businesses. Many were recent migrants to California, attracted by job opportunities in aerospace. Bee Gathright herself had arrived from Iowa, after World War II, taking a job as an executive secretary at Douglas Aircraft in Santa Monica. Orange County's 800 square miles lie at the geographic center of the Southern California basin, and large lemon and orange groves dominated the economy until the 1940s. The Second World War and Cold War defense-related spending accelerated Orange County's growth as companies like Hughes Aircraft, Autonetics, and Beckman Instruments created over 30,000 new manufacturing jobs in defense and electronics between 1950 and the early 1960s. The strong demand for housing spurred a highly profitable construction boom and a roaring real estate market. By 1960, over 700,000 people lived in Orange County, an increase of nearly 400 percent since 1940, and the population doubled again to almost 1.5 million by 1970.

While Barry Goldwater's 1964 campaign had ignited great enthusiasm in Orange County, his national defeat forced conservatives to consider how they might shed the "extremism" label and put more emphasis on winning office. In 1966 they succeeded in electing Ronald Reagan as governor. A former Hollywood actor and New Deal liberal, Reagan had evolved in the 1950s into an effective conservative spokesman and a prominent Republican Party activist. His gubernatorial campaign stressed limiting state support for welfare and other social services, while expanding state power to enforce law and order.

Reagan's electoral success in California, as well as Richard Nixon's election as president in 1968, signaled an important new turn for American conservatives in the 1970s. They still championed anticommunism, but no longer engaged in the kind of loose talk about using nuclear weapons that had hurt Goldwater. They attacked the growth of "big government," but no longer spoke openly about repealing popular New Deal programs like Social Security. Instead, they responded to the concerns over "social issues" that increasingly troubled and mobilized Orange County's grass-roots activists. These issues were largely defined by a "backlash" against the antiwar movement, counterculture, feminist activism, and urban riots, and an emphasis on so-called family issues, in which opposition to sex education, obscenity, abortion rights, and gay liberation were all linked together. On the economic side, conservatives began to tap a deep well of resentment over rising property taxes and high inflation.

Two of the central themes of this new conservatism found powerful expression in Orange County and resonated with millions of Americans well beyond it. One was the so-called tax revolt led by Howard Jarvis, a flamboyant campaigner long active in Southern California conservative circles. Saying he had been energized and inspired by local taxpayer-protest meetings, Jarvis told his supporters, "Lower taxes and less government became my holy grail. . . . The only way to cut government spending is not to give them the money in the first place." Jarvis relied on local networks to gather 1.3 million signatures to get his Proposition 13 on the ballot—a constitutional amendment that slashed the property tax rate from 3 percent to 1 percent of a home's market value and strictly limited future tax increases. After its passage in 1978, the "tax revolt" soon spread to other states and attracted millions to the conservative message of limiting government and lowering taxes.

Orange County was a center of the second new force reshaping conservatism, the spectacular growth of "born again" evangelical Christianity. Fundamentalist sects had long been associated with the rural poor of the South, but Orange County's religious revival demonstrated how educated professionals and middle-class suburbanites were also turning to "born again" Christianity in their search for spirituality and meaning, as a rejection of "permissiveness," and as a way to assert order amidst rapid cultural and social change. One of the most successful fundamentalist ministers was the Reverend Chuck Smith, who pioneered the use of Christian folk music, adopted countercultural symbols and motifs, and conducted mass ocean baptisms in Corona del Mar. By 1978 his mother church in Costa Mesa, Calvary Chapel, had 25,000 members. They found community not only in Sunday services, but also in a wide range of tightly organized activities: Bible study groups, summer retreats, "singles' fellowships," prayer breakfasts, and "Christian" consumer culture, which allowed people to simultaneously embrace faith, modern business techniques, and worldly goods.

The political implications of the new evangelicalism became clear by the late 1970s. Most fundamentalist preachers tied their sermons and prophesies to conservative political themes, especially fears about the decline of morality and of American power in the world. Reverend Chuck Smith warned that "the decline of the economy and government of the United States will open the doors to the rise of the anti-Christ to world power."

Newly politicized Christian voters worked diligently to elect Ronald Reagan President in 1980. In Orange County they helped Reagan get 68 percent of the vote, the most lopsided victory of any large county in the nation. For Bee Gathright, the former Goldwater supporter who by then had shifted her energies to Christian missionary work, Reagan's victory provided a national vindication of her years of grass-roots activism. For her, as for so many others in Orange County, the "Christian movement" and the conservative movement had become one and the same.

THE OVEREXTENDED SOCIETY

In the 1970s Americans faced an unfamiliar combination of skyrocketing prices, rising unemployment, and low economic growth. Economists termed this novel condition "stagflation." By 1975, the unemployment rate had reached nearly 9 percent, its highest level since the Great Depression, and it remained close to 7 percent for most of the rest of the decade. Inflation, meanwhile, reached double digits.

The United States had come to a turning point in its economic history. Emerging from World War II as the most prosperous nation in the world and retaining this status through the 1960s, the country suddenly found itself falling behind Western Europe and Japan. Polls conducted at the end of the 1970s revealed that a majority of Americans believed that conditions would worsen.

WHAT EXPLAINS the weakness of the U.S. economy in the 1970s?

A TROUBLED ECONOMY

In October 1973 gasoline prices nearly doubled, jumping from 40¢ to nearly 70¢ per gallon. Several states responded to the shortage by introducing rationing programs.

The oil crisis began suddenly, although it had been decades in the making. The United States, which used about 70 percent of all oil produced in the world, had found the domestic supply sufficient until the late 1950s. But rising demand had outstripped national reserves, and by 1973 the nation was importing one-third of its crude oil, mainly from the Middle East. In that year, following the Arab-Israeli War, oil prices skyrocketed. On October 17, the **Organization of Petroleum Exporting Countries (OPEC)**, a cartel of mainly Arab oil producers, announced an embargo on oil shipments to Israel's allies, including the United States.

President Nixon responded to the embargo by creating an "energy czar" and paving the way for the creation of the Department of Energy in 1977. He ordered a 10 percent reduction in air travel and appealed to Congress to lower speed limits on interstate highways to 55 miles per hour and to extend daylight-saving time into the winter months.

With the cost of gasoline, oil, and electricity up, many other prices also rose, from apartment rents and telephone bills to restaurant checks. As oil prices continued to rise through the 1970s, many Americans also began to look suspiciously at the pricing practices of U.S. oil companies. Whatever the causes, the oil crisis played a major role in the economic downturn.

Organization of Petroleum Exporting Countries (OPEC) Cartel of oil-producing nations in Asia, Africa, and Latin America that gained substantial power over the world economy in the mid- to late-1970s by controlling the production and price of oil.

The economic downturn, according to many experts, had deeper roots in the failure of the United States to keep up with the rising industrial efficiency of Western Europe and Japan. Manufacturers from Asia, Latin America, and Europe now offered consumers cheaper and better products, including automobiles, long considered the monopoly of Detroit. U.S. automakers, determined to reduce costs, turned to "outsourcing"—that is, making cars and trucks from parts produced cheaply abroad and imported into the United States as semifinished materials (which were subject to a lower tariff than finished goods.) In high-tech electronics, the United States scarcely competed against Japanese-produced televisions, radios, tape players, cameras, and computers. An AFL-CIO leader complained that the United States was becoming "a nation of hamburger stands . . . a country stripped of industrial capacity and meaningful work."

The situation in agriculture was even more grim. The huge increase in oil prices translated into higher gasoline and fertilizer costs, forcing farmers to

 # MAP EXPLORATION

To explore an interactive version of this map, go to **http://www.prenhall.com/faraghertlc/map30.1**

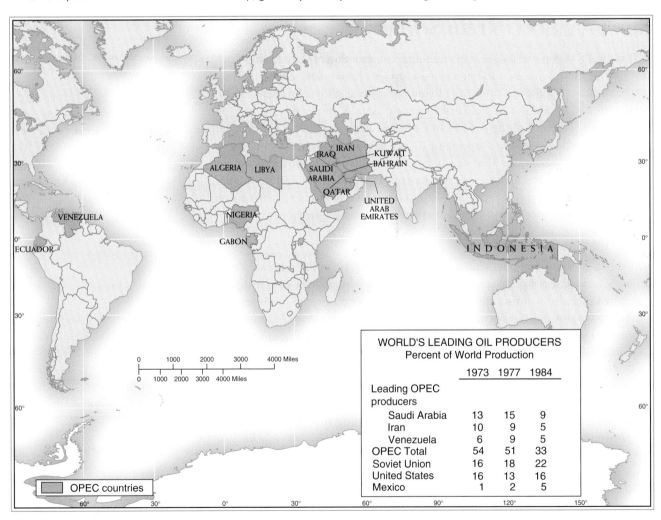

WORLD'S LEADING OIL PRODUCERS Percent of World Production			
	1973	1977	1984
Leading OPEC producers			
Saudi Arabia	13	15	9
Iran	10	9	5
Venezuela	6	9	5
OPEC Total	54	51	33
Soviet Union	16	18	22
United States	16	13	16
Mexico	1	2	5

MAP 30-1
World's Leading Oil Producers

WHY DID OPEC's share of world oil production drop between 1973 and 1984?

borrow heavily from banks. Soon the high interest rates on borrowed money threw many family farmers into a state of permanent indebtedness. When overseas sales declined at the end of the 1970s, tens of thousands defaulted on loans and lost their farms to banks and credit companies, ending a way of life generations old.

BLUE-COLLAR BLUES

In past decades labor unions had typically responded to inflation by negotiating new contracts or, if necessary, striking for higher pay. But while factories closed, the National Labor Relations Board increasingly ruled in favor of management, making the organization of new union locals far more difficult. Between 1970 and 1982 the AFL-CIO lost nearly 30 percent of its membership. Union-backed measures now routinely failed in Congress, despite the Democratic majority.

Typical of hard times, women in increasing numbers sought jobs to support their families. By 1980 more than half of all married women and nearly 60 percent of mothers with children between the ages of six and seventeen were in the labor force. Yet despite these statistical changes, women had lost ground relative to men. In 1955 women earned 64 percent of the average wages paid to men; in 1980 they earned only 59 percent. The reason for this dip was that women were clustered in the clerical and service trades where the lowest wages prevailed.

African American women made some gains. Through Title VII of the Civil Rights Act, which outlawed work place discrimination by sex or race, and the establishment of the Equal Employment Opportunity Commission to enforce it, they managed to climb the lower levels of the job ladder. By 1980, Northern black women's median earnings were about 95 percent of white women's earnings.

In contrast, Hispanic women, whose labor force participation leaped by 80 percent during the decade, were restricted to a very few poorly paid occupations. Puerto Ricans found jobs in the garment industry of the Northeast; Mexican Americans more typically worked as domestics or agricultural laborers in the Southwest. Neither group earned much more than the minimum wage.

SUNBELT/SNOWBELT COMMUNITIES

By the 1970s the **Sunbelt** offered a rare showplace of American prosperity. It boasted a gross product greater than many nations and more cars, television sets, houses, and even miles of paved roads than the rest of the United States. Large influxes of immigrants from Latin America, the Caribbean, and Asia combined with the shift of Americans from the depressed Northeast to boost the region's population.

This increase had been made possible by a huge outlay of federal funds, including defense spending and the allocation of Social Security funds. The number of residents over the age of sixty-five increased by 30 percent during the 1970s, reaching 26 million by 1980. Armed with retirement packages won decades earlier, huge "golden age" migrations created new communities in Florida, Arizona, and southern California.

The South witnessed a dramatic turnaround in demographic and economic trends. While manufacturing and highly subsidized agribusiness flourished, Southern cities reversed the century-long trend of out-migration among African Americans. The Southwest and West changed yet more dramatically. Aided by air conditioning, water diversions, public improvements, and large-scale development, California became the nation's most populous state; Texas moved to third, behind New York. Former farms and deserts were turned almost overnight into huge metropolitan areas by the automobile and suburbs. Phoenix grew from 664,000 in 1960 to 1,509,000 in 1980, Las Vegas from 127,000 to 463,000.

IMAGE KEY

for pages 830–831

a. A piece of the fallen Berlin Wall.

b. President Ronald Reagan and First Lady Nancy Reagan dance at his first inaugural ball at the Smithsonian Institute on January 21, 1981.

c. Nesting dolls of Communist or Russian leaders Boris Yeltsin, Mikhail Gorbechev, Leonid Brezhnev, Nikita Khruschev, Joseph Stalin, Vladimir Lenin, and Czar Nicholas II.

d. The black flying wing design of the stealth bomber resembles a bat.

e. Traders on the floor of the New York Stock Exchange on Monday, October 19, 1987. The Dow Jones Industrial Average plunged more than 500 points for the biggest one-day loss in history.

f. Abortion rights advocate Inga Coulter stands next to pro-life protester Elizabeth McGee during clashing demonstrations outside the Supreme Court building.

g. Three of the American hostages held in Iran arriving from Tehran at the Rhein-Main Airbase in Germany on 1/21/81.

h. An Hispanic female student raises her hand in class.

i. Mikhail Gorbachev and Ronald Reagan sign the INF treaty at the White House.

Sunbelt   The states of the American South and Southwest.

MAP EXPLORATION

To explore an interactive version of this map, go to
http://www.prenhall.com/faraghertlc/map30.2

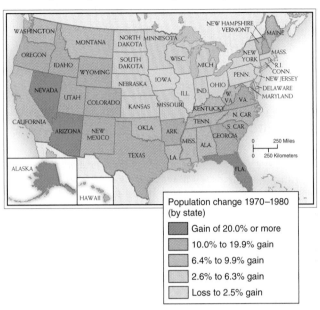

Population change 1970–1980 (by state)

- Gain of 20.0% or more
- 10.0% to 19.9% gain
- 6.4% to 9.9% gain
- 2.6% to 6.3% gain
- Loss to 2.5% gain

MAP 30-2

Population Shifts, 1970–1980   Industrial decline in the Northeast coincided with an economic boom in the Sunbelt, encouraging millions of Americans to head for warmer climates and better jobs.

HOW WERE the changes in population between 1970 and 1980 reflected in the American economy?

Much of the Sunbelt wealth tended to be temporary or sharply cyclical, producing a boom-and-bust economy of sudden expansion and disordered sprawl. Corporate office buildings in cities such as Houston emptied almost as fast as they filled. Income was also distributed very unevenly. Older Hispanic populations made only modest gains, while recent Mexican immigrants and Indian peoples suffered from a combination of low wages and poor public services. The Sunbelt states concentrated their tax and federal dollars on strengthening police forces, building roads or sanitation systems for the expanding suburbs, and creating budget surpluses, in contrast to eastern and midwestern states that continued to spend significantly on public housing, education, and mass transit.

The "Snowbelt" (or "Rustbelt") states meanwhile suffered severe population losses accompanying the sharp decline of industry. Of the nineteen metropolitan areas that lost population during the 1970s, all were old manufacturing centers, topped by New York, Cleveland, Pittsburgh, Boston, Philadelphia, and Buffalo.

A feeling of defeat intensified in the aging industrial cities of the Monogahela River valley in Western Pennsylvania. Since the late ninteeenth century, "Mon Valley" had proudly stood as the steelmaking center of the nation and much of the world. With the decline of steel production, however, major firms such as U.S. Steel increased investments in overseas mining and mineral processing companies, some of which worked closely with foreign steelmakers. This policy of "disinvestment" had a devastating impact on the people and communities who for generations had helped build the nation's basic industries. During the 1980s the Mon Valley lost 30,000 people, or 10 percent of its population.

New York City offered a more spectacular example. A fiscal crisis in 1975 forced liberal mayor Abraham Beame to choose between wage freezes for public employees and devastating cuts and layoffs. Eventually, with the municipal government teetering on the brink of bankruptcy, he chose both. In response to cutbacks in mass transit and the deterioration of municipal services, a large sector of the middle class fled. At the same time, the proportion of poor people rose from 15 percent in 1969 to nearly 25 percent fourteen years later.

"LEAN YEARS" PRESIDENTS: FORD AND CARTER

Gerald R. Ford and Jimmy Carter presided over not only a depressed economy, but also a nation of disillusioned citizens. Replacing Nixon in August 1974, Gerald Ford reassured the public that "our long national nightmare is over"—then quickly pardoned Nixon for all the federal crimes he may have committed. The pardon reinforced public cynicism toward government and Ford in particular.

Ford, who issued more vetoes of major bills than any other president in the twentieth century but saw Congress override most of them, struck most Americans as a pleasant person of modest ability. First Lady Betty Ford was the shining star of the White House. She broke ranks with other Republicans to champion the Equal Rights Amendment. She also won praise for her courage in discussing her mastectomy for breast cancer and her voluntary entry into a substance abuse clinic for a drinking problem.

Ford banked on his incumbency for the 1976 election and welcomed Senator Robert Dole of Kansas as his running mate. Democrats chose Jimmy Carter, a former one-term governor of Georgia, who depicted himself as an antipolitician, an outsider, and someone who was independent of the Washington establishment. When Carter told his mother he was running for president, she reportedly asked, "President of what?"

A "born again" Christian, Carter had been born in Plains, Georgia, in 1924. A successful Southern politician, Carter promoted regional development. In seeking the nomination, he declined to call himself a liberal, offering instead personal integrity as his chief qualification for the nation's highest office.

Carter campaigned as a moderate on domestic policy issues. Counting on support from both conservative and Southern voters who would ordinarily vote Republican, he defended existing entitlement programs while opposing Senator Edward Kennedy's call for comprehensive health coverage. He capitalized on Ford's unpopular Nixon pardon and, with his running mate Senator Walter Mondale of Minnesota, won with just over 50 percent of the popular vote and a 297-to-240 margin in the Electoral College.

In office, Carter seemed to many observers enigmatic, even uninterested in the presidency. His most successful innovation, **deregulation** of the airlines, brought lower fares for millions of passengers. But by freeing banks from congressional control, he inadvertently encouraged bad investments, outright fraud, and a round of disastrous bank failures. Inflation proved to be his worst enemy. As older Americans could recognize, half of all the inflation since 1940 had occurred in just ten years. Carter could not deliver on his promise to turn the economy around. By the time he left office in 1980, a majority of those polled agreed that "the people running the country don't really care what happens to you."

MAP EXPLORATION

To explore an interactive version of this map, go to
http://www.prenhall.com/faraghertlc/map30.3

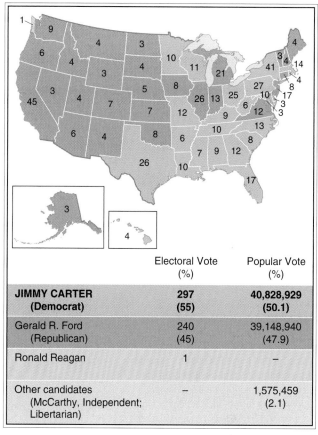

	Electoral Vote (%)	Popular Vote (%)
JIMMY CARTER (Democrat)	**297** **(55)**	**40,828,929** **(50.1)**
Gerald R. Ford (Republican)	240 (45)	39,148,940 (47.9)
Ronald Reagan	1	–
Other candidates (McCarthy, Independent; Libertarian)	–	1,575,459 (2.1)

MAP 30-3

The Election of 1976   Incumbent Gerald Ford could not prevail over the disgrace brought to the Republican Party by Richard Nixon. The lingering pall of the Watergate scandal, especially Ford's pardon of Nixon, worked to the advantage of Jimmy Carter, who campaigned as an outsider to national politics. Although Carter and his running mate Walter Mondale won by only a narrow margin, the Democrats gained control of both the White House and Congress.

WHY DID Ford pardon Nixon? Did it cost him the election?

COMMUNITIES AND POLITICS

The mass demonstrations of the 1960s gave way in the 1970s to a style of political mobilization centered squarely in communities. Unlike national elections, which after 1968 registered increasing voter apathy, local campaigns brought a great many people to the voting booth and into newly organized voluntary associations.

THE NEW URBAN POLITICS

In many cities, new groups came into political power. In several college towns, such as Berkeley, California, and Eugene, Oregon, both of which had been centers of political activism during the 1960s, student coalitions were formed to secure seats for their candidates on city councils. In 1973 labor unions, college students, and community groups in Madison, Wisconsin, elected a former student activist to the first of three terms as mayor.

WHAT WERE the major social and economic trends in America's cities in the 1970s and 1980s?

Deregulation   Reduction or removal of government regulations and encouragement of direct competition in many important industries and economic sectors.

Affirmative action   A set of policies to open opportunities in business and education for members of minority groups and women by allowing race and sex to be factors included in decisions to hire, award contracts, or admit students to higher education programs.

29–9
Jimmy Carter, The "Malaise" Speech (1979)

Geronimo, **1981, by** Victor Orozco Ochoa. During the 1970s public murals appeared in many cities, often giving distinctive expression to a community's racial or ethnic identity. The murals, painted in the mid-1970s on the outside of the Centro Cultural de la Raza in San Diego, were among the most striking. After vandals ruined one section, Ochoa, whose grandmother was Yaqui, replaced it with this enormous representation of Geronimo, surrounded by figures of contemporary Chicano cultural life.

Untitled, *Geronimo* mural. Victor Orozco Ochoa

African American candidates scored impressive victories during the 1970s. The newly elected African American mayor of Atlanta, Maynard Jackson, concluded that "politics is the civil rights movement of the 1970s." By 1978, 2,733 African Americans held elected offices in the South, ten times the number a decade earlier. Voters had elected African American mayors in New Orleans and Atlanta. In other parts of the country, black mayors, such as Coleman Young in Detroit, Richard Hatcher in Gary, and Tom Bradley in Los Angeles, held power along with many minor black officials.

Other racial or ethnic groups advanced more slowly, rarely in proportion to their actual numbers in the population. Mexican Americans had already won offices in Crystal City, Texas, and in 1978 took control of a major city council, in San Antonio, for the first time. They also scored electoral victories in other parts of Texas and in New Mexico and developed strong neighborhood or ward organizations in southern California. Puerto Ricans elected a handful of local officials in New York, mostly in the Bronx. Asian Americans advanced in similar fashion in parts of Hawai'i.

The fiscal crises of the 1970s nevertheless undercut these efforts to reform municipal government. Most new officials found themselves unable to make the sweeping changes they had promised during their campaigns. Community-based job programs could not counteract the effects of factory shutdowns and the disappearance of industrial jobs. **Affirmative action** programs aroused cries of "reverse discrimination" from angered whites who felt that minorities' progress had been registered at their expense. Conservatives put forward their own candidates, charging that government at all levels favored minorities, the jobless, and criminals over the law-abiding, hardworking, tax-paying majority.

THE CITY AND THE NEIGHBORHOOD

The Community Development Act of 1974, signed by President Ford, combined federal grant programs for cities into a single program and put mayors and city managers directly in charge of spending. With grants totaling $8.4 billion over three years, city governments could allocate funds as they saw fit and encourage citizens to take part in local planning. Groups of preservationists organized to save historic buildings and public spaces, to form land trusts for acquiring and refurbishing old houses, and to turn vacant lots into neighborhood parks.

Local and national foundations joined federal agencies in funding Community Development Corporations (CDCs) through a series of antipoverty agencies. These community groups promoted "development banks" that would facilitate "sweat equity"—that is, the granting of low-interest mortgage loans to buyers willing to rebuild or refurbish dilapidated housing. They also acted to prevent local banks from closing when a neighborhood became mainly black.

In 1979 President Carter's National Commission on Neighborhoods recommended the strenthening of local institutions "to reorganize our society . . . to a new democratic system of grass-roots involvement." But advocacy groups often learned to their dismay that foundations and federal agencies with money to spend resisted local decision making. While the economy worsened, mortgages moved out of reach for most buyers, and rents in many locations doubled. Local preservationists' dreams sometimes became nightmarish. "Gentrification" often accompanied restoration, with poor residents displaced by the more prosperous Americans who craved the increasingly fashionable old homes.

THE ENDANGERED ENVIRONMENT

On March 28, 1979, a series of mechanical problems and judgment errors at the nuclear generating facility at Three Mile Island (TMI), near Harrisburg, Pennsylvania, led to the formation of a dangerously explosive hydrogen bubble and posed the danger of a catastrophic core meltdown. After the news broke, nearly 150,000 residents fled their homes. Ten days later, the Nuclear Regulatory Commission announced that any danger of explosion had passed, but what had seemed an isolated event in one community had already grown into a regional phenomenon with national repercussions. Massive demonstrations against nuclear power followed the accident, concluding in a rally of more than 200,000 people in New York City. Groups organized in many communites to defeat referendums to fund new nuclear power facilities or rallied around candidates who promised to shut down existing ones. Of the ninety-six under construction and the thirty more planned at the time of the TMI crisis, only a handful were completed.

Earlier in the 1970s, the discovery of high rates of cancer and birth defects in Love Canal, near Buffalo, New York, had offered compelling evidence of a growing danger to many American communities. Here toxic wastes dumped by the Hooker Chemical Laboratory had oozed into basements and backyards, and homemaker Lois Gibbs organized a vigorous publicity campaign to draw attention to the grim situation. Meanwhile, outraged Florida residents realized that the damming of the Everglades for sugar production and housing developments, undertaken by the Army Corps of Engineers decades earlier, had degraded thousands of acres of wilderness, eliminating natural filtration systems and killing millions of birds and other species.

Even before the energy crisis, many Americans had begun to make changes in their own ways of living. Many families began to save glass bottles and newspapers for reuse. Some began to reduce or eliminate their consumption of beef, since beef is far more costly and uses more resources to produce than grain. Backyard vegetable gardens became popular, as did grocers who stocked organic foods.

The environmentalist movement grew stronger in long-standing organizations, such as the Audubon Society and the Wilderness Society. The Sierra Club, formed in 1892 as a small society of Western mountain hikers, grew to 100,000 members in

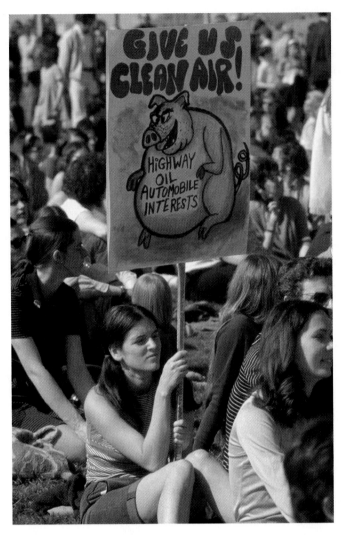

Senator Gaylord Nelson of Wisconsin, hoping to direct some of the energy of the anti–Vietnam War protests into environmental activism, organized the first Earth Day, which was celebrated on April 22, 1970. On that day, 20 million Americans demonstrated for a healthy and sustainable environment. Their protest against the deterioration of the environment led to the creation of the Environmental Protection Agency and marks the birth of the modern environmental movement.

Photo by Dennis Brack. Black Star (470/2584)

1970 and to 500,000 over the next decade. New groups sprang up in response to the energy crisis, often devoted to developing renewable energy sources such as solar power.

Cutting across nearly all population groups and regions, environmentalists reached such traditionally conservative areas as the Deep South with warnings of the dangers of toxic wastes, the destruction of wetlands, and the ruin of fishing industries. Sometimes campaigns succeeded in blocking massive construction projects, such as nuclear energy plants; more often they halted small-scale destruction of a natural habitat or historic urban district. These campaigns made the public more aware of the consequences of private and government decisions about the environment.

Responding to organized pressure groups, Congress passed scores of bills designed to protect endangered species, reduce pollution caused by automobile emissions, limit and ban the use of some pesticides, and control strip-mining practices. The Environmental Protection Agency (EPA), established in 1970, grew to become the federal government's largest regulatory agency, employing more than 10,000 people by the end of the decade.

Environmentalists enjoyed only limited success in bringing about large-scale changes in policy. Cities often avoided congressional mandates for reduction in air pollution by requesting lengthy extensions of deadlines for compliance. Despite the introduction of lead-free gasoline, the air in major metropolitan areas grew no better in the long run because automobile traffic increased at a fast pace. Environmentalists lost an important campaign with the approval of the Alaskan Pipeline, 800 miles of pipe connecting oil fields with refining facilities.

SMALL-TOWN AMERICA

A host of unresolved problems, ranging from air pollution to rising crime rates to higher taxes, encouraged a massive exodus from the nation's cities. Between 1970 and 1975, for every 100 people relocating to metropolitan areas, 138 moved out. Newer residential communities in small towns and in formerly rural areas grew at a fast pace, attracting retirees and others seeking solace or security.

Government programs such as mortgage guarantees and low-interest financing on individual homes promoted these large "low-density" developments of single-family houses. In many regions, the countryside gradually disappeared into "exurbia," a trend that population experts Peter A. Morison and Judith P. Wheeler attributed to the American "wish to love one's neighbor but keep him at arm's length." Opinion polls suggested that many Americans wanted to live in a small town that was not a suburb but was still no more than thirty miles from a major city.

Soon even small towns developed their own suburbs, usually moderate-income tracts of ranch houses squeezed between older wood-frame colonial or Victorian farmhouses. Federal subsidies for the construction of sewerage and water lines, originally intended to aid rural communities, now became springboards for further development. Ironically, shopping malls on former farmland drained commercial activity from the small-town centers, channeling the benefits of development to chain stores rather than to local merchants.

Some communities organized to oppose these trends. Following the publication of E. F. Schumacher's *Small Is Beautiful* (1973), groups of people began to question the advantages of "bigness" and its toll on humanity. They principally sought to rebuild communities on a smaller scale and therefore campaigned to preserve the environment by opposing further development and the construction of new highways, nuclear energy generating plants, and toxic dumps. In Vermont, liberal "hippies" and "back-to-the-landers" joined traditionally conservative landowners to defeat a 1974 gubernatorial plan to attract developers. In other locales, such as the Berkshire Mountains of Massachusetts, community land trusts were organized to encourage common ownership of the land. "From coast to coast," the *New York Times* reported, "environmental, economic and social pressures have impelled hundreds of cities and towns to adopt limitations on the size and character of their populations." To encourage public discussion of land-use issues, President Carter created the Small Community and Rural Development Policy group. Many small towns, especially those in the Plains states, meanwhile collapsed from failing family farms and small businesses, leaving rundown schools, inadequate medical care, and abandoned movie theaters and grocery stores. Only nursing homes and funeral parlors continued to thrive.

THE NEW CONSERVATISM

Sizable numbers of taxpayers resented the tax hikes required to fund government programs that benefited minorities, provided expanded social services for the poor, or protected the environment at the expense of economic development. In 1978 California voters staged a "taxpayers' revolt," approving Proposition 13, which cut property taxes and government revenues for social programs and education. In other economically hard-pressed urban areas, white voters who resented the gains made by African Americans and Latinos formed a powerful backlash movement. By the end of the decade, the only substantial increase in voter participation was among conservatives.

WHAT EXPLAINS the rise of the New Right in the 1980s?

THE NEW RIGHT

The largest New Right constituency united behind major conservative religious and political leaders to promote what they viewed as traditional values. Evangelical Christians became the backbone of key organizations such as the National Conservative Political Action Committee and, most especially, Moral Majority.

Conservative political organizations were among the first to employ direct-mail campaigns. Greater success came from the work of televangelists. By the late 1960s, televangelists such as Pat Robertson and Jim Bakker frequently mixed conservative political messages with appeals to prayer. Falwell's *Old-Time Gospel Hour* was broadcast over 200 television stations and 300 radio stations each week. Christian broadcasters generally endorsed Falwell's faith that "the free-enterprise system is clearly outlined in the Book of Proverbs of the Bible." By the end of the 1970s more than 1,400 radio stations and 30 TV stations specialized in religious broadcasts that reached an audience of perhaps 20 million weekly.

The Reverend Jerry Falwell formed the Moral Majority as a political lobbying group to advocate tough laws against homosexuality and pornography, to promote a reduction of government services (especially welfare payments to poor families), and to increase spending for a stronger national defense.

Jesse Helms was the first major politician to appeal directly to the New Right and to build his own impressive fundraising empire with its help. A North Carolina

QUICK REVIEW

The Conservative Critique

- Free markets work better than government programs.
- Government intervention does more harm than good.
- Government assistance saps the initiative of the poor.

Roe v. *Wade* U.S. Supreme Court decision (1973) that disallowed state laws prohibiting abortion during the first three months (trimester) of pregnancy and establishing guidelines for abortion in the second and third trimesters.

Gallup Poll on the Equal Rights Amendment, 1975

By 1973 thirty of the thirty-eight states required to ratify the ERA had done so. Although the amendment ultimately failed to achieve ratification and died in June 1982, public support was strong. In the 1976 presidential campaign, the platforms of both Democrats and Republicans included planks favoring its passage.

The Gallup Poll: Public Opinion, 1935–1974 (New York: Random House, 1974)

Asked of those who said they had heard of or read about the Equal Rights Amendment: Do you favor or oppose this amendment?	
Favor	58%
Oppose	24%
No opinion	18%
By Sex	
Male	
Favor	63%
Oppose	22%
No opinion	15%
Female	
Favor	54%
Oppose	25%
No opinion	21%
Interviewing Date 3/7–10/1975, Survey #925-K	

journalist who had fought the integration of public schools and defended the Ku Klux Klan, he had often attacked Martin Luther King Jr. as a Communist-influenced demagogue. Helms entered national politics as a Goldwater supporter in 1964 and ran for the Senate in 1972. Carried to victory with Nixon's success in North Carolina, Helms immediately promoted a host of conservative bills as well as federal support for regional tobacco interests. He introduced legislation to allow automobile owners or dealers to disconnect mandatory antipollution devices. He also defended the Watergate break-ins as necessary to offset the "traitorous conduct" of antiwar activists. By 1978 he had raised $8.1 million, the largest amount ever, for his successful reelection campaign. Helms built a powerful, loyal, and wealthy following.

The political surge rightward gained intellectual respectability from neoconservatives, former liberals who blamed the social movements of the 1960s for the demoralization of the nation. The American Enterprise Institute and the Heritage Foundation, heavily supported by major corporations, established major research centers for conservative scholars. These and other foundations also funded campus publications attacking welfare programs, affirmative action, and environmentalism.

ANTI-ERA, ANTIABORTION

The New Right rallied support for a balanced budget amendment to the Constitution, sought unsuccessfully to return prayer to the public schools, and endorsed the Supreme Court's approval of the death penalty in 1977. Practically all the New Right's campaigns emphasized restoration of the "traditional family values" undermined, they alleged, by the women's liberation movement.

The defeat of the Equal Rights Amendment (ERA) stood at the top of the New Right agenda. Approved by Congress in March 1972, nearly fifty years after its introduction (see Chapter 22), the ERA stated: "Equality of rights under the law shall not be denied or abridged by the United States or by any State on account of sex." Endorsed by both the Democratic and Republican Parties, the amendment appeared likely to be ratified by the individual states. Nearly all mainstream women's organizations, including the Girl Scouts of America, endorsed the ERA. Even the AFL-CIO retracted its long-standing opposition and endorsed the amendment.

Cued by this groundswell of support in favor of the ERA, the New Right swung into action. Phyllis Schlafly, a self-described suburban housewife and popular conservative lecturer, headed the STOP ERA campaign, describing the amendment's supporters as "a bunch of bitter women seeking a constitutional cure for their personal problems." The New Right mounted large, expensive campaigns in each swing state and overwhelmed pro-ERA resources. Although thirty-five states had ratified the ERA by 1979, the amendment remained three votes short of passage. Despite a three-year extension, the ERA died in 1982.

The New Right also waged a steady campaign against abortion, which the women's liberation movement had defined as a woman's right rather than a mere medical issue. In 1973 the Supreme Court had ruled in *Roe* v. *Wade* that state laws decreeing abortion a crime during the first two trimesters of pregnancy constituted a violation of a woman's right to privacy. Opponents of *Roe* rallied for a constitutional amendment defining conception as the beginning of life and arguing that the "rights of the unborn" supersede a woman's right to control her own body. The Roman Catholic Church organized the first antiabortion demonstrations after the Supreme Court's decision and sponsored the formation of the National Right to Life Committee, which claimed 11 million members by 1980.

Antiabortion groups also picketed Planned Parenthood counseling centers, intimidating potential clients. They rallied against government-subsidized day-care centers and against sex education programs in public schools. A small minority turned to more extreme actions and bombed dozens of abortion clinics.

"THE ME DECADE"

The shift in the political winds of the 1970s registered not only the rise of the New Right, but also the disengagement of a sizable number of Americans from politics altogether. In 1976 novelist Tom Wolfe coined the phrase the "Me Decade" to describe an era obsessed with personal well-being and emotional security. Health foods and diet crazes, a mania for physical fitness, and a quest for happiness through therapy involved millions of middle-class Americans. Historian Christopher Lasch provided his own label for this enterprise in the title of his best-selling book *The Culture of Narcissism: American Life in an Age of Diminishing Expectations* (1978).

The rise of the "human potential movement" provided a vivid example of this trend. The most successful was Erhard Seminars Training (EST), a self-help program blending insights from psychology and mysticism. Founded by Werner Erhard (a former door-to-door seller of encyclopedias), the institute taught individuals to form images of themselves as successful and satisfied. Through sixty hours of intensive training involving playacting and humiliation, participants learned one major lesson: "You are the one and only source of your experience. You created it." Priced at $400 for a series of two weekend sessions, EST peaked at 6,000 participants per month, grossing $25 million in revenue in 1980.

Transcendental meditation (TM) promised a shortcut to mental tranquility and found numerous advocates among Wall Street brokers, Pentagon officials, and star athletes. Techniques of TM were taught in more than 200 special teaching centers and practiced by a reputed 350,000 devotees.

Religious cults also formed in large numbers during the 1970s. The Unification Church, founded by the Korean Reverend Sun Myung Moon, extracted intense personal loyalty from its youthful disciples, dubbed by the media as "Moonies." Moon's financial empire, which included hundreds of retail businesses and the conservative *Washington Star*, proved highly lucrative and kept his church solvent despite numerous lawsuits. By contrast, Jim Jones's People's Temple, an interracial movement organized in the California Bay Area, ended in a mass murder and suicide when Jones induced more than 900 of his followers to drink cyanide-laced Kool-Aid in a remote retreat in Guyana in 1978.

Popular music expressed and reinforced many of these trends. The songs of community and hope common in the late 1960s gave way to songs of nostalgia, despair, or nihilism. Bruce Springsteen, whose lyrics lamented the disappearance of the white working class, became the decade's most popular new rock artist. At the same time, heavy metal bands such as Kiss, as well as punk and new wave artists underscored themes of decadence and futility. Meanwhile country and western

---

> *Would you favor or oppose a law that would permit a woman to go to a doctor to end pregnancy at any time during the first three months?*
>
> | | |
> |---|---|
> | Favor | 40% |
> | Oppose | 50% |
> | No opinion | 10% |
>
> Interviewing Date 11/12–17/1969, Survey #793-K, Question #4, Index #54
>
> *The United States Supreme Court has ruled that a woman may go to a doctor to end pregnancy at any time during the first three months of pregnancy. Do you favor or oppose this ruling?*
>
> | | |
> |---|---|
> | Favor | 47% |
> | Oppose | 44% |
> | No opinion | 9% |
>
> Interviewing Date 3/8–11; 3/15–18/1974, Survey #894-K; 895 -K

Gallup Polls on Abortion: 1969, 1974

During the 1960s, numerous American women began to demand control over their own reproductive processes and the repeal of legislation in place in all fifty states rendering abortion illegal. The American Institute of Public Opinion surveyed Americans in 1969, when abortion was still illegal, and again in 1974, one year after *Roe* v. *Wade,* the Supreme Court ruling that struck down state laws prohibiting abortion during the first three months of pregnancy.

The Gallup Poll: Public Opinion, 1935–1974 (New York: Random House, 1974).

29–7
Roe v. *Wade* (1973)

music hit its peak with crossover hits and numerous new all-C&W radio stations. Charismatic stars like Willie Nelson sang melodic refrains reeking of loneliness and nostalgia and appealing to older, white, working-class Americans.

ADJUSTING TO A NEW WORLD

HOW DID the Iran hostage crisis affect the election of 1980?

In April 1975 the North Vietnamese struck Saigon and easily captured the city as the South Vietnamese army, now without U.S. assistance, fell apart. All fighting stopped within a few weeks, and Saigon was renamed Ho Chi Minh City. Vietnam was reunited under a government dominated by Communists. For many Americans, this outcome underscored the futility of U.S. involvement in the Vietnam War.

By the mid-1970s a new realism seemed to prevail in U.S. diplomacy. Presidents Ford and Carter, as well as their chief advisers, acknowledged that the cost of fighting the Vietnam War had been too high, speeding the decline of the United States as the world's reigning superpower. The realists shared with dissatisfied nationalists a single goal: "No More Vietnams."

A THAW IN THE COLD WAR

The military defeat in Vietnam forced the makers of U.S. foreign policy to reassess priorities. The United States must continue to defend its "vital interests," declared Ford's secretary of state Henry Kissinger, but must also recognize that "Soviet-American relations are not designed for tests of manhood." Both nations had experienced a decline of power in world affairs. And both were suffering from the already enormous and relentlessly escalating costs of sustaining a prolonged Cold War.

At the close of World War II, the United States could afford to allocate huge portions of its ample economic resources to maintaining and enlarging its global interests. Soon, however, military and defense expenses began to grow at a much faster rate than the economy itself. Whereas the Korean War had cost around $69.5 billion, the Vietnam War cost $172.2 billion. Clandestine operations, alliance building, and weapons production accounted for many billions of dollars more.

Military spending at this level eventually took its toll on the American economy, especially as the federal government increasingly relied on deficit spending in an attempt to cover the bill. The federal debt, which stood at $257 billion in 1950, had jumped to $908 billion by 1980, and an increasingly large part of the federal budget went to paying just the interest on this debt. At the same time, military spending diverted funds from programs that could have strengthened the economy. The results were disastrous. While the United States endured falling productivity levels and rates of personal savings, and a disappearing skilled work force, other nations rushed ahead.

The Soviet Union, whose economy suffered even greater setbacks from defense spending, joined the United States in moving toward détente. The signing of SALT I, the first Strategic Arms Limitation Treaty, during Nixon's administration, followed by the U.S. withdrawal from Vietnam, encouraged new efforts to negotiate on strategic arms control. In November 1974, Ford and Soviet leader Leonid Brezhnev met in Vladivostok to set the terms of SALT II, and President Carter secured the final agreement in 1979. However, the treaty failed to win confirmation from the Senate when the Soviet Union invaded Afghanistan in December 1979.

Although repeated conflicts in the third world continued to slow the pace toward détente, leaders in both the United States and the Soviet Union usually recognized that their economic well-being depended on a reduction in defense spending.

FOREIGN POLICY AND "MORAL PRINCIPLES"

When he took office, President Carter presented his lack of experience in foreign affairs as an asset. "We've seen a loss of morality," he noted, "and we're ashamed." The "soul" of his policy would be an "absolute" commitment to human rights.

Carter condemned policies that allowed the United States to support "right-wing monarchs and military dictators" in the name of anticommunism. In 1976 a powerful human rights lobby pressured Congress to pass a bill that required the secretary of state to report annually on the status of human rights in all countries receiving aid from the United States and to cut off assistance to any country with a record of "gross violations." Carter's secretary of state, Cyrus R. Vance, and the assistant secretary for human rights and humanitarian affairs, Pat Derrian, worked to punish or at least to censure repressive military regimes in Brazil, Argentina, and Chile. For the first time, leading U.S. diplomats spoke out against the South African apartheid regime.

In line with this policy, Carter attempted to institute reforms at the Central Intelligence Agency (CIA), particularly to halt the blatant intervention in the affairs of foreign governments. He appointed Admiral Stansfield Turner, a Rhodes scholar, as director and ordered a purge of the "rogue elephants" who had pursued covert operations in Southeast Asia during the Vietnam War. "The CIA must operate within the law," Carter insisted. Under Turner, however, these reforms remained incomplete; they later proved temporary.

President Carter signs the Middle East Peace Treaty with Egyptian President Anwar Sadat and Israeli Prime Minister Menachem Begin, in Washington, D.C., March 1979. President Carter had invited both leaders to Camp David, the presidential retreat in Maryland, where for two weeks he mediated between them on territorial rights to the West Bank and Gaza Strip. Considered Carter's greatest achievement in foreign policy, the negotiations, known as the Camp David Peace Accords, resulted in not only the historic peace treaty, but also the Nobel Peace Prize for Begin and Sadat.

CORBIS

Carter nearly triumphed in the Middle East. Early in his administration, Carter met privately with Israeli prime minister Menachem Begin to encourage conciliation with Egypt. When negotiations between the two countries stalled in 1978, Carter brought Begin together with Egyptian president Anwar el-Sadat for a thirteen-day retreat at Camp David, Maryland.

The **Camp David Accords**, signed in September 1978, set the formal terms for peace in the region. Egypt became the first Arab country to recognize Israel's right to exist, as the two nations established mutual diplomatic relations for the first time since the founding of Israel in 1948. In return, Egypt regained control of the Sinai Peninsula, including important oil fields and airfields. In 1979 Begin and Sadat shared the Nobel Prize for Peace.

But disappointment lay ahead. Carter staked his hopes for regional peace on the final achievement of statehood, or at least political autonomy, for Palestinians in a portion of their former lands now occupied by the Israelis. The accords specified that Israel would eventually return to its approximate borders of 1967. However, although Begin agreed to dismantle some Israeli settlements in the Sinai, the Israeli government continued to sponsor more and more Jewish settlements, expropriating Palestinian holdings. The final status of the Palestinians remained in limbo, as did that of Jerusalem, which many Christians and Muslims felt should be an autonomous holy city. Meanwhile Sadat grew increasingly isolated within the Arab world. In 1981 he was assassinated by Islamic fundamentalists.

Carter scored his biggest moral victory in foreign affairs by paving the way for Panama to assume the ownership, operation, and defense of the Panama Canal Zone. Negotiations with Panama had begun during Johnson's administration, following riots by Panamanians against U.S. territorial rule in their country. Carter pressured the Senate to ratify new treaties in 1978 (by a vote of 68 to 32) that would turn the Panama Canal over to Panama by the year 2000.

(MIS)HANDLING THE UNEXPECTED

Mired in problems inherited from his predecessors, Carter often found himself disoriented by contradictory advice. Carter's Secretary of State Cyrus Vance recommended well-planned negotiations to soothe Soviet–U.S. relations and resolve disagreements with third world nations. But national security adviser Zbigniew Brzezinski, a bitterly anti-Communist Polish exile, adhered to Cold War policies and interpreted events in even remote sections of Africa or South America as plays in a zero-sum game: wherever the United States lost influence, the Soviet Union gained, and vice versa. Despite Carter's commitment to human rights, he allowed U.S. policy to resume Cold War postures.

In 1979 the overthrow of the brutal Nicaraguan dictatorship of Anastasio Somoza, long-time ally of the United States, left Carter without a succcessor to support. When the new Sandinista revolutionary government pleaded for help, Congress turned down Carter's request for $75 million in aid to Nicaragua. Meanwhile, in El Salvador, the Carter administration continued to back a repressive government even after the assassination of Oscar Romero, a Catholic archbishop and opposition leader. Following the rape and murder of four U.S. Catholic church women, apparently by the ultra-right Salvadoran armed forces trained in the United States, peace activists and other Americans pleaded with Carter to withhold further military aid. Conservatives meanwhile demanded yet more funds to bolster the repressive anti-Communist regime.

African nations vacillated between allying with the United States and courting the Soviet Union. In this tricky political territory, UN ambassador (and former civil rights leader) Andrew Young, the first major African American diplomat assigned to Africa, could not persuade Carter to recognize the antiapartheid gov-

Camp David Accords Agreement signed by Israel and Egypt in 1978 that set the formal terms for peace in the Middle East.

ernment of Angola, which had invited 20,000 Cuban troops to help in its fight against South African–backed rebels. Nor did Carter's and Young's verbal criticisms of the South African regime, unaccompanied by economic sanctions, satisfy black Africans. After Carter fired Young for having met secretly with officials of the Palestine Liberation Organization (PLO), the president proved even less effective in negotiating with antiapartheid leaders.

The Soviet invasion of Afghanistan produced a major stalemate. In December 1979, 30,000 Soviet troops invaded their neighbor to put down a revolt by Islamic fundamentalists against the weakening Soviet-backed government. The invasion succeeded mainly in heating up the civil war, which the American press quickly labeled the "Russian Vietnam." As the war bogged down, Americans heard familiar stories, this time of Soviet soldiers using drugs and expressing disillusionment with their government.

President Carter responded to these events with his own corollary to the Monroe Doctrine. The so-called Carter Doctrine asserted the determination of the United States to protect its interests in yet another area of the world, the Persian Gulf. Carter acted on the advice of Brzezinski, who believed that the Soviet Union would soon try to secure for itself a warm-water port on the gulf, an area rich in oil and now vital to U.S. interests. The president backed up his increasingly hard-line policies by halting exports of grain and high technology to the Soviet Union, supporting Afghani resistance against the Russians, and by cancelling American participation in the 1980 Moscow Olympics.

By the end of Carter's term, conservatives had swamped liberals within the Democratic Party. With the economy still hurting from the effects of Cold War spending, Carter called for ever-larger increases in the military budget. He also signed Presidential Directive 59, guaranteeing the production of weapons alleged necessary to win a prolonged nuclear war. The prospect of peace and **détente** dried up.

THE IRAN HOSTAGE CRISIS

On November 4, 1979, Iranian fundamentalists seized the U.S. embassy in Tehran and held fifty-two American employees hostage for 444 days. This event made President Carter's previous problems seem small by comparison.

For decades, U.S. foreign policy in the Middle East had depended on a friendly government in Iran. After the CIA had helped to overthrow the reformist, constitutional government and installed the Pahlavi royal family and the shah of Iran in 1953, millions of U.S. dollars had poured into the Iranian economy and the shah's armed forces. President Carter had toasted the shah for his "great leadership" and overlooked the rampant corruption in government and a well-organized opposition. But, by early 1979, a revolution led by Islamic fundamentalist Ayatollah Ruholla Khomeini had overthrown the shah.

After Carter had allowed Mohammad Reza Pahlavi, the deposed shah, to enter the United States to be treated for cancer in November, a group of Khomeini's followers retaliated, storming the U.S. embassy and taking the American staff as hostages.

Cyrus Vance assured Carter that only negotiations could free the Americans. Caught up in a reelection campaign and lobbied by Brzezinski for decisive action, Carter ordered U.S. military forces to stage a nighttime helicopter rescue mission. But a sandstorm caused some of

Détente (French for "easing of tension.") Used to describe the new U.S. relations with China and the Soviet Union in 1972.

QUICK REVIEW

Hostages

◆ November 4, 1979: Iranian fundamentalists seized U.S. embassy in Tehran.

◆ Fifty-two Americans held hostage for 444 days.

◆ Crisis doomed the Carter presidency.

Iranians demonstrate outside the U.S. Embassy in Tehran, raising a poster with a caricature of President Carter. The Iran hostage crisis, which began November 8, 1979, when a mob of Iranians seized the U.S. embassy in Tehran, contributed to Carter's defeat at the polls the following year. Fifty-two embassy employees were held hostage for 444 days.

AP/WideWorld Photos

MAP EXPLORATION

To explore an interactive version of this map, go to
http://www.prenhall.com/faraghertlc/map30.4

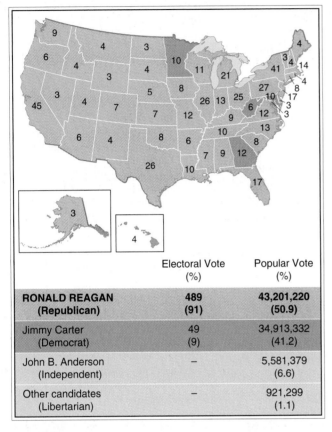

	Electoral Vote (%)	Popular Vote (%)
RONALD REAGAN (Republican)	**489** **(91)**	**43,201,220** **(50.9)**
Jimmy Carter (Democrat)	49 (9)	34,913,332 (41.2)
John B. Anderson (Independent)	–	5,581,379 (6.6)
Other candidates (Libertarian)	–	921,299 (1.1)

MAP 30-4

The Election of 1980   Ronald Reagan won a landslide victory over incumbent Jimmy Carter, who managed to carry only six states and the District of Columbia. Reagan attracted millions of traditionally Democratic voters to the Republican camp.

WHAT ATTRACTED many Democratic voters to Ronald Reagan?

30–2
Ronald Reagan, First Inaugural Address (1981)

WHAT ECONOMIC

assumptions underlay

"Reaganomics"?

the aircraft to crash and burn, leaving eight Americans dead, their burned corpses displayed by the enraged Iranians. Short of an all-out attack, which surely would have resulted in the hostages' death, Carter had used up his options.

The political and economic fallout was heavy. Cyrus Vance resigned, the first secretary of state in sixty-five years to leave office over a political difference with the president. The price of oil rose by 60 percent. Carter had failed in the one area he had proclaimed central to the future of the United States: energy. He had also violated his own human rights policy, which was intended to be his distinctive mark on American foreign affairs.

THE 1980 ELECTION

Carter's prospects for reelection appeared to rest on his conduct of international affairs. If he only could put his human rights policy on a firm ground, move toward lasting peace in the Middle East, or strike a bargain with the Soviets on arms limitation, he might restore voter confidence. If not, his presidency would end after a single term.

Ultimately, Carter's bid for renomination depended more on his incumbency than on his popularity. Delegates at the Democratic National Convention unenthusiastically endorsed Carter along with running mate Walter Mondale. On the Republican side, former California governor Ronald Reagan had been building his campaign since his near nomination in 1976. Former CIA director and Texas oil executive George H. W. Bush, more moderate than Reagan, became the Republican candidate for vice president. The Moral Majority placed itself squarely in Reagan's camp, and Senator Jesse Helms's Congressional Club contributed $4.6 million to the campaign.

Reagan repeatedly asked voters, "Are you better off now than you were four years ago?" Although critics questioned Reagan's competence, the attractive, soft-spoken actor shrugged off criticisms while spotlighting the many problems besetting the country.

The Republican ticket cruised to victory. Carter won only 41.2 percent of the popular vote to Reagan's 50.9 percent, 49 votes in the Electoral College to Reagan's 489. The Republicans won control of the Senate for the first time since 1952 and with the largest majority since 1928. Still, barely half of the eligible voters turned out in the 1980 election, bringing Ronald Reagan into office with a mandate of a thin 25 percent.

THE REAGAN REVOLUTION

THE GREAT COMMUNICATOR

Ronald Reagan was born in 1911 and raised in the small town of Dixon, Illinois. His father was a salesman and an alcoholic who had a tough time holding a job. His strong-willed mother was a fundamentalist Christian who kept the family together despite frequent moves. A job with the Works Progress Administration for Reagan's father had helped the family survive the hard times of the Great Depression. Encouraged by his mother, Reagan began acting in church plays and in productions at Eureka College, from which he graduated in 1932.

In 1937 Reagan began a Hollywood acting career that lasted for a quarter-century. Although he was never a big star, on screen he appeared tall, handsome, and affable. In later years, he credited his political success to his acting experience. He told one interviewer: "An actor knows two important things— to be honest in what he's doing and to be in touch with the audience. That's not bad advice for a politician either."

While serving as president of the Screen Actors Guild from 1947 to 1952, Reagan began to distance himself from New Deal liberalism by becoming a leader of the anti-Communist forces in Hollywood. In 1954 he became the host of a new national television program, General Electric Theater, and began a long stint as a national promoter for GE. In this role he made numerous speeches celebrating the achievements of corporate America and emphasizing the dangers of big government, excessive liberalism, and radical trade unions."

Reagan switched his party affiliation to the Republicans and became a popular fundraiser and speaker for the California GOP (Grand Old Party—Republican Party). He took a leading role in conservative Republican Barry Goldwater's 1964 presidential campaign. A televised address on Goldwater's behalf thrust Reagan himself to national prominence. At the core of Reagan's conservative message was an attack on big government. He lashed out at a growing bureaucracy and celebrated the achievements of entrepreneurs unfettered by government regulation or aid.

Ronald and Nancy Reagan at the Inaugural Ball, January 20, 1981. The Reagans, supported by a circle of wealthy conservative friends from the business world and Hollywood, brought a lavish style to the White House that helped define the culture of the 1980s.

Photo by Dennis Brack. Black Star (1-81-8930)

With the financial backing of a group of wealthy, conservative Californians, Reagan defeated Democratic governor Edmund G. Brown in 1966 and won reelection in 1970. As governor, he cut the state welfare rolls, placed limits on the number of state employees, and funneled a large share of state tax revenues back to local governments. He vigorously attacked student protesters and black militants, thereby tapping into the conservative backlash against the activism of the 1960s.

REAGANOMICS

During the Reagan presidency, supply-side economic theory, dubbed "Reaganomics," dominated the administration's thinking and helped redirect American economic policy. Supply-side theorists urged a sharp break with the Keynesian policies that had been dominant since the New Deal era (see Chapter 24). Keynesians traditionally favored moderate tax cuts and increases in government spending to stimulate the economy and reduce unemployment during recessions. By putting more money in people's pockets, they argued, greater consumer demand would lead to economic expansion.

By contrast, supply-siders called for simultaneous tax cuts and reductions in public spending. This combination, they claimed, would give private entrepreneurs and investors greater incentives to start businesses, take risks, invest capital, and thereby create new wealth and jobs. Whatever revenues were lost in lower tax rates would be offset by revenue from new economic growth. At the same time, spending cuts would keep the federal deficit under control and thereby keep interest rates down.

Reagan quickly won bipartisan approval for two key pieces of legislation based on these ideas. The **Economic Recovery Tax Act of 1981** cut income and corporate taxes by $747 billion over five years. For individuals, the act cut taxes across the board. It also reduced the maximum tax on all income from 70 percent to 50 percent, lowered the maximum capital gains tax—the tax paid on profitable investments—from 28 percent to 20 percent, and eliminated the distinction between earned and unearned income. This last measure proved a boon to the small, richest fraction of the population that derives most of its income from rent, dividends, and interest instead of from wages.

With the help of conservative Southern and Western Democrats in the House, the administration also pushed through a comprehensive program of spending cuts, awkwardly known as the Omnibus Reconciliation Act of 1981. This bill mandated cuts of $136 billion in federal spending for the period 1982–1984, affecting more than 200 social and cultural programs. The hardest hit areas included federal appropriations for education, the environment, health, housing, urban aid, food stamps, research on synthetic fuels, and the arts. The conservative coalition in the House allowed only one vote on the entire package of spending cuts, a strategy that allowed conservatives to slash appropriations for a wide variety of domestic programs in one fell swoop.

While reducing spending on domestic programs, the Reagan administration greatly increased the defense budget. During the 1980 election campaign, Reagan's calls to "restore America's defenses" helped reinforce the public perception that President Carter had dealt ineffectively with the Iran hostage crisis. Once in office he greatly accelerated a trend already under way during the last two years of the Carter presidency: a sharp increase in defense spending. Over all, the Reagan budgets for military spending totaled $1.6 trillion over five years and indicated a significant shift in federal budget priorities under his administration.

Meanwhile, the Reagan administration created a chilly atmosphere for organized labor. In the summer of 1981, some 13,000 federal employees, all members of the Professional Air Traffic Controllers Organization (PATCO), went on strike. The president retaliated against the strikers by firing them, and the Federal Aviation Administration started a crash program to replace them. Conservative appointees to the National Labor Relations Board and the federal courts toughened its antiunion position.

Reagan appointed conservatives to head the Environmental Protection Agency, the Occupational Safety and Health Administration, and the Consumer Product Safety Commission. These individuals abolished or weakened hundreds of rules governing environmental protection, workplace safety, and consumer protection, all in the interest of increasing the efficiency and productivity of business. The deregulatory fever dominated cabinet departments as well. Secretary of the Interior James Watt opened up formerly protected wilderness areas and wetlands to private developers. Secretary of Transportation Andrew L. "Drew" Lewis Jr. eliminated regulations passed in the 1970s aimed at reducing air pollution and improving fuel efficiency in cars and trucks.

Following the tenets of supply-side economics, the Reagan administration weakened the Antitrust Division of the Justice Department, the Securities and Exchange Commission, and the Federal Home Loan Bank Board. Large corporations, Wall Street stock brokerages, investment banking houses, and the savings and loan industry were all allowed to operate with a much freer hand than ever before. By the late 1980s, the unfortunate consequences of this freedom would become apparent in a series of unprecedented scandals in the nation's financial and banking industries.

Economic Recovery Tax Act of 1981
A major revision of the federal income tax system.

THE ELECTION OF 1984

As the 1984 election approached, many Americans expressed doubts about the Reagan administration's defense initiatives. Polls showed that more than 70 percent of Americans favored a nuclear freeze with the Soviet Union. Many observers noted that Reagan also appeared politically vulnerable for his economic policies and cutbacks in social programs.

Hoping to win back disgruntled voters, Democrats chose Carter's vice president, Walter Mondale, as their nominee. As a former senator from Minnesota, Mondale had close ties with the party's liberal establishment and also the support of its more military-minded wing. At the Democratic National Convention, Mondale named Representative Geraldine Ferraro of New York as his running mate, a first for women in American politics. Charismatic speakers such as the Reverend Jesse Jackson, a dynamic disciple of Martin Luther King Jr., and Governor Mario Cuomo of New York stirred the delegates and many television viewers with their appeals to compassion, fairness, and brotherhood.

Opinion polls showed Mondale running even with Reagan, but the president's enormous personal popularity, along with the booming economy, overwhelmed the Democratic ticket. While Mondale emphasized the growing deficit and called attention to Americans who were left out of prosperity, Reagan cruised above it all. It was "morning again in America," his campaign ads claimed. In one of the biggest landslides in American history, Reagan won 59 percent of the popular vote and carried every state but Minnesota and the District of Columbia.

30–5
T. Boone Pickens, "My Case for Reagan" (1984)

RECESSION, RECOVERY, FISCAL CRISIS

Over the course of his two terms in office, Reagan's economic policies had mixed results. In 1982 a severe recession, the worst since the 1930s, gripped the nation. The official unemployment rate reached nearly 11 percent, or more than 11.5 million people. Another 3 million had been out of work so long they no longer actively looked for jobs and were therefore not counted in official statistics. But by the middle of 1983 the economy had begun to recover, and unemployment dropped to about 8 percent while inflation fell below 5 percent. The stock market boomed, pushing the Dow Jones industrial average from 776 in August 1982 to an all-time high of 2,722 in August 1987. The administration took credit for the turnaround, hailing the supply-side fiscal policies that had drastically cut taxes and domestic spending. But critics pointed to other factors: the Federal Reserve Board's tight-money policies, an energy resource glut and a consequent sharp drop in energy prices, and the billions of dollars pumped into the economy for defense spending.

Few doubted, however, that the supply-side formula intensified an ominous fiscal crisis. Although President Reagan had promised to balance the federal budget, his policies had the opposite effect. The national debt grew from $907 billion in 1980 to over $2 trillion in 1986, more than the federal government had accumulated in its entire previous history. Expenditures for paying just the interest on the national debt reached 14 percent of the annual budget in 1988, double the percentage set aside for that purpose in 1974.

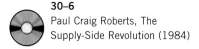

30–6
Paul Craig Roberts, The Supply-Side Revolution (1984)

In the Reagan years the fiscal crisis became a structural problem with newly disturbing and perhaps permanent implications for the American economy. Big deficits kept interest rates high, as the government drove up the cost of borrowing the money it needed to pay its own bills. Foreign investors, attracted by high interest rates on government securities, pushed up the value of the dollar in relation to foreign currencies. The overvalued dollar made it difficult for foreigners to buy American products, while making overseas goods cheaper to American consumers. Basic American industries—steel, autos, textiles—thus found it difficult to compete abroad and at home. In 1980, the United States still enjoyed a trade surplus of $166 billion. By 1987 the nation had an indebtedness to foreigners of $340 billion. Since World War I, the United States had been the world's leading creditor; in the mid-1980s it became its biggest debtor.

In late 1986, the Securities and Exchange Commission (SEC) uncovered the biggest stock scandal in history, in the process revealing the inner workings of high finance in the 1980s. Ivan Boesky, one of the nation's leading stock speculators, admitted to using confidential information about upcoming corporate takeovers to trade stocks illegally. Just two years earlier the dapper Boesky had made more than $100 million on just two deals. Now he agreed to cooperate with SEC investigators.

The biggest fish caught in their net was Michael Milken, a Boesky ally. An investment banker for Drexel Burnham Lambert, Milken perfected the art of corporate raiding through creative manipulation of debt. He showed how enormous profits could be earned from weak firms that were tempting targets for takeovers and mergers. Their debt could be used as tax write-offs; less efficient units could be sold off piecemeal; and more profitable units could be retained, merged, or sold again to form new entities. Instead of borrowing from banks, Milken financed his deals by underwriting high-yield, risky "junk bonds" for companies rated below investment grade. Investors in turn reaped huge profits by selling these junk bonds to hostile-takeover dealers.

Milken and other corporate raiders reshaped the financial world, setting off the greatest wave of buying and selling in American business history. Milken himself made a staggering $550 million in one year alone. Just before filing for bankruptcy in 1990, Drexel Burnham Lambert paid its executives $350 million in bonuses—almost as much as it owed its creditors. Milken was eventually convicted of insider trading and stock fraud and sent to prison.

On Wall Street, the bull market of the 1980s ended abruptly in the fall of 1987. After reaching its new high of 2,722 at the end of August, the Dow Jones average of thirty leading industrial stocks began to slide downward and then crashed. On October 19, the Dow lost almost 23 percent of its value. The panic on the trading floors recalled the pandemonium set off by the stock market crash of 1929.

BEST OF TIMES, WORST OF TIMES

WHY DID the gap between rich and poor grow in the 1980s?

The celebration of wealth, moneymaking, and entrepreneurship dominated much of popular culture, politics, and intellectual life in the 1980s. But grimmer realities lay under the surface. A variety of measures strongly suggested that the nation had moved toward greater inequality, that the middle class was shrinking, and that poverty was on the rise. Two of the most cherished basic assumptions about America—that life would improve for

Share of Total Net Worth of American Families		
	1983	**1989**
Richest 1 percent of families	31%	37%
Next richest 9 percent	35	31
Remaining 90 percent	33	32

Source: *New York Times*, April 21, 1992, from Federal Reserve Survey of Consumer Finances.

most people and their children, and that membership in the comfortable middle class was available to all who worked for it—looked shaky by the end of the decade.

THE CELEBRATION OF WEALTH

The very wealthy did extremely well during the 1980s. In 1989, the richest 1 percent of American households accounted for 37 percent of the nation's private wealth—up from 31 percent in 1983, a jump of almost 20 percent. This top 1 percent owned more than the bottom 90 percent of Americans.

Other affluent Americans also made huge gains. In 1980 the top 5 percent of families earned 15.3 percent of the nation's total income. By 1992 their share had grown to 17.6 percent, an increase of 15 percent; their average income was $156,000 a year. In 1980 the top 20 percent of families earned 41.6 percent of the nation's total. By 1992 their share had grown to 44.6 percent, an increase of about 7 percent, with an average income of $99,000 a year. In contrast, the bottom 40 percent of families had 16.7 percent of aggregate income in 1980. By 1992 their share had declined to 14.9 percent, a drop of nearly 2 percent, with an average income of about $16,500 a year.

A TWO-TIERED SOCIETY

During the 1960s, despite the diversion of federal funds to military spending during the Vietnam War, President Johnson's Great Society had brought a higher standard of living to many Americans. By the time Carter took office in 1977, the sinking economy was undercutting these gains. Reagan's supply-side policies enlivened the economy but at the same time widened the gap between rich and poor.

The number and percentage of Americans in poverty grew at an alarming rate. Since the mid-1970s, most of the new jobs clustered in low-paying service and manufacturing sectors and less than half of them paid more than the $11,611 poverty-level income for a family of four. In 1979 the government classified about 26.1 million people as poor, 11.7 percent of the total population; by 1992 the number of poor had reached 36.9 million, or 14.5 percent of the population, and nearly 22 percent of all American children under eighteen lived in poverty.

The widening gap between rich and poor was sharply defined by race. By 1992, 33 percent of all African Americans lived in poverty, as did 29 percent of Hispanics (the rate was especially high among Puerto Ricans, yet low among Cuban Americans). The majority of African Americans, six out of ten, lived in central cities with high unemployment rates, and the bleak prospects took a toll especially on the young. A black child was twice as likely as a white child to die before reaching his or her first birthday and four times more likely to be killed between the ages of one and four. Among black teenagers, the unemployment rate topped

Number of Poor, Rate of Poverty, and Poverty Line, 1979–1992

	1979	1992
Millions of poor	26.1	36.9
Rate of poverty	11.7%	14.5%
Poverty line (family of four)	$7,412	$14,335

Source: U.S. Bureau of the Census, *Current Population Reports: Consumer Income*, Series P-60, Nos. 161 and 185, 1988, 1993. U.S. federal data compiled by Ed Royce, Rollins College.

29–8
Ione Malloy, *Southie Won't Go*
(1975)

29–6
Swann v. *Charlotte-Mecklenburg Board of Education* (1971)

40 percent; the few jobs available to them were among the lowest paid in the economy. Meanwhile, the high school dropout rate skyrocketed, and the number of serious crimes, such as burglary, car theft, and murder, perpetrated by children between the ages of ten and seventeen increased at an alarming rate.

Moreover, opportunities for advancement into the middle class were dwindling. By 1980 fewer black students attended integrated schools than in 1954, except in the South, where about half the black students did. The turnabout resulted in part from increasing opposition by white parents to court-ordered school busing, which had served since *Brown* v. *Board of Education* as the principal means of achieving racial balance in urban school systems. During the 1980s the busing controversy nearly disappeared because federal judges hesitated to mandate such programs. But more important was the change in the racial composition of American cities. As a consequence of "white flight" to the suburbs, big-city school systems were serving mainly African American and Latino children, making the issue of integration moot.

New legal rulings closed off important routes to employment in the professions. A 1978 U.S. Supreme Court decision dealt a sharp blow to affirmative action. To ensure acceptance of a minimum number of minority students, the University of California at Davis Medical School had established a quota system under affirmative action guidelines. In 1973 and 1974 the school denied admission to Allan Bakke, a white student. Bakke sued the university for "reverse discrimination," claiming his academic record was better than that of the sixteen minority students who were admitted. The U.S. Supreme Court handed down a five-to-four decision on June 18, 1978, stating that the use of an "explicit racial classification" in situations where no earlier discrimination had been demonstrated violated the equal protection clause of the Fourteenth Amendment. The Court ordered the University of California to admit Bakke to its medical school. During the 1980s, therefore, affirmative action programs could operate only when "a legacy of unequal treatment" could be proved.

THE FEMINIZATION OF POVERTY

Despite a growing rate of labor force participation, the majority of women gainfully employed earned less than a living wage. Even if employed, women usually lost ground following a divorce, especially as new no-fault divorce laws lowered or eradicated alimony. Moreover, the majority of men defaulted on child-support payments within one year after separation. Whereas divorced men enjoyed a sizable increase in their standard of living, divorced women suffered a formidable decline. During the 1970s alone, the number of poor families headed by women increased nearly 70 percent.

A sharp rise in teenage pregnancy reinforced this pattern. Many of these mothers were too young to have gained either the education or skills to secure jobs that would pay enough to support themselves and their children. Even with Aid to Families with Dependent Children (AFDC) payments and food stamps, it was impossible for these single mothers to keep their families above the poverty line. By 1992, female-headed households, comprising 13.7 million people, accounted for 37 percent of the poor. African American and Latino women and their children had by far the highest poverty rates.

EPIDEMICS: DRUGS, AIDS, HOMELESSNESS

Drug addiction and drug trafficking took on frightening new dimensions in the early 1980s. The arrival of "crack," a cheap, smokable, and highly addictive form of cocaine, made that drug affordable to the urban poor. As crack addiction spread, the drug trade assumed alarming new proportions both domestically and internationally. Crack ruined hundreds of thousands of lives and led to a dramatic increase in crime rates. Studies showed that over half the men arrested in the nation's largest cities tested positive for cocaine. The crack trade spawned a new generation of young drug dealers who were willing to risk jail and death for enormous profits. In city after city, drug wars over turf took the lives of dealers and innocents, both caught in the escalating violence.

The Reagan administration declared a highly publicized "war on drugs," a multibillion-dollar campaign to bring the traffic under control. Critics charged that the war on drugs focused on supply from abroad when it needed to look at demand here at home. They urged more federal money for drug education, treatment, and rehabilitation. Drug addiction and drug use, they argued, were primarily health problems, not law enforcement issues.

In 1981 doctors in Los Angeles, San Francisco, and New York began encountering a puzzling new medical phenomenon. Young homosexual men were dying suddenly from rare types of pneumonia and cancer. The underlying cause was found to be a mysterious new viral disease that destroyed the body's natural defenses against illness, making its victims susceptible to a host of opportunistic infections. Researchers at the Centers for Disease Control (CDC) in Atlanta called the new disease **acquired immune deficiency syndrome (AIDS)**. The virus that causes AIDS is transmitted primarily in semen and blood. Full-blown AIDS might not appear for years after initial exposure to the virus. Thus, one could infect others without knowing one had the disease. Although tests emerged to determine whether one carried HIV, there was no cure. The majority of early AIDS victims were homosexual men who had been infected through sexual contact. Many Americans, thus, perceived AIDS as a disease of homosexuals. But other victims became infected through intravenous drug use, blood transfusions, heterosexual transmission, or birth to AIDS-carrying mothers.

AIDS provoked fear, anguish, and anger. It also brought an upsurge of organization and political involvement. In city after city, the gay community responded to the AIDS crisis with energy and determination. Most gay men changed their sexual habits, practicing "safe sex" to lessen the chances of infection. The Reagan administration, playing to antihomosexual prejudices, largely ignored the epidemic. One important exception was Surgeon General C. Everett Koop, who urged a comprehensive sex education program in the nation's schools.

Homelessness emerged as a chronic social problem during the 1980s. Often disoriented, shoeless, and forlorn, growing numbers of street people slept over heating grates, on subways, and in parks. Homeless people wandered city sidewalks panhandling and struggling to find scraps of food. Winters proved especially difficult. In the early 1980s, the Department of Housing and Urban Development placed the number of the nation's homeless at between 250,000 and 350,000, but advocates for the homeless estimated that the number was as high as 3 million.

Who were the homeless? Analysts agreed that at least a third were mental patients who had been discharged from psychiatric hospitals amid the deinstitutionalization trend of the the 1970s. Many more were alcoholics and drug addicts

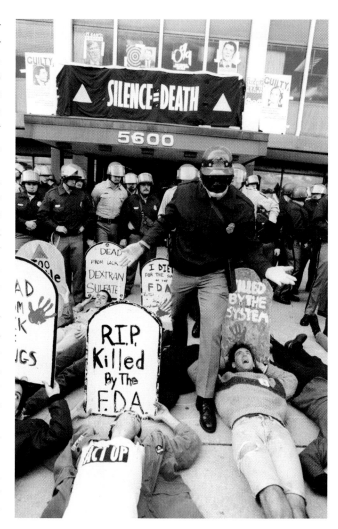

In May 1987, members of the Lesbian and Gay Community Services in Downtown Manhattan organized ACT-UP. Protesting what they perceived to be the Reagan administration's mismanagement of the AIDs crisis, they used nonviolent direct action, which often took the form of dramatic acts of civil disobedience. ACT-UP grew to more than 70 chapters in the United States and the world.
AP/Wide World Photos

Acquired immune deficiency syndrome (AIDS) A complex of deadly pathologies resulting from infection with the human immunodeficiency virus (HIV).

unable to hold jobs. But the ranks of the homeless also included female-headed families, battered women, Vietnam veterans, AIDS victims, and elderly people with no place to go. Some critics pointed to the decline in decent housing for poor people and the deterioration of the nation's health-care system as a cause of homelessness.

REAGAN'S FOREIGN POLICY

THE EVIL EMPIRE

In the early 1980s, the Reagan administration made vigorous anti-Communist rhetoric the centerpiece of its foreign policy. In a sharp turn from President Carter's focus on human rights and President Nixon's pursuit of détente, Reagan described the Soviet Union as "an evil empire . . . the focus of evil in the modern world." The president denounced the growing movement for a nuclear freeze, arguing that "we must find peace through strength."

Administration officials argued that the nation's military strength had fallen dangerously behind that of the Soviet Union during the 1970s. Critics disputed this assertion, pointing out that the Soviet advantage in intercontinental ballistic missiles (ICBMs) was offset by American superiority in submarine-based forces and strategic aircraft. Nonetheless, the administration proceeded with plans to enlarge America's nuclear strike force.

In 1983 President Reagan introduced an unsettling new element into superpower relations when he presented his **Strategic Defense Initiative (SDI)**, the plan for a space-based ballistic-missile defense system that journalists dubbed "Star Wars," after the popular Hollywood film series. This proposal for a five-year $26 billion program promised to give the United States the capacity to shoot down incoming missiles with laser beams and homing rockets. To critics, the plan seemed unworkable, impossibly expensive, and likely to destabilize existing arms treaties. The Reagan administration pressed ahead, spending $17 billion in research before the president left office—without achieving any convincing results.

THE REAGAN DOCTRINE AND CENTRAL AMERICA

Declaring the "Vietnam syndrome" over, the president confidently reasserted America's right to intervene anywhere in the world to fight Communist insurgency. The Reagan Doctrine, as this declaration was later called, assumed that all political instability in the third world resulted not from indigenous factors such as poverty or corruption but from the pernicious influence of the Soviet Union. It found its most important expression in Central America, where the United States hoped to reestablish its historical control over the Caribbean basin.

On the economic front, the Caribbean Basin Initiative (CBI) promised to stimulate the Caribbean economy by encouraging the growth of business corporations and a freer flow of capital through $350 million in U.S. aid. Yet Congress refused to play by the rules of free trade, placing stiff tariffs and quotas on imports of shoes, leather goods, and sugar competing with U.S. products. Many Latin American business leaders opposed key parts of the CBI, such as generous tax breaks for foreign investors. They feared that once large multinational corporations entered their markets, the CBI would strengthen the kind of chronic economic dependency that had shaped so much of the region's past.

In El Salvador, the Reagan administration continued to support the repressive regime. Military aid jumped from $6 million in 1980 to $82 million in 1982, and El Salvador received more U.S. economic assistance than any other Latin

---

HOW DID Reagan explain and justify U.S. policy in Central America?

30-4
Ronald Reagan, Address to the National Association of Evangelicals (1983)

30-3
Ronald Reagan, Speech to the House of Commons (1982)

30-7
Bill Chappell, Speech to the American Security Council Foundation (1985)

Strategic Defense Initiative (SDI) President Reagan's program, announced in 1983, to defend the United States against nuclear missile attack with untested weapons systems and sophisticated technologies.

American country. By 1983 right-wing death squads, encouraged by military elements within the regime, had tortured and assassinated thousands of opposition leaders. The election in 1984 of centrist president José Napoleón Duarte failed to end the bloody civil war. Some 53,000 Salvadorans, more than one out of every hundred, lost their lives in the conflict.

In Nicaragua, the Reagan administration claimed that the revolutionary Sandinista government posed "an unusual and extraordinary threat to the national security." U.S. officials accused the Sandinistas of shipping arms to antigovernment rebels in El Salvador. In December 1981, Reagan approved a $19 million CIA plan arming and organizing Nicaraguan exiles, known as **Contras**, to fight against the Sandinista government. As Reagan escalated this undeclared war, the aim became not merely the cutting of Nicaraguan aid to Salvadoran rebels, but also the overthrow of the Sandinista regime itself.

In 1984 the CIA secretly mined Nicaraguan harbors. When Nicaragua won a judgment against the United States in the World Court over this violation of its sovereignty, the Reagan administration refused to recognize the court's jurisdiction in the case and ignored the verdict. Predictably, the U.S. covert war pushed the Sandinistas closer to Cuba and the Soviet bloc. Meanwhile, U.S. grass-roots opposition to Contra aid grew more vocal and widespread. A number of U.S. communities set up sister city projects offering humanitarian and technical assistance to Nicaraguan communities. Scores of U.S. churches offered sanctuary to political refugees from Central America.

In 1984 Congress reined in the covert war by passing the Boland Amendment, introduced by Democratic representative Edward Boland of Massachusetts. It forbid government agencies from supporting "directly or indirectly military or paramilitary operations" in Nicaragua. Denied funding by Congress, President Reagan turned to the National Security Council to find a way to keep the Contra war going. Between 1984 and 1986, the NSC staff secretly ran the Contra assistance effort, raising $37 million in aid from foreign countries and private contributors, creating the largest mercenary army in hemispheric history. In 1987 the revelation of this unconstitutional scheme exploded before the public as part of the Iran-Contra affair, the most damaging political scandal of the Reagan years.

GLASNOST AND ARMS CONTROL

Meanwhile, momentous political changes within the Soviet Union led to a reduction in East–West tensions and ultimately the end of the Cold War itself. Soviet premier Leonid Brezhnev, in power since 1964, died toward the end of 1982. His successors, Yuri Andropov and Konstantin Chernenko, both died after brief terms in office. But in 1985 a new, reform-minded leader, Mikhail Gorbachev, won election as general secretary of the Soviet Communist Party. Although a lifelong Communist, Gorbachev represented a new generation of disenchanted party members. He initiated a radical new program of economic and political reform under the rubrics of *glasnost* (openness) and *perestroika* (restructuring).

Gorbachev and his advisors opened up political discussion and encouraged criticism of the Soviet economy and political culture. The government released longtime dissidents like Andrei Sakharov from prison and took the first halting steps toward profit-based, private initiatives in the economy. This "new thinking" inspired an unprecedented wave of diverse, often critical perspectives in Soviet art, literature, journalism, and scholarship.

In Gorbachev's view, improving the economic performance of the Soviet system depended first on halting the arms race. Over 10 percent of the Soviet GNP (gross national product) went to defense spending, while the majority of its citizens

Contras Nicaraguan exiles armed and organized by the CIA to fight the Sandinista government of Nicaragua.

Glasnost Russian for "openness" applied to Mikhail Gorbachev's encouragement of new ideas and easing of political repression in the Soviet Union.

Perestroika Russian for "restructuring," applied to Mikhail Gorbachev's efforts to make the Soviet economic and political systems more modern, flexible, and innovative.

still struggled to find even the most basic consumer items in shops. Gorbachev thus took the lead in negotiating a halt to the arms race with the United States.

The historical ironies were stunning. Reagan had made militant anticommunism the centerpiece of his administration, but between 1985 and 1988 he had four separate summit meetings with the new Soviet leader. In October 1986, he and Gorbachev met in Reykjavík, Iceland, but this summit bogged down over the issue of SDI. Reagan refused to abandon his plan for a space-based defensive umbrella. Gorbachev insisted that the plan violated the 1972 Strategic Arms Limitation Treaty (SALT I) and that SDI might eventually allow the United States to make an all-out attack on the Soviet Union.

After another year of tough negotiating, the two sides agreed to a modest treaty that called for comprehensive, mutual, on-site inspections. It provided an important psychological breakthrough. At one of the summits a Soviet leader humorously announced, "We are going to do something terrible to you Americans—we are going to deprive you of an enemy."

THE IRAN-CONTRA SCANDAL

In 1987 the revelations of the Iran-Contra affair laid bare the continuing contradictions and difficulties attending America's role in world affairs. The affair also demonstrated how overzealous and secretive government officials subverted the Constitution and compromised presidential authority under the guise of patriotism.

The Middle East presented the Reagan administration with its most frustrating foreign policy dilemmas. In October 1983 a terrorist bombing in marine barracks in Lebanon killed 241 American servicemen, and the administration pulled the marines out of Lebanon, shying away from a long-term commitment of U.S. forces in the Middle East.

Terrorist acts, including the seizing of Western hostages and the bombing of commercial airplanes and cruise ships, redefined the politics of the region. These were desperate attempts by small sects, many of them splinter groups associated with the Palestinian cause or Islamic fundamentalism, to inhibit U.S. support of Israel. The Reagan administration insisted that behind international terrorism lay the sinister influence and money of the Soviet bloc, the Ayatollah Khomeini of Iran, and Libyan leader Muammar el-Qaddafi. In the spring of 1986 the president, eager to demonstrate his antiterrorist resolve, ordered the bombing of Tripoli in a failed effort to kill Qaddafi.

As a fierce war between Iran and Iraq escalated, the administration tilted publicly toward Iraq to please the Arab states around the Persian Gulf. But in 1986 Reagan's advisors began secret negotiations with the revolutionary Iranian government. They eventually offered to supply Iran with sophisticated weapons for use against Iraq in exchange for help in securing the release of Americans held hostage by radical Islamic groups in Lebanon.

Subsequent disclosures elevated the arms-for-hostages deal into a major scandal. Some of the money from the arms deal had been secretly diverted into covert aid for the Nicaraguan Contras. The American public soon learned the sordid details from investigative journalists and through televised congressional hearings held during the summer of 1987. In order to escape congressional oversight of the CIA, Reagan and CIA director William Casey had essentially turned the National Security Council, previously a policy-coordinating body, into an operational agency. Under the direction of National Security Advisors Robert McFarlane and later Admiral John Poindexter, the NSC had sold TOW and Hawk missiles to the Iranians, using Israel as a go-between. Millions of dollars from these sales were then given to the Contras in blatant and illegal disregard of the Boland Amendment.

QUICK REVIEW

Iran-Contra

- 1986: Reagan opened secret negotiations with Iran.
- Agreed to sell arms in exchange for help freeing hostages.
- Some of the proceeds were used to illegally fund Nicaraguan Contras.

In the televised congressional hearings, NSC staffer and marine lieutenant colonel Oliver North emerged as the figure running what he euphemistically referred to as "the Enterprise." North defiantly defended his actions in the name of patriotism. Some Americans saw the handsome and dashing North as a hero; most were appalled by his and Poindexter's blithe admissions that they had lied to Congress, shredded evidence, and refused to inform the president of details in order to guarantee his "plausible deniability." A blue-ribbon commission led by former senator John Tower of Texas concluded that Reagan himself "did not seem to be aware" of the policy or its consequences. But the Tower Report offered a stunning portrait of a president who was at best confused and far removed from critical policy-making responsibilities.

Ultimately, the Iran-Contra investigation raised more questions than it answered. The full role of CIA director Casey, who died in 1987, particularly his relationships with North and the president, remained murky. The role of Vice President George H. W. Bush remained mysterious as well, and it would return as an issue in the 1992 presidential election. Both North and Poindexter were convicted of

CHRONOLOGY

1973 *Roe* v. *Wade* legalizes abortion.

Arab embargo sparks oil crisis in the United States.

1974 Richard Nixon resigns presidency; Gerald Ford takes office.

President Ford pardons Nixon and introduces antiinflation program.

1975 Unemployment rate reaches nearly 9 percent.

South Vietnamese government falls to communists.

Antibusing protests break out in Boston.

1976 Percentage of African Americans attending college peaks at 9.3 percent and begins a decline.

Jimmy Carter is elected president.

1977 President Carter announces human rights as major tenet in foreign policy.

1978 *Bakke* v. *University of California* decision places new limits on affirmative action programs.

Camp David meeting sets terms for Middle East peace.

California passes Proposition 13, cutting taxes and government social programs.

1979 Three Mile Island nuclear accident threatens a meltdown.

Nicaraguan Revolution overthrows Anastasio Somoza.

Iranian fundamentalists seize the U.S. embassy in Tehran and hold U.S. citizens hostage for 444 days.

Soviets invade Afghanistan.

1980 Inflation reaches 13.5 percent.

Ronald Reagan is elected president.

1981 Reagan administration initiates major cuts in taxes and domestic spending.

Military buildup accelerates.

AIDS is recognized and named.

1982 Economic recession grips the nation.

1983 Reagan announces the Strategic Defense Initiative, labeled "Star Wars" by critics.

241 marines killed in Beirut terrorist bombing.

1985 Mikhail Gorbachev initates reforms— *glasnost* and *perestroika*—in the Soviet Union.

1986 Iran-Contra hearings before Congress reveal arms-for-hostages deal and funds secretly and illegally diverted to Nicaraguan rebels.

felonies, but their convictions were overturned by higher courts on technical grounds. Reagan held fast to his plea of ignorance. When pressed on what had happened, he repeatedly claimed, "I'm still trying to find out."

In December 1992, following his reelection defeat and six years after the scandal broke, President George H. W. Bush granted pardons to six key players in the Iran-Contra affair. The Bush pardons made it unlikely that the full truth about the arms-for-hostages affair would ever be known.

Conclusion

The success of conservatives to halt and in some cases actually reverse key trends in American politics, from Franklin Roosevelt's New Deal to Lyndon Johnson's Great Society, was made possible by the legacy of the Cold War and the trauma of defeat in Vietnam. But it also owed a great deal to a deepening anxiety of the public about cultural changes and a growing pessimism about the ability of politicians to offer solutions, especially at the national level. Those community activists struggling to extend the protest movements of the 1960s into an updated, comprehensive reformism encompassing such issues as feminism, ecology, and affirmative action readily recognized that the liberal era had ended.

President Ronald Reagan, a charismatic figure who sometimes invented his own past and seemed to believe in it, offered remedies for a weary and nostalgic nation. By insisting that the rebellious 1960s had been a terrible mistake, lowering national self-confidence along with public morals and faith in the power of economic individualism, he successfully wedded the conservatism of Christian fundamentalists, many suburbanites, and Sunbelt voters with the more traditional conservatism of corporate leaders. In many respects, the Reagan administration actually continued and added ideological fervor to the downscaling of government services and upscaling of military spending already evident under President Jimmy Carter, while offering supporters the hope of a sweeping conservative revolution.

In the end, critics suggested, supporters of Ronald Reagan and Reaganism could not go back to the 1950s—just as the erstwhile rebels of the 1960s could not go back to their favorite era. Economically, conservatives achieved many of their goals, including widespread acceptance of sharper economic divisions within society and fewer restraints on corporations and investments. But socially and culturally, their grasp was much less secure.

Summary

The Overextended Society In the 1970s, American society was in transition. The economy was shaken by a variety of domestic and international forces. The hard times hit the working class the hardest. Two very different regions were evident. The Sunbelt appeared prosperous but was subject to boom and bust cycles while the Snowbelt showed signs of severe decline. The policies of Presidents Ford and Carter failed to improve economic conditions.

Communities and Politics Political mobilization in the 1970s focused on communities. Minorities gained political power and political office, but reforms were difficult due to fiscal problems. A mix of federal government, community organizations, and philanthropic foundations sponsored initiatives to rebuild the cities.

In addition, environmental crises shocked communities and the nation, stimulating the environmental movement. Retirees and urban problems fueled growth in small towns, but some residents protested against new subdivisions.

The New Conservatism The expansion of government and the drive to promote so-called traditional values led to the creation of the New Right. Evangelical Christianity played a strong role in this movement that opposed liberal issues. Another political trend of the seventies was disengagement from politics in favor of personal growth and self-indulgence. Popular culture reflected these new trends.

Adjusting to a New World After the Vietnam War, U. S. foreign policy was reassessed. Economic and other considerations led to a thaw in the Cold War. President Jimmy Carter's defense of human rights introduced morality into American foreign policy and helped negotiate a major Middle East agreement between Israel and Egypt. He also set the stage for Panama to gain ownership and control of the Panama Canal but backed repressive dictators in Central America in certain cases. A major problem for Carter was handling unexpected developments in Central America, Africa, and Central Asia. His biggest challenge was the Iran hostage crisis. Carter was renominated more because he was the incumbent than because he was popular. Ronald Reagan easily won the 1980 election.

The Reagan Revolution Ronald Reagan attempted to reshape the American political and social scene along conservative lines. His ability to communicate with the American people made him extremely popular. In domestic affairs, he stressed supply-side economics but his reductions were countered by massive defense spending. Reagan supported business interests over labor favoring deregulation of business. The economic recovery helped Reagan win a landslide victory in 1984. Reagan's economic policies had mixed results as the nation moved from a brief recession to a recovery to a fiscal crisis due to the rising national debt. The stock scandals of the late 1980s also affected the economy.

Best of Times, Worst of Times Entrepreneurship and moneymaking dominated the 1980s but the celebration of wealth was not shared by all. Affluent Americans tended to do well, but a two-tiered society was developing. The gap between the rich and poor widened and the opportunities to climb to middle-class status diminished. Minorities and women were particularly hard hit by the economic gap. Other issues also affected the nation. Drug use became more widespread. AIDS was a new disease that achieved epidemic proportions. Homelessness became a chronic problem.

Reagan's Foreign Policy Reagan wanted to restore America's world leadership. His strong anticommunism dominated his foreign policy. In Central America, the Reagan administration engaged in covert activities to stem communist influence. Changes occurred with the opening up of Soviet society to discussion and change. Gorbachev headed negotiations to end the arms race and Reagan responded positively. But the Iran-Contra scandal tarnished the Reagan administration, leading to several resignations and convictions for illegal acts.

REVIEW QUESTIONS

1. Evaluate the significance of the major population shifts in the United States from the 1940s through the 1970s. What was their impact on local and national politics?

2. Discuss the connections between the energy crisis and the rise of the environmental movement.

3. Why was the 1970s dubbed the "Me Decade"? Interpret the decline of liberalism and the rise of conservative political groups. How did these changes affect the outcome of presidential elections?

4. Was the Iran hostage crisis a turning point in American politics or only a thorn in Carter's reelection campaign? How did Iran-Contra affect the Republicans?

5. Describe the central philosophical assumptions behind Reaganomics. What were the key policies by which it was implemented? To what extent were these policies a break with previous economic approaches?

6. Evaluate Reagan's foreign policy. How did it differ from Carter's approach to foreign affairs?

7. Analyze the key structural factors underlying recent changes in American economic and cultural life. Do you see any political solutions for the growth of poverty and inequality?

KEY TERMS

Acquired immune deficiency syndrome (AIDS) (p. 855)
Affirmative action (p. 838)
Camp David Accords (p. 846)
Contras (p. 857)
Deregulation (p. 837)
Détente (p. 847)
Economic Recovery Tax Act of 1981 (p. 850)

Glasnost (p. 857)
Organization of Petroleum Exporting Countries (OPEC) (p. 833)
Perestroika (p. 857)
Roe v. *Wade* (p. 842)
Strategic Defense Initiative (SDI) (p. 856)
Sunbelt (p. 835)

RECOMMENDED READING

Lee Edwards, *The Conservative Revolution: The Movement That Remade America* (2000). Traces the rise of modern political conservatism from its origins in Cold War anticommunism. A longtime conservative activist and writer, Edwards credits much of Reagan's success in office to the presence of a stong, vital, and grass-roots conservative movement.

Frances FitzGerald, *Way Out There in the Blue: Reagan, Star Wars, and the End of the Cold War* (2000). A well-documented study of the conservative mood that made Star Wars both credible and popular among conservatives. FitzGerald provides a sweeping historical context for Star Wars with special attention given to the impact of the Cold War on traditional isolationism.

Angela Howard and Sasha Ranae Addams Tarrant, eds., *Reaction to the Modern Women's Movement, 1963 to Present* (1997). A collection of essays covering a wide variety of topics concerning the rise of antifeminism. The editors include excerpts from the writings of leading conservatives and analysis by historians.

John Karaagac, *Between Promise and Policy: Ronald Reagan and Conservative Reformism* (2000). Assesses Reagan's major polities, such as increased funding for federal government and regulatory reform, in light of his professed conservative ideals. Karaagac argues that Reagan wielded ideology as a political weapon to gain support for his programs while acting pragmatically and with a good deal of flexibility on particular issues.

Michael B. Katz, *Improving Poor People: The Welfare State, the "Underclass," and Urban Schools as History* (1995). Provides a broad overview of the history of urban poverty, welfare policy, and public education. Katz examines the "underclass" debates of the 1970s as a function of the interaction between politics and economics within the postindustrial inner city.

William M. LeoGrande, *Our Own Backyard: The United States in Central America, 1977–1992* (1998). Assesses the efforts of the Reagan adminstration to gain congressional approval for funding counterrevolutionary operations in El Salvador and Nicaragua. LeoGrande, a former congressional advisor, based his well-documented and detailed study on declassified State Department records, interviews, as well as conventional published sources.

Melani McAlister, *Epic Encounters: Culture, Media, and U.S. Interests in the Middle East, 1945–2000* (2001). A close reading of American popular culture, including films, television news broadcasts, museum exhibits, and fiction, representing relationships between the Middle East and the United States. McAlister considers the importance of the abundance of oil and the Islamic religion of the Middle East as factors shaping U.S. foreign policy.

Lisa McGirr, *Suburban Warriors: The Origins of the New American Right* (2001). Traces the resurgence of American conservatism by analyzing issues that galvanized grass-roots middle-class activism in 1960s and 1970s Southern California.

Bruce J. Schulman, *The Seventies: The Great Shift in American Culture, Society, and Politics* (2001). Examines the move away from the public-spirited universalism that characterized the New Deal and civil rights movement toward the sovereignty of the free market and celebration of private life. With a geopolitical twist that emphasizes the increasing importance of the Sunbelt, Schulman argues that the conservative 1980s actually began a decade earlier.

Judith Stein, *Running Steel, Running America: Race, Economic Policy, and the Decline of Liberalism* (1998). Discusses the impact of the decline of the U.S. steel industry on its large African American labor force. Stein analyzes trade policy, especially under Carter, that benefited foreign steel producers and led to the closing of American plants.

Robert A. Strong, *Working in the World: Jimmy Carter and the Making of American Foreign Policy* (2000). A collection of nine case studies of international affairs covering Carter's presidency. Strong's goal is not to provide new insight into the central crises of the era but to open a window to the range of presidential responsibilities in the diplomatic arena.

Andrew Szasz, *EcoPopulism: Toxic Waste and the Movement for Environmental Justice* (1994). A careful analysis of a turning point in federal regulation of toxic waste. Szasz shows how the prevention of pollution, previously considered a local issue, through strengthened state and federal regulations became a national issue and a springboard for the environmental movement.

Winifred D. Wandersee, *On the Move: American Women in the 1970s* (1988). A highly readable overview of the changes that brought American women into political life but also kept them at the margins of power. This study includes a close description of the National Organization for Women as well as media personalities, such as Jane Fonda, who gave feminism a public face.

. . . the looks on the faces of the people
coming out of the city that day will haunt me forever . . .
everyone was the same color . . . dust white . . .
women crying . . . men crying . . . we must never forget
the men and women that died that day . . .
—*John McNamara,* The September 11 Digital Archive, *April 13, 2002*

Black smoke billows through lower Manhattan during
the collapse of the World Trade Center.

31

TOWARD A TRANSNATIONAL AMERICA

SINCE 1988

WHAT EVENTS led to the

collapse of communism in Eastern Europe?

WHAT FACTORS

contributed to the economic boom

of the 1990s?

Other 9.3%
Europe 11.4%
Asia 25.4%
Latin America 53.9%

WHAT WERE the major divisions in

American society at the end of the twentieth century?

HOW DID the threat of

international terrorism transform the

American political landscape in the

first decade of the twenty-first century?

AMERICAN COMMUNITIES
The World Trade Center, New York, as a Transnational Community

TELMO ALVEAR HAD QUIT HIS JOB AS A BUSBOY IN AUGUST 2001 to become a waiter at Windows on the World, a restaurant on the 106th and 107th floors of the North Tower of the World Trade Center (WTC) that was once described by New York magazine as "the most spectacular restaurant in the world." The posh restaurant was huge and elegant. Designed originally as part of a private club for the WTC's business clients, Windows on the World could accommodate as many as 1,000 people. In the decade after it opened in 1976, Windows was one of the most successful restaurants in the world, earning revenues that topped $20 million a year. Much of its success came from its fabulous menu, originally planned in consultation with James Beard, one of the world's most renowned chefs. In the early 1990s, the reputation of Windows began to slip, and following a terrorist attack on the WTC in February 1993, the restaurant closed. But by the time Alvear found a job there, Windows on the World was once again thriving. Celebrity chef Michael Lomonaco was in charge, earning for the restaurant the Visitors Choice Award of "Grand Prize for Best Restaurant Overall." With views on a clear day extending for forty-five miles, and with a wine cellar and liquor stock that was modestly named "The Greatest Bar on Earth," Windows had become a prime tourist attraction and a popular dining spot for some of the most powerful international traders and merchants in the world. "It's more than a restaurant," one reviewer enthused. "It's a New York experience."

And so it was. Not just Windows on the World but the entire World Trade Center had come to represent both the best and worst of New York City, the commercial capital of the world. The twin skyscrapers, which were designed to be the tallest in the world, were audacious. Completed in 1973 at a cost of $400 million, they rose 110 stories above ground and occupied a thirteen-square-block site in Lower Manhattan, conveniently close to Wall Street and the New York Stock Exchange. When the WTC was first built, many New Yorkers, including distinguished architects, complained that the mammoth, boxy structures destroyed the city's unrivaled skyline. They stood too self-assuredly, critics charged, as tasteless monuments to commerce, wealth, and ambition. But over the years, the WTC became a preeminent symbol of the glory of New York and, by extension, the United States. The image of the twin towers was emblazoned on t-shirts and captured on postcards and sold to tourists from all over the world. The WTC provided office space to hundreds of businesses and government agencies and served as a workplace for more than 50,000 people.

The people who worked in the twin towers constituted a remarkable transnational community. Although many were native New Yorkers, a large number were relative newcomers. Alvear himself was one in a huge wave of Hispanic immigrants who had been transforming New York City since 1990. Immigrating from Ecuador as a teenager, he represented what census takers term "other Hispanics"—immigrants from South and Central America and the Caribbean who had replaced the Puerto Ricans and Cubans as the city's Hispanic majority. Alvear lived with his wife Blanca and their one-year-old son in Queens and spent his hours away from work at soccer games and dance clubs.

At his job, Alvear worked with and served people from a wide array of national backgrounds. Those who worked at Windows on the World proudly described themselves as a "little United Nations" because they represented just about every nation of the world and spoke nearly as many languages. Representing a wide range of cultures, they were well prepared to deal with the restaurant's equally diverse patrons, tourists from around the world and international traders and executives with offices in the WTC.

The Port Authority of New York and New Jersey, which owned the WTC, rented space primarily to tenants engaged in international commerce. Importers, exporters, freight handlers, steamship lines, oil traders, and insurance organizations were among the long-term renters. Many were multinational businesses, the majority with home offices in the United States, but a sizable number represented financial or commercial operations from Latin America, Asia, Africa, and Europe. American-based firms such as Verizon Communications, Morgan Stanley, and the Oppenheimer Funds occupied several floors. But Fuji Bank of Japan, Thai Farmers Bank, Zim-American Israeli Shipping Company, and the Bank of Taiwan also had offices there. To promote transnational exchanges, the World Trade Institute, on the 55th floor of the North Tower, sponsored training courses in world trade, seminars for international businesspeople, and even language classes. Many of these firms chose to rent space in the WTC not because their businesses benefited directly from physical proximity to other international traders, but because an address at the WTC offered visibility to firms seeking a high profile in the world of commerce. The WTC offered firms the prestige of working in New York's most imposing landmark, a symbol of American wealth and power.

On September 11, 2001, two commercial jetliners hijacked by terrorists crashed into both towers of the World Trade Center and within an hour both towers had collapsed. Telmo Alvear, who usually worked the night shift, had been covering for a friend that *morning. At age twenty-five he perished, along with nearly eighty members of the Hotel and Restaurant Workers Union who, like Alvear, were serving a special breakfast meeting. Nearly 3,000 people—citizens of the United States and eighty other nations— died that day. Uncounted were an unknown number of homeless New Yorkers who had sought what they believed to be a safe haven in the cavernous underground spaces of the WTC.*

The WTC symbolized, if any building could, the confidence of American leadership in an era when national borders seemed to melt away. It also symbolized the transnationalism that many believed laid the foundation for a new world order based on the democratic liberalism that Americans treasured. Its vulnerability to surprise attack suggested the fragile nature of the swiftly changing society.

A NEW WORLD ORDER

Between 1989 and 1991, Americans watched with amazement as the Soviet empire disintegrated, and the Cold War came to an end. But contrary to expectations, this dramatic event did not bring world peace. The end of the Cold War let loose a multitude of furies in the form of renewed nationalism, ethnic and religious conflict, and widening divisions between the world's rich and poor. Just as dramatically, as the old geopolitical order disappeared, ideological rivalry shifted to the Middle East and other areas in the world where Islamic militants had forcefully turned against the West.

THE COLLAPSE OF COMMUNISM

The reforms initiated by Mikhail Gorbachev in the mid-1980s, known as *perestroika*, and, more immediately, the failed Soviet war in Afghanistan led to the dissolution of the Soviet Union and to the end of Communist rule throughout Eastern Europe. Beginning in June 1989, when Poland held its first free elections since the close of World War II in 1945, prodemocracy demonstrations forced out long-time Communist leaders in Hungary, Czechoslovakia, Bulgaria, and Romania. Most dramatic of all were the events in East Germany. The Berlin Wall, which for thirty years had loomed as the ultimate symbol of Cold War division, came down on November 9, 1989. Hundreds of thousands of East Germans immediately rushed into West Berlin. Popular protest intensified, paving the way for German reunification the following year.

Political changes in the Soviet Union came more slowly, accompanied by such drastically reduced living standards that successful transition to a liberal market economy and democratic political system was uncertain. In March 1989 the Soviet Union held its first open elections since 1917, and a new Congress of People's Deputies replaced the old Communist Party–dominated Supreme Soviet. In the next elections the following year, hundreds of party officials went down in defeat in key Russian cities. In August 1991 party hard-liners made a final attempt to hold on to the old order and staged a coup, placing President Gorbachev under house arrest. Although the coup quickly failed, most of the fifteen republics had meanwhile announced their withdrawal from the Soviet Union. Gorbachev found he could no longer control the government. On Christmas Day 1991 the weary and bitter president of the USSR resigned and recognized the new Commonwealth of Independent States.

WHAT EVENTS led to the collapse of communism in Eastern Europe?

Constructed by the Port Authority of New York and New Jersey in the early 1970s, the World Trade Center provided office space to businesses from around the world. The 110-story twin towers dominated the skyline of Lower Manhattan.

© Joseph Sohm; Visions of America/CORBIS (JS1262341)

Operation Desert Storm U.S. military campaign to force Iraqi forces out of Kuwait.

QUICK REVIEW

The Fall of Gorbachev and the Soviet Union

- ◆ August 1991: Old-line communists attempted a coup against Gorbachev.
- ◆ Boris Yeltsin organized the successful resistance to the plotters.
- ◆ Gorbachev resigned and all fifteen Soviet republics declared their independence.

30–9
George Bush, Address to the Nation Announcing Allied Military Action in the Persian Gulf (1991)

U.S. Marines swept into Kuwait City, March 1991. After six weeks of intensive bombing and less than five days after the start of a massive ground offensive, U.S. and allied forces overwhelmed the Iraqi army and ended Saddam Hussein's occupation of Kuwait.

Photo by Patrick Downs. © Los Angeles Times. Reprinted by permission

The Soviet Union had dissolved, marking the end of the great superpower rivalry that had shaped American foreign policy and domestic politics for nearly a half-century. President Bush described the end of the Cold War as an event of "biblical proportions." Many scholars have agreed that the changes rivaled the collapse of European empires during World War I and the rise of the Cold War after World War II.

WAR IN THE MIDDLE EAST

On August 2, 1990, 120,000 Iraqi troops backed by 850 tanks swept into neighboring Kuwait and quickly seized control of that tiny monarchy with its rich oil fields. The motives of Saddam Hussein, Iraq's military dictator, were mixed. Like most other Iraqis, Hussein believed that oil-rich Kuwait was actually an ancient province of Iraq that had illegally been carved away by British imperial agents in the 1920s as part of the dismemberment of the Ottoman Empire. Control of Kuwait would give Saddam Hussein control of its huge oil reserves, as well as Persian Gulf ports for his landlocked country. Just emerging from an exhausting and inconclusive eight-year war with Iran, Iraqis also bitterly resented Kuwait's production of oil beyond OPEC quotas, which had helped send the world price of oil plummeting from the highs of the 1970s and early 1980s.

The United States responded swiftly to news of the invasion. Its first concern was that Saddam Hussein might also attack Saudi Arabia, which the United States had defined as vital to its interests as far back as 1943. On August 15, President George H. W. Bush ordered U.S. forces to Saudi Arabia and the Persian Gulf, calling the action Operation Desert Shield. By the middle of October, some 230,000 American troops had been sent to the Persian Gulf.

In early November, President Bush announced a change in policy to what he called "an offensive military option," and the U.S. troop deployment quickly doubled and reached 580,000 by January 1991. Administration officials now demonized Saddam Hussein as another Adolf Hitler. The UN sanctions failed to budge Hussein from Kuwait, and the drift to war now looked inevitable. In January 1991, Congress narrowly passed a joint resolution authorizing the president to use military force.

After a last-minute UN peace mission failed to break the deadlock, President Bush announced, on January 16, 1991, the start of Operation Desert Storm. U.S-led air strikes began forty-two days of massive bombing of Iraqi positions in Kuwait, as well as Baghdad and other Iraqi cities. The ground war, which began on February 24, took only 100 hours to force Saddam Hussein's troops out of Kuwait. Hussein's vaunted military machine—the fourth largest army in the world—turned out to be surprisingly weak. U.S. forces lost only 184 dead, compared to nearly 100,000 Iraqi deaths, mostly from the bombing.

Almost every community in the United States sent men and women to the Gulf, and the vast majority supported **Operation Desert Storm.** Unlike the media coverage of the Vietnam War, television news reports showed virtually no blood or death. The Pentagon required "military escorts" to accompany all reporters and carefully regulated the release of silent film footage documenting precision bombing runs. Air strikes looked more like video games than bombing attacks, and military officials insisted that the bombing had been limited to Iraqi military targets. But subsequent investigations revealed massive numbers of targeting errors and the devastation of Iraq's infrastructure, from its communications network to its water system.

Victory in the Gulf War rekindled national pride in many people of the United States. But for the 18 million people of Iraq, it produced the worst possible outcome. The ecological damage in the Gulf region was extensive and long-lasting. Oil fires burned out of control. Human rights groups reported an appalling toll among civilians.

The limits of military power to solve complex political and economic disputes became clear in the aftermath of victory. The **Persian Gulf War** failed to dislodge Saddam Hussein, who remained in power despite CIA attempts to overthrow him and repeated bombings of Iraqi military positions. Trade sanctions did little to weaken his rule, although the economic boycott, which brought increasing hardship to the civilian population, eventually divided the Western powers, leaving the United States and Great Britain isolated in their sanctions against Iraq.

Moreover, regional tensions worsened in the aftermath of the war. In order to gain support from Egypt, Syria, Jordan, and Saudi Arabia to conduct military operations against Iraq, U.S. diplomats had promised to forge a just peace between the Palestinians and Israelis. President Clinton undertook secret negotiations culminating in a Declaration of Principles in Oslo, Norway, in 1993, which for the first time promised security for the Israelis and self-rule for the Palestinians. For their role in this process, Israeli prime minister Itzakh Rabin and Palestinian leader Yassar Arafat were jointly awarded a Nobel Peace Prize. But the assassination of Rabin by an Israeli religious fundamentalist, the continuing buildup of Israeli "settlements" in the occupied West Bank of the Jordan River, and the resulting violence on both sides deprived Clinton of a major diplomatic triumph.

The repercussions of the Gulf War were long-lasting. The leading U.S. ally in the region, the oil-rich kingdom of Saudi Arabia, had served as the launching pad for the invasion of Iraq, and following the war the Saudis had allowed the continuing presence of U.S. troops and weapons. This occupation of Saudi territory, which included Islamic holy sites, intensified the hatred of Americans among many Muslims and prompted appeals for revenge.

Among those actively opposed to the U.S. role in the region was Saudi millionaire Osama bin Laden, just a few years earlier a close ally of the United States during the Russian invasion of Afghanistan. He now turned squarely against his former arms suppliers and CIA contacts. Using his own funds and a tribal network, bin Laden built his shadowy Al Qaeda organization, training small groups in terror tactics to be used against Western interests, particularly to force American troops out of the Middle East.

PEACEKEEPING IN THE BALKANS

The immediate victory in the Persian Gulf and a six-month surge of popularity did little to help President Bush when faced with a formidable candidate, William Jefferson Clinton. Unlike Bush, the last of the World War II veterans to enter the White House, Arkansas governor Clinton belonged to the Vietnam War generation and had opposed U.S. military intervention in Southeast Asia. The electorate awarded him 43 percent of the votes, compared to Bush's 38 percent, and gave the moderate Democrat a solidly Democratic House and Senate.

Despite this strong mandate, Clinton did not enjoy an easy transition. Heightened ethnic nationalism and religious fundamentalism continued to fill the vacuum left by the collapse of communism. Across the globe, from Africa to the Middle East, the Indian subcontinent, and beyond, civil wars created massive civilian casualties and new waves of refugees.

With the collapse of communism, Yugoslavia had quickly fallen to pieces when four of its six states declared independence. Ethnic and religious rivalry

Persian Gulf War   War initiated by President Bush in reponse to Iraq's invasion of Kuwait.

Young Author Ziata Filipoviic sits among the rubble of a building in Sarajevo, Bosnia and Herzgovina.

Boulata Alexandra/Sipa

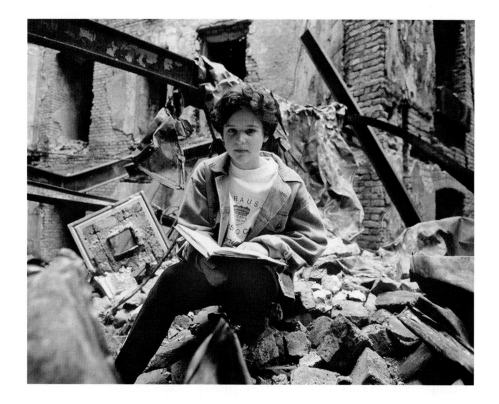

among Serbs, Croats, and Muslims living in **Bosnia** erupted into a violent civil war. Bush and his foreign policy advisors, seeing no threat to American interests, opposed U.S. military intervention. But as reports of "ethnic cleansing"—forced removal and murder of Croats and Muslims by Bosnian Serbs—increased, and as the numbers of refugees grew, Clinton, with congressional support, prepared to act. By late summer 1995, U.S. and NATO fighter pilots were bombing Serbian strongholds in Bosnia. After negotiating with Yugoslavian president Slobodan Milosevic, on November 27 Clinton announced the Dayton Accords, an agreement drawn up in Dayton, Ohio, and signed in Paris, that called for a federated, multiethnic state of Bosnia. An International Protection Force, one-third of whom were U.S. troops, was then installed as peacekeepers.

The worst foreign crisis of Clinton's presidency erupted in **Kosovo**, a Serbian province about 160 miles east of Italy, across the Adriatic Sea. Milosevic, a Serb nationalist, had terminated the autonomy of the province shortly after he took office in 1989, and in response the ethnic Albanians living there organized their own government and declared their independence the following year. While preoccupied by the civil war in Bosnia, Milosevic paid comparatively little attention to Kosovo. However, in 1997, the virtual collapse of the government of neighboring Albania changed the situation dramatically. Armed Albanians poured into Kosovo and joined the rebel forces. Clashes between Serbs and Albanians intensified, and the fighting soon spread to neighboring Macedonia and to Albania itself.

President Clinton once again attempted to negotiate, but he failed to resolve the problems through diplomacy. After NATO authorized air strikes, he addressed Americans on March 24, 1999, stating that U.S. armed forces had that day joined their allies to attack Serbian forces in Kosovo. On June 10, after a little more than two months of intensive bombing, he reported that the Serbian army was withdrawing from Kosovo and "for the first time in seventy-nine days, the skies over Yugoslavia are silent."

Bosnia A nation in southeast Europe that split off from Yugoslavia and became the site of bitter civil and religious war, requiring NATO and U.S. intervention in the 1990s.

Kosovo Province of Yugoslavia where the United States and NATO intervened militarily in 1999 to protect ethnic Albanians from expulsion.

His country in ruins, and voted out of office, Slobodan Milosevic became the first head of state to be brought to trial for war crimes and crimes against humanity by the International War Crimes Tribunal in 2001. Meanwhile, in the Balkans, nationalist and ethnic conflicts continued to flare up, and U.S. peacekeepers remained.

CHANGING AMERICAN COMMUNITIES

The dark side of the post–Cold War era seemed to be offset during the 1990s by the unprecedented surge of the U.S. economy and the inclusion of millions of new immigrants, who easily found places for themselves within the rapidly expanding service sector. The patterns of growth indicated a dynamic shift toward a postindustrial economy based upon high technology, wherein today's worker with a high degree of skill and entrepreneurial initiative might be tomorrow's millionaire. After a recession, which had plagued Bush's presidency, bottomed out in 1994, Americans settled in to enjoy record profits, low unemployment rates, and unsurpassed prosperity.

THE BOOM YEARS

The economy rather than foreign affairs had fueled the 1992 presidential election campaign. Republicans took credit for forcing the fall of communism and reviving America's military strength, but they had also promised to cut government spending and balance the budget. In 1985, the Republican Congress had enacted, amid great fanfare, the Balanced Budget and Emergency Deficit Reduction Act, more popularly known as **Gramm-Rudman** after its principal authors, Senators Phil Gramm and Warren Rudman. The act mandated automatic spending cuts if the government failed to meet fixed deficit reduction goals leading to a balanced budget by 1991. But just as Bush was about to take office in 1989, many of the nation's savings and loan institutions, which had been deregulated by Reagan, collapsed. Then, on Friday, October 13, 1989, the stock market took its worst nose dive since 1987, signaling the beginning of a major recession. With the national debt reaching an astronomical $4 trillion, the paradoxes of the Reagan-Bush years had become readily apparent.

In the Democrats' campaign headquarters a sign humorously reminded the staff: "It's the economy, stupid." Candidate Bill Clinton promised economic leadership, including deficit reduction and a tax cut for the middle class. He also effectively adopted many of the conservative themes that had proved so advantageous to Republicans over the past twelve years. He called for "responsibility" on the part of recipients of social programs, spoke of the importance of stable families, promised to be tough on crime and to reduce the bureaucracy, and stressed the need for encouraging private investment to create new jobs. Economic issues also fueled the independent campaign of Texas billionaire H. Ross Perot, who with his folksy East Texas twang argued that a successful businessman such as himself was better qualified to solve the nation's economic woes than Washington insiders.

The Clinton administration succeeded in breaking the political gridlock caused by the traditional Democratic resistance to the "economic discipline" urged by Republicans. He pursued a strategy his advisors called "triangulation," positioning himself above and between the interests of warring Democrats and Republicans. For example, despite his attacks on the Republicans as radicals, Clinton opposed his own party's efforts to block a Republican plan to dismantle the federal welfare system in place since the New Deal. The new legislation—the Welfare

WHAT FACTORS
contributed to the economic boom of the 1990s?

Gramm-Rudman   Law that mandated automatic spending cuts if the government failed to meet fixed deficit reduction goals leading to a balanced budget by 1991.

Republican President George Bush, Democrat Bill Clinton, and Independent H. Ross Perot debated the issues on television three times during the 1992 presidential campaign. Bush emphasized the "character" issue by hammering away at Clinton's failure to serve during the Vietnam War. Clinton focused on the plight of the "forgotten middle class," many of whom had deserted the Democratic party. Perot appealed to voter frustration with the two major parties.

Corbis/Sygma (280232)

North American Free Trade Agreement (NAFTA) Agreement reached in 1993 by Canada, Mexico, and the United States to substantially reduce barriers to trade.

World Trade Organization (WTO) International organization that sets standards and practices for global trade, and the focus of international protests over world economic policy in the late 1990s.

Reform Act—abolished the sixty-year-old Aid to Families with Dependent Children program (AFDC). Poor mothers with dependent children would now have access to aid for only a limited period and only if they were preparing for or seeking work. When Congress passed the act in August of 1996, Clinton held a public signing ceremony and declared "an end to welfare as we know it."

President Clinton pushed two major trade agreements through Congress that built on efforts by the Reagan and Bush administrations to expand markets and encourage "free trade." Approved in November 1993, the **North American Free Trade Agreement (NAFTA)** eased the international flow of goods, services, and investments among the United States, Mexico, and Canada by eliminating tariffs and other trade barriers. Supplemental agreements called for cooperation on environmental and labor concerns. The stated goal of NAFTA was to improve productivity and living standards through a freer flow of commerce in North America. It created the largest free-trade zone in the world, comprising 360 million people and an annual gross national product of $6 trillion.

In 1994 Congress also approved the General Agreement on Tariffs and Trade (GATT), which slashed tariffs on thousands of goods throughout the world and phased out import quotas imposed by the United States and other industrialized nations. It also established the **World Trade Organization (WTO)** to mediate commercial disputes among 117 nations.

Critics and supporters of NAFTA and GATT argued over whether the agreements would encourage global competition, thereby boosting American export industries and creating new high-wage jobs for American workers, or simply erode the American industrial base and accelerate environmental degradation. Cities on the U.S.–Mexican border, such as Tijuana and San Diego, were clear beneficiaries, but the downside was considerable. New *maquiladora* (factories and assembly plants) lacked pollution controls and spewed tons of toxic wastes into the air and groundwater. Despite the boost from NAFTA, the Mexican peso collapsed, and only a $20 billion bailout of the Mexican economy directed by executive order from the White House on January 31, 1995, prevented a serious depression there.

Perhaps the greatest stimulus to Clinton's economic policy was the soaring stock market of the 1990s, with "tech stocks" leading the way. The record highs of the Bush years, when the Dow Jones index of thirty industrials approached 4,000, paled by comparison to the leap in 1999 when the Dow hit 10,000 in March and then peaked above 11,000 in May. The market remained volatile during the decade, but profits were extraordinarily high. Annual returns on investments, generally under 6 percent during the 1970s, had risen to more than 18 percent.

The down side of the economic boom was nearly invisible. Productivity had risen sharply since the 1970s while labor costs had actually declined, hoisting profits to new levels. But critics observed that while a corporate official had earned around twenty or thirty times the pay of a blue-collar worker at the same company a few decades earlier, corporate executive income was more than two hundred times greater than that of a blue-collar employee. Moreover, "downsizing" became a common strategy for increasing profit levels or defeating negative trends. In the blue-collar sector, industrial jobs continued to disappear as factories closed or companies moved production of textiles, auto parts, and even electronics across borders or overseas. By the second half of 1999, the "dot-com" **Internet**-related stocks began to tumble, and economic analysts began to wonder if the business cycle had indeed been rendered obsolete.

SILICON VALLEY

Much of the growth of the 1990s was attributed to the consolidation of the "new economy," a phrase coined by economists in the 1970s to characterize the increasing importance of the service sector, corporate restructuring, and globalization. During the peak years of the new economy, a thirty-by-ten-mile strip of Santa Clara County, California, emerged as both the real and symbolic capital of the most important sector of the new economy—microelectronics. As late as 1960 this region was the major processor of fruits and vegetables in the world; forty years later one-third of the valley's work force were employed by high-tech companies.

Dubbed "**Silicon Valley**" in 1971 after the semiconductor chip, which is made of silicon, and which became the basic building block of modern microelectronics, the region flourished thanks to its unique combination of research facilities, investment capital, attractive environment, and a large pool of highly educated people. At first, military contracts predominated, but the consumer electronics revolution of the 1970s fueled an explosive new wave of growth. Silicon Valley firms gave birth to pocket calculators, video games, home computers, cordless telephones, digital watches, and almost every other new development in electronics. It became home to more than 1,700 high-tech firms that specialized in gathering, processing, or distributing information or in manufacturing information technology.

Internet   The system of interconnected computers and servers that allows the exchange of email, posting of Web sites, and other means of instant communication.

Silicon Valley   The region of California including San Jose and San Francisco that holds the nation's greatest concentration of electronics firms.

Companies like Atari, Apple, and Intel achieved enormous success and became household names. Silicon Valley boasted the greatest concentration of new wealth in the United States.

By the end of the century, Silicon Valley had become a continuous sprawl of two dozen cities between San Francisco and San Jose and the home and workplace of a diverse population. The managers and engineers, nearly all of whom were white males, had settled in affluent communities such as Palo Alto, Mountain View, and Sunnyvale. Manual workers on assembly lines and in low-paying service jobs clustered in San Jose and Gilroy. Most of these were Latino, African American, Vietnamese, Cambodian, and Filipino men and women who constituted a cheap, nonunionized labor pool with an extremely high turnover rate.

The prime example of the new economy, Silicon Valley was also part of a global enterprise. Its firms were closely linked to the microelectronic industry of the greater Pacific Rim. The end of the Cold War and the accompanying decline in military spending in the United States forced high-tech firms in California into greater competition on the world market and especially against similar companies in Japan, Korea, China, and Malaysia. But many American companies protected themselves against such competition by owning and managing a large share of the plants in these countries.

By the end of the century, the rate of growth showed signs of slowing, as did the infusion of new venture capital into high-tech industries. Young entrepreneurs throughout the Pacific Rim found it more difficult to start successful new companies and to make the leap from a small, start-up company to a large corporation. By this time, scarcity in housing, traffic jams, and an inflated cost of living were already leading many companies and individuals to move out of Silicon Valley.

AN ELECTRONIC CULTURE

The technological developments produced in Silicon Valley helped reconfigure cultural life in the United States and the world. Revolutions in computers and telecommunications merged telephones, televisions, computers, cable, and satellites into a global system of information exchange. The new technologies changed the way people worked and relaxed, made the nation's cultural life more homogeneous, and played a greater role than ever in shaping politics.

The twin arrivals of cable and the videocassette recorder (VCR) expanded and redefined the power of television. By the end of the 1980s pay cable services and VCRs had penetrated roughly two-thirds of American homes. The VCR revolutionized the way people used their television sets, allowing them to organize program watching around their own schedules. Hollywood studios began releasing movies on videotape, and the rental and sale of movies for home viewing quickly outstripped ticket sales at theaters as the main profit source for filmmakers.

In 1981, a new cable channel called MTV (for Music Television) began airing videos of popular music stars performing their work. The intent was to boost sales of the stars' audio recordings, but the music video soon became a new art form in itself. Artists who best exploited music video, such as Madonna and Michael Jackson, achieved international superstar status. MTV also helped transform smaller, cult musical forms, such as rap and heavy metal, into giant mass-market phenomena. MTV pioneered an imaginative visual style, featuring rapid cutting, animation, and the sophisticated fusion of sound and image.

More than ever, television drove the key strategies and tactics defining American political life. Politicians and their advisers focused intently on a candidate's television image. Issues, positions, and debate all paled alongside the key question: How did it look on television? Fewer citizens voted or took an active role in campaigns, and most relied on television coverage to make their choices. Thus creating an effective television "character" emerged as perhaps the most crucial form of political discourse.

Perhaps no aspect of the electronics culture was more revolutionary than the creation of cyberspace, the conceptual region occupied by people linked through computers and communications networks. It began with ARPANET, the first computer network, which was created by the Department of Defense in the early 1970s. Computer enthusiasts known as "hackers" created unexpected grass-roots spinoffs from ARPANET, including electronic mail, computer conferencing, and computer bulletin board systems. In the mid-1980s the boom in cheap personal computers capable of linking to the worldwide telecommunications network began a population explosion in cyberspace. By then, tens of thousands of researchers and scholars at universities and in private industry were linked to the Internet—the U.S. government-sponsored successor to ARPANET—through their institutions' computer centers. The establishment of the **World Wide Web** and easy-to-use browser software such as Netscape, introduced in 1994, made the "information highway" accessible to millions of Americans with few computer skills and created a popular communications medium with global dimensions.

By the beginning of the new century, the Census Bureau estimated that more than half of all households had at least one computer and more than 40 percent were connected to the Internet. Nearly 85 percent of classrooms in public schools were online. At work, Americans spent an average of 21 hours per week online. At home, they spent an average of 9.5 hours per week online, gaining access to the Web from independent service providers such as America Online and Earthlink. For a flat monthly fee users could play games, send electronic mail, discuss issues in public forums, and purchase a huge array of goods and services, ranging from books and airline tickets to automobiles and psychotherapy sessions.

These new information technologies gave birth to a media community that transcended national boundaries. During the 1980s, exports from Hollywood to the rest of the world doubled in value. The number of hours of television watched throughout the world nearly tripled. MTV was broadcast to an estimated 250 million households throughout the world. By the mid-1990s there were more television sets in China than in the United States. The growth of cable was phenomenal; in the Netherlands, for example, 98 percent of households received programming by cable.

THE NEW IMMIGRANTS AND THEIR COMMUNITIES

The 2000 census showed that the nation's population during the 1990s grew by 32.7 million, a number greater than that of any other decade in U.S. history. Even the 1950s, which witnessed the post–World War II baby boom, could not compete against a decade marked by a huge number of immigrants and a birthrate that surpassed the death rate. At the beginning of the new millennium, Americans numbered 281.4 million.

The 2000 census confirmed what many Americans had observed over the previous decade in their communities and workplaces. The face of the nation was perceptibly changing and changing on a scale that compared to the first decades of the twentieth century when immigration from Europe peaked. At the turn of the twenty-first century, more than a third of the

World Wide Web   A part of the Internet designed to allow easier navigation of the network through the use of graphical user interfaces and hypertext links between different addresses.

Continent of Birth for Immigrants, 1990–2000

By 2000, the number of foreign-born residents and their children—56 million according to the Census Bureau—had reached the highest level in U.S. history.

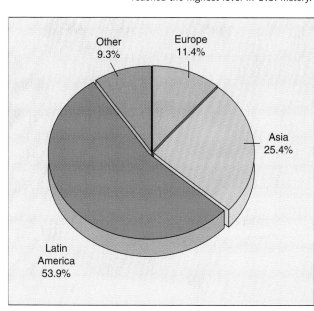

nation's population growth came from the influx of new immigrants. Although three-quarters of the newcomers joined many other Americans in flocking to the Sunbelt states, headed by California, Texas, and Florida, they not only helped to reverse population loss in such major urban centers as New York and Chicago and slow the decline in Rustbelt cities like Cleveland, Detroit, and Milwaukee, but also for the first time in any census, they played a major role in the population increase in all fifty states.

The Immigration Act of 1965, passed almost unnoticed in the context of the egalitarian political climate created by the civil rights movement, had revolutionary consequences, some of them unintended. The act abolished the discriminatory national origins quotas that had been in place since the 1920s. It also limited immigration from the Western Hemisphere for the first time, while giving preferences to people from the nations of the Eastern Hemisphere who had specialized job skills and training. This provision created the conditions for Asian immigrants to become the fasting growing ethnic group in the United States. But in setting limits on Western Hemisphere immigration, the 1965 act tempted many thousands of people from Latin American to enter the United States illegally. By the mid-1980s, growing concern over "illegal aliens" had become a hotly debated political issue, particularly in the Southwest. The Immigration Reform and Control Act of 1986 marked a break with the past attempts to address this problem. Instead of mass deportation programs, the law offered an amnesty to all undocumented workers who had entered the country since 1982. Four years later, additional revisions of this act enlarged the quota of immigrants, once again giving priority to skilled and professional workers. Hispanics and Asians benefited from these changes in immigration law. Within the twenty fastest growing cities, the number of Hispanics and Asians increased by approximately 70 percent.

According to the 2000 census, Hispanics were the nation's largest minority group among those 17 and younger. They represented a generation of nearly 12.3 million, the majority living in California and the Southwest.

Photograph by Jose L. Pelaez. Corbis/Stock Market (0-067-0130)

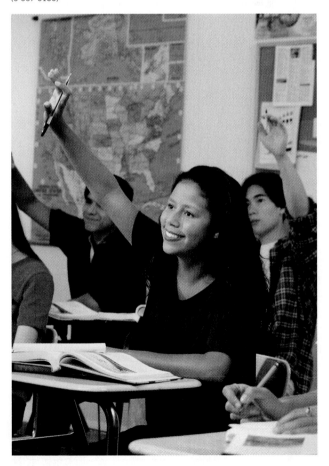

Demographers predicted that Hispanics, who had grown from 22.4 million in 1990 to 35.3 million in 2000, according to census data, would replace African Americans as the largest minority group in the nation by the middle of the twenty-first century. By 1990 Hispanics had already formed over a third of the population of New Mexico, a quarter of the population of Texas, and over 10 percent of the populations of California, Arizona, and Colorado. Nearly a million Mexican Americans lived in Los Angeles alone.

The 2000 census showed that Mexicans were the largest Hispanic group in the United States, at 20.6 million and representing nearly 60 percent of the total Hispanic population. The boom of the U.S. economy in the 1990s, with service, agricultural, and even factory jobs readily available, had provided a significant "pull" for these newcomers. But other factors encouraged many immigrants to make an often difficult and dangerous sojourn. First, a drop in worldwide oil prices followed by the deflation of the Mexican national currency dramatically lowered living standards in Mexico in the mid-1990s. The North American Free Trade Agreement (NAFTA) and the greater integration of the U.S. and Mexican economies brought new jobs, but often with increasingly expensive living conditions. Tens and perhaps hundreds of thousands of Mexicans worked in the United States temporarily while planning a permanent move north, with or without legal documentation.

After settling across the border, most new Mexican Americans struggled in low-wage and often dangerous jobs such as meat-packing or construction, and they were more likely to die from workplace injuries than other workers. Through education and success in business, a significant number achieved middle-class status and wealth, but almost 20 percent of Mexican Americans lived below the poverty line. They tended to live in segregated neighborhoods and were less likely than non-Hispanic whites to have health insurance or to own their own homes.

Puerto Rican–born population jumped from 100,000 to roughly 1 million. However, during the 1990s, this trend had begun to reverse, their numbers falling by 12 percent. The smaller but highly influential Cuban population declined even more, by 27 percent. Meanwhile, other Latin populations grew at an extraordinary rate of 50 percent. The Mexican-born population more than doubled, and Filipinos, who often speak Spanish as a first language, increased by 27 percent. Immigrants from the Dominican Republic, now second in population size only to Puerto Ricans, dominated sizable sections of Washington Heights and Brooklyn, while immigrants from various countries in Central and South America created new communities throughout the greater metropolitan region.

The cultural implications for all Americans, not just new New Yorkers, were far-reaching. Children born to the new immigrants of the 1980s and 1990s, despite increasing neighborhood segregation by race, played on the streets together, attended the same schools and often married outside their racial group. In the 2000 census, 6.8 million Americans nationwide listed themselves as multiracial. Identities blurred as popular entertainment created new mixes of traditions and styles. "World beat" music (heavily influenced by "Afro-Pop"), *Alternalatiano* (alternative Latin music—a mixture of salsa and merengue), Tejano, Reggae, and other music in fusion mixtures became as common in Manhattan or Los Angeles as in Mexico City or Rio. By the 1990s, the West Indian carnival held annually in Brooklyn at the end of summer had become the most popular ethnic festival in Greater New York City.

Although smaller in number than Hispanics, Asians were the fastest growing racial group in the United States. The number of Asian Americans soared from 7.3 million in 1990 to approximately 10.2 million in 2000. With a steady flow of professionals and workers skilled in technology into their communities, Chinese Americans maintained their status as the largest Asian ethnicity in the United States. However, other groups grew at faster rates, particularly Indo Americans (from the subcontinent of India), whose numbers doubled during the 1990s to 1.68 million to become the third-largest Asian group. Meanwhile Japanese Americans, once the largest and most influential members of the pan-Asian community, declined. Immigration from Japan had virtually ceased during the decade, while many young Japanese Americans married someone of a different race.

Like earlier immigrant groups, new Americans from Korea, Vietnam, and the Philippines tended to cluster in their own communities and maintain a durable group identity. As a whole, Asian Americans made mobility through education a priority, along with pooling family capital and labor to support small businesses. Newcomers selected communities with job opportunities or where family members and friends had previously settled. This "chain migration" is illustrated by the large

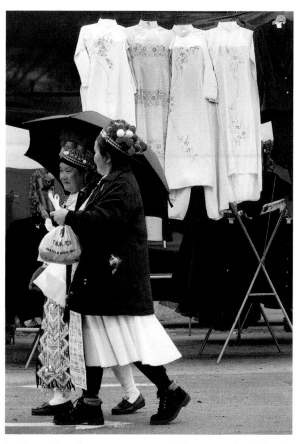

Immigrants from Hmong were among the fastest growing Asian groups in the United States in the 1990s. In Minnesota, they were the leading Asian group coming to the state. The Hmong brought traditional clothing as well as entertainments, food, and sports and established more than 400 businesses in the Minneapolis-St. Paul region.

Photograph by *The Merced Sun-Star*. AP/Wide World Photos (6090567)

numbers of Hmongs, a tribal group from Laos, living in Minneapolis and St. Paul. The stream of Hmongs began with church-sponsored refugee programs and then gained momentum as more and more family members followed. As one of the nation's leading states in the resettlement of refugees, Minnesota saw its total Asian population triple, increasing during the 1980s from 26,000 to 78,000, and then nearly doubling in the next decade.

A NEW AGE OF ANXIETY

WHAT WERE the major divisions in American society at the end of the twentieth century?

Despite the prosperity of the 1990s, many Americans experienced an uneasiness that resembled the anxiety of the mid-twentieth century when the world seemed on the brink of nuclear destruction. The threat of communism had expired along with the Cold War, but doubts and fears about the fate of their own society had multiplied. So many changes had occurred in just the last three decades of the century that a sense of permanence had disappeared. The new economy had transformed the way Americans worked and played. The new wave of immigration had dramatically altered the demographic landscape. Even the way the nation's leaders conducted themselves appeared not only new but also potentially hazardous to the moral order. In addition, many Americans had begun to fear for their personal safety, even within their own communities.

THE RACIAL DIVIDE

In the spring of 1992 an upheaval in Los Angeles offered the starkest evidence that racial tensions had not eased. The spark that ignited the worst riot of the century was outrage over police brutality. A year earlier, Rodney King, a black motorist, had been pulled from his vehicle and severely beaten by four white police officers. An amateur videotape of the incident was widely aired on television news programs. When, despite this graphic evidence, a jury acquitted the officers of all but one of eleven counts of assault, several minority communities erupted in anger. Rioters swept through South Central Los Angeles and nearby Koreatown, looting and burning businesses. Fifty-one people were killed, more than $850 million in damage was reported, and about 500 buildings were destroyed before L.A. police and National Guard troops restored order.

More than a quarter-century after the uprising in Watts, the situation in Los Angeles seemed more desperate than ever to most African Americans. The poverty rate in South Los Angeles was 30.3 percent, more than twice the national average. The unemployment rate for adult black males hovered around 40 percent, and a quarter of the population was on welfare. Drug dealing and gang warfare had escalated, reflecting the sense of despair among young people.

The events in Los Angeles exposed the deep animosity among various groups—so much so that observers referred to the event as a "multicultural riot." Almost 2,000 Korean businesses were destroyed, and Koreans angrily accused the police of making no effort to defend their stores. The division was sharpest, though, between white people and the minority populations. "We are all quite isolated in our own communities," a resident of Westwood, a mostly white middle-class neighborhood, explained. "We don't know and don't care about the problems in the inner cities. Driving to work every day most of us don't even know where South Central is—except many of us saw the fires from that direction when we were stuck in traffic."

The situation in Los Angeles was not unique. The 2000 census showed that segregation was on the rise, not only in cities but also in their surrounding sub-

QUICK REVIEW

Los Angeles Riots

- Spring 1992: Riots sparked by acquittal of officers in Rodney King case.
- Fifty-one people were killed and $850 million in damage was reported.
- Riots exposed ethnic and economic divisions in the city.

In March of 1991, arson and looting occurred in Los Angeles after the Rodney King verdict led to acquittal of four police officers on the charges of using undue force to subdue him after a traffic stop.

Gethy Images, Inc. Liaison.

urbs. For example, in the Atlanta region, which claimed the largest share of black suburbanites in the nation (26 percent), the percent living separately from whites had increased from 52 percent in 1990 to nearly 60 percent by 2000. Similarly, in the nation's schools, the gains from the civil rights era were diminishing and, in some communities, disappearing altogether. A report released in 2001 showed that, despite the increasing racial and ethnic diversity of the nation's youth, segregation was becoming more pronounced in grades K–12.

The publicity generated by the arrest of Rodney King fed several major controversies concerning the U.S. criminal justice system. Racial disparities were pronounced, with ethnic and racial minorities accounting for approximately two-thirds of state prison inmates. Based on these figures, the Bureau of Justice estimated that 28 percent of African American men would enter a state or federal prison during their lifetimes.

Various civil liberties groups reviewed these statistics and concluded that African Americans were not necessarily more prone to criminal activity but were far more likely to be stopped, searched, arrested, convicted, and given harsher penalties than white Americans. Critics singled out the practice of "racial profiling" whereby police disproportionately stopped African Americans and Latinos as the most likely offenders. By the end of the decade, in a review of various data nationwide, the National Institute of Drug Abuse estimated that although 12 percent of illegal drug users were black, they now made up 50 percent of all drug possession arrestees. By this time, "driving while black" had become a news item in all the major media, leading to the introduction of a bill into the U.S. Senate in 1999 to collect statistics on traffic stops.

THE FORCES OF FEAR

During the 1990s and first years of the new century, anxiety about terrorism and random violence escalated. Within their own borders, Americans were actually far safer from terrorist attacks than the citizens of many other countries. Nevertheless, two events—the attack on the World Trade Center in 1993 and the destruction of the federal building in Oklahoma City in 1995—alerted Americans to danger at home.

Rescue workers carried an injured man from the rubble of the U.S. Embassy in Nairobi, Kenya. A terrorist bomb killed more than 100 people and injured more than 1,600 on August 8, 1998

© AFP/CORBIS (FT0047338)

On February 26, 1993, a small group associated with Osama bin Laden bombed the World Trade Center in New York City. The terrorists used a rented van to deliver explosives that demolished an underground parking lot, killed six people, and injured more than a thousand others. Taken in retaliation for U.S. policies in the Middle East, the attack was the most destructive act of terrorism committed within the United States to that time. Despite increased surveillance of terrorist groups, bin Laden's organization struck another lethal blow. On August 7, 1998, car bombings of U.S. embassies in Nairobi, Kenya, and Dar es Salaam, Tanzania, injured more than 5,500 people and killed 225.

The bombing of the Alfred P. Murrah Federal Building in Oklahoma City raised an entirely different specter: terrorism by self-described patriotic Americans. The perpetrators represented the extremist wing of the New Right, the superpatriot movement, which included groups of people who set up "survivalist" encampments in rural areas and organized themselves into armed militias. Inspired by author William Pierce's *Turner Diaries* (1978), which predicted a revolt of "Aryans" against people of color and the federal government, the patriots found their martyrs in the Branch Davidians and their revenge in Oklahoma.

Two years earlier, on February 28, 1993, agents of the FBI and the Federal Bureau of Alcohol, Tobacco, and Firearms (ATF) had conducted a "search and arrest" operation against the Branch Davidians that turned deadly. Their object was David Koresh, the leader of the obscure religious sect who was suspected of stockpiling illegal firearms and ammunition. After a round of shots, which took the lives of four ATF agents and six Branch Davidians, Koresh's heavily armed followers barricaded themselves in their compound in Waco, Texas. Fifty-one days later, on April 19, government agents brought their siege to a fiery end. Nine Davidians managed to escape the flames engulfing their buildings, while seventy-six others, including twenty-one children, perished.

On April 19, 1995, Timothy McVeigh and his accomplices took revenge for the tragedy in Waco. Shortly after 9:00 A.M., a bomb went off in the federal office

Korean, Arab, and French small businesses serve the diverse populations of American cities.

Robert Brenner/Photo Editor

building in Oklahoma City, killing 168 people, including 19 children, and injuring more than 500 others. They had chosen April 19, the anniversary of the federal raid at Waco, as their "Date of Doom." Arrested within hours of the bombing on a misdemeanor traffic violation, McVeigh was charged in connection with the crime just three days later. After a trial in federal court and demonstrations both for and against the death penalty, he was executed in June 2001.

Terrorism continued, with many of the attacks politically or ideologically motivated. For example, medical clinics that provided abortion services to women became a prime target. Often the motivation for acts of domestic terror eluded even experts on the subject. Workers suspended from their jobs, fathers separated from their children, as well as individuals with grudges against the government turned to violence. One of the most highly publicized cases occurred in Littleton, Colorado, a mostly white, middle-class suburb of Denver. On April 20, 1999, two students at Columbine High School, armed with semiautomatic handguns, shotguns, and explosives, opened fire, killing one teacher and twelve of their classmates before killing themselves.

THE CULTURE WARS

In the 1980s and 1990s, moral and social issues, many observers noted, were replacing long-standing political markers such as religion, ethnicity, and socio-economic class. Whereas the "New Democrats" of Clinton's administration and conservative Republicans differed little on their perception of the appropriate size and power of the federal government, they were at loggerheads over what constituted American values. Thus, what one scholar described as "the struggle to define America" became hotly contested in the 1990s, with politics increasingly centered in discussions about reproductive rights and reproductive technology, homosexuality and gay rights, the curriculum in public schools, codes of speech and standards in the arts, gun control, scientific developments such as cloning, genetic alteration, and fetal tissue research, and even the validity of Darwin's theory of evolution.

The increasing racial and ethnic diversity of American society, as well as the expansion of rights for groups such as women and gays, had become the impetus for a broad and controversial movement known as **multiculturalism**. Unlike earlier conceptions of America as a "melting pot," new metaphors such as "salad bowl" or "mosaic" became popular expressions that emphasized the unique attributes and achievements of formerly marginal groups and recent immigrants. This celebration of diversity played a big part in the campaign strategy of Bill Clinton, and he won a large share of votes by tailoring his appeals to specific groups. Like other Democrats, he received upward of 80 percent of black votes, but he won more votes from Latinos and Asian Americans than any other candidate in American history. On college campuses, multiculturalism marked the high point of the curricular reform that had been ongoing since the late 1960s and early 1970s, when specialized programs in women's studies and African American studies were launched (see Chapter 29).

For many conservatives, multiculturalism had replaced communism as the nation's most dangerous enemy, and they rallied to reinstate what they called universal truths and traditional moral values. University of Chicago professor Allan Bloom's best-selling *The Closing of the American Mind* (1987), for example, argued that the new lesson plans failed to prepare Americans for the responsibility of preserving their democratic legacy.

The culture wars were not restricted to the academic world. Americans divided sharply over many issues, including immigration policy. In 1994, a referendum on California's ballot, **Proposition 187**, called for making all undocumented aliens ineligible for any welfare services, schooling, and nonemergency medical care, and it required teachers and clinic doctors to report illegal immigrants to the police. Proposition 187 passed by a three to two margin, but it was immediately challenged in the streets and in the courts. In 1998, after several years of legal wrangling, a Los Angeles federal district court judge ruled that Proposition 187 unconstitutionally usurped federal authority over immigration policy. In June 2001, the U.S. Supreme Court ruled that immigrants are entitled to the same protection by the Constitution as that afforded to citizens.

But the national debate over immigration policy, in which economic issues and racial fears were deeply entangled, continued unabated in California and elsewhere. As one Stanford law professor who had worked to overturn Proposition 187 put it: "Some people genuinely worry about the problem of too many immigrants in a stagnant economy. But for most, economics is a diversion. Underneath it is race."

A similar backlash gathered steam against gays. A major controversy erupted around a push for the legal recognition of marriage for same-sex couples. Although the first lawsuits dated to the early 1970s, in May 1993 the Supreme Court of Hawai'i ruled that the laws barring same-sex couples from getting a marriage license were discriminatory and, therefore, in violation of the state constitution. This highly controversial decision prompted conservative state legislators to propose an amendment to the state constitution barring same-sex marriages, which the Hawai'ian voters overwhelmingly approved in 1998. Meanwhile, several Republicans in the U.S. Congress, fearing that if any state recog-

Multiculturalism Movement that emphasized the unique attributes and achievements of formerly marginal groups and recent immigrants.

Proposition 187 California legislation adopted by popular vote in California in 1994, which cuts off state-funded health and education benefits to undocumented or illegal immigrants.

nized same-sex marriages all other states would be forced to recognize these marriages as legal, sponsored legislation to deny recognition to these unions. In 1996, President Clinton signed the **Defense of Marriage Act**, which specified that gay couples would be ineligible for spousal benefits provided by federal law. By the end of the century, more than thirty states had enacted similar legislation. Vermont, however, stood alone, becoming the first state to recognize civil unions, allowing same-sex couples to receive many, although not all, of the legal benefits of marriage.

At the end of the century, the antiabortion movement took a new turn by opposing government financing of an area of scientific research that had been growing in importance since the birth of the first test-tube baby in 1981—embryonic stem cell research. Because these microscopic clusters of cells have the potential to grow into any tissue in the body, embryonic stem cells hold promise, scientists believe, for refurbishing or replacing damaged tissues or organs and therefore might prove useful in treating or perhaps even curing diseases such as diabetes, Parkinson's, and Alzheimer's. Conservatives opposed this research because it involves the destruction of human embryos, usually derived from the excess products of *in vitro* fertilization processes and scheduled for disposal by fertility clinics. In 1995, in response to pressure from conservative groups such as the National Right to Life Committee, Congress enacted legislation banning the use of federal funds for research that involves the destruction of human embryos. However, in his last year in office, Clinton loosened the ban and thereby generated another round of controversy. Most conservative groups remained firm in their opposition, agreeing with the United States Conference of Catholic Bishops, which insisted "that the government must not treat any living human being as research material, as a mere means for benefit to others."

HIGH CRIMES AND MISDEMEANORS

During the 1994 election campaign, the Republicans targeted the key item in Clinton's liberal agenda, reform of the nation's health-care system. President Clinton had appointed Hillary Rodham Clinton to head a task force charged with preparing a sweeping legislative overhaul of health care. The task force sought a political middle ground between conservative approaches, which stressed fine-tuning the system by making private insurance available to all, and more liberal approaches, which would have the federal government guarantee health care as a right. Powerful forces such as the Chamber of Commerce, the National Association of Manufacturers, and most Republicans immediately attacked the proposal. The Health Insurance Association of America spent millions of dollars on negative advertisements. In August, as the 1994 election campaign moved into its final phase, the president conceded that his proposal had died in Congress.

Voter turnout was light in most areas, but the majority who voted turned firmly against Clinton. Republicans gained control of both the House and Senate for the first time in forty years—a disaster of historic proportions for Clinton and the Democratic Party. Congress was now dominated by a new breed of younger, ideologically more conservative Republicans led by the new House Speaker, Newt Gingrich of Georgia.

Gingrich, first elected to Congress in 1978, had quickly won a reputation as a formidable polemicist for the Republican Party's far right. With his scathing denunciations of big government and celebration of entrepreneurship, Gingrich challenged Clinton as the key figure setting the nation's political agenda. His priorities were expressed in a set of proposals labeled the "**Contract with America.**" Invoking the "hundred days" of Franklin D. Roosevelt's New Deal in 1933 (see

Defense of Marriage Act Act which specified that gay couples would be ineligible for spousal benefits provided by federal law.

Contract with America Platform proposing a sweeping reduction in the role and activities of the federal government on which many Republican candidates ran for Congress in 1994.

Chapter 24), Gingrich promised to bring all these proposals to a vote in the House within a hundred days. The House did indeed pass much of the "Contract," including a large tax cut, an increase in military spending, cutbacks in federal regulatory power in the environment and at the workplace, a tough anticrime bill, and a sharp reduction in federal welfare programs.

Differences with the Senate, however, and the threat of presidential veto ultimately thwarted Gingrich's plans and created conditions that allowed President Clinton to make a political comeback. In December 1995 the Republican-controlled Congress forced a shutdown of the federal government rather than accede to President Clinton's demand for changes in their proposed budget. The result was a public relations disaster for the Republicans. Gingrich's reputation plummeted, and after little more than a year as Speaker he had become one of the most unpopular figures in American politics.

Meanwhile, Clinton undercut the Republicans by adapting many of their positions to his own. He endorsed the goal of a balanced federal budget and declared, in his January 1996 State of the Union message, that "the era of big government is over." With such deft maneuvers, the president set the theme for his 1996 reelection campaign, portraying himself as a reasonable conservative and the Republicans in Congress as conservative radicals.

While the Republican contender, Robert Dole of Kansas, majority leader of the Senate, waged an inept campaign for president, Clinton and his staff crafted a brilliant and well-funded one. Confounding the predictions of the political pundits who had pronounced his political death, the president won a resounding reelection victory in November 1996. He won 49 percent of the popular vote compared to Dole's 41 percent and carried thirty-three states.

During his second term as president, Clinton had to answer many questions about his moral conduct. Real estate deals involving both him and Hillary Rodham Clinton blew up into a major scandal known as **Whitewater**. More predictive of troubles ahead, a former Arkansas state employee, Paula Jones, charged Clinton with sexual assault during his gubernatorial term. Attorney General Janet Reno, under extreme pressure from conservatives, appointed an independent counsel, former judge Kenneth Starr, to investigate allegations. But in the summer of 1998, Starr delivered to the House Judiciary Committee a report focusing on an extramarital affair that the president conducted with a young White House intern, Monica Lewinsky. Starr's report outlined several potential impeachable offenses, including false testimony under oath, witness tampering, and obstruction of justice, all allegedly committed by the president to keep his relationship with Lewinsky secret.

After agreeing to testify before a grand jury empaneled by Starr—a first for an American president—Clinton made an extraordinary television address to the nation. He defended his legal position and attacked the Starr inquiry as politically motivated. The Congress and the American people at large fiercely debated the nature of the charges against the president: Were they truly impeachable—"high crimes and misdemeanors" as the Constitution put it—or merely part of a partisan political effort to overturn the election of 1996? For only the third time in history, in October 1998, the House of Representatives voted to open an inquiry into possible grounds for the impeachment.

Whitewater Arkansas real estate development in which Bill and Hillary Clinton were investors; several fraud convictions resulted from investigations into Whitewater, but evidence was not found that the Clintons were involved in wrongdoing.

Republicans hoping to reap a wholesale victory from the scandal in the fall elections were bitterly disappointed. Contrary to predictions and traditions in off-term elections, the president's party added seats, trimming the Republican majority in the 105th Congress. Higher than expected turnout from such core constituencies as union members and African Americans (especially in the South) also contributed to the unexpectedly strong Democratic showing. The election also brought a shakeup in the Republican leadership. Newt Gingrich, under pressure from Republican colleagues angry about a campaign strategy that had narrowly focused on Clinton's impeachment problem, announced his resignation as Speaker of the House and from his seat in Congress.

In the aftermath of the 1998 election, most politicians and analysts, and indeed most Americans, believed the impeachment inquiry to be at a dead end. But the House Judiciary Committee, after raucous televised debate, voted to bring four articles of impeachment—charging President Clinton with perjury, obstruction of justice, witness tampering, and abuse of power—to the full House. Neither the 1998 election results, nor polls showing a large majority of Americans opposed to removing the president, curbed the Republican determination to push impeachment through the House and then on to the Senate for trial. On February 12, 1999, the Senate trial concluded with the president's acquittal.

THE NEW MILLENNIUM

At the beginning of the twenty-first century, citizens, politicians, and business and religious leaders had to rethink their basic assumptions about the American way of life. American society had become more stratified along lines of race and income. New immigrant groups, especially from Asia and Latin America, had changed the face of the nation's communities, schools, and workplaces. New media technologies had made cultural life more homogenized and caused the manipulation of image to become more crucial than ever to both politics and entertainment. The New Economy, service oriented and high tech, had fundamentally altered the way many Americans did business and earned a livelihood, and it depended not only on American consumers heavily burdened with debt, but also on an expanding global market.

HOW DID the threat of international terrorism transform the American political landscape in the first decade of the twenty-first century?

The end of the Cold War had reconfigured global politics, ending the bilateralism that had dominated international affairs since the end of World War II. The United States alone held fast to its superpower status, but this achievement did not necessarily make Americans more secure or safe. The old enemy, Soviet communism, was succeeded by more fanatic, less predictable foes. It was clear that international terrorism was emerging as a persistent threat, as witnessed by yet another terrorist attack, the October 12, 2000, bombing of the USS *Cole* in Aden, Yemen, which cost the lives of seventeen American sailors.

THE ELECTION OF 2000

After a relatively dull campaign season, the 2000 election played out as high drama. Voters went to the polls as usual on election day, watched as late-night television newscasters projected a victory for the Democratic candidate, Clinton's vice president Al Gore, and then woke up the next morning to learn that perhaps the winner was not the vice president but his Republican opponent, Governor George W. Bush of Texas, son of former president George H. W. Bush. It was clear that Gore and his running mate, Connecticut Senator Joseph Lieberman, had won the popular vote, although by the closest margin since John F. Kennedy defeated Richard Nixon in 1961. In doubt was the number of votes in the Electoral College. At 2:15 A.M., the pollsters who had projected Gore as the winner changed their minds. The cliffhanger in Florida had finally ended with the state's decisive twenty-five electoral votes earmarked for the Republicans. By morning Gore had called Bush to concede. The *New York Times*, however, ran a guarded headline "Bush Appears to Defeat Gore." Only a few hundred votes in Florida gave Bush the edge, and in cases where the margin is so narrow Florida law mandates a machine recount in all sixty-seven counties. Gore soon retracted his concession, putting voters into suspense until the middle of December, when the vice president finally ended his campaign.

Such a spectacular ending to the 2000 campaign could not have been foreseen from the primaries. As the son of a former president, George W. Bush had run a low-key campaign, calling himself a "compassionate conservative" who cared about the underdog and the nation's educational system. He nevertheless did not swerve from the Republican agenda that President Reagan had shaped: tax cuts, strong military defense, and the overhaul of Social Security and Medicare. He also promised relief from environmental regulations, new judicial appointments that would eventually limit reproductive rights, and the restoration of morality to public life. Albert Gore Jr., also the son of a prominent politician, carried the burden of association with Bill Clinton and waged an uphill battle. More notable was his running mate, Lieberman, the first Jewish candidate for vice president. Dick Cheney, who had served prominently in the senior Bush's administration, balanced the younger Bush's relative lack of experience in federal government. The emergence of consumer advocate Ralph Nader as Green Party candidate added spice to an often dull campaign.

The 2000 campaign played out as the first disputed presidential election since 1876, when Democrat Samuel J. Tilden, who won the popular vote, charged his Republican opponent, Rutherford B. Hayes, with fraudulent vote counting. A similar question of legitimacy hung over the 2000 election. After Florida completed its machine recount of votes, the Democrats requested a hand tally in selected counties where the ballots were in dispute. The Republicans responded by suing in the Miami district court to prohibit the manual recounting. Meanwhile Florida election officials, mainly Republicans, set November 14 as the date to certify the election results, thereby disallowing the returns on overseas ballots which might favor Al Gore. In turn, Democrats sued to extend the deadline. Eventually, appeals by both parties reached the Florida Supreme Court and finally the U.S. Supreme Court, which voted 5 to 4 along partisan lines to halt the counting. Time had run out, and on December 12 Gore conceded defeat. With less fanfare than usual, George W. Bush took the oath of office in January 2001.

MAP EXPLORATION

To explore an interactive version of this map, go to
http://www.prenhall.com/faraghertlc/map31.1

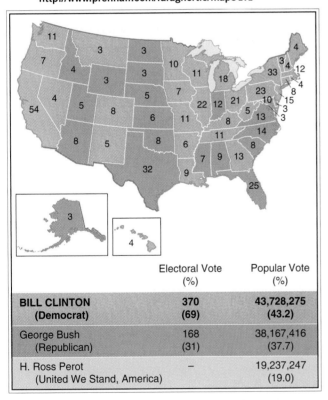

	Electoral Vote (%)	Popular Vote (%)
BILL CLINTON (Democrat)	**370** **(69)**	**43,728,275** **(43.2)**
George Bush (Republican)	168 (31)	38,167,416 (37.7)
H. Ross Perot (United We Stand, America)	–	19,237,247 (19.0)

MAP 31-1

The Election of 2000 The 2000 presidential election was the closest one in U.S. history and the first one to be decided by a decision of the Supreme Court.

WHY DID the framers of the Constitution create the electoral college? Does the election of 2000 support the argument for direct election of presidents?

A GLOBAL COMMUNITY?

Beginning in the 1970s, social scientists began to study and debate the degree to which people throughout the world were affected by events happening far from their homelands. The big questions concerning globalization centered on political economy. Now that communism has collapsed, they asked, would a steady expansion of free trade among nations create the basis for a global community?

There were many answers to this question. Some observers argued that the interpenetration of markets and cultural patterns—the enormous sales of Hollywood movies in China, for example—set the stage for other exchanges. Others argued that the global economy depended less on "interpenetration" than "domination" of the marketplace by the

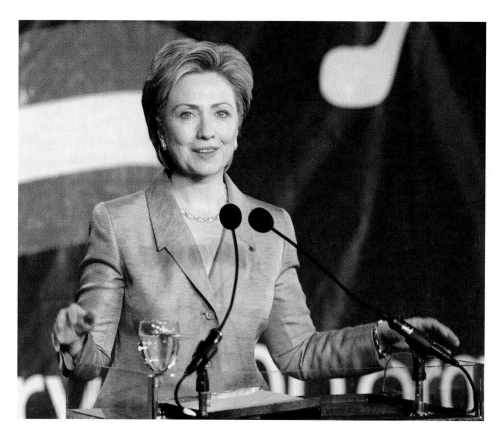

First Lady and New York State U.S. Senator-elect Hillary Rodham Clinton addresses supporters during her victory rally. Senator Clinton made history in the election of 2000 by becoming the first First Lady ever to be elected to public office.

AP/Wide World photos

industrialized nations. Whereas physical occupation of territory defined the form of colonialism that prevailed before World War II, a new "colonialism" had come into existence since the 1960s that relied on a few multinational corporations controlling distant economies throughout the world. To back up this argument, they referred to a UN report that estimated that about 90 percent of the multinational corporations that did business worldwide were headquartered in the industrialized nations of North America, Europe, and Japan. Known collectively as the Triad, the consortium of these nations, home to only 15 percent of the world's population, produced nearly 75 percent of the world's goods by the late 1990s. Some traditional economists discounted the significance of these developments, insisting that trading activities date to the earliest civilizations and that well-organized transnational economies were the hallmark of the Industrial Age.

What made the current trend toward "globalization" distinctive was, therefore, not the rate of growth but the absolute volume and character of the exchange. Revenues from multinational corporations grew phenomenonally at the end of the twentieth century. Because the member nations of the Triad were homes to the world's largest multinational corporations, they also reaped the largest share of the wealth. A UN annual human development report stated that "global inequalities in income and living standards have reached grotesque proportions." The report offered statistics showing that the gap in wealth between the upper 20 percent and the world's poorest people was at the end of the nineteenth century 30 to 1; by 1990 it reached 60 to 1; and by the end of the century it had widened to 74 to 1.

While many political observers and scholars predicted that globalization would bring both free markets and democracy to more and more of the world's people, others became increasingly skeptical. At the turn of the twenty-first century, an international protest movement emerged that targeted the most powerful organization in the global economy, the World Trade Organization (WTO) and the International Monetary Fund (IMF), or World Bank. In November 1999, thousands of protestors converged in Seattle, Washington, site of the annual meeting of the WTO, only to be pushed back by local police. In response, the WTO formulated new procedures for its meetings, secreting delegates behind walls and banning demonstrations from the area near future sites. Nevertheless, confrontations continued, the most dramatic occurring at a meeting of delegates from the eight leading industrial nations in Genoa, Italy, in 2001, which resulted in the death of one protestor.

Experts on globalization could not agree if the trend toward a single international market challenged traditional notions of national sovereignty and laid the foundation for global democracy or if the post–Cold War world order was increasingly challenged by civil wars, ethnic and religious clashes, and the breakup of nation-states.

TERRORIST ATTACK ON AMERICA

On September 11, 2001, hijackers, armed only with knives and box cutters, crashed two jetliners (one into each of) New York's World Trade Center towers, while a third jetliner slammed into the Pentagon in Virginia. A fourth plane, diverted from its terrorist mission by courageous passengers, hurtled to the ground near Pittsburgh. In all, 246 people perished in the four planes. At the sites of the attack, the damage was devastating. At the Pentagon, which had been built to withstand terrorist attacks, a

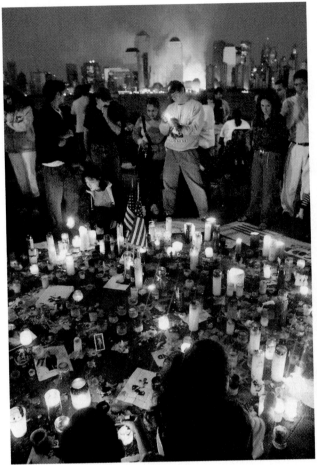

By the evening of September 11, groups of people across the nation gathered in candlelight vigils to honor the victims of the terrorist attacks. President Bush declared September 14 a National Day of Prayer and Remembrance.

© Reuters New Media Inc./CORBIS

huge explosion followed by fierce fires destroyed a large section of the defense complex. The death toll soon reached 184, including 59 people who had been on board the hijacked airliner. In New York, the number of lives lost was, as Mayor Rudolph W. Giulani said, "horrendous." The collapse of the twin towers, most likely caused by the intense fires propelled by the planes' jet fuel, brought death to thousands, including hundreds of police and rescue workers who had dashed into the buildings to help. At the end of the day, the New York City Fire Department had lost 350 firefighters, nearly thirty times the number ever lost by the department in a single incident. The nation watched in horror as the events vividly unfolded in live newscoverage on TV. The stark images of the second plane hitting the WTC, the dramatic collapse of the buildings, and the fear on the faces of thousands fleeing the sites were replayed over and over again on televisions throughout the world.

While the media recalled Pearl Harbor, President Bush declared the deadly attacks an act of war and vowed to hunt down those responsible for the "evil, despicable acts of terror." Congress, with only one dissenting vote, granted him power to take whatever steps necessary. The Department of Justice began what it described as the largest and most intensive investigation ever conducted, and the president issued a blanket warning to all nations who harbor terrorists. Secretary of State Colin Powell stated clearly, "You're either with us or against us." For the first time ever, NATO invoked the mutual defense clause in its founding treaty, which in effect supported any U.S. military response.

Observers described Bush's response as the defining moment of his presidency, as it was for the lives of many Americans. A patriotic surge found flags displayed on homes and cars—even painted on the faces of children. Millions of

Americans rushed to donate blood, and thousands traveled to New York to assist rescue efforts. Prayer vigils were held in churches, synagogues, and mosques, as well as in public buildings and parks. Millions of dollars were soon raised for the relief effort and to assist the families of those who perished.

Many businesses, especially those in the travel, entertainment, or hazardous materials industries, were closed in the days following the attack. Perhaps most dramatic was the unprecedented shutdown of all airports in the United States, stranding thousands around the world. Service returned several days later at greatly

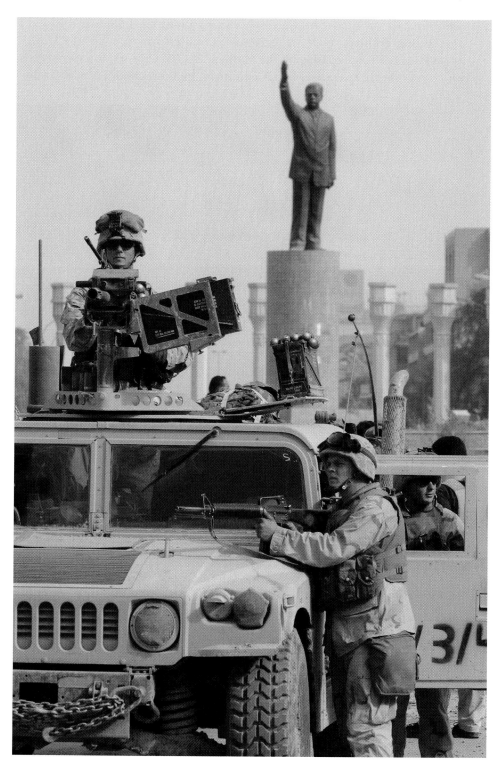

U.S. troops move into the center of Baghdad. A statue of deposed dictator Saddam Hussein is seen in the background. The statue was later toppled by troops and dragged through the streets by the Iraqi citizenry.

Peter Arnold Inc.

reduced levels and with enhanced security. President Bush created a new Cabinet-level agency, Homeland Security, charged with coordinating the efforts of more than forty other agencies to protect Americans against terrorists and to respond to any such attacks. He also allocated millions of dollars to boost the budgets of the Department of Defense, the CIA, and the FBI.

The day following the highly coordinated terrorist attack, President Bush identified the Saudi Arabian Osama bin Laden as the prime suspect. Administration officials linked the airline hijackers, all presumed to be Islamic fundamentalists, to his Al-Qaeda network, which apparently had dispatched them to train at American flight schools. In 1998, bin Laden had issued a decree that granted religious legitimacy to all efforts to expel the United States from the lands of Islam in the Middle East. His network of terrorist cells, which reportedly operated in sixty countries, had directed rage at what they

President George W. Bush, along with British Prime Minister Tony Blair, assembled a "coalition of the willing" to invade Iraq and depose Saddam Hussein.

AP/Wide World Photos.

CHRONOLOGY

1981 MTV and CNN start broadcasting as cable channels.

1986 Immigration Reform and Control Act addresses concerns about illegal aliens.

1987 Allan Bloom publishes *The Closing of the American Mind*.

1988 Indian Gaming Regulatory Act allows Indian tribes to operate gambling establishments.

George H.W. Bush is elected president.

Terrorist attack on Pam Am plane over Lockerbie, Scotland.

1989 Tiananmen Square demonstration in China.

Communist authority collapses in Eastern Europe.

1990 August: Iraqi invasion of Kuwait leads to massive U.S. military presence in the Persian Gulf.

1991 January–February: Operation Desert Storm forces Iraq out of Kuwait.

Operation Rescue launched in Wichita, Kansas.

Soviet Union dissolves into Commonwealth of Independent States.

1992 Rodney King verdict sparks rioting in Los Angeles.

UN holds first Earth Summit.

Bill Clinton is elected president.

1993 Terrorist bombing of World Trade Center kills six people.

Federal agents conduct seige of Branch Davidian compound in Waco, Texas.

Clinton administration introduces comprehensive health-care reform, but it fails to win passage in Congress.

Congress approves the North American Free Trade Agreement.

1994 Republicans win control of Senate and House for first time in forty years.

Congress approves the General Agreement on Tariffs and Trade.

Congress passes the Comprehensive AIDS Revenue Emergency Act.

Congress passes Defense of Marriage Act.

California voters approve Proposition 187.

1995 Bombing of Alfred P. Murrah Federal Building in Oklahoma City kills 168 people.

Clinton announces Dayton Accords to mediate civil war in Bosnia.

1996 Congress passes Welfare Reform Act.

Congress enacts the Antiterrorism and Effective Death Penalty Act.

President Bill Clinton is reelected.

1997 Kyoto Protocol endorsed by European Union, but not United States.

1998 U.S. embassies in Kenya and Tanzania bombed by terrorists.

House of Representatives votes to impeach President Clinton, but vote fails in Senate.

1999 United States joins NATO forces in Kosovo.

Protesters disrupt meetings of the World Trade Organization in Seattle.

2000 USS *Cole* bombed by terrorists.

2001 George W. Bush becomes president after contested election.

Terrorists attack World Trade Center and Pentagon.

United States begins military campaign in Afghanistan.

believe to be the global arrogance of the United States—its accumulation of unprecedented wealth when poverty and hopelessness extended across the Middle East.

With bin Laden presumed to be hiding in Afghanistan and supported by the ruling Taliban government, President Bush insisted that the Taliban regime hand over the terrorists "or they will share in their fate." He dispatched U.S. aircraft carriers to join the U.S. forces already assembled in the Persian Gulf region and mobilized reservists for a possible invasion. On October 7, he ordered the first air strikes in Afghanistan, with the stated goal of destroying Al-Qaeda's terrorist training camps and bringing down the Taliban government that was shielding bin Laden.

CONCLUSION

Although the attack on the WTC and the Pentagon stunned and infuriated most Americans, it represented only the most destructive in the series of terrorist attacks that had been levied against the United States since the 1980s. In 1999, the U.S. Commission on National Security/Twenty-first Century, established by Congress to evaluate the nation's defense systems, had concluded that "America will become increasingly vulnerable to hostile attack on our homeland" and that "Americans will likely die on American soil, possibly in large numbers." The security promised by the end of the Cold War seemed more elusive than ever. By early 2002, the Taliban government had collapsed much sooner than anticipated by U.S. military advisors. However, the war continued. President Bush, who had asked Americans to be patient "in understanding that it will take time to achieve our goals," broadened the scope and declared a world-wide war on terrorism.

SUMMARY

A New World Order The collapse of communism did not bring an era of peace. Conflicts broke out in the Middle East and the Balkans that involved the United States militarily. The aftermath of the Gulf War was worsening tensions in the Middle East.

Changing American Communities The recession and budget deficits of the late 1980s helped Bill Clinton win the 1992 election. Clinton broke the gridlock between Democrats and Republicans to pass legislation on welfare reform and trade. The economy boomed with growth occurring through the consolidation of the new economy epitomized by Silicon Valley. Developments in media and information technology helped create an electronic culture. Another trend was a large increase in immigration, especially from Latin America and Asia, that led to the development of new communities and cultural expressions.

A New Age of Anxiety The economic prosperity did not touch every American. Significant numbers of African Americans and Latinos lived in poverty and were subject to greater police scrutiny and imprisonment. Tensions rose between various groups raising the issue of race. At the same time, terrorist attacks grew more violent and frequent, with tragic consequences. Amid this turbulence, a debate emerged between conservatives and liberals over multiculturalism, abortion, gay rights, and evolution. In government, the election of young conservative Republicans who gained control of Congress in 1994 created conflict with the Clinton administration. Clinton won reelection but soon was embroiled in scandals on sex allegations and eventually in impeachment proceedings.

The New Millennium George W. Bush won the hotly disputed election of 2000. He showed a conservative bent by calling for a tax cut and strong military defense. The globalization movement focused on the economy, and the power of multinational corporations in the United States, Europe, and Japan prompted criticisms. The terrorist suicide attacks on the World Trade Center and the Pentagon led to the declaration of a war on terrorism and heightened security in the United States.

REVIEW QUESTIONS

1. Is the United States entering a "new era" in the twenty-first century? What effects have the globalized economy and the fall of the Soviet Union had on American political life?

2. How is the "new" economy different from the "old" economy? How has it reshaped American business and financial practices? Explain the relationship between the new economy and electronic media, such as the Internet and cable television.

3. Evaluate the presidency of Bill Clinton. Compare his domestic and foreign policies to those of the Republican presidents who preceded and followed him in office. What was the impact of the scandals that plagued his presidency?

4. Describe the major demographic trends revealed by the 2000 census. Identify the racial and ethnic groups with the greatest gains in population. How have various legislation acts since 1965 affected immigration to the United States? How have communities changed as a result of the influx of new immigrants?

5. The concept of globalization is highly controversial. Are borders between nations "melting away" as some scholars contend? How does this concept square with the description of the United States as the single superpower in the world? Does this concept apply primarily to economics, or is it useful for discussing issues related to culture, media, the environment, and population trends?

6. Earlier scholars predicted that the end of the Cold War would bring peace and promote democracy throughout the world. Events, beginning with the Persian Gulf War, have instead suggested a new basis for international affairs. Describe the importance of regional and ethnic conflicts in the Middle East and Central Europe.

KEY TERMS

Bosnia (p. 870)

Contract with America (p. 883)

Defense of Marriage Act (p. 883)

Gramm-Rudman (p. 871)

Internet (p. 873)

Kosovo (p. 870)

Multiculturalism (p. 882)

North American Free Trade Agreement (NAFTA) (p. 872)

Operation Desert Storm (p. 868)

Persian Gulf War (p. 869)

Proposition 187 (p. 882)

Silicon Valley (p. 873)

Whitewater (p. 884)

World Trade Organization (WTO) (p. 872)

World Wide Web (p. 875)

RECOMMENDED READING

Angus Kress Gillespie, *Twin Towers: The Life of New York City's World Trade Center* (1999). A detailed history of the buildings, including the political background and the process of design and construction. Gillespie traces the emergence of the World Trade Center as a popular symbol of New York City and center of international commerce.

Mark S. Hamm, *Apocalypse in Oklahoma: Waco and Ruby Ridge Revenge* (1997). Provides a succinct overview of the events leading to the bombing of the federal building in Oklahoma City in 1995, seeing it as an act of murderous revenge.

David Held, ed., *A Globalizing World? Culture, Economics, Politics* (2000). Four essays addressing various aspects of globalization. This slim volume offers a concise summary of the major theories of globalization and compares the contemporary situation with previous eras.

Neil Howe, *Millennials Rising: The Next Generation* (2000). An optimistic assessment of the generation of Americans who were born in or after 1982 and projections for their future. Howe surveys statistics as well as cultural trends and concludes that the rising generation shows a return to conservative family values and a respect for rules.

William G. Hyland, *Clinton's World: Remaking American Foreign Policy* (1999). Evaluates the first post–Cold War president's decisions with regard to the major international events of the 1990s. Examines the developing policies toward Russia and Asia. Hyland offers a fairly negative assessment.

Robert K. Kaplan, *The Coming Anarchy: Shattering the Dreams of the Post–Cold War* (2000). Nine essays on international affairs that provide an often disturbing assessment of the prospects for peace. Kaplan discusses the rise of ethnic conflict in regions such as Sierra Leone, Russia, and India and weighs the signficance of increasing tribalistic warfare, the breakdown of central government authority in several nations, and the rise in crime in post-Communist countries.

Judith Millwer, Stephen Engelberg, and William Broad, *Germs: Biological Weapons and America's Secret War* (2001). Beginning with the use of salmonella to poison food in Oregon in 1984, this book narrates the history of biological warfare in the last half of the twentieth century. The authors, veteran reporters for the *New York Times*, argue that the United States is ill equipped to protect its citizens against a serious biological attack.

Jill Nelson, ed., *Police Brutality: An Anthology* (2000). Twelve essays written by scholars, activists, and writers that discuss, from a variety of perspectives, police presence in American communities. Several essays focus on the broad historical dimensions of this issue, tracing the roots back to the time of slavery.

New York Times staffwriters, *The Downsizing of America* (1996). A well-researched account detailing the devastating impact of corporate "downsizing" on American communities and families.

Howard Rheingold, *The Virtual Community* (1994). Very thoughtful examination of the promises and problems posed by the new computer-based technologies associated with "virtual communities."

Micah L. Sifry and Christopher Cerf, eds., *The Gulf War Reader* (1991). An excellent collection of historical essays, government documents, and political addresses that provides a comprehensive overview of the Persian Gulf War.

Janet Thomas, *The Battle in Seattle: The Story Behind and Beyond the WTO* (2000). An impassioned, eyewitness account by a participant in the 1999 demonstrations against the World Trade Organization, which the author describes as a "global tailspin at the end of the century."

APPENDIX

The Declaration of Independence

When in the course of human events it becomes necessary for one people to dissolve the political bands which have connected them with another and to assume, among the powers of the earth, the separate and equal station to which the laws of nature and of nature's God entitle them, a decent respect to the opinions of mankind requires that they should declare the causes which impel them to the separation.

We hold these truths to be self-evident, that all men are created equal; that they are endowed by their Creator with certain unalienable rights; that among these are life, liberty, and the pursuit of happiness. That, to secure these rights, governments are instituted among men, deriving their just powers from the consent of the governed; that, whenever any form of government becomes destructive of these ends, it is the right of the people to alter or to abolish it, and to institute a new government, laying its foundation on such principles, and organizing its powers in such form, as to them shall seem most likely to effect their safety and happiness. Prudence, indeed, will dictate that governments long established should not be changed for light and transient causes; and, accordingly, all experience hath shown that mankind are more disposed to suffer, while evils are sufferable, than to right themselves by abolishing the forms to which they are accustomed. But when a long train of abuses and usurpations, pursuing invariably the same object, evinces a design to reduce them under absolute despotism, it is their right, it is their duty, to throw off such government and to provide new guards for their future security. Such has been the patient sufferance of these colonies, and such is now the necessity which constrains them to alter their former systems of government. The history of the present King of Great Britain is a history of repeated injuries and usurpations, all having, in direct object, the establishment of an absolute tyranny over these States. To prove this, let facts be submitted to a candid world:

He has refused his assent to laws the most wholesome and necessary for the public good.

He has forbidden his governors to pass laws of immediate and pressing importance, unless suspended in their operation till his assent should be obtained; and, when so suspended, he has utterly neglected to attend to them.

He has refused to pass other laws for the accommodation of large districts of people, unless those people would relinquish the right of representation in the legislature, a right inestimable to them and formidable to tyrants only.

He has called together legislative bodies at places unusual, uncomfortable, and distant from the depository of their public records, for the sole purpose of fatiguing them into compliance with his measures.

He has dissolved representative houses, repeatedly for opposing, with manly firmness, his invasions on the rights of the people.

He has refused, for a long time after such dissolutions, to cause others to be elected; whereby the legislative powers, incapable of annihilation, have returned to the people at large for their exercise; the state remaining, in the meantime, exposed to all the danger of invasion from without and convulsions within.

He has endeavored to prevent the population of these States; for that purpose, obstructing the laws for naturalization of foreigners, refusing to pass others to encourage their migration hither, and raising the conditions of new appropriations of lands.

He has obstructed the administration of justice by refusing his assent to laws for establishing judiciary powers.

He has made judges dependent on his will alone for the tenure of their offices and the amount and payment of their salaries.

He has erected a multitude of new offices and sent hither swarms of officers to harass our people and eat out their substance.

He has kept among us, in time of peace, standing armies, without the consent of our legislatures.

He has affected to render the military independent of, and superior to, the civil power.

He has combined with others to subject us to a jurisdiction foreign to our Constitution and unacknowledged by our laws, giving his assent to their acts of pretended legislation—

For quartering large bodies of armed troops among us;

For protecting them by mock trial, from punishment for any murders which they should commit on the inhabitants of these States;

For cutting off our trade with all parts of the world;

For imposing taxes on us without our consent;

For depriving us, in many cases, of the benefit of trial by jury;

For transporting us beyond seas to be tried for pretended offences;

For abolishing the free system of English laws in a neighboring province, establishing therein an arbitrary government, and enlarging its boundaries, so as to render it at once an example and fit instrument for introducing the same absolute rule into these colonies;

For taking away our charters, abolishing our most valuable laws, and altering, fundamentally, the powers of our governments.

For suspending our own legislatures and declaring themselves invested with power to legislate for us in all cases whatsoever.

He has abdicated government here by declaring us out of his protection and waging war against us.

He has plundered our seas, ravaged our coasts, burnt our towns, and destroyed the lives of our people.

He is, at this time, transporting large armies of foreign mercenaries to complete the works of death, desolation, and tyranny already begun with circumstances of cruelty and perfidy scarcely paralleled in the most barbarous ages, and totally unworthy the head of a civilized nation.

He has constrained our fellow citizens, taken captive on the high seas, to bear arms against their country, to become the executioners of their friends and brethren, or to fall themselves by their hands.

He has excited domestic insurrections amongst us and has endeavored to bring on the inhabitants of our frontiers, the merciless Indian savages, whose known rule of warfare is an undistinguished destruction of all ages, sexes, and conditions.

In every stage of these oppressions, we have petitioned for redress in the most humble terms; our repeated petitions have been answered only by repeated injury. A prince whose character is thus marked by every act which may define a tyrant is unfit to be the ruler of a free people.

Nor have we been wanting in attention to our British brethren. We have warned them, from time to time, of attempts made by their legislature to extend an unwarrantable jurisdiction over us. We have reminded them of the circumstances of our emigration and settlement here. We have appealed to their native justice and magnanimity, and

we have conjured them, by the ties of our common kindred, to disavow these usurpations, which would inevitably interrupt our connections and correspondence. They, too, have been deaf to the voice of justice and consanguinity. We must, therefore, acquiesce in the necessity which denounces our separation, and hold them, as we hold the rest of mankind, enemies in war, in peace, friends.

We, therefore, the representatives of the United States of America, in general Congress assembled, appealing to the Supreme Judge of the world for the rectitude of our intentions, do, in the name and by the authority of the good people of these colonies, solemnly publish and declare, that these united colonies are, and of right ought to be, free and independent states: that they are absolved from all allegiance to the British Crown, and that all political connection between them and the state of Great Britain is, and ought to be, totally dissolved; and that, as free and independent states, they have full power to levy war, conclude peace, contract alliances, establish commerce, and to do all other acts and things which independent states may of right do. And, for the support of this declaration, with a firm reliance on the protection of Divine Providence, we mutually pledge to each other our lives, our fortunes, and our sacred honor.

THE CONSTITUTION OF THE UNITED STATES OF AMERICA

We the people of the United States, in order to form a more perfect union, establish justice, insure domestic tranquillity, provide for the common defense, promote the general welfare, and secure the blessings of liberty to ourselves and our posterity, do ordain and establish this Constitution for the United States of America.

ARTICLE I

SECTION 1.   All legislative powers herein granted shall be vested in a Congress of the United States, which shall consist of a Senate and House of Representatives.

SECTION 2.   1. The House of Representatives shall be composed of members chosen every second year by the people of the several States, and the electors in each State shall have the qualifications requisite for electors of the most numerous branch of the State legislature.

2. No person shall be a representative who shall not have attained to the age of twenty-five years, and been seven years a citizen of the United States, and who shall not, when elected, be an inhabitant of that State in which he shall be chosen.

3. Representatives and direct taxes[1] shall be apportioned among the several States which may be included within this Union, according to their respective numbers, which shall be determined by adding to the whole number of free persons, including those bound to service for a term of years, and excluding Indians not taxed, three fifths of all other persons.[2] The actual enumeration shall be made within three years after the first meeting of the Congress of the United States, and within every subsequent term of ten years, in such manner as

they shall by law direct. The number of representatives shall not exceed one for every thirty thousand, but each State shall have at least one representative; and until such enumeration shall be made, the State of New Hampshire shall be entitled to choose three, Massachusetts eight, Rhode Island and Providence Plantations one, Connecticut five, New York six, New Jersey four, Pennsylvania eight, Delaware one, Maryland six, Virginia ten, North Carolina five, South Carolina five, and Georgia three.

4. When vacancies happen in the representation from any State, the executive authority thereof shall issue writs of election to fill such vacancies.

5. The House of Representatives shall choose their speaker and other officers; and shall have the sole power of impeachment.

SECTION 3.   1. The Senate of the United States shall be composed of two senators from each State, chosen by the legislature thereof,[3] for six years; and each senator shall have one vote.

2. Immediately after they shall be assembled in consequence of the first election, they shall be divided as equally as may be into three classes. The seats of the senators of the first class shall be vacated at the expiration of the second year, of the second class at the expiration of the fourth year, and of the third class at the expiration of the sixth year, so that one third may be chosen every second year; and if vacancies happen by resignation, or otherwise, during the recess of the legislature of any State, the executive thereof may make temporary appointments until the next meeting of the legislature, which shall then fill such vacancies.[4]

---

[1]See the Sixteenth Amendment.
[2]See the Fourteenth Amendment.

[3]See the Seventeenth Amendment.
[4]See the Seventeenth Amendment.

3. No person shall be a senator who shall not have attained to the age of thirty years, and been nine years a citizen of the United States, and who shall not, when elected, be an inhabitant of that State for which he shall be chosen.

4. The Vice President of the United States shall be President of the Senate, but shall have no vote, unless they be equally divided.

5. The Senate shall choose their other officers, and also a president pro tempore, in the absence of the Vice President, or when he shall exercise the office of the President of the United States.

6. The Senate shall have the sole power to try all impeachments. When sitting for that purpose, they shall be on oath or affirmation. When the President of the United States is tried, the chief justice shall preside: and no person shall be convicted without the concurrence of two thirds of the members present.

7. Judgment in cases of impeachment shall not extend further than to removal from office, and disqualification to hold and enjoy any office of honor, trust or profit under the United States: but the party convicted shall nevertheless be liable and subject to indictment, trial, judgment and punishment, according to law.

SECTION 4. 1. The times, places, and manner of holding elections for senators and representatives, shall be prescribed in each State by the legislature thereof; but the Congress may at any time by law make or alter such regulations, except as to the places of choosing senators.

2. The Congress shall assemble at least once in every year, and such meeting shall be on the first Monday in December, unless they shall by law appoint a different day.

SECTION 5. 1. Each House shall be the judge of the elections, returns and qualifications of its own members, and a majority of each shall constitute a quorum to do business; but a smaller number may adjourn from day to day, and may be authorized to compel the attendance of absent members, in such manner, and under such penalties as each House may provide.

2. Each House may determine the rules of its proceedings, punish its members for disorderly behavior, and, with the concurrence of two thirds, expel a member.

3. Each House shall keep a journal of its proceedings, and from time to time publish the same, excepting such parts as may in their judgment require secrecy; and the yeas and nays of the members of either House on any question shall, at the desire of one fifth of those present, be entered on the journal.

4. Neither House, during the session of Congress, shall, without the consent of the other, adjourn for more than three days, nor to any other place than that in which the two Houses shall be sitting.

SECTION 6. 1. The senators and representatives shall receive a compensation for their services, to be ascertained by law, and paid out of the Treasury of the United States. They shall in all cases, except treason, felony, and breach of the peace, be privileged from arrest during their attendance at the session of their respective Houses, and in going to and returning from the same; and for any speech or debate in either House, they shall not be questioned in any other place.

2. No senator or representative shall, during the time for which he was elected, be appointed to any civil office under the authority of the United States, which shall have been created, or the emoluments whereof shall have been increased, during such time; and no person holding any office under the United States shall be a member of either House during his continuance in office.

SECTION 7. 1. All bills for raising revenue shall originate in the House of Representatives; but the Senate may propose or concur with amendments as on other bills.

2. Every bill which shall have passed the House of Representatives and the Senate, shall, before it become a law, be presented to the President of the United States; If he approves he shall sign it, but if not he shall return it, with his objections, to that House in which it shall have originated, who shall enter the objections at large on their journal, and proceed to reconsider it. If after such reconsideration two thirds of that House shall agree to pass the bill, it shall be sent, together with the objections, to the other House, by which it shall likewise be reconsidered, and if approved by two thirds of that House, it shall become a law. But in all such cases the votes of both Houses shall be determined by yeas and nays, and the names of the persons voting for and against the bill shall be entered on the journal of each House respectively. If any bill shall not be returned by the President within ten days (Sundays excepted) after it shall have been presented to him, the same shall be a law, in like manner as if he had signed it, unless the Congress by their adjournment prevent its return, in which case it shall not be a law.

3. Every order, resolution, or vote to which the concurrence of the Senate and the House of Representatives may be necessary (except on a question of adjournment) shall be presented to the President of the United States; and before the same shall take effect, shall be approved by him, or being disapproved by him, shall be repassed by two thirds of the Senate and House of Representatives, according to the rules and limitations prescribed in the case of a bill.

SECTION 8. 1. The Congress shall have the power

1. To lay and collect taxes, duties, imposts, and excises, to pay the debts and provide for the common defense and general welfare of the United States; but all duties, imposts, and excises shall be uniform throughout the United States.

2. To borrow money on the credit of the United States;

3. To regulate commerce with foreign nations, and among the several States, and with the Indian tribes;

4. To establish a uniform rule of naturalization, and uniform laws on the subject of bankruptcies throughout the United States;

5. To coin money, regulate the value thereof, and of foreign coin, and fix the standard of weights and measures;

6. To provide for the punishment of counterfeiting the securities and current coin of the United States;

7. To establish post offices and post roads;

8. To promote the progress of science and useful arts, by securing for limited times to authors and inventors the exclusive right to their respective writings and discoveries;

9. To constitute tribunals inferior to the Supreme Court;

10. To define and punish piracies and felonies committed on the high seas, and offenses against the law of nations;

11. To declare war, grant letters of marque and reprisal, and make rules concerning captures on land and water;

12. To raise and support armies, but no appropriation of money to that use shall be for a longer term than two years;

13. To provide and maintain a navy;

14. To make rules for the government and regulation of the land and naval forces;

15. To provide for calling forth the militia to execute the laws of the Union, suppress insurrections and repel invasions;

16. To provide for organizing, arming, and disciplining the militia, and for governing such part of them as may be employed in the service of the United States, reserving to the States respectively, the appointment of the officers, and the authority of training the militia according to the discipline prescribed by Congress;

17. To exercise exclusive legislation in all cases whatsoever, over such district (not exceeding ten miles square) as may, by cession of particular States, and the acceptance of Congress, become the seat of the government of the United States, and to exercise like authority over all places purchased by the consent of the legislature of the State in which the same shall be, for the erection of forts, magazines, arsenals, dockyards, and other needful buildings; and

18. To make all laws which shall be necessary and proper for carrying into execution the foregoing powers, and all other powers vested by this Constitution in the government of the United States, or any department or officer thereof.

SECTION 9. 1. The migration or importation of such persons as any of the States now existing shall think proper to admit, shall not be prohibited by the Congress prior to the year one thousand eight hundred and eight, but a tax or duty may be imposed on such importation, not exceeding ten dollars for each person.

2. The privilege of the writ of habeas corpus shall not be suspended, unless when in cases of rebellion or invasion the public safety may require it.

3. No bill of attainder or ex post facto law shall be passed.

4. No capitation, or other direct, tax shall be laid, unless in proportion to the census or enumeration hereinbefore directed to be taken.[5]

5. No tax or duty shall be laid on articles exported from any State.

6. No preference shall be given by any regulation of commerce or revenue to the ports of one State over those of another: nor shall vessels bound to, or from, one State be obliged to enter, clear, or pay duties in another.

7. No money shall be drawn from the treasury, but in consequence of appropriations made by law; and a regular statement and account of the receipts and expenditures of all public money shall be published from time to time.

8. No title of nobility shall be granted by the United States: and no person holding any office of profit or trust under them, shall, without the consent of the Congress, accept of any present, emolument, office, or title, of any kind whatever, from any king, prince, or foreign State.

SECTION 10. 1 No State shall enter into any treaty, alliance, or confederation; grant letters of marque and reprisal; coin money; emit bills of credit; make any thing but gold and silver coin a tender in payment of debts; pass any bill of attainder, ex post facto law, or law impairing the obligation of contracts, or grant, any title of nobility.

2. No State shall, without the consent of the Congress, lay any imposts or duties on imports or exports, except what may be absolutely necessary for executing its inspection laws: and the net produce of all duties and imposts laid by any State on imports or exports, shall be for the use of the treasury of the United States; and all such laws shall be subject to the revision and control of the Congress.

3. No State shall, without the consent of the Congress, lay any duty of tonnage, keep troops, or ships of war in time of peace, enter into any agreement or compact with another State, or with a foreign power, or engage in war, unless actually invaded, or in such imminent danger as will not admit of delay.

ARTICLE II

SECTION 1. 1. The executive power shall be vested in a President of the United States of America. He shall hold his office during the term of four years, and, together with the Vice President, chosen for the same term, be elected, as follows:

2. Each State shall appoint, in such manner as the legislature thereof may direct, a number of electors, equal to the whole number of senators and representatives to which the State may be entitled in the Congress: but no senator or representative, or person holding any office of trust or profit under the United States, shall be appointed an elector.

The electors shall meet in their respective States, and vote by ballot for two persons, of whom one at least shall not be an inhabitant of the same State with themselves. And they shall make a list of all the persons voted for, and of the number of votes for each; which list they shall sign and certify, and transmit sealed to the seat of the government of the United States, directed to the president of the Senate. The president of the Senate shall, in the presence of the Senate and House of Representatives, open all the certificates, and the votes shall then be counted. The person having the greatest number of votes shall be the President, if such number be a majority of the whole number of electors appointed; and if there be more than one who have such majority, and have an equal number of votes, then the House of Representatives shall immediately choose by ballot one of them for President; and if no person have a majority, then from the five highest on the list the said House shall in like manner choose the President. But in choosing the President, the votes shall be taken by States, the representation from each State having one vote; a quorum for this purpose shall consist of a member or members from two thirds of the States, and a majority of all the States shall be necessary to a choice. In every case after the choice of the President, the person having the greatest number of votes of the electors shall be the Vice President. But if there should remain two or more who have equal votes, the Senate shall choose from them by ballot the Vice President.[6]

3. The Congress may determine the time of choosing the electors, and the day on which they shall give their votes; which day shall be the same throughout the United States.

4. No person except a natural born citizen, or a citizen of the United States, at the time of the adoption of this Constitution,

---

[5]See the Sixteenth Amendment.

[6]Superseded by the Twelfth Amendment.

shall be eligible to the office of President; neither shall any person be eligible to the office who shall not have attained to the age of thirty-five years, and been fourteen years a resident within the United States.

5. In case of the removal of the President from office, or of his death, resignation, or inability to discharge the powers and duties of the said office, the same shall devolve on the Vice President, and the congress may by law provide for the case of removal, death, resignation or inability, both of the President and Vice President, declaring what officer shall then act as President, and such officer shall act accordingly until the disability be removed, or a President shall be elected.

6. The President shall, at stated times, receive for his services a compensation which shall neither be increased nor diminished during the period for which he shall have been elected, and he shall not receive within that period any other emolument from the United States, or any of them.

7. Before he enter on the execution of his office, he shall take the following oath or affirmation:—"I do solemnly swear (or affirm) that I will faithfully execute the office of President of the United States, and will to the best of my ability, preserve, protect and defend the Constitution of the United States."

SECTION 2.   1. The President shall be commander in chief of the army and navy of the United States, and of the militia of the several States, when called into the actual service of the United States; he may require the opinion in writing, of the principal officer in each of the executive departments, upon any subject relating to the duties of their respective offices, and he shall have power to grant reprieves and pardons for offenses against the United States, except in cases of impeachment.

2. He shall have power, by and with the advice and consent of the Senate, to make treaties, provided two thirds of the senators present concur; and he shall nominate, and by and with the advice and consent of the Senate, shall appoint ambassadors, other public ministers and consuls, judges of the Supreme Court, and all other officers of the United States, whose appointments are not herein otherwise provided for, and which shall be established by law; but the Congress may by law vest the appointment of such inferior officers, as they think proper, in the President alone, in the courts of laws, or in the heads of departments.

3. The President shall have power to fill up all vacancies that may happen during the recess of the Senate, by granting commissions which shall expire at the end of their next session.

SECTION 3.   He shall from time to time give to the Congress information of the state of the Union, and recommend to their consideration such measures as he shall judge necessary and expedient; he may, on extraordinary occasions, convene both Houses, or either of them, and in case of disagreement between them with respect to the time of adjournment, he may adjourn them to such time as he shall think proper; he shall receive ambassadors and other public ministers; he shall take care that the laws be faithfully executed, and shall commission all the officers of the United States.

SECTION 4.   The President, Vice President, and all civil officers of the United States, shall be removed from office on impeachment for, and conviction of, treason, bribery, or other high crimes and misdemeanors.

ARTICLE III

SECTION 1. The judicial power of the United States shall be vested in one Supreme Court, and in such inferior courts as the Congress may from time to time ordain and establish. The judges, both of the Supreme and inferior courts, shall hold their offices during good behavior, and shall, at stated times, receive for their services, a compensation, which shall not be diminished during their continuance in office.

SECTION 2.   1. The judicial power shall extend to all cases, in law and equity, arising under this Constitution, the laws of the United States, and treaties made, or which shall be made, under their authority;—to all cases of admiralty and maritime jurisdiction;—to controversies to which the United States shall be a party;[7]—to controversies between two or more States;—between a State and citizens of another State;—between citizens of different States;—between citizens of the same State claiming lands under grants of different States, and between a State, or the citizens thereof, and foreign States, citizens or subjects.

2. In all cases affecting ambassadors, other public ministers and consuls, and those in which a State shall be party, the Supreme Court shall have original jurisdiction. In all the other cases before mentioned, the Supreme Court shall have appellate jurisdiction, both as to law and fact, with such exceptions, and under such regulations as the Congress shall make.

3. The trial of all crimes, except in cases of impeachment, shall be by jury; and such trial shall be held in the State where the said crimes shall have been committed; but when not committed within any State, the trial shall be such place or places as the congress may by law have directed.

SECTION 3.   1. Treason against the United States shall consist only in levying war against them, or in adhering to their enemies, giving them aid and comfort. No person shall be convicted of treason unless on the testimony of two witnesses to the same overt act, or on confession in open court.

2. The Congress shall have power to declare the punishment of treason, but no attainder of treason shall work corruption of blood, or forfeiture except during the life of the person attained.

ARTICLE IV

SECTION 1. Full faith and credit shall be given in each State to the public acts, records, and judicial proceedings of every other State. And the Congress may by general laws prescribe the manner in which such acts, records and proceedings shall be proved, and the effect thereof.

SECTION 2.   1. The citizens of each State shall be entitled to all privileges and immunities of citizens in the several States.[8]

2. A person charged in any State with treason, felony, or other crime, who shall flee from justice, and be found in another State, shall on demand of the executive authority of the State from which he fled, be delivered up to be removed to the State having jurisdiction of the crime.

---

[7]See the Eleventh Amendment.
[8]See the Fourteenth Amendment, Sec. 1.

3. No person held to service or labor in one State under the laws thereof, escaping into another, shall, in consequence of any law or regulation therein, be discharged from such service or labor, but shall be delivered up on claim of the party to whom such service or labor may be due.[9]

SECTION 3.   1. New States may be admitted by the Congress into this Union; but no new State shall be formed or erected within the jurisdiction of any other State, nor any State be formed by the junction of two or more States, or parts of States, without the consent of the legislatures of the States concerned as well as of the Congress.

2. The Congress shall have power to dispose of and make all needful rules and regulations respecting the territory or other property belonging to the United States; and nothing in this Constitution shall be so construed as to prejudice any claims of the United States, or of any particular State.

SECTION 4.   The United States shall guarantee to every State in this Union a republican form of government, and shall protect each of them against invasion; and on application of the legislature, or of the executive (when the legislature cannot be convened) against domestic violence.

ARTICLE V

The Congress, whenever two thirds of both Houses shall deem it necessary, shall propose amendments to this Constitution, or, on the application of the legislatures of two thirds of the several States, shall call a convention for proposing amendments, which in either case shall be valid to all intents and purposes, as part of this Constitution, when ratified by the legislatures of three fourths of the several States, or by conventions in three fourths thereof, as the one or the other mode of ratification may be proposed by the Congress; Provided that no amendment which may be made prior to the year one thousand eight hundred and eight shall in any manner affect the first and fourth clauses in the ninth section of the first article; and that no State, without its consent, shall be deprived of its equal suffrage in the Senate.

ARTICLE VI

1. All debts contracted and engagements entered into, before the adoption of this Constitution, shall be as valid against the United States under this Constitution, as under the Confederation.[10]

2. This Constitution, and the laws of the United States which shall be made in pursuance thereof; and all treaties made, or which shall be made, under the authority of the United States, shall be the supreme law of the land; and the judges in every State shall be bound thereby, any thing in the Constitution or laws of any State to the contrary notwithstanding.

3. The senators and representatives before mentioned, and the members of the several State legislatures, and all executive and judicial officers, both of the United States and of the several States, shall be bound by oath or affirmation to support this Constitution; but no religious test shall ever be required as a qualification to any office or public trust under the United States.

ARTICLE VII

The ratification of the conventions of nine States shall be sufficient for the establishment of this Constitution between the States so ratifying the same.

Done in Convention by the unanimous consent of the States present the seventeenth day of September in the year of our Lord one thousand seven hundred and eighty-seven, and of the independence of the United States of America the twelfth. In witness whereof we have hereunto subscribed our names.

[Signatories' names omitted]

Articles in addition to, and amendment of, the Constitution of the United States of America, proposed by Congress, and ratified by the legislatures of the several States, pursuant to the fifth article of the original Constitution.

Amendment I
[First ten amendments ratified December 15, 1791]

Congress shall make no law respecting an establishment of religion, or prohibiting the free exercise thereof; or abridging the freedom of speech, or of the press; or the right of the people peaceably to assemble, and to petition the government for a redress of grievances.

Amendment II

A well regulated militia, being necessary to the security of a free State, the right of the people to keep and bear arms, shall not be infringed.

Amendment III

No soldier shall, in time of peace be quartered in any house, without the consent of the owner, nor in time of war, but in a manner to be prescribed by law.

Amendment IV

The right of the people to be secure in their persons, houses, papers, and effects, against unreasonable searches and seizures, shall not be violated, and no warrants shall issue, but upon probable cause, supported by oath or affirmation, and particularly describing the place to be searched, and the persons or things to be seized.

Amendment V

No person shall be held to answer for a capital or otherwise infamous crime, unless on a presentment or indictment of a grand jury, except in cases arising in the land or naval forces, or in the militia, when in actual service in time of war or public danger; nor shall any person be subject for the same offense to be twice put in jeopardy of life or limb; nor shall be compelled in any criminal case to be a witness against himself, nor be deprived of life, liberty, or property, without due process of law; nor shall private property be taken for public use, without just compensation.

Amendment VI

In all criminal prosecutions, the accused shall enjoy the right to a speedy and public trial, by an impartial jury of the State and district wherein the crime shall have been committed, which district shall have been previously ascertained by law,

---

[9]See the Thirteenth Amendment.
[10]See the Fourteenth Amendment, Sec. 4.

and to be informed of the nature and cause of the accusation; to be confronted with the witnesses against him; to have compulsory process for obtaining witnesses in his favor, and to have the assistance of counsel for his defense.

Amendment VII

In suits at common law, where the value in controversy shall exceed twenty dollars, the right of trial by jury shall be preserved, and no fact tried by a jury shall be otherwise reexamined in any court of the United States, than according to the rules of the common law.

Amendment VIII

Excessive bail shall not be required, nor excessive fines imposed, nor cruel and unusual punishments inflicted.

Amendment IX

The enumeration in the Constitution of certain rights shall not be construed to deny or disparage others retained by the people.

Amendment X

The powers not delegated to the United States by the Constitution, nor prohibited by it to the States, are reserved to the States respectively, or to the people.

Amendment XI [January 8, 1798]

The judicial power of the United States shall not be construed to extend to any suit in law or equity, commended or prosecuted against one of the United States by citizens of another State, or by citizens or subjects of any foreign State.

Amendment XII [September 25, 1804]

The electors shall meet in their respective States, and vote by ballot for President and Vice President, one of whom, at least, shall not be an inhabitant of the same State with themselves; they shall name in their ballots the person voted for as President, and in distinct ballots, the person voted for as Vice President, and they shall make distinct lists of all persons voted for as President and of all persons voted for as Vice President, and of the number of votes for each, which lists they shall sign and certify, and transmit sealed to the seat of the government of the United States, directed to the President of the Senate;—The President of the Senate shall, in the presence of the Senate and House of Representatives, open all the certificates and the votes shall then be counted;—The person having the greatest number of votes for President, shall be the President, if such number be a majority of the whole number of electors appointed; and if no person have such majority, then from the persons having the highest numbers not exceeding three on the list of those voted for as President, the House of Representatives shall choose immediately, by ballot, the President. But in choosing the President, the votes shall be taken by States, the representation from each State having one vote; a quorum for this purpose shall consist of a member or members from two thirds of the States, and a majority of all the States shall be necessary to a choice. And if the House of Representatives shall not choose a President whenever the right of choice shall devolve upon them, before the fourth day of March next following, then the Vice President shall act as President,

as in the case of the death or other constitutional disability of the President. The person having the greatest number of votes as Vice President shall be the Vice President, if such number be a majority of the whole number of electors appointed, and if no person have a majority, then from the two highest numbers on the list, the Senate shall choose the Vice President; a quorum for the purpose shall consist of two thirds of the whole number of Senators, and a majority of the whole number shall be necessary to a choice. But no person constitutionally ineligible to the office of President shall be eligible to that of Vice President of the United States.

Amendment XIII [December 18, 1865]

SECTION 1. Neither slavery nor involuntary servitude, except as a punishment for crime whereof the party shall have been duly convicted, shall exist within the United States, or any place subject to their jurisdiction.

SECTION 2. Congress shall have power to enforce this article by appropriate legislation.

Amendment XIV [July 28, 1868]

SECTION 1. All persons born or naturalized in the United States, and subject to the jurisdiction thereof, are citizens of the United States and of the State wherein they reside. No State shall make or enforce any law which shall abridge the privileges or immunities of citizens of the United States; nor shall any State deprive any person of life, liberty, or property, without due process of law; nor deny to any person within its jurisdiction the equal protection of the laws.

SECTION 2. Representatives shall be apportioned among the several States according to their respective numbers, counting the whole number of persons in each State, excluding Indians not taxed. But when the right to vote at any election for the choice of electors for President and Vice President of the United States, representatives in Congress, the executive and judicial officers of a State, or the members of the legislature thereof, is denied to any of the male inhabitants of such State, being twenty-one years of age, and citizens of the United States, or in any way abridged, except for participating in rebellion, or other crime, the basis of representation there shall be reduced in the proportion which the number of such male citizens shall bear to the whole number of male citizens twenty-one years of age in such State.

SECTION 3. No person shall be a senator or representative in Congress, or elector of President and Vice President, or hold any office, civil or military, under the United States, or under any State, who having previously taken an oath, as a member of Congress, or as an officer of the United States, or as a member of any State legislature, or as an executive or judicial officer of any State, to support the Constitution of the United States, shall have engaged in insurrection or rebellion against the same, or given aid or comfort to the enemies thereof. But Congress may by a vote of two thirds of each House, remove such disability.

SECTION 4. The validity of the public debt of the United States, authorized by law, including debts incurred for payment of pensions and bounties for services in suppressing insurrection or rebellion; shall not be questioned. But neither the United States nor any State shall assume or pay any debt or obligation incurred in aid of insurrection or rebellion against the United States, or any claim for the loss or emancipation of any slave; but all such debts, obligations, and claims shall be held illegal and void.

SECTION 5.   The Congress shall have the power to enforce, by appropriate legislation, the provisions of this article.

Amendment XV [March 30, 1870]

SECTION 1. The right of citizens of the United States to vote shall not be denied or abridged by the United States or by any State on account of race, color, or previous condition of servitude.

SECTION 2. The Congress shall have power to enforce this article by appropriate legislation.

Amendment XVI [February 25, 1913]

The Congress shall have power to lay and collect taxes on incomes, from whatever source derived, without apportionment among the several States, and without regard to any census or enumeration.

Amendment XVII [May 31, 1913]

The Senate of the United States shall be composed of two senators from each State, elected by the people thereof, for six years; and each senator shall have one vote. The electors in each State shall have the qualifications requisite for electors of the most numerous branch of the State legislature.

When vacancies happen in the representation of any State in the Senate, the executive authority of such State shall issue writs of election to fill such vacancies: Provided, That the legislature of any State may empower the executive thereof to make temporary appointments until the people fill the vacancies by election as the legislature may direct.

This amendment shall not be so construed as to affect the election or term of any senator chosen before it becomes valid as part of the Constitution.

Amendment XVIII[11] [January 29, 1919]

After one year from the ratification of this article, the manufacture, sale, or transportation of intoxicating liquors within, the importation thereof into, or the exportation thereof from the United States and all territory subject to the jurisdiction thereof for beverage purposes is thereby prohibited.

The Congress and the several States shall have concurrent power to enforce this article by appropriate legislation.

This article shall be inoperative unless it shall have been ratified as an amendment to the Constitution by the legislatures of the several States, as provided in the constitution, within seven years from the date of the submission hereof to the States by Congress.

Amendment XIX [August 26, 1920]

The right of citizens of the United States to vote shall not be denied or abridged by the United States or by any State on account of sex.

Congress shall have the power to enforce this article by appropriate legislation.

Amendment XX [January 23, 1933]

SECTION 1.   The terms of the President and Vice President shall end at noon on the 20th day of January and the terms of Senators and Representatives at noon on the 3d day of January, of the years in which such terms would have ended if this article had not been ratified; and the terms of their successors shall then begin.

SECTION 2.   The Congress shall assemble at least once in every year, and such meeting shall begin at noon on the 3d day of January, unless they shall by law appoint a different day.

SECTION 3.   If, at the time fixed for the beginning of the term of President, the President-elect shall have died, the Vice President-elect shall become President. If a President shall not have been chosen before the time fixed for the beginning of his term, or if the President-elect shall have failed to qualify, then the Vice President-elect shall act as President until a President shall have qualified; and the Congress may by law provide for the case wherein neither a President-elect nor a Vice President-elect shall have qualified, declaring who shall then act as President, or the manner in which one who is to act shall be selected, and such person shall act accordingly until a President or Vice President shall have qualified.

SECTION 4. The Congress may by law provide for the case of the death of any of the persons from whom, the House of Representatives may choose a President whenever the right of choice shall have devolved upon them, and for the case of the death of any of the persons from whom the Senate may choose a Vice President whenever the right of choice shall have devolved upon them.

SECTION 5.   Sections 1 and 2 shall take effect on the 15th day of October following the ratification of this article.

SECTION 6.   This article shall be inoperative unless it shall have been ratified as an amendment to the Constitution by the legislatures of three-fourths of the several States within seven years from the date of its submission.

Amendment XXI [December 5, 1933]

SECTION 1.   The Eighteenth Article of amendment to the Constitution of the United States is hereby repealed.

SECTION 2.   The transportation or importation into any State, Territory, or possession of the United States for delivery or use therein of intoxicating liquors in violation of the laws thereof, is hereby prohibited.

SECTION 3.   This article shall be inoperative unless it shall have been ratified as an amendment to the Constitution by conventions in the several States, as provided in the Constitution, within seven years from the date of the submission thereof to the States by the Congress.

Amendment XXII [March 1, 1951]

No person shall be elected to the office of the President more than twice, and no person who has held the office of President, or acted as President, for more than two years of a term to which some other person was elected President shall be elected to the office of the President more than once.

---

[11]Repealed by the Twenty-first Amendment.

But this article shall not apply to any person holding the office of President when this article was proposed by the Congress, and shall not prevent any person who may be holding the office of President, or acting as President, during the term within which this article becomes operative from holding the office of President or acting as President during the remainder of such term.

This article shall be inoperative unless it shall have been ratified as an amendment to the Constitution by the legislatures of three-fourths of the several States within seven years from the date of its submission to the States by the Congress.

Amendment XXIII [March 29, 1961]

SECTION 1. The District constituting the seat of Government of the United States shall appoint in such manner as the Congress may direct.

A number of electors of President and Vice President equal to the whole number of Senators and Representatives in Congress to which the District would be entitled if it were a State, but in no event more than the least populous State; they shall be in addition to those appointed by the States, but they shall be considered, for the purposes of the election of President and Vice President, to be electors appointed by a State; and they shall meet in the District and perform such duties as provided by the twelfth article of amendment.

SECTION 2. The Congress shall have power to enforce this article by appropriate legislation.

Amendment XXIV [January 23, 1964]

SECTION 1. The right of citizens of the United States to vote in any primary or other election for President or Vice President, for electors for President or Vice President, or for Senator or Representative in Congress, shall not be denied or abridged by the United States or any State by reason of failure to pay any poll tax or other tax.

SECTION 2. The Congress shall have power to enforce this article by appropriate legislation.

Amendment XXV [February 10, 1967]

SECTION 1. In case of the removal of the President from office or of his death or resignation, the Vice President shall become President.

SECTION 2. Whenever there is a vacancy in the office of the Vice President, the President shall nominate a Vice President who shall take office upon confirmation by a majority of both Houses of Congress.

SECTION 3. Whenever the President transmits to the President pro tempore of the Senate and the Speaker of the House of Representatives his written declaration that he is unable to discharge the powers and duties of his office, and until he transmits to them a written declaration to the contrary, such powers and duties shall be discharged by the Vice President as Acting President.

SECTION 4. Whenever the Vice President and a majority of either the principal officers of the executive departments or of such other body as Congress may by law provide, transmit to the President pro tempore of the Senate and the Speaker of the House of Representatives their written declaration that the President is unable to discharge the powers and duties of his office, the Vice President shall immediately assume the powers and duties of the office as Acting President.

Thereafter, when the President transmits to the President pro tempore of the Senate and the Speaker of the House of Representatives his written declaration that no inability exists, he shall resume the powers and duties of his office unless the Vice President and a majority of either the principal officers of the executive departments or of such other body as Congress may by law provide, transmit within four days to the President pro tempore of the Senate and the Speaker of the House of Representatives their written declaration that the President is unable to discharge the powers and duties of his office. Thereupon Congress shall decide the issue, assembling within forty-eight hours for that purpose if not in session. If the Congress, within twenty-one days after receipt of the latter written declaration, or, if Congress is not in session, within twenty-one days after Congress is required to assemble, determines by two-thirds vote of both Houses that the President is unable to discharge the powers and duties of his office, the Vice President shall continue to discharge the same as Acting President; otherwise, the President shall resume the powers and duties of his office.

Amendment XXVI [June 30, 1971]

SECTION 1. The right of citizens of the United States who are eighteen years of age or older to vote shall not be denied or abridged by the United States or by any State on account of age.

SECTION 2. The Congress shall have power to enforce this article by appropriate legislation.

Amendment XXVII[12] [May 7, 1992]

No law, varying the compensation for services of the Senators and Representatives, shall take effect until an election of Representatives shall have intervened.

---

[12]James Madison proposed this amendment in 1789 together with the ten amendments that were adopted as the Bill of Rights, but it failed to win ratification at the time. Congress, however, had set no deadline for its ratification, and over the years—particularly in the 1980s and 1990s—many states voted to add it to the Constitution. With the ratification of Michigan in 1992 it passed the threshold of 3/4ths of the states required for adoption, but because the process took more than 200 years, its validity remains in doubt.

PRESIDENT AND VICE PRESIDENT

1. George Washington (1789)
   John Adams (1789)

2. John Adams (1797)
   Thomas Jefferson (1797)

3. Thomas Jefferson (1801)
   Aaron Burr (1801)
   George Clinton (1805)

4. James Madison (1809)
   George Clinton (1809)
   Elbridge Gerry (1813)

5. James Monroe (1817)
   Daniel D. Thompkins (1817)

6. John Quincy Adams (1825)
   John C. Calhoun (1825)

7. Andrew Jackson (1829)
   John C. Calhoun (1829)
   Martin Van Buren (1833)

8. Martin Van Buren (1837)
   Richard M. Johnson (1837)

9. William H. Harrison (1841)
   John Tyler (1841)

10. John Tyler (1841)

11. James K. Polk (1845)
    George M. Dallas (1845)

12. Zachary Taylor (1849)
    Millard Fillmore (1849)

13. Millard Fillmore (1850)

14. Franklin Pierce (1853)
    William R. King (1853)

15. James Buchanan (1857)
    John C. Breckinridge (1857)

16. Abraham Lincoln (1861)
    Hannibal Hamlin (1861)
    Andrew Johnson (1865)

17. Andrew Johnson (1865)

18. Ulysses S. Grant (1869)
    Schuyler Colfax (1869)
    Henry Wilson (1873)

19. Rutherford B. Hayes (1877)
    William A. Wheeler (1877)

20. James A. Garfield (1881)
    Chester A. Arthur (1881)

21. Chester A. Arthur (1881)

22. Grover Cleveland (1885)
    T. A. Hendricks (1885)

23. Benjamin Harrison (1889)
    Levi P. Morgan (1889)

24. Grover Cleveland (1893)
    Adlai E. Stevenson (1893)

25. William McKinley (1897)
    Garret A. Hobart (1897)
    Theodore Roosevelt (1901)

26. Theodore Roosevelt (1901)
    Charles Fairbanks (1905)

27. William H. Taft (1909)
    James S. Sherman (1909)

28. Woodrow Wilson (1913)
    Thomas R. Marshall (1913)

29. Warren G. Harding (1921)
    Calvin Coolidge (1921)

30. Calvin Coolidge (1923)
    Charles G. Dawes (1925)

31. Herbert C. Hoover (1929)
    Charles Curtis (1929)

32. Franklin D. Roosevelt (1933)
    John Nance Garner (1933)
    Henry A. Wallace (1941)
    Harry S. Truman (1945)

33. Harry S. Truman (1945)
    Alben W. Barkley (1949)

34. Dwight D. Eisenhower (1953)
    Richard M. Nixon (1953)

35. John F. Kennedy (1961)
    Lyndon B. Johnson (1961)

36. Lyndon B. Johnson (1963)
    Hubert H. Humphrey (1965)

37. Richard M. Nixon (1969)
    Spiro T. Agnew (1969)
    Gerald R. Ford (1973)

38. Gerald R. Ford (1974)
    Nelson A. Rockefeller (1974)

39. James E. Carter Jr. (1977)
    Walter F. Mondale (1977)

40. Ronald W. Reagan (1981)
    George H. Bush (1981)

41. George H. Bush (1989)
    James D. Quayle III (1989)

42. William J. Clinton (1993)
    Albert Gore (1993)

43. George W. Bush (2001)
    Richard Cheney (2001)

PRESIDENTIAL ELECTIONS (CONTINUED)

Year	Number of States	Candidates	Party	Popular Vote*	Electoral Vote†	Percentage of Popular Vote
1789	11	GEORGE WASHINGTON	No party designations		69	
		John Adams			34	
		Other Candidates			35	
1792	15	GEORGE WASHINGTON	No party designations		132	
		John Adams			77	
		George Clinton			50	
		Other Candidates			5	
1796	16	JOHN ADAMS	Federalist		71	
		Thomas Jefferson	Democratic-Republican		68	
		Thomas Pinckney	Federalist		59	
		Aaron Burr	Democratic-Republican		30	
		Other Candidates			48	
1800	16	THOMAS JEFFERSON	Democratic-Republican		73	
		Aaron Burr	Democratic-Republican		73	
		John Adams	Federalist		65	
		Charles C. Pinckney	Federalist		64	
		John Jay	Federalist		1	
1804	17	THOMAS JEFFERSON	Democratic-Republican		162	
		Charles C. Pinckney	Federalist		14	
1808	17	JAMES MADISON	Democratic-Republican		122	
		Charles C. Pinckney	Federalist		47	
		George Clinton	Democratic-Republican		6	
1812	18	JAMES MADISON	Democratic-Republican		128	
		DeWitt Clinton	Federalist		89	
1816	19	JAMES MONROE	Democratic-Republican		183	
		Rufus King	Federalist		34	
1820	24	JAMES MONROE	Democratic-Republican		231	
		John Quincy Adams	Independent-Republican		1	
1824	24	JOHN QUINCY ADAMS	Democratic-Republican	108,740	84	30.5
		Andrew Jackson	Democratic-Republican	153,544	99	43.1
		William H. Crawford	Democratic-Republican	46,618	41	13.1
		Henry Clay	Democratic-Republican	47,136	37	13.2
1828	24	ANDREW JACKSON	Democrat	647,286	178	56.0
		John Quincy Adams	National Republican	508,064	83	44.0
1832	24	ANDREW JACKSON	Democrat	687,502	219	55.0
		Henry Clay	National Republican	530,189	49	42.4
		William Wirt	Anti-Masonic	} 33,108	7	} 2.6
		John Floyd	National Republican		11	

* *Percentage of popular vote given for any election year may not total 100 percent because candidates receiving less than 1 percent of the popular vote have been omitted.*

† *Prior to the passage of the Twelfth Amendment in 1904, the electoral college voted for two presidential candidates; the runner-up became Vice-President. Data from Historical Statistics of the United States, Colonial Times to 1957 (1961), pp. 682–683, and The World Almanac.*

PRESIDENTIAL ELECTIONS   (CONTINUED)

Year	Number of States	Candidates	Party	Popular Vote	Electoral Vote	Percentage of Popular Vote
1836	26	MARTIN VAN BUREN	Democrat	765,483	170	50.9
		William H. Harrison	Whig		73	
		Hugh L. White	Whig	739,795	26	
		Daniel Webster	Whig		14	49.1
		W. P. Mangum	Whig		11	
1840	26	WILLIAM H. HARRISON	Whig	1,274,624	234	53.1
		Martin Van Buren	Democrat	1,127,781	60	46.9
1844	26	JAMES K. POLK	Democrat	1,338,464	170	49.6
		Henry Clay	Whig	1,300,097	105	48.1
		James G. Birney	Liberty	62,300		2.3
1848	30	ZACHARY TAYLOR	Whig	1,360,967	163	47.4
		Lewis Cass	Democrat	1,222,342	127	42.5
		Martin Van Buren	Free Soil	291,263		10.1
1852	31	FRANKLIN PIERCE	Democrat	1,601,117	254	50.9
		Winfield Scott	Whig	1,385,453	42	44.1
		John P. Hale	Free Soil	155,825		5.0
1856	31	JAMES BUCHANAN	Democrat	1,832,955	174	45.3
		John C. Frémont	Republican	1,339,932	114	33.1
		Millard Fillmore	American ("Know Nothing")	871,731	8	21.6
1860	33	ABRAHAM LINCOLN	Republican	1,865,593	180	39.8
		Stephen A. Douglas	Democrat	1,382,713	12	29.5
		John C. Breckinridge	Democrat	848,356	72	18.1
		John Bell	Constitutional Union	592,906	39	12.6
1864	36	ABRAHAM LINCOLN	Republican	2,206,938	212	55.0
		George B. McClellan	Democrat	1,803,787	21	45.0
1868	37	ULYSSES S. GRANT	Republican	3,013,421	214	52.7
		Horatio Seymour	Democrat	2,706,829	80	47.3
1872	37	ULYSSES S. GRANT	Republican	3,596,745	286	55.6
		Horace Greeley	Democrat	2,843,446	*	43.9
1876	38	RUTHERFORD B. HAYES	Republican	4,036,572	185	48.0
		Samuel J. Tilden	Democrat	4,284,020	184	51.0
1880	38	JAMES A. GARFIELD	Republican	4,453,295	214	48.5
		Winfield S. Hancock	Democrat	4,414,082	155	48.1
		James B. Weaver	Greenback-Labor	308,578		3.4
1884	38	GROVER CLEVELAND	Democrat	4,879,507	219	48.5
		James G. Blaine	Republican	4,850,293	182	48.2
		Benjamin F. Butler	Greenback-Labor	175,370		1.8
		John P. St. John	Prohibition	150,369		1.5
1888	38	BENJAMIN HARRISON	Republican	5,447,129	233	47.9
		Grover Cleveland	Democrat	5,537,857	168	48.6
		Clinton B. Fisk	Prohibition	249,506		2.2
		Anson J. Streeter	Union Labor	146,935		1.3

* Because of the death of Greeley, Democratic electors scattered their votes.

PRESIDENTIAL ELECTIONS (CONTINUED)

Year	Number of States	Candidates	Party	Popular Vote	Electoral Vote	Percentage of Popular Vote
1892	44	GROVER CLEVELAND	Democrat	5,555,426	277	46.1
		Benjamin Harrison	Republican	5,182,690	145	43.0
		James B. Weaver	People's	1,029,846	22	8.5
		John Bidwell	Prohibition	264,133		2.2
1896	45	WILLIAM MCKINLEY	Republican	7,102,246	271	51.1
		William J. Bryan	Democrat	6,492,559	176	47.7
1900	45	WILLIAM MCKINLEY	Republican	7,218,491	292	51.7
		William J. Bryan	Democrat; Populist	6,356,734	155	45.5
		John C. Woolley	Prohibition	208,914		1.5
1904	45	THEODORE ROOSEVELT	Republican	7,628,461	336	57.4
		Alton B. Parker	Democrat	5,084,223	140	37.6
		Eugene V. Debs	Socialist	402,283		3.0
		Silas C. Swallow	Prohibition	258,536		1.9
1908	46	WILLIAM H. TAFT	Republican	7,675,320	321	51.6
		William J. Bryan	Democrat	6,412,294	162	43.1
		Eugene V. Debs	Socialist	420,793		2.8
		Eugene W. Chafin	Prohibition	253,840		1.7
1912	48	WOODROW WILSON	Democrat	6,296,547	435	41.9
		Theodore Roosevelt	Progressive	4,118,571	88	27.4
		William H. Taft	Republican	3,486,720	8	23.2
		Eugene V. Debs	Socialist	900,672		6.0
		Eugene W. Chafin	Prohibition	206,275		1.4
1916	48	WOODROW WILSON	Democrat	9,127,695	277	49.4
		Charles E. Hughes	Republican	8,533,507	254	46.2
		A. L. Benson	Socialist	585,113		3.2
		J. Frank Hanly	Prohibition	220,506		1.2
1920	48	WARREN G. HARDING	Republican	16,143,407	404	60.4
		James M. Cox	Democrat	9,130,328	127	34.2
		Eugene V. Debs	Socialist	919,799		3.4
		P. P. Christensen	Farmer-Labor	265,411		1.0
1924	48	CALVIN COOLIDGE	Republican	15,718,211	382	54.0
		John W. Davis	Democrat	8,385,283	136	28.8
		Robert M. La Follette	Progressive	4,831,289	13	16.6
1928	48	HERBERT C. HOOVER	Republican	21,391,993	444	58.2
		Alfred E. Smith	Democrat	15,016,169	87	40.9
1932	48	FRANKLIN D. ROOSEVELT	Democrat	22,809,638	472	57.4
		Herbert C. Hoover	Republican	15,758,901	59	39.7
		Norman Thomas	Socialist	881,951		2.2
1936	48	FRANKLIN D. ROOSEVELT	Democrat	27,752,869	523	60.8
		Alfred M. Landon	Republican	16,674,665	8	36.5
		William Lemke	Union	882,479		1.9
1940	48	FRANKLIN D. ROOSEVELT	Democrat	27,307,819	449	54.8
		Wendell L. Willkie	Republican	22,321,018	82	44.8

PRESIDENTIAL ELECTIONS   (CONTINUED)

Year	Number of States	Candidates	Party	Popular Vote	Electoral Vote	Percentage of Popular Vote
1944	48	FRANKLIN D. ROOSEVELT	Democrat	25,606,585	432	53.5
		Thomas E. Dewey	Republican	22,014,745	99	46.0
1948	48	HARRY S. TRUMAN	Democrat	24,105,812	303	49.5
		Thomas E. Dewey	Republican	21,970,065	189	45.1
		J. Strom Thurmond	States' Rights	1,169,063	39	2.4
		Henry A. Wallace	Progressive	1,157,172		2.4
1952	48	DWIGHT D. EISENHOWER	Republican	33,936,234	442	55.1
		Adlai E. Stevenson	Democrat	27,314,992	89	44.4
1956	48	DWIGHT D. EISENHOWER	Republican	35,590,472	457*	57.6
		Adlai E. Stevenson	Democrat	26,022,752	73	42.1
1960	50	JOHN F. KENNEDY	Democrat	34,227,096	303†	49.9
		Richard M. Nixon	Republican	34,108,546	219	49.6
1964	50	LYNDON B. JOHNSON	Democrat	42,676,220	486	61.3
		Barry M. Goldwater	Republican	26,860,314	52	38.5
1968	50	RICHARD M. NIXON	Republican	31,785,480	301	43.4
		Hubert H. Humphrey	Democrat	31,275,165	191	42.7
		George C. Wallace	American Independent	9,906,473	46	13.5
1972	50	RICHARD M. NIXON‡	Republican	47,165,234	520	60.6
		George S. McGovern	Democrat	29,168,110	17	37.5
1976	50	JIMMY CARTER	Democrat	40,828,929	297	50.1
		Gerald R. Ford	Republican	39,148,940	240	47.9
		Eugene McCarthy	Independent	739,256		
1980	50	RONALD REAGAN	Republican	43,201,220	489	50.9
		Jimmy Carter	Democrat	34,913,332	49	41.2
		John B. Anderson	Independent	5,581,379		
1984	50	RONALD REAGAN	Republican	53,428,357	525	59.0
		Walter F. Mondale	Democrat	36,930,923	13	41.0
1988	50	GEORGE BUSH	Republican	48,901,046	426	53.4
		Michael Dukakis	Democrat	41,809,030	111	45.6
1992	50	BILL CLINTON	Democrat	43,728,275	370	43.2
		George Bush	Republican	38,167,416	168	37.7
		H. Ross Perot	United We Stand, America	19,237,247		19.0
1996	50	BILL CLINTON	Democrat	45,590,703	379	49.0
		Robert Dole	Republican	37,816,307	159	41.0
		H. Ross Perot	Reform	7,866,284		8.0
2000	50	GEORGE W. BUSH	Republican	50,459,624	271	47.9
		Albert Gore, Jr.	Democrat	51,003,328	266	49.4
		Ralph Nader	Green	2,882,985	0	2.7
2004	50	GEORGE W. BUSH	Republican	59,117,523	286	51.1
		John Kerry	Democrat	55,557,584	252	48.0
		Ralph Nader	Green	405,623	0	0.3

* Walter B. Jones received 1 electoral vote.

† Harry F. Byrd received 15 electoral votes.

‡ Resigned August 9, 1974: Vice President Gerald R. Ford became President.

ADMISSION OF STATES INTO THE UNION

State	Date of Admission	State	Date of Admission
1. Delaware	December 7, 1787	26. Michigan	January 26, 1837
2. Pennsylvania	December 12, 1787	27. Florida	March 3, 1845
3. New Jersey	December 18, 1787	28. Texas	December 29, 1845
4. Georgia	January 2, 1788	29. Iowa	December 28, 1846
5. Connecticut	January 9, 1788	30. Wisconsin	May 29, 1848
6. Massachusetts	February 6, 1788	31. California	September 9, 1850
7. Maryland	April 28, 1788	32. Minnesota	May 11, 1858
8. South Carolina	May 23, 1788	33. Oregon	February 14, 1859
9. New Hampshire	June 21, 1788	34. Kansas	January 29, 1861
10. Virginia	June 25, 1788	35. West Virginia	June 20, 1863
11. New York	July 26, 1788	36. Nevada	October 31, 1864
12. North Carolina	November 21, 1789	37. Nebraska	March 1, 1867
13. Rhode Island	May 29, 1790	38. Colorado	August 1, 1876
14. Vermont	March 4, 1791	39. North Dakota	November 2, 1889
15. Kentucky	June 1, 1792	40. South Dakota	November 2, 1889
16. Tennessee	June 1, 1796	41. Montana	November 8, 1889
17. Ohio	March 1, 1803	42. Washington	November 11, 1889
18. Louisiana	April 30, 1812	43. Idaho	July 3, 1890
19. Indiana	December 11, 1816	44. Wyoming	July 10, 1890
20. Mississippi	December 10, 1817	45. Utah	January 4, 1896
21. Illinois	December 3, 1818	46. Oklahoma	November 16, 1907
22. Alabama	December 14, 1819	47. New Mexico	January 6, 1912
23. Maine	March 15, 1820	48. Arizona	February 14, 1912
24. Missouri	August 10, 1821	49. Alaska	January 3, 1959
25. Arkansas	June 15, 1836	50. Hawaii	August 21, 1959

DEMOGRAPHICS OF THE UNITED STATES

POPULATION GROWTH

Year	Population	Percent Increase
1630	4,600	
1640	26,600	478.3
1650	50,400	90.8
1660	75,100	49.0
1670	111,900	49.0
1680	151,500	35.4
1690	210,400	38.9
1700	250,900	19.2
1710	331,700	32.2
1720	466,200	40.5
1730	629,400	35.0
1740	905,600	43.9
1750	1,170,800	29.3
1760	1,593,600	36.1
1770	2,148,100	34.8
1780	2,780,400	29.4
1790	3,929,214	41.3
1800	5,308,483	35.1
1810	7,239,881	36.4
1820	9,638,453	33.1
1830	12,866,020	33.5
1840	17,069,453	32.7
1850	23,191,876	35.9
1860	31,443,321	35.6
1870	39,818,449	26.6
1880	50,155,783	26.0
1890	62,947,714	25.5
1900	75,994,575	20.7
1910	91,972,266	21.0
1920	105,710,620	14.9
1930	122,775,046	16.1
1940	131,669,275	7.2
1950	151,325,798	14.5
1960	179,323,175	18.5
1970	203,302,031	13.4
1980	226,542,199	11.4
1990	248,718,301	9.8
2000	281,421,906	13.1

Source: *Historical Statistics of the United States* (1975); *Statistical Abstract by the United States* (2001).
Note: Figures for 1630–1780 include British colonies within limits of present United States only; Native American population included only in 1930 and thereafter.

WORK FORCE

Year	Total Number Workers (1000s)	Farmers as % of Total	Women as % of Total	% Workers in Unions
1810	2,330	84	(NA)	(NA)
1840	5,660	75	(NA)	(NA)
1860	11,110	53	(NA)	(NA)
1870	12,506	53	15	(NA)
1880	17,392	52	15	(NA)
1890	23,318	43	17	(NA)
1900	29,073	40	18	3
1910	38,167	31	21	6
1920	41,614	26	21	12
1930	48,830	22	22	7
1940	53,011	17	24	27
1950	59,643	12	28	25
1960	69,877	8	32	26
1970	82,049	4	37	25
1980	106,940	3	43	23
1990	125,840	3	45	16
2000	140,863	2	47	12

Source: *Historical Statistics of the United States* (1975); *Statistical Abstract of the United States* (2001).

VITAL STATISTICS (IN THOUSANDS)

Year	Births	Deaths	Marriages	Divorces
1800	55	(NA)	(NA)	(NA)
1810	54.3	(NA)	(NA)	(NA)
1820	55.2	(NA)	(NA)	(NA)
1830	51.4	(NA)	(NA)	(NA)
1840	51.8	(NA)	(NA)	(NA)
1850	43.3	(NA)	(NA)	(NA)
1860	44.3	(NA)	(NA)	(NA)
1870	38.3	(NA)	9.6 (1867)	0.3 (1867)
1880	39.8	(NA)	9.1 (1875)	0.3 (1875)
1890	31.5	(NA)	9.0	0.5
1900	32.3	17.2	9.3	0.7
1910	30.1	14.7	10.3	0.9
1920	27.7	13.0	12.0	1.6
1930	21.3	11.3	9.2	1.6
1940	19.4	10.8	12.1	2.0
1950	24.1	9.6	11.1	2.6
1960	23.7	9.5	8.5	2.2
1970	18.4	9.5	10.6	3.5
1980	15.9	8.8	10.6	5.2
1990	16.7	8.6	9.8	4.7
1997	14.6	8.6	8.9	4.3

Source: *Historical Statistics of the United States* (1975); *Statistical Abstract of the United States* (1999).

RACIAL COMPOSITION OF THE POPULATION

(IN THOUSANDS)

Year	White	Black	Indian	Hispanic	Asian/Pacific Islander
1790	3,172	757	(NA)	(NA)	(NA)
1800	4,306	1,002	(NA)	(NA)	(NA)
1820	7,867	1,772	(NA)	(NA)	(NA)
1840	14,196	2,874	(NA)	(NA)	(NA)
1860	26,923	4,442	(NA)	(NA)	(NA)
1880	43,403	6,581	(NA)	(NA)	(NA)
1900	66,809	8,834	(NA)	(NA)	(NA)
1910	81,732	9,828	(NA)	(NA)	(NA)
1920	94,821	10,463	(NA)	(NA)	(NA)
1930	110,287	11,891	(NA)	(NA)	(NA)
1940	118,215	12,866	(NA)	(NA)	(NA)
1950	134,942	15,042	(NA)	(NA)	(NA)
1960	158,832	18,872	(NA)	(NA)	(NA)
1970	178,098	22,581	(NA)	(NA)	(NA)
1980	194,713	26,683	1,420	14,609	3,729
1990	208,727	30,511	2,065	22,372	2,462
2000	211,461	34,658	2,476	35,306	10,642

Source: U.S. Bureau of the Census, U.S. *Census of Population: 1940*, vol. II, part 1, and vol. IV, part 1; *1950*, vol. II, part 1; *1960*, vol. I, part 1; *1970*, vol. I, part B; and *Current Population Reports*, P25-1095 and P25-1104; *Statistical Abstract of the United States* (2001).

IMMIGRATION BY THE ORIGIN

(IN THOUSANDS)

Period	Europe	Americas	Asia
1820–30	106	12	—
1831–40	496	33	—
1841–50	1,597	62	—
1851–60	2,453	75	42
1861–70	2,065	167	65
1871–80	2,272	404	70
1881–90	4,735	427	70
1891–1900	3,555	39	75
1901–10	8,065	362	324
1911–20	4,322	1,144	247
1921–30	2,463	1,517	112
1931–40	348	160	16
1941–50	621	355	32
1951–60	1,326	997	150
1961–70	1,123	1,716	590
1971–80	800	1,983	1,588
1981–90	762	3,616	2,738
1991–2000	1,100	3,800	2,200

Source: Historical Statistics of the United States (1975); *Statistical Abstract of the United States* (1991); Population Estimates Program, Population Division, U.S. Census Bureau, April 2001.

GLOSSARY

1938 Fair Labor Standards Act Act that established the first federal minimum wage (25 ¢ an hour) and set a maximum work week of forty-four hours for all employees engaged in interstate commerce.

Acquired immune deficiency syndrome (AIDS) A complex of deadly pathologies resulting from infection with the human immunodeficiency virus (HIV).

Actual representation The practice whereby elected representatives normally reside in their districts and are directly responsive to local interests.

Affirmative action A set of policies to open opportunities in business and education for members of minority groups and women by allowing race and sex to be factors included in decisions to hire, award contracts, or admit students to higher education programs.

Alamo Franciscan mission at San Antonio, Texas that was the site in 1836 of a siege and massacre of Texans by Mexican troops.

Albany Regency The tightly disciplined state political machine built by Martin Van Buren in New York.

Alien and Sedition Acts Collective name given to four acts passed by Congress in 1798 that curtailed freedom of speech and the liberty of foreign residents in the United States.

Alliance for Progress Program of economic aid to Latin America during the Kennedy administration.

Allies In World War I, Britain, France, Russia, and other belligerent nations fighting against the Central Powers but not including the United States.

Almanac A combination calendar, astrological guide, and sourcebook of medical advice and farming tips.

American Colonization Society Organization, founded in 1817 by antislavery reformers, that called for gradual emancipation and the removal of freed blacks to Africa.

American Federation of Labor (AFL) Union formed in 1886 that organized skilled workers along craft lines and emphasized a few workplace issues rather than a broad social program.

American Indian Movement (AIM) Group of Native-American political activists who used confrontations with the federal government to publicize their case for Indian rights.

American Society for the Promotion of Temperance Largest reform organization of its time dedicated to ending the sale and consumption of alcoholic beverages.

American system A technique of production pioneered in the United States that relied on precision manufacturing with the use of interchangeable parts.

American System The program of government subsidies favored by Henry Clay and his followers to promote American economic growth and protect domestic manufacturers from foreign competition.

Annapolis Convention Conference of state delegates at Annapolis, Maryland, that issued a call in September 1786 for a convention to meet at Philadelphia to consider fundamental changes.

Anti-Federalists Opponents of the Constitution in the debate over its ratification.

Appeal to the Colored Citizens of the World Written by David Walker, a published insistence that "America is more our country, than it is the whites'—we have enriched it with our blood and tears."

Archaic period The period roughly 10,000 to 2,500 years ago marked by the retreat of glaciers.

Articles of Confederation Written document setting up the loose confederation of states that comprised the first national government of the United States.

Athapascan A people that began to settle the forests in the northwestern area of North America around 5000 B.C.E.

Atlantic Charter Statement of common principles and war aims developed by President Franklin Roosevelt and British Prime Minister Winston Churchill at a meeting in August 1941.

Axis powers The opponents of the United States and its allies in World War II.

Aztecs A warrior people who dominated the Valley of Mexico from 1100–1521.

Bacon's Rebellion Violent conflict in Virginia (1675–1676), beginning with settler attacks on Indians but culminating in a rebellion led by Nathaniel Bacon against Virginia's government.

Bank War The political struggle between President Andrew Jackson and the supporters of the Second Bank of the United States.

Battle of New Orleans Decisive American War of 1812 victory over British troops in January 1815 that ended any British hopes of gaining control of the lower Mississippi River Valley.

Battle of the Bulge German offensive in December, 1944 that penetrated deep into Belgium (creating a "bulge"). Allied forces, while outnumbered, attacked from the north and south. By January, 1945, the German forces were destroyed or routed, but not without some 77,000 Allied casualities.

Bay of Pigs Site in Cuba of an unsuccessful landing by fourteen hundred anti-Castro Cuban refugees in April 1961.

Beaver Wars Series of bloody conflicts, occurring between 1640s and 1680s, during which the Iroquois fought the French for control of the fur trade in the east and the Great Lakes region.

Benjamin Franklin's Plan of Union Plan put forward in 1754 calling for an intercolonial union to manage defense and Indian affairs. The plan was rejected by participants at the Albany Congress.

Beringia A subcontinent bridging Asia and North America, named after the Bering Straits.

Berlin blockade Three-hundred-day Soviet blockade of land access to United States, British, and French occupation zones in Berlin, 1948–1949.

Bill for Establishing Religious Freedom A bill authored by Thomas Jefferson establishing religious freedom in Virginia.

Bill of Rights A written summary of inalienable rights and liberties.

Black codes Laws passed by states and municipalities denying many rights of citizenship to free black people before the Civil War.

Black Hawk 1832 war in which federal troops and Illinois militia units defeated the Sauk and Fox Indians led by Black Hawk.

Black Panther Political and social movement among black Americans, founded in Oakland, California, in 1966 that emphasized black economic and political power.

Black Power Philosophy emerging after 1965 that real economic and political gains for African Americans could come only through self-help, self-determination, and organizing for direct political influence.

Bleeding Kansas Violence between pro– and antislavery forces in Kansas Territory after the passage of the Kansas-Nebraska Act in 1854.

Blitzkrieg German war tactic in World War II ("lightning war") involving the concentration of air and armored firepower to punch and exploit holes in opposing defensive lines.

Bolsheviks Member of the Communist movement in Russia that established the Soviet government after the 1917 Russian Revolution.

Bonus Army Unemployed veterans of World War I gathering in Washington in 1932 demanding payment of service bonuses not due until 1945.

Bosnia A nation in southeast Europe that split off from Yugoslavia and became the site of bitter civil and religious war, requiring NATO and U.S. intervention in the 1990s.

Boston Massacre After months of increasing friction between townspeople and the British troops stationed in the city, on March 5, 1770, British troops fired on American civilians in Boston.

Boston Tea Party Incident that occurred on December 16, 1773, in which Bostonians, disguised as Indians, destroyed £9,000 worth of tea belonging to the British East India Company in order to prevent payment of the duty on it.

Brown v. Board of Education Supreme Court decision in 1954 that declared that "separate but equal" schools for children of different races violated the Constitution.

Cahokia One of the largest urban centers created by Mississippian peoples, containing 30,000 residents in 1250.

Californios Californians of Spanish descent.

Calvinist theology of predestination Belief that God has predestined certain individuals to be saved and others to be damned.

Caminetti Act 1893 act giving the state the power to regulate the mines.

Camp David Accords Agreement signed by Israel in Egypt in 1978 that set the formal terms for peace in the Middle East.

Carpetbaggers Northern transplants to the South, many of whom were Union soldiers who stayed in the South after the war.

Central Intelligence Agency (CIA) Agency established in 1947 that coordinates the gathering and evaluation of military and economic information on other nations.

Central Powers Germany and its World War I allies in Austria, Italy, Turkey, and Bulgaria.

Chinese Exclusion Act Act which suspended Chinese immigration, limited the civil rights of resident Chinese, and forbade their naturalization.

Civil Rights Act 1866 Act that gave full citizenship to African Americans.

Civil Rights Act of 1964 Federal legislation that outlawed discrimination in public accommodations and employment on the basis of race, skin color, sex, religion, or national origin.

Clans Groups of allied families.

Clayton Antitrust Act of 1914 Replaced the old Sherman Act of 1890 as the nation's basic antitrust law. It exempted unions from being construed as illegal combinations in restraint of trade, and it forbade federal courts from issuing injunctions against strikers.

Clovis tradition A powerful new and sophisticated style of tool making, unlike anything found in the Old World.

Coercive Acts Legislation passed by Parliament in 1774; included the Boston Port Act, the Massachusetts Government Act, the Administration of Justice Act, and the Quartering Act of 1774.

Cold war The political and economic confrontation between the Soviet Union and the United States that dominated world affairs from 1946 to 1989.

Committee of Safety Any of the extralegal committees that directed the revolutionary movement and carried on the functions of government at the local level in the period between the breakdown of royal authority and the establishment of regular governments.

Committee on Public Information (CPI) Government agency during World War I that sought to shape public opinion in support of the war effort through newspapers, pamphlets, speeches, films, and other media.

Committees of Correspondence Committees formed in Massachusetts and other colonies in the pre-Revolutionary period to keep Americans informed about British measures that would affect the colonies.

Compromise of 1850 The four-step compromise which admitted California as a free state, allowed the residents of the New Mexico and Utah territories to decide the slavery issue for themselves, ended the slave trade in the District of Columbia, and passed a new fugitive slave law to enforce the constitutional provision stating that a slave escaping into a free state shall be delivered back to the owner.

Compromise of 1877 The Congressional settling of the 1876 election which installed Republican Rutherford B. Hayes in the White House and gave Democrats control of all state governments in the South.

Confederate States of America Nation proclaimed in Montgomery, Alabama, in February 1861, after the seven states of the Lower South seceded from the United States.

Congregationalists Members of Puritan churches governed by congregations.

Congress of Industrial Organizations An alliance of industrial unions that spurred the 1930s organizational drive among the mass-production industries.

Congress of Racial Equality (CORE) Civil rights group formed in 1942 and committed to nonviolent civil disobedience.

Congressional Reconstruction Name given to the period 1867–1870 when the Republican-dominated Congress controlled Reconstruction-era policy.

Conspicuous consumption Highly visible displays of wealth and consumption.

Constitutional Convention Convention that met in Philadelphia in 1787 and drafted the Constitution of the United States.

Constitutional Union Party National party formed in 1860, mainly by former Whigs, that emphasized allegiance to the Union and strict enforcement of all national legislation.

Continental Army The regular or professional army authorized by the Second Continental Congress and commanded by General George Washington during the Revolutionary War.

Continental Congress Convention of delegates from the colonies that first met to organize resistance to the Intolerable Acts.

Contract with America Platform proposing a sweeping reduction in the role and activities of the federal government on which many Republican candidates ran for Congress in 1994.

Contras Nicaraguan exiles armed and organized by the CIA to fight the Sandinista government of Nicaragua.

Copperheads A term Republicans applied to Northern war dissenters and those suspected of aiding the Confederate cause during the Civil War.

Council of Economic Advisors Board of three professional economists established in 1946 to advise the president on economic policy.

Counterculture Various alternatives to mainstream values and behaviors that became popular in the 1960s, including experimentation with psychedelic drugs, communal living, a return to the land, Asian religions, and experimental art.

Coureurs de bois French for "woods runner," an independent fur trader in New France.

Covenant Chain An alliance between the Iroquois Confederacy and the colony of New York which sought to establish Iroquois dominance over all other tribes and thus put New York in an economically and politically dominant position among the other colonies.

Coxey's Army A protest march of unemployed workers, led by Populist businessman Jacob Coxey, demanding inflation and a public works program during the depression of the 1890s.

Cuban missile crisis Crisis between the Soviet Union and the United States over the placement of Soviet nuclear missiles in Cuba.

Culpeper's Rebellion The overthrow of the established government in the Albermarle region of North Carolina by back-country men in 1677.

Dawes Severalty Act An 1887 law terminating tribal ownership of land and allotting some parcels of land to individual Indians with the remainder opened for white settlement.

D-Day June 6, 1944, the day of the first paratroop drops and amphibious landings on the coast of Normandy, France, in the first stage of Operation Overlord during World War II.

Declaration of Independence The document by which the Second Continental Congress announced and justified its decision to renounce the colonies' allegiance to the British government.

Declaration of Sentiments The resolutions passed at the Seneca Falls Convention in 1848 calling for full female equality, including the right to vote.

Declaratory Act Law passed in 1776 to accompany repeal of the Stamp Act that stated that Parliament had the authority to legislate for the colonies "in all cases whatsoever."

Defense of Marriage Act Act which specified that gay couples would be ineligible for spousal benefits provided by federal law.

Democrats Political party formed in the 1820s under the leadership of Andrew Jackson; favored states' rights and a limited role for the federal government.

Denmark Vesey's conspiracy The most carefully devised slave revolt in which rebels planned to seize control of Charleston in 1822 and escape to freedom in Haiti, a free black republic, but they were betrayed by other slaves, and seventy-five conspirators were executed.

Deregulation Reduction or removal of government regulations and encouragement of direct competition in many important industries and economic sectors.

Détente (French for "easing of tension.") Used to describe the new U.S. relations with China and the Soviet Union in 1972.

Dingley Tariff of 1897 Act which raised import duties to an all-time high.

Dixiecrat States' Rights Democrats.

Dred Scott decision Supreme Court ruling, in a lawsuit brought by Dred Scott, a slave demanding his freedom based on his residence in a free state, that slaves could not be U.S. citizens and that Congress had no jurisdiction over slavery in the territories.

Eastern Front The area of military operations in World War II located east of Germany in eastern Europe and the Soviet Union.

Economic Recovery Tax Act of 1981 A major revision of the federal income tax system.

Edmunds Act 1882 act that effectively disfranchised those who believed in or practiced polygamy and threatened them with fines and imprisonment.

Edmunds-Tucker Act 1887 act which destroyed the temporal power of the Mormon Church by confiscating all assets over $50,000 and establishing a federal commission to oversee all elections in the Utah territory.

Emancipation Proclamation Decree announced by President Abraham Lincoln in September 1862 and formally issued on January 1, 1863, freeing slaves in all Confederate states still in rebellion.

Embargo Act Act passed by Congress in 1807 prohibiting American ships from leaving for any foreign port.

Emergency Banking Act 1933 act which gave the president broad discretionary powers over all banking transactions and foreign exchange.

Empresarios Agents who received a land grant from the Spanish or Mexican government in return for organizing settlements.

Encomienda In the Spanish colonies, the grant to a Spanish settler of a certain number of Indian subjects, who would pay him tribute in goods and labor.

Engagés Catholic immigrants to New France.

Enlightenment Intellectual movement stressing the importance of reason and the existence of discoverable natural laws.

Enumerated goods Items produced in the colonies and enumerated in acts of Parliament that could be legally shipped from the colony of origin only to specified locations.

Environmental Protection Agency Federal agency created in 1970 to oversee environmental monitoring and cleanup programs.

Equal Pay Act of 1963 Act that made it illegal for employers to pay men and women different wages for the same job.

Era of Good Feelings The period from 1817 to 1823 in which the disappearance of the Federalists enabled the Republicans to govern in a spirit of seemingly nonpartisan harmony.

Espionage Act Law whose vague prohibition against obstructing the nation's war effort was used to crush dissent and criticism during World War I.

Farmers' Alliance A broad mass movement in the rural South and West during the late nineteenth century, encompassing several organizations and demanding economic and political reforms.

Federal Highway Act of 1956 Measure that provided federal funding to build a nationwide system of interstate and defense highways.

Federal Reserve Act The 1913 law that revised banking and currency by extending limited government regulation through the creation of the Federal Reserve System.

Federal Trade Commission (FTC) Government agency established in 1914 to provide regulatory oversight of business activity.

Federalism The sharing of powers between the national government and the states.

Federalists Supporters of the Constitution who favored its ratification.

Female Moral Reform Society Antiprostitution group founded by evangelical women in New York in 1834.

Feudalism A medieval European social system in which land was divided into hundreds of small holdings.

Field Order 15 Order by General William T. Sherman in January 1865 to set aside abandoned land along the Southern Atlantic coast for forty-acre grants to freedmen; rescinded by President Andrew Johnson later that year.

Fifteenth Amendment Passed by Congress in 1869, guaranteed the right of American men to vote, regardless of race.

Fireside chat Speeches broadcast nationally over the radio in which President Franklin D. Roosevelt explained complex issues and programs in plain language, as though his listeners were gathered around the fireside with him.

First Continental Congress Meeting of delegates from most of the colonies held in 1774 in response to the Coercive Acts.

The Congress endorsed the Suffolk Resolves, adopted the Declaration of Rights and Grievances, and agreed to establish the Continental Association.

Food and Drug Act Act that established the Food and Drug Administration (FDA), which tested and approved drugs before they went on the market.

Forest Management Act 1897 act which, along with the National Reclamation Act, set the federal government on the path of large-scale regulatory activities.

Frame of Government William Penn's constitution for Pennsylvania which included a provision allowing for religious freedom.

Free silver Philosophy that the government should expand the money supply by purchasing and coining all the silver offered to it.

Free speech movement Student movement at the University of California, Berkeley, formed in 1964 to protest limitations on political activities on campus.

Freedmen's Bureau Agency established by Congress in March 1865 to provide social, educational, and economic services, advice, and protection to former slaves and destitute whites; lasted seven years.

Freedom Summer Voter registration effort in rural Mississippi organized by black and white civil rights workers in 1964.

French and Indian War The last of the Anglo-French colonial wars (1754–1763) and the first in which fighting began in North America. The war ended with France's defeat.

Fugitive Slave Law Part of the Compromise of 1850 that required the authorities in the North to assist Southern slave catchers and return runaway slaves to their owners.

Gabriel's Rebellion Slave revolt that failed when Gabriel Prosser, a slave preacher and blacksmith, organized a thousand slaves for an attack on Richmond, Virginia, in 1800.

Gang System The organization and supervision of slave field hands into working teams on Southern plantations.

General Land Revision Act of 1891 Act which gave the president the power to establish forest reserves to protect watersheds against the threats posed by lumbering, overgrazing, and forest fires.

Geneva Accord Accord that called for reunification and national elections in Vietnam in 1956.

GI Bill Legislation in June 1944 that eased the return of veterans into American society by providing educational and employment benefits.

Gilded Age Term applied to late nineteenth-century America that refers to the shallow display and worship of wealth characteristic of that period.

Glasnost Russian for "openness" applied to Mikhail Gorbachev's encouragement of new ideas and easing of political repression in the Soviet Union.

Gospel of wealth Thesis that hard work and perseverance lead to wealth, implying that poverty is a character flaw.

Gramm-Rudman Law that mandated automatic spending cuts if the government failed to meet fixed deficit reduction goals leading to a balanced budget by 1991.

Grandfather clauses Rules that required potential voters to demonstrate that their grandfathers had been eligible to vote; used in some Southern states after 1890 to limit the black electorate.

Grange The National Grange of the Patrons of Husbandry, a national organization of farm owners formed after the Civil War.

Granger laws State laws enacted in the Midwest in the 1870s that regulated rates charged by railroads, grain elevator operators, and other middlemen.

Great Awakening North American religious revival in the middle of the eighteenth century.

Great Awakening Tremendous religious revival in colonial America striking first in the Middle Colonies and New England in the 1740s and then spreading to the Southern colonies.

Great Compromise Plan proposed at the 1787 Constitutional Convention for creating a national bicameral legislature in which all states would be equally represented in the Senate and proportionally represented in the House.

Great Depression The nation's worst economic crisis, extending through the 1930s, producing unprecedented bank failures, unemployment, and industrial and agricultural collapse.

Great Migration Puritan emigration to North America between 1629 and 1643.

Great Migration The mass movement of African Americans from the rural South to the urban North, spurred especially by new job opportunities during World War I and the 1920s.

Great Society Theme of Lyndon Johnson's administration, focusing on poverty, education, and civil rights.

Great Uprising Unsuccessful railroad strike of 1877 to protest wage cuts and the use of federal troops against strikers; the first nationwide work stoppage in American history.

Half-Way Covenant Plan adopted in 1662 by New England clergy to deal with the problem of declining church membership, allowing children of baptized parents to be baptized whether or not their parents had experienced conversion.

Harlem Renaissance A new African American cultural awareness that flourished in literature, art, and music in the 1920s.

Hepburn Act Act that strengthened the Interstate Commerce Commission (ICC) by authorizing it to set maximum railroad rates and inspect financial records.

Hispanic-American Alliance Organization formed to protect and fight for the rights of Spanish Americans.

Holocaust The systematic murder of millions of European Jews and others deemed undesirable by Nazi Germany.

Homestead Act Law passed by Congress in May 1862 providing homesteads with 160 acres of free land in exchange for improving the land within five years of the grant.

Homestead Act of 1862 1862 act which granted a quarter section (160 acres) of the public domain free to any settler who lived on the land for at least five years and improved it.

Horizontal combination The merger of competitors in the same industry.

House of Burgesses The legislature of colonial Virginia. First organized in 1619, it was the first institution of representative government in the English colonies.

House Un-American Activities Committee (HUAC) Originally intended to ferret out pro-Fascists, it later investigated "un-American propaganda" that attacked constitutional government.

Immigration Act 1921 act setting a maximum of 357,000 new immigrants each year.

Imperialism The policy and practice of exploiting nations and peoples for the benefit of an imperial power either directly through military occupation and colonial rule or indirectly through economic domination of resources and markets.

Indentured Servants Individuals who contracted to serve a master for a period of four to seven years in return for payment of the servant's passage to America.

Indian Removal Act President Andrew Jackson's measure that allowed state officials to override federal protection of Native Americans.

Industrial Revolution Revolution in the means and organization of production.

Initiative Procedure by which citizens can introduce a subject for legislation, usually through a petition signed by a specific number of voters.

Intercourse Act Basic law passed by Congress in 1790 which stated that the United States would regulate trade and interaction with Indian tribes.

International Bank for Reconstruction and Development (World Bank) Designed to revive postwar international trade, it drew on the resources of member nations to make economic development loans to governments for such projects as new dams or agricultural modernization.

International Monetary Fund (IMF) International organization established in 1945 to assist nations in maintaining stable currencies.

Internet The system of interconnected computers and servers that allows the exchange of email, posting of Web sites, and other means of instant communication.

Interstate Commerce Commission (ICC) The 1887 law that expanded federal power over business by prohibiting pooling and discriminatory rates by railroads and establishing the first federal regulatory agency, the Interstate Commerce Commission.

Intolerable Acts American term for the Coercive Acts and the Quebec Act.

Irreconcilables Group of U.S. senators adamantly opposed to ratification of the Treaty of Versailles after World War I.

Island hopping The Pacific campaigns of 1944 that were the American naval versions of the Blitzkrieg.

Issei The first generation of Japanese to come to America starting in the late1800s.

Jay's Treaty Treaty with Britain negotiated in 1794 in which the United States made major concessions to avert a war over the British seizure of American ships.

Jim Crow laws Segregation laws that became widespread in the South during the 1890s.

John Brown's raid New England abolitionist John Brown's ill-fated attempt to free Virginia's slaves with a raid on the federal arsenal at Harper's Ferry, Virginia, in 1859.

Judicial review A power implied in the Constitution that gives federal courts the right to review and determine the constitutionality of acts passed by Congress and state legislatures.

Judiciary Act of 1789 Act of Congress that implemented the judiciary clause of the Constitution by establishing the Supreme Court and a system of lower federal courts.

Kachinas Impersonations of the ancestral spirits by Southwest Indians.

Kansas-Nebraska Act Law passed in 1854 creating the Kansas and Nebraska Territories but leaving the question of slavery open to residents, thereby repealing the Missouri Compromise.

King George's War The third Anglo-French war in North America (1744–1748), part of the European conflict known as the War of the Austrian Succession.

King Philip's War Conflict in New England (1675–1676) between Wampanoags, Narragansetts, and other Indian peoples against English settlers; sparked by English encroachments on native lands.

King William's War The first Anglo-French conflict in North America (1689–1697), the American phase of Europe's War of the League of Augsburg.

King William's War The first of a series of colonial struggles between England and France; these conflicts occurred principally on the frontiers of northern New England and New York between 1689 and 1697.

Knights of Labor Labor union founded in 1869 that included skilled and unskilled workers irrespective of race or gender.

Know-Nothings Name given to the antiimmigrant party formed from the wreckage of the Whig Party and some disaffected Northern Democrats in 1854.

Korean War Pacific war started on June 25, 1950, when North Korea, helped by Soviet equipment and Chinese training, attacked South Korea.

Kosovo Province of Yugoslavia where the United States and NATO intervened militarily in 1999 to protect ethnic Albanians from expulsion.

Ku Klux Klan Perhaps the most prominent of the vigilante groups that terrorized black people in the South during Reconstruction era, founded by the Confederate veterans in 1866.

Land Ordinance of 1785 Act passed by Congress under the Articles of Confederation that created the grid system of surveys by which all subsequent public land was made available for sale.

Landrum-Griffin Act 1959 act that widened government control over union affairs and further restricted union use of picketing and secondary boycotts during strikes.

League of Nations International organization created by the Versailles Treaty after World War I to ensure world stability.

League of Women Voters League formed in 1920 advocating for women's rights, among them the right for women to serve on juries and equal pay laws.

Lecompton constitution Proslavery draft written in 1857 by Kansas territorial delegates elected under questionable circumstances; it was rejected by two governors, supported by President Buchanan, and decisively defeated by Congress.

Legal Tender Act Act creating a national currency in February 1862.

Lend-Lease Act An arrangement for the transfer of war supplies, including food, machinery, and services to nations whose defense was considered vital to the defense of the United States in Word War II.

Liberal Republicans Disaffected Republicans that emphasized the doctrines of classical economics.

Liberty Bonds Interest-bearing certificates sold by the U.S. government to finance the American World War I effort.

Liberty Party The first antislavery political party, formed in 1840.

Limited Nuclear Test-Ban Treaty Treaty, signed by the United States, Britain, and the Soviet Union, outlawing nuclear testing in the atmosphere, in outer space, and under water.

Lincoln-Douglas debates Series of debates in the 1858 Illinois senatorial campaign during which Douglas and Lincoln staked out their differing opinions on the issue of slavery.

Loyalists British colonists who opposed independence from Britain.

Lynching Execution, usually by a mob, without trial.

Manifest destiny Doctrine, first expressed in 1845, that the expansion of white Americans across the continent was inevitable and ordained by God.

Manumissions Grant of freedom to slaves by individual masters.

Marbury v. Madison Supreme Court decision of 1803 that created the precedent of judicial review by ruling as unconstitutional part of the Judiciary Act of 1789.

Market revolution The outcome of three interrelated developments: rapid improvements in transportation, commercialization, and industrialization.

Marshall Plan Secretary of State George C. Marshall's European Recovery Plan of June 5, 1947, committing the United States to help in the rebuilding of post–World War II Europe.

Massachusetts Bay Company A group of wealthy Puritans who were granted a royal charter in 1629 to settle in Massachusetts Bay.

Mayflower Compact The first document of self-government in North America.

McCarthyism Anti-Communist attitudes and actions associated with Senator Joe McCarthy in the early 1950s, including smear tactics and innuendo.

Medicare Basic medical insurance for the elderly, financed through the federal government; program created in 1965.

Mercantilism Economic system whereby the government intervenes in the economy for the purpose of increasing national wealth.

Mesoamerica The region stretching from central Mexico to Central America.

Mexican-American War War fought between Mexico and the United States between 1846 and 1848 over control of territory in southwest North America.

Middle Passage The voyage between West Africa and the New World slave colonies.

Militarism The tendency to see military might as the most important and best tool for the expansion of a nation's power and prestige.

Minutemen Special companies of militia formed in Massachusetts and elsewhere beginning in late 1744.

Missouri Compromise Sectional compromise in Congress in 1820 that admitted Missouri to the Union as a slave state and Maine as a free state and prohibited slavery in the northern Louisiana Purchase territory.

Monroe Doctrine Declaration by President James Monroe in 1823 that the Western Hemisphere was to be closed off to further European colonization and that the United States would not interfere in the internal affairs of European nations.

Monroe Doctrine In December 1823, Monroe declared to Congress that Americans "are henceforth not to be considered as subjects for future colonization by any European power."

Morrill Act of 1862 Act by which "land-grant" colleges acquired space for campuses in return for promising to institute agricultural programs.

Morrill Land Grant Act Law passed by Congress in July 1862 awarding proceeds from the sale of public lands to the states for the establishment of agricultural and mechanical colleges.

Morrill Tariff Act Act that raised tariffs to more than double their prewar rate.

Muckraking Journalism exposing economic, social, and political evils, so named by Theodore Roosevelt for its "raking the muck" of American society.

Multiculturalism Movement that emphasized the unique attributes and achievements of formerly marginal groups and recent immigrants.

My Lai Massacre Killing of twenty-two Vietnamese civilians by U.S. forces during a 1968 search-and-destroy mission.

Nat Turner's Revolt Uprising of slaves in Southampton County, Virginia, in the summer of 1831 led by Nat Turner that resulted in the death of fifty-five white people.

Nation of Islam (NOI) Religious movement among black Americans that emphasizes self-sufficiency, self-help, and separation from white society.

National Aeronautics and Space Administration (NASA) Federal agency created in 1958 to manage American space flights and exploration.

National American Woman Suffrage Association (NAWSA) The organization, formed in 1890, that coordinated the ultimately successful campaign to achieve women's right to vote.

National Association for the Advancement of Colored People Interracial organization co-founded by W. E. B. DuBois in 1910 dedicated to restoring African-American political and social rights.

National Bank Act Act prohibiting state banks from issuing their own notes and forcing them to apply for federal charters.

National Defense Education Act (NDEA) 1958 act that allocated $280 million in grants for state universities to upgrade their science facilities, created $300 million in low-interest loans for college students, and provided fellowship support for graduate students planning to go into college and university teaching.

National Industrial Recovery Act 1933 act which was meant to be a systematic plan for economic recovery.

National Labor Relations Act Act establishing Federal guarantee of right to organize trade unions and collective bargaining.

National Reclamation Act 1902 act which added 1 million acres of irrigated land to the United States.

National Security Council (NSC) The formal policymaking body for national defense and foreign relations, created in 1947 and consisting of the president, the secretary of defense, the secretary of state, and others appointed by the president.

National Security Council Paper 68 (NSC-68) Policy statement that committed the United States to a military approach to the Cold War.

Nationalists Group of leaders in the 1780s who spearheaded the drive to replace the Articles of Confederation with a stronger central government.

Nativism Favoring the interests and culture of native-born inhabitants over those of immigrants.

Neutrality Act of 1939 Permitted the sale of arms to Britain, France, and China.

New Deal coalition Coalition that included traditional-minded white Southern Democrats, big-city political machines, industrial workers of all races, trade unionists, and many Depression-hit farmers.

New deal The economic and political policies of the Roosevelt administration in the 1930s.

New Freedom Woodrow Wilson's 1912 program for limited government intervention in the economy to restore competition by curtailing the restrictive influences of trusts and protective tariffs, thereby providing opportunities for individual achievement.

New Frontier John F. Kennedy's domestic and foreign policy initiatives, designed to reinvigorate sense of national purpose and energy.

New Jersey Plan Proposal of the New Jersey delegation for a strengthened national government in which all states would have an equal representation in a unicameral legislature.

New Lights People who experienced conversion during the revivals of the Great Awakening.

Niagara movement African American group organized in 1905 to promote racial integration, civil and political rights, and equal access to economic opportunity.

Nisei U.S. citizens born of immigrant Japanese parents.

Nonimportation movement A tactical means of putting economic pressure on Britain by refusing to buy its exports to the colonies.

North American Free Trade Agreement (NAFTA) Agreement reached in 1993 by Canada, Mexico, and the United States to substantially reduce barriers to trade.

North Atlantic Treaty Organization (NATO) Organization of ten European countries, Canada, and the United States who together formed a mutual defense pact in April 1949.

Northwest Ordinance of 1787 Legislation that prohibited slavery in the Northwest Territories and provided the model for the incorporation of future territories into the union as co-equal states.

Nullification A constitutional doctrine holding that a state has a legal right to declare a national law null and void within its borders.

Nullification Crisis Sectional crisis in the early 1830s in which a states' rights party in South Carolina attempted to nullify federal law.

Office of Economic Opportunity (OEO) Federal agency that coordinated many programs of the war on poverty between 1964 and 1975.

Old Lights Religious faction that condemned emotional enthusiasm as part of the heresy of believing in a personal and direct relationship with God outside the order of the church.

Omaha Act of 1882 Act which allowed the establishment of individual title to tribal lands.

Open Door American policy of seeking equal trade and investment opportunities in foreign nations or regions.

Open shop Factory of business employing workers whether or not they are union members; in practice, such a business usually refuses to hire union members and follows antiunion policies.

Operation Desert Storm U.S. military campaign to force Iraqi forces out of Kuwait.

Operation Overlord United States and British invasion of France in June 1944 during World War II.

Operation Torch The Allied invasion fo Axis-held North Africa in 1942.

Oregon Trail Overland trail of more than two thousand miles that carried American settlers from the Midwest to new settlements in Oregon, California, and Utah.

Organization of Petroleum Exporting Countries (OPEC) Cartel of oil-producing nations in Asia, Africa, and Latin America that gained substantial power over the world economy in the mid- to late 1970s by controlling the production and price of oil.

Panic of 1857 Banking crisis that caused a credit crunch in the North; it was less severe in the South, where high cotton prices spurred a quick recovery.

Pan-Indian military resistance movement Movement calling for the political and cultural unification of Indian tribes in the late eighteenth and early nineteenth centuries.

Patriots British colonists who favored independence from Britain.

Pendleton Civil Service Reform Act A law of 1883 that reformed the spoils system by prohibiting government workers from making political contributions and creating the Civil Service Commission to oversee their appointment on the basis of merit rather than politics.

Peninsular Campaign Union offensive led by McClellan with the objective of capturing Richmond.

Pentagon Papers Classified Defense Department documents on the history of the United States's involvement in Vietnam, prepared in 1968 and leaked to the press in 1971.

Pequot War Conflict between English settlers and Pequot Indians over control of land and trade in eastern Connecticut.

Perestroika Russian for "restructuring," applied to Mikhail Gorbachev's efforts to make the Soviet economic and political systems more modern, flexible, and innovative.

Persian Gulf War War initiated by President Bush in reponse to Iraq's invasion of Kuwait.

Pilgrims Settlers of Plymouth Colony, who viewed themselves as spiritual wanderers.

Pleistocene Overkill Intensified hunting efforts brought on in response to lowered reproduction and survival rates of large animals.

Plessy v. Ferguson Supreme Court decision holding that Louisiana's railroad segregation law did not violate the Constitution as long as the railroads or the state provided equal accommodations.

Poll taxes Taxes imposed on voters as a requirement for voting.

Popular sovereignty A solution to the slavery crisis suggested by Michigan senator Lewis Cass by which territorial residents, not Congress, would decide slavery's fate.

Populist movement A major third party of the 1890s formed on the basis of the Southern Farmer's Alliance and other reform organizations.

Predestination The belief that God decided at the moment of Creation which humans would achieve salvation.

Preparedness Military buildup in preparation for possible U.S. participation in World War I.

Progressive era An era in the United States (roughly between 1900 and 1917) in which important movements challenged traditional relationships and attitudes.

Prohibition A ban on the production, sale, and consumption of liquor, achieved temporarily through state laws and the Eighteenth Amendment.

Proposition 187 California legislation adopted by popular vote in California in 1994, which cuts off state-funded health and education benefits to undocumented or illegal immigrants.

Proprietary colony A colony created when the English monarch granted a huge tract of land to an individual or group of individuals, who became "lords proprietor."

Protective association Organizations formed by mine owners in response to the formation of labor unions.

Protestant Reformation Martin Luther's challenge to the Catholic Church, initiated in 1517, calling for a return to what he understood to be the purer practices and beliefs of the early church.

Protestants All European supporters of religious reform under Charles V's Holy Roman Empire.

Puritans Individuals who believed that Queen Elizabeth's reforms of the Church of England had not gone far enough in improving the church. Puritans led the settlement of Massachusetts Bay Colony.

Putting-out system Production of goods in private homes under the supervision of a merchant who "put out" the raw materials, paid a certain sum per finished piece, and sold the completed item to a distant market.

Quakers Members of the Society of Friends, a radical religious group that arose in the mid-seventeenth century. Quakers rejected formal theology, focusing instead on the Holy Spirit that dwelt within them.

Quartering Act Acts of Parliament requiring colonial legislatures to provide supplies and quarters for the troops stationed in America.

Quasi-War Undeclared naval war of 1797 to 1800 between the United States and France.

Quebec Act Law passed by Parliament in 1774 that provided an appointed government for Canada, enlarged the boundaries of Quebec, and confirmed the privileges of the Catholic Church.

Queen Anne's War American phase (1702–1713) of Europe's War of the Spanish Succession.

Radical Republicans A shifting group of Republican congressmen, usually a substantial minority, who favored the abolition of slavery from the beginning of the Civil War and later advocated harsh treatment of the defeated South.

Rancherias Dispersed settlements of Indian farmers in the Southwest.

Recall The process of removing an official from office by popular vote, usually after using petitions to call for such a vote.

Reconquista The long struggle (ending in 1492) during which Spanish Christians reconquered the Iberian peninsula from Muslim occupiers.

Reconstruction Act 1877 act that divided the South into five military districts subject to martial law.

Red Scare Post–World War I public hysteria over Bolshevik influence in the United States directed against labor activism, radical dissenters, and some ethnic groups.

Redemptioner Similar to an indentured servant, except that a redemptioner signed a labor contract in America rather than in Europe.

Referendum Submission of a law, proposed or already in effect, to a direct popular vote for approval or rejection.

Renaissance The intellectual and artistic flowering in Europe during the fourteenth, fifteenth, and sixteenth centuries sparked by a revival of interest in classical antiquity.

Republican Party Party that emerged in the 1850s in the aftermath of the bitter controversy over the Kansas-Nebraska Act, consisting of former Whigs, some Northern Democrats, and many Know-Nothings.

Republicanism A complex, changing body of ideas, values, and assumptions, closely related to country ideology, that influenced American political behavior during the eighteenth and nineteenth centuries.

Republicans Party headed by Thomas Jefferson that formed in opposition to the financial and diplomatic policies of the Federalist party; favored limiting the powers of the national government and placing the interests of farmers over those of financial and commercial groups.

Roe v. Wade U.S. Supreme Court decision (1973) that disallowed state laws prohibiting abortion during the first three months (trimester) of pregnancy and establishing guidelines for abortion in the second and third trimesters.

Roosevelt Corollary President Theodore Roosevelt's policy asserting U.S. authority to intervene in the affairs of Latin American nations; an expansion of the Monroe Doctrine.

Royal Proclamation of 1763 Royal proclamation setting the boundary known as the Proclamation Line.

Rush-Bagot Treaty of 1817 Treaty between the United States and Britain that effectively demilitarized the Great Lakes by sharply limiting the number of ships each power could station on them.

Sabbatarianism Reform movement that aimed to prevent business on Sundays.

Sand Creek Massacre The near annihilation in 1864 of Black Kettle's Cheyenne band by Colorado troops under Colonel John Chivington's orders to "kill and scalp all, big and little."

Santa Fé Trail The 900-mile trail opened by American merchants for trading purposes following Mexico's liberalization of the formerly restrictive trading policies of Spain.

Scalawags Southern whites, mainly small landowning farmers and well-off merchants and planters, who supported the Southern Republican party during Reconstruction.

Second Bank of the United States A national bank chartered by Congress in 1816 with extensive regulatory powers over currency and credit.

Second Great Awakening Religious revival among black and white Southerners in the 1790s.

Sedition Act Broad law restricting criticism of America's involvement in World War I or its government, flag, military, taxes, or officials.

Segregation A system of racial control that separated the races, initially by custom but increasingly by law during and after Reconstruction.

Selective Service Act The law establishing the military draft for World War I.

Self-determination The right of a people or a nation to decide on its own political allegiance or form of government without external influence.

Seneca Falls convention The first convention for women's equality in legal rights, held in upstate New York in 1848.

Separatists Members of an offshoot branch of Puritanism. Separatists believed that the Church of England was too corrupt to be reformed and hence were convinced they must "separate" from it to save their souls.

Seven Years' War War fought in Europe, North America, and India between 1756 and 1763, pitting France and its allies against Great Britain and its allies.

Shakers The followers of Mother Ann Lee, who preached a religion of strict celibacy and communal living.

Sharecropping Labor system that evolved during and after Reconstruction whereby landowners furnished laborers with a house, farm animals, and tools and advanced credit in exchange for a share of the laborers' crop.

Shays's Rebellion An armed movement of debt-ridden farmers in western Massachusetts in the winter of 1786–1787. The rebellion created a crisis atmosphere.

Sheppard-Towner Act The first federal social welfare law, passed in 1921, providing federal funds for infant and maternity care.

Sherman Antitrust Act The first federal antitrust measure, passed in 1890; sought to promote economic competition by prohibiting business combinations in restraint of trade or commerce.

Sherman Silver Purchase Act 1890 act which directed the Treasury to increase the amount of currency coined from silver mined in the West and also permitted the U.S. government to print paper currency backed by the silver.

Silicon Valley The region of California including San Jose and San Francisco that holds the nation's greatest concentration of electronics firms.

Sixteenth Amendment of 1913 Authorized a federal income tax.

Slaughterhouse cases Group of cases resulting in one sweeping decision by the U.S. Supreme Court in 1873 that contradicted the intent of the Fourteenth Amendment by decreeing that most citizenship rights remained under state, not federal, control.

Slave Codes A series of laws passed mainly in the Southern colonies in the late seventeenth and early eighteenth centuries to defend the status of slaves and codify the denial of basic civil rights to them.

Social Darwinism The application of Charles Darwin's theory of biological evolution to society, holding that the fittest and wealthiest survive, the weak and the poor perish, and government action is unable to alter this "natural" process.

Social Security Act of 1935 Act establishing federal old-age pensions and unemployment insurance.

Solid South The one-party (Democratic) political system that dominated the South from the 1890s to the 1950s.

Sons of Liberty Secret organizations in the colonies formed to oppose the Stamp Act.

Southern Christian Leadership Conference (SCLC) Black civil rights organization founded in 1957 by Martin Luther King Jr. and other clergy.

Southern Farmers' Alliance The largest of several organizations that formed in the post-Reconstruction South to advance the interests of beleaguered small farmers.

Southern Manifesto A document signed by 101 members of Congress from Southern states in 1956 that argued that the Supreme Court's decision in *Brown* v. *Board of Education of Topeka* itself contradicted the Constitution.

Specie Circular Proclamation issued by President Andrew Jackson in 1836 stipulating that only gold or silver could be used as payment for public land.

Stamp Act Congress October 1765 meeting of delegates sent by nine colonies, held in New York City, that adopted the Declaration of Rights and Grievances and petitioned against the Stamp Act.

Stamp Act Law passed by Parliament in 1765 to raise revenue in America by requiring taxed, stamped paper for legal documents, publications, and playing cards.

States' rights Favoring the rights of individual states over rights claimed by the national government.

Strategic Arms Limitation Treaty Treaty signed in 1972 by the United States and the Soviet Union to slow the nuclear arms race.

Strategic Defense Initiative (SDI) President Reagan's program, announced in 1983, to defend the United States against nuclear missile attack with untested weapons systems and sophisticated technologies.

Student Nonviolent Coordinating Committee (SNCC) Black civil rights organization founded in 1960 that drew heavily on younger activists and college students.

Students for a Democratic Society (SDS) The leading student organization of the New Left of the early and mid-1960s.

Suffrage The right to vote in a political election.

Sugar Act Law passed in 1764 to raise revenue in the American colonies. It lowered the duty from 6 pence to 3 pence per gallon on foreign molasses imported into the colonies and increased the restrictions on colonial commerce.

Sunbelt The states of the American South and Southwest.

Taft-Hartley Act Federal legislation of 1947 that substantially limited the tools available to labor unions in labor-management disputes.

Tammany Society A fraternal organization of artisans begun in the 1780s that evolved into a key organization of the new mass politics in New York City.

Tariff of 1789 Apart from a few selected industries, this first tariff passed by Congress was intended to raise revenue and not protect American manufacturers from foreign competition.

Tariff of 1789 Apart from a few selected industries, this first tariff passed by Congress was intended to raise revenue and not protect American manufacturers from foreign competition.

Tea Act of 1773 Act of Parliament that permitted the East India Company to sell through agents in America without paying the duty customarily collected in Britain, thus reducing the retail price.

Tejanos Persons of Spanish or Mexican descent born in Texas.

Temperance Reform movement originating in the 1820s that sought to eliminate the consumption of alcohol.

Tenements Four– to six-story residential dwellings, once common in New York, built on tiny lots without regard to providing ventilation or light.

Tennessee Valley Authority (TVA) Federal regional planning agency established to promote conservation, produce electric power, and encourage economic development in seven Southern states.

Tenure of Office Act Act stipulating that any officeholder appointed by the president with the Senate's advice and consent could not be removed until the Senate had approved a successor.

The Albany movement Coalition formed in 1961 in Albany, a small city in southwest Georgia, of activists from SNCC, the NAACP, and other local groups.

The Toleration Act Act passed in 1661 by King Charles II ordering a stop to religious persecution in Massachusetts.

Thirteenth Amendment Constitutional amendment ratified in 1865 that freed all slaves throughout the United States.

Timber Culture Act 1873 act which allotted homesteaders an additional 160 acres of land in return for planting and cultivating 40 acres of trees.

Tonkin Gulf resolution Request to Congress from President Lyndon Johnson in response to North Vietnamese torpedo boat attacks in which he sought authorization for "all necessary measures" to protect American forces and stop further aggression.

Tories A derisive term applied to Loyalists in America who supported the king and Parliament just before and during the American Revolution.

Townshend Revenue Acts Acts of Parliament, passed in 1767, imposing duties on colonial tea, lead, paint, paper, and glass.

Trail of Broken Treaties 1972 event staged by the American Indian Movement (AIM) that culminated in a week-long occupation of the Bureau of Indian Affairs in Washington, D.C.

Trail of Tears The forced march in 1838 of the Cherokee Indians from their homelands in Georgia to the Indian Territory in the West.

Transcontinental Treaty of 1819 Treaty between the United States and Spain in which Spain ceded Florida to the United States, surrendered all claims to the Pacific Northwest, and agreed to a boundary between the Louisiana Purchase territory and the Spanish Southwest.

Transoceanic migrations A population migration across oceans.

Treaty of Fort Laramie The treaty acknowledging U.S. defeat in the Great Sioux War in 1868 and supposedly guaranteeing the Sioux perpetual land and hunting rights in South Dakota, Wyoming, and Montana.

Treaty of Ghent Treaty signed in December 1814 between the United States and Britain that ended the War of 1812.

Treaty of Greenville Treaty of 1795 in which Native Americans in the Old Northwest were forced to cede most of the present state of Ohio to the United States.

Treaty of Paris The formal end to British hostilities against France and Spain in February 1763.

Treaty of Tordesillas Treaty negotiated by the pope in 1494 to resolve the territorial claims of Spain and Portugal.

Truman Doctrine Doctrine pronounced in President Harry Truman's statement in 1947 that the United States should assist other nations that were facing external pressure or internal revolution.

Underwood-Simmons Act of 1913 Reform law that lowered tariff rates and levied the first regular federal income tax.

Union League Republican party organizations in Northern cities that became an important organizing device among freedmen in Southern cities after 1865.

United States Constitution The written document providing for a new central government of the United States.

Valley Forge Area of Pennsylvania approximately twenty miles northwest of Philadelphia where General George Washington's Continental troops were quartered from December 1777 to June 1778 while British forces occupied Philadelphia during the Revolutionary War.

Versailles Treaty The treaty ending World War I and creating the League of Nations.

Vertical integration The consolidation of numerous production functions, from the extraction of the raw materials to the distribution and marketing of the finished products, under the direction of one firm.

Virginia Company A group of London investors who sent ships to Chesapeake Bay in 1607.

Virginia Plan Proposal calling for a national legislature in which the states would be represented according to population.

Virtual representation The notion that parliamentary members represented the interests of the nation as a whole, not those of the particular district that elected them.

Volstead Act The 1920 law defining the liquor forbidden under the Eighteenth Amendment and giving enforcement responsibilities to the Prohibition Bureau of the Department of the Treasury.

Voting Rights Act Legislation in 1965 that overturned a variety of practices by which states systematically denied voter registration to minorities.

War Hawks Members of Congress, predominantly from the South and West, who aggressively pushed for a war against Britain after their election in 1810.

War Industries Board (WIB) The federal agency that reorganized industry for maximum efficiency and productivity during World War I.

War of 1812 War fought between the United States and Britain from June 1812 to January 1815 largely over British restrictions on American shipping.

War on poverty Set of programs introduced by Lyndon Johnson between 1963 and 1966 designed to break the cycle of poverty by providing funds for job training, community development, nutrition, and supplementary education.

War Powers Act Gave the U.S. president the power to reorganize the federal government and create new agencies; to establish programs censoring news, information, and abridging civil liberties; to seize foreign-owned property; and award government contracts without bidding.

Watergate A complex scandal involving attempts to cover up illegal actions taken by administration officials and leading to the resignation of President Richard Nixon in 1974.

Welfare capitalism A paternalistic system of labor relations emphasizing management responsibility for employee well-being.

Whigs The name used by advocates of colonial resistance to British measures during the 1760s and 1770s.

Whiskey Rebellion Armed uprising in 1794 by farmers in western Pennsylvania who attempted to prevent the collection of the excise tax on whiskey.

Whitewater Arkansas real estate development in which Bill and Hillary Clinton were investors; several fraud convictions resulted from investigations into Whitewater, but evidence was not found that the Clintons were involved in wrongdoing.

Wilmot's Proviso The amendment offered by Pennsylvania Democrat David Wilmot in 1846 which stipulated that "as an express and fundamental condition to the acquisition of any territory from the Republic of Mexico . . . neither slavery nor involuntary servitude shall ever exist in any part of said territory."

Wobblies Popular name for the members of the Industrial Workers of the World (IWW).

Woman's Christian Temperance Union (WCTU) Women's organization whose members visited schools to educate children about the evils of alcohol, addressed prisoners, and blanketed men's meetings with literature.

Women's Educational and Industrial Union Boston organization offering classes to wage-earning women.

World Trade Organization (WTO) International organization that sets standards and practices for global trade, and the focus of international protests over world economic policy in the late 1990s.

World Wide Web A part of the Internet designed to allow easier navigation of the network through the use of graphical user interfaces and hypertext links between different addresses.

XYZ Affair Diplomatic incident in 1798 in which Americans were outraged by the demand of the French for a bribe as a condition for negotiating with American diplomats.

Yalta Conference Meeting of U.S. President Franklin Roosevelt, British Prime Minister Winston Churchill, and Soviet Premier Joseph Stalin held in February 1945 to plan the final stages of World War II and postwar arrangements.

Yeoman Independent farmers of the South, most of whom lived on family-sized farms.

TEXT CREDITS

PHOTO CREDITS

of the Concord Museum, Concord, MA and the archives of the Lexington Historical Society. David Bohl, photographer; f. anne S.K. Brown Military Collection, John Hay Library, Brown University; g. Benjamin West, 1783 "American commissioners of Preliminary Negotations"; h. Library of Congress.

Chapter 8 Image Key: a, Harry N. Abrams, Inc.; b. Courtesy of the Historical Soceity of Pennsylvania Collection, Atwater kent Museum of Philadelphia; c. Corbis/Bettmann; d. Gallery of the Republic; e. Francis Kemmelmeyer "General George Washington Reviewing the Western Army at Fort Cumberland the 18th of October 1794," after 1794. Oil on paper backed with linen. Dimensions, 18-1/8 × 23 1/8. Courtesy of Winterthur Museum; g. White House Historical Association; h. The Library Company of Philadelphia.

Chapter 9 Image Key: a. Corbis/ Bettmann; b. from the collection of Mac G. and Janelle C. Morris Collection; c. Getty Images–Hutton Archive Photos; d. Smithsonian Institution photo no. 95-3550; e. Museum of the City of New York/Corbis; f. Library of Congress; g. © Bettmann/Corbis; h. John Wesley Jarvis, Black Hawk and His Son, Whirling Thunder, 1833. Oil on cavas. 23 × 30. Gilcrease Museum, Tulsa, Oklahoma; i. Getty Images Inc.–Hulton Archive Photos.

Chapter 10 Image Key: a. national Numismatic Collection/Smithsonian Institution; b. Corbis/Bettmann; c. Library of Congress; d. Getty Images; e. Thomas Coke Ruckle, Fairview Inn or Three Mile House on Old Frederick Road, c. 1829?, watercolor on paper. Collection of the Maryland Historical Society, Baltimore, MD.; f. The Bridgeman Art Library International Ltd.; g. Crockett Almanac, 1841, Prints and photographs division, Library of Congress.

Chapter 11 Image Key: a. Tina Chambers, Dorling Kindersley Media Library; b. Corbis/Bettmann; c. The Granger Collection, New York; d. Library of Congress; e. Library of Congress; f. Dorling Kindersley Media Library; g. Collection of the New York Historical Society; h. William Gladstone; i. Corbis Bettmann; j. Hunter Museum of Art, Chattanooga, TN; k, Library of Congress.

Chapter 12 Image Key: a. Library of Congress; b. Center for Lowell History; c. The New York Public Library, Research Libraries/Art Resource; d. American Textile History Museum; e. Library of Congress; f. Lowell Historical Society; g. Library of Congress; h. Getty Images, Inc.–Taxi.

Chapter 13 Image Key: a. Courtesy of the New York Historical Society, New York City; b. The Granger Collection; c. The Granger Collection; d. © Bettmann/Corbis; e. The Granger Collection; f. Winterthur Museum; g. Library of Congress; h. the Granger Collection; i. Omni-photo Communications, Inc.

Chapter 14 Image Key: a. Geoff Brightling, Dorling Kindersley Media Library; b. Getty Images Inc.–Hutton Archive Photos; c. Albert Bierstadt, "The Oregon Trail," Private collection/Bridgeman Art Library International Ltd., New York; d. Peter Anderson, Dorling Kindersley Media Library; e. Lynton Gardinier, Dorling Kindersley Media Library; f. © Christie's Images Inc. 2004; g. the Walters Art Museum, Baltimore; h. The Granger Collection; I. Collection of the New York Historical Society, New York City.

Chapter 15 Image Key: a. Corbis NY; b. Courtesy of the Library of Congress; c. Corbis NY; d. Corbis/Bettmann; e. Library of Congress; f. Library of Congress; g. Illinois State Historical Library; h. the Granger Collection; i. Getty Images Inc.–PhotoDisc.

Chapter 16 Image Key: a. Getty Images Inc.–Photodisc; b. National Archives and Records Administration; c. Dorling Kindersley Media Library; d. Dorling Kindersley Media Library; e. Dorling Kindersley Media Library; f. the Granger Collection, New York; g. Valentine Museum Library, Richmond, VA; h. Corbis/Bettmann; i. Getty Images Inc.–Hulton Archive Photos; j. Center of Military History, U.S. Army.

Chapter 17 Image Key: a. William Gladstone; b. no source; c. Corbis/ Bettmann; d. Specials Collection, Musselman Library, Gettysburg College, Gettysburg, PA; e. Library of Congress; f. the Granger Collection, New York; g. Library of Congress; h. Library of Congress; i. the Picture Bank, Frank & Marie Therese Wood Print Collection.

Chapter 18 Image Key: a. Lynton Gardiner, Dorling Kindersley Media Library; b. The Granger Collection, New York; c. Dave King © Dorling Kindersley Media Library; d. Dorling Kindersley Media Library; e. Library of Congress; f. Idaho State Historical Society; g. Nebraska State Historical Society, Solomon D. Butcher Collection; h. Library of Congress; i. Library of Congress.

Chapter 19 Image Key: a. Library of Congress; b. Lewis W. Hine, George Eastman House; c. Corbis/Bettmann; d., The Granger Collection, New York; e. Collection of the New York Historical Society, New York City; f. The Granger Collection, New York; g. Ford Motor Company.

Chapter 20 Image Key: a. Picture Research Consultants; b. Library of Congress; c. The Granger Collection; d. the Granger Collection, New York; e. Library of Congress; f. Corbis/Bettmann; g. the Granger Collection; h. Library of Congress; I. Library of Congress; j. Library of Congress; k. Harvard University; Library of Congress.

Chapter 21 Image Key: a. Corbis/Bettmann; b. Corbis/Bettmann; c. the Granger Collection, New York; d. Corbis/Bettmann; e. Indiana Historical Society; f. The original Paterson Pageant Program on which this drawing appeared is part of the collection of the American labor Museum/Botto House National Landmark. The poster is a copy of the program cover; g. Corbis/Bettmann; h. the Granger Collection.

Chapter 22 Image Key: a. Corbis/Bettmann; b. Getty Images Inc.–Hulton Archive Photos; c. Corbis/Bettmann; d. Richard Ward, Dorling Kindersley Media Library; e. The Granger Collection; f. Library of Congress; g. The Granger Collection; h. National Archives and Records Administration; i. the Granger Collection, New York.

Chapter 23 Image Key: a. Getty Images Inc.–Hulton Archive Photos; b. Corbis/Bettmann; c. Getty Images–Photodisc; d. C. Squared Studios, Getty Images, Inc. Photodisc; e. Wisconsin Historical Society; f. Campbell Soup Company; g. W.A. Swift Photograph Collection, Archives and Special Collections, Ball State University.

Chapter 24 Image Key: a. Corbis/Bettmann; b. Corbis/Bettmann; c. SuperStock, Inc.; d. Corbis/Bettmann; e. Getty Images, Inc. Photodisc; f. Brown Brothers; g. Corbis/Bettmann; h. The Granger Collection © Estate of Ben Shahn/Licensed by VAGA New York; i. Isaac Soyer, "Employment Agency" Oil on canvas. The Whitney Museum of American Art.

Chapter 25 Image Key: a. Andy Crawford, Dorling Kindersley Media Library; b. Corbis/Bettmann; c. Andy Crawford, Dorling Kindersley Media Library; d. the Granger Collection, New York; e. Getty Images Inc.–Hulton Archive Photos; f. Corbis/Bettmann; g. Reiger Communications, Inc.; h. Library of Congress; i. National Archives And Records Administration; j. The Granger Collection, New York.

Chapter 26 Image Key: a. Corbis/Bettmann; b. Getty Images/Time Life Pictures; c. Corbis/Bettmann; d. Getty Images Inc.–Hulton Archive Photos; e. Getty Images/Time Life Pictures; f. Corbis/Bettmann; g. Corbis/ Bettmann; h. Corbis/Bettmann; i. AP/Wide World Photos; j. Corbis/Bettmann.

Chapter 27 Image Key: a. Corbis/Bettmann; b. Getty Images Inc.–Hulton Archive Photos; c. Dorling Kindersley Media Library; d. Getty Images Inc.–Photodisc; e. Bernard Hoffmann/Life Magazine© 1950 Time Pix; f. Sondak, Getty Images, Inc.–Taxi; g. Retna, Ltd.; h. © Springer/Bettmann/Corbis; i. Library of Congress; j. AP/Wide World Photos.

Chapter 28 Image Key: a. Library of Congress; b. Corbis/Bettmann; c. John F. Kennedy Library; d. Library of Congress; e. Dorling Kindersley Media Library; f. Corbis/Bettmann; g. Corbis/Bettmann; h. Corbis/Bettmann.

Chapter 29 Image Key: a. © Royalty-Free/Corbis; b. © Royalty-Free/Corbis; c. © John Paul Filo/Hulton Archive Photos; d. George Meany Memorial Archives; e. AP/Wide World Photos; f. Corbis/ Bettmann; g. Corbis/Bettmann; h. Bernie Boston; i. AP/Wide World Photos; j. AP/Wide World Photos.

Chapter 30 Image Key: a. Telepress Syndicate Agency, Corbis/Bettmann; b. Ron Edmonds, Corbis/Bettmann; c. Corbis/Bettmann; d. Dorling Kindersley Media Library; e. AP/Wide World Photos; f. Joe Marquette, AP/Wide World Photos; g. Corbis/Bettmann; h. Jose L. Pelaez, Corbis/Stock Market.

Chapter 31 Image Key: a. Doug Katner, SIPA Press; b. Author supplied; c. Dorling Kindersley Media Library; d. Dorling Kindersley Media Library; e. Dorling Kindersley Media Library; f. Dorling Kindersley Media Library; g. Dorling Kindersley Media Library; h. Getty Images, Inc.–Agence France Presse; i. Barbara Gauntt/The Clarion-Ledger; j. Author supplied; k. Stephen Crowley, New York Times Pictures.

INDEX

U.S. HISTORY DOCUMENTS CD-ROM

SINGLE PC LICENSE AGREEMENT AND LIMITED WARRANTY

READ THIS LICENSE CAREFULLY BEFORE OPENING THIS PACKAGE. BY OPENING THIS PACKAGE, YOU ARE AGREEING TO THE TERMS AND CONDITIONS OF THIS LICENSE. IF YOU DO NOT AGREE, DO NOT OPEN THE PACKAGE. PROMPTLY RETURN THE UNOPENED PACKAGE AND ALL ACCOMPANYING ITEMS TO THE PLACE YOU OBTAINED THEM.

1. GRANT OF LICENSE and OWNERSHIP: The enclosed computer programs <<and data>> ("Software") are licensed, not sold, to you by Pearson Education, Inc. publishing as Pearson Prentice Hall ("We" or the "Company") and in consideration of your purchase or adoption of the accompanying Company textbooks and/or other materials, and your agreement to these terms. We reserve any rights not granted to you. You own only the disk(s) but we and/or our licensors own the Software itself. This license allows you to use and display your copy of the Software on a single computer (i.e., with a single CPU) at a single location for academic use only, so long as you comply with the terms of this Agreement. You may make one copy for back up, or transfer your copy to another CPU, provided that the Software is usable on only one computer.

2. RESTRICTIONS: You may not transfer or distribute the Software or documentation to anyone else. Except for backup, you may not copy the documentation or the Software. You may not network the Software or otherwise use it on more than one computer or computer terminal at the same time. You may not reverse engineer, disassemble, decompile, modify, adapt, translate, or create derivative works based on the Software or the Documentation. You may be held legally responsible for any copying or copyright infringement that is caused by your failure to abide by the terms of these restrictions.

3. TERMINATION: This license is effective until terminated. This license will terminate automatically without notice from the Company if you fail to comply with any provisions or limitations of this license. Upon termination, you shall destroy the Documentation and all copies of the Software. All provisions of this Agreement as to limitation and disclaimer of warranties, limitation of liability, remedies or damages, and our ownership rights shall survive termination.

4. LIMITED WARRANTY AND DISCLAIMER OF WARRANTY: Company warrants that for a period of 60 days from the date you purchase this SOFTWARE (or purchase or adopt the accompanying textbook), the Software, when properly installed and used in accordance with the Documentation, will operate in substantial conformity with the description of the Software set forth in the Documentation, and that for a period of 30 days the disk(s) on which the Software is delivered shall be free from defects in materials and workmanship under normal use. The Company does not warrant that the Software will meet your requirements or that the operation of the Software will be uninterrupted or error-free. Your only remedy and the Company's only obligation under these limited warranties is, at the Company's option, return of the disk for a refund of any amounts paid for it by you or replacement of the disk. THIS LIMITED WARRANTY IS THE ONLY WARRANTY PROVIDED BY THE COMPANY AND ITS LICENSORS, AND THE COMPANY AND ITS LICENSORS DISCLAIM ALL OTHER WARRANTIES, EXPRESS OR IMPLIED, INCLUDING WITHOUT LIMITATION, THE IMPLIED WARRANTIES OF MERCHANTABILITY AND FITNESS FOR A PARTICULAR PURPOSE. THE COMPANY DOES NOT WARRANT, GUARANTEE OR MAKE ANY REPRESENTATION REGARDING THE ACCURACY, RELIABILITY, CURRENTNESS, USE, OR RESULTS OF USE, OF THE SOFTWARE.

5. LIMITATION OF REMEDIES AND DAMAGES: IN NO EVENT, SHALL THE COMPANY OR ITS EMPLOYEES, AGENTS, LICENSORS, OR CONTRACTORS BE LIABLE FOR ANY INCIDENTAL, INDIRECT, SPECIAL, OR CONSEQUENTIAL DAMAGES ARISING OUT OF OR IN CONNECTION WITH THIS LICENSE OR THE SOFTWARE, INCLUDING FOR LOSS OF USE, LOSS OF DATA, LOSS OF INCOME OR PROFIT, OR OTHER LOSSES, SUSTAINED AS A RESULT OF INJURY TO ANY PERSON, OR LOSS OF OR DAMAGE TO PROPERTY, OR CLAIMS OF THIRD PARTIES, EVEN IF THE COMPANY OR AN AUTHORIZED REPRESENTATIVE OF THE COMPANY HAS BEEN ADVISED OF THE POSSIBILITY OF SUCH DAMAGES. IN NO EVENT SHALL THE LIABILITY OF THE COMPANY FOR DAMAGES WITH RESPECT TO THE SOFTWARE EXCEED THE AMOUNTS ACTUALLY PAID BY YOU, IF ANY, FOR THE SOFTWARE OR THE ACCOMPANYING TEXTBOOK. BECAUSE SOME JURISDICTIONS DO NOT ALLOW THE LIMITATION OF LIABILITY IN CERTAIN CIRCUMSTANCES, THE ABOVE LIMITATIONS MAY NOT ALWAYS APPLY TO YOU.

6. GENERAL: THIS AGREEMENT SHALL BE CONSTRUED IN ACCORDANCE WITH THE LAWS OF THE UNITED STATES OF AMERICA AND THE STATE OF NEW YORK, APPLICABLE TO CONTRACTS MADE IN NEW YORK, EXCLUDING THE STATE'S LAWS AND POLICIES ON CONFLICTS OF LAW, AND SHALL BENEFIT THE COMPANY, ITS AFFILIATES AND ASSIGNEES. THIS AGREEMENT IS THE COMPLETE AND EXCLUSIVE STATEMENT OF THE AGREEMENT BETWEEN YOU AND THE COMPANY AND SUPERSEDES ALL PROPOSALS OR PRIOR AGREEMENTS, ORAL, OR WRITTEN, AND ANY OTHER COMMUNICATIONS BETWEEN YOU AND THE COMPANY OR ANY REPRESENTATIVE OF THE COMPANY RELATING TO THE SUBJECT MATTER OF THIS AGREEMENT. If you are a U.S. Government user, this Software is licensed with "restricted rights" as set forth in subparagraphs (a)-(d) of the Commercial Computer-Restricted Rights clause at FAR 52.227-19 or in subparagraphs (c)(1)(ii) of the Rights in Technical Data and Computer Software clause at DFARS 252.227-7013, and similar clauses, as applicable.

Should you have any questions concerning this agreement or if you wish to contact the Company for any reason, please contact in writing: Legal Department, Prentice Hall, 1 Lake Street, Upper Saddle River, NJ 07450 or call Pearson Education Product Support at 1-800-677-6337.